ALSO BY ELIZABETH DREW

Washington Journal: The Events of 1973–1974
American Journal: The Events of 1976
Senator

Elizabeth Drew

PORTRAIT OF AN ELECTION

The 1980 Presidential Campaign

Simon and Schuster • NEW YORK

Most of the material in this book appeared originally in *The New Yorker*,
in slightly different form.

Copyright © 1981 by Elizabeth Drew, Inc.
All rights reserved
including the right of reproduction
in whole or in part in any form
Published by Simon and Schuster
A Division of Gulf & Western Corporation
Simon & Schuster Building
Rockefeller Center
1230 Avenue of the Americas
New York, New York 10020

SIMON AND SCHUSTER and colophon are trademarks of Simon & Schuster
Designed by Irving Perkins Associates
Manufactured in the United States of America

1   2   3   4   5   6   7   8   9   10

Library of Congress Cataloging in Publication Data

Drew, Elizabeth.
Portrait of an election.

Includes index.
1. Presidents—United States—Election—1980.
2. United States—Politics and government—1977–
1981.   I. Title.
E875.D73   324.973′0926   81-9339
AACR2
ISBN 0-671-43034-3

FOR DAVID

Contents

Introduction

EVERY TIME we choose a President, we are taking our fate in our hands, and therefore each Presidential election is an awesome process—sometimes absurd, sometimes tedious, sometimes cause for despair, but still awesome. Moreover, politics is a very particular and, to my mind, fascinating art form. And there is a mysterious interplay of human nature and events in the process by which we choose our Presidents—an alchemy that defies predictions and form charts.

A Presidential election year is not the frozen past but the historical hinge between what has gone before and what follows. A Presidential election is a repository of accumulated hopes and frustrations, a period in which the public's feelings that have lurked beneath the surface, or been right out there, are explored—and exploited—by the political practitioners. It is also revelatory of what is to come: if we look carefully, we can learn a great deal about the person who becomes our President and about the kind of Administration he brings with him. He is, during the campaign, more exposed than he will be after he goes behind the White House gates, to be even more sheltered and spoken for by others.

A journalist who watches an election up close has a chance to see the people who involve themselves in it—the candidates and their advisers—as they try to shape it and are shaped by it, try to outwit and outmaneuver their opponents and are outwitted and outmaneuvered, fumble for the right combination of things to be said (and not said) and moves to be made. One has an opportunity to see, and try to understand, how people in politics think, calculate, react—and to capture how it looks and feels. This sort of journalism can constitute a history of a period—an account of the realities of the time, unguided, and also undistorted, by hindsight.

As a journalist covering the 1980 election for *The New Yorker,* I tried to

11

look at the election from different angles of vision: to see the principal participants coping with a variety of situations; to listen to the strategists as they groped their way along; to understand as much as possible about human nature in these circumstances; and to learn as much as possible about the rich subject of the practice of politics. I tried also to understand and record the erratic interconnections between events and human efforts, and to get across something of what is involved in running for the highest office in such a large and complex country, particularly at a time when, domestically and internationally, so many things are so perplexing and frustrating. I tried to capture the participants as they attempted to appeal both to what they deemed to be the national constituency and to the many special constituencies, as they sought to follow thought-out strategies and also got caught up in situations they could not anticipate, as they tried to resolve the political equations and to cope with the extraordinary demands—internal and external—while they followed the course charted by their own (and others') ambitions. And I tried, of course, to understand what happened.

This book is intended to provide a portrait of the period, beginning in mid-November, 1979; to give the feel of it—how it looked and sounded and seemed—at the time; and to provide insight into the events and the major figures. The appendix consists of strategy memorandums prepared by Reagan's pollster, Richard Wirthlin, and Carter's pollster, Patrick Caddell, in the course of the campaign, showing how these men saw things at the time, and the advice they were giving their candidates.

As the story proceeded, it was told from different perspectives. Various characters and themes appear and reappear, and as the story unfolds the election can be seen not as a succession of isolated and inchoate events but as a total picture. Seen as a whole, the picture is much more coherent than many people thought at the time and also different from the way it is often interpreted and remembered.

—Elizabeth Drew

NOTE: The first chapter was written as of November 15th, 1979; the second, as of December 27th, 1979; the third, January 24th, 1980; the fourth, February 21st, 1980; the fifth, March 13th, 1980; the sixth, April 3rd, 1980; the seventh, May 1st, 1980; the eighth, June 12th, 1980; the ninth, July 31st, 1980; the tenth, August 28th, 1980; the eleventh, September 18th, 1980; the twelfth, October 2nd, 1980; the thirteenth, October 9th, 1980; the fourteenth, November 20th, 1980.

CHAPTER 1

Beginnings ─────────────

SIMPLY STATED, there has never been anything like it in Washington before. The struggle over the Presidential nomination between President Carter and Senator Edward M. Kennedy established, rapidly, an atmosphere that re sembles nothing so much as a civil war. A city obsessed with politics in any event was suddenly presented with not just an ordinary contest for a nomination but a brutal struggle for very high stakes between two very determined, powerful, and combative men, each backed by very determined, combative forces. The struggle had seemed theoretically possible for some time, but its actuality turned out in short order to be of a magnitude and nature that had not been imagined. There have been challenges to Presidents from within their own parties in recent years, but no challenger in memory has occupied such an important base of power in Washington. The struggle tears at loyalties, friendships, even families. Meanwhile, Republican candidates occasionally troop across the Washington stage to define, declare, or otherwise further their ambitions. And—as befits any Presidential-election season, only this time more so—others here make their calculations of what to do, what would be the best position to have been in at the right time. And, of course, the speculation about how it will all come out goes on with great intensity, irrespective of the fact that such speculation is futile. Suddenly the campaign has backed up on us. For some time, there had been preliminaries in the year before an election, but it became clear early this fall that these were no longer the preliminaries.

Morris Udall has adopted what he calls Udall's Law. Udall's Law is that all the pet theories on the front-runners and the favorites a year before the election are neat, simple, cold, logical, and wrong. There are innumerable examples of the validity of this law, but they do nothing to diminish the speculation. The prevailing view about what is going to happen in both parties shifts with remarkable swiftness. This week's certainty is, while utterly different from, no less certain than, last week's certainty. The speculation about the Democrats ran, in a matter of a few weeks: Kennedy will clobber Carter. No, wait a minute, Kennedy has liabilities, and Carter and his people are good at campaigning—in fact, that is what they are good at. No, Kennedy is going to clobber Carter—early. Wait, Kennedy's liabilities are real, and serious. On the Republican side, it has run: Reagan has it. No, Reagan is too old, Connally is overtaking him. No, Connally has too many liabilities; it's still Reagan, or, if not Reagan, Howard Baker; watch out for George Bush. The political tag that is applied to Baker is that, as the saying goes, he "looks good on paper." But the thing is, the candidates do not run on paper.

A number of things are forgotten, it seems, amid the speculation. Events that were by no means inevitable are given a retrospective inevitability. Carter had some good fortune in the early stages of the 1976 nomination struggle and, as it happens, had real trouble, even though he had no single strong opponent, toward the end of it; he very nearly lost the election. Many people who are suddenly remembering what gifted politicians the Carter people are seem to be overlooking the fact that if they were such gifted politicians they would not be in their present pickle. The speculation takes place in a vacuum. It does not, because it cannot, anticipate the kinds of goofs, *gaffes,* accidents, and outside events that have changed the course of past campaigns. It does not, cannot, take into account the changing, intuitive judgments that the public makes as the candidates are subjected to extended scrutiny. The sheer number of candidates in a primary can affect the outcome. As can the turnout. Even the weather. It seems to be widely forgotten that we did not know the result of the 1976 election until 3:46 A.M. the following day.

The Kennedy candidacy had a certain inevitability, and it remained for Carter to provide the opportunity. Kennedy sometimes says that he would have been content to serve out his years in the Senate, and, of course, he colors his decision to run as one made with the greatest reluctance. But the idea that Edward Kennedy might someday run for President has been around him for a long, long time—since even before either of his brothers was assassinated. It has been an open subject since 1968—twelve years before the 1980 election. Therefore, there were at least twelve years during which Kennedy had to weigh the decision, assess his options and opportunities, and listen to invited and uninvited counsel. The legacy was there, bringing with it some combination of opportunity, obligation, and ambition. Kennedy spent a long time "keeping his options open," as they say, even while he temporarily foreclosed them. He gave consideration to running for

President in 1968—there was a great deal of sentiment in favor of his doing so—and then, briefly, to running as the Vice Presidential candidate with George McGovern in 1972. At one point, he even gave consideration to running with Carter in 1980. The theory was that by having served as Vice President he would be "sanitized" with respect to the personal problems that shadow his public life—that the voters would get used to thinking of him in Presidential terms. One old friend of Kennedy's says, "He's walked around the question of his candidacy for a long time; a good power operator is always walking around that kind of question, sensing the possibilities." Yet sixteen years (or perhaps twenty if a Republican is elected in 1980 and is strong enough to be re-elected) is a long time for a politician to keep himself "viable," even if he is a Kennedy. Other politicians, with their own ambitions, might not cooperate in this long-range planning. There are some younger Democrats—such as Senators Gary Hart, of Colorado, and Joseph Biden, of Delaware—who give off signs that they have ambitions of their own.

There are a number of people who tell of conversations with Kennedy over the past couple of years in which he gave implicit or explicit indications that he was thinking seriously of running this time. And there were the overt acts: the breaking of the Kennedy tradition of live-and-let-live with Republican senators from Massachusetts when, in 1978, Kennedy backed the Democrat, Paul Tsongas, over Edward Brooke, putting Tsongas, who won, in a position to look after Kennedy's interests; the hiring, in December, 1978, of Carl Wagner, a political organizer in his early thirties (Wagner, who is from Iowa, is presumably not an expert on Massachusetts, and is generally believed to be one of the best political organizers in the country); the seizing of the opportunity to bring the Democratic Party's constituent groups to their feet at the Party's 1978 midterm conference in Memphis and to reinforce his hold on them by making a speech ostensibly about health insurance but actually attacking the President's emphasis on military spending at the expense, Kennedy charged, of social programs; the decision to give some interviews this past July, ten years after the event, about the incident at Chappaquiddick.

As matters turned out, those particular interviews, apparently given in the hope that they would make the subject go away, or would at least provide a test of its virulence, were virtually obliterated from the public mind, coming as they did during the week that the President gave what has come to be known as his "malaise" speech (in which he said that he would try to be a better President but also that the nation was suffering from a crisis of the spirit) and the Administration engulfed itself in the chaos of mass resignations and firings. It was during that period that the President began his decline to an all-time low, for any President, in the polls, which also indicated in the first week in August that Kennedy enjoyed a two-to-one lead over Carter. Many Democratic politicians on Capitol Hill were frantic over the possibility of having to run with Carter at the head of the ticket. There was a great deal of talk in the cloakrooms about what might happen if the Republicans were to take over the Senate. There was a strong feeling on Capitol Hill in July that the Carter Administration had collapsed. Kennedy was presented with a mixture of duty and opportunity: if there were to be a Republican sweep, the Senate would be at least a markedly changed place, several of his allies might be defeated, and, for some time to come, the atmosphere would be a poor one for his issues and his politics. At some point, one becomes tired of turning things over in the mind, of weighing familiar factors. It was during August, by his own account, that Kennedy made the decision to run.

Carter also unwittingly played a hand in the timing of Kennedy's entry into the race. For some time, Kennedy had expressed to friends a concern about avoiding the problem of being charged with opportunism—as his brother Robert was when he entered the 1968 race after Eugene McCarthy demonstrated in New Hampshire that Lyndon Johnson was vulnerable—if he waited until someone else showed Carter to be vulnerable. Moreover, the later he entered the race, the more serious the problems of organizing a campaign would be. And so, after Labor Day, with the timing still uncertain, Kennedy began to drop public hints about his decision. (This had the effect of keeping alive the "Draft Kennedy" movement and of keeping people who might join or support his campaign at the ready.) The rationale for his running, he said, was Carter's failure of leadership. The probability of his candidacy had two effects, one of which was expected, the other not necessarily so. The expected effect was that when Kennedy the candidate, as opposed to Kennedy the theoretical candidate, was measured against Carter, the gap between them in the polls would narrow. (It was also expected that, in any event, Carter's rating would not stay at such a low point.) The unexpected effect was that the Carter Administration, perhaps because it was faced with the prospect of a Kennedy challenge, gave indications that it had learned something. Several of its legislative goals began to come to fruition in Congress. Who gets credit for this is subject to some debate, but Carter was looking more "Presidential." So, lest the rationale slip away, the timing of Kennedy's entry into the race was advanced. (Kennedy announced his candidacy on November 7th.) Also, it was clear that the Carter people had for some time been working on their campaign. Politicians, generally speaking, are not patient people, and their very competitiveness makes it difficult for them to stand back once they have decided to wage a fight. Moreover, Kennedy has a hyperactive personality, as many politicians do, and, seeing that he was in for a real fight, once he had decided to go ahead with it he wanted to go ahead with it.

On the morning of Thursday, October 18th, at eight o'clock, Gerald Ford is having breakfast at the Sheraton-Carlton Hotel with a group of reporters. Here is a former President of the United States, looking well, if a bit older than when he left office, sitting around with a bunch of reporters, talking like one of the guys. Actually, this sort of thing came naturally to Ford during his many years as a member of the House of Representatives. The question at the moment is what he plans to do about running for the Presidency again. Ford lost his race for the Presidency in 1976 in the worst possible way—narrowly. There are many what-ifs to live with after that. Now he would like to be President again, if only he didn't have to run for the nomination. Before 1976, Ford had never run for office in anything larger than a congressional district, and he especially disliked having to slug it out with Reagan in the primaries. At that time, he had the appurtenances of the Presidency to help him along, and still he almost lost the nomination to Reagan. Ford is leading what many would consider the good life—Palm Springs, Vail, well-paid speeches, an ample income, respectful treatment as a former President. Campaigning for the nomination would make him just one of the pack and subject him to the accompanying indignities. He is said by friends to enjoy receiving attention when he appears in golf tournaments or gives speeches, and being told that things were better when he was President and that he ought to run again—and also to enjoy titillating people with hints that he might indeed run. The problem is that all that might be spoiled if he actually ran. Ford's preference is to wait until a few months into next year to see what happens, and then decide what to do. He is one of the would-be candidates who seem to turn up in every election hoping that "lightning will strike." But it hasn't in a long time, and the possibility that it will has become less likely, given the way the nominating system has evolved. Recently, Ford met in Palm Springs with some of his political advisers, who went over the dates and details of primaries and filing deadlines, and so on, with him. They advised him that if he delayed his decision it would only make it more difficult for others who wanted to oppose Reagan, and might well guarantee Reagan the nomination. Ford was also told that if he waits too long it will be too late for him. So the question most on the reporters' minds this morning is what Ford intends to do. He is asked if he is planning to run.

"It's getting more enjoyable on the outside than it was on the inside," he answers, smiling. "If I came here as a candidate, I'd have to be answering tough questions. Now I don't come here having to make some point, having to seduce you. I'm seeing good friends, old acquaintances. Isn't that a nice way to spend a morning?"

The question is repeated in another form.

Ford suggests that the press is trying to stir something up. "I'm exactly today where I was a year ago, two years ago," he says. "I will speak out on SALT, other issues. That doesn't indicate I'm sitting in a smoke-filled room with charts and experts, scheming. If something happens, it happens. I'm a fatalist." And he adds, "I never say 'never' in politics."

In answer to still a third question on the subject, he says, "Only as the primaries progress there might be some switching, but it's too early to honestly say that. Nobody's had a primary yet. . . . We haven't really had a voter test."

The questions and the answers continue along the same line.

"I'm not a candidate, I'm not," he insists. "Somehow you all don't believe it. On the other hand, if a scenario developed, I'd have to take another look at it."

The next day, Ford calls a press conference on Capitol Hill, on short notice, and announces that he has made "a firm decision not to become an active candidate." He also says that he would be available if the Republican Convention were to be deadlocked but says he thinks chances of that are "very remote."

Every Presidential campaign causes a large number of people—politicians whose own fortunes might be affected, people with visions of serving in the White House or in some other high-level government job (some are quite specific in their own minds quite early), strategists for various interest groups, people to whom it is important to have the right connections, and other investors in power—to try to calculate what's in it for them to go which way, and where they want to have been when. This can get very tricky, but never more so than in the situation created by the Carter-Kennedy struggle. The calculations are essentially unsentimental and take a number of forms.

A Democratic senator, over lunch in the Senate Dining Room in mid-October, when Kennedy's candidacy seemed certain but was not yet official: "Some of the enthusiasm for Ted's candidacy up here has waned a bit. Carter's low point was just after Labor Day, and Ted's high point was right up until he made his move." When, following its August recess, Congress returned to Washington in early September, many were convinced that Carter was finished. August hadn't gone much better for him than July had (the furor over Andrew Young and the P.L.O. while Carter floated down the Mississippi, the imbroglio over the Soviet troops in Cuba). In mid-September, an Associated Press–NBC News poll showed his approval rating at nineteen. Even members of the House, who, because they run every two years, feel they are closer to their constituents than senators are, and so generally consider themselves more immune to the fate of the top of the Presidential ticket, were worried. One House Democrat said to me at the time, "A lot of us could lose, *and Carter isn't worth it*."

The Democratic senator continued, "Once it became clear Ted would run, people started attacking him, and others started to consider problems they'd brushed aside. People here still think he'll be the nominee, but not as easily as before. Carter's people obviously did a professional job in Florida." This was just after Carter won, narrowly, a non-binding preliminary caucus vote in Florida on October 13th against an unofficial Kennedy organization. (Only thirty-four thousand people participated, and the contest was largely one of logistics.) "A lot of people feel that while there has been a lot of ineptness and clumsiness in the Carter Administration, Carter's tried to do the right thing, and he made some tough decisions in the Cuban mess and got out of it not too badly. The conjecture up here is that Kennedy does well in New England, Carter does well in the South, and in the end Kennedy takes New York, Pennsylvania, and California. Up here, people feel that those big states are where the Democrats need the help next year. The feeling is that Carter would help in the South but Ted would help in the big states with a whole pile of House seats that could determine the ideology of the House, and would also make a big difference in the Senate."

I asked him if such a calculation assumed that Kennedy would, if he was nominated, win in November.

"No," he replied. "It doesn't assume that he wins, but it does assume that his candidacy will cause a big turnout—and of minorities, such as blacks and Chicanos—that can determine the outcome of other races. Low turnouts have been hurting the Democrats."

There is another side to that assumption. Some Southern Democrats are unenthusiastic about a Kennedy race for the very reason that some Northern Democrats are eager for it.

There is still another side. One Southern senator said to me recently, "It's almost a wash for Southern senators. He'll bring out the poor and blacks, who vote in small numbers, and that's a plus. On the other hand, the people who feel intensely against him will also be brought out, and that will hurt some in the South."

I spoke to another Democratic senator—one who is partial to Kennedy and is not running for re-election in 1980. "The first thing to remember is that everybody's looking out for themselves," he said. "Some would feel that maybe they're better off with Carter—that it's a different kind of campaign if he's the nominee. They may be able to survive Carter; they may not be able to survive Kennedy. I think a guy figures, 'My voting record is different from Kennedy's. Kennedy is too liberal; philosophically, I'm more attuned to Carter. I don't have to defend Carter's positions as against my positions.' I think Carter's game frightens them a little—his saying last June, 'I'm going to whip his ass.' They know it's going to be a tough campaign; they worry about Chappaquiddick. There's something else: politicians are very timid guys. They're not sure they want a guy who comes on as strong as Ted does. They worry about what happens with the rising of the decibels. Politicians used to like excitement; now most of them are gray, want to play it safe. They're afraid of the special interests—the gun lobby, the anti-abortionists. Those groups are the mouthy people, and all the mouthy people are going to be against Kennedy. There is a feeling Kennedy would arouse the dogs in a campaign, and a lot of politicians don't want the excitement."

Another Democratic senator explained the Capitol Hill calculations as follows: "There's a powerful compulsion when you're up for a House or Senate seat to take yourself out of the Presidential thing. Everyone's consumed by their own fortunes. They need the help of everyone. For them to risk alienating any faction at this stage would be highly unusual."

I asked him about the shift in climate that had occurred on Capitol Hill not long after Kennedy made it clear that he would run.

He replied, "I think some of those who were wanting Kennedy to head the ticket are sobering up as they see how tough it's going to be and how tough an experience Ted is going to be subjected to. These guys want to stand off and see how that storm is weathered. They all get colder feet; there is an impetus to hold back and make sure that their original thesis survives the test. The two most obvious factors that changed the climate were, one, that the Kennedy challenge makes the Carter people pull themselves together, and, two, that the Carter people are getting to what they're good at—campaigning, rather than governing. Also, what you see coming out is sympathy for Carter and the desire for regular order, the natural inclination of regular Democrats to be discomfited by a fight. They say they're for Ted, but 'Why now? Why not 1984?' If they're state chairmen or other Party officials, they themselves are threatened: they could be thrown out if there's a split. The safest haven for them is the regular order. So there's a large element of wait-and-see on Kennedy."

A Democratic senator who is up for re-election said to me, "I really think it would be a distraction from my campaign for me to endorse either of them. I won't want to go into every meeting—I attend seven or eight a day —and be asked, 'Why are you supporting President Carter, when he's bought that crazy oil-company philosophy and lifted price controls and is letting the oil companies rip us off?' Or 'Why are you supporting Kennedy, with his crazy spending programs?' I think half of my time would have to be devoted to a defense of my position on the Presidential race. Still, I realize that I'm going to have to answer questions on whether I agree with Kennedy or Carter on this or that."

Some Democrats on Capitol Hill would prefer Kennedy to Carter as President because they see him, for all the talk about his liberalism, as a pragmatic politician, as someone they can work with, as someone who understands Congress and knows how to work within it. Some would prefer Carter because they are not certain they want a President who is good at working with them, who might reduce their independence.

Politicians on Capitol Hill noticed that Carter attended a World Series game with House Speaker Thomas P. O'Neill and asked him to be the chairman of the Democratic Convention—an offer that O'Neill accepted. "That's smart long-run politics," said one senator who is not partial to Carter. "It shows that they're thinking several months ahead, that they're laying in acorns for the winter." Obviously, O'Neill, a Massachusetts man, has ties that pull him to Kennedy, but, as an old-fashioned Democrat, he is loyal to the President. As Speaker of the House, he is better off not taking any position. His being made chairman of the Convention freed him from pressures to choose, and for that he was said to be grateful.

When I went to see one Democratic senator in late October, Senator Daniel Inouye, Democrat of Hawaii, was coming out of the senator's office. Inouye, who is up for re-election in 1980, had stopped by to ask the senator to attend a "Friends of Carter/Mondale" dinner that evening. The senator had declined.

Word of maneuvers in the struggle travels quickly through the cloakrooms of Capitol Hill. And it travelled quickly one day that Jimmy Carter had telephoned Senator Dale Bumpers, Democrat of Arkansas, and said that he and Rosalynn had just been talking about Bumpers and his wife, Betty, at breakfast that morning. And that the President added that he hoped Bumpers would be with him. Bumpers told the President that he was not making any commitments. What gave the story special point was that Bumpers, a moderate Southerner and a former governor, who is up for re-election to the Senate in 1980, is widely considered a good possibility to be Kennedy's running mate. The penchant for speculation is such that discussions of who Kennedy's running mate would be began in September.

Dan Rostenkowski, a Democratic representative from Illinois, is the chief deputy majority whip of the House and one of the most important Democratic members. For years, he was, in effect, Mayor Richard Daley's ambassador to Washington, and now, like other Chicago politicians and the remains of the Cook County organization, he has a tenuous relationship with the city's mayor, Jane Byrne. When I go to see Rostenkowski in late October, Mayor Byrne has indicated publicly that she will support Carter, and both Carter and Kennedy are making a big thing of trying to win her support. (Some people in the Carter camp have warned that Mrs. Byrne is highly unpredictable, and that it is very likely that if she finally endorses someone it will be Kennedy, so Carter should not make such a big thing of it.) Therefore, Dan Rostenkowski is on the spot. It is said that he wants to "stay loose." (So do some others in Cook County, for reasons of their own. When Carter went to Chicago recently for a Democratic fund-raising dinner, Roman Pucinski, formerly a member of Congress and now a Chicago alderman, commented to a reporter, "We're just startin' to squeeze the guy.") Rostenkowski has been telling people in the Carter and Kennedy camps that he's going to wait to see what O'Neill is going to do—that, after all, O'Neill is part of the leadership and he himself is part of the leadership.

Rostenkowski is a large man, with reddish hair and a husky voice. "Carter is the contrast now of what he's been for the last three years," he says. "He's being aggressively political. Where's he been? I'm happy that he's seen that Washington politics has to be played maybe with a kid glove, but the hand has to be in the glove. He's starting to be a President. When he came to Washington, he wanted his aides to get around Washington in taxis. You had the Ways and Means Committee"—Rostenkowski is a member—"waiting around one day because Mike Blumenthal couldn't get a cab."

I point out that Blumenthal, the former Secretary of the Treasury, like all Cabinet members, had a limousine available for official appointments.

Rostenkowski says, "Well, if it wasn't Mike, it was some Treasury official. I've had some strong conversations with the President about this. He's started to play 'Hail to the Chief' now, but he never should have stopped playing it. This is Carter's last campaign. That's how he'll have to go at it —no holds barred. You're starting to get people to choose sides. Everybody is going to start making assessments about what they've had under Carter and what it would be like under Kennedy. Some of my colleagues are starting to say Carter hasn't been that bad."

I ask him if people in the House have been shifting their assessments.

Rostenkowski replies, "I think the realization of fighting an incumbent President who has become the candidate, has become more aggressive as President—the realization that they're not going to roll Jimmy Carter over —is making some people sit back. On the other hand, it's so much more convenient for a candidate running for re-election to run on a platform of new hope, new ideas, new leadership. They could do that with Carter in 1976. A candidate could do that with Brown, with Kennedy, but a candidate running with Carter now would have to defend what Carter has done. The fellow that's running for re-election that doesn't have the comfort of my district"—Rostenkowski got more than eighty percent of the vote in each of the last three elections—"the tenure that I have, may want to talk about the dreams of tomorrow."

What, then, I ask, does a member of Congress do?

"He's going to play the string out as long as he possibly can," Rostenkowski replies. "He'll avoid identification with one candidate or another as long as possible. He wants to be on the winner's side. Under the conditions that exist today, you can't blame him." He leans forward in his chair and adds, "Besides, if you're good at your job, even if you're on the losing side, the winner needs you."

Following my visit with Rostenkowski, Jane Byrne endorsed Kennedy, thus beating out the Cook County Central Committee, which was also planning to endorse him; Rostenkowski had lunch at the White House with the President; Rostenkowski tried to delay an endorsement of Kennedy by the Cook County organization; the organization endorsed Kennedy. After all this happened, Rostenkowski said to me, "The organization was premature. We don't know how the voters are going to react to Kennedy. For me, it's very hard to drop an incumbent President. But I'll support what the committee has done. I've always done that. But I've also always run as a delegate on their slate. This time, I won't do that. I'm not running as committed, uncommitted. I'm not running, period."

I asked one prominent mayor who had endorsed Carter why he had done so. He replied, "The White House can do me a lot of good over the next few months, and if he loses I can't believe Kennedy's not going to need me."

A Democratic senator says over the phone, "I'm staying out of it, out of sheer cowardice."

An important labor leader, at a dinner, says he's staying neutral. "I have other fish to fry," he says. If the President has a serious challenger, the labor leader's bargaining power with the President—and with the challenger—is increased. "The more the merrier," he says, smiling. The assumption of the union leaders who are remaining neutral—the group includes, as of now, the leaders of the A.F.L.–C.I.O. and the United Auto Workers—is that the rank and file will largely support Kennedy. But the leaders have their own exigencies. A number of wage settlements are coming up in which the Administration will play a role; for the U.A.W., there was the question of federal financial aid for the Chrysler Corporation. (Early this month, the Administration recommended a federal loan guarantee to Chrysler.) Vice President Mondale has been expending a good deal of effort with union executive boards, trying to rekindle the old Humphrey ties. (Recently—actually, on the day Kennedy made his formal announcement that he was a candidate—Muriel Humphrey, Hubert Humphrey's widow, stood on the White House lawn, with Mondale by her side, and announced that she supported the Carter-Mondale ticket.) As for the Administration's decision to help Chrysler, a U.A.W. official says, "Strauss and Mondale were very cagey. They took the leadership up to the mountaintop and showed them how good the goodies are." Some union people find themselves making calculations not unlike those made by members of Congress. As it happens, eight positions in the U.A.W. leadership are opening up next year. Elections of delegates to the U.A.W. convention are to be held next spring, around the time of several important primaries. A U.A.W. official says, "If a guy figures that what he wants is to be vice president of the union, he might drag his heels on the Presidential thing, because otherwise it might complicate his life. Therefore, some guys who would be for Kennedy are not declaring."

A man I know here works for someone of some importance in the Administration and is also close to someone who is close to Kennedy. This man feels he must take care how much time he spends with his friend, and under what circumstances, so as not to make his boss, to whom he is utterly loyal, uneasy.

There are many levels to the Democrats' struggle in Washington. One is the obvious strategic and public-relations considerations in the Kennedy camp's luring away of Administration officials. A certain amount of this was to be expected, because the Administration is, after all, made up largely of Democrats, and a certain number of them have old ties to Kennedy, or would like to have future ones. In recognition of this, Jody Powell, the President's press secretary, having bitterly attacked Dick Clark, the former Democratic senator from Iowa, for leaving his job as ambassador-at-large in charge of refugee affairs to join the Kennedy camp, hedged against eventualities by telling reporters in a background briefing that, of course, more "defections" were expected. The Administration has made it clear that people in it are expected not just to try to govern but also to support the President's re-election. Some people are willing to do the first but are less enthusiastic about the second. People working at agencies far removed from the White House tell of hearing that their political loyalties have been inquired about. Married couples who work for the Administration have to consider the effect on the career of one partner if the other leaves to work for Kennedy. What the Administration will have a hard time doing anything about is that Kennedy has for a long time been the recipient of memorandums and information from people within the Administration who are dissatisfied with certain policies.

By comparison, Republicans are almost mellow. I went to see a moderate Republican senator one afternoon in October. He said he went along with the general assumption that his party's nomination was Reagan's unless Reagan did something to lose it. He continued, "I don't find the divisive quality to this campaign that I have found to every one of our other campaigns since 1964."

I asked him what he thought was the reason for this.

"It may just be that it's early," he replied. "But I also think that the terrible divisiveness of 1976, and the fact that most people say that that's what cost the G.O.P. the White House, has been a sobering experience."

I suggested that if I had said to him four years ago that Ronald Reagan was going to be the nominee of his party he would not have been sitting there so calmly.

"At that point, he wasn't," he replied. "Besides, I'm not about to be a part of allowing the Party to become just a Sunbelt club. This is one of the things we've got to thrash out."

It seems that the moderate Republicans are in part bowing to what might be the inevitable and, if they are up for re-election, trying to avoid the wrath of the Party's conservatives, and perhaps even work out a deal with Reagan, who might need them. (Thus, Jacob Javits, of New York, who is up for re-election, said on "Face the Nation" in September that he could live with any of the candidates, including Reagan.)

On Thursday, October 25th, George Bush is addressing a luncheon of the Washington Press Club at the Sheraton-Carlton Hotel, in the same room where Ford had breakfast with reporters a week ago. (Not far away, John Anderson, a House Republican from Illinois, who has also declared for the Presidency, is addressing the National Press Club.) Bush is virtually nowhere in the polls now, and few people give him a chance. His supporters here say that he is doing well in Iowa (where he has spent a great deal of time), in Puerto Rico, and even in New Hampshire. Bush has held a larger number of important jobs than most people who run for the Presidency—director of the C.I.A., head of the United States mission in Peking, Ambassador to the United Nations, Republican Party chairman, representative from Texas—and he was among those who were thought to be considered for the Vice Presidency when Richard Nixon had to fill the vacancy left by Spiro Agnew. Such a string of experiences is likely to leave a man thinking he is at least as well qualified to be President as others who make the attempt. (Elliot Richardson, who outdoes Bush in number of government jobs held, and is another story, has also had that thought.) Bush is tall and handsome and has a slightly crooked smile, and reporters who have travelled with him come away saying that he is a very nice man, but they also say they can't much remember what he said. As he goes about seeking Republican support, Bush stresses his experience as a Texas businessman over his roots in New England, where he grew up.

Today, Bush begins by making some not terribly funny remarks, in a game attempt at self-deprecating humor. It is as if he felt he may be just a bit too elegant, a bit too patrician, a bit too polished for what people expect in politicians, and he must show that he can be one of the boys. Then he swings into his prepared statement, in which he describes the 1980s as "the most dangerous decade in the past forty years." He points out that Carter ran as a candidate "who talked love and trust," and says he hopes that the fact that Carter is now viewed as "weak and ineffective" has not "given decency a bad name." And then, in case Kennedy turns out to be the problem, he attacks what he calls "the Camelot syndrome in modern media politics." He outlines his own economic program: limit the growth of spending, remove the excesses of regulation, build productivity by cutting taxes, balance the budget. He makes a jab at John Connally, without mentioning his name. This is a little convention that Republicans, at least for the time, are observing. He points out that Teddy Roosevelt didn't say, "Talk tough and carry a swagger stick." He says that the "true toughness" is "mental toughness," and that the American people know this, and that this is why "I'm going to win the nomination and the Presidency next year."

Bush is not a compelling speaker—though today he is trying to pump more enthusiasm, definiteness, into his speaking style. As he reaches the close of his prepared remarks, he says, "Some others might be more exciting orators. But we're not trying to elect a class valedictorian; we're trying to elect somebody who can restore confidence in this country—run it." And he gives his definition of leadership, which is what all the candidates seem to be saying they are for: "experience; conviction; the ability to inspire confidence in the people you lead; the ability to disagree and still command respect; the ability to persuade without bullying; enough humility to avoid the unnecessary error; the ability to attract excellence and to bring out the best those people can offer."

As Bush answers questions, he again tries to persuade the audience to take him seriously: "I know I'm going to win this nomination. You just watch."

He is asked if he is gaining ground in the Republican race.

"There is great evidence that it's getting better," he says. "You had no reason to take me seriously a year ago. Now today you do, some of you grudgingly." He says this with good humor. He points out that he has been winning "straw polls" in Iowa; there have been six thus far, and Bush has won them all.

In 1975, Jimmy Carter, who until then had been little noticed, won a straw poll in Iowa, and so now some are taking that as the model. "We've got a classy game plan, the best grass-roots organization in these early states," Bush says, "and that's how you build name recognition." He grows animated and waves his arms. "I'm going to win it by seeing very little of you and a hell of a lot of Iowa and New Hampshire."

On Wednesday, October 31st, two days after Kennedy's brother-in-law Stephen Smith announced the formation of a Kennedy for President Committee, Kennedy's Senate office, Room 2241 of the Dirksen Office Building, is a madhouse. Job applicants, tourists crowd the reception room. One of two women who handle the phones (the line is often busy these days) is politely thanking someone for offering Kennedy a place to stay during the campaign. Former Kennedy staff members are coming back. Roles in the campaign are still being sorted out. Telephones have not yet been installed in the campaign headquarters in downtown Washington. Campaign strategists are scattered around the city. There are logistical problems to be solved, advance people to be suddenly found and sent into the field. There are questions of baggage handling and hotel rooms. The travel schedule keeps changing. Strategists are still sorting out the requests for appearances and their own ideas as to when Kennedy should appear where. The schedulers have to mesh the political exigencies with commitments already made and with the Senate duties that Kennedy will still want to perform.

Kennedy will go to West Virginia and Buffalo this coming weekend, and so far sixty-three reporters, an exceptional number for any political figure except a President, have signed up to go along. When Carter was flying around Iowa in January, 1976, only a handful of reporters accompanied him. What will amount to about a sixteen-million-dollar effort (just for the primaries), involving fifty states and four hundred and thirty-five congressional districts, suddenly has to be assembled. The idea that the Kennedys have a "well-oiled machine" at the ready is mistaken, as it was in 1968. Kennedy people stress how much of a head start the White House has had; they say that winning Iowa will be very difficult. (When it appeared that his surrogate forces would lose Florida, Kennedy said that Iowa would be the first real test.) At this point in the campaign, each side has reason both to play up its chances (so as to attract, or hold, people and donors and psychological edge) and to play them down (so as not to create expectations that are not fulfilled), and at this point both sides are doing both.

In one corner of a large room where eight people are working, in Kennedy's Senate office suite, Carey Parker, Kennedy's chief legislative assistant, is getting together "issues books" for the campaign—black notebooks containing material on Kennedy's record, the issues on which he is likely to be challenged, the issues on which he will challenge Carter. Parker, who is in his mid-forties, is a tall, thin, soft-spoken man; he has worked for Kennedy for ten years and is generally considered one of the most brilliant staff people on Capitol Hill. There have been numerous meetings over the past few weeks to discuss which issues to stress. The consensus is that the main themes are "leadership," the economy, and energy, but the questions are how to develop and illustrate the leadership theme, and how specific to get on the other issues. This is one big challenge of the Kennedy campaign: his differences with Carter on the issues are not enormous; what he has to assert is that he is more likely to get things done. To the extent that it can, the Carter campaign will try to hold Kennedy to the issues, suggesting that there is really no rationale for his candidacy.

The Kennedy campaign plan at this point is to see how the speech formally announcing his candidacy—which is now being worked on—goes, and then to have Kennedy make a speech to dispel the idea that there are not differences between Carter and Kennedy on the economy and to show that Kennedy would be better able to carry out policies than Carter is. The need to demonstrate that one is a better leader is an easier thing to understand than to commit to paper as a strategy. Kennedy's hopes lie in the possibility that people will simply assimilate this idea almost unconsciously. Carter's hopes lie in the possibility that they will not.

Kennedy's people assume that he will be attacked as a big spender, as soft on defense, as someone who talked about national health insurance but could not get a bill on it out of subcommittee (Kennedy and the Carter Administration never agreed on a bill, in part because they didn't want to); the Kennedy people know there will be at least oblique attacks on his character. Ways of handling all these charges are being prepared. Kennedy's voting record is being combed for inconsistencies, on the assumption that a similar exercise is being conducted at the White House. And the Kennedy forces figure that Carter will have his own vulnerability on the matter of shifting positions.

Some people in the Carter camp think that Kennedy made a mistake in his speech in Memphis last December when he criticized Carter's plans to increase military spending—by three percentage points over inflation—and to hold down increases for social programs. Mondale countered the next day with a speech in which he said that an anti-inflation program is also a social program. In the weeks following the Memphis meeting, the Carter Administration found more money for social programs, and Kennedy issued a press release in which he said he approved the Administration's attempt to hold the new budget deficit to less than thirty billion dollars. In September of this year, the political climate surrounding the issue of defense spending having changed, Kennedy joined other senators in voting for a three-percent increase in defense spending for 1980. (The vote was seventy-eight to nineteen. The Senate also went on record, by a much narrower vote, in support of increases in 1981 and 1982 of five percentage points over inflation—a move that Kennedy opposed, as did Carter.) At this point, an early speech is planned to deal with the idea that Kennedy may be "soft on defense."

Carter and Kennedy will, to some degree, be trying to adopt each other's constituencies. For some time, the Carter strategy has been to hew to the middle, figuring that in the final election that is where most of the voters are. Now Carter must do what he can to hold the Party's constituent groups. Kennedy must march toward the center, so as to avoid, the theory goes, winning the nomination only to lose the general election, and he must try to do so without being labelled a hypocrite and losing some of his troops. The Kennedys have always been pragmatic politicians. John Kennedy's Presidential campaign was criticized for being devoid of content. Robert Kennedy was accused of expediency when he talked about "law and order" in the course of the 1968 Indiana primary.

At the end of the day on which I have been to Kennedy's office, I talk to Jody Powell at the White House. He has just come from a meeting to plan the President's speech, scheduled for December 4th, announcing his candidacy for re-election. The President and his aides are described by a number of people as more upbeat than they have been in a long time. It is said that the Kennedy challenge got their juices flowing—that the President emerged from a period of self-pity, which had lasted through much of the summer, of feeling trapped by matters he could not control, and of believing that there was indeed "malaise" in the land and that it was in part his fault.

There is a belief that matters are going better for the Administration in Congress. Carter and his associates are glad to be back to campaigning. One of Carter's advisers says that Kennedy drew out Carter's combativeness, making him a better President and a better candidate. They have felt for some time that Kennedy is more vulnerable than the polls and much of the public commentary have indicated; some of the Carter people have been spelling out sequences of events which had Carter winning. But the pressures of trying to govern—Carter will be judged on his record and is eager to show that he can get things done—and also campaign impinge on the White House. "It's hard," says one person who works there. "You're pursuing the course that has been determined on certain issues, implementing the President's policies, and, on the other hand, trying to anticipate what the opposition is going to do, and develop strategies so that you're not always on the defensive. There's a lot to think about and strategize about and anticipate. A good deal of thought has gone into the elements of what we expect Kennedy's approach and issues are going to be, and how to anticipate those and how to respond." Moreover, the President is facing another round of budget-making decisions that, given current economic restraints and inflation, are going to cause even more agonizing choices than last year's exercise did, and risks of antagonizing constituent groups. Because of the political situation, one of the President's advisers says, this year's budget process is "more poignant."

In my conversation with Powell, he says, "The announcement speech is a forcing mechanism for the basic approach for the whole campaign writ large: What is your basic approach? What do you choose to emphasize? We clearly forced Kennedy to move before he wanted to move. That's a problem for him and also a problem for us. They seem to be wanting to take one more run at the 'stampede' number—that the Carter people had might as well throw up their hands and quit. They tried that in September, and they're having one more shot at it now. Clearly, neither Jane Byrne nor Dick Clark wanted to do what they did the way they did it."

I ask him how he knows this.

"It just makes sense," he replies. "Neither of them looked very good." Powell points out with pleasure a news story that appeared in the Atlanta *Constitution* that day saying that Kennedy had invited the Reverend Martin Luther King, Sr., to his office and asked for his support, and that King, who has supported Carter, declined. Powell says, "I'm sure they've got a few more salted away somewhere. We've got to prevent him from creating the stampede picture over the next two to three weeks. We have one thing that will beat it—the straw poll in Iowa next Saturday." (Carter, as had been expected, won the straw poll, conducted at a dinner in Ames. The results were based on which side got more supporters to buy tickets. The Kennedy people, expecting defeat, played the event down.) Powell continues, "And we have one or two other things in mind. If we can brake the stampede this time, then he's got to have a second act. Right now, he's on a 'Look at me; don't I just sorta make you feel better' sort of thing. There's got to be more to it than that. If they can't get the bandwagon rolling, then he's losing his rationale for running. As long as the myth that the nomination was his for the asking was credible, that's one thing. Then there is no party-splitting fight, because there is no fight. But now he no longer has a rationale—or not the rationale he said."

Powell returns to the subject of the considerations shaping the President's campaign. "What we're really dealing with in its bluntest terms," he says, "is what should the President say about himself. Others could say other things. What contrasts should we draw? Kennedy clearly would like to avoid the drawing of issues. We've done some work on where he might choose to go when he has to deal with specifics. That's one of the reasons I get the feeling they're not as ready as they'd like to be. There are some real inconsistencies, and some important things on which he's endorsed what we've done on energy and the economy. By their saying they don't want to stress issues, but leadership, that not only plays to Kennedy's strength—the strong, forceful Kennedy thing, and the nostalgia thing—but he's also trying to run away from the record. You can try to define the campaign by not having the record an issue, but you can't try to change the record, and that's what they've tried to do, and that guarantees that the record becomes an issue."

I ask Powell if he thinks Kennedy is vulnerable on, for example, defense.

He replies, "He's vulnerable on that basic trust-and-confidence issue. He's one thing today and something else tomorrow, and that's his basic weakness anyway—trust and confidence, all the sort of personal baggage. So why would they give us a chance to go after him on that kind of issue? You have to ask yourself how much of that is the sort of thing you want to get into, and is it a legitimate thing to get into. It clearly is a legitimate thing to deal with someone who is inconsistent, who fuzzes things up, who runs for President and has said things that don't fit together. That goes to a basic question about the person."

Room 318, the Senate Caucus Room, November 1st. Howard Baker is announcing his Presidential candidacy. A large number of Republican senators are here, some because they support him, some out of courtesy—he is, after all, the Senate Minority Leader. Baker tried to be Vice President, beginning in 1968, and he, too, was among those mentioned as a replacement for Agnew, and after Ford passed him over in 1976 he said, "If I ever run for national office again, it won't be for Vice President." Baker, too, has had to move up his timing. He apparently hoped to star in the Senate debate on the SALT treaty and then announce his candidacy, but the SALT treaty has been delayed in getting before the Senate, and he has been advised that he had better get an organization together, that the other candidates are not sitting around.

One of the senators here to witness the announcement is William Cohen, of Maine, who for some time has been promoting the idea that Howard Baker is the moderates' best hope of saving the Party from the conservatives. This Saturday, there will be a "straw poll" in Maine, and Cohen has worked hard to see to it that Baker wins. A number of Presidential candidacies have been launched in the Caucus Room, but this is also, of course, where Baker became famous for his role in the Ervin-committee hearings on Watergate—a role that remains marked by controversy. Some see Baker as gifted at legislative compromise; others wonder whether he has any compass. Today, he is wearing a navy-blue suit, a white shirt, and gold-rimmed glasses. He begins straightforwardly: "I am a candidate for President of the United States." A banner on the marble wall behind him bears his name and his slogan, which is presumably meant to carry a subliminal message: "TOUGH. HONEST. RIGHT FOR THE 80's."

Baker says, "Throughout our history, days of trouble have turned into years of pride through a renaissance of the American spirit." He says that "we will recover in pride—but only if we are honest enough to admit our peril." He says that America has lost its "margin for error." He says that "our superiority in strategic arms . . . is gone." He says that our abundance of energy is gone, that our advantage in productivity and our confidence in the future are gone. Like Bush, he swipes at his opponents without using names. He says, "It is obvious that one of five men will be our next President." Then he says, "Surely we know we cannot withstand still more Washington inexperience." (Carter, Reagan.) He says that "government by ideological reflex, left or right, will not bring the unity we need." (Reagan, Kennedy.) He says that "a President cannot govern without trust and . . . trust never comes from bluster." (Connally.) He says, "And surely we know that we need a leader for tomorrow if the goal is a new generation of confidence." (Baker.) He continues, "So I offer myself for the job with humility, but as well with the personal certainty that I am ready." He lists some more of his qualifications: that he can "give us the confidence to stand tall again;" can "curb useless regulation and spending . . . assure energy independence . . . cope with inflation;" that he can provide tax relief; that he is articulate enough, tough enough, honest enough, compassionate enough, young enough, and experienced enough. He asks that he be judged on his performance on Watergate and in the forthcoming SALT debate, and he makes it definite that he will work to defeat the treaty. Some of the Republican senators withhold their applause when he says this. "I don't honestly know whether I can beat both Jimmy Carter and Teddy Kennedy on this treaty," he says, and he concludes, "Watch me. Judge me. Then come with me. Let's reach for the future and make it ours."

During the question period, he says that his comments were not aimed at any of the other candidates.

He is asked if his opposition to the SALT treaty is politically motivated, and is part of an effort to make amends to the Republican right for having supported the Panama Canal treaties. It is a question to which the response is not likely to be "Yes."

"No," he says. He says, "I'm dedicated to the SALT process," and "I'm convinced we got outbargained on this treaty and it should be amended;" he calls for the sorts of amendments that the Administration says would require renegotiation of the treaty.

He acknowledges that Reagan is the front-runner.

He is asked where he thinks he might be able to beat Reagan.

After a long pause, he says, "I would have to overtake him by the time we're in the middle primaries. There are lots of states out there and I have lots of plans."

On the evening of Sunday, November 4th (one year before the election), at a party where political journalists and campaign strategists are gathered, the Bush man is jubilant—and surprised—that Bush won the Maine straw poll last night, defeating Baker and six others. He says that the Bush campaign will have to get Baker out early, so that someone can become the alternative to Reagan early and that that person won't be Connally. The Connally man agrees with the Bush man that Baker has virtually no organization and that there is feuding among his strategists. The Connally man says that Connally will come within eleven points of the front-runner in New Hampshire, and that that person might be Bush, not Reagan. The Reagan man says that Reagan's biggest challenge as front-runner is to live up to expectations—not to falter—and that the plan is to announce the candidacy relatively late, lie low, win the nomination in about three months, and then take a respite until the final campaign. The Reagan man also suggests that the Reagan people in Maine threw votes to Bush so as to knock out Baker and Connally.

There is also much talk at the party about an interview, scheduled to be aired tonight, that Kennedy has given to CBS. It is already known that in the interview Kennedy stumbled around on some answers, did not seem to have his thoughts together, and provided some unsatisfying ones about Chappaquiddick. One question tonight is whether the interview will turn out to have been a small matter or a major event. Earlier today, the news came that the American Embassy in Teheran had been seized and that a large number of Americans had been taken hostage by students who demanded that the Shah of Iran be returned from the United States to Iran. Tonight, the implications of this incident are not yet clear, nor is there any way of knowing now whether it is an incident or a larger thing.

On Monday, November 5th, two days before Kennedy is to formally announce his candidacy, I have an interview with him over lunch in his office. During the past weekend, he has made a campaign trip to Charleston, West Virginia, and to Buffalo, and today he seems tired and has a slight cold. The wind of opinion has taken a sudden shift, and this week's certainty is that Kennedy will have no easy time of it in trying to defeat Carter.

Much is being made of his performance on the CBS special about him that was on the air last night. It was not to be expected that he would have anything new to say about Chappaquiddick—he cannot by this time—and it had been known all along, and written, that Kennedy often speaks in incomplete sentences. So did his brother Robert. Edward Kennedy has an unusual articulate/inarticulate ratio. In delivering formal speeches, he can be eloquent, and in private conversation he can be barely comprehensible, but he can also be comprehensible in private conversation and in interviews and highly articulate in spontaneous give-and-take on the Senate floor. Now that he is an actual candidate, rather than an abstraction, however, things that had been known about him but perhaps, as one of his colleagues has suggested, brushed aside are viewed differently. The Kennedy camp expected that once he became a candidate his liabilities would receive greater scrutiny, but it is doubtful whether they were prepared for the force and suddenness with which the wind would shift. It was assumed that on

Chappaquiddick the questions would be the same, and that the answers, satisfying or not, would be the same, and that there might be one more round of stories on the subject, and that then, as the campaign got under way, attention would turn elsewhere. One of Kennedy's aides says it is a good thing that now they can take the campaign on the road, have him deal with audiences—which they presume him to be good at—and start shaping and refining the issues, seeing what works, and forcing the White House to respond. "We've been in a kind of sitzkrieg," the aide says.

I ask Kennedy if he is relieved that the campaign is getting under way.

"I've really never second-guessed the decision," he replies. "I made up my mind this summer. I suppose there was a set of circumstances that could have altered it or changed it. I'm actually relieved that the final aspects of the campaign have started. I think I had some consideration that I could remain in the Senate during the debates on windfall profits and SALT, but quite clearly the acceleration of interest in the campaign, and the Administration's actions, and the need to organize, and the firmness in my own mind led me to accelerate the announcement. The issue wasn't Carter's standing in the Party or in the country. There were many people who came and spoke to me about his standing. The issue was the *reason* for that standing—it was the realization, from my own evaluation and discussions, that the standing was because of a failure to come to grips with the concerns of Americans. If his position in the polls had been the result of his setting forth visions for this country and coming to grips and setting forth in a bold and compassionate way, then no matter where he was in the polls I would not have run. I would have stood on the barricades with him."

I ask him whether the campaign is proving rougher than he expected.

"No," he replies. "I knew it would be a hard and difficult campaign. I knew, obviously, that I'd be tested on my positions on issues and my vision for this country as well as on personal matters."

I ask him if he expected so much attention to the last.

He replies, "Yes, I did. I expected that there would be—I also knew that there was nothing new that would develop about those aspects, because, obviously, if there was anything new that would come out, it would end the candidacy effectively."

I ask him how damaging he thinks these personal issues are.

"It's hard for me to make any assessments," he replies.

I ask him if he feels he has a problem in establishing a rationale for his campaign.

"I'll spell that out in my announcement statement, and effectively so," he replies. "That's what the purpose of the statement will be. I think we'll be effective in doing that in the next few weeks and months. I think the differences will be both implicit and explicit in the statement, in running for the Presidency, and will develop in the course of the campaign."

I ask him if he sees a political problem in trying to appeal to the traditional Democratic constituency groups and also trying to win a general election.

"I don't think so," he replies. "The central concern in the country is not only who is bearing the burden of the failure to deal effectively with inflation —the needy and the elderly and the disadvantaged—but I think there is a sense across the spectrum that a vision of America is not being spelled out, that the goals are not being established, that there is not effective coordination of the government and galvanization of the people. Meanwhile, there is talk about 'malaise' of the people—that the problems are too difficult to deal with—from our national leadership. The former analysis is much more consistent not only with the people who are bearing the burden but with the overwhelming majority of the people, who feel that there is a failure.''

I ask Kennedy if he thinks there is a danger that he might raise expectations too high.

He replies, ''I think people are very realistic about the complexity of the problems. People understand there is no magic solution, that no single piece of legislation will solve the problems. What they want is a feeling of progress in which they are involved—that you don't overpromise, that you don't try to solve the problems with massive programs but that you involve them and there is a sense that we're moving along on these issues. And that doesn't exist in this country today.''

Does he, then, I ask, concede that the problems are more complicated now than they were before?

''I don't know that they're more complicated,'' he replies. ''People have been led to believe it. Fighting our way out of the Articles of Confederation into the Constitution. The Depression. I don't think they're necessarily so. They are complicated, but as Americans were involved in other parts of our history and faced up to the challenges, I think they want to be involved today in facing up to the challenges, and they're not being asked to do it. The President's speech in July''—the ''malaise'' speech—''made a significant impact on my thinking about the next four years: the way the President looks at the American people and the future.''

I return to the question of raising expectations too high.

''I think Americans always have responded best when they're challenged,'' Kennedy replies. ''Obviously, the question is how one perceives leadership: obviously, it's releasing the enormous forces in this society who want to be productive and be involved in the solution of the problems. A leader wants to be able to release those energies and play a critical role in setting out the agenda. I think those forces out there—the elderly, youth, church groups—have a synergistic effect on each other, and that moves this nation. The energy is what's involved in moving this country to come to grips with these problems. I don't think that's overpromising; I think it's releasing the energy and the hope to deal with these problems in a positive and constructive way.''

I ask him about the view that there are deeper divisions among groups in this country than ever before, and that each group is getting more sophisticated in finding methods to push its view, thus making consensus on many issues hard to achieve.

"I agree with that," Kennedy replies. "And I think those groups are strengthened. And when you don't have clearly established a vision and sense of direction for this country, then it releases those forces. This country doesn't stand still. One of the failures of this Administration has been to fail to recognize that this country wants to see a President do well, that the Congress wants to see a President do well, and that they want to see someone who can work with the institutions. If there is a perception in the institutions that there is not a direction, not national goals, then the regionalism, narrow self-interest, special interests contaminate the purposes of our society. I think having set out a vision and purpose and goal for this country, it's important to develop a team that can work on these goals and work with the institutions that can impact them. That's not been there. I think the challenge is that American people who have confidence in themselves, confidence in their country, are perhaps cynical and skeptical about their country. The challenge is whether they would have a sense of confidence during the next twelve months that you're able to establish these directions and play a part in setting these goals."

Is he, I ask, talking about some sort of formal goals setting process?

He replies, "I'm not talking just about a listing of programs. I started last week, on my trip, and will address in a serious way the major matters that face this country, and establish the agenda for the next four years—a vision for the country, standards for the nation."

On November 8th, Jerry Brown comes to Washington to announce his Presidential candidacy at the National Press Club, another place from which a number of candidacies have been announced. Brown has almost been forgotten in all the uproar. The polls show him behind both Kennedy and Carter. In what does not appear to be a marvellous public-relations stroke, on the lectern that he stands behind is a poster that says "wow! BROWN NOW." What shows up on the television screens is his head and "wow!" In his statement, he says, "My principles are simple: Protect the earth, serve the people, and explore the universe." NBC shows him being asked what he thinks his chances are. He says that the odds are one in three. "One in three?" he is asked. He replies, "One in three. There's Kennedy and there's Carter and there's me."

CHAPTER 2

Diversion

THE WAY outside developments can whang into a Presidential campaign and spin it around—upending assumptions, calculations, strategies—has certainly been demonstrated by the events in Iran. How lasting the effects will be, and even exactly what they are, remain questions, but it is clear that the end of the crisis will not be the end of the argument over it. Some controversy is guaranteed by the nature of this Presidential campaign—in particular, the set of candidates—and the historical context in which the events occurred. Iran touched a number of raw nerves, produced by cumulative frustrations and by assumptions that such a thing could not have happened if the United States had not been seen to be militarily weak and irresolute and if our foreign policy had not been suffering from a near-fatal case of idealism.

At the same time, the crisis threw into relief several of the questions that were moving to the foreground in any event as the political year 1980 approached. Undoubtedly, this campaign will have its equivalents of former F.B.I. Director Clarence Kelly's window valances, but other kinds of issues that were in the background in 1976 were becoming inescapable: what the lessons of Vietnam really are, what it is within our power to do, what the function of military strength is, how to come to grips with energy realities. There was now dramatic evidence that nations with nowhere near our military strength will make weapons of commodities that they hold and we need; that there are situations that render our missiles meaningless and cannot be fixed by a dozen men in trenchcoats; that our dependence on foreign supplies of oil is literally dangerous.

Even as President Carter's political fortunes rose, largely—not entirely, the White House would argue—as a result of his handling of the situation in Teheran, it seemed clear that other issues that had been pushed out of the political discussion, such as the economy and the President's overall record, would return. And it seemed likely that even if the hostages were got out alive Carter would be subject to cross fire on Iran once the crisis was over. From one side, there would be more questions about why the Shah was allowed into the United States in the first place (he was admitted for surgery in New York in late October, and he is now in Panama), and, going further back in history, about why we had supported the Shah for so long and become so closely identified with him, and even about the purposes and consequences of our role in the overthrow of Mohammed Mossadegh, the last elected leader of Iran, and the reinstallation of the Shah on the throne. From the other side would come questions about why we had not supported the Shah more firmly, and why we did not take tougher actions after the hostages were seized. And once the problem of the hostages was resolved, there could be a whole new row over what further actions the United States should take against Iran. At the White House, the general belief was that if the President succeeded in getting the hostages out alive it would ill behoove some critics—for which read Edward Kennedy—to quibble over the details of how the whole mess had come about. "That would be seen as sour grapes," Jody Powell said in a conversation I had with him in mid-December. As for the criticism that would come from the Republicans, White House people said, that would be applicable only in the general election—and this was not the problem at the moment.

When I talked to Jody Powell, he was eager to point out that the President's rise in the polls was not simply a result of his handling of the Iranian crisis. "Clearly, up to now, from a political standpoint, the way the President has conducted himself has had a favorable impact, and at the same time its impact on how it affects us vis-à-vis Kennedy has been overstated," he said. "The press lays it all to Iran. You don't have to be too bright to look back and see that that won't cut." He then reached for a report of an ABC News poll of Democratic state chairmen which indicated that the greatest rise in support for Carter, as opposed to Kennedy, among that group—from that of a slight minority to a substantial majority—occurred before the hostages were seized.

I have also heard the theory at the White House that the Iranian crisis will have a lasting effect, because while voters do not necessarily expect a President to be "Presidential" all the time, they want him to be so some of the time, and until Iran, Carter had been in danger of failing to appear so any of the time. Some senior advisers to the President were concerned that White House aides might be drawing too much comfort from the President's sudden good political fortune. One adviser told me, "People are getting too cocky here. Too many people are going around with smiles on their face. A lot of us are saying Iran is going to be over; it could turn to dust; Kennedy is going to get his act together—soon." Some advisers had mixed feelings about the late-December polls that showed Carter well ahead of Kennedy. They took comfort from indications that Kennedy's own problems contributed to the disparity; they worried about the burdens put on Carter now that he was no longer the underdog. But they also found the shifting fortunes advantageous as they went about the business of trying to peel off support of local politicians from Kennedy, organizing delegate slates, and raising money.

One could also sense in the White House more than a little tension—an awareness that a single misstep or misstatement could bring the roof down on everybody's head. Powell and Hodding Carter, the State Department spokesman, confer daily about what the press—and the world—will be told. Each statement by the press officers is a potential foreign-policy pronouncement; each reaction to each statement by whoever appears to be speaking for whatever group in Iran must be carefully measured. Powell told me, "The potential impact of misstatements is much more serious than is normally the case. The nuance game gets more serious and deadly with the passage of time. The press and the public are all past the one-two-three-fours of it. Take this thing about Iran's having an international tribunal. Having taken previous positions about show trials, the question is, Does this or does this not fall into that category? We may not know and the press does or does not know, but come the end of the day, when the networks and the newspapers have their deadlines, there is likely to be an attempt to force an answer."

There was also some question as to how long, in any event, the President would be able to capitalize on the political fortune the Iranian crisis had brought him. At what point would he seem not measured in his response but weak? At what point would he appear to be exploiting the event? At what point would people want to hear more about other issues that are bothering them? As the crisis dragged on, the widely accepted moratorium on criticism of his actions was likely to expire. Carter is not the first President to be tempted to play Commander-in-Chief politics, but the exercise can become a bit obvious. On weekends during the crisis, the President and Mrs. Carter, according to a White House aide, have been making at least sixty calls each to potential supporters in the early-caucus and early-primary states. Many calls have also been made during the week, when there was time. From these calls and from other methods of testing public opinion, the White House concluded as the year ended that the public's patience was running out.

Washington is a fickle place, and as the fortunes of the Democratic rivals shifted, however temporarily, politicians and other investors in power adjusted. Some politicians were less eager than before to have Kennedy make appearances with them. More people turned up at the White House annual Christmas ball for Congress than had in recent years. This gave members of Congress an opportunity to shake the President's hand and then tell their constituents that they had been to the White House to see the President, and that he was holding up well in the crisis. One White House aide says, "They like to pass responsibility to the President in a crisis. They've been amazingly supportive, because the American people are supportive. But they'll be quick to cut when it's over." Frank Moore, the President's assistant for congressional liaison, who has come under a fair amount of criticism from Congress, said to me in mid-December, "You go up to the Hill now, it's like you're a rock star. People are coming up to you—they all have a message for you to give the President. They say they were talking to a Rotary Club and praised the President and people cheered. Of course, next week they may dodge you. They've read the polls, and they say, 'Of course, we've supported you all along.' " During the period just after it became clear that Kennedy would challenge the President, and the common assumption was that it was all over for Carter, three wives of White House aides compared notes and found that in each case their invitations had dropped substantially. Sure enough, Carter's rise in the polls arrested the decline in their social lives.

Kennedy's comments in a television interview in early December criticizing the Shah and saying that he should not be given permanent residence in the United States, and the reaction to them, were examples both of the kinds of unanticipated things that can happen in campaigns and of the way they can be magnified out of proportion. The White House, of course, made the most of Kennedy's statement, and on the day after he made it there seemed to be few Administration officials or Republican candidates who were not before television cameras deploring what Kennedy had said. Lost in all the noise was the context in which he said it: after a series of answers in which he restated his support of the President's handling of the crisis, he made the remarks in answer to a question about whether the Shah should be permitted to remain in the United States. Ronald Reagan had just said that he should be. Also, the Shah had just been moved to Lackland Air Force Base, in Texas, and the President had declined comment on whether he would be allowed to stay in this country.

Kennedy apparently thought that his answers would be taken as a whole, which was a misjudgment. But whatever the wisdom, timing, or impact of his remarks, the amount of fuss they stirred was a phenomenon in itself. Such things have happened before: in 1967, when George Romney explained a shift of position on the Vietnam War by saying that he had been "brainwashed" by United States generals and diplomats during a trip there; in 1972, when Edmund Muskie, exhausted and upset over attacks on his wife, wept before the press in New Hampshire; and in 1976, when Gerald Ford said, "There is no Soviet domination of Eastern Europe." The press lands on such statements and gives them almost as much importance, sometimes as much, as everything else the candidate has been saying. Sometimes the incident is interpreted as an example of a fundamental characteristic of the candidate (and sometimes this is accurate), but it is fairly difficult to get through a campaign without making some slip, and much of the press watches for, and even welcomes, such an event. It's big news, and grounds for extensive analysis. A few words can alter the outcome of a Presidential campaign.

Kennedy's people, of course, put the best interpretation they could on the event, saying that when the subsequent debate over the whole issue took place Kennedy would be seen as having been ahead of the others on the question of the Shah. But they were frustrated by the extended crisis and eager for the subject to change. The Kennedy campaign was premised on the idea that Carter was not a leader; then, of all things, just as the campaign began, he was being hailed as one. Peter Edelman, who is in charge of issues at Kennedy's Washington campaign headquarters, said to me in mid-December, "With all the problems in getting this campaign off the ground, it's very clear that the major factor in the polls is Iran. We all know that these things are extremely evanescent. There are very serious questions that are going to be asked when this is over. It's quite possible it will turn out not to have had an effect. It's also possible that Carter will galvanize himself, but I find it very hard to believe that the man who has been so ineffective during almost three-fourths of his term of office is going to find his definition, his style, and leave his mark on the American people."

In December, the anxiety at the Kennedy headquarters was apparent— not just over what Iran was doing to the campaign but also over what Kennedy himself was doing to it. There was a morale problem: people who had joined up thinking they were about to ride the crest of a wave were adrift. They found themselves not being greeted triumphantly but having to explain, defend. Kennedy himself seemed to have been thrown off stride. Even some of his partisans noticed that he was not performing up to his capacity on the campaign trail. And each failure to live up to his prior billing was given great significance. A man who had become accustomed during his entire career to receiving praise for his political acumen and ability suddenly, according to press reports, could do nothing right. A man who used to be able to bring crowds to their feet, suddenly, it was said, could hardly deliver a speech. Each slip of the tongue was reported, which made him more self-conscious, which led to further slips of the tongue, which increased the reporting of such incidents. Whereupon, at the urging of his staff, he began to read his speeches, which led to wooden delivery and loss of contact with his audiences.

Even a candidate who starts out confident can be shaken by such things. And virtually each day Kennedy was faced with what was probably the most painful criticism of all: that he was not as good as his brothers. All his life, it seemed, he had been measured against them, and now, in the largest and most visible test, he was held to be falling short. This could not help his confidence. One thing Kennedy cares about a great deal is his legacy. One theory about the problems he had at the beginning of the campaign is that he is, simply, tense about running for the Presidency, discomfited by the pressure to live up to the memories of his brothers.

When I stop by the Kennedy headquarters, a former Cadillac showroom at Twenty-second and N streets, campaign workers—numbering about seventy-five—are going about their business. The large plate-glass windows that used to display automobiles are covered over with blue paper on which is lettered in white "Kennedy '80!" The lettering seems deliberately amateurish, to give the look of spontaneity. To enter the headquarters, one goes around to a side door and through a room where cars used to be driven in, and in the reception area, on a door leading to a stairway, is a sign saying "Insurance & Settlement. Caution—Step Up."

The campaign organization fills two floors. Partitions are still being constructed, and campaign workers are still introducing themselves to each other. Outside, a truck from Metropolitan Office Furniture is delivering furniture. On the second floor, workers in the scheduling office are yelling at each other, but then schedulers are always yelling at each other. Also on the second floor are two rooms where people have begun to work on delegate selection: one room contains six people who collect information from various regions of the country on a daily basis and feed it to the people in the other room, who help make the strategic decisions. Another office holds the people handling the advance work for Kennedy's appearances. In one room, I find Dick Clark, sitting in front of a large map of Iowa. Downstairs, in a section of what was once one large showroom, are people handling finances (including the complexities of complying with the federal campaign-finance laws), two pressrooms, rooms where volunteers work, and offices for the issues staff. The floors are linoleum, and the walls are cream-colored except for patches of green that seem to have escaped the last paint job.

Carl Wagner, the director of field operations, has put together a calendar of the day-by-day actions necessary to meet the delegate-selection laws of the various states from January until the Party Convention, in August; it is twenty pages long. There are actions that must be taken in almost two-thirds of the states in January and February. For example, the Pennsylvania primary is not until late April, but delegate slates have to be filed in January. So while the outside world focusses on Iowa and New Hampshire, Wagner and others must focus on those states plus Maine, Minnesota, Massachusetts, Florida, Georgia, Alabama, California, Connecticut, South Carolina, South Dakota, North Carolina, Wisconsin, Kansas, Vermont, Nebraska, Ohio, Maryland, Rhode Island, and Illinois. The top campaign officials must settle the problems that arise constantly as people demand decisions on who is going to be in charge in a certain state and as people take offense at these decisions. As I tour the headquarters, campaign officials, insistently and somewhat uneasily, say things like "It's all coming together now."

Stephen Smith, Kennedy's brother-in-law and campaign chairman, sits in a large office on the second floor. Smith has a taut, wiry body and speaks in a low voice. He talks in a sort of stream, and often looks down or away, so it is sometimes hard to hear him; upon request, he will repeat in a louder voice what he has just said, and then return to his low monotone. "It's about ready to start working here," he says when I stop in to see him. "We need to flesh things out, but now at least we're all under one roof." He says there was criticism at the outset of John Kennedy's campaign, in 1960, and of Robert Kennedy's, in 1968, and he talks of the enormously increased difficulty of starting up a campaign now, under the new rules. He also says, "The Iranian thing has had a great impact, obviously."

As Smith talks, a television set in his office shows Carter speaking to a group in the East Room of the White House. Smith points to the set and refers to "the terrific ability of the Presidency to affect a campaign." He says, "Frankly, Lyndon Johnson was supposed to be pretty heavy-handed, but I've never seen anything like what's going on now, with the way they're using federal funds to affect the campaign. Senator Kennedy's candidacy has caused several cities and states to get funds. I think all those people are very appreciative. Things that wouldn't have been done are being done in a very prompt and generous fashion."

Smith says this with a thin smile. "In the end, the basic question about the Iranian crisis is whether it was necessary for the Shah to be here. Obviously, there will be a rather careful examination of all that. I don't know why he's here. Do you? At the same time, the economy is not good; people are concerned about inflation and unemployment. The attitude of the business world toward Edward Kennedy is the same that they had toward John Kennedy in '60 and Robert Kennedy in '68." Smith talks about hiring more people—especially blacks and Chicanos—and says that every time a name is mentioned in print the Carter people try to hire that person. He says that things are coming along well in Iowa and New Hampshire. "We're out in the field in a pretty good way in a short period of time," he says. "I don't think there's another figure in the country who could have put it together in a month. The problems are the product of what I've just described. Who else goes out from a dead stop with fifty or sixty reporters along? It's gotten a focus nobody else has gotten. John Kennedy couldn't make a farm speech in Wisconsin in 1960. It was painful. We've got a candidate who had to deal with too much too quickly."

One theory held among Republicans is that Kennedy's remarks about the Shah were a boon to Ronald Reagan. According to this reasoning, Reagan was vulnerable for having suggested that the Shah should be permitted to remain in the United States, and in the furor over Kennedy's remarks people simply forgot about what Reagan had said. There is also the theory that, at least in the short term, the Iranian crisis helped Reagan by pushing him offstage, which is essentially where John Sears, his campaign manager, prefers him to be. The extent to which Reagan has been able to stay ahead while staying behind the scenes has frustrated the other Republican candidates' camps. "The clock is running, and he's able to hold on to his lead," the manager of another candidate said to me recently. Members of the other camps had looked forward to Reagan's coming under scrutiny in the first weeks after he formally announced his candidacy, in mid-November. And Reagan had begun to fumble: he had trouble explaining his new idea for a "North American accord" between the United States, Canada, and Mexico, and seemed uninformed about aid to New York City. But then along came Iran, and Kennedy.

David Keene, who is the political director of George Bush's campaign, feels that Iran has worked to benefit Bush most, in a couple of ways. For one thing, he says, as the most recent of a series of international crises, Iran will cause the voters to focus on the candidates' credentials in the fields of foreign affairs and defense, and, Keene argues, the C.I.A. has returned to good repute.

Keene also argues that the combination of Iran, Bush's defeat of Howard Baker in a Maine straw vote in early November, and Connally's poor showing and Bush's good showing (compared with expectations, which is what counts) in a Florida straw vote in mid-November—Connally came in a far second to Reagan and not very far ahead of Bush—worked to Bush's benefit. "The last visible political events in 1979 were Bush victories," Keene said to me over lunch. "And Iran has not hurt that, and momentum in politics is based on the last thing you did. Of course, it could all collapse in January. But there has been no heavy political coverage since those victories, because Iran has dominated the public mind. If there were a straw poll tomorrow, no one would pay much attention to it. And since it's harder to get people to pay attention, it's harder for people like Baker and Connally to play catch-up."

Keene, who is thirty-four, is baby-faced and pleasant. He was the national chairman of Young Americans for Freedom, he has worked for Spiro Agnew and James Buckley, and he was a regional coordinator of Reagan's 1976 campaign. I asked him what sort of post-Iran debate he foresaw.

"Even if Carter gets the hostages out alive, there will still be an attack on him," he replied. "There will be a great temptation for Republicans to do that. Exactly what happens will depend on a reading of the public. The public may be tired of it. But there will probably be a lot of talk from the candidates once it's over about how did we get into it, how can we avoid Irans. And, necessarily, whoever gives the speech will have to put part of the blame on Carter. The Republican argument is probably going to be couched in the larger question, Why is the United States powerless in an increasingly chaotic world? I don't necessarily agree that that's the right question, but I think it's the one that will be asked. The basic question is going to be, Did American foreign policy in one way or another lead to it? That can come from the left or the right. Did support for the Shah lead to it, or did failure to support the Shah lead to it? I think Carter is going to get it from both sides."

I asked Keene if he thought that the argument that the Shah could have been maintained in power by the United States was a persuasive one.

"I don't think the argument that he could have been maintained in power is salable in that way," he replied. "But as the world becomes more chaotic I think people are more willing to choose among unattractive alternatives. Some of the naïveté is gone. The old ways of making choices are gone: the old bipolar world, where the Russians were the bad guys and we were the good guys; or the human-rights standard, where this guy put too many people in jail, so he's bad; or is the ruler a left-winger or a right-winger? The human-rights standard is not valid anymore. It was used to pick on our allies rather than their allies, because we could bring pressure on ours.

"In the case of Iran, we said the Shah was a bad man who tortured people and had a secret police, all of which was true, but, on the other hand, the Shah was overthrown in part because he was too liberal and his modernization assailed the old religious bastions. The irony was you'd see the Iranian coeds demonstrating here in favor of the Ayatollah and against the Shah because he was oppressive, but if they went home they'd be told to put on a veil. There's that, on the one hand—that what appears to be true turns out not to be true. It becomes clear that we withdraw our support from the Shah because he is a bad man and nobody wins. The Iranians didn't win, the coeds didn't win, and we certainly didn't win. And the whole world is destabilized." (An argument is also made that by encouraging the Shah to hang on as long as he did we made it more difficult for moderates to take his place, but that is another subject.)

"The point is, it's all muddled," Keene continued. "It's not ideological. The world we are entering is more dangerous than the old world, partly because there are lunatics out there. The Soviets were bad people but were rational. They have a world view and a goal that may be antithetical to our interests, but it's like chess players moving their pawns in a very dangerous chess game. There are only so many moves. But an ayatollah will upset the chessboard."

I asked Keene how politicians could argue convincingly that all this could be brought under control.

"I'm not sure I know," he replied. "In fact, I'm certain I don't. But if you're dealing with a public that has reached certain conclusions about what a dangerous world it is, they're more likely to face unattractive trade-offs. We've swung in recent years from the overblown realpolitik of the Kissinger period to the naïve human rights of the Carter period, and it seems that neither is appropriate in this particular kind of world."

But, I asked him, wouldn't the candidates simplify these questions?

"I don't think they can successfully do so," he replied. "I don't think the public sees the world as a place where the simple things work anymore. If you look at the poll data on Iran, you see no consensus on what ought to be done. That's why Carter has been able to get the unity he has. If there had been a substantial percentage wanting to send in the Marines, he couldn't have held it."

I asked him if he thought it was a salable proposition that Iran happened because we are weak.

He replied, "No, I don't think they'd be able to sell to the public that this all happened because we're weak—it's precisely the madman who can tie up a giant. Or that a SWAT team would be able to prevent it. Or that if we doubled the defense budget no one would take hostages. I don't think people are willing to buy that."

In mid-December, John Connally arrived in Washington and had breakfast with a group of reporters. Connally has a number of things to be frustrated about at the moment: his campaign is generally said to be going nowhere, which does not help his campaign get anywhere; the Iran crisis has forced him to keep quiet about the sort of thing he normally would have something to say about. He has raised a great deal of money—eight million dollars, more than any other Republican candidate—but his problem is how to turn that cash into popular support. Connally is a proud man and, it seems, a congenitally confident man. When things don't go right for him, it just doesn't seem right. At the breakfast, Connally is, as usual, well dressed, coiffed, and manicured.

He is asked if he is still certain that Kennedy will be the Democratic nominee.

He smiles and replies, "I must say my confidence has been shaken a little bit. I'm impressed by the President's rise in the polls. But I don't think I'm deceived by it, any more than y'all are. It's a reflection of support for the President as a result of patriotism in the country." He says that once the crisis over the hostages ends, there will be "the spectre of inflation, high interest rates, and all the rest," and a drop in the President's standing in the polls. But while Carter is dealing with the hostage problem, "I'm certainly going to support him," Connally says. "I'm not going to criticize or second-guess or suggest alternative modes of action." He says that he has been critical of Senator Kennedy's remarks about the Shah.

He is asked what he thinks our approach to foreign policy should be once Iran is resolved.

He replies, "I think we are going to have to take a different look at it. I don't know what my views would be. I haven't had enough time to look at it." This is odd. Connally is usually a man of definite opinions. "I don't know what my views would be. I haven't had enough time to think about it, time to confer with people about it. But let me put it this way. Our foreign policy has been based on military strength. I don't think that's going to be sufficient. We're going to have to have a foreign policy that's broader than that. We're going to have to rebuild our military strength. We're going to have to rebuild our economic strength, re-establish the soundness of the dollar. It has to be based on political and psychological factors that emphasize our system of government and our way of life in contrast with the Soviet Union and the Communist way of life.

"We're going to have to quit having fear of saying things because the

Communists might not like it. Take the boat people fleeing Vietnam. We don't ask why they're boat people. We don't talk about the atrocities. We don't say the Communists did it. We just ask other people to help. We're going to have to make up our minds that we're going to believe in the system and defend the system, and we can't let the Communists outmaneuver us in the developing nations of the world." He says that if he were in the Senate today he would not vote for the SALT agreement. He defends a speech he gave in October on the Middle East; the speech set off a furor, essentially because he appeared to make a connection between our interest in defending Israel and our interest in obtaining oil. Now Connally says, "I never suggested we ought to equate oil to Israel," and he says that he did not call for a Palestinian state. It is always a problem when a candidate has to do a lot of explaining and defending of something he has said.

Then Connally says that he is going to renounce the use of federal matching funds for his campaign. Acceptance of such funds places a limit on the amount that can be spent in each state—and such is Connally's political condition that he must spend a lot, early—and also on the overall amount that can be spent. Connally says that he is opposed to the federal campaign-finance laws—as someone who can raise a lot of money, he can afford to be —and as he denounces them agitatedly he gets confused about what they are. He talks about the fact that he has been unable to purchase time from the networks for television appearances, except for two five-minute spots from CBS. He is clearly exercised. "How are you going to compete in this area?" he asks. "How are you going to compete against Ronald Reagan? He's been running for ten years and spent about twenty-five million dollars." He adds, "I anticipate that I'm going to beat him in some primaries before Illinois. In order to be credible, I'm going to have to beat him." The Connally strategy is now pinned on defeating Reagan somewhere in the South.

A reporter asks Connally about reports that he is upset about having been unable to cut into Reagan's lead in 1979.

"I'm not disappointed, but it's clear he's far, far ahead," he says. "I thought if we could spend about a million dollars on TV in October and November we could cut into his lead. We haven't been able to do that, so I'm frustrated. But we have gained some—in Iowa, New Hampshire, and so on. But I am disappointed—and will be until I'm running Number One in every state in the union." He says that Reagan "has created an image in the minds of people that he thinks how they do." He goes on, "They think he does. They don't know what he really thinks, except on the Panama Canal."

He returns to the question of Carter and the polls. "The polls have changed, but it's basically an aberration," he says. "It's a surge of patriotism of the American people toward a President in a time of crisis. That's all it is. I think it's obvious the American people were dissatisfied with the President. I think once the Iran crisis is over he'll be right back to where he was. Maybe I'll be critical of him, but I don't think maliciously so or in a partisan fashion.''

For the most part, Congress has proceeded routinely during the Iran crisis; there has been little else it could do. However, Iran has affected Congress's agenda. By the time the hostages were taken, no one was expecting Senate action on the SALT II treaty to be completed by the end of 1979, but Iran created an atmosphere in which Senate leaders did not even dare bring the treaty up. It was not that there was any logical connection between SALT and Iran, but the mood created by the crisis made it seem unpropitious to bring up an agreement whose prospects were in doubt in any event.

This was the second time the treaty had been pushed back on the calendar by an external event—the first being the discovery of Soviet troops, or whatever, in Cuba in August—and there is, of course, no guarantee that some other unpleasantness will not occur in 1980. The treaty's supporters had hoped to get consideration out of the way before the election year. Not that SALT would ever be quarantined from politics, but at least the political ingredient might be diluted. One Senate aide says, ''There is practically no one in the Senate who would be hurt by voting against SALT. There are several who might feel they would be hurt by voting for it. The closer the vote to election time, the greater the fear.'' There was also a concern among SALT supporters that the Administration itself would be more distracted in an election year.

Both SALT supporters and opponents are uncertain about the treaty's prospects once it is brought up; some supporters tend to give the most optimistic ''counts'' to the press. Both sides have been organizing for the battle for some time, and some supporters took heart when Robert Byrd, the Senate Majority Leader, assumed a major role in setting strategy. With his approval, a committee of Senate staff members has been organized to devise strategies and arguments. The Administration's effort to win votes for the treaty by coming forward with an increase in the defense budget which three months earlier it said was not necessary had questionable results. Those whom the increases were designed to mollify turned out to be not so mollified: as people in such positions often do, they raised their price. There remained questions about what, exactly, all the new equipment and so on that the Administration was now proposing was for. (Very little of it had to do with the strategic balance.) Among the items included in the increase was additional money for a Rapid Deployment Force, but the Administration did not make clear what sorts of contingencies this force might be used for.

In briefing reporters on the new defense budget, Zbigniew Brzezinski, the President's national-security adviser, said that it marked the end of the ''Vietnam complex.'' It was unclear what policy was to follow. The delays changed the psychological atmosphere surrounding the treaty: if SALT was unimportant enough to be put off for so long, and other issues took precedence, perhaps it was not so important. And to some supporters the treaty had become so costly in terms of increases in weaponry that it seemed less and less worth the fight. (The problem for them with giving up on the treaty on those grounds was that the treaty's defeat would probably lead to still greater increases in spending for defense.)

And while Congress got fairly far along on the President's energy program by the year's end, no one seriously argued that the program would equip the United States to deal with the potential losses of supplies that now seemed more possible than before.

Congress had planned to adjourn from December 21 to January 21, but then arranged to be technically, if not actually, in session, to avoid the appearance of unseemliness by being absent so long at such a time. This maneuver was also designed to head off any attempt by the President to be "Presidential" by calling them back into session.

As the Christmas season approached, the President participated in the traditional Christmas activities and other formal functions at the White House. At the annual lighting of the Christmas tree, the President lit only the top light on the big tree, saying that the rest of the lights would be turned on when the hostages were returned. The mansion, with its Christmas decorations, was particularly beautiful; it looked like the kind of place that might have been worth all the effort that Jimmy and Rosalynn Carter had made to get there. There was no way of knowing what the next Christmas there would be like for them. The President, for all his surface cheer, seemed a trapped man, his fate, like that of the Americans held in Teheran, hostage to the unpredictable, conflicting, confusing voices from Iran. Each time an official in Teheran said something vaguely encouraging, the official lost his job or was overruled by a statement from Ayatollah Khomeini, in Qum. It was perhaps the strangest form of diplomatic negotiation any government had ever tried to carry on, and the frustration of our own officials was obvious.

At the annual Christmas party for the press, on a Thursday evening, as the President and Mrs. Carter stood in a long receiving line, the President occasionally voiced optimism that the hostages would be released soon. Arrangements had just been completed that day for the Shah to leave the United States for Panama, but the news did not break until the next weekend. On Sunday, the Iranian Foreign Minister said that the Shah's departure made possible the release of some of the hostages by Christmas and that he hoped none of them would be tried, and on Monday Khomeini appeared to contradict him. That evening, the President held a state dinner for Margaret Thatcher, the British Prime Minister, and, despite the strain and disappointment—his emotion showed as the Prime Minister, in her toast, referred to the hostages—went through with a festive evening that ended with the singing of Christmas carols in the East Room.

CHAPTER 3

Kennedy _____

WHEN EDWARD M. KENNEDY set off for a week's campaigning in Iowa in early January, he and his closest advisers understood that far more than the outcome of the state's Democratic precinct caucuses was at stake. By then, it was recognized within his campaign organization, despite what was being said publicly, that what was at risk politically was not only the result in Iowa but, perhaps, the entire enterprise of the Kennedy challenge to President Carter.

On the day Kennedy left for Iowa, one of his advisers told me that, despite what was being said publicly, before long the Kennedy campaign could collapse. Among other things, it was running out of money. If Kennedy did poorly in Iowa, contributors were not likely to be lining up. Politicians whose support had been expected were holding back. Moreover, the Kennedy people knew, on the basis of their own soundings in Maine and their poll in New Hampshire, where the next contests would be held, that it was not at all certain Kennedy would do so well in those states. "We could easily lose Maine and New Hampshire—why not?" the adviser said. And at the moment Kennedy was in terrible trouble in Illinois, whose primary, the first of the large industrial states' contests, would be held on March 18th. As for Iowa, the Kennedy organization's own poll there, taken in December and being kept secret, showed Kennedy losing by almost three to one among those who said they planned to attend the Iowa precinct caucuses.

The caucuses were the first of four steps in choosing the state's fifty delegates to the Democratic National Convention; the fourth step will not come until mid-June. As Kennedy began his Iowa swing, one of his advisers told me bluntly that it was possible Kennedy would lose to Carter there by two to one—a dire prediction, and one that turned out to be accurate. What the people in Kennedy's organization were saying publicly was that their goal was simply to hold Carter to less than fifty percent of the vote. It was assumed, incorrectly, that the size of the vote for "Uncommitted" and for Jerry Brown would make fifty percent impossible. They wanted people to accept the premise they put forth: that, given international events, and given Carter's refusal to join the political debate, and given Carter's history of ties to Iowa, this was the best that Kennedy could be expected to do. They said that Kennedy would do well in the large industrial states, whose primaries would begin in the spring, and that, after all, "it will be a long year." But in fact they knew there was some question whether the campaign would make it to those industrial states.

Within the Kennedy organization, there was an assumption that the protective bubble around Carter—a bubble produced by the crises in Iran and Afghanistan—would burst, but there was concern that it would not burst in time. (On December 27th the Soviet Union invaded Afghanistan. The following day, the President cancelled the debate, sponsored by the Des Moines *Register,* scheduled for early January.) And, for all their complaints about the difficulty of joining issue with Carter, members of the Kennedy camp also recognized that questions about Kennedy's personal life were having far greater impact on the campaign than had been anticipated. "Chappaquiddick and the whole moral question have hurt him very badly with the American public, and maybe irreparably," one of his advisers said to me in early January. "It isn't that they don't think he would be a better leader than Carter—our polls indicate that even a lot of people voting for Carter feel that he would be. They're just bothered by these other things. They don't trust his judgment. Everybody underestimated it—inside, outside the campaign. People thought it was going to be a big problem, but they didn't see it as a determining factor. It may already be fatal."

Another problem for Kennedy was that the Kennedy campaign's polls indicated that the public did not react well to personal attacks on President Carter: that people believed that Carter was a decent man who was trying hard. The feeling within the Kennedy campaign was that some of Kennedy's direct attacks on Carter had misfired. This raised the question of what, exactly, Kennedy could say. And it was also recognized that Kennedy had yet to establish a rationale for his candidacy. The original rationale had, of course, been—as of last summer—that Carter was on the ropes, his poll ratings at an all-time low for any President, and his Administration in chaos. Now, with Carter doing very well in the polls, Kennedy had to establish a new rationale. He also had to find coherent themes for his campaign. And he had to pull himself together as a campaigner. The Kennedy campaign had a good organization in place in Iowa, but more was needed in order to motivate people to actually go to the precinct caucuses to vote for him. At the time Kennedy left for Iowa, the motivation was not believed to be there. It was up to Kennedy, through what he did that week, to provide it.

But almost lost in all the talk about organization and themes and polls and who-is-going-to-win-where was the high drama of what this effort was really all about: a fight for enormous stakes, the Presidency of the United States. Not just any fight but one between two men who had everything to lose; between a man who had scrapped from out of nowhere to gain the Presidency and one about whom it had long been assumed that the position was his for the asking; between a man of modest origins and an American prince; a struggle of Shakespearean dimensions. Other men could run for the Presidency and lose and go their ways, with whatever degree of disappointment or bitterness. But Edward Kennedy, the last of the Kennedy brothers, was, in making this challenge, laying on the line a legend, and a legacy for which he felt responsible. Once he had decided to run, he had opened himself to the most painful public scrutiny and to a contest that was far more difficult than had been imagined. He and his rival had already undergone an extraordinary reversal in the political standings. His failure, if it came to that, would be of a different magnitude, historically and personally, from that of others. It was with all of this hanging over him that Kennedy set off for Iowa.

The theory behind Kennedy's swing through Iowa, which was to last six days and was his fifth trip there since the campaign began, was that he should go not only to the largest cities, where he had already spent some time, but also to the medium-sized cities and to some of the rural areas around the larger cities. The belief was that the Kennedy campaign was well organized in the cities (it had backing from the United Auto Workers and the International Association of Machinists) and that Carter was stronger in the rural and small-town areas, which account for about half the precinct delegates, and therefore Kennedy had to try to cut into Carter's rural strength and then give one last boost to the organizations in the cities.

Kennedy was scheduled to return only one more day after this week: his campaign officials wanted him (and the numerous members of his family who have been in the state) out of the way, so that they could devote their energies to organizing; the one day was to consist simply of stops at airports, where he would appear before the media. This week, Kennedy was scheduled to make twenty stops in all. On his previous trips, he spent nine days in Iowa and made twenty-three stops. In 1976, only thirty-eight thousand five hundred Democrats, or seven percent of the eligible Democratic voters, attended the precinct caucuses. As it happened, "Uncommitted" received the most votes, but Carter came in second and claimed victory, the press went along, and Carter was on his way.

Carter's discovery of the potential of the Iowa precinct caucuses—until then largely ignored by the candidates and the press—started a whole new industry. (This year, the turnout was two and a half times what it was in

1976.) Iowa may send to the Democratic Convention only fifty of the three thousand three hundred and thirty-one delegates—about a sixth as many as New York will send—but these precinct caucuses have become important because people think they are important. Moreover, when Kennedy realized that the unofficial organization backing him would lose a non-binding preliminary caucus vote in Florida last October, he said, apparently without giving it much consideration, that Iowa—where the "Draft Kennedy" movement was strong—would be the first real test. After a while, he stopped saying that.

On Wednesday, January 9th, the third day of Kennedy's swing through Iowa, he is touring small towns south of Des Moines. Yesterday, he travelled north of the capital. Today began in Indianola, a town of about ten thousand people, with a stop at the Crouse Café and then at a farm. In the county in which Indianola is situated, four hundred and eighty-seven people participated in the 1976 precinct caucuses, and it will elect 1.27 percent of the state's delegates to the National Convention. Kennedy is being accompanied by his wife, Joan, and their two eldest children—Kara, who is nineteen, and Teddy, who is eighteen. As Kennedy, dressed in a gray tweed overcoat, and his wife, dressed in a bright blue-white-and-red plaid coat, toured the farm, which was covered with two inches of snow, Kennedy asked polite questions about the age of a combine, about hog prices, about how much hogs eat and where their feed comes from. He didn't seem very comfortable with this small talk, but it is essential, of course, to show an interest in farming here, and such visits also provide "visuals" for TV.

After meeting in the white clapboard farmhouse for a half-hour with about six farm couples, Kennedy came out and talked briefly to the press. He has opposed President Carter's move, which the President announced in a television address last Friday evening, to impose an embargo on the sale of grain to the Soviet Union in retaliation against the Soviet invasion of Afghanistan. (The invasion occurred just when the Iranian crisis was beginning to drag on in a way that might have caused people to become bored with it or impatient with the President's handling of it. And, at least so far, Carter is the recipient of a kind of wartime support in the Afghanistan crisis. He has called the invasion "the most serious foreign-policy crisis since World War II.") Iowa would, of course, be especially hard hit by the embargo, and, moreover, Carter had promised in 1976 that he would not embargo grain. Kennedy needs issues against Carter, and in several respects he is in irons. Frontal attacks on foreign policy are still considered out of bounds (especially in the case of Iran, on which Kennedy got in so much trouble for making critical remarks about the Shah), as are attacks on Carter himself. The international crises and Carter's rise in the polls have diverted public attention from the question of the competence of the Carter White House.

The grain embargo looked to the Kennedy people like an opening, and they jumped in. But there is some question how the issue will actually fall out across the state: some conservative political organizations and the American Farm Bureau Federation have supported the embargo, and even Lowell Gose, the president of the Iowa Farmers Union and a Kennedy supporter, has said he was "taking another look" at his decision to support Kennedy, because of Kennedy's position on the embargo. Gose said, "It's the only thing President Carter can do." The issue is subject to strange crosswinds: Iowa is heavily dependent on its agricultural economy—farm-equipment dealers, bankers, and exporters are involved as well as farmers —and the farm segment of the state has an intuitive dislike for embargoes. On the other hand, there is a sense of patriotism which tempers the farmers' anger this time (previous embargoes were imposed to hold down prices) and even a certain amount of pride that when it comes to retaliating against the Soviet Union they are the ones with the weapon. Yesterday, Jody Powell attacked Kennedy for opposing the embargo and said that a search of Kennedy's record turned up no evidence of past opposition to embargoes. When Kennedy was asked about this by reporters outside the farmhouse, he said, "We've never had those votes in the Congress of the United States. I've stated my position on this: it's going to hurt the taxpayers and the farmers and it won't stop the transgressors. All it means is that the Soviets are going to eat a little more chicken and a little less meat."

Now, shortly before noon, Kennedy is doing a walking tour of a drugstore, a bank, a drygoods store, and a ten-cent store in Knoxville. (Three hundred and four people in this county participated in the 1976 Democratic caucuses, and it will elect .99 percent of the state's delegates to the National Convention.) He tours the Baker Drug Store, accompanied by his wife and children and by Secret Service agents, a few reporters who form the press "pool" for the event, a television crew, and the mayor of Knoxville.

Kennedy asks the woman behind the cash register, "How's business been?"

She replies, "Very good." The woman asks him, "How do you like Knoxville?"

"Nice. Nice," Kennedy replies. And he adds, smiling, "Nice and cool." It is two degrees outside.

As he walks up and down the aisles, past the Max Factor cosmetics and the Russell Stover candy, Kennedy makes small talk, somewhat stiffly, with the few customers in the store, and says his familiar "How *ah* you? Good to *see* you." For all the Irish pol in him, Kennedy is not an easy conversationalist with people he does not know. Hubert Humphrey, for example, would have flooded this drugstore with talk. Every once in a while, Kennedy says to someone, "Say hello to Joan." It is not at all routine for Presidential candidates' wives to tour with their husbands, but it was felt that Joan Kennedy's presence was required, for obvious reasons.

As he continues his tour, a number of Iowans ask Kennedy how he likes the cold weather. "Love it, love it," he replies, laughing.

Then Kennedy goes to the 4 Corner Bingo Parlor for a meeting with people whom his organization has identified as actual or potential support-ers, and anyone else who has happened to turn up, out of curiosity. Now Kennedy has removed his overcoat and, wearing a navy-blue suit, sits be-hind a table in the front of the room. This is a calculated strategy. Some of his advisers had argued that Kennedy's natural, booming stump style might be fine for a union hall but would not work before the middle-class people of Iowa, particularly rural Iowa, and that it was also, as the expression goes, "too hot" for television. So a new approach has been devised. Ken-nedy is to sit in a chair, rather than stand at a lectern, and is to talk for just a few minutes and then take questions.

This is, in effect, the third approach of the campaign: the early stump speeches caused problems, because Kennedy seemed uncertain about his themes and sometimes stumbled when he spoke, and this was given great play in the press; then he read speeches, and came across as wooden. Most Presidential candidates take some time working out their themes and ap-plause lines, largely out of sight of the press. Some, as Jimmy Carter did in 1975, have almost a full year before the press starts paying much attention. But Kennedy had no choice but to start out full blast and in full view. And, as experienced a politician as he was, he was not prepared for this experi-ence. Kennedy can be one of the most effective stump speakers in politics today, but, for one reason or another, he has not yet made good use of that talent since he started running for President, and now the impression is abroad that he can't talk at all.

Another reason for this new approach is that Kennedy's very celebrity—that which his competitors have feared and envied—has its drawbacks: it is believed by Kennedy's people to cause a certain sense of remoteness among the voters here. Even the glamour seems to work against him, make people suspicious. So the idea of these meetings is to let people see him up close—to present him not as a movie star who has landed in their midst but as a nice family man who wants to meet them and talk things over with them. People tend to think of Carter as a family man, religious, a good man; of Kennedy as a man from a different world and with a questionable past. (The Carter campaign is running a thirty-second television ad that has Carter saying, "I don't think there's any way you can separate the responsibility of being a husband or a father or a basic human being from that of being a good President. . . . What I do in the White House is to maintain a good family life, which I consider crucial to being a good President.") So Ken-nedy has to try to back off from his glamour and campaign one-to-one, humble, just folks. But that is Carter's routine. Some within Kennedy's campaign organization do not agree with this new approach. They argue that he should be more forceful wherever he goes, because that is what he's most natural with and therefore best at.

Now Kennedy goes into his little talk. He introduces his wife and his children, who are seated behind him. He has before him note cards listing, in a word or two, the themes he wants to touch on, but he talks virtually without reference to the notes. He looks very young (the lines in his face are not visible at a distance), although, at forty-seven, he is older than his two brothers were when they sought the Presidency, even older than John Kennedy was when he died. He speaks slowly, carefully, deliberately. "I come to your community because I believe what happens in Knoxville and other small towns and villages of Iowa is very important to the future of our country," he says. "I had looked forward, my friends, to debating the President of the United States in Des Moines, to having an exchange of ideas. I think that would have been valuable for the people of Iowa and the people of the United States." He points out that he accepted the invitation to debate Carter in Iowa when he himself was far ahead in the polls. As the time for the debate approached, the polls had switched around and Kennedy needed the debate, which undoubtedly was one of the reasons Carter cancelled out. Now Kennedy hopes to make an issue of that. "Let me just touch on some of the matters that we would have touched on in that debate," he says, and he urges his audience to watch a half-hour television ad that his campaign will be running statewide at six-thirty next Monday evening. Ordinarily, a campaign would not go to such an expense in a caucus state, but this contest is different. The Carter campaign is also running a half-hour ad.

In Kennedy's ad and in his little talks this week, he will stress the themes that were developed and honed during meetings over the Christmas holidays to prepare for the debate (and for the ad). The essential theme is that under Carter events are out of control domestically and internationally; the sub-theme is that there must be a renewal of the American spirit, so that we can get on with dealing with our problems. Another theme is the rationale for Kennedy's candidacy: Iowans, in particular, are believed to be troubled by the idea of insurgency, and to wonder why Kennedy did not wait.

Now, to answer the question in an anticipatory rather than a defensive way, he says, "I think one of the questions on the minds of Iowans is why I challenged the President of our own party. I campaigned for Mr. Carter in 1976, and I worked on his legislative program in the last three years. But in the last year I became very concerned about the failure of the Administration to deal with the problems facing Americans at home." After talking about energy and the economy, he adds that he also became concerned about "the failures of foreign policy," and he continues, "I think people would have asked why is it that American hostages are held, that American Embassies are burned, that there are Cuban troops in Africa and Soviet troops in Cuba and Soviet troops in Afghanistan. I can remember when our allies and our adversaries respected the United States."

On the basis of what he has said in the past, it would seem that Kennedy knows it's all a bit more complicated than that; and what he has just said could comfortably have been said by Ronald Reagan or John Connally. But now is not the time for complexities, it appears, and Kennedy is using whatever he can. He goes on to say that American foreign policy "has been lurching from crisis to crisis," and that it is "constantly reacting to events." He attacks the grain embargo as a response to the invasion of Afghanistan. "We can show the Soviets we're strong by beefing up our military presence in Southwest Asia, and stopping the sale of sophisticated technology to the Soviet Union; we can provide military assistance to countries in that part of the world"—steps that the Carter Administration is taking—"but I don't think food ought to be a weapon." He is applauded.

He moves to another theme—another way of going after Carter, which takes into account the polls' showing that people think Carter is trying hard. "Secondly, I think good intentions are not enough when dealing with the central concerns of Americans," he says, and he identifies the central concern as inflation. The idea is to try to go at Carter through issues rather than through attacks that can be construed as directed at the President personally. He points out that four years ago the inflation rate was less than five percent and now it is thirteen percent, and that then interest rates were six percent and now they are fifteen percent, and he goes on to spell out what those statistics mean in "human terms"—that high interest rates make it difficult for people to buy homes, for young families to get started, for people to send their children to college, and for the elderly to pay rising home-heating bills and to purchase prescription drugs. He says, "One mark of a society is how it treats its elderly people." He gets applause. "Now, my friends, I don't believe inflation is inevitable," he says, and as he continues he starts speaking more rapidly and his voice becomes louder, as if he were edging toward his natural style. "There are no problems—energy problems, health-care problems—that we cannot deal with. After all, this is America, and we have faced up to such problems effectively." Now he talks with more emotion: "There is no reason we cannot face up to those problems and restore respect and dignity for the United States." He gets applause, and then, realizing that he has strayed from the plan, he lowers his voice and says, "We're getting all excited here." And he cuts off his talk and asks for questions.

He is asked what his position is on defense. The Carter Administration has tried to portray him as "weak" on defense.

"We need a defense to meet our national-security interests," he says. "We need to strengthen conventional forces, but I am opposed to gold-plating." He adds, in an effort to get the argument away from one simply over numbers, "I don't think more is necessarily better; I don't think less is better. Better is better."

A woman asks him what he would do about establishing more faith in the federal government.

Kennedy replies, "This means to me more than just good slogans," and he draws an analogy with what he has said about defense. "What we need is not more government or less government but better government. Four years ago, we had a candidate who ran against Washington, against the institutions. What we need is a working partnership between the Congress and the American people and the President. I think the American people would like to see that." This is another of Kennedy's themes: that he would be better able than Carter to work with the institutions to get things done. The essential challenge for Kennedy, which he approaches in a number of ways, is to get across the idea that he would be the better leader.

This is the idea at the heart of his campaign—not his differences with Carter over energy policy or national health insurance. The problem is how to show that one is a better leader; essentially, that is something people have to feel intuitively. People ask what the differences are between his policies and Carter's policies, but that is not really the point. The word "leadership" has become a cliché in this Presidential campaign, but there is something to the idea: that a President should have a capacity for, and even enjoy, the gritty business of working with and fighting with the political institutions, of marshalling coalitions and taking on interest groups; and that he should be able to set the agenda and stay on a steady course and command the attention of the people. But this is a difficult thing for a candidate to spell out. Kennedy is onto something, but is also a bit trapped in the position of seeming to say that with a little more oomph we can get things done, that with him things would be, well, better.

A questioner points out that Rosalynn Carter has been a big part of the Carter Presidency, and asks what part Joan Kennedy would play.

"I'll let her speak for herself," Kennedy responds, and the audience applauds.

Mrs. Kennedy, obviously nervous, approaches the microphone and says, hesitantly, "This wasn't rehearsed." She goes on, "I have done a great deal of campaigning with my husband and for my husband—for seventeen years, as a matter of fact. All I want to do is be a very good campaigner. I would very much like to be First Lady, but that's a long way down the road." Joan Kennedy is obviously a fragile and vulnerable woman, and one cannot help wondering about the cost of this. The members of the audience applaud her heartily, as if they had been pulling for her, and Kennedy himself leads the applause. She is treated as if she were a frail creature.

After taking a couple more questions, Kennedy thanks the audience and says, "If it's agreeable with you—I see a lot of people getting hungry here —we would like to greet you. Let me again say how much I need your help at those caucuses. I hope you'll take the time, and I pledge to you, when I am elected President I'll try to be the very best President the United States has ever had." While the Kennedys shake hands with those present—about three hundred and fifty people—campaign workers hold Kentucky Fried Chicken buckets in which people are to drop cards they have been given to fill out, indicating that they will support Kennedy at the precinct caucuses or help with his campaign. These people will be called later. Getting people to a precinct caucus traditionally is no easy thing. They have to show up at a specified time—8 P.M.—sometimes after travelling long distances, and, in front of their neighbors, take a position for a candidate, rather than simply cast a ballot in the privacy of a polling booth. In the caucus balloting, people supporting different candidates stand in different parts of the room, and because of the requirement for having the votes of fifteen percent of those present in order to win delegates to the county convention, horse-trading and recombining go on. Actually, Iowa has had one of the highest turnouts for caucus voting; the national average for caucus states in 1976 was just under four percent.

Here in Knoxville, the crowd had applauded Kennedy, but with no great outburst of enthusiasm. It is hard to tell what that means. These are stolid, rural people, not given to emotional displays, and Kennedy was not being natural, and there is some question whether it would have worked if he had been. One can better imagine Jimmy Carter talking to them quietly, talking of their shared origins, telling them that their values are his values, and getting their quiet assent. Jimmy Carter isn't in Iowa now, of course, but he is present. He spent a great deal of time here in 1975 when he was stealing a march on his rivals, staying in homes and making his bed. Since his election, he has returned to the state several times—he rather spectacularly took his summer vacation on a Mississippi River boat here last year—and Iowans have been especially cultivated. In 1978, there was an Iowa Day at the White House, commemorating the second anniversary of Carter's "victory," and on many other occasions a large number of Iowans have been invited to briefings and dinners at the White House. And the President has been assiduously phoning Iowans in recent weeks. This morning's Des Moines *Register* has a story headlined "FROM THE BLUE, CARTER PHONES IOWA TRUCKER," which tells of Carter's calling Thomas Pelham, of Marshalltown, Iowa, who, it turns out, is not even a Democrat. (Pelham is quoted as saying, "We had a nice chat, I guess. No big deal, though. . . . It's kind of funny. He knew all about me. He asked me about being a truck driver and things like that.") Kennedy has been making calls, too, but not to the degree Carter has, and these handshaking sessions are as close as he can come to catching up with Carter's years of personal courtship of Iowans.

At Kennedy's next stop, at the Y Community Center in Oskaloosa (three hundred and seventy-three people voted in the 1976 Democratic precinct caucuses in this county, which has .84 percent of the state's delegates). Kennedy seems a bit more comfortable with his new approach, and develops some of his themes further. This time, he sits in a chair on a low platform (the idea is that he should not be on a stage, removed from the audience), with just a microphone in front of him—no table. A fairly large crowd has gathered—so large that an overflow has to listen to him from another room.

He still talks slowly, in a sort of singsong. His arms are folded as he talks. He asks, "Why is it that we don't have more notice about these challenges to the United States' prestige and influence?" He says, "You see, I don't believe that inflation is inevitable in the United States of America. I reject that view. There are some of those in government today who say, 'Well, it's a difficult problem.' Sure, it's a difficult problem; but we can deal effectively with it, and we can fashion an energy policy that is going to be fair and equitable.'' He criticizes the Administration's policy of decontrolling the price of oil, and he holds up a pamphlet published by the Community Services Administration (the remains of the old poverty program) which tells people how to stay warm: ''It talks about if you don't have long johns or pajamas which you can wear under your clothes for warmth, then you can use cloth or newspaper.'' He says that every other industrial nation in the world is effective in dealing with its problems. He talks about restoration of respect for the United States—''the American eagle, which in the one hand holds the olive branch and in the other hand holds the arrows.''

Other politicians have used this symbol, but they were not the sort who shared Kennedy's politics. Kennedy rolls the domestic and foreign issues into one ball and hurls it, gently, at Carter by saying, ''What I'm basically talking about is for the United States to regain a control over its own destiny. Good intentions are really not enough. What we really have to do is to establish a vision for this nation of ours, what we have to do is marshal the forces within this country and develop a working partnership between the executive and the Congress and the American people, to come to grips with the central problems of our time.'' He is applauded politely.

In the question period, he is asked what his energy program is. He says that he opposes the Administration's eighty-eight-billion-dollar synthetic-fuel program, because it is untested, and that he would support a more modest program and would encourage more conservation. He says it is ''incredible'' that oil refiners haven't been called in to the White House and asked to roll back the price of home-heating oil. He calls for an increase in productivity and for a reduction of regulation ''over economic areas of our economy'' (he does not explain this, but he did work for the airline deregulation that was passed by Congress and he has worked on trucking deregulation), and he calls for a program to develop foreign trade. He talks about the inflationary impact of the decontrol of oil and gas. He tells, as he often does, of how the oil companies said they needed decontrol—''that means taking all the controls off the oil and letting the sheikhs in the Middle East set the price for oil overseas and, effectively, natural gas overseas''—as an incentive to find more oil and gas, and says, ''And what does Mobil Oil do with the profits they received from decontrol? They go out and buy Montgomery Ward department store.'' And he adds—he clearly knows that it is an effective line, because he has used it earlier in the campaign—''Now, how much oil do you think they're going to find drilling in the aisles of Montgomery Ward department store?'' (Actually, Mobil bought Montgomery Ward in 1976, before oil was decontrolled.) He calls for a more rigorous anti-trust policy. And he calls for moving toward a balanced budget—he is trying to overcome his image as a ''spender''—and adds, his voice trailing off, ''We're doing that by statute in the Congress of the United States. We should be balanced by 1981 under a budget resolution which I have supported.'' He does not explain how a balanced budget is to be achieved.

In the area of foreign policy, Kennedy says, ''we need a spokesperson, which ought to be the President of the United States, who speaks with a single voice, not a Secretary of State who speaks with one voice and a national-security adviser who speaks with another voice.''

The way Kennedy talks about foreign policy fits a number of ideologies. It is his way of dealing with his problem of talking about foreign policy at all right now. One of his advisers says, "I think the public is getting tired of surprises, and senses the Administration is either naïve or knows better.'' But because of the constraints on attacking Carter, Kennedy does not take advantage of the opening that Carter provided when he told a television interviewer on New Year's Eve that the Soviet move into Afghanistan "has made a more dramatic change in my opinion of what the Soviets' ultimate goals are than anything they've done in the previous time that I've been in office." Kennedy is also still weighing the question of how strongly he should attack the grain embargo. And because of the constraints, and because of the furor over his remarks criticizing the Shah of Iran, Kennedy does not take up the question of how the mess in Iran came about. His own record and the remarks of his associates indicate that he is critical of our past support for the Shah, and of the Shah's being let into the United States for treatment—at least, without precautions being taken to protect the Embassy in Teheran. Instead, he tosses the seizing of the hostages into his list of things he says came about simply because of the decline in respect for the United States. Of course, there are many who subscribe to this theory and other (Republican) politicians who suggest it, but Kennedy's record indicates that his thinking runs along quite different lines—or, at least, that it used to.

The adviser continues, "There are a lot of things about which you can find fault, but at the moment I think people are genuinely concerned about the hostages, and now the Administration is calling Afghanistan the greatest crisis since World War II. So, although they're worried, they historically look to a President in this kind of situation, and if, the first thing out of the box, a political candidate starts to tear into him, it's a very difficult business. I don't think for a moment it's altered the rationale for his candidacy. If anything, it's underlined the foundation. But the question is, What can you do for the moment? If the surprises continue, then the obligation might fall the other way—to talk about these things more directly. It's a tough call in a campaign. You look like you're carping or criticizing. That's the toughest thing right now.''

After three events in Oskaloosa, Kennedy goes on to Ottumwa, where he addresses a crowd of about seven hundred and fifty gathered at the Ottumwa High School. (Joan Kennedy has left to return to Boston.) Four years ago, only five hundred and twenty-seven people attended the county's Democratic precinct caucuses, and the county elects 1.67 percent of the state's Convention delegates. Once again, there is no way of knowing whether people are here because they support Kennedy or because they simply want to see him. This crowd, which contains labor people—there is a John Deere plant here, organized by the U.A.W.—as well as farmers, shows more enthusiasm for him than the others today have shown, and Kennedy responds. What he says is not very different from what he has been saying all day, but it sounds different. There is a symbiotic and somewhat mysterious relationship between speaker and audience: as the audience responds to the speaker, the speaker becomes more confident and his delivery improves, and the audience responds; when the audience does not respond, it is difficult for the speaker to work up any enthusiasm, or even deliver a speech very well.

Now, standing before this audience, Kennedy speaks more forcefully than he has all day, and he adds some new touches, but one still senses that he is holding something in. He says, alluding to Carter's famous speech of last July, "I refuse to accept that there's a malaise in the spirit of the American people. I have not found it to be so." He says that next week "the eyes of America will be on Iowa." He says that he has travelled five thousand miles in Iowa during the last nine weeks. He says, "I think that this is going to be a judgment not only on the past but really on the future of our nation. I'm not satisfied with the status quo. I do not believe that we should accept the status quo in foreign policy or domestic policy for the period of the next four years. And I do not believe that the American people want the acceptance of the status quo." He talks about what they want of a President, and he concludes, "And I believe very sincerely that we in this country that have the natural resources in abundance, have the greatest political system that has ever been described by mankind and womankind, that we who have the genius to unlock the atom and to put man's footprints on the moon"—now his voice is rising as it has not all day—"that none of the problems that we are facing here today in the United States can defy our application and our commitment and our energy and our efforts. And that is why I am a candidate." He receives enthusiastic applause.

Kennedy has come closer to his natural style now, and several of the reporters who have travelled with him for some time say that this is the best speech he has given so far. But does it make any difference now? It is as if he were finding himself again. He isn't actually saying very much, but he is hitting on themes, touching nerves—in some instances not very responsibly, in others in a way meant to inspire. Like his brothers, he is appealing to the national spirit. In an odd way, Kennedy here and Carter in his "malaise" speech were getting at the same point—that the nation's morale must be lifted if we are to get on with things; and there is something to it, but Carter mishandled his material. When Kennedy finishes his speech, he offers to shake hands with everyone in the audience, and for the next hour and fifteen minutes he does so. After this, he will fly to Wisconsin to attend a fund raiser this evening in the little resort town of Delavan for Les Aspin, a member of the House of Representatives who has supported Kennedy's candidacy. What he is doing is incredibly gruelling, but, having started at all, he has no choice.

These days, Kennedy doesn't generate the excitement that John Kennedy did or the electricity that Robert Kennedy did, and now he's being advised not to try to stir the excitement that he in his own way can, and he is following that advice. The reputedly most natural and experienced politician of the Kennedy brothers is being programmed and reprogrammed. When he's at his best, he goes with his instincts, speaks from his gut, and can also be very funny. Now he seems battened down and unnatural. Kennedy enjoys politics and loves a good political fight, and now he is going around essentially with his hands tied behind him—in part by circumstance and in part by choice. From time to time, he expresses his frustration to his aides. ("Geez, when can we go out there and have some fun?") Occasionally, briefly, the naturalness comes through—a quick bit of banter with an audience. But the feeling that one gets is of a man on the defensive, tentative, explaining himself. He is asking his audience for help because he really needs it. There is no way of knowing now whether what he is doing will work; in any event, this is not, as yet, a joyous quest.

On Thursday, January 10th, Kennedy is in Springfield, Illinois. Each time he goes to Iowa, the campaign tries to make a stop in Illinois, because some of the media there reach Iowa and also because Kennedy has big problems in Illinois. The support of Mayor Jane Byrne, of Chicago, which both Kennedy and Carter sought and Kennedy won, has turned out to be costly. Along with the Mayor's support came the considerable number of political enemies she has acquired. As Chicago's problems have grown, so have the Mayor's—and Kennedy's; and her demands for power within the Kennedy campaign have made for awkwardnesses. Meanwhile, the Carter organization in Illinois, headed by lieutenants of Vice President Mondale, has been merrily lining up support.

Kennedy, in his answers to questions at the fund raiser last night, spoke with more feeling than before on this trip about why he is for national health insurance, and in defense of his liberal record. Asked why all he wanted to do was "spend, spend, spend," Kennedy showed some annoyance at the question—his campaign assumes that certain questions are planted by the Carter organization—and then he said, "I'm proud of a record in the United States Senate of seventeen years of being a voice for the voiceless and a source of strength for the weak in our society. I'm proud of a record of working with the handicapped and the disadvantaged in our society. And I am proud of the record in the Congress of the United States of trying to help those who have been shunted aside in our society. I run for the Presidency with that record, and I'm proud of it." He went on to deal in a vague way with the argument that new approaches are needed, saying, "Now, having said that, I do believe that as we come to grips with the problems of the 1980s we need new solutions to the problems that we're facing. And we need solutions to the problems, to these issues and questions, that are going to take the best minds and the most concerned individuals in our society. And I'm open-minded about the ways that we should proceed and the way that we can proceed in order to meet the challenges of our time.''

Today, in Springfield, he has held one press conference, met with some labor leaders, and addressed a U.A.W.–sponsored meeting of senior citizens and a large meeting of supporters and others who have expressed interest in his campaign, including about two dozen state legislators. In both of his addresses this morning, he seemed to grow more assured and more comfortable. His theme line became more precise: "The issue that is really before us as a people is whether we are going to continue a policy of drift here at home and a policy of lurching from crisis to crisis overseas." Like entertainers, politicians and others who speak publicly with some frequency try out lines to see how they go over, polish them, work on the timing. When they see that a line works well, they incorporate it in their repertoire.

When Kennedy spoke before the political group, he jokingly commended the legislators for their courage in showing up, and cracked that Neil Goldschmidt, the Secretary of Transportation, was outside taking down their license numbers. (After Mayor Byrne endorsed Kennedy, Goldschmidt said that he would look for opportunities to deny discretionary federal funds to Chicago.)

At this morning's press conference, Kennedy failed, as he has all along, to explain how, except for the grain embargo, his handling of the crisis in Afghanistan would have been any different from Carter's. In fact, he has specifically agreed with Carter's other moves—cutting off the sale of sophisticated technology to the Soviet Union and strengthening our military presence in the area and our ties with China.

He was asked about a poll taken by WBBM-TV in Chicago and released early this year which showed Carter defeating Kennedy among Illinois Democrats by sixty-nine percent to eighteen percent, and among Cook County Democrats by seventy-three percent to fifteen percent.

Kennedy replied, "I'm encouraged by the way the campaign is going in Illinois, and I think we'll do better."

Asked if he found the poll believable, he said, "I don't question that . . ." His answer trailed off.

Now, in the early afternoon, he is holding another "press opportunity." (The earlier one was added on to give local reporters time to make deadlines.)

He is asked what he thinks of the idea, which Carter broached in his Friday-night television appearance, that the United States might not participate in the Olympics in Moscow next summer, as planned.

He replies, "I think the best way of participating in the Olympics is to go to Moscow and whip their—" He stops and smiles. When, last June, Carter said to a group of congressmen that if Kennedy ran he would "whip his ass,'' the Carter White House made sure that the world knew he had said it. At the time, the world generally assumed that this was a case of bravado.

Kennedy is asked about his previous statements that Iowa would be the first real test, and whether, if he loses, his campaign is in jeopardy.

He replies, "I say that Iowa is clearly important. I think that the President has to gain at least fifty percent of the vote in that state or it would be a clear reflection that at least half of the Democrats would support an uncommitted slate . . . or are supporting Governor Brown or supporting my own candidacy." He has been telling reporters recently that Iowa is not a real test, and that there probably cannot be one until the hostages are released and the subjects of energy and the economy can be debated—unless the hostage situation goes on too long.

Kennedy and his associates are painfully aware that people around the country are reading the polls and withholding their contributions and endorsements and hedging their bets. The hope is that if Carter wins, his margin will not be so great and the Kennedy people will be able to say that, given international events and so on, Kennedy did not do so badly. Among those whose endorsements had been expected, and are still being awaited, are Governor Hugh Carey, of New York; Senator Henry Jackson, of Washington; and Senator Harrison Williams, of New Jersey. Some people encouraged Kennedy to run and then said that they would have to wait and see or, recently, said that this is no time for them to split with the President. One of Kennedy's associates says, "He has to wonder, 'Where are my troops?' It's not just the endorsements—what's even more important is someone's word. That's what's discouraging."

Kennedy dodges a question about whether he agrees with Brown's charge that Carter is exploiting the hostage situation, responding that he thinks a debate would illuminate the important issues.

He is asked about remarks made by Vice President Mondale in Iowa today which, the reporter says, suggest that Kennedy and others who are not supporting the grain embargo are not patriotic.

Kennedy seems surprised by this. "I would certainly reject that suggestion," he says, and he adds that he has never supported the use of food as a weapon. He says that there are other ways for the United States to show its resolution.

Kennedy is standing on a platform in the front of a room at the Springfield Hilton, where he has just addressed his political supporters. He has answered the reporters' questions with an air of certainty, even sternness. Now some of the shadows over his campaign materialize into questions.

A reporter says, "Millions of Americans cringed when they found out that Ted Kennedy was going to run for President. . . . I say that sincerely, because of what happened to your two brothers. I'm wondering, How do you live with that every day? People just don't understand how you can take it."

As the question is asked, Kennedy's jaw tightens and he stares off into space, and then he replies, hesitantly, "Well, I'm mindful of the dangers of remaining in public life. I've been extremely fortunate in having the cooperation and the support of the Secret Service, which I and my family are very grateful for, and they're an outstanding group of men and women." And he goes on, "And so, uh, we're getting our message across and hope to be able to do that in the course of the campaign," and so on.

The same reporter says, "A recent poll, Senator, said that fifty-five percent of the American people think that you handled Chappaquiddick improperly," and he asks Kennedy how he would respond.

Once again, Kennedy's jaw has gone tight, and he replies, "I would hope that the issues which affect people's lives will be the issues which will be the most decisive in the course of the campaign. I believe that will be the case."

Don Rothberg, of the Associated Press, ends the press conference, and Kennedy says to the press, quickly, "Thank you very much," and hurries off the platform.

On the campaign plane, on the way from Springfield to Omaha, Nebraska, just across the Missouri River from Council Bluffs, Iowa, Kennedy relaxes in a front compartment over a lunch of cold cuts while his aides work on a statement in reply to Mondale. The plane, a leased 727, is equipped with phones and office machinery and is of the sort usually used only by Presidential nominees. Although members of the press are charged two hundred and twenty-five percent of first-class fare (this also covers ground transportation and such amenities as coffee in the pressrooms), Kennedy aides say that the plane is very costly to the campaign and is part of what is draining the treasury. (After the Iowa caucus, the campaign switched to commercial and charter flights.) The Kennedy campaign started out big, perhaps top-heavy—a large staff of experienced and expensive people, a large plane, and a large group to handle logistics. During these flights, Kennedy ordinarily confers with aides, makes phone calls, or prepares for his next stop, but from time to time he needs to simply relax. Given everything he has been through and is going through, he is remarkably resilient. He also appears to have more sheer physical stamina than most candidates. Today, Kennedy has a glass of wine before lunch and a cigar afterward (he finds that the cigar is dried out, and makes a rueful remark about that being just one more thing one has to put up with in a campaign), and these, plus some casual conversation, help him to unwind a bit, to put a little normality into his schedule.

It is clear that Kennedy knows he's in trouble in Iowa, and he seems a bit surprised that the Administration has sent so many people after him there. Rosalynn Carter, Vice President and Mrs. Mondale, Secretary of Agriculture Robert Bergland, and even Muriel Humphrey are campaigning there against him this week. Obviously, the Administration would like to beat him as badly as possible, and perhaps even knock him out of the race soon. Despite all the apparatus and all the aides and all the advisers—of which there may be too many—the fate of the campaign lies with him. A misstep, an ill-considered statement could end the whole thing, and only he can put himself over. No matter how surrounded a candidate is, he is essentially on his own. And sometimes the more surrounded he is the greater the possibilities for confusion are, and the greater the strain, and the less the opportunity for peace.

While Kennedy is having lunch, a phone on the wall next to him rings—loudly—and an aide takes the message. Another aide is calling from Washington to say that it is urgent that Kennedy phone a certain senator who is concerned about a certain provision on the criminal-code-reform bill that Kennedy is sponsoring. Kennedy says that he will make the call from the ground. Now he wants to go over with his aides his response to Mondale. Of all things, the question of "patriotism" has entered the campaign. Mondale is a decent man, and not the sort to throw such charges around lightly, and there is some question as to what he actually meant to say. But he is an experienced politician, well schooled in implications. After Mondale said that those who opposed the embargo were pursuing "the politics of the moment," and that supporting the embargo was "the patriotic thing to do," reporters pressed him about whether he was saying that Kennedy was unpatriotic, and Mondale, instead of simply putting an end to the matter, said, "I've said what I've said." Actually, Kennedy and Mondale, while they have never been close—their temperaments are different—get on amiably and were frequently allied in the Senate. Had the political fates arranged themselves otherwise, the two men could be allies today. There are really no great differences between them on the issues, but, as it happens, because Mondale and Kennedy represent the same constituency within the Democratic Party, Mondale is used by the Carter Administration to take Kennedy on within that constituency. A "press opportunity" is on the schedule when the plane sets down in Omaha (whose media reach into Iowa), and now Kennedy is preparing an answer to the inevitable question about Mondale's remarks.

At the airport, Kennedy opens with remarks about how happy he is to be in Omaha, and then comes the inevitable question. Kennedy replies firmly, carefully, without reference to notes, "I would reject any suggestion about questioning my patriotism. I have too high a regard for Vice President Mondale to question his decency or his loyalty or his patriotism, and nothing that happens during the course of this campaign will alter the high regard that I have for the Vice President." He is apparently trying to show that he is not interested in personal brawls, is above such things. He continues, "But, as one who took strong dissent to the war in Vietnam and was joined by the Vice President in that dissent, I am used to the suggestion that unless we conform with Administration policy one might be suggested—one might make the point that someone is somehow unpatriotic." (Actually, Kennedy did not publicly oppose the war until February, 1968—two years later than his brother Robert did—and Mondale did not oppose it until September, 1968.) Kennedy continues, "I don't think the farmers of Iowa or Nebraska who believe as I do that the grain embargo will harm the farmers and the taxpayers and the people of this country more than it will harm the Soviet Union, the transgressors in Afghanistan, are unpatriotic. There are many farmers, many public officials in Iowa, who share my view. There are many members of the Congress and Senate who share my view, and I think those people are loyal Americans but Americans who take serious exception to this aspect of Administration policy. And I don't think that I or the members of my family need a lecture by Mr. Mondale or anyone else about patriotism." It is a skillful statement, touching a number of bases, and delivered coolly and with dignity—without forced indignation or outrage.

The "patriotism" story made tonight's news. The television correspondents who follow Kennedy say they have trouble getting on the air unless there is a story about some contretemps involving Kennedy and the White House. So, across the country, not many people know what Kennedy is saying. Yet there are two campaigns going on simultaneously—one for precinct delegates in Iowa and one for national opinion. People seem to be more aware that he said "fam farmily" last fall, and that he can stumble around when he speaks—which he has essentially stopped doing in his public appearances—than of anything else about the campaign he is conducting. And there is a time lag: two of the networks ran stories about his verbal stumbling after it had greatly diminished. ABC talked about it in its story on Kennedy tonight. (ABC also ran Mondale's charge but not Kennedy's response.) He still uses a number of "uh"'s in answers to questions and on occasion when he is getting warmed up in a speech—this is a habit —and sometimes his syntax gets confused. But Kennedy, who can be both inarticulate and articulate, is still being portrayed as essentially inarticulate on the trail, when that is no longer the case.

In the gym of the Lewis Central Middle School in Council Bluffs, in the early evening, a band is playing before Kennedy enters—band music usually raises the spirits of a political crowd—and the crowd gives him a warm welcome, and Kennedy himself seems buoyed by the enthusiastic reception. He raises his fist in the air happily and breaks into a big smile. He is given a blue-and-white T-shirt, and he holds it in the air and says playfully, his voice rising to a roar by the time he reaches the end of the sentence, "I was just saying to myself as I travelled six thousand miles that what I really wanted was a Lewis Central T-shirt." (Now his Iowa mileage has gone from five thousand to six thousand miles.) He continues, "I may not have been able to debate President Carter this week"—he is smiling broadly, and his voice is going up in pitch as well as volume—"but I have a Lewis Central T-shirt." This is one form of Kennedy's humor. It is a kind of playful, high-spirited humor, a rambunctious humor, as compared with a dry wit or a contextual humor. It is robust, and he gives the impression that he is thoroughly enjoying himself. There is also a streak of self-mockery, and of recognition of the absurdity of situations he is in. Kennedy can be quiet, and thoughtful, but he also needs humor: he enjoys banter and kidding and being kidded.

Tonight, he stands at a lectern and gives his talk confidently and vigorously and without any apparent reference to notes, and the crowd, of about five hundred people, is utterly still and attentive. He says, "There are those who question whether any of us should express any dissent from Administration policy." He says, "I think we can bring a restoration of the American dream," and he links this to, and develops, a theme he began working in Ottumwa. He appeals to Iowans' pride in their state, in their educational system (which is one of the best in the country), in their sense of themselves as a hardworking people, in their agricultural productivity, and he says, "So I believe that the people of Iowa are going to send an important message to this country." He concludes, his voice ringing, his rhetoric carrying unmistakable echoes of John Kennedy, "My fellow citizens, we have been effective over the history of this nation in coming to grips with the challenges which are before us, and I, for one, refuse to believe that we cannot do the same for the problems that we're facing here at home. . . . We can establish a goal and a vision for America; we can marshal the resources of this country and the most important resources of the genius and the technology of its people, and the willingness to supply those energies in a direction to respond to the challenges of our time. And I think that we can see the restoration of the United States as a proud and noble country that is a source of strength for its friends and the world, and is respected by its adversaries. That is what I want to achieve. That is why I hope that you're here this evening: because you share this kind of dream with me for this country and for what this country can mean for the people around the world. . . . That's what I believe that this election is about. . . . I hope that together that we can send a message to this country about what we want to achieve for it here at home and around the world. Daniel Webster, one of the great senators, who held the seat from Massachusetts and whose seat I hold, said it best a number of years ago when he said, 'Let us develop the resources of our land, promote its interest, let those of us of our generation perform something worthy to be remembered.' My fellow citizens in Council Bluffs, my fellow citizens in Iowa, my fellow citizens across this land, let it be said of our generation that we, too, have performed something worthy to be remembered."

The band starts playing, and suddenly over the loudspeaker comes Kennedy's voice saying, "We're not leaving until I've shaken the hand of all of you." So, as he has done at every meeting, he shakes the hand of everyone in the audience who wishes to greet him. Kara Kennedy, who has been travelling with him all this time, stands beside him, also shaking hands. Teddy, Jr., is elsewhere in Iowa. Kennedy has chronic back trouble—his back was broken in a plane crash in 1964—and is frequently in pain, and when he stands for these long receiving lines a Secret Service agent holds the back of a chair against Kennedy's back, for support. Also, because of the obvious dangers that his campaign runs, a doctor, who serves on the staff of the health subcommittee Kennedy heads, and a nurse, who is specially trained in emergency procedures, travel with him on the campaign. Both are unobtrusive, and are not identifiable by their dress or by what they carry, but both are usually near him. There is also an ambulance nearby.

At the Best Western Village Inn, where the Kennedy entourage is staying for the night, Kennedy meets with about a hundred and seventy people—farmers and their wives. Council Bluffs is said to be a conservative area, and the land outside the city is sparsely populated. The area is also substantially Catholic, and no one is sure how the Catholic vote will go in the caucuses. At the motel, Kennedy stands in the front of the room and talks to the farmers quietly, telling them, "I've come tonight to learn." He tells them that he has served in the Senate for seventeen years and that he comes from an agricultural state—one that is number one in cranberries—but that perhaps he shouldn't even mention that in the presence of men and women who have worked a lifetime in rural areas.

Kennedy is no expert on agriculture, so it is probably just as well that he keeps his remarks brief and tells this audience that he has come to learn. He does talk about his opposition to the grain embargo, and he recites his "lurching from crisis to crisis" criticism of foreign policy, and says, "I think it ought to be very clear to the Soviets that we as a society will not permit any interruption of our oil supply in the Middle East and that any movement toward that interruption would mean the involvement of a major armed conflict." He talks to this audience, as he has to several others, about Leonard Trachta, a farmer in Marion whom he met on a previous trip to Iowa and who told him that he and his wife had each worked for a dollar a day during the Depression, and that now he has a successful farm but his children are having financial difficulties in trying to get started in farming. Leonard Trachta is a Kennedy staple; political campaigns are always delighted to come upon such anecdotal material. Kennedy talks about the importance of family life on a farm, and remarks that "as one who grew up in a large family with strong ties to each other and to their parents" he finds it "tragic" that, for economic reasons, some families cannot stay together on farms.

He asks the group for comments—"one of the important elements of a Presidential campaign is the educational process"—but for a while no hands go up. Finally, he is asked some questions. He has been joined just before this event by his son Patrick, who is twelve. Patrick is a small, strawberry-haired, freckle-faced child, and when someone gets up to ask Kennedy a question, Kennedy sends Patrick to him with a microphone and then has him bring it back for his reply. When one farmer asks Kennedy how he feels about the longshoremen who are boycotting the loading and unloading of cargo to and from the Soviet Union, Kennedy pauses, smiles, and says, as

Patrick returns with the microphone, "Take your time, Patrick, in getting it back." Kennedy gets out an answer to the effect that longshoremen are frustrated, just as farmers are. Some of the farmers finally express their frustration with Administration policy, which is undoubtedly what Kennedy wants them to do.

Some of Kennedy's answers to questions seem better informed than others. A senator, simply through issues that come up before his committees and on the Senate floor, picks up a lot of information, much of it necessarily superficial. Kennedy is conversant with a wide range of subjects, up to a point. He has picked up a lot over the years, and he is a studious senator—he often holds briefings with his staff and with outsiders at his home in Washington, mornings and evenings. He is known for selecting a good staff and for calling extensively on outsiders to get their ideas. Sometimes he seems to have thought something through and be on point, and sometimes he seems to have a cluttered mind. Sometimes he will seem to have a particle of an idea he has picked up somewhere.

On Friday morning, the Des Moines *Register*'s poll shows Carter leading Kennedy by more than two to one—fifty-seven percent to twenty-five percent—among the state's Democrats. Brown has the support of four percent, and fourteen percent say they are uncommitted. There can be a difference, as the paper points out, between Democrats in general and those who will attend the precinct caucuses. Its December poll showed Kennedy and Carter each receiving the support of forty percent of the respondents, and in August Kennedy led Carter, forty-nine percent to twenty-six percent. The most recent poll results had been expected by the Kennedy people, but there is some difference between expectation and reality. Among other things, the poll can demoralize their troops, and act as a disincentive to attend the caucuses. Now Kennedy has two more days here this week to try to rally his troops and convince people it is worthwhile going to those caucuses to vote for him.

This morning, Kennedy toured another farm, outside Council Bluffs, and then flew to Cedar Rapids, and then his motorcade brought him to Iowa City, where the University of Iowa is situated. The area is one of the most liberal in the state, so it is useful for Kennedy to make a stop here. The students are between semesters, and it was felt that Kennedy should deliver a substantive speech here, so he speaks in the School of Pharmacy auditorium on health insurance. In the audience are campaign workers as well as medical personnel of the university. For some curious reason, he reads his speech—health insurance is something he knows how to talk about—and his delivery is wooden and flat. It is hard to see what good this performance will do him.

In the question period, he is asked again about the Olympics, and this time he says, "The best response is for American athletes to go to the Olympics and win gold medals." He is applauded.

A young woman reads a question to the effect that he is campaigning on the issue of leadership and yet in his seventeen years in the Senate he didn't even get a health-care bill out of subcommittee, and she asks, "What kind of leadership is that?"

Her charge is one that the Carter people often make, and Kennedy remarks, smiling, "That sounds like a direct quote from Mr. Carter." A reply to this question has long since been prepared, and now Kennedy gives it: A bill to provide national health insurance was before the Finance Committee —not the committee that covers health—for eight of the last ten years. Beyond that, he says, for seven of those last ten years "we had a President who was strongly opposed to it." He continues, "I thought in 1976 we elected a President who was strongly in favor of it." Carter promised the U.A.W. during the 1976 primaries that he would support national health insurance, and received the union's support. Kennedy then points out that the Carter Administration proposed only a first phase of national health insurance, only a few months ago. (There were extensive negotiations between Kennedy and the Administration on a bill, but it seems that neither side really wanted to reach agreement.) Kennedy concludes, "We need the kind of leadership that can get that sort of program passed." He is applauded. Kennedy has been, in fact, widely considered one of the most effective senators, but somehow his campaign has failed to get that across. Perhaps because his organization does not now choose to stress the kinds of issues that Kennedy has for the most part been working on.

Then Kennedy goes to a pressroom that has been set up upstairs. What is on most reporters' minds, and is undoubtedly on Kennedy's mind, is what he will say in response to the poll. But the first question is about what he means when he calls for deploying conventional forces in the Middle East.

He says he is talking about "naval forces," and goes on for a bit about them.

Then he is asked a question about the poll.

He laughs, and says, "And, furthermore, the naval force should have . . ." and then he answers the question. He is clearly prepared for it. "Well, this is a time of considerable volatility in the polls here in this state and across the country," he says. ("Volatility" has become one of the much used terms in this election.) He cites concern for the hostages, the invasion of Afghanistan, and says, "And this doesn't mean that in my travels around the country that the American people do not want to have these issues debated and discussed, and they want, I find, American foreign policy debated and discussed. During the period of the last days here in Iowa, we've been well and warmly received. I think we've got a good organization. I think there's increasing questions of the Administration's program in embargoing the grain. . . . I think that the people in Iowa and around this country want foreign policy discussed, they want it debated, they want domestic policy discussed. And I'm satisfied that we'll have strength here in Iowa." He talks firmly, as if he were determined to project a strong—not a worried—figure. "I'm unable to predict to a mathematical degree what that strength would be. But it seems apparent to me that, given the results of this poll and the other activities of the Administration, that President Carter has to do considerably better than fifty percent of the caucus vote. And I think that anything less than that would certainly be considered to be a questioning of our foreign policy and our domestic policy." He has just raised the ante.

He is asked, "How are you going to be able to get back into this race if the President remains in the White House saying that he cannot get out and campaign, he cannot debate the issues because of the international crisis?"

He replies, "I don't question that the inability that I have had to engage the President in debate on foreign policies, on the series of crises that American foreign policy has seen over the period of these past recent years, the continued growth of inflation and interest rates over the past years, the inability to have a thoughtful debate and discussion of these issues between the President and myself obviously makes it more difficult, more compli-cated to get our message across. I accepted a debate when I had a substan-tial lead in the polls, because I thought that it was important for the American people to have the chance to examine the candidates, to listen to their views, and to debate these issues. Now that's been denied in Iowa. But I can't believe that the American people are going to continue to permit 1980 to go by without a serious discussion and debate of these issues."

He is asked, "When do you expect to win in an election against President Carter?"

He replies, "The important election to win is the Democratic-nomination election. I'm still optimistic about the ultimate result at the Democratic Convention."

He is asked, "Do you expect President Carter to win in Iowa?"

He replies, "The President clearly must get fifty percent or above in terms of the caucuses or that would be a major setback."

I have an interview with Kennedy as he rides in a motorcade in the late afternoon from Moline, Illinois—one of the "Quad Cities," on the Missis-sippi River border between Illinois and Iowa—to Clinton, Iowa, more than an hour away. Tonight, Kennedy will make a swing around the Quad Cities area. During the two-hour break this afternoon at a Moline Holiday Inn, which was decorated to give one the effect of being somewhere in Polynesia, Kennedy took a swim (the pool is smack in the lobby), made phone calls (including one to congratulate the new mayor of Lewiston, Maine, and several to Iowans, some of whom support him, some whose support he is seeking), helped Patrick with his homework, and then took off for this evening's events. According to his staff, Kennedy seldom naps.

In the car, Kennedy is smoking a cigar and seems relaxed. He and his travelling staff display a certain equanimity—at least publicly—that is strik-ing in the light of the roller coaster they have been on. Some interpret this as betraying a lack of determination on the candidate's part, but I have seen no signs of that.

I ask Kennedy if he has found it more frustrating to get through to people than he expected.

He replies, "I'd say the fact of Iran and the incursion into Afghanistan have preoccupied the news and the media since our campaign." A characteristic of the way Kennedy talks is that sometimes his words set him at some distance from himself; he uses such terms as "our campaign" and "the candidacy," and so on. "So that obviously had a very significant impact on our ability to come to grips with the campaign—the announcement statements; the principal stories about the campaign getting started. We've really been hard put to get the focus and attention on the issues of the time. But my own sense is it's inevitable, because the hostages will be released—or, with the growing frustration with the failures of current policies. We need a debate on traditional Democratic issues in a Democratic forum." Kennedy is clearly counting on the idea that he has a stronger base in the Democratic Party than Carter has. "Now, when that's going to come I can't tell you."

I ask him if he thinks there is any chance that it will come too late.

He replies, "My own sense of it, from what I see in the faces out there and what the polls show, is that the sense of wholehearted support for foreign policy is cracking—outside of concern for the hostages." Kennedy must be especially careful on this subject. "As well it might. It must."

But, I ask, don't some of his problems go back to the beginning of the campaign (the attention to his propensity to talk in half-sentences at times; the resurgence of interest in Chappaquiddick)?

"Certainly some," he replies. "I never felt the campaign would ultimately be judged by the problems at the beginning. I understand that impressions can be set at the beginning and they have to be dealt with. But I've always felt if we could get focus on these other issues and what I could achieve as President, then we could get attention on the main questions I'm trying to raise." And then he gives, as he often does in formal interviews, a rote answer. "I think the question for 1980 is the future as well as the past three years. Fine with me. I welcome that. But I think we have to look at the past as well as the future."

I ask him how much he thinks the early impressions are still the problem.

"It's difficult to judge," he replies. "You look at various kinds of studies, you can find what you want in them. Looking at the Harris poll, you see a broad base of support on the economy, even though the polls have gone down in my standing vis-à-vis the President. The way people view my candidacy—I'm not the best one to judge that."

I ask him how he sorts out all the conflicting advice he gets on what works and what doesn't work and what the polls mean.

"I don't," he replies. "The basic reason for the candidacy, which I've stated in different ways, with varying effectiveness, is the drift at home and abroad. That's the sum and substance of it. You can vary that. You can say, 'Twelve years of Republicans in the White House is enough' and get people cheering, or you can say, 'Things are out of control and it's time to get in control,' and you get a nod. You try in a campaign to do different things.''

I ask him if a nod is good or bad.

''That's a good thing, too,'' he replies. ''I can't tell you whether you get more votes for the nod or more votes with a cheer. Some would characterize one as 'shrill' and the other as 'dull.' I think some approaches have been more successful than others, but I can't tell you at this time which. It depends to a great extent on the group and the time and the audience you're communicating with.''

I ask him whether, when he made up his mind last summer that he was going to run, he ever dreamed that Carter would be as high in the polls as he is now. (Last August, Kennedy was leading Carter among Democrats by fifty-three percent to twenty-one percent nationwide; last December, Carter was leading Kennedy by forty-eight percent to forty percent.)

''I didn't expect so, no,'' Kennedy says, and he pauses, looking off into space. He continues, ''I've been around in public life long enough to know that anything can happen. I never assumed gaining the nomination or winning the election would be easy. I never assumed that.'' And then he laughs a brief laugh, and says, ''And I don't assume it now.''

I return to the question of whether he thinks there are impressions of him that must still be overcome.

He replies, ''There's always a start-up time in a campaign, as there was in our campaign. You're moving from a legislator very involved in the details of legislation to a national political campaign. It's like getting your equipment one day and playing in the Super Bowl the second day. I had always felt that we would have to start hitting our stride from the debate on, and I felt confident we would. I've felt we're making important progress. The campaign is settling down; people are learning their responsibilities, and the campaign is better at communicating my thoughts and hopes for the country. But we still have a long way to go for the nomination.''

Switching to what he has been saying about foreign policy, I ask him what leads him to make the argument that a failure of respect for the United States brought about the seizing of the hostages.

Kennedy replies, ''My sense of foreign policy is that it has to be certain and predictable and understandable to our people and give a sense of confidence to our allies and is respected by our adversaries.'' This is what he has been saying on the stump. He continues with some of the other things he has been saying: about the need for one foreign-policy spokesman, for better intelligence and better understanding of the intelligence, and for a strong economy at home to back up foreign policy. He says, ''Now, our principal adversary is the Soviet Union, and that relationship has to be one of cooperation—arms control and trade—and areas of competition. And that has to be understood. Built into that policy has to be incentives and disincentives—incentives to cooperate and disincentives to compete." Kennedy gets very involved as he talks about this. "In the campaign, they say, 'What would you do about Afghanistan?,' and that's important, but there's a broader question that has to do with predictability and incentives and disincentives. The adversary has to know what the disincentives are. We've said there never would be a grain embargo; the Soviet Union had to assume there wouldn't be one. The President went on TV and said the status quo in Cuba was unacceptable and later he said it was acceptable. So in the case of Afghanistan any warning given to the Soviet Union isn't going to have credibility; the Soviet Union is always looking for targets of opportunity. That dimension has been missing in our foreign policy." (He has mused in private conversation about his visit with Soviet President Leonid Brezhnev in September of 1978, and his feeling from that that the United States had been too unpredictable in its dealings with the Soviet Union. He cites the Administration's failure to push to conclusion negotiations for a comprehensive test-ban treaty; he says that we switched negotiating strategies on SALT, and that we did not warn the Soviet Union that our approval of the SALT II treaty would be linked to Soviet actions.)

I ask Kennedy again how he relates the seizing of the hostages to a lack of respect for the United States.

Again he doesn't answer. He talks about terrorism and attacks on our embassies "which have occurred five times in recent months," and associates these with "actions taken by our Administration in at least flirting with terrorist organizations such as the Palestine Liberation Organization," and he talks about the importance of being sensitive to the Third World. In fact, the Administration is now under some criticism for having been too much so.

I ask Kennedy how he thinks he can get the idea across that he would be a better leader than Carter.

He replies, "We'll see, know more as the thing goes on. We've tried to spell out what we would do with wage-price guidelines, and they say, 'You agree with Administration policy.' But, just as in the Super Bowl analogy, you can have the same plays, but how they're executed depends on the players you send in. It's a question of how you implement them and marshal the forces."

When Kennedy enters the gym of North Catholic School in Clinton this evening, the Clinton High School rock band is playing, and he is cheered enthusiastically. Patrick and Kara are with him, and, as he does everywhere, Kennedy introduces his children, who join him in shaking hands at the end of events. Kennedy is, in fact, quite close to his children, who live with him. He has assumed extensive responsibilities for his extended family; with these, his Senate duties, and the political demands on him even before he ran, he has lived under a great deal of pressure. There are about a thousand people here, and two hundred more—the overflow—are gathered in the bingo hall of the nearby church. Clinton calls itself Iowa's eastern-most city; today's campaign has crossed Iowa from its western border to its eastern one. (In 1976, four hundred and fifty-nine people participated in the Clinton County Democratic precinct caucuses, and the county elects 1.9 percent of the state's delegates.) As Kennedy stands before this audience, he appears to be in a good mood. The sitting-down, subdued-voice period is over, and he seems happier. This kind of greeting obviously buoys him. Tonight's events, like tomorrow's, are pep rallies, and he responds to the crowd's enthusiasm. It is now shortly after six o'clock.

"How many of you are hungry?" Kennedy calls out. He gets some cheers and laughs. "You want a short speech?" he asks, smiling.

"No-o-o-o," says the crowd.

He praises the rock band: "We could hear them all the way back in the Quad City area." And he praises the St. Mary's High School championship basketball team. He says, "I bet you didn't know that we *knewwwww* about the St. Mary's team back in the United States Senate. But you'd be *amaaaazed* at what you learn when you run for President."

Kennedy has a big, carrying voice. It is a different voice from that of either of his brothers, and his speaking style is different from either of theirs. John Kennedy had a cultivated delivery style, which he had developed over time, and his pitch was relatively high; and Robert Kennedy had a somewhat thin, reedy voice. Edward Kennedy has a power of delivery that, when it is fully employed, makes his voice seem to come from deep within his barrel chest. And his style is more that of the old-fashioned orator, in mannerisms and in tone. When it all works, Kennedy can command a room; he seems to be quite aware of this power and to enjoy using it. Sometimes it seems to come out of his strong streak of competitiveness: he sometimes goes at a speech as if he were an athlete determined to do his damnedest.

Now he says, "I, for one, reject the suggestion that the American people are in a malaise." He continues, "I believe they want to get control over their own destiny." He is warming to this theme. "I come from a family and a tradition that believes that we can come to grips with the problems of our time; and that's the spirit of the people of Iowa." And now he seems to be finding still stronger voice, and to be polishing his close: "My friends in Clinton, we can send a very clear message from the heartlands of America that the people of Iowa, that the people of Clinton, are prepared to march again." And then he offers to shake hands with everyone who is here.

We arrive at Muscatine, the next stop, after a motorcade ride of an hour and fifteen minutes, and are a half-hour late. (Mondale was crisscrossing this same area today.) The handshaking did it, and then some phone calls. A little problem that arose during the meeting in Clinton was that Tom Southwick, Kennedy's press secretary, received a call from the Des Moines *Register* asking for a response to another White House charge alleging an inconsistency in Kennedy's record on food embargoes, and the Kennedy people had to rebut the charge. Southwick has complained to me that the Carter White House tends to release things of this kind just before newspaper deadlines, giving the Kennedy people little time to prepare a response. Kennedy may deplore the fact that the Carter Administration reacts to events, but that is what his campaign must do.

The event in Muscatine is at another Holiday Inn with a pool in the lobby. Another large crowd has gathered, a country band is playing stomping music, and some families in pajamas are getting a glimpse of all this from their rooms overlooking the pool. Clinton and Muscatine are relatively rural areas, and the Kennedy people feel that the Carter people have not made inroads there. There are a number of Chicano farm workers in the Muscatine area, and Kennedy is introduced enthusiastically by José Olvera, a lawyer and a Kennedy leader in this area. Kennedy comes on jovially and shouts, "Viva José!" The warmth of the crowd seems to energize him still more. This is more his kind of crowd than the ones he faced earlier this week. Again he jokes with his audience. He sometimes seems to be bordering on making fun of the place he is in, but the audiences don't seem to take it that way. "We had a meeting in Davenport and had a question-and-answer period, and you know what they asked? 'When are you going to Muscatine?' "

When Kennedy gets going onstage, he puts on a performance—moves about and jokes, as a professional comedian would, and with a professional's timing, and then he throws himself into his speech. He tells the audience in Muscatine that he accepted the invitation to debate Carter "when I was far ahead in the standings, the poll standings," and, for what seems the first time, he gets applause when he goes through his litany of foreign-policy crises we have been "lurching" among. As the audience cheers, Kennedy says, "Pour it on, Ted," and then he pauses and says, "Who said that?" Pause. "Patrick?" He is letting himself go, and having a good time. It is as if he has said to himself, "The hell with it," and just decided to let 'er rip—and have some fun. Whether it is the hour, or the crowd, or a final breaking out from the constraints—or all three—is hard to tell. Now his big voice is filling the Holiday Inn; from time to time, an arm chops the air or shoots upward. He pauses for effect, and sometimes bobs his head quickly in agreement with what he is saying. His face becomes flushed. From time to time, his voice cracks. He allows just enough time for the applause. By now, his speaking is extemporaneous. He refers to the fact that many people in the audience are of Spanish origin, and he talks of his work in the Senate for bilingual education (Mondale was also a major sponsor of such legislation) and for bilingual-voting rights. Again he rejects "malaise." He says, "The challenge of America is the challenge of hope."

After he has concluded his remarks and is being cheered, he shouts into the microphone, "No one's going to leave here tonight until they shake my hand!" Kennedy is certainly going at it now, but there is no way of knowing, as he does so, what it means. What the candidate himself does is only a part of the equation, and it is impossible to tell at the moment what part. And even if he does well in Muscatine tonight, does it matter? How different would Kennedy's situation be now if his campaign had got off to a better start and if he had not been thrown off stride by the shaky beginning? Was there, all along, too much in his background for him to overcome? Has the attention to his background been in proportion? How much difference, really, have the foreign-policy crises made? Is he, for all his previous popularity, well suited as an actual candidate for these times? These questions will be mulled over, but the answers may never be known. As Kennedy puts on his performance, there is not even any way of knowing what difference it will make to the people standing here watching him, or even why they are here. A campaign gropes along through a great many mysteries and uncertainties.

When Kennedy arrives at the cafeteria of Marycrest College, in Davenport, about forty minutes late, his sisters Pat Lawford and Jean Smith are bouncing up and down on the stage—as they must have done twenty years ago—leading the crowd in cheers of "We want Ted!" Outside, there are a few right-to-life protesters, carrying signs saying such things as "SAVE THE UNBORN." Inside the hall, "God Bless America" is sung, and then Kennedy, grinning, leads the audience in shouting "We want Ted!" This is a crowd of about three hundred caucus organizers, and Kennedy says, "I want to find out if there are any Democratic precinct leaders who are going out to those precinct caucuses," and he gets a big cheer.

By now, Kennedy's voice is about gone, and he asks for a glass of water. These are the committed people, and they want him to cheer them on, and he does that, and they, in turn, cheer him on. He speaks briefly—he can tell that they are already enthusiastic—praising Iowa again. He says of his campaign, "We're going to continue it not only all over Iowa but also all the rest of the states of this country up until the Democratic nomination, where we're going to"—and now he pounds the lectern—"*get the nomination.*" He's clearly pleased, enjoying the fight. As the evening goes on, he gets looser and looser. It is now nearly eleven o'clock. He says, smiling, "Don't look at the clock. They'll serve breakfast here." The crowd laughs. "I refuse to accept the comments and the statements of Mr. Carter when he talks about 'malaise,' " he says, and the crowd cheers. This may be the first time he has mentioned Carter by name this week. "I say no malaise," and then, more insistently, "No malaise." The audience cheers, and begins to chant "We want Ted!" He concludes, "And on the caucus day we'll show the Des Moines *Register* what a real poll is." The audience cheers and shouts.

While Kennedy shakes hands with the audience, Don Rothberg, of the Associated Press, informs Tom Southwick that Carter has agreed to appear on "Meet the Press" on Sunday, January 20th. Southwick seems a bit stunned, and then he says, "I certainly find it exceedingly curious that he can find time to do that and he can't find time to come out to Iowa to debate." He points out that the Des Moines *Register* offered to hold the debate in Washington, and the White House declined that, too. Southwick says, "I assume he expects all the international crises to be resolved by then." After the rally, Kennedy holds a meeting with a small group in the same building and returns to the Holiday Inn in Moline shortly after midnight.

Today—Saturday, the last day of Kennedy's swing through Iowa—the campaign will cross the state again, this time from east to west, and then double back east, to Des Moines and then to Waterloo, where Kennedy will appear at a dinner with Mondale and Brown. Yesterday, Rosalynn Carter, Joan Mondale, Muriel Humphrey, and Ruth Carter Stapleton, one of the President's sisters, all appeared in Waterloo. The headline on today's Des Moines *Register* is "600% MORE GASOHOL IS CARTER'S '81 GOAL." The production of gasohol is, of course, very important to Iowa's corn growers.

Today, Kennedy will appear at "Kennedy caucuses"—meetings in the larger cities at which potential voters will be seated by precinct, so that organizers can see who turns out and who doesn't, and at which people will be rehearsed in caucus procedures. At the first meeting of the day, at Prairie Senior High School, in Cedar Rapids, most people straggle in too late to arrange themselves by precinct. Kennedy enters and calls out "Good morning!" and that livens the group up. "Isn't this a lovely way to spend a Saturday morning?" he says. He introduces Kara and Patrick, and then he says, "Is Ray Ratcliff in the audience? Where's Ray—is he here? There he is, right back there. Now, I know all of you are going to go out and knock on doors this weekend. Well, I hope you don't talk to Ray before you do. Because I understand that he's already been bitten by two dogs during the course of his knocking on doors and fallen through one porch." The audience laughs. And then Kennedy goes into his talk, and he gets applause for his litany about foreign policy. This morning, he is talking at about middle volume. He stresses the word "party" in these Party meetings, as opposed to his appearances before rural audiences, and says, "Members of our party are concerned about what has been happening in domestic policy." He says, "We hear the Administration talking about malaise in the spirit of America. Well, they ought to spend more time out in Iowa."

In Mason City, in the north-central part of the state, Kennedy holds his second rally of the day, at the North Iowa Fairgrounds. Mason City is the River City of *The Music Man*. First, he meets with precinct captains in the Fair boardroom, and then, in a corner of a large room where a flea market is being held, he gives a television interview to a reporter from a local station. When he is asked in the interview at what point he would go to war over Afghanistan or Iran, he says, "Well, I don't think there's a point now in considering if we go to war," and he continues, "What is important for the Soviets to understand is that we cannot afford interruption of the oil lifeline to the United States and to the Western world that comes through

Southwest Asia. That is a vital link which is absolutely essential for our security interest, and that can be unimpaired. I don't think there's a value or use now to talk about war, but we have very important strategic interests in that area of the world and they must be maintained, and they will be maintained." Asked if he would support a naval blockade against Iran, he says, "No, at this time."

At the rally, which is in a large building that holds exhibits at fair time, about six hundred people are gathered. (In this county, eight hundred and sixty-two people participated in the 1976 Democratic caucuses.) A band is playing "Mountain Dew," and there are signs around the hall that say "Mason City Loves Ted." Kennedy has been told that this group needs firing up and would like a little more talk about issues. He says, "Quite frankly, I do not believe that we ought to expect that the farmer is going to bear the burden for failures of American policy." In a new twist on his foreign-policy section, he says, "I believe this country is strong. I believe that in other times in our history that the Soviet Union has respected American strength and American influence and American prestige." In an unmistakable echo of John Kennedy, he says, "I believe we can do better. And I believe the people in Iowa think we can do better. And I think the American people believe that we can do better to bring about a restoration of the prestige of the United States."

He gives his full speech here today, and he goes at it fully. He leans into the lectern; he bobs his head for emphasis of certain points; he jabs his finger in the air in indignation. It is as if he had been warming up all week for this speech; in fact, it is probably the case that the earlier ones did help him warm up for this one.

"And I believe," he cries, "you care about this state and about its future and about the future of our country." And then, speaking slowly, and with full voice, he says, "The people of Iowa want to respond to the challenges that are before us, whether on the farm or in the cities of this great state. The people of Iowa, I believe, share with me a feeling that we can control our own destiny, here at home and overseas. The people of Iowa, I believe, share with me a feeling that rampant inflation and soaring interest rates are not the inevitable history of the American economy. The people of Iowa share with me a sense that we can bring about a restoration of the sense of respect for our country overseas. And so I come to you today to ask for your help and for your support as we, as a people and as a party, restore and regain our own destiny over our economy, over the energy policy, over the central challenges that we face at home and the central challenges that we face overseas. And I hope that ten days from now that the people of Iowa will send a message to the rest of this country and to the rest of the world that the people of Iowa believe the American dream is alive and well; that America still means hope for future generations; that there are no problems that we face here at home that defy our attention and our resolution. There are different issues in this campaign, but there is only one question—whether the citizens of Iowa and the rest of this country are prepared to see this great nation of ours respond to the challenges that we face in the 1980s at home and abroad the way that we have responded before. I ask you to join me in facing up to the challenges that we are facing here. Together, I think that we can make a better community for our children and a better future for all the people of this great land.''

Shortly before five o'clock, Kennedy is on the stage at the Civic Center in Des Moines. He is almost an hour behind schedule. At his last appearance, in Sioux City, at the western end of the state, he seemed to become stronger still in his delivery of his theme. (At Sioux City, for the second time on this trip, a few right-to-lifers carried posters protesting Kennedy's support of federal funding for abortions for those covered by Medicaid.) He then gave a local television interview in which he said, "If we were unable to get the Soviet Union troops out of Cuba, which the Administration said was unacceptable, I'm not sure the Soviets would pay much attention when the Administration tells them to get their troops out of Afghanistan."

Here in Des Moines, before perhaps a thousand people (who are sitting by precinct), he is introduced enthusiastically, and the audience gives him his most enthusiastic welcome of the week. He walks slowly to the front of the stage like a boxer, one fist raised in the air. Now Kennedy begins, at full volume, *"My fellow Democrats."* He is at home. He makes essentially the same points he has made all week—about foreign policy, about the fact that there has been no debate. This is his fourth speech of the day, and he speaks more forcefully than ever. His confidence appears to have returned. Now he attacks the grain embargo in more detail than before and goes after Secretary Bergland. Secretaries of Agriculture are always good campaign targets. He has returned to saying that he has traveled five thousand miles in Iowa, rather than six thousand. He talks about the economic statistics and the "human dimension" of those statistics. He leans into the lectern and, in a full, strong voice, says, "The Administration suggests that these issues are complicated and difficult to resolve. Of course they are. But Mr. Carter also suggests that there's a *malaaaaaaaise* in the spirit of the American people. Well, I will tell you. I have not found that to be true, in talking to farmers, in talking to working people, in talking to the elderly and talking to the young, of the people of Iowa. I find a state that is proud of itself. I see a state that is unsurpassed in the field of agriculture; number one in corn, number one in soybeans—a rich agricultural state that is proud of what it contributes to the strength and vitality of this great economy and of feeding the people here in the United States and around the world."

The audience applauds him when he praises the state's educational system, and Kennedy steps back a bit and just lets it applaud. And then he goes into his conclusion, throwing his bulk into it: "If America means anything, America means hope. And the dream still lives in Iowa, and I believe that it lives in the length and breadth of this nation." And then he fairly bellows, *"Weeeeee'll show* the Des Moines *Register* what an Iowa poll is really like." As the audience cheers, whistles, and applauds, he starts to take his seat and then comes forward again on the stage and, smiling, waves his fist in the air and circles the stage; he is acting "the champ" and at the same time mocking himself, and showing his exuberance.

Kennedy's plane arrives at Waterloo shortly before seven and taxis up and parks right behind Mondale's—a large blue-and-white one that says "UNITED STATES OF AMERICA." Waterloo is a factory town, with meat-packing and farm-machinery plants. It is a Democratic town, and the Kennedy and Carter camps are fighting hard over it. Carter did well here in 1976 and has the support of the National Education Association—which has supported him ever since, in 1976, he promised a Department of Education —and the Communications Workers of America; Kennedy has the U.A.W. and the Machinists. Kennedy talks to some precinct leaders at the Ramada Inn, changes, and then, at eight o'clock, enters the U.A.W. hall, where tonight's dinner, a fund raiser for the Black Hawk County Democratic Party, is to be held. He receives loud cheers. The Kennedy people insisted that the dinner be held in this hall, rather than a larger one—as the Mondale people demanded—figuring that this U.A.W. setting would give them an advantage. There will be a contest for applause, and each camp is saying that the event is "stacked" in favor of the other. People are seated at long tables, eating a dinner of pork chops, baked potatoes, and salad. Around the hall are blue-and-white Kennedy campaign posters and green-and-white signs saying "SUPPORT EDUCATION. VOTE CARTER-MONDALE" and "CWA —CARTER-MONDALE." A band is playing a combination rock/country music, and Kennedy makes his rounds of the room, shaking hands. There is a good deal of commotion.

Kennedy receives more cheers when he goes up on the platform where he and the others are to sit at a long table, but then he seems to realize he will be sitting there alone through Mondale's and Brown's entrances, so he goes back down and circles the room some more. The sponsors of this event don't seem to have figured out how to get the stars onstage. Mondale arrives next, also to cheers, and his entourage looks puzzled about what he is supposed to do, and he, too, starts circling the room, and then stands on a chair, so that people can see him. A few minutes later, Brown just wanders onto the platform. He is applauded politely. Finally, all three are seated on the left, facing the audience—Mondale at the end, then Kennedy, then Brown. Local Party officials are on the right. A group in the audience starts a cheer for Kennedy, and Kennedy, smiling, waves his fist in the air, urging them on, and then another group starts to cheer for Carter.

Kennedy and Mondale laugh at the cheering contest—they have to. Brown looks bemused. Actually, the feeling in the room is one of good humor; this is not the kind of angry cheering contest one sometimes witnesses at party Conventions. The people here are excited—after all, they have landed three major figures for their dinner. The democratic process is working in Waterloo tonight. After lengthy speeches by the local officials, it finally comes time for each of the featured attractions to give a twenty-minute speech. When the master of ceremonies says that it's time for "the more serious part of the program," Kennedy leads the audience in applause. Then, when the master of ceremonies says, "There's one burning question on all of our minds," someone from the audience shouts "Where's Linda?" —referring to Brown's famous friend Linda Ronstadt—and Kennedy breaks up into laughter, and Mondale laughs, and then, after some hesitation, Brown smiles.

Brown's turn is first, and he begins by saying that "in view of the fact we did not have an opportunity in Des Moines to answer questions," he will simply use his time to answer questions from the audience. Trust Brown to reorder the universe. Mondale has a prepared speech text, and Kennedy has some notes. Now Brown has, in effect, challenged the others; the Kennedy camp had not ruled out that Brown would suggest a debate, but it had not expected this. Brown has not made a real effort in Iowa; he became interested in it only after the possibility of the debate arose. Brown answers questions about the Olympics ("Except in the rarest of circumstances, we should not attempt to use the Olympics as a political issue") and on a variety of other subjects. Sometimes he uses an answer to make arguments that are not quite to the point, and he talks quickly, spilling out a number of ideas. He makes no attempt to get the audience worked up. He is applauded from time to time, and Mondale and Kennedy watch him carefully. At times, Mondale goes over his speech text, adjusting to the new circumstances, and at one point Kennedy engages in signalling with one of his aides—apparently about a new strategy. At another point, Kennedy and Mondale confer; in an odd way, they are comrades here. During the preliminaries, Kennedy seemed to have an easier time joking with him than with Brown. Kennedy and Mondale are more like each other than either of them is like Brown—or, for that matter, Carter. At one point, a man in the audience complains to Brown about the fact that Carter has not debated, and Brown responds, "How do I formulate that into a question? Is it: Can we, should we, and how do we get President Carter to debate?" The audience cheers, and Kennedy joins in and then stands, laughing, and leads the cheers. Brown criticizes the grain embargo. He says, "General Patton used to say, 'The point is not to die for your country but make sure your adversary dies for his,' " and he concludes with brief remarks.

When Kennedy begins, he says, full-voiced, smiling broadly, "First of all, I have something to give my good friend Fritz Mondale." He holds up a red jersey. "A New England Patriots *football* shirt. I present it as one good patriot to another." The jersey has white lettering on the back that says "FRITZ 2." Mondale laughs, and the whole patriotism matter has been defused. (Mondale had already said that he had not intended to question Kennedy's patriotism.) Then Kennedy tells about how, when it was thought that Carter might send Mondale as a surrogate to the debate, he tried to figure out who could act as a surrogate for him. He says that he thought of someone who in the Senate had supported national health insurance, a man who had opposed grain embargoes, and he goes on through the list of things that describe Mondale's record; the audience, having caught on, laughs as Kennedy builds to his conclusion: "But then I was reminded by Fritz that he was already representing someone else." Kennedy has entertained the audience, and has reminded everyone in two ways that Mondale is only number two. Then Kennedy says, "I've been getting along pretty well with the Administration"—pause—"lately." The audience laughs. "All I have to do is talk about a particular problem or an issue and the Administration comes in the area and awards those grants." Laughter. Pause. "And if you haven't gotten plenty here in Waterloo, you ought to make your applications now—before next week." More laughter. He tells of having mistakenly mentioned the Wabash Railroad, which no longer exists—"and, what do you know, it got a three-and-a-half-million-dollar loan." He delivers these and other stories with energy, and he gives the impression that he is having a wonderful time, and it has an infectious effect on the audience.

Then he says that he will make a few remarks, answer some questions, and close with some remarks. He has adjusted to Brown's setting of the agenda. He talks about his travels in Iowa, and his disappointment that the debate did not take place, and the questions he thinks are on people's minds about domestic and foreign policy. He gets in his remarks about hostages being seized and embassies burned, and Cuban troops in Africa and Soviet troops in Cuba and Soviet troops in Afghanistan. He says, "There is no excuse—there is no excuse—for the United States not to have a foreign policy in the period of the 1980s that has the support of the American people and the confidence of our allies, and is respected by our adversaries."

Kennedy goes on with his standard comments about economic statistics and what they mean and how one of the "tests of our civilization is whether we as a society can insure that the elderly people who have contributed so much to our society will be able to live their golden years in peace and dignity." He is talking passionately now, his face flushed. Sometimes he pounds the lectern. His hair is beginning to fall onto his forehead. Kennedy tamps down the audience's applause with his hands—he doesn't have time. "We see the clock moving," he says, and he says he wants to take questions.

He is asked whether the Russians can be trusted.

He replies, "American policy should not be made upon trusting the Soviet Union." He talks about "cooperation and competition." He says that he has supported an arms-limitation agreement. "Not because I'm interested in doing a favor for the Soviet Union, and not because I trust the Soviet Union. If the SALT agreement cannot meet the national-security interests of the United States, it should be rejected by the Senate of the United States. My own belief is that it does meet the national-security interests of the United States."

He is asked whether he favors a Rapid Deployment Force, which the Administration is proposing.

"I feel strongly we need to beef up the capability of our conventional forces," he replies. He says that half of our ships can't arrive in ports on time, half our planes can't take off on time. He thinks we have units that are "combat ready"—he names some combat units—and he says, "I'm not convinced that we have to develop some new type of capability other than beefing up or strengthening our existing conventional forces."

Then he is asked about why he has not been able to get health insurance out of his subcommittee, and as soon as the questioner, who phrases the question almost precisely the way it was phrased in Iowa City yesterday, has said a few words, Kennedy says, "You know what's coming, gang."

He gives the same answer he gave yesterday, only this time with more fervor. He says, "The only way—the only way—that the United States will be able to join the other countries of the world in relieving their citizens of the fear of financial ruin because of illness or sickness is if you're going to have a President who is going to be at the ramparts to try to achieve it." The U.A.W., of course, champions national health insurance. Again, he stops the applause and continues talking. He talks, as he has before, about the good medical coverage that senators receive, and about the illnesses that his family has suffered—his father's stroke, his son Teddy's cancer, his son Patrick's asthma. He says, with his big voice booming, "There isn't a family in this room, let alone a handful of families in this country, that could assure their families of the kind of excellent-quality health care that this member of the United States Senate was able to achieve for his family." He pounds the lectern again. "I reject the thought that there is a family in Iowa that shouldn't be entitled for their families —should their families be struck with the same kind of illness and sickness that my family was struck by— that should not be entitled to the same kind of excellence and quality of health care." And he is cheered.

And then he puts his all into his concluding remarks. His conclusion is the culmination of his efforts this week to find his voice, and now he is eloquent. He delivers it as if it were coming from somewhere deep within him. This will be his last such appearance in Iowa. "I am a candidate for the President of the United States because I have a sense of hope for the future of our nation. I reject the counsel of the voices, no matter how high in government, that talk about a *malaaaaaise* of the spirit." (As it happens, so did Mondale when Carter's "malaise" speech was being debated at Camp David last July. Now Mondale is expressionless.)

Kennedy continues, "I haven't seen it in Iowa. And I haven't seen it in ten weeks of travelling the length and breadth of this nation. I think the people of Iowa share the belief that I do that America means hope and that America means opportunity, that everyone who's in this room wants to try and improve our community and improve our state and improve our country, so that we can pass a greater country on to our children." The room is utterly still. He says, "In eight days from now, the people of Iowa will gather in the caucuses, and there will be people on one side of the room and people on the other side of the room. I'm asking the people, the Democrats of Iowa, to walk across that room and to join with us, join with us and try to insure that this great nation of ours can come to grips with the problems that we're facing today, the problems of inflation and the problems of energy, and the problems of restoring American foreign policy to the place of respect and dignity that it has always had in our proudest moments.'' And now his voice somehow gains more power, and—like an opera singer who reaches in there for that last reserve of strength for the end of an aria—he hurls out his closing: "And then we will send a message to the rest of this country and to the rest of this world that America is on the move again.'' Then he changes to his fighting tone and adds, "I ask you to join me and show the Des Moines *Register* what a real Iowa poll is like.''

Mondale begins by joking, "Tonight, Waterloo is not just a Democratic city. It has become the center of the civilized world.'' Mondale, too, tells some jokes that go over well, and then he says, "I come to you as an old, seasoned Hubert Humphrey progressive Democrat,'' and he adds that "contrary to what someone suggested, this is a progressive, compassionate, and caring President, in the finest traditions of the Democratic Presidents of our country.'' As he did at the Party's midterm conference in Memphis in December of 1978, Mondale is fighting Kennedy for the traditional Democratic constituency. As he did then, he gives an impassioned defense of Carter's record. He is doing the best he can with what he's got, and he gets applause, but he does not stir the excitement that Kennedy did.

But all three men, each in his way, have done well tonight. Mondale refutes Kennedy on foreign policy. When Mondale praises Carter for having "proposed the most progressive national-health-insurance plan that has ever been proposed by a sitting President,'' Kennedy smiles at the relativity of Mondale's claim. When Mondale says that he wants to bring up "the issues of Presidential character,'' Kennedy's jaw tightens. Mondale gets worked up as he delivers his remarks, and makes a couple of verbal slips that would probably be big news if Kennedy had made them. Mondale speaks for twenty minutes, although he had said he intended to take questions, and when he is out of time he says again that he will take a few questions. Brown leans over to say something to Kennedy, and then, after Mondale goes on for a few minutes, Kennedy looks displeased. There are limits to good fellowship. Especially when the stakes are as high as they are now. Under the good spirits, there has been a certain tension, and now it surfaces. The master of ceremonies confers with Brown and Kennedy, and, looking worried, finally tells Mondale that his time is up, and Mondale quickly concludes his remarks.

After Kennedy's plane takes off from Waterloo to return to Washington, Kennedy, in shirt sleeves, his tie loosened, comes back to the press section of the plane. He talks about the evening and jokes with the press. He looks tired now. He has done all he can, and now he needs to unwind. One reporter kids him about changing his mileage in Iowa from five thousand to six thousand and then back to five thousand. He laughs, and says that he was told he had to stick to five thousand, because that is what he says in his forthcoming television ad. When a reporter, mocking a radio announcer, jokes over the plane's intercom that this week Dick Drayne, who used to be Kennedy's press secretary and is now a campaign adviser and turned up in Iowa this week, "slipped into Iowa with two suitcases of verbs and complete sentences," Kennedy roars with laughter.

Shortly after midnight, I talk with Kennedy for a few minutes in his front compartment. Patrick is sitting across from him, doing homework.

I ask Kennedy if he enjoyed the evening.

"It was a good evening," he replies. "I kind of thought it would be, anyway."

I ask him why.

He replies, "You feel both comfortable and motivated. You don't think there will be any surprises, or events that can't be turned to advantage." He shrugs. "It's a question of give your talk or give answers. It's all the same thing. I thought the audience set the mood: the Democratic Party searching and seeking a President, in a small room. The Democratic Party in the heartland of the country. It was really the heart of the Democratic Party that was there. It's so different from the kinds of events you usually get to appear at—a Sunday interview show, a debate, which is sanitized. There's an earthiness and liveliness of the Party that reflected itself tonight."

I ask Kennedy if he feels any less frustrated than he did at the beginning of the week.

He pauses, and then he says, "I think it went well this week." By now, his voice is hoarse and he is obviously tired. "I feel that the issues which motivated my involvement in the campaign—that really hasn't changed. There's been a lot of analysis of the campaign and the candidate, but nothing has altered. I feel the same interests and concerns that I've felt the whole time. There's been a settling down of the campaign, and I think there has been a settling down of the candidate as well. I think it's been a good week."

Kennedy's plane arrives at Dulles Airport, which is an hour out of Washington, shortly before 2 A.M., Eastern time. When Kennedy walks into the terminal, he is greeted by about a hundred campaign workers; some are holding welcome-home signs. They know it has been a gruelling week for him. Kennedy seems a bit startled, and moved. He jokes, "I thought it was the right-to-lifers." He thanks them for coming and shakes their hands, and as he starts to leave the terminal he says to them, "I have good news from Iowa. We had a good week." They cheer. And then he says, "As I told them in Mason City, we'll show them what a real Iowa poll is."

CHAPTER 4

Bush

On a Monday morning in early February, George Bush is touring the Baron Machine Company, in Laconia, New Hampshire, in the central part of the state. Bush's motorcade left the Nashua Holiday Inn at 7 A.M. and drove for two hours to get here for this, the first of two plant tours he will make today—his forty-seventh day of politicking in New Hampshire. Thirty-eight of those forty-seven days were in 1979, and, in addition, Bush made several stops at political events in this state in 1978, as he quietly began his long march. In all, George Bush spent three hundred and twenty-nine days on political travel in 1979, which may be a record.

He began planning his Presidential campaign in the fall of 1977, three full years before the election. His extensive efforts in Iowa paid off: he won the primary there and is now the subject of a great deal of attention. He himself claims that he has "Big Mo"—for momentum. (Carter defeated Kennedy in Iowa, fifty-nine percent to thirty-one percent.) This is his third trip to Laconia. Now Bush, a tall, slim man, cheerfully tours the plant, which has ninety employees. He has shed his green parka and is wearing a dark-gray suit; the sleeves of a navy cardigan show at his wrists. Bush moves swiftly through the plant, approaching each worker, saying "I'm George Bush" or "I want to say hello. I'm George Bush." Sometimes he chats for a minute or two. He is trailed by Hugh Gregg, a former governor of New Hampshire, who managed Ronald Reagan's 1976 campaign in the state and is running Bush's campaign here this time. Gregg hands out campaign leaflets. Bush's campaign slogan is "A President we won't have to train," and his pamphlet stresses his résumé—two terms as a congressman; almost two years as

Ambassador to the United Nations; chairman of the Republican National Committee from January 1973 until September 1974, during the height of Watergate; chief of the United States Liaison Office in Peking for a little over a year; and director of the Central Intelligence Agency for a year. The pamphlet has a picture of Bush jogging. Ronald Reagan is, of course, the main obstacle in Bush's way to the nomination, and though Bush does not mention Reagan's age he does say things like "I do my three miles every day. I think I'm philosophically and mentally up for two terms in the eighties." Bush goes about this plant tour as thoroughly as he has gone about the rest of his campaign. Sometimes he spots a worker and heads for him, saying, "How about this guy? Can we snag him?"

As he does all this, Bush gives the impression that he can't think of anything that would be more fun. When Jimmy Carter (on whose 1976 campaign Bush's is closely modelled) did much the same thing, one saw determination, even obsessiveness, but no hint of enjoyment. After a quick tour of the second plant, a clothing factory just a few yards away, Bush stands out front and, in answer to a reporter's question about what was the point of the tours, says, "That was very pleasant. It's just a part of what we've been doing. I don't know—I enjoy it. It's relaxing in a sense. You want to get in there and meet people. They're very pleasant, whether they agree with you or not. The plant things we've done—people are very open-minded. It doesn't hurt a darn thing to learn about the productivity of a little plant like this." Given the speed with which he went through the plants and what he did when he was there, it's hard to see how he could have learned very much. "We've been through quite a few plants now, and you get a much better perception of what that's about. But if, obviously, you garner some votes, that's what it's all about."

It appears that George Bush really does enjoy this sort of thing. His does not seem the forced good humor that shows through in so many candidates' smiles. George Bush is enthusiastic. One of his aides told me recently that Bush's enthusiasm is often, but should not be, mistaken for naïveté. He comes across as a nice man, casual, easygoing, but there is obviously a purposefulness, a drivenness, that has propelled him all those miles all those days. And Bush also has a protective coloration of another sort. There seems to be some mystery about his political philosophy, but another of his aides explained it to me simply enough: Bush is a conservative, but his Connecticut-preppy-Ivy-League style (he grew up privileged in Connecticut and attended Andover and Yale), which he has not shaken despite years in the oil business in Texas and years in Texas politics, colors the conserva-tiveness with moderation. If he and John Connally or he and Ronald Reagan say the same thing, it sounds different. (Bush and Connally, both from Houston, are said to detest each other, and their rivalry has divided Repub-lican circles in Texas.) It is also a deliberate part of the Bush campaign's strategy to scramble the image. Bush began with a base among members of the Party establishment and is now trying to expand that base. The strategy has been to try to defeat Reagan without alienating Reagan's following and to attract Reagan backers without alienating the Republican Party's more moderate wing. One of Bush's strategists told me that after Iowa about half of Bush's new support was being drained from Reagan.

To overcome any idea that Bush is simply a nice guy who went to Yale and who jogs, who has travelled in Eastern elite circles and may be a touch "soft," his campaign stresses that he is "hard" on defense issues and that he is a war hero—while serving as a Navy pilot, he was shot down in the Pacific. (His campaign pamphlet also describes him as a "hard hitting first baseman" on his Yale baseball team.) To offset the conservatism on defense and domestic issues, the campaign also points out that he has supported civil rights, the Equal Rights Amendment, and certain good-government proposals. One of his strategists said to me, "You look for issues that overlap different wings of the Party, or issues that make conservatives happy but don't bother moderates, such as some civil-liberties issues—but no social ones—or Taiwan; and you try to find some moderate issues that don't alienate conservatives, such as conservation. Conservatives want two things: a strong defense and less government. On those, Bush is conservative. Frankly, it's good that the other issues don't make a lot of people mad anymore, so he has the best of both worlds."

At noon, Bush is speaking before a luncheon of the Lakes Region Chamber of Commerce in Laconia. He has already addressed a public reception in Laconia and done a walking tour of the town—a fast in-and-out of several shops. About three hundred people are gathered at this luncheon. He says much the same thing he said to the group this morning. He tells this group, "People say, 'Isn't it an awful system where you have to go out and campaign the way you do?' People asked me at the factory this morning, 'Why do you do that?' " And then he answers, "You learn from that. I'll be a better President because I've had to work harder than the others, had to see the full planting cycle in Iowa, or come here and see the job New Hampshire is doing in diversification of energy sources, or whatever it is." Of course, Bush, like Carter in 1975, was in a position to devote a full year before the election year to campaigning. And, like Carter, he probably had to if he was to get anywhere.

Bush likes to point out that before the Iowa precinct caucuses he was an "asterisk" in the polls. As of now, on the basis of having won in Iowa, he is considered a hot prospect for the Presidency. Still, very little is known about him: how his mind works, what he really thinks, what grasp he has of the hard questions about governing. Like Carter four years ago, he is saying very little, trying to remain as inoffensive as possible. He is picking his way carefully among the minefields that lie in the path of a Presidential candidate, and trying to avoid the terrific ideological fights at which Republicans are adept. He is painting a picture by the numbers.

Bush has a standard upbeat litany, and now he tells the audience, "I believe in the integrity of the process. I believe our institutions can still cope. I believe that we can still solve problems. And so, fundamentally, I am an optimist, I am an idealist." He does add that "there are tons of problems, of course," and he attacks Carter for having presided over an increase in inflation. He has a certain way that he does this, and it goes over well with audiences. He says that when Carter came to office inflation was four and eight-tenths percent. He says that Carter said in his campaign, " 'I'm going to do something about this.' " Pause. "He did. It's thirteen percent the last year." At this, Bush's arm shoots into the air. "He made it a lot worse." He says, "I know these problems are complicated. There's no quick, simple, easy fix for the Middle East."

This seems to be aimed at Connally; David Keene, Bush's political director, told me last fall that one of the problems with the speech Connally gave on the Middle East in October was that it appeared to suggest that one man had the formula for resolving such a complex situation. Bush goes on to say that there are no simple solutions "to the Persian Gulf, to the relationship in the Pacific where you have a very aggressive Soviet Union backing Vietnam, taking over Laos, Cambodia, and threatening Thailand." He says, "These are tough problems. I just believe if we emphasize the fundamentals that we can go about solving the problems. But I see that glass that is half full and not half empty."

He tells the audience, "I am convinced if we try something we haven't done for many, many years, try to emphasize the fundamentals in economics, get away from the Keynesian economists that say the way you do it is spend yourself into prosperity, move away from that, limit the growth in spending, still improve education, still help those people that are destitute —in training, whatever it is, but you can still help. But you can't grow recklessly in the public sector. And you've got to have some meaningful growth in the private sector, so you hold the growth in spending." He says that he is against "excesses of regulation." But he also says, "If I found people burying toxic wastes in a brutal way—midnight buriers, they're called—if you found them, full force of the law against them, of course."

When Bush talks about "excessive regulation," he uses the example of the new federal regulation requiring that manufacturers equip cars with air bags. (Actually, this is optional; manufacturers may install automatic safety belts instead, which is what most are expected to do.) Bush says, "When I back out of my garage and hit a neighbor, I don't want to be engulfed in an air bag." (In fact, air bags inflate only upon severe collision and don't work when a car is in reverse.)

The third fundamental economic point, Bush says, in addition to cutting the growth in spending and reducing regulation, is cutting taxes. He points out that twenty-one percent of the gross national product goes into taxes, and he suggests that the amount should go back to eighteen percent, where it was "when Gerald R. Ford was in office." He calls for tax cuts to stimulate investment, suggesting a cut of twenty billion dollars—half to individuals, in order to stimulate savings, and half to business. He says that federal spending should grow by less than the rate of inflation. These formulas have been floating around Capitol Hill. Bush does not say what else he would do about inflation, of which federal spending is only one component—how large a component is much debated—or where he would make cuts in federal spending.

Then he says, "In foreign affairs, again, emphasize fundamentals." He says, "I grew up in New England. I saw how so-called Yankee ingenuity, Yankee integrity, all that kind of thing—there's something to that." He says that in West Texas, where he first moved when he went into the oil business, "your word of honor's your bond." He says, "That concept is a valid concept in relations between people; it's a valid concept in relationships between nations. And we don't need to threaten countries, we don't need to bully our allies, but we've got to keep our word—our word of honor internationally must be kept." He talks of how the United States led Chancellor Helmut Schmidt of West Germany to believe that it would deploy a neutron weapon and then changed its mind. He says, "You don't look like you're willing to pull back on a commitment in the Middle East in order for a hoped-for economic gain. You don't look like you're going to pull your troops unilaterally out of Korea and say to the Japanese and the South Koreans and those ASEAN countries"—Association of South East Asian Nations—"like Indonesia and Malaysia and the Philippines, 'Look, we don't really care about the stability of the Pacific.' You cannot make decisions that shake up your staunch allies—you want to keep your word. Secondly, morality in foreign policy, of course." He says, "I don't know if all of you feel like I do, but I'm sick and tired of being asked to apologize for *our* failures, for *our* lack of compassion, for *our* misunderstandings."

Bush's talk is being well received. He's simplifying, of course, but then many candidates do that. But Bush does not give the impression that he has given hard thought to hard questions. He comes across as likable, reasonable. It is an American likableness, the American regular guy. At fifty-five, he is youthful-looking; his somewhat crooked smile makes him seem pleasant when he talks, and sometimes an eyebrow is cocked. When he gets going in speeches, a lock of his brown hair falls to his forehead. His voice is a bit high, and he talks loud and very fast, conveying a sense of urgency— as if he is trying very hard to get across his enthusiasm about what he is saying. He seems eager, and his eagerness conveys a certain weakness. He often drops one shoulder or the other as he speaks, and he uses gestures that seem out of proportion to what he is saying or to the real force, as opposed to the volume, with which he is saying it. The gestures seem unnatural; the clear impression is that he has been told he is too bland, and is working to overcome the problem. Arms shoot out and up, sometimes out of sync with what he is saying; he jumps about, as if he had been told that standing still is dull.

He says, "I learned, as your Ambassador to China, Ambassador to the U.N., head of the C.I.A.—I saw the world as it is." He says that he sees "a Soviet Union that wants superiority, not parity." He says, "I've said it incessantly, and, some people said, at political risk—and I think I can do it protecting the rights of Americans: we'd better strengthen the Central Intelligence Agency and our intelligence capability." He is applauded. There was a time when Bush's polls indicated that his identification with the C.I.A. might be a liability; now times have changed and, to Bush's good fortune, his identification with the C.I.A. is turning out to be a plus.

Now Bush criticizes Carter for cutting from Ford's defense budget the B-1 bomber and the MX mobile-missile system. (Actually, Congress held up the B-1 until Carter could decide whether to go ahead with it, and he cancelled it on the ground that the cruise missile was a preferable weapon, an action Congress approved; he slowed down the MX in order to review its basing system, which was subsequently changed—and may be changed again—but the MX is under way.) Bush says that a strong defense "will be the best possible deterrent to Soviet aggression." He does not explain how he would cut federal spending, increase the defense budget, and reduce taxes. He says, "I believe in fundamentals, like family and religious conviction." Bush and his wife, Barbara, have been married thirty-five years and have five children; the family is apparently close-knit. He says, "I'm not a cynic." He tells the audience, "I lived in a Communist country. Fascinating! I know those Chinese leaders, perhaps as well as anybody in this country. . . . I saw the Great Wall. I like Chinese art. I appreciate the simplicity of the Chinese people. But after my wife and I were there for a while, we saw what it was like to live in a country devoid of the freedom which you and I have taken for granted every day of our lives."

He says, "Yes, I believe in service, and, yes, I believe in the integrity of the process, and I'm not so newfangled that these old-fashioned values have lost meaning for me." (This morning, when he made this point he said, "Some write that off as patrician or old-fashioned.") There is every reason to believe that Bush does indeed believe in service as much as he says he does. He refers often to his father, Prescott Bush, who was a Republican senator from Connecticut for ten years, and to the fact that his father instilled in him a sense of service. Prescott Bush was a partner in Brown Brothers Harriman and then served in the Senate. He was respected and well liked but did not leave any particular mark. One interesting thing about George Bush is that he took off for West Texas—he later moved to Houston —to make it on his own. Bush did make his own fortune in the oil business. Now he concludes, "I want to keep countries around the world that want to be free—are free and want to stay free—and this is why I want to be President and this is why I need your help and, very frankly, this is why I feel deep inside now that I am going to be the next President of the United States."

During the question period, he is asked what he would have done about Afghanistan, and he says, "If certain items had been left in the budget, and turn around the perception of pulling back, it probably or could well have forestalled the brutality of Soviet aggression. We must strengthen our ability to project conventional force." He adds, "I don't think the Soviets want conventional or strategic war with the United States." When he was asked this morning whether he thought the Administration had overreacted to the invasion of Afghanistan, he replied, "Very candidly, I don't think there was an overreaction. I think there was a belated recognition that the Soviet Union is not seeking parity—it is seeking superiority." Then he says, "We've got to keep commitments. We've got to make the Saudis understand that we are not taking lightly the matter of revolution in Yemen. We have got to avail ourselves of the bases that have been offered in Oman, Kenya, and Somalia—not to permanently station people there, I don't want that, because I don't want to see the Soviets drawn down into the Middle East. We've got to reassure Israel that our commitment is not only a moral but a strategic commitment. And we have to help Pakistan. And these are the things, some of which, incidentally, Carter has belatedly, belatedly done."

Bush tells audiences that he supported the volunteer Army, that he is not yet sure a draft is needed but that if there is one it should be equitable, and that, as a strong supporter of the Equal Rights Amendment, he thinks women should be included. He says that the burden of the draft should fall equally on a Ph.D. candidate and a ghetto kid. (Bush also tells audiences, when he is asked, that he opposes a constitutional amendment prohibiting abortion—but this is an issue that he and his managers would prefer to avoid.)

Now he is asked about a poll in yesterday's Boston *Globe* which indicated that he was ahead of Reagan in New Hampshire. His answer is ambivalent —deliberately so. His advisers have cautioned him to stop saying, as he has been lately, that he is going to win New Hampshire and go all the way, to stop talking about his "momentum." They fear this will set expectations too high, and also may cause the troops to slack off. He says, "It shows we've come a long way. I was an asterisk about four months ago. But there's no complacency. We've got a long way to go these last three weeks. I'm going to work hard." He waves his fist in the air. The people in the audience applaud enthusiastically.

Bush rides in the press bus to the next stop, about forty-five minutes away. He sits toward the rear, surrounded by reporters, and he is, for the most part, relaxed, direct—more natural and less forced than in his stage performances. And many of the people in Bush's immediate entourage are pleasant and candid and have a sense of humor. His is not the buttoned-up, tense sort of campaign that surrounds so many candidates. Sometimes Bush shows a certain edginess when he is pressed on a question. After a brief display of this edginess when reporters ask him why he is not more specific on such things as how he would cut inflation ("I don't think it's vague"), he calmly agrees that his description of how he would reduce inflation is "quite general."

When a reporter asks Bush if he thinks it is getting to be time to be more specific, he replies, "It could be. Indeed, I've asked a couple of people to take a good look at the budget."

When a reporter suggests that there is a hazard to getting specific, Bush replies, "Yeah, there's a hazard to it. There's a hazard to being too general, too. I listen very carefully to the questions I'm asked by the people of Iowa, the people of New Hampshire. I listen to the amount of specificity they're asking for."

Someone asks him why he does not spell out more of an energy policy. (In answer to questions from audiences, Bush says that he is for the windfall-profits tax, provided there is a "plowback" to the oil industry, to be used for further exploration.)

"I was asked about it at one of those earlier meetings today," Bush replies. "You know, you get up there and somebody says, 'You got to hurry up and get out of here; it's three minutes of.' "

Someone asks Bush, "What is your biggest worry, your biggest problem in New Hampshire?"

Bush replies, "Reagan." It is part of the Bush strategy to ignore Howard Baker, with whom he is presumed to be competing for the same voters. The Bush strategy is to get Baker out of the race as soon as possible, and meanwhile have voters see the real competition as one between Reagan and Bush. Bush's campaign does resemble Carter's 1976 campaign in some respects, but in another one it's different. He is organized for further down the line. His organization now has people in place in forty states, and, unlike Ford's in 1976, it has not overlooked the Western states, which were more or less left to Reagan by default.

Bush is asked about criticism that he is bland.

"I'm awfully bland, I admit," he replies. Then, as if he had thought over this concession, he says, " 'Bland' has a troubling connotation to me. It means I'm dull compared to some of those charismatic so-and-sos. I was never as bland as you people said I was. I don't know if I want to be charismatic or not. It used to be a good word. Ted Kennedy ruined it for me." He talks about his distaste for political labels, settles for the idea that he would like to be seen as a "moderate conservative," and then says, "What I hope people perceive is reasonableness. That you think through positions. That I'm thoughtful."

The press wants specificity, but specificity has killed off many a candidate, so it is in the nature of Presidential politics that many—not all—candidates see spelling out precisely what they would do about complicated issues as a trap to be avoided at all costs. "Position papers" are published for those earnest enough to pursue the question of where a candidate stands on certain issues, but even the position papers put out by the Bush campaign are, for the most part, general and unremarkable. It is hard to see how, having spent so much time on the road, he would have had time to think through what he had not already thought through, or how he can think things through now. If a candidate hasn't developed a coherent philosophy and a set of programs before he hits the road, it's too late. After that, he is at the mercy of advisers and events.

Like some others in public life, Bush seems propelled by a combination of duty and ambition. He accepted a couple of thankless assignments: chairmanship of the Republican National Committee during Watergate (leaving his U.N. assignment) and directorship of the C.I.A. during a time of turmoil in the agency (leaving his post in China). When he was given all his jobs by Presidents Nixon and Ford, it was generally assumed that it was not because he was especially outstanding but because he was dependable, safe, and willing. His was a name that was always on lists. He was one of those considered when Nixon had to select a replacement for Spiro Agnew. Still, people who are not Bush partisans give him good marks for the job he did at the C.I.A. One man who was involved with the congressional investigation of the agency at the time says that Bush was a good listener, that he was open to suggestion, that when there was a problem he heard people out and then tried to work out a solution, that he handled relations with Congress well, that he helped restore morale at the agency. I asked this man how smart he thought Bush was. He replied, "Not terribly. But I'm not sure what that means. He's smart enough to listen to people who know more than he does, and he works hard. I can't tell how wise he is." This man also pointed out that Bush did not stay in the C.I.A. job very long and that any appraisal is based on a short record.

A Republican senator who thinks Bush did a good job at the C.I.A. and likes him very much—who describes him as a decent, friendly, open person —requested anonymity when I asked how deep Bush is. He said, "I have trouble answering that, as well as I've known him. He's obviously an able person, but he's been extraordinarily lucky. He's kept moving. Sooner or later when you're in a job, you make a mistake. The real question is how you confront that mistake. He's never had that test, so there's no way to judge his depth or his character in that context. Whether he can do what the Carter Administration fails to do, which is to take a problem and carry it through to its third or fourth consequence—whether George thinks in those terms I'm not sure. When you look at what he has said, he doesn't seem to have composed his thoughts. They seem random, or scattered. They look jumbled. They don't seem pulled together in a program or philosophy. He kind of puts up the arguments and leaves them there. There's no guide to what he would do as President."

Tonight, Bush is addressing a large crowd at Plymouth State College. This afternoon, he spoke to two more public gatherings, and now he seems more worked up than he has been all day. He says most of the same things he did earlier, with a few additions. As he did at the earlier meetings, he says, "I'm an optimist." When he talks about holding down the growth in federal spending, he says we should "still be compassionate, still help people less fortunate than ourselves, but do it by emphasizing our fundamental economic strength." He says, "The answers are relatively simple, but they must be steadfastly pursued."

When Bush talks about "Jimmy Carter's inflation," he gets big applause. When he talks about "excessive regulation," he waves a fist in the air and says that regulatory legislation should be more tightly drawn. Then he spreads his arms and says, "People say, 'Nobody can do anything about it.' " He says he would "get rid of people who are put in there who are always leaning over on the far side of the regulatory process." At a meeting this afternoon, he referred to such people as "McGovern-type regulators." Tonight, when he talks about the air bag he shrinks back as if in horror at the idea of having one. This afternoon, he said something a bit surprising when he was talking about the air bag. He said, "I worry that I'm going to feel like I do about life sometimes—you know, kind of engulfed by it." Usually, Bush gives the impression of a man who is personally secure and confident, a man who has been blessed by life—even though he has had both personal sorrow (a young daughter died of leukemia) and public reverses (the loss of two races for the Senate) and has suffered on occasion from an ulcer. It is not out of the question for a person who is truly secure to run for the Presidency, but the question of what drives people who make the race to go through what they do, especially these days, does arise. When Bush talks about giving tax credits to those who train people for jobs instead of using government programs to train people, he thrusts his fist in the air and shouts, "How much better to do that!" Having listed his "fundamentals" on economic policy—hold down inflation, decrease regulation, and increase investment incentives—he says, "If we try those three fundamentals— Oh, there are so many more!" He says, as he has been saying all day, "Centralized answers don't work."

On foreign policy, he avoids whipping up passions or fears about the current state of relations between the United States and the Soviet Union. He says again that he does not believe that the Soviet Union wants war, but he adds, "When they see us as naïve, when they see us as weak, when they see us as vacillating, I think they're going to take a step forward." He says that he is opposed to the Strategic Arms Limitation Talks agreement. He says he would support a subsequent SALT agreement if it made deep cuts and if he was satisfied that it was completely verifiable.

Of the Panama Canal treaties he says, "My concern with Panama was not the fact that we tried to address ourselves to the long-held charge that we were colonialists, U.S. flags flying in a swath through the other person's country. Mine was the perception of pulling back from a defense commitment, with others looking at us and saying, 'Well, the U.S. isn't really committed to the defense of the Isthmus as much as it used to be.' "

SALT and the Panama Canal treaties are, of course, important to the Republican right. Bush says, "Jimmy Carter wakes up three years into his Presidency, sees naked aggression in Afghanistan, and says, 'Hey, I don't think we can trust the Soviet Union.' " He pounds the lectern and says,

"Come on!" And, waving a finger in the air, he shouts, "That's too long. Too long." Again the forcefulness does not seem natural. He seems more convincing when he talks naturally, as he does when he is not onstage. Sometimes, particularly when he gets worked up, he stumbles and gets his syntax confused, but then he catches himself and goes on. Sometimes he uses words in such a way that he ends up saying the opposite of what he means—he'll state something in the affirmative when he means the negative —and occasionally it is totally unclear what he is trying to say. It is hard to tell at this point whether this is a man who could lead people. Audiences— at least, these audiences—like him, and seem to sense a certain decency and straightness. He does not have a commanding presence, but perhaps he does not need one. Politicians can acquire "Presidentialness" by virtue of being viewed in the context of being President. They can also lose it. Of course, when people consider any candidate, they must also consider the others; the choice in a Presidential election is often among not the ideal but the available.

Bush goes into an explanation of why he believes we should have supported—as the C.I.A. did for a time, until Congress intervened—the forces of Jonas Savimbi in Angola (Savimbi was also backed by South Africa) against forces backed by the Soviets and the Cubans. He says, "I believe that we have always had a moral foreign policy. We may have made mistakes, but Presidents, Republican or Democrat, I cannot assign immorality as an indictment. I just don't believe it. I think we've been generous. I think we've been fair. I think we've been extraordinarily compassionate to countries around the world." And then he says, "And so you have to try to effect change, and stand up for your fundamental, moral, human-rights beliefs, but you also have to be realistic—and you have to recognize sometimes that if we just continue to push and shove and change things that sometimes the person that we were supporting previously and then stopped supporting may be gone, that you may be faced with a situation where you then have less human rights and your total strategic interests are diminished."

Bush appears to be referring to Iran; this echoes a conversation I had last fall with David Keene about the subject. Bush says, "I don't want to wake up seeing diminished strategic interests coupled with less human rights." And then he talks about Vietnam: "We had Vietnam. It divided us. We're asked to accept a rather revisionist view and impression of the United States and of our purpose. What's happened in Vietnam today has made our purpose more clear, less uncertain. We got out of Vietnam. Vietnam indeed is unified. The lack of freedom of the press in the South that we used to hear a lot about is no problem anymore, because there's no press at all there. They've taken over Cambodia and they've taken over Laos and they've brutalized the ethnic Chinese in their own country and we realize that this isn't a nice, peace-loving nation that's trying to live harmoniously within their own borders—it's something very different. But that divided our country, for very understandable reasons.'' He concludes, talking about running for President, "It's worth it, *believe me*. People say to me, 'Isn't it awful you've got to do this?' It's not awful at all. It's a *fantastic system,* because we are the most decent, fairest, most honorable country, and I want to be a part of the answer, not a part of the problem.''

There are a number of questions from the audience. One young man says, "The focus of your TV campaign is on your experience. When you look at your credentials, you spent as long in foreign policy as Jimmy Carter did in the governor's mansion. If we already invested three national budgets on Jimmy Carter's education, why blow another two trillion dollars on yours?''

Bush stares aside for a moment and then answers calmly, "One thing you learn about this is you're no longer as inhibited as your parents taught you about talking about yourself." And then he talks about having been shot down during the Second World War—he usually works this in in his appearances. He talks about his experience in Congress and in foreign affairs. And then he says, "I also know something different than Carter. I know what I don't know." And he is applauded.

Bush often says that he would select better people than Carter did. Another questioner asks him who his advisers would be. Bush says that this is a good question but he's not far enough along in the race to answer it, and he suggests that people look at the list of members of his steering committee. The steering committee, of three hundred and fifty people, includes politicians—members of Congress, former members of Congress, and former governors; former Cabinet officers, ambassadors, and National Committee chairmen; people from the academic, industrial, and financial worlds; retired military officers; and the requisite sports figures and entertainers (Earl Blaik and Tom Seaver, Lionel Hampton and Tammy Grimes). Bush has attracted many of the Party's mandarins, all-rightniks, and stars. Among those who support his candidacy are such people as Henry Cabot Lodge, Clare Boothe Luce, George Romney, and Hugh Scott. Among the members of Congress on the steering committee are Representatives Millicent Fenwick, of New Jersey; Bill Frenzel, of Minnesota; and Barber Conable, of New York, the committee chairman. As Bush's candidacy became increasingly plausible, Bush became increasingly attractive to investors in power. Even Henry Kissinger, who had once all but endorsed John Connally, came knocking.

Another questioner says, "I'm one of those poor, unfortunate people who every time I go to the polls I don't so much vote for one person as I vote against another one. You've taken shots at Jimmy Carter and other politicians and they're doing the same with you, right? What's so special about George Bush that his miracles he's talking now are not going to fade away when he gets to the White House, if he does?''

Bush replies, "They're not miracles. They're fundamentals. And the very fact that you are so cynical you think they're miracles troubles me, because what we haven't done is try these fundamentals. There's nothing so special about me except I have a deep conviction about our country, and based on experience, as a matter of fact, that we can solve these problems. I'm not so cynical that I go into the polls always to vote against somebody." He pounds the lectern and shouts, *"Come on! Cheer up a little bit!"* He says, "My perception of the Presidency is that a person can make a difference." He concludes, "I'll end where I began. I'm an idealist. I firmly believe that the United States can solve any problem, do anything it sets its sights to, to help people at home and to help countries around the world that want to be free."

Tuesday, Worcester, Massachusetts. This morning, Bush toured one insurance company here—he gave a talk to the officers and then the employees on each of four floors—and at noontime, trailing camera crews, reporters, and aides, landed in the cafeteria of another insurance company. This afternoon, he is to hold a press conference in Boston, where he will be endorsed by Elliot Richardson. There was a time, until not long ago, when Richardson, whose list of jobs held is even longer than Bush's, considered being a candidate himself. Richardson's endorsement was originally scheduled to take place after the New Hampshire primary, so that it would have special impact on Massachusetts, whose primary follows New Hampshire's by a week. Richardson embodies the Eastern, Brahmin wing of the Party, and his endorsement was to show that Bush has, as one of his managers said to me, "broad appeal." The timing was advanced after Edward Brooke, the former Republican senator from Massachusetts, endorsed John Anderson. The Bush aide told me that Anderson is a worry, because he is attracting activists—"people who will make more than their share of phone calls per day."

The Bush people want to narrow the number of candidates as soon as possible, and the problem, the Bush aide explains, is that it is still possible for what he termed "conscience candidates," such as Anderson, to remain in the race. Also today, in Washington, William Ruckelshaus will endorse Bush. Ruckelshaus was the Deputy Attorney General who was fired after Richardson, then the Attorney General, resigned on that famous Saturday night when Nixon ordered them to fire Special Prosecutor Archibald Cox. Bush was chairman of the Republican National Committee during these goings on. When he is asked today what role he played then, he says, "I was in the foxhole, waiting for other shoes to drop."

I have an interview with Bush in his car as he rides from Worcester to Boston. I ask him about his concept of the Presidency, and of how one can bring about change. I point out that he talks about the importance of getting a Republican Congress, and ask how, aside from that, he envisions working with the interest groups and the institutions—dealing with the paralysis that affects so much public policy no matter who is President.

He replies, "In the first place, having been in the Congress and been around the White House, I am not so naïve as to think that a Republican President, if dealing with two halves of the Congress controlled by Democrats, would have it easy. I do think one obvious place to begin would be with your legislative liaison.'' He says he has heard that Carter's legislative-liaison office has not been effective. He continues, ''I think it's got to be a combination of a strong liaison office and a mandate with which you're elected, where you move very fast to try to get certain kinds of changes, because as time sets in you're against a hostile Congress. The further away you get from your election, the more contentious and divided things can be.''

I ask him again about the broader question of how to get things done in the context of the number of interests.

''I think you take a position and spell it out,'' he says. ''Clearly, if you've been elected you'll have some popular support and you've got to mobilize that. You've got to have the people react; you have to lead in such a way that someone follows. Some of it, I don't know, leadership to me is kind of, it's an abstract thing, all right, but I think I could mobilize people to do things, encourage contact with Congress. But there's no institutional change that's going to do that; there's no way we can fine-tune institutions to do it unless, as I say, you improve your legislative liaison. It's going to have to be spelling out a path and staying with it and having people think you're right more than you're wrong and that you're sincere, that you believe what you say. You see, I don't think people are in quest of ideological conformity. I don't think they're looking for someone that agrees with them on absolutely everything. I think they're looking for reason, I think they're looking for conviction, I think they're looking for integrity. If I am elected President, I will have demonstrated that I can get people fired up to vote for me, and I will use whatever that is that got me elected to get 'em fired up to get their Congress to do what it is they wanted when they voted for me. I think I can do that, I just believe that.''

''So you think you have some feel for working with, or taking on and fighting, the interest groups that do make it so tough?''

''Sure I could do it. I'm not saying it would be a cinch, at all. I'm sure there will be battles with labor or certain elements in the business community or special interests in the regulatory field, but I think I can get things done—not everything I wanted done. I worry about this kind of fractionation, special-interest constituency, the rise of the single-purpose groups, but I also see a certain decline in some of that. Ralph Nader today is less effective than Ralph Nader was ten years ago. I think people are waking up on some of that. I'm a great believer in the pendulum theory. We talk about it too much, but I really believe that. I think it swings over on some things and then has a way of coming back to a certain common-sense, reasonable norm, and that the country's demonstrated that. I really believe—and I haven't articulated it as well as I want—that the late sixties and the seventies were an anomaly. I really feel that we've had a confluence of things that made us unsure of ourselves. One of them was the election of a very decent, honorable fellow who didn't have a feel for the way the system or government or Washington works. I can sit down with Lane Kirkland"—the president of the A.F.L.–C.I.O.—"and say, 'Lane, what price do we agree on?' and try to start from there, and then when you get to the contentious ones, O.K., you will have eliminated a lot of points before you have to fight on whatever else remains. I've always been able to talk to people I disagree with; I can talk to them agreeably and still not knuckle under and do it someone else's way. There's a certain reason to leadership, it seems to me. Now, toughness is sometimes reaching an impasse and getting your way over screaming, kicking, tough opposition, I understand that, but I don't think you start off by assuming that the way you demonstrate leadership or toughness is the destruction of someone who disagrees with you. You start with the assumption that you're dealing with reasonable people. Now, when you wake up and find out you're not, you don't wait too long. You treat adversaries with a certain respect, and you prevail because you've convinced them that you're more reasonable in your position and that position is the way it's going to be and that you're the President of the United States, like it or not, and you need cooperation. Do you ever compromise? Sure. But you don't start by assuming that if this guy differs with me on that I'm going to crush him."

"When did you decide to run for President?"

"Well, I started thinking a long time ago—I mean, like, hasn't everybody thought about being President for years? It's been a cumulative, kind of emerging process, and some of it was looking around at possible opposition, without arrogance, saying, 'Look, I think I'd be a better President than these people.' Feeling, 'Well, I've had the experience.' A certain confidence mounted as I surveyed the field. It just evolved."

I ask Bush if, when he talks about human rights and how we can end up with a regime that is worse than the one we had been critical of, he is saying that we should have tried to maintain the Shah in power.

"Well, I'm not saying that now or discussing Iran now, because I want to avoid doing what I was critical of Kennedy for doing. So let's wait until the hostages are back to tell you what I'm saying."

"Well, it seems that you allude to Iran in your comments."

"Well, you could go across the country or across the world and talk about the changes where we end up—Nicaragua is a good example where I think the jury is still out—as to whether we're going to be worse off or better off in terms of human rights, and where I worry that our strategic interests would be diminished."

I return to the idea that he has been referring to Iran, at least indirectly, in his public comments.

"I could have, but I'd prefer not to go any further than what I've said, because I just don't want to go into— Here they are, trying to determine some tribunal for the Shah at the U.N., and I just don't want to inadvertently go further than I may have inadvertently gone. But ask me a hypothetical question and maybe I can help you with the answer.''

"Do you think there are instances in which we have—''

"Undermined a friend?''

"Yes.''

"Yes. We failed to try to shape events in any way. I'm unclear on Iran; I'm unclear on the Huyser mission.'' (According to press reports, General Robert Huyser, the deputy chief of United States forces in Europe, was sent to Iran as the Shah's regime was crumbling and urged the Iranian military not to try to block the revolution.) "If it's, as it appears, that Huyser was sent to keep the military in the barracks and keep them from doing anything at all—if we intervened in that way—I'll certainly have something to say about it later on. I'll have the benefit of hindsight, which I think is a good thing.''

"Do you think the Shah could have been maintained in power?''

"I'm not sure about the Shah being maintained; I'm not sure that's our role. We're not dealing, in a lot of these situations, with just nice, unsupported, indigenous uprisings. You're not. You're dealing with things which are stimulated from the outside in one way or another. The Communist dogma talks about it—both the support and export of revolution—and we don't seem to understand that, or if we do understand it we don't want to be troubled by it.''

"Isn't there going to be a lot of cross fire over Iran eventually?''

"Yeah, there is. I suppose I'll be to some degree a reluctant dragon, because there's going to be plenty of room for criticism. Gosh, what this country's being put through—all of this is a very tough period.''

"Is the burden of the Vietnam comments that you made last night, and that I know you've made earlier in the campaign, that that is a war you would have waged?''

"No, just the opposite; it's a war that divided this country. No—not the opposite. It's a war where we were asked to believe that we were immoral in our purpose by some in this country. Many of our young people were taught that we were immoral, that this was an indigenous civil war and that these were peace-loving people that, once unified, and once free of outside intervention, would live at peace with their neighbors and would respect free institutions. You remember arguments about how the press in South Vietnam wasn't free. Our journalists said, 'Wait a minute, they're muzzling the press.' The whole concept was if we were just out of there you'd have a free, united, peaceful society. You don't have that, you've got something very different, and I think what you've got, particularly with the boat people, really kind of manifests the fact that we weren't immoral in trying to preserve some self-determination for the South. Now, if your question is, 'Should we have been involved in the way we were involved in it?'—with the benefit of hindsight, I don't think so.''

"What do you mean, 'in the way'?''

"Just getting in there and getting bogged down in a land war in Asia."

"Getting in there at all? I'm just trying to get clear what it is you're saying."

"Just getting in there the way we were involved."

"In other words, if you're going to get in, do it with more strength?"

"Don't get into a situation in which you put yourself into a virtually unwinnable position. In hindsight, that appears what we got into."

"Would you have got in?"

"When?"

"Is it a war you would have fought at all?"

"Would I have ever tried to help South Vietnam stay free by any means?"

"By military means."

"Not knowing what I know now."

"Because, as you know, there are those who argue that if we'd used more force we would have been able to do more. Is that your argument?"

"I answered your question."

"Well, I'm not sure. Because one argument over Vietnam is either we shouldn't have got in or if we did get in we should have done it with more force."

"Clearly, my view is, in hindsight, if we were going to be in there we ought not to have had such a limited— You know, where we held back and cut off support for the effort. We ended up in a way where we were not able to keep the South free from what now is brutality. And so we didn't do it right once we got in there. I don't think there's any question about that. I supported the President on the war; I didn't feel we were immoral in our purpose then. And yet if you give me the benefit of hindsight and you talk about a divided country and you talk about a wave of mobilization of world opinion—part of the mobilization fed on our own perception of ourselves among certain elements—no, I think it was very divisive and unproductive. But that's not a choice a President has; he can't always know the outcome and make the judgment."

"I just wanted to be sure we cleared this up, so that I understand what it is that you're saying."

"I'm trying to make a very different point about Vietnam, and you don't want to let me off; it's just you want me to make another point. You have any idea what point I'm trying to make?"

"Yes, I do. But the implications of it weren't entirely clear. In that same vein, when you talk about the Panama Canal, that we gave the appearance of retreating on a commitment, does that mean that you would not have—"

"It means that I have opposed the Panama Canal treaty the way it resolved itself."

"What does that last phrase mean?"

"Well, it means without a permanent treaty where we worked out arrangements to keep more of a continued defense presence in Panama. I

don't believe that that Latin-American solidarity we saw at the treaty signing was solidarity.''

"So if it had come down to their refusing to have a treaty providing a
military presence, then you wouldn't have had one?''

"Take some time. It was the same as tearing up our treaty with Taiwan.
Take time, resolve it in a better way, later.''

"You end some of your appearances, as you did last night, with words to
the effect that we should help any countries in the world that want to be
free. How far do you extend that, and to what kind of—''

"It's too hypothetical to answer that. We want to be a beacon of freedom
to countries—and we have rather limited capabilities. If we are widely and
credibly viewed as strong and as a deterrent to Soviet aggression, we'll be
fulfilling to a large degree that challenge. There are still countries that probably would like to be free and where undoubtedly majorities of the people
would like to be free that aren't, and we can still be a beacon of freedom to
those people. And—who knows?—someday we might see the extension of
freedom. It would be a marvellous concept to think that would be possible
—more human rights, more freedom, less dictatorial control.''

We talk about SALT for a while. Bush spells out his concern about
verification: that his real concern is over why the Soviet Union is unwilling
to share certain information.

Then I say, "Let me ask you an economic question for a minute, and then
I'll let you alone, if you want to be left alone.''

"Forever.'' He smiles a thin smile when he says this.

"You got into this whole thing. It comes with the territory," I said,
smiling back.

"How much has to, though?'' Bush asks this quizzically.

I decide to follow up on these indications that he is not as overjoyed with
campaigning as he usually says he is. "I guess more than you expected. Is
it all, in that sense, more demanding or more difficult or more unpleasant
than you expected?''

"No, it's not more unpleasant than I would have thought. You're talking
to a guy who's been tempered by two assignments that were helpful in this
regard—the C.I.A. during the Church Committee hearings, chairman of the
Republican Party in Watergate times. I was tempered. I've still got plenty
to learn. But I'll tell you, the unfortunate thing is I find myself like a zone-
defense man—I find myself playing much more defense than I would have
had I not been through those experiences and had the country not been
through what it's been through. And so maybe I don't tell you the neat
joke I heard that's funny but maybe slightly— If somebody just wanted to
make it wrong they could, and ruin my character in the process. So I'm
less— But that's all right; you gotta play by the rules you don't set up. So
people say you're bland or you're uncharismatic or you're— You know,
probably that's true, because I'm defensive in some ways. Not with voters,
not with people in a plant. I think it feels great going through that; I really

do. I felt better when I left that cafeteria than when I went in. I learned stuff. I've learned to be, hopefully, respectful; hopefully, available—but cautious.''

"Other than that, is it different from what you thought it might be?''

"No, it's a lot of fun.''

"You do seem to have a good time with it.''

"I do. Isn't that awful? I really enjoy it, and I say 'awful' only because I'm just beginning to wonder what the hell's happening to me, you know, but I really do enjoy it. I loved going through that cafeteria, kidding with them and learning stuff and sitting and chatting and trying to be responsive to the person and yet have a concern for what concerns them. I mean it when I say I'm better. I'll be better, more sensitive, stronger, from things like that. And there *is* the smell of the greasepaint and that other crap; there's some of that. I mean, this is very different today. There was a time nobody'd stand out in even hot weather to see me. I was all alone four months ago, and here people are waiting. And there's a certain forward adrenaline feeling there that exists today. Hopefully, there will be more of them. Maybe not; maybe I'll be lousy and they'll go away, but that's part of the fun of it. Part of it is the process itself. It's a good process. I love going to those things in New Hampshire in those town halls and seeing different kinds of people. I liked it when there were ten people, so I guess it's not just the adrenaline. People don't understand things about me. I think they sit around scratching their head—'Why does a guy like this in his Botany 800 Brooks Brothers suit think this is any fun?' I mean, look at an individual, look at a stereotype, look at a mold, and understand that— I don't agree with it.''

"Do you think your temperament is different from most people's?''

"Hell, I like people. I liked them in West Texas, and I was taken from one culture and—oomp—put right down in the middle of another. Taken from a prep school here and plunked into Squadron 86-C or whatever the heck it was at Chapel Hill—completely different. And I mean I feel that about people, so I hope I can convey it to them. But I can understand that people are inclined in this world to deal in stereotypes and just make everyone fit a mold, or fit a label. I don't want to be a part of it, and I'm not just being politically clever when I say I don't want to get into these molds, 'cause these damn labels mean different things to different people—they really do. You go into a black church in Texas and you say I'm a conservative, and they'll nod and they'll want balanced budgets and they'll want less taxes; they damn sure don't want inflation. But that's not what they think about when they say 'conservative'—they think the status quo in race; it has a historic negative connotation to them. It's probably less true today, but that's been true over the last thirty, forty years. I've been involved in politics for thirty years in Texas. And it's a good lesson. Why do it? Particularly in the Republican Party, where we *thrive* on everybody being labelled. One guy's out there to prove I'm a moderate. Why? 'Cause he thinks that'll finish me off. Somebody else's out there to prove I'm a right-winger. Why? 'Cause then he can garner in the other factions.

"We're dealing all the time in being determined, as politicians in our party, to fractionate a minority party. I just won't be any part of that. I'd rather have you conclude what I am if you can figure it out after listening to me. You know, I don't know what you'd say. If you'd say, 'Well, I don't care what you say, or how you couch it in rhetoric, you're a conservative' —fine, that's your conclusion. Somebody else might look at it and conclude just the opposite. So why should I be out there worrying about all that, especially when the words mean different things to different people? Labelling. I hate it. Back in 1966, I ran for Congress, and some guy says, 'Hey, try this one— Labels are for cans, not for people.' And I tried it and it didn't go anywhere—nobody thought it was very funny, and I stopped saying it. But I cite it only because it's not something new with me. It's something I've felt a long time. And I'm not sure it's bad politics, either. It may prove to be, but I don't think so. It may prove to be good politics.''

CHAPTER 5

Reagan

SHORTLY BEFORE noon on Friday, February 29th, Ronald Reagan and his wife, Nancy, arrive at the airport just outside Sarasota, Florida. It is suddenly dawning on a lot of people, in the wake of his unexpectedly thorough defeat of George Bush in New Hampshire earlier this week, that Reagan might in fact be the Republican Party's nominee. Assumptions about what will happen in politics bloom and fade rapidly. And memories are short. For some time, it had been assumed that Reagan might well be the nominee, because no one could figure out which candidate could stop him. Then it was assumed that he was too old, too blunder-prone, simply too improbable. Reagan could still make a big mistake and some candidacy could pull itself together to stop him, but as of this moment, as he arrives here in Florida, neither has happened.

Another assumption has been that if Reagan is the Republican nominee the election of a Democrat is certain. That's exactly what people thought when Reagan first ran for governor of California, in 1966. He won by almost a million votes, in a state that was heavily Democratic and whose Republican tradition was liberal to moderate, and he was re-elected four years later by a half-million votes. He had a strong instinct for what would attract traditionally Democratic blue-collar votes. Moreover, the great waves of national discontent have been moving in Reagan's direction: discontent with inflation and with "big government," with our powerlessness in certain international situations, and with our lack of military superiority over the Soviet Union. Reagan is at once a very familiar figure and a remote one, accessible and at the same time inaccessible. And his campaign has been going through turmoil: on the day of his New Hampshire triumph, he fired John Sears, his campaign manager, and two of Sears's allies, and the campaign has already spent two-thirds of the money allowed under the federal spending laws. Reagan has been the object of a tactical and ideological struggle among the people who would make him President. The question is where—or even who—he is in all this.

Reagan has, of course, been the conservatives' beau ideal for years now; he has a gift for speaking to what is bothering them. He is the titular leader of that wing of the Republican Party which took over in 1964 and changed the Party's politics and its culture: the East yielded power to the West; large Eastern financial interests to small businesses and shopkeepers in the South and Southwest; Wasps to blue-collar workers and Catholics. The Reagan wing can also draw on young voters of the sort who once supported George Wallace. (In 1968, Wallace received twice as much support as Eugene McCarthy among young voters.) That wing of the Party forms Reagan's base and makes him the only Republican candidate who started with such a committed following.

In New Hampshire, the Reagan campaign took advantage of the fact that Bush's image, if not his politics, made him appear to represent the old Eastern elite, and left in ruins Bush's strategy of trying to bridge the great divide in the Party. Gerald Carmen, Reagan's New Hampshire campaign manager, ran what approached a class war there. He told the Boston *Globe,* "There are more of us than there are of them." One of Sears's stratagems had been to try to soften the edges on Reagan's conservative picture, on the theory that this would make Reagan more electable. That was the idea behind Reagan's choosing Richard Schweiker as his running mate in 1976 and behind some of the early strategies for 1980. The struggle over Sears's role had gone on for some time, and Sears lost out for a number of reasons, only one of them ideological. Sears had insisted on too much power and made too many important enemies in the Reagan camp, including some who had been closest to Reagan for many years. And, finally, Nancy Reagan turned on him.

Sears was one of the few people able to tell Reagan that he shouldn't say certain things. Reagan's natural inclination when he campaigns is to do what he is most comfortable with: say things that fire up his natural following. The problem is that when he follows his inclination to take the red-flag issues to the conservatives, the moderates see red flags. Sears was trying to prevent some of this. One of the victors in the power struggle told me that the strategy of keeping Reagan under wraps in Iowa (making few appearances and declining to participate in a debate with the other Republican candidates), which has been attributed to Sears, and to which Reagan's defeat there is ascribed, was generally agreed on in the Reagan camp. But Reagan was not comfortable in his cotton batting, and many of the faithful were feeling let down and were complaining to the Reagan camp. These people were useful allies to the Old Guard in the power struggle. Reagan began to follow his own instincts in the final days before the New Hampshire primary. Afterward, he and those who supported such an approach felt vindicated.

On the way from the Sarasota airport to his first stop, I have an interview with Reagan—the first of two today. I ask him if the description of him as perhaps the most conservative major figure in this campaign is an accurate one. Talking to Reagan can be something like grappling with a wet cake of soap. He is pleasant enough, and responsive, even garrulous, but he often follows much the same script that he does onstage, and many of his answers slide away.

Now he responds, "I have always deplored labels, because I don't think they are fairly descriptive. Everybody has his own definition when they hear the word as to what they think that word means. I would just prefer to go on the specific issues and on the record of what I did in California. For example, is it ultraconservative that when I began, the state income tax in California began with the first two thousand dollars of a family's earnings, and when I left, it began with the first eight thousand dollars? Or that almost instantly when I took office I called in the prison director and we introduced in California the conjugal visit?"

Reagan was, in fact, a more moderate governor of California than his campaign rhetoric would suggest. This is attributed at least in part to strong countervailing forces—the Democratic legislature, the state's liberal traditions, and the strong professional state government. One of his former opponents says, "He fought with the symbolic liberal institutions—the state-university system, welfare groups, Cesar Chavez—and on the rest he struck a bargain." It has also been said that he was not a very energetic governor, particularly in his second term—that he seemed bored. Reagan is often described as not particularly interested in getting in and coping with the push and pull of politics.

I ask Reagan where he thinks the idea that he is so conservative comes from, then, and whether he would prefer that that were not the impression people had.

"No," he replies. "I suppose it's conservative to the extent that I don't believe in big, centralized federal government. I believe that the federal government has attempted to do far too many things—that there are federal programs that should be returned to the states, along with the tax resources to pay for them. I believe that the federal government is too interventionist. I believe in the free marketplace." In his 1976 campaign, Reagan got into some difficulty by proposing that the federal government return ninety billion dollars' worth of programs to the states, to be continued there or not, and only later amended that to say that the taxes to pay for the programs would also be returned to the states. When I ask him what, other than a saving in overhead, his transfer of programs to the states would accomplish, he talks about the diversity of the nation and suggests that mayors should have more discretion in the use of federal funds. When I ask him if he thinks there should be federal standards to require certain equities on the part of the state and local governments, Reagan replies, "There are areas that properly belong to the federal government. For example, I have no quarrel with there being a federal Food and Drug Administration. It began around the turn of the century, when we lost a great many people—as a matter of fact, soldiers in the Spanish-American War—through poisoned canned meat. That's fine. Government exists to protect us from each other. But as the years have gone on and the bureaucracy grows, as bureaucracies do, we find that they have gone far beyond protecting us from poisonous or harmful substances, and they have now set themselves up as the doctor and decided that they will tell us what medicines are effective." And then he gives what he obviously feels to be an absurd example. This is a standard Reagan technique—the ridiculous example, sometimes of dubious origin or accuracy. We begin to talk about Reagan's anti-inflation program but, having arrived at the first stop, agree to resume later.

In Sarasota, Reagan is holding a "press availability" beside Sarasota Bay, just outside the hall where there will be a rally later. The sky is clear, and the scene is a lovely one and will look good on television. A large number of Republicans—the highest concentration in the state—are clustered in the Gulf Coast area of Florida that Reagan will cover today. The only problem with this setting is that occasionally Reagan's answers to questions are drowned out by a powerboat or an airplane. Nancy Reagan stands beside him, looking, as she always does, perfect—relentlessly neat and composed—and her expression, as always, is one of fixed adoration. She is wearing a bright-pink Adolfo knit suit, a fuchsia blouse, and pumps that blend with the blouse. Mrs. Reagan's fixed stare can give the impression that that is all there is to her, but this is definitely not the case; she is a true conservative believer, an influence on her husband, and a power in the campaign. The Reagans are obviously very close, and are frequently seen holding hands. Reagan is wearing a blue-gray tweed suit, just short of flashy, with double vents; a white handkerchief is folded in his breast pocket. Just as George Bush looks Eastern and John Connally looks Texan, Ronald Reagan looks Western.

Reagan is asked his reaction to the recently renewed rumors that Gerald Ford might enter the race.

"Well, what can I say?" he replies. "The race is open to anyone who wants to enter."

He is asked whether he thinks that Ford's candidacy would be a formidable one.

Reagan smiles, and replies, "It was the last time." (Still, Ford was the incumbent, and had used the incumbency, and Reagan went into the Republican Convention with just eighty fewer delegates than were committed to Ford.) He says that Ford had told him that he would not enter the primaries but that if the Convention was deadlocked he would answer a draft. Reagan continues, "That's the only word I've had, and that was directly from him."

He is asked about a statement he made in the course of a debate with

Republican opponents in South Carolina last night to the effect that marijuana is the most dangerous drug in America. He says that what he said was that a great many scientific people have come to the conclusion that it is one of the most dangerous drugs, and that one of the latest findings is that "a marijuana cigarette probably is several times the cancer hazard for lung and throat cancer that a tobacco cigarette is."

A reporter remarks that a person doesn't have to smoke as many marijuana cigarettes to get the desired effect.

Nancy Reagan pokes her husband and whispers, "You wouldn't know."

Ronald Reagan says, "I wouldn't know."

A reporter points out that this is the hundred-and-eighteenth day that the hostages have been held in Iran, and asks Reagan whether he would have handled the matter differently.

Reagan says that the Administration apparently believed that when the United Nations commission to investigate Iranian grievances was established the hostages would be released, and that then more concessions were demanded. He says, "And each time our government has taken up the negotiating of those additional salami slices. And I believe once you think you have made a deal you have to say to the captors, 'This is all you get. There are no further concessions to be made.' If you don't do that, as long as they have the hostages they can just keep on demanding concessions until you're grovelling on the ground."

He is asked if Iran couldn't then just say that they would keep the hostages indefinitely, and he replies, "Well, there comes the time when a government has got to be willing to set a date for their release and let them know privately what the option will be if they are not released as of that date."

He is asked if our government could do that now.

He says, "I think we should have done it back about the end of the first or second week that they were held."

After this press conference, the Reagans will attend a fund-raising brunch, and Reagan will give an interview to a local radio station, which has carried his syndicated three-minute weekday commentaries. (During campaigns, the commentaries have to be dropped because of equal-time laws.) About two hundred stations across the country have been carrying those commentaries for years—which hasn't hurt his political career.

Now, in the early afternoon, Reagan is standing on a stage in a large auditorium, with a large American flag as a backdrop. Behind him is the Riverview High School Kiltie Band, which played "The Stars and Stripes Forever" when the Reagans entered the hall. Over the years, the Reagan campaigns have done better than any other at appropriating the patriotic symbols. His rallies are draped in red-white-and-blue bunting. Reagan supporters wear straw boaters with red-white-and-blue bands that say "Reagan." His posters are red-white-and-blue, and this year's shows

Reagan smiling his crinkly-eyed smile over a picture of the White House. The slogan is "Let's Make America Great Again."

Onstage as well as up close, Reagan looks fine. The blue eyes are clear, the apple cheeks give an impression of health. His recent triumph seems to have invigorated him, given him a certain buoyancy. There do appear to be some new wattles about his chin, which show up more in some camera shots than in others. Reagan delivers his message in a jaunty style, his head tilted slightly to one side. He often smiles the crinkly-eyed smile. He is a polished performer, as well he might be. The voice is husky-silky. There are no oratorical glissandos or gestures—he doesn't need them. Reagan's standard approach now is to make a few brief remarks and then take questions from the audience, in what he refers to as a "dialogue." The brevity of the remarks relieves him of the burden of developing a thought at any length, and the question-and-answer session enables him at once to seem accessible to "the people" and to turn the situation to advantage. Sometimes he uses his four-by-six index cards, sometimes not. He has his lines down well by now.

Today, he begins with a couple of audience-warming jokes and then says that Carter took what he himself had described as "minor crises" when he took office—inflation and energy—and turned them into "major disasters." Reagan's solution for inflation is balancing the budget and cutting tax rates by a third over three years (this is a version of the Kemp-Roth proposals that have been floating around in Congress) and reducing regulation of business. He says, "General Motors has to employ twenty-three thousand three hundred full-time employees just to fill out government paperwork and comply with government regulations." The audience gasps. (Like several Reagan examples, this one is technically accurate but gives a misleading impression. Actually, according to General Motors, about twenty-four thousand eight hundred of its employees work full time at complying with federal, state, and local regulations, but the great majority of these are workers involved in engineering work on pollution-control, fuel-economy, and safety standards and on regulation of plant facilities—air- and water-pollution standards and safety standards. Even according to the company, about five thousand—out of more than five hundred thousand—General Motors employees are involved in government "paperwork," which includes such subjects as taxes.)

Reagan says, "Balancing the budget is like protecting your virtue: all you have to do is learn to say no." In propounding his tax cuts, he employs a curious mixture of liberal Democratic and conservative Republican thought. He points out—as Democrats did against Gerald Ford—that each percentage-point increase in unemployment costs twenty billion dollars, mainly in unemployment compensation and lost tax revenues. Harking back to the sort of Keynesian economics that most Republicans deplore, he points out that a tax cut proposed by John Kennedy and enacted in 1964 stimulated the economy. But the Kennedy tax cut was employed to stimulate a sluggish economy, whereas recently the problem has been that the economy is overheated. Therefore, unless Reagan is contemplating making cuts in government spending in combination with his tax cuts (as the latest version of Kemp-Roth proposes)—and he does not mention this—what he suggests is, by most reckonings, inflationary. He says that the President says, "The good days in America are over." Waving toward the high school band behind him, Reagan says, "I want to believe that someday these young people back here can know the same freedom that we knew in this country when we were their age." The audience applauds and cheers.

As for energy, he says, "They say, 'Turn down the thermostat, drive less, or don't drive at all.' " He says that there was no energy problem "from the days of the horseless carriage until 1971," and that "from 1971 until the present, we have had increasing scarcity and skyrocketing prices." And he says, "Well, the simple difference is in 1971 the government injected itself into the energy industry." He asks, "Is it too difficult to suggest that we go back to what we were doing for seventy-one years and set the oil industry loose?" (The Nixon Administration imposed price controls on oil in 1971, as part of its total wage-price freeze, and kept them on oil when the other controls were removed; it imposed controls on allocations of oil in 1973, during the Arab embargo. Reagan is correct in saying that the system by which the government allocates refinery products, which is scheduled to expire in 1981, has led to distortions in distribution; the Carter Administration is phasing out controls on the price of oil.) Reagan suggests that there really is no energy problem. "Two-thirds of the oil is still down there . . . but government won't let them charge the price." It is true that when companies drill for oil they tend to extract only one-third of the oil in the ground; the rest has been considered too expensive to recover. No one knows how much will be recovered once price controls are removed.

Reagan says, as he often does in his appearances, that "the oil geologists in this country, the leading men, have told me that there is more oil yet to be found than we have taken out of the ground." He says, "The U.S. Geological Survey says that the potential for Alaska alone is greater than the proven reserves of Saudi Arabia. And yet our government has taken two hundred and fifty thousand square miles of Alaska and has said, 'That's a preserve; you cannot even look at that to find out if there's oil underneath that ground.' " (The United States Geological Survey estimates that Alaska has proven reserves of slightly over nine billion barrels of oil and potential reserves of between twelve and forty-nine billion additional barrels, while Saudi Arabia has proven reserves of a hundred and sixty-five billion barrels. The American Petroleum Institute estimates that if all the potential oil in the United States—onshore, offshore, in Alaska—were recovered, production would increase by four million barrels a day; currently, the United States imports eight million barrels a day.)

Reagan criticizes the Carter Administration for having held up the development or deployment of various weapons, and says, "Today, we are not equal to the Soviet Union, and that is why they were able to cross into Afghanistan." (The United States had vast strategic superiority over the Soviet Union when Soviet troops went into Hungary, not long after the Eisenhower Administration had enunciated a policy of "massive retaliation," and the United States still held a clear lead when the Soviets invaded Czechoslovakia twelve years later.) "We have betrayed our friends and appeased our enemies," he says. Then he says, "There will be no more Taiwans and no more Vietnams." The audience cheers.

When Reagan says that he will take questions, he says that he will take them mainly from people close to the stage—there are several indications that he is hard of hearing.

In answers to questions, he says that he is against a peacetime draft, for equal rights but against the Equal Rights Amendment. He says that the E.R.A. would put the issue in the courts "that have given us forced busing and some of the other decisions with regard to crime that we have."

A woman asks how and when we will stop helping the Soviet Union— Reagan has said we're still providing the Russians with technology that can be used for military purposes—and he replies, "When we get some people in the State Department who recognize that the Soviet Union is embarked on a goal that they have never retreated from, and that is to communize the entire world, and maybe then we'll stop helping them destroy us."

He is asked about his idea for a "North American accord" between the United States, Canada, and Mexico, and he gives a vague answer. This idea was offered at the beginning of his campaign, but he couldn't explain it very well and then it largely disappeared.

He closes by saying that as governor of California for eight years he held the second-largest executive job in the United States, and that he took the state's budget from bankruptcy to a surplus and gave the citizens rebates amounting to five billion seven hundred million dollars. (This amount is in dispute, as is the origin of the "rebate." According to the state's Office of Legislative Analysts, most of the rebate was tax relief initiated by the legislature. Reagan also sponsored substantial tax increases during his tenure, and both state spending and taxing more than doubled.) "We stopped the bureaucracy growth cold in its tracks, and we can do it in Washington, and I want nothing more in my life than to do that," Reagan says. He is given an ovation, and while a collection is taken up, the audience sings "God Bless America."

As before, Reagan's mind appears to be a grab bag of clippings and "facts" and anecdotes and scraps of ideas. People who have worked for him describe him as an intelligent man with an open mind but strong political instincts of his own. He is inclined toward uncomplicated concepts: a balanced budget, a strong defense, patriotism. He is in tune with what he conceives to be mainstream American thinking, because he shares it. There are people around him who hold highly conservative philosophies and can follow an argument through. Reagan seems to pluck from his briefings some facts and ideas that might be useful, but he does not seem to have thought things through. And sometimes when he gets out beyond his facts and his idea scraps, he flounders.

He does not seem comfortable with the more complicated economic concepts he has been fed. Still, one man, a Democrat who had frequent clashes with Reagan when he was governor, says that Reagan has a conventional mind but does have his own insights and is confident about his own judgments. "He's not programmed," this man told me recently. "He's not simply an actor who reads his lines. He tends to go for the politically effective, and he has a strong instinct for the microphone and the cameras and how things will go over." Thus the famous "I paid for this microphone, Mr. Breen," at the Nashua, New Hampshire, debate with Bush. Reagan appeared to know just what he was doing. (This event, where Reagan, who invited the other Republican candidates to join in the two-man debate staged by the Nashua *Telegraph,* and made Bush, who objected, appear the chump, has been considered the decisive factor in the New Hampshire primary. Actually, Reagan was beginning to pull ahead shortly before that.) The Democrat continued, "He's not a fool. The national media underestimate him."

Most candidates, one way or another, appeal to people's frustrations and disappointments. Reagan also speaks to their resentment. Maybe it is his mellifluous manner and nice-guy appearance, but he seems to stop short of arousing the guttural hatred that George Wallace or Spiro Agnew did. Of course, some of the social issues they played upon have died away. Still, in his way, Reagan does strike several of the same chords. When he does, it does not come across as mean, because Reagan does not come across as a mean man. With him, it comes across smoothly. As he was in 1976, he is the candidate of indignation. And now he has added the politics of nostalgia. With him, he is saying, we can go back to the days when things were simpler. He offers simple answers. Reagan has a certain plausibility when he does this, because he is himself a figure of nostalgia. Reagan can talk all he wants about what a competent governor he was, but he evokes, deliberately, it seems, the Hollywood myth: of John Wayne or Jimmy Stewart—or Ronald Reagan—riding into town and setting things right.

Mid-afternoon. Reagan addresses a large crowd in an indoor shopping mall. Red-white-and-blue bunting adorns the platform, and little Cub Scouts holding little American flags stand in front of it. He says, "There are many of us in this crowd who can remember not too many years ago when no country on earth would have even dared take fifty Americans hostage and hold them for a hundred and eighteen days," and he receives big cheers. He says, "We have a group of elitists in Washington who have no more faith and trust in the American people, and they think they must control our destiny, make all the rules, tell us how to run our lives and our businesses. And it is time to have a President who will take the government off the people's backs and turn the great genius of the American people loose once again.'' He gets Pakistan and Afghanistan mixed up, and admits to the crowd that he does that sometimes. He says that if we just let the oil companies drill away, ''we'll be back where we were and happy again.'' If Reagan is right about the energy problem, an awful lot of people are terribly wrong. This time, he ends by waving his arm toward the Cub Scouts— young people are among his props—and saying that we want the kind of country in which ''these young people will know the freedom that we knew when we were their age.''

In an interview with Reagan on the way to the next stop, I begin by asking him about his anti-inflation program. (Reagan assiduously waves to every- one along his route. I hesitated to begin the interviewing until we had pulled away from the shopping mall and his waving had subsided, but Reagan urged me to proceed. ''Go ahead. I'll wave—I can do it at the same time.'') When I asked him in our earlier conversation how he knew that his proposed tax cut would not increase the deficit, he cited the example of the Kennedy tax cut, drawing on material used by Congressman Jack Kemp, Republican of New York, and Senator William Roth, Republican of Delaware, to make their point. Some economists argue that, aside from the fact that the Ken- nedy tax cut was aimed at a slow economy, the cut was only one factor that led to increased revenue; another was that our participation in Vietnam was beginning to build. Reagan also said to me then that the result of the recent cut in taxes on capital gains is that ''in the very first year the government ended up getting more revenue at the lower rate than they did at the higher.'' However, the cut was enacted in 1978, and since the tax returns for 1979 are not yet in, there is no way to know this. In its original version, the Kemp-Roth plan was simply to cut personal-income-tax rates by approx- imately one-third; the theory was that it would not increase the deficit, because it would stimulate the economy enough to pay for itself, and that it would not be inflationary, because by encouraging people to work and in- vest more it would increase supply enough to satisfy the increased demand (the ''Laffer curve''). Few economists agreed; and when Republicans went about the country during the 1978 congressional campaign promoting the idea, the public didn't buy it. The Republicans then regrouped, and rede- signed the concept so that it combined the tax cuts with cuts in government spending, and a second Kemp-Roth proposal was introduced in January, 1979. But when I now ask Reagan if, when he talks about cutting taxes by one-third over three years, he is also talking about making equivalent cuts in government spending, he says that he is not, and he goes on to use examples and figures that Republicans used when they defended the original Kemp-Roth proposal. These days, Republicans in Congress, including Roth, are not talking much about even the revised proposal; their emphasis is on budget cuts, not tax cuts. Kemp says that he and Reagan, whom he has been advising, put a higher priority on cutting taxes and that this is what separates Reagan from what Kemp terms the ''Eisenhower-Nixon-Ford- Bush'' Republican economic orthodoxy.

I refer to Reagan's comments about Iran this morning and ask him what kind of "option" he thinks might be effective.

He replies, "Well, this is the thing that all of us on our side have refused to speculate on, for two reasons. That, you see, should be done in private. You don't want to suggest something that might be in the planning and you louse it up, or you don't want to be in the position of telling in advance what you're going to do. But you also don't want to do something that might bring further harm to the hostages. I would have to be in the position to sit there with the National Security Council or with the Joint Chiefs of Staff and say, 'All right, now, what are all the things that are possible?' " He says he understands that the sort of raid the Israelis staged at Entebbe would not be possible. "But what we're talking about is what if there were some pressure points that Iran can't stand? A blockade of their ports, or a mining of their ports—whatever. I'm only saying these are examples of all the types of things you would explore. I think for a long time we've made the mistake of telling enemies and potential enemies what we won't do. If you remember, Lyndon Johnson was frequently asked, 'Would we use nuclear weapons in the Vietnam War?' And no one wants to use nuclear weapons. But Lyndon Johnson would say, 'No, under no circumstances would we ever use nuclear weapons.' Well, you really should let the enemy go to bed every night wondering whether you will. You only have to go back to the Korean War, when Eisenhower was elected President. There were many appeals for armistice talks, and Ike, as a new President, said, 'I'm going to review our potential with regard to the use of weapons,' and made it very plain what he was talking about. And almost instantly the North Vietnamese agreed to the Panmunjom talks."

"You mean the North Koreans?"

"The North Koreans."

I ask Reagan what he meant when he said at an earlier rally that there should be "no more Vietnams."

"What I meant by that was never again must this country ever ask young men to fight and die in a war we're afraid to let them win." He tells me a story he says a Vietnam veteran told him the other day about being fired at by people dressed as Buddhist monks and having to get permission from Washington to fire back.

"Are you saying that you wouldn't have gone in or that we should have gone in and fought it in a way to win?"

"I was one who never believed we should have gone in," he says. "I've always believed in the MacArthur dictum that you don't get involved in a land war in Asia. But the troops were sent in; once we sent them in, then you have made a commitment to the men you're asking to fight that you are going to give them every resource to win this thing and get them home as soon as possible. And that's where the difference lay."

I ask Reagan if he thinks we can regain military superiority over the Soviet Union.

"Yes," Reagan replies. "I think the Soviet Union is probably at the very limit of its military output. It has already had to keep its people from having so many consumer goods. Instead, they're devoting it all to this military buildup. I think it's the greatest military buildup the world has ever seen. I think it tops what Hitler did. And therefore, when people talk about an arms race, this doesn't mean that the Soviet Union escalate to twice what they're doing now. We're the ones who have actually played along with the treaties and, if anything, actually reduced our weapons.'' He continues, ''Now, what I think the Russians would fear more than anything else is a United States that all of a sudden would hitch up our belt and say, 'O.K., Buster, we've tried this other way. We are now going to build what is necessary to surpass you.' And this is the last thing they want from us, an arms race, because they are already running as fast as they can and we haven't started running.''

''Where are you going to get the money to pay for this military buildup?''

''Out of the economy.''

When Reagan talks about defense, he sometimes uses examples—such as the fact that a high percentage of Soviet bombers could get through to the United States—that sound alarming but are beside the point. Defense planners, starting with the Nixon period, decided that the real issue was missiles, not bombers.

When I ask him how he would work with the interest groups and institutions in Washington, Reagan says, ''I know how hard it's going to be, because, again, I had a Democratic legislature. But I also found that in many instances in the major things—don't do this with the little things—you work with them, you try to work with them, you compromise, you get as much as you can get. In other words, I'll settle for half a loaf and try for the second half later. But on the major things I took the case to the people, and sometimes it is necessary to make the legislature see the light, you make them feel the heat. This was how we got our welfare reform. They held out for months—in fact, they refused to allow me to present the welfare reform to a joint session of the legislature. That was like banning a book in Boston—that made me a best-seller. Everybody wanted to hear the speech they wouldn't listen to. One day, the leader of the opposition came into my office with his hands above his head, smiling, and he said, 'Stop those cards and letters.' He sat down, and we negotiated out the welfare reform.''

Going back to where I began with him, I ask him how, since he is seen as a conservative, he would broaden his base so as to be able to govern.

Again, he refers to California, pointing out that he won by a million votes in a state that was heavily Democratic. He continues, ''And I think the same thing is evident here. In New Hampshire, I noticed how the networks post people outside the polling place to ask them who they vote for. Well, the other night I was watching that, and I saw that, contrary to the usual Republican country-club, big-business image, they were finding that the more affluent had voted for Bush, and I had the working people. And I think this has always been true. That's what I had in California.''

''And this could happen nationally?''

"I think so, because I think there are millions of Democrats who may not call themselves conservatives, but they've come to realize the federal government's big social solutions just don't work."

We arrive at Sun City Center, a retirement community, almost forty-five minutes late; another large crowd has gathered to await him. Reagan is elated. "Oh, boy, they're here, aren't they?" he says as he starts waving.

Reagan, once more surrounded by red, white, and blue, tells the Sun City Center Republican Club, "Inflation is caused by government, and government can make it go away. It's as simple as that." He talks of the hostages held in Iran and of the American Ambassador being held hostage in Colombia, and says, "Since 1968, there have been sixty-three assassinations of American diplomatic personnel or non-diplomatic but Americans internationally by terrorist groups." He talks of ninety-some kidnappings, six hundred and some bombings. He says, "All of these things have happened to a United States that most of you can remember, as I do remember, a United States that even where an American was on business, or on vacation, or wherever, and got caught in some little country that was having a revolution, or got caught in a war, all that the American had to do was pin to his lapel a little American flag and he could walk right through that war and nobody would lay a finger on him. Well, I want to see that United States back in the world again." He is cheered.

Asked about whether the Shah should have been allowed into this country, he says, "I don't think there would have been a necessity to admit him into this country. Had the right Administration been there or done what was right, the United States would not have pulled the rug out from a thirty-seven-year ally." About the allegations of torture during the Shah's regime, Reagan says, "Is it any different than what Algeria is doing? Is it any different than what Iraq is doing? There are different parts of the world with different customs than ours." He says that he and Nancy had lunch with the Shah in Teheran, and explains that the Shah's major problem was that he was trying to modernize Iran and he divided up the land; he says that the Shah gave away his own land, and that "the mullahs were the other big landowners—maybe that's one of the reasons why they're mad at him."

There being no young people to embrace in his closing, he closes with: "I would like nothing better than to be the leader of this country, a leader whose idea was to remove the shackles and the roadblocks that hold down this great people by government and turn the genius of America once again to be the great country that we were."

Tampa. Reagan has attended a fund raiser and given a television interview, and is now speaking at his last rally of the day, at the Holiday Inn. More red, white, and blue. Another band. Before Reagan arrived, a master of ceremonies explained to the audience that since "this is a media event," the people with Reagan posters should be down front, in sight of the cameras. At these events, the posters face the cameras, not Reagan. The day has been a long one, leaving the impression that no one is to question the man's stamina. Stamina aside, there is, for all the nice-guy, easy demeanor, and underlying toughness. And also a shrewdness. Any doubts that he can be a very determined man should have been overcome four years ago. And his recent victory and the adulation of the crowds have helped propel him along. Reagan does not disappoint his audiences, nor they him. As the day has gone on, he has said many of the same things, but he also seems to have drawn closer and closer to his old self.

Tonight, he suggests that "we reimplement the Tenth Article of the Bill of Rights—that part of the Constitution that says the federal government shall do only those things specifically called for in the Constitution," and he receives huge applause. He asks, "Isn't it time now that we deliver a message to the world that this great industrial giant here is going to rebuild its military forces to the point that there will be no country on earth . . ." and his conclusion is drowned out as the audience stands and cheers. It stands and cheers again when, returning to a line that was one of his most effective ones in 1976, he says, "Yes, if we can get the federal government out of the classroom, maybe we can get God back in." He says that he wants to be President not so that he can hear "Hail to the Chief" and not for the perquisites. But, he says, "I do hunger for that job, because I believe that with the experience I've had I could turn once again to the people of this country and help remove the shackles and the roadblocks that government has put on the people of this country and once again unleash the great power of the American people to go forward . . ." and once more his words are drowned in cheers.

CHAPTER 6

The President

TRYING TO run for re-election and govern at the same time is, as the Carter Administration has been finding out, a far more complex proposition than might have been imagined. The advantages of incumbency are many, of course, but there are disadvantages. While other candidates accuse the President of hiding out in the White House, he has to lay his policies on the line; he has to act. Other people in the vast reaches of his government can cause him political problems. It is in the nature of the Presidency, unless a President has made a decision to serve for only one term, that re-election considerations will affect policy. And it is a requirement of governing that the political implications of actions be considered: without such considerations, effective governing is not possible. But, to the extent that the two are distinguishable, the Carter Administration has indicated more of an interest in politics than in governing. The challenge from Senator Edward Kennedy appears, for a number of reasons, to have raised this interest to a new level.

The President, an intensely competitive man (even for a politician), is said to see himself as running against the Kennedy legend. Kennedy has always aroused a certain resentment among some other politicians. Carter is not the first President to view the Kennedys as a threat—Johnson and Nixon did the same thing. And there has always been a strong feeling among the Carter group that the Carter Administration has never really been accepted as legitimate by the Democratic Party establishment and "Washington." The Kennedy candidacy, more than any other conceivable one, seemed a direct challenge to that legitimacy.

Certain insights and strategies have governed the Carter re-election cam-

122

paign from the outset—and the outset was quite some time ago. Beginning in the fall of 1978, those who would play a major role in the campaign for the election to be held two years later began to meet at the Georgetown house shared by Patrick Caddell, the President's pollster, and Tim Kraft, then the President's appointments secretary and now his national campaign manager. Among those at the meetings were Hamilton Jordan, then the President's top assistant and now his chief of staff; Jody Powell, the President's press secretary; Caddell; Kraft; and Gerald Rafshoon, the President's media adviser. They arrived at a four-part strategy: start early; anticipate the toughest possible opposition; run everywhere; and spend carefully.

For planning purposes, the group assumed that Kennedy would run. The Kennedy spectre over the White House had long been reflected in actions and conversations there. Jordan made it a point to read everything about the Ford campaign in 1976, looking for precedents for an incumbent's campaign. He also studied what Gerald Ford had done to try to keep Ronald Reagan out of the race in 1976, on the theory that these efforts had backfired—had succeeded only in egging Reagan on, and had also suggested that Ford was vulnerable—and that similar behavior was to be avoided. (Carter's "I'm going to whip his ass" comment last June was a deviation from this policy. Until then, in response to the innumerable questions about how Carter viewed the prospects of a Kennedy candidacy the President had politely observed that the Senator had said he would support him.)

Meanwhile, no chances were being taken. By the spring of 1979, months before Kennedy is said to even have made up his mind, the Carter campaign had field organizations in Iowa, New Hampshire, and Florida. When the Draft Kennedy movement in Florida went to work to win a non-binding caucus vote in October, the Carter organization was ready. Carter won. This victory, in turn, hastened Kennedy's entry into the race—before he and his organization were ready.

Jordan was of the view that Kennedy would have more drawbacks as a candidate than was generally appreciated, and Caddell had an insight that became the core of the President's renomination strategy: the voters must be made to feel that when they cast their vote in a primary they were voting in a general election. In a primary, voters might register a protest vote—"send a message"—but in a general election they were choosing a President. The idea, then, was that they must be made to feel that in deciding whether to vote for Carter or Kennedy they were deciding which one they preferred as President. This way, Kennedy was less likely to become the vehicle of people's frustrations against the incumbent Administration, as some primary challengers in the past had been, and would be measured as a potential President.

The focus was to be on Kennedy himself as much as possible. The media campaign was designed to fit this strategy. The Carter slogan was "A Solid Man in a Sensitive Job." The advertising spots stressed what was seen as Carter's strength with the electorate—the view of him as a man of good character, honest, a family man—and, of course, they not very subtly went at what was seen as Kennedy's vulnerability. On the other hand, Carter's strategists realized that Kennedy was seen as a strong leader—a point on which Carter was vulnerable. One of Carter's strategists said to me recently, "If you're President, there are things you can do about this. It's much harder to do something about character problems." The President's strategists were also of the view that people have lower expectations of a President now—think there are things beyond any President's control—and believe we have changed Presidents too often. This is what Caddell terms "the is-it-worth-the-moving-expense? syndrome." Four years ago, Carter ran on the theme of "a fresh face": his inexperience was a credential. Now the theme is "experience."

Many of these things were discussed at a meeting at Camp David late last October that was attended by the President's key strategists and the President himself. Carter is said to have agreed with the idea that the primary contest could be made to be seen as a general election. Caddell believes that Kennedy fell into the trap laid for him by starting off his campaign essentially on the proposition that if the people would simply substitute him for Carter, things would somehow be better. "That invited the public to take a close look at Kennedy," Caddell says.

One of the decisions made at the Camp David meeting was that the most important thing for the President to do to enhance his chances of renomination was to be seen as being "Presidential." One of the participants at the meeting says, "There was acceptance of the idea that Carter would win or lose based on how he was seen doing his job in the White House, far more than on what he did on the campaign trail." The following week—on November 4th, one year before Election Day—the hostages were seized in Iran. One of Carter's strategists says, "The perception of his handling of Iran and Afghanistan had more impact than anything we could have done —tripled or squared."

Actually, in both the public polls and Caddell's private polls, Carter's standing had begun to improve earlier in the fall. Of course, it had been at an all-time low for any President. Also, even before the international events some things occurred that made Carter look better. One was the visit of Pope John Paul II to Washington, in October—of which Carter took full advantage. The other was Carter's speech at the dedication of the Kennedy Library in Boston, on October 20th. By that time, it was clear that Kennedy would be running, and the competitive instincts of Carter and his team were aroused. ("Kennedy will make Carter a better campaigner," one of Carter's advisers said to me then.) And Carter, a notably poor public speaker, walked right into Kennedyland and gave a speech that, given the circumstances, was hailed as a triumph. But there was something in Carter's improvement in the polls that Caddell considered ominous. His soundings indicated to him that the President's improvement, which grew and deepened in December and January, had to do with more than just the international crises: that it involved a more positive view of how Carter, roundly dismissed as "inept" last summer, was handling his job—a sense that he had learned. Caddell found that what he terms the "attitudinal reactions" were similar to those in 1977, Carter's first year in office. Caddell uses as a measurement "semantic differentials," in which he measures responses to word pairings to describe someone—such as warm/cold and effective/ineffective. "Attitudes toward him improved enormously," Caddell said to me a couple of weeks before the New York primary. "At the heart of it seemed to be a perception that he had changed—that he was different from what he was before. That could be very dangerous politically. Sometimes it's better to have people angry and disappointed in you, rather than think you've become something different and then have them come back to thinking, My God, it's the same Jimmy Carter."

Another early decision—taken at a weekend retreat of White House and campaign officials on the Eastern Shore of Maryland late last August, when things looked pretty grim for Carter—was to pursue an "endorsement strategy." The thinking behind this was not what it seemed; a widespread assumption was that it was a rerun of Edmund Muskie's strategy, in 1972, of seeking the endorsement of Democratic political leaders on the theory— which turned out to be mistaken—that the voters would follow.

The theory behind the Carter campaign's endorsement strategy was that in the light of all the talk that Carter was a loser and would drag the Democratic Party to defeat, and that the Party was rising up and demanding that Kennedy run, it was important to show that some important political leaders were standing by Carter. "We had to show that they didn't all believe that if the President was nominated the Party would take a bath," one of the strategists says. This effort culminated in a dinner that was held in October at the Hyatt Regency Hotel in Washington and attended by about five hundred people, including almost two hundred elected officials (over a hundred members of the House, twenty-five senators, several mayors and governors, and various state and county officials). Following that, there was a continuing effort to win endorsements—among other reasons, to keep Kennedy from winning them. One campaign official said to me recently, "The appeal to mayors was simple: 'Here's what the President has done for cities—don't you agree?' " Many mayors and others realized they had little to lose: that the Carter Administration had its hand on certain taps and that in the event Kennedy was nominated he would need their support.

A special group, operating out of the office of Jack Watson, the President's assistant for intergovernmental affairs (meaning liaison with mayors and governors), has worked to help the mayors and governors see what is in their interest. The work that Watson has done over the years in cultivating governors and mayors has proved most beneficial to the campaign. Some time ago, the White House people decided to make more effective political use of the "discretionary" funds in federal programs. Sometimes it was just a matter of deciding who should get credit—a certain congressman, a senator, a mayor, a governor—for a federal grant or loan, and making sure that the President was mentioned. Sometimes it was more than that.

As the campaign got under way, Watson's group kept an eye on the calendar and tried to make sure that the Administration missed no opportunity to make an opportune announcement. Thus, when the Small Business Administration decided, just before the Maine precinct caucuses and the New Hampshire primary, to designate five New England states an "economic dislocation area" because of the lack of snow this winter, enabling businesses to receive low-cost loans (White House aides insist that the timing was just a coincidence), it was arranged that New Hampshire's governor, Hugh Gallen, make the announcement, and stories about it were in the papers while Vice President Mondale and Mrs. Carter were campaigning in the area. And when a certain mayor needed some persuading to support the President, campaign aides could ask Watson's office what might be done by way of speeding a project along, finding some discretionary money— CETA (Comprehensive Employment and Training Act) money, money for urban parks.

By this spring, a decision had been made within the campaign that perhaps the political use of projects had received too much publicity and was beginning to backfire. And there was some question about how much good such efforts did, at least as far as the voters were concerned. For example, a major issue in Maine politics for years had been whether Loring Air Force Base, near Presque Isle, would be kept open, and in late October the Administration announced that it would be kept open permanently. In January, Mondale, who had worked hard on the matter, attended a Chamber of Commerce "appreciation" dinner at the Loring base. A week before the Maine precinct caucuses, Mondale returned for an appearance at Presque Isle. This was an area that the Carter-Mondale campaign thought it should carry in any event. Kennedy carried the area. The practice of making well-aimed, well-timed grants and loans continues, but more quietly. The theory is that the elected officials, if not the public, will be grateful.

There was also established within the White House a group called the "reaction committee," which met every afternoon to decide whether and how to rebut whatever charges Kennedy was making. The group would consider such questions as who should make the response—the Vice President, the First Lady, Powell, a Cabinet officer—and in what forum. Richard Moe, the Vice President's chief of staff, was put in charge of the group, and among its members were David Rubenstein, deputy to Stuart Eizenstat, assistant to the President for domestic affairs and policy; Rex Granum, deputy press secretary; Gail Harrison, assistant to the Vice President for domestic policy; Bert Carp, also of Eizenstat's staff; and Martin Franks, who is in charge of research for the Carter/Mondale Presidential Committee. (Franks served as an administrative assistant to and for a time lived with John Tunney, a former Democratic senator from California, who is one of Kennedy's closest friends—a fact that the Carter people believe has made the Kennedy people nervous.) Sometimes Powell was involved; sometimes people with expertise in a particular subject were invited to join in. When Kennedy gave his speech at Georgetown University one morning in late January and laid out specific policy differences with the Administration, the reaction committee, including Powell, went to work earlier than usual. (Some people at the White House could not for the life of them understand why Kennedy made the speech so early in the day, giving them plenty of time to prepare a response.)

The group decided to refrain from engaging Kennedy on the issues—despite some eagerness to do so—in order to avoid drawing attention to them and elevating them. So Powell, at his regular afternoon briefing, simply offered the observation that Kennedy's defeat in Iowa had driven him to the left and he would have difficulty squaring some of the things he had said with his previous record. The official response was drafted for the campaign committee, which issued a statement declaring, among other things, that the speech represented Kennedy's "latest attempt to develop a rationale for his candidacy."

The following day, Robert Strauss, the committee's chairman, referring to the Kennedy speech, remarked in Richmond, "I talked with the President about twenty minutes last night, and, I'm almost embarrassed to say, it never came up." Some campaign aides thought that Strauss should have got an Academy Award for that. After a while, the reaction committee decided that people weren't paying much attention to what Kennedy was saying, and as the New York primary—which had the campaign organization worried—approached, the group became a sort of New York committee: making sure that everything that could be done in the state was being done, that the multitude of government representatives who were sent to the state did not talk at cross-purposes, and that everyone who needed to be sent was sent.

The President's remaining in the White House was more a situation that evolved than a strategy that was decided upon, and its consequences were unwelcome to many of the President's political advisers. It began when Carter cancelled a scheduled four-day campaign trip at the end of November and then, in early December, cancelled his appearance at a fund-raising dinner in Washington where he was to announce his candidacy and instead made a brief statement in the East Room of the White House. In both cases, the rationale that was offered was that the President did not wish to be distracted from his search for a solution to the hostage crisis. Even then, some people around the President warned that he should be careful not to get caught in the position of saying that he would undertake no political appearances as long as the hostages were being held. At that point, Kennedy was considered a serious threat, and Carter was warned that to stay away from the voters too long might be disastrous. One of the President's political advisers says, "When he cancelled those appearances in November and

December, no one dreamed he'd still be in the White House in March." When the question arose whether the President should participate in the debate in Iowa in January, his political advisers were actually divided. Some thought that since Kennedy was now appearing vulnerable, the President had everything to lose by getting up on a stage with him—and also with Jerry Brown, whose debating skills they especially feared. Others thought that the President could hold his own and that his failure to appear would be politically costly, and also that the debate offered a "window" out of a strategy they might come to regret. "Our discussion was not in terms of the hostages," says one political adviser. This person says that while the President came to his conclusion largely on the ground that he should not give the appearance of returning to business as usual, "he also had a political inkling that it might be better to stay out of the debate." Once the debate decision was made, and put on the basis of the hostages, the policy was set. Another of the President's advisers says, "The strategy became strategy not when it happened—when the President first cancelled his appearances —but six weeks later."

There is reason to believe the political advisers when they say that they wish the President had been campaigning outside the White House—that the same enthusiasm cannot be generated in his absence, that the trappings (Air Force One and all that) are politically helpful out there. Many have felt that, for all the television time a President can command, Carter simply wasn't visible enough. But the strategy had become a trap. (On the other hand, some White House aides suggested privately that there was some risk that when the President did campaign he might—especially in the face of a Kennedy challenge—display a certain mean streak that he evidenced in 1976. When Hubert Humphrey finally said he would not enter the race, Carter couldn't help saying he was sorry because he would have liked to show that he could beat him.) There was also strong evidence, based on conversations with White House aides, that, whatever happened with regard to the hostages, the White House had settled on a policy of not joining Kennedy—and Brown—in a debate. They indicated that if the hostages were released and the President hit the road, there would still be a disinclination to debate. Meanwhile, the reluctance to debate made it all the more important that the President not be seen as making "political" appearances.

There were, of course, advantages to having the President stay home. He could appear Presidential, while Kennedy appeared to be racing around the country yapping. Kennedy could make ten appearances a day and perhaps earn a minute and a half on television that night—and there were many nights, especially during the foreign crises, when he was not on at all— while Carter was more likely to get on the air simply by holding a meeting, greeting some athletes. One of the President's aides said to me in early February, "I know from 1976 how frustrating it is to go to twenty towns a day and make six charges and that night see on television only the President signing a bill and hardly working up a sweat." There were also less obvious advantages. This same aide said, "We have the luxury, which we didn't have in the '76 campaign, of planning what we want to do that day and, since we aren't shuttling through the sky, having excellent communications. The President can say in the morning, 'I want to say this today,' the speech writers can work on it, advance notice can be given to the press, the press can be briefed, and the President can say it at four o'clock—in time to get on the air. When you're flying around, the work can't get done that well. You can't have the wide consultations; you can't get the reporters briefed; the candidate can't be as well prepared. When you're here, you can get on the air just by being seen with someone who is prominent—you don't even have to say anything. When you're on the road, the story is you're campaigning and how you're doing and the mistakes you're making."

One evening that week, all three networks reported the President's call to the Canadian Prime Minister, Joe Clark, to thank him for Canada's help in obtaining the release of some Americans from Iran; two of the networks reported Carter's sending Muhammad Ali to Africa to secure support for the boycott of the Moscow Olympics; two networks reported on Kennedy, both focussing on his campaign troubles. The White House also believed that the nature of the surrogates it could send out to campaign for the President gave him an edge. Mrs. Carter and Vice President Mondale, of course, carried the brunt of the campaigning. Almost all the Cabinet officers —the exceptions were Secretary of State Cyrus Vance, Attorney General Benjamin Civiletti, and Defense Secretary Harold Brown—were out campaigning, and so were members of the White House senior staff. A White House aide said to me earlier this year, "Kennedy may have twenty-six relatives out there, but he doesn't have big-name people with a lot of power talking to people. A labor group would rather hear the Secretary of Labor than Caroline Kennedy." The White House also figured that having Rosalynn Carter out campaigning at a time when Joan Kennedy was visibly struggling to gain composure as a campaigner was an asset of several dimensions. "We have a *wife* out there," the aide said. He also pointed out that by not having the President campaign a good bit of money was being saved.

Just as the Carter campaign is being run by essentially—in fact, almost exactly—the same people who ran the 1976 campaign (Jordan, Powell, Caddell, Rafshoon, and, to a lesser extent, Kraft and Strauss), so the White House is dominated by the small group that dominated it before last summer's noisy shake-ups and reorganization. In both cases, Jordan remains the most powerful of the President's aides, and in both cases there are Jordan and Powell and then everyone else. Mrs. Carter is also, of course, a most important influence, and because she and Mondale have been on the front lines of the campaign, what they say about that has some authority. The talents of some of Mondale's staff have become more fully appreciated, and used.

On most Monday evenings, there is a campaign meeting in the residence side of the White House, with the President, the Vice President, Mrs. Carter, Jordan, Powell, Caddell, Rafshoon, Strauss, Kraft, Moe, Sarah Weddington, an assistant to the President, and Philip Wise, the President's appointments secretary, in attendance. Other meetings and conversations go on, of course, all the time. Strauss, while he is the titular head of the campaign, does not really run it. In a sense, no one really runs the Carter campaign; it is a collegial undertaking, not without its strains. Strauss acts on behalf of the campaign, makes appearances, raises money, offers advice, keeps in touch with his vast network, speaks for the President—all of which is quite valuable. The Kennedy campaign has no counterpart. Nor did Kennedy begin with a team that had had the experience of working together through a Presidential campaign, as the Carter group had. When one of the Carter political strategists was telling me what an advantage this prior experience was for the Carter campaign, I asked him about the fact that Carter barely won the 1976 nomination and nearly lost the election. "We learned from that experience," he replied. And then he added (this was shortly before the New York primary), "Of course, we haven't really been tested yet."

Jordan's attention to the campaign, and to his duties as chief of staff, has been somewhat fitful. For a brief period following his designation last summer as chief of staff, he gave a spurt of interviews in which he acknowledged that his image could stand some improving and pledged that he and the way the White House was run would change. But then came the investigation into allegations that Jordan had used cocaine, and, according to his friends, there followed a period in which he seemed distracted from his job. Subsequently, when he had started giving more attention to his White House duties, and to the campaign, he became a sort of desk officer for the Iranian problem—partly because the President needed a trusted confidant to carry out a sensitive job (and apparently no one else was as trusted) and partly because Jordan had become buddies with Omar Torrijos Herrera, the head of the government of Panama, during the long fight over the Panama Canal Treaties. The Iran assignment took him both to Panama and to Paris. And Jordan adopted the policy of having very little contact with the press and staying out of the public eye. According to his friends, this was not just because he was carrying out sensitive assignments but also because he felt that he had been burned by the press and his image was not helpful to the President.

The chore of shaping up the management of the White House was turned over to Alonzo McDonald, the former managing director of McKinsey & Company, the management-consulting firm, who was brought into the White House to act as staff director. McDonald has succeeded in imposing a little more order in some matters, but he is largely a target of derision (within the White House, he is widely referred to as Gonzo), because of his incessant process memos (they say such things as "Of course, we must accomplish these tasks in an orderly and professional manner") and his efforts to impose business-management techniques on an institution that, by its nature, leaving aside the current crowd, does not lend itself to them. The requirements of political action, in its broadest sense, cannot be made to fit "Program Evaluation and Review Technique [PERT] charts" or "critical path analysis." McDonald has worked out an elaborate chart for the preparation of Presidential speeches, rating the importance of a speech (from A to D) and its difficulty (from 1 to 4), and setting forth the subject, themes, and tone. For example, Mrs. Carter's greeting of the Pope in Boston was rated an A-4; the subject was listed as "Welcome;" the theme was "Introduction to American People;" and the specified tone was "Uplift/Eloquent/Emotional." A Presidential toast for President López Portillo of Mexico was rated B-2; the subject was identified as "U.S./Mexican Relations;" and the specified tone was "Warm/Neighborly."

Cabinet meetings, which once were held weekly, are now infrequent. According to several witnesses, there has been no noticeable increase in efforts by the White House to manage the government. The new, bold, unconventional approaches to governing that were supposed to emerge from the sessions at Camp David last July never seemed to come to pass. By this spring, almost half the staff members of the congressional-liaison office were out working on the campaign in various states. Since, technically, campaign work is not supposed to take place at the White House or on White House time (a technicality all Administrations blink at—as, to some extent, they must), in the past few months various members of the White House staff have been taking leaves of absence, using up compensatory time, or deciding that they would take vacations in such places as Iowa, New Hampshire, Illinois, and New York.

There were major disputes within the White House over the political implications of some of the most fateful decisions that the President has made this year, and there were also a number of politically alarming moments, even before New York. One of those moments was caused by the tone and the nature of the President's State of the Union speech. There was serious disagreement over whether the President should call for draft registration: the major proponent was the President; the opponents were a number of the people—including Mondale, Eizenstat, and Caddell—who advise the President on domestic and political matters. Jordan and Powell are said to have favored it. Vance and Brown are characterized as not having been much involved in the dispute, and Zbigniew Brzezinski, the President's national-security adviser, as favoring registration but not arguing very strenuously for it. Brzezinski was more concerned with other aspects of the speech. The idea was suggested at a meeting with the President, but a number of people at the White House apparently did not think that anything would come of it. Then the proposal turned up in a draft of the speech that the President himself had worked on at Camp David. The opponents argued that registration was not necessary—the Selective Service had just completed a report saying as much. They also argued that it was a poor idea politically: Caddell, who is described by others as having been nearly beside himself about the matter, argued that it would alienate the very groups that provide volunteers for campaigns. Eizenstat wrote a memorandum saying that registration was neither necessary nor advisable. Mondale argued against the idea. A number of junior staff members opposed it. Initially, the President wanted to call for immediate registration, but eventually he was persuaded to start with a proposal for simply revitalizing the Selective Service system.

The opponents of the whole idea argued against it up until shortly before the President gave his speech, and at one point they thought they had the President convinced—but it turned out that they had simply misread one version of the toned-down proposal. The President, says one of those who were in on the argument, *felt very strongly about it*. The public explanation was that this was one way to show the Soviet Union that the United States intended to be firm in its response to the invasion of Afghanistan. But there is also reason to believe that the President, and perhaps some of his advisers, saw a political attraction in the idea: that Kennedy would be sure to oppose it (as he did, in his Georgetown speech), and that this would be another way of identifying him with the left fringe of the Democratic Party, and also as "soft" on the Soviet Union.

Shortly after the State of the Union speech, one White House aide said to me, with some excitement, that now they would have Kennedy three for three: that he had opposed the embargo on the sale of grain to the Soviet Union, that he had opposed the boycott of the Olympics, and that now he would oppose registration. Kennedy had taken the first two positions during the campaign in Iowa, where the President defeated him by a two-to-one margin—a greater margin than the White House had expected. The campaign statement issued after Kennedy's Georgetown speech said, "First he opposed the grain embargo. Next, [he] opposed an Olympic boycott. Now he opposes draft registration. . . . If Senator Kennedy is not willing to support actions which show the Soviets we mean business, what would he do?" A White House aide talked to reporters in the same vein, and this made its way onto the television news. CBS reported that "officials" said, "What is he prepared to do to stand up to the Russians?"

The long-standing differences between Brzezinski and the State Department over how to deal with the Soviet Union continue, and they affected the deliberations over the tone of the State of the Union speech. There was agreement within the Administration that there should be a sharp response to the Soviet invasion; the differences were over not only the tone of the response but also the degree to which it should reverse the course of foreign policy. Brzezinski, who was predisposed to see events in terms of the rivalry of the United States and the Soviet Union, and eager to take actions that would challenge the Soviets, had his moment after the invasion of Afghanistan. He wanted to characterize the invasion as a critical juncture in the two-power struggle and as defining the situation in the Persian Gulf. He is portrayed—by people who do not agree with him, and not just in the State Department—as having seen the Afghanistan invasion as an opportunity to make fundamental changes in our dealings with the Soviet Union. The State Department, for its part, was anxious to retain what people there refer to as the "framework" of our foreign policy—concern with the internal structure of nations in the Persian Gulf region and elsewhere in the Third World, concern with regional conflicts, a continuation of the effort to achieve arms control, prevention of a total rupture in our dealings with the Soviet Union. Each side got some of what it wanted, but, according to neutral witnesses of the battle, Brzezinski, who had the more dynamic position, essentially prevailed. One person at the State Department said to me not long ago, "I do sympathize with the President; it's easier to enunciate questions in terms of the superpowers than in terms of countries' internal problems." He added, "A political campaign doesn't make it especially easy to maintain a nuanced and balanced policy." The confusion that followed the President's enunciation of a "Persian Gulf doctrine" was indicative of the way foreign policy has sometimes been conducted: moves are made without sufficient preparation or before the next moves or the consequences are thought through. For example, much was made, very publicly, of our renewed interest in an alliance of sorts with Pakistan, and, very publicly, we were rejected.

Some of the President's domestic and political advisers were also concerned about the tone of the State of the Union speech and its emphasis of the superpower conflict, and several thought the President's description of the Afghanistan invasion as "the most serious threat to the peace since the Second World War" hyperbolic, and one that might lead to later difficulty. But there is also good reason to believe that some domestic and political advisers were not disturbed by these things, and that to them as well as to the President the tone of the speech was good politics. Since Carter's first year in office, Jordan has been worried that the President may have made foreign-policy and defense moves that cumulatively might cause him to appear too "dovish," and give him domestic political problems. It is a fact that Carter, Jordan, and Powell come from a state with a political tradition of stressing military might—the tradition of Richard Russell, Carl Vinson —and that Carter supported the war in Vietnam for quite a long time. When Lieutenant William Calley was convicted of the murder of civilians at My Lai, Carter, as Governor of Georgia, declared "American Fighting Man's Day" and issued a proclamation urging Georgians to display the flag and turn their automobile headlights on during the day.

There is no reason to doubt that Carter's effort to achieve an arms-control agreement with the Soviet Union has been sincere. (The effort to achieve Senate approval of the treaty this year has been abandoned.) But there is evidence that Carter's pledge, when he was running for the nomination in 1976, to cut the defense budget was one of a number of things he did to woo the Party's liberals. When the President was preparing his State of the Union speech, he was in some trouble for having backed down on the question of the Soviet troops in Cuba; the White House believed that public support of his handling of the hostage problem was running out (he had been remarkably successful in getting across the idea that military action would be in vain); the public was moving away from his early positions on questions of defense and the Soviet Union; and he was under increasing criticism that he had led us into weak foreign and defense policies. It was inevitable that these things would be taken into consideration in the State of the Union speech, particularly in a Presidential-election year.

As it turned out, the speech put the President in jeopardy in the tests in Maine and New Hampshire that followed. Early in the campaign planning, Hamilton Jordan realized that there was a chance in Maine for what, it then seemed, would be interpreted as an upset of Kennedy in New England. The thinking went that Maine voters are independent types and would not automatically be for Kennedy; that relations between Edmund Muskie and Kennedy were cool at best, and Muskie could be counted on to help; and that since Maine would hold caucuses, rather than a primary, the Carter people would have an advantage, because they were good at organizing for caucuses. Moreover, Carter had won the Maine caucuses in 1976. The idea was that the attempt in Maine would be low-key—low-profile, as they say. They hoped to take the Kennedy people by surprise. But after the Iowa caucuses the press began to focus on Maine, and so did Kennedy, who now needed to do well there; the Carter people regrouped, tripled the budget for Maine, added staff, and decided to invest a fair amount of their resources in the media there. This turned out to be an important strategic decision, because Kennedy made a major effort in the state, and, significantly, received a lot of help from volunteers—busloads of students from out of state—who were upset about registration. Carter won, but the press focus was on how close Kennedy had come (four points). "We won the election but lost the interpretation," one Carter campaign strategist said to me afterward.

Just after Maine, the Carter people found that Kennedy's strength was growing in New Hampshire, which would hold its primary slightly more than two weeks later, and they believed that New Hampshire was, after Massachusetts, the state in which Kennedy was most likely to do well. And Caddell's surveys in New Hampshire were turning up some very interesting, disturbing, and, in retrospect, foreboding things.

In measuring how Carter is doing in a given state, Caddell keeps track of two sets of numbers. One is the surface numbers that any poll might find— how people say they are going to vote. The other is the "adjusted figures," indicating where the voters might actually end up, which Caddell arrives at after respondents have been asked a set of questions that force them to reconsider their preference. This polling enables him to see the way the voters seem to be moving. (Kennedy, strapped for resources, has had nothing like this. For some time, Kennedy has had no professional polling at all

—only some volunteer polling.) Caddell found that while the surface figures showed Carter holding a substantial lead over Kennedy in New Hampshire, the adjusted figures showed him only five points ahead. He found that Carter's lead was shrinking partly because of the economy, partly because Kennedy's campaign was taking hold, and also, he noticed, because a substantial number of voters were disturbed by the President's reaction to the invasion of Afghanistan and all the talk of war. His surveys also showed that New Hampshire voters were moving toward a "primary" rather than a "general election" vote—that they were considering casting a protest vote against Carter. Several steps were taken to counter this. Caddell's polls indicated that one of the points that had the greatest impact on voters whose support for Carter was "soft" and on those who were potential defectors (these are separate categories) was Carter's successful negotiation of the Middle East peace treaty last year. The surveys also found that a lot of people had forgotten about the event but that when they were reminded of it, it suggested to them that Carter can get things done and, more important, that he is a man of peace.

Fortunately for Carter, a press conference had been scheduled for the evening of February 13th, three days after the Maine caucuses—his first press conference in eleven weeks. (In the beginning of his Administration, Carter made a point of holding a press conference about every two weeks.) The February press conference was put to several uses. New Hampshire voters like to see the candidates—expect to be cultivated by them—and the press conference was a way for Carter to undercut the idea, which was taking hold, that he was hiding out in the White House. And he took several opportunities to stress the point that he was seeking peaceful solutions to the international crises. ("We must convince the Soviet Union, through peaceful means, *peaceful* means, that they cannot invade an innocent country with impunity.") The word "peace" recurred many times. He emphasized that he had not called for and did not anticipate calling for a draft. Also, Carter, angered by Kennedy's charge that the Administration was moving to establish a United Nations commission on Iran only because Kennedy had urged that it do so, attacked Kennedy strongly for this. ("His statements have not been true, they've not been accurate, and they've not been responsible, and they've not helped our country.") Carter's anger was a real anger, apparently, but the demonstration of it was calculated. Caddell's figures showed afterward that Kennedy's "negatives"—questions about his credibility and dependability—went up.

Also to deal with the "war talk" problem in New Hampshire, Carter's advertising was changed. One of the "negative" radio spots was pulled off the air. This one charged Kennedy with saying one thing and doing another on several issues, including defense (it said that in the past he had supported several defense cuts), and it was believed to be hurting Carter with the "peace" voters. While Rafshoon worked up two new television spots, another one, referred to as the "peace spot," was run. This spot shows Carter at a "town meeting" in Elk City, Oklahoma, in March, 1979. A woman stands up and says, choking with emotion, that she wants to make a comment: that she is the mother of three teen-age boys and she wants to thank Carter for his role as a peacemaker. And then the crowd erupts into a standing ovation. Carter has a look of humble pride. A narrator says, "People have disagreed with President Carter on various issues, but on one point there is absolute agreement stretching all across the nation. More than any other President in recent times, this man has been a peacemaker."

One of the new spots shows scenes at the Camp David summit, the signing of the peace treaty, and Carter telling the Cabinet, "To get peace in the Middle East is more important than my being re-elected." The narrator says, "More than most Presidents in recent times, the President has been a peacemaker, and he has not forgotten that we are still the last, best hope on earth," and after still another scene of the treaty-signing the narrator says, "President Jimmy Carter: Peacemaker."

The other new spot, referred to as the "two things" ad, shows a ballot with the names of the candidates, and the narrator says, "A man brings two things to a Presidential campaign. He brings his record, and he brings himself. . . . In the voting booth, the voter must weigh both record and character before deciding. Often it's not easy, and the voter winds up asking, 'Is this the person I really want in the White House for the next four years?' A man brings two things to a campaign: his record and himself." And then the spot shows a hand checking off Carter. Mondale began virtually every campaign appearance in New Hampshire with references to Carter as a steady man, a peacemaker. Within a week, Carter went back up in the adjusted figures to an eleven-point lead over Kennedy, or forty-nine to thirty-eight —which is how the New Hampshire primary turned out. One campaign strategist says, "We were rolling down the hawk trail, and Caddell pulled us off." Caddell says, "Presidential politics is always about images."

The "run everywhere" strategy has turned out to be crucial. There were several theories behind it. In 1976, the Carter campaign was able to "leapfrog"—organize in a few states at a time, and, when one primary or caucus was completed, pack up and move to a state whose contest was farther down the calendar. The thinking this time was that, as the incumbent, Carter had to have a presence in every state—that organizers, state politicians, other politicians, and the press would be looking for that presence. (At the outset, the Kennedy people were talking about "running everywhere," too, but the money wasn't there.) By mid-March of this year, the Carter-Mondale organization had over three hundred paid staff members in the field and about half as many full-time volunteers. The total campaign staff was around four hundred and fifty—a quite sizable organization. There were around sixty full-time, paid staff people in Illinois alone. Having people in the various states not only helps with organizing and canvassing but also provides a capacity for building crowds for a candidate—or, in this case, his surrogates. One of the campaign strategists says, "All of that may not amount to more than five or ten percent of the vote, but in a close race that's what makes the difference." Another factor in the strategy was that if the campaign did turn out to be a long one, the more states the Carter people were organized in early, the better. This would provide some security if things did not go well at first: because of proportional representation —a candidate can lose a primary or a caucus and still get some portion of the delegates—it paid to make an effort to pick up delegates wherever possible.

One insight that Caddell and Jordan had was that making a real effort in Vermont would be worthwhile: the Vermont primary took place on the same day as the Massachusetts primary, and they figured that a victory there might take some of the glow off the probable Kennedy victory in Massachusetts. (Caddell pointed out that Vermont was a very Protestant state, with fewer blue-collar voters than either New Hampshire or Massachusetts.) And so on election night, when the anchormen were telling us about Kennedy's first victory, in his "home state" of Massachusetts, they were also pointing out that "next door" Carter had defeated Kennedy seventy-four to twenty-six percent.

On February 22nd, the Friday before the New Hampshire primary, the Consumer Price Index went up to eighteen and two-tenths percent—almost four and a half points above the figure for the previous month. The Producer Price Index (formerly the Wholesale Price Index) for January had already gone to twenty and seven-tenths percent. The bond market was in disarray. On Monday, February 25th, the day before the New Hampshire primary, the President told a group of out-of-town editors that his current economic policies "suit me fine." One of his campaign strategists says, "We did not view that as helpful politically or economically." The President also said of his policies, "The tuning of those and the enhancement of those is something that we intend to do," but this remark was generally overlooked. As a matter of fact, the President had met with his economic advisers on Sunday evening, and a review of the Administration's economic policy was under way. The Administration was in still another trap: caught between its acceptance of the fact that it was necessary to take action to try to break the inflation fever, so as to calm people down, and its reluctance to take action that might be costly in the forthcoming primaries in two large industrial states—Illinois and New York. In a way, this was yet another form of a tension that had existed in Administration policy all along: the tension between trying to avoid offending the Democratic Party's constituent groups (with the spectre of Kennedy behind them) and trying to conduct a domestic policy that would be suitable for a general election.

In the fall of 1980, when the budget for the fiscal year 1981 was being planned, there was some discussion of whether the President should try to achieve a balanced budget then—as he had promised during his 1976 campaign. Some people in the Office of Management and Budget suggested that, given the political danger of the inflation issue, the budget should be balanced—even at the risk of inflaming the Democratic constituent groups—

and taxes should be cut when the inflationary fever cooled down. (Among other things, inflation was causing increases in people's income taxes.) The President was said to have been interested in the idea but to have been argued out of it by a number of his advisers. Some said that the President was already moving toward a very restrictive fiscal policy (the most restrictive since 1973), that his Administration was forecasting a recession (as were most economists), and that he was already lowering the deficit significantly from the one he inherited. (The deficit he inherited from Ford was forty-four billion dollars, and that was being decreased to an estimated fifteen billion eight hundred million for fiscal 1981.) Stuart Eizenstat and Vice President Mondale, taking the sort of position they generally took in such arguments, said that the budget was already very tight and that there could be trouble with the constituent groups if it was cut further. Several dispassionate outside economists also felt that the fiscal policy represented in the budget was a tight one, that there was essentially no real growth in spending, and that in real terms the national debt was being decreased. Approximately sixty-seven billion dollars of the budget was going toward paying interest on the debt; if interest rates were not so high, the budget would have shown a surplus. In the end, the Administration produced what the late Arthur Okun, the economist, termed a "muddle-through election-year budget": it didn't make very drastic changes, and it didn't make very many groups very angry. The Democratic interest groups were relatively calm: they had been steeled for the worst and carefully attended to by the White House, and many of their concerns had been taken care of.

But a substantial body of opinion had been building in the country behind the idea of a balanced budget, and Congress was feeling the pressure. Even members of Congress who did not believe that a balanced budget would make much difference in the cost-of-living figures—and the economists' computers said that it would not—began to back the idea. Moreover, they understood, as the Administration finally did, that a balanced budget had taken on a psychological importance. Some Administration officials insist that in December the public was not ready to accept a balanced budget; but some people (Democrats) on Capitol Hill argue that the Administration had miscalculated the mood of the public and Congress, and need not have put itself through two budget exercises within three months. One Administration official pointed out to me that since most members of Congress do not face primary challenges, they were looking to the politics of November, while the President was faced with a different political situation.

One of the ironies and difficulties of this whole business is that in reality those whom the interest groups represent are as disturbed about inflation as anybody else, but the groups themselves do not want to make the sacrifices. The person who is upset about inflation and the person who is upset about the loss of a certain government grant, loan, or service are often the same person. Some members of the Administration expected inflation to rise in January—largely as the consequences of increased oil prices spread through the economy—but no one expected the rise to be so explosive or so pervasive. As people borrowed to keep up, inflation cycled upward. And the recession refused to arrive. The unusual executive-congressional deliberations that ensued on how to cut the budget were in part an exercise in getting each other to share responsibility for the unpleasantness, and in part an effort by the Administration to insure that whatever it came up with would succeed in Congress, where the interest groups would wage their fight. I asked one White House man whether the President could not still take political credit if he came up with budget reductions that Congress did not approve. "No," he replied. "Because then the President wouldn't look like a leader."

While the serious deliberations were going on within the White House over what to do about the economy, there were also serious deliberations over when and how to announce whatever was decided. The President's political advisers were virtually unanimous in their hope that any unpleasant news about budget cuts could be put off until after the Illinois and New York primaries. The thinking of some went that if they could wait until after Illinois and New York, by then Kennedy might well be out of the race, and the Administration would have until November to pacify the Democratic constituent groups—mayors, governors, labor, blacks—that were likely to be angered by the cuts. One political adviser said to me then, "I think we've all said to him, 'Couldn't you wait until after New York?' "

To some extent, the decision about the timing of the new anti-inflation proposals was affected by an ostensibly unrelated matter—the vote in the United Nations Security Council on Saturday, March 1st, condemning Israel for its settlements on the West Bank and in Gaza, and calling for their dismantling. After some frantic meetings on Monday, the White House issued its strange statement that evening that the vote had been an error, and Administration officials explained to reporters that the President had been under the impression that all references to East Jerusalem had been removed. They also pointed out that after the vote they had expressed reservations about the section calling for the dismantling of the settlements. The Administration's explanation that the whole thing resulted from a "communications failure" between the President and Vance, and Vance's assumption of the blame, did no good. As it happens, a copy of the resolution had been before the President, but Administration officials told reporters later that the President hadn't read it. A copy was also before the staff of the National Security Council. It has never been satisfactorily explained how it was that no one on the large staff of the National Security Council bothered to keep track of what was going on. Taken by itself, the United Nations vote, controversial as it was, might not have been such a monumental thing. It had the impact it did because it brought back, powerfully, an impression of the Carter Administration that was most politically damaging. "We're back to the 'incompetence' problem," a White House aide said to me mournfully at the time. That such a thing might come about is precisely what Caddell had feared when the President's standing began to improve last fall.

On Friday, March 7th, the Producer Price Index was at nineteen and one-tenth percent—not much better than the previous month's figure. Some of the President's political advisers began to sense that Kennedy was picking up ground, that the issue of the economy was beginning to cause the President more political damage—and Caddell's "numbers" bore these things out. In the White House, a consensus developed that as a result of the United Nations vote and inflation the Administration was caught in what one aide described to me at the time as "a downdraft," and that it was politically as well as economically necessary to take action on the economy before the Illinois and New York primaries.

A consensus also developed that the budget must be balanced. Some steps to achieve that were rejected as out of the question in an election year. (For example, it is generally agreed that the Consumer Price Index reflects mortgage-interest rates to an excessive degree; and many government "entitlement" programs, such as Social Security, are required by law to rise by the same amount as the Consumer Price Index. But the Administration hadn't the least interest in attempting to change the way the Consumer Price Index is computed, or the laws by which entitlement programs work, in an election year. When I asked one White House aide, somewhat facetiously, why these approaches weren't taken, he replied, "Are you kidding?") Wage and price controls were ruled out: the President has said he is against them, and, besides, Kennedy is for them (as are a few members of the President's entourage). There was a flurry of meetings at the White House on the first weekend in March, and it was decided that the President would present his economic proposals in the coming week.

Then there were innumerable discussions about how to "package" his presentation. Some of the President's political advisers—including Rafshoon, Caddell, Jordan, and Powell—were searching for a way for the President to give a speech on the inflation problem without becoming identified with the inflation problem. They recalled the problem that the President had been faced with last July, when he cancelled a speech on energy and then, ten days later, gave one about "malaise" (with energy thrown in): his previous energy speeches had done him little good politically. One of the political strategists explained to me in the course of these deliberations, "When the President gives a speech about something that is a negative, it associates him with something that is a negative." He continued, "Every time Carter has given a speech about inflation, it hasn't helped inflation, and has therefore hurt Carter. The White House is accused of P.R.-ing so much. There are some things you don't want to P.R." But the Vice President, Eizenstat, and the President's economic advisers—"the substance people," as they are derisively referred to by one of the political strategists—wanted the President to give a televised address before a Joint Session of Congress, to get the most attention for his new program. (Some of them also thought that this would be politically wise—would show the President "taking charge.")

But one political adviser remarked to me at the time, "There aren't a lot of applause lines in a speech on budget cuts and credit controls." Finally, Thomas P. O'Neill, Jr., the Speaker of the House, advised the White House that the President should not make such a big deal of doing such an unpopular thing, and this is said to have influenced Mondale. Some people in the House think this advice may have reflected O'Neill's own feeling that the new budget exercise was an almost entirely political one and would therefore be done in the worst possible way. The Speaker, an unreconstructed liberal, believed that the only excuse for the exercise was to calm the financial markets, and he took a dim view of the whole idea.

The final "packaging" was designed to achieve a number of objectives. The President delivered his speech in the East Room on Friday afternoon before a friendly group—Cabinet officers, some members of Congress, and other invited guests. (There was not a drop of applause until the President concluded.) The political aides figured that the networks would not choose to televise the speech and that, even if they did, not many people would be watching in the middle of the afternoon. (But they did televise it.) Then, the thinking went, by holding a televised press conference that evening, the President could announce the essentials of his new program and change the subject by taking questions on other matters. The President's advisers believe that the President is at his best at press conferences.

The whole argument over how the President was to deliver a speech on what had become a national crisis, and the nature of the speech itself, typified what even some people inside the Administration consider a fundamental problem: that the President and some of the people around him are excessively technocratic—lack a sense of how to maneuver and set in motion large forces, lack the sense of theater that the Presidency requires. It was this problem, above all, that set off the sessions at Camp David last summer, after which everything was supposed to change. Even some of the President's supporters were dismayed that he had not already got himself across as someone who was in there battling inflation. "Can you find our energy-conservation program?" one of the President's advisers asked me not long ago. The many shifts of direction have dismayed members of Congress who generally support the President. They are pleased that there have been no Mayaguezes and feel that the Administration is essentially an enlightened and humane one. A certain historical relativity is applied, and they remember that the Constitution has not been assaulted, and they are relieved that, whatever the fits and starts of foreign policy, there has been a general exercise of restraint. The problem for other politicians who would like to defend the Administration's policies is that they are not sure, from week to week, what it is they are supposed to defend.

It appears to be the case that it was not technically possible for the Administration to produce all the numbers for the new budget by the time the President made his speech; it is the case that more information about the nature of the budget cuts could have been released before the Illinois and New York primaries. As things turned out, in trying to have it both ways the Administration got it both ways: enough was known about the cuts to make people angry, and the withholding of more detail was seen as a cynical move.

On the day after the New York primary, more information about the budget cuts was released. As the final decisions on the new budget were being made, Eizenstat succeeded in persuading the economic advisers to salvage five hundred million dollars for "financially hard-pressed cities" that were going to lose other funds as a result of the cuts. Robert Giaimo, Democrat of Connecticut and the chairman of the House Budget Committee, dubbed this the "Jimmy Carter New York primary amendment," and a few days before the primary the committee rejected it. And in the course of the week that the final decisions about the economic speech were being debated, the U.N. mission to Iran failed.

Before the Illinois and New York primaries, it was clear from conversations with numerous people involved in the President's campaign—including "the substance people"—that they were worried about the effects of the recent string of events on the forthcoming contests. There was far less concern about Illinois than about New York, because the President had been holding such a commanding lead in Illinois, but there was concern that if that lead should slip, this would have an impact on New York. The Illinois campaign was supervised by James Johnson, the Vice President's executive assistant, and he and his colleagues had a splendid time turning Mayor Jane Byrne's endorsement of Kennedy into as large an albatross as possible. For months, the campaign worked to peel away other Illinois politicians and isolate the Mayor, and the Carter people understood the importance, because of the way the Illinois primary works, of having major local figures run as their delegates. A man named Todd Renfrow, an important downstate county leader, may have received as many calls from President Carter as Menachem Begin has. The division between the Mayor and the late Mayor's oldest son, Richard (Richie) Daley, was exploited. Surrogates trooped through the state to take on Kennedy. On the Monday before the primary, Charles Duncan, the Secretary of Energy, was in downstate Illinois, where there is a lot of coal, swapping charges with the Kennedy people over whether the Carter Administration or Kennedy was more anti-coal. The whole thing took on a rather slapstick quality, and Carter, of course, clobbered Kennedy, defeating him two to one. The delegate-count margin was even greater—a hundred and sixty-three to sixteen.

Before the Illinois primary, the Carter campaign began to offer to the media an internal memorandum indicating that it was mathematically impossible for Kennedy to win. It said, in a "disaster scenario," that even if Carter lost Illinois, New York, Connecticut, Wisconsin, Pennsylvania, Michigan, California, Ohio, New Jersey, and Rhode Island by fifty-five percent to forty-five percent, it was still mathematically possible—because of proportional representation and because of Carter's strength in Southern, border, and Western states—for Carter to win. For a while, it was almost impossible to have a conversation with anyone involved in the Carter campaign without hearing about "the arithmetic." It was clear that the Carter people were trying to literally talk Kennedy out of the race. They asked everyone who would listen, If Kennedy lost Illinois and New York, what would be the point of his staying in? He would succeed, they said (with striking uniformity), only in dividing the Party, and helping to elect a Republican. (The Carter people were disappointed that Gerald Ford did not enter the Republican race and do some party-dividing of his own.) Moreover, they said, the Party needed to raise money for both the Presidential and the congressional elections, and the Kennedy campaign was simply diverting energies from this task. "And for what?" Jody Powell asked me, in exasperation, one afternoon. One White House aide told me then that it was hoped that after the New York primary Senator Wendell Ford, Democrat of Kentucky, who is the chairman of the Democratic Senatorial Campaign Committee, would put the case to Kennedy that by continuing to campaign he was jeopardizing the re-election chances of many of his Senate colleagues and increasing the possibility that the Republicans would take over the Senate in 1981. (All along, White House aides have seemed remarkably aware of which senators have, from time to time, urged Kennedy to get out of the race.)

Still, the President's advisers were clearly alarmed about New York. They realized well in advance that Kennedy just might win it—though not by the margin that he did. And if Kennedy won, they thought, it would delay his departure from the race, and that would be inconvenient. By early March, Caddell had noticed that the President's position in New York was deteriorating—as a result of inflation, the U.N. vote, and the failure to get a resolution of the hostage problem. At a meeting at the White House on the evening of Monday, March 10th, Caddell presented to the assembled group, which included the President and Mrs. Carter, two sets of figures. One set showed that the President was doing well against Kennedy in New York and Connecticut in a head-to-head poll. The adjusted figures, indicating voters' reactions to questions about the President's performance and their responses to attitudinal questions about the candidates, showed that the vote in New York was very close and that there could be trouble in Connecticut.

The figures also showed that the President was not doing well in upstate New York, where he should have been strong. Moreover, the Carter people felt that New York was not naturally hospitable ground for the President. (Carter came in fourth there in 1976.) Whereas, in the words of one of the President's strategists, "on spending, the Democratic Party nationally looks like the Republican Party four years ago," New York Democrats were considered to be more concerned about cuts in federal programs. Caddell's findings showed that New Yorkers who vote in Democratic primaries were less concerned about traditional mores than were voters elsewhere.

It was decided to send in more surrogates—Robert Strauss, the Vice President, the First Lady, Stuart Eizenstat, and Philip Klutznick, the Secretary of Commerce and a former head of the World Jewish Congress. It was decided that it was important to work hard to keep Mayor Koch mollified and, as one of the President's people put it, to "up-hit" the U.N. vote, by stressing that the incident showed that the President had the courage to admit a mistake. More organizers were sent in, especially upstate. Rafshoon ordered up a whole new set of media spots, attacking Kennedy head-on; they attacked his wage-and-price-control proposal, and they attacked him —in ads that ran upstate—as having opposed certain defense expenditures, and also as a spender. Rafshoon had noticed that Kennedy had been receiving a great deal of media time in New York simply by being in the state, and that sometimes he was on the air, attacking the President, for as long as ten minutes. And so four days before the primary the President granted five separate ten-minute interviews to New York City television stations.

Another of the President's political strategists said to me not long before the primary, "We're going to try to be aggressive about reminding people about the Camp David accords. You'll see a lot of television of Begin, Sadat, and Carter." A White House ceremony marking the first anniversary of the signing of those accords was set for the Sunday before the New York primary; the actual anniversary was the day after the primary. And just as White House people were telling me about how the President was now going to concentrate on the inflation fight, that now he would be more visible on the subject—talking to groups, jawboning, and the like—in order to demonstrate his leadership ("Foreign policy is going to take less of his time and inflation more"), the White House announced on the Wednesday before the New York primary that the President would be meeting in April with Begin and Sadat.

The meetings were to be an attempt to salvage the talks between Egypt and Israel about autonomy for the West Bank and Gaza, a subject that had been postponed at Camp David. It was essentially because the talks were at an impasse, and because Israel was continuing to establish settlements, that the vote was cast at the U.N. So the President was in still another bind: how to take actions that would keep his Camp David triumph from fading without infuriating the Jewish constituency. When the meetings with Begin and Sadat were announced—an announcement that took people at the State Department by surprise—one of the President's political advisers said to me, smiling, "It's fine with me if the talks are announced before New York and held afterward."

Someone who has observed all of this at somewhat close hand explained to me, "What you have is a highly competitive man in a race against the Kennedy legend, as he sees it, with the potential of being seen as fiddling while Rome burns. So things have to be done to give the appearance of action and command—on Afghanistan, the Middle East, the economy. What you've been seeing is someone trying to take full advantage of the White House and incumbency for political purposes, with few political options. So he has to figure out how to keep the focus on the White House and give a sense of command and strength. The list of options becomes pretty clear. And there is a pretty high threshold of what you have to do to be credible. You can't get away with inviting too many hockey teams to the White House. You have to take real problems, with high visibility, and show command and action. The problem of having a limited number of options is that some of the things you do look a little bit strange."

As the New York primary approached, one could almost feel the increasing apprehension and tension at the White House. At a meeting on Wednesday, the day after the Illinois primary and six days before the New York primary, Caddell informed the President, Mrs. Carter, and the other political advisers that the President now trailed Kennedy in the adjusted figures in New York, and that there were strong indications that there would be a protest vote. By the following weekend, the adjusted figures were even worse for the President, and, most alarming for the White House, the question of "character" was dropping in significance—rapidly. Moreover, a number of people at the White House were tired, strung out. They continued to be faced with problems—the economy, Iran—that they simply couldn't get behind them. And Kennedy would not go away. Worse, the press was beginning to write stories commending Kennedy for gallantry in adversity.

When I went to see Jody Powell one afternoon that week, he was in a perfectly terrible mood. He talked about how the press was acting as if the primary contest were all over, when in fact it was not. The problem was that the White House was once again caught in trying to have it both ways: Powell himself had just given a briefing to the press about "the arithmetic." I asked Powell why he was in such a bad mood. One reason it is valuable to listen to Powell is that he and the President are close and have some similar traits, and Powell often reflects the President's thinking. He said, "I think politically we're going to end up all right. But watching this thing sort of reconfirms my worst suspicions. You've got Teddy being literally carried from one primary to another by his supporters in the Fourth Estate and getting away with the rawest sort of demagoguery and being held to no scrutiny whatsoever."

In the aftermath of Kennedy's victory in New York (he defeated Carter fifty-nine percent to forty-one percent, and also beat Carter in Connecticut on the same day), some of the President's strategists concluded that there had been too much talk about "the arithmetic"—leading too many people to think that it was indeed all over. This, they concluded, had encouraged the newspaper stories about how gallant Kennedy was in defeat, and may have led some voters to think it didn't matter what they did. They also decided that it was bad psychology and bad politics to be putting it about that the President would more or less back into the nomination because of the numbers—that he would somehow be renominated by a fluke. They said publicly that a lot of events came together that were not likely to recur—

the U.N. vote, the budget cuts, the flight of the Shah to Egypt on the previous weekend—and largely this is what they believed.

They also placed a good bit of blame on Cyrus Vance for his testimony before congressional committees on the Thursday and Friday before the primary, which seemed to indicate that the Carter Administration still supported the essence of the U.N. resolution. Vance was simply stating the Administration's policy, but afterward the White House considered the testimony impolitic and quite untimely. (Key advisers to the President had gone over the testimony in the hope of limiting its impact on New York, but they later decided, in hindsight, that they should have focussed on postponing the whole thing until after the primary.) Two days after the primary, there appeared in the Washington *Post* a story that pointed to Vance's alleged role in the New York debacle; the story was clearly inspired by the White House and read like an invitation to Vance to resign.

The President's strategists agreed that the President must begin to make more "nonpolitical" appearances outside the White House, that he had to be seen as taking charge more, that Kennedy had to be made the issue again, and that they had to make the case once more of why Carter was the better man for the job. They also agreed that, somehow, they had to generate some good news. The President's strategists realized that what had really gone wrong was that their initial strategy had, at least for the moment, collapsed. They figured that, perhaps in part as a result of the President's own previous victories, people were now willing to cast a "protest" vote for Kennedy. What they feared was that too many people might start to actually prefer Kennedy as President.

During the week between the New York and Wisconsin primaries, they did their all to try to establish that New York and Connecticut had been a fluke, not a trend. The President denounced Mobil Oil, accusing the company of violating government price guidelines and overcharging customers. Mondale increased his number of appearances in Wisconsin, and more campaign workers were sent in. After it was made clear over the weekend before the vote that new moves on Iran were in the works, the President went to great lengths to generate timely good news, by announcing at 7:20 A.M. on the day of the primary, in time for the television news programs, a "positive step"—that the government of Iran had declared its intention of taking custody of the hostages from the militants.

The President's substantial victory in Wisconsin had the campaign strategists talking once again about the mathematical odds facing Kennedy, which they said had now increased. They were already gearing up for the contest against Kennedy in Pennsylvania—which both sides considered extremely important, and which has the Carter people worried—at the end of April. And they had also begun to plan for the contingency that even if Kennedy arrived at the Convention with too few delegates, he would, by making fights over the platform and the Convention rules, challenge Carter for the nomination there.

CHAPTER 7

Anderson _____

ON MONDAY, April 21st, three days before John Anderson formally announced that he was withdrawing from the Republican Presidential contest and was exploring the feasibility of running as an independent, I talked to him at his home about the course he was taking. I had been having brief conversations with Anderson and his wife, Keke, during the past ten days, while he pondered what to do. Obviously, Anderson was pleased with his rather sudden celebrity and with the fact that his style of politics had caught on with a substantial number of voters, and he found the idea of running as an independent "very attractive." And he was clearly tempted, as people in politics tend to be, by those telling him he was needed—as a voice and as an alternative.

The mixture of duty, ego, and seduction which motivates politicians is difficult to sort out. But Anderson is a proud man and a reflective one, and it was clear from the earlier conversations that he did not wish to end up appearing a quixotic fool or a "spoiler"—or being the man whose candidacy gave the election to Ronald Reagan. Some of his Republican friends, people who are in philosophical agreement with him, cautioned him that he should not lightly challenge the nominee of his own party. Some friends warned him that, instead of retiring as a man who had had a respected twenty-year career in the House of Representatives and had done something striking in the Republican primaries, and who could still be a voice, he risked going down in history as a man who had become overambitious and, moreover, in the process had elected Ronald Reagan, or had even caused the election to be thrown into the House of Representatives.

In our earlier conversations, Anderson would cite polls indicating the public's dissatisfaction with the idea of being left with the choice of Reagan or Carter, and would talk of the people who had importuned him to run. He would ask what would happen if he was not in place to make the run and by the fall Carter was in terrible political trouble and Reagan had come unravelled as a candidate. He had tried to rest and think these things over during a brief trip to California but found himself surrounded by too many people. Then he spent a week in Washington thinking some more, taking some time with his children (the Andersons have four daughters and a son, ages eight to twenty-six), and talking the question over with his family, friends, and advisers. But he was also faced with the physical reaction that sets in when a candidate stops running: exhaustion and the emotional letdown that follows an uncommon effort. So on the weekend before he made his announcement, he went to Florida for another rest. By this time, he had made up his mind to begin a series of steps leading to an independent candidacy, and on Monday, in a number of meetings with advisers, he refined the approach further. They discussed the timing and the nature of the effort he would make. Deadlines for filing to get on the ballot in certain states were approaching—some already had slipped by—and therefore if he was to go at all, he had to get going. The exploratory process was to lead to a decision by early June on whether actually to run as an independent. What Anderson was setting up, at least as he and his associates outlined it, was a process that he could stop at any time—if it appeared feckless or seemed to be leading to the election of Reagan.

The intention was that the Anderson campaign would be an unconventional one. As he described it, it seemed to be the sort of campaign that was bound to be tried eventually and one that, as it happens, suits Anderson's own personality and style as well as his political exigencies. There would be less running around and more time given to gathering ideas and developing thoughts on the issues. The candidate would be offered as someone who had actually thought about important questions and said what he thought. The nature of conventional campaigning has reached the point where this could turn out to be an arresting idea. Moreover, it was decided that Anderson would offer a "national unity" ticket, trying to rally people in both parties as well as those alienated by both, by holding out the idea that an Anderson Administration would draw on people of excellence, irrespective of party. But before Anderson could persuade others to say they would serve with him, or could attract the kind of person he would want as a running mate—a respected Democrat, moderate Republican, or independent—he would have to be able to persuade them that his candidacy had a serious chance of success. So while the lawyers researched the question of how many ballots he could get on, and planned lawsuits if necessary to get on some, Anderson had to set in motion the process of running. At this point, there was no way that anyone, including Anderson, could know what the result would be, for Anderson or the country. It was possible that he would end up a footnote; it was also possible that what he did would affect the history of the country, and some people did not rule out the possibility that he could actually win.

When I meet Anderson at his modest, split-level home in Bethesda, Maryland, a suburb of Washington (Secret Service cars are parked outside), late Monday afternoon, he is tanned but looks tired and is strangely subdued. He moves about slowly. Anderson is not a very lighthearted man in any event. He is good-humored but not particularly humorous—not given to banter or to telling stories. The mien that he presents to the world is, as he is, fundamentally serious.

We sit in Anderson's den—Anderson, a slight man, looking somewhat shrunken as he sits in a stiff-backed chair in a corner, in his shirt-sleeves. He sips a Scotch and also smokes a cigarillo—something he does, Mrs. Anderson has told me, only when he is particularly tense or troubled. Mrs. Anderson, a trim, dark-haired woman, dressed this afternoon in brown corduroy pants and a beige sweater, sits in on the interview from time to time. She sits in on, and often joins in, most of Anderson's interviews, and his strategy sessions as well. She is a strong-willed, outspoken woman, and no one doubts that she is an important influence on her husband. She denies that she encouraged her husband to make the race as an independent, but friends of theirs say that she did. Today, Mrs. Anderson is relatively quiet; it turns out that she is bothered, even hurt, by recent newspaper articles that have portrayed her as a noisy, pushy woman. Actually, there is a sort of innocence about the Andersons—a kind of simplicity, an uncomplicatedness. And all of this is new to them. Both of them, in their way, are direct, because it is in their nature to be so. The public Andersons—at least, thus far—are essentially the same as the private Andersons.

I ask Anderson if he is tired, and he replies, "No, not tired—had a long day, with a lot of conversation." There had been meetings throughout the day at the Madison Hotel with his campaign advisers, including David Garth, the media consultant. "We talked about what steps we should take to really come to a final decision, which we have not done yet."

Then Anderson begins a sort of monologue. "I'm not physically tired, but you've got to be emotionally and mentally drained from making a decision like this. It really is a watershed." Long pause. He looks off into space. "You're turning away from twenty years of party loyalty. And you know the disapprobation that will come down on your head. The chairman of the Republican National Committee has already said I'm on an ego trip, and others will call me a Benedict Arnold. There comes a time in a man's life when obeisance to party has to give way to something else. I'm under no illusions about the tempest and the travail, and even the torment, that you go through." He is speaking slowly, apparently just letting his thoughts come out. Though Anderson is talking dramatically, it seems that this is not an act, that he is truly discomfited by what he might be getting into. "I don't know whether I'll turn out to be Sisyphus—pushing a boulder up a hill, that will come crashing down. And I'm essentially a conservative person. I don't make rash decisions. And the Republican Party is a conservative party, and I will be met with less than approbation by what has been my constituency for a long time. The country is in so much political turmoil, and there is so much skepticism of politicians, and I'll be seen as a self-seeker—as someone deciding things on a basis other than St. Augustine. That doesn't sound like a very exhilarating mood, does it, on the eve of entering the field of battle?'' Pause. Silence. ''What is the greatest fear that men have? I suppose it's the fear of the unknown; and where my path will lead me when it's over, who can say? I don't pretend to know. And yet you get to a point where you are driven by some inner compulsion—and it isn't entirely generated by your own spirit. It's also the ceaseless pounding of people from one end of the country to the other saying, 'Do it, John, do it.' It's not derring-do; that's not my nature. I have the same qualms and fears and trepidations that any man should have, and yet''—slight pause—''I'm going to do it.

''Why am I going to do it? I'm not even sure of the answer to that question. Not out of any lust for power. Not for personal gain. It may bring me more unhappiness than anything in my life. But I don't see anybody else willing to do it. I see senior members of my party, with which I've always identified, trading an endorsement of Reagan for a seat at the Convention, and I see old friends endorsing Reagan.'' He shakes his head. ''It makes me wonder. But the system has to keep on operating, and I guess that can happen if one man is willing to put his body on the line, and that means sacrifice a lot of friendships, upset a lot of people, and do what has to be done. But we've heard a lot about leadership in this campaign. Maybe that's what leadership is all about: chart a course in the campaign, and only when it's all over will we know whether it's all been worth it—and that's six and a half months from now. But I have to believe that there's nothing wrong —indeed, that there's something fundamentally right—about giving people a choice. A lot of people feel disenfranchised. I don't want to go so far as to say, as some are suggesting, that there's victory in defeat, but it might come to that. But I guess no great venture in the history of humankind has ever been launched without the person who had the responsibility of launching it being assailed by some self-doubt. What you have to do, I guess, is look at what the result would be if you didn't make the effort, and then be strengthened by the thought that if you didn't make the effort the outcome would be worse than if you did. And then you have to hope that over six months the results would be successful with more than the eighteen percent who now say they would be unhappy if they had no other choice but Reagan and Carter. Eighteen percent is a lot. That *is* a few million people. I guess it all boils down to: Do you stand for something, or do you stand for nothing? Do you make the decision Howard Baker made yesterday: endorse your erstwhile opponent in the name of party unity?'' Yesterday, Baker met Reagan in Philadelphia and endorsed him.

Now Mrs. Anderson, who has joined us and has sat silently through the monologue, answers the phone. She turns to her husband and relays the question she has been asked: "Is it true you have asked Moynihan to be your running mate?" Anderson looks surprised, but he apparently doesn't have to tell her the answer. As he shakes his head, Keke Anderson tells the caller, "There is no truth to that."

Anderson resumes. "Do you sacrifice everything on the altar of party unity so you are united behind a man who you don't really feel, if elected, is going to have the answers to the nation's problems? Do you take the risk of stumbling through another four years of disarray in the country and disenchantment with the democratic process? Or I guess then if you reject that argument, you make the argument that what you need is a little creative disunity. I don't think what I'm doing is any more disunifying than what Teddy Kennedy is doing."

The phone rings again. The Associated Press says that ABC is going with the Moynihan story and wants to know if it's true. Mrs. Anderson tells the caller, "There's nothing to it. He's not thinking about things like that now."

Anderson continues, "I guess people find it hard to understand that a man is not so consumed by the push to be President. I know they will say it's a bolt from the Party. But why should loyalty to a party at a time of national crisis be the highest sum of total virtues of a man who wants to serve his country? It isn't that I don't appreciate the stabilizing influence of the two-party system. But 1980 isn't 1976 or 1972. It's unique. It sounds like you're taking refuge in the last refuge of scoundrels—patriotism—but you're trying to offer another choice. How do you escape the epithet of 'the messiah complex'—that you think you're the only one who can save the country? There are loads of men and women out there, but where are they? But there still are going to be those people who think that the two-party system is so sacred that anyone who rocks the boat is less than a true American.

"I don't want to sound like I'm bereft of friends, and I don't want to sound like I've had my head turned by the siren call and am influenced only by those on the fringes who are upset with the existing order. But there is something wrong with the nominating process. Far less than a quarter of those who are eligible will have expressed their choice. If you want a healthy democracy, you have to have participation by as many people as possible." Pause. Silence. "But there's a loneliness in all this that I don't think anyone can appreciate. You can talk to the political consultants and talk to all the venders to political campaigns, and you always have the nagging thought that their advice might have something to do with the services they render rather than an objective view of the independent candidacy. And I'm only human, all too human, and I'm aware of those who will say it's all egotism, he's off on a frolic of his own. Of course, there is egotism in every politician, and I suppose there is some in me."

Now the New York *Post* calls about the Moynihan rumor. Mrs. Anderson says, "There is no truth to that at all."

It is growing dark in the den. I ask Anderson how his decision evolved.

He replies, "I think it pretty much evolved since the first of April, the Wisconsin primary, where we ran third, with twenty-eight percent. I mean, we came to the end of the line." The subject of an independent candidacy had been in the air since before the Wisconsin primary, but Anderson had said then, as he had to, that he was thinking only about running in the Republican primaries. "It had been our strategy to start strong in the East and go into the Midwest and demonstrate that in the heartland of the Republican Party we had strength. And I must say that I thought that thirty-seven percent was pretty good in the state of Illinois, where I was little known except in a little district in a corner of the state—a district of four hundred and sixty thousand people in a state of almost twelve million—but it was interpreted as a defeat." Anderson has represented the city of Rockford and its surrounding rural area, in the northwest corner of the state. He himself was among those who stressed that since Illinois was his home state, he should do well there. "And when we were unable to put together a victory in Wisconsin, with a crossover vote, we were through. I knew that. We weren't on the ballot in Pennsylvania."

Through a staff oversight, the filing deadline for the Pennsylvania primary was missed. When I saw Anderson ten days ago, he was upset about that. He also indicated then that he was reluctant to go through more Republican primaries, only to get beaten. Now he says, "And the next state is a hardrock Republican state—Indiana. So what do you do? We began casting around for an alternative. The polls came out with eighteen to twenty percent supporting the idea of my running as an independent. Then you get interested. I'm aware of all the cynics who say, Yes, but when it gets closer to Election Day the eighteen percent will go down to five percent—but I've got six months to try to say the things that will convince people that for the first time in history they ought to vote for an independent. Can I do it? I don't know. Can I find the words? Can I find the wisdom? Can I kindle the spark that may be lying in the psyche of the people? I don't know. Will I have the ideas? I don't know. We're so much a prisoner of events. Who knows what will happen in Iran? Reagan, with his slickly packaged campaigns, talking about tax cuts and all the rest—maybe that's what the people will want. I'm going to have to preach a very tough line. I'll have to talk about sacrifice."

Mrs. Anderson wrinkles her nose.

Anderson says to her, "I know you don't like that word."

She says, "I like 'cooperation.' "

He replies, "That's a soporific; that's a soporific."

Anderson continues, "I've talked in my speeches about the need to toughen up at home. I don't know how you get out of this inflation and recession without more people giving up something."

Mrs. Anderson says, "People are already sacrificing."

Anderson replies animatedly, "They're not; they're not. They're accommodating."

"I'll go along with that," Mrs. Anderson says quietly.

Anderson says, "They may be giving up going out to dinner one night a week or a trip to Miami. I don't think they've begun to sacrifice."

"What do you mean by sacrifice?" Mrs. Anderson asks.

Her husband replies, "Giving up, giving up some of the things they enjoy. I don't think people have begun to sacrifice. No, it's the poor who are sacrificing, and it's them we harp on when we look at the budget and decide where to cut. We let people have deductions for investing in real estate that appreciates every year, but we don't want to spend on food stamps. People don't look on interest deductions as welfare. They don't look on a one-and-a-half-billion-dollar loan guarantee to Chrysler as welfare—that's an investment. But these arguments aren't going to win you the votes of the middle class, are they? And, you see, they feel pinched, and to some extent they are, but they don't realize how real the poverty is to a person who's trying to get along on a welfare check of three hundred dollars a month, and can't invest in a money-market certificate."

Anderson and I return to the question of how his decision developed.

He says, "It was after Wisconsin that I realized that what everyone told me when I began was really true: that there was no way within the universe of the Republican Party that I would be nominated. I guess I really thought that all my talk about a new coalition of the American people, and talking tough, would catch on. Now, you would be justified in asking, If it didn't catch on then, would it catch on in a general election? I don't know. But without being a prophet of doom and gloom I have to say that I have felt in my bones for some time that we were heading for a much deeper recession than the Administration was talking about. There's something basically, basically wrong with the American economy. Something has happened to the American dream. It's not working. And I guess that's going to be the basis of my campaign: that the old easy assumptions that we've always made don't work. We're still talking about doing things at the margins—cut taxes a little, gin up the economy a little. I don't think so. I think we have to make fundamental changes in the structure of our economy. Of course, energy is a big part of my campaign, as you know."

I ask Anderson if he has any thoughts about how to make fundamental changes in the structure of our economy, and he says that he has been talking to Felix Rohatyn, the New York financier, who has been writing and speaking on this subject, and that he plans to talk to others.

"Will you have time to think these things through?" I ask.

He replies, "I plan to take the time. That's how my campaign will be different from the others. I'll have no Republican chicken dinners to attend. I won't be invited. I'll have time to sit down and talk economics and other subjects, and if after that I'll be able to find the fora to dispute Ronald Reagan that we have more oil under the ground than we have used, that all we have to do is cut everyone's taxes thirty percent—whether I can find the fora to express the ideas, I don't know. Without being querulous about it, that's the problem with an independent campaign. Maybe if I come up with enough interesting ideas they'll catch fire. The power of ideas is enormous, and if I don't come up with some new ideas, what am I doing? I'd might as well stay home and rake the yard and play with my eight-year-old daughter. I've just got to bank on the idea that people are tired of old platitudes and the old ideas, that they will listen. I have to say there's some question—when you see that Reagan got fifty percent of the vote in New Hampshire by railing against government and high taxes. He subverted the thinking of the state.

"So the auguries are not that favorable at the moment. But as things get worse, which I think they will before they get better, and as people hear the old ideas, if I can somehow package my ideas in a way that makes sense to people, I've just got to have confidence that people will listen. I keep returning to the quote of Emerson 'Nothing astonishes men so much as common sense and plain dealing.' Maybe if I can talk common sense I can inspire a constituency." Pause. Silence. "I'm not sure. I'm not sure. Maybe that's asking too much. I'm clearly under no illusion that it will be easy."

An important question about Anderson is how he would be at governing if he should get to the Presidency. Some people have misgivings, because of his independent style in the House of Representatives. It has been partly a matter of his politics, partly his personality. Anderson has been a member of probably the loneliest group in Congress—the moderate and liberal Republicans in the House of Representatives. Being a member of that segment of the minority party brings pressures that wear down many people. For various reasons, the peer pressures in the Senate to go along with Party positions is not as great. But even some moderate Senate Republicans, like their House counterparts, begin to lose their edge, go gray. Somehow, this did not happen to Anderson. But he was often frustrated by his situation, and depressed by what he saw happening to his party. He considered quitting in 1978 but, faced with a well-financed right-wing renomination challenge, made the fight, and then decided to retire from the House in 1980. Rather than go quietly or run for the Senate, he took a flyer at running for President. Anderson's position in the House was complicated by the fact that until last summer he was a member of the House Republican leadership —chairman of the Republican Conference, the third-ranking leadership office. The fact that he remained in that position at all reflects the respect, albeit some of it grudging, of his colleagues. Even many of those who don't much like him—who resent his somewhat schoolmasterish, righteous style —respect his intellectual power and his oratorical skills.

But Anderson has been an introvert in an institution that values extroversion. He is not one for going to the gym and swapping stories with the boys or for engaging in the purposeful conviviality of Capitol Hill. And even some of Anderson's friends say that he made things unnecessarily difficult for himself—that on occasion he needlessly took a position that was at odds with that of his party, or took the position in a manner that rankled others needlessly. "John is difficult to help," says one of his House colleagues who defends him within that body. "He lacks tact." The question is whether Anderson would have the taste, or the capacity, for the kind of humoring, wheedling, and cajoling that a President is presumed to need. One of his congressional friends and admirers says, "John is not a political animal, never has been. That's both one of his great qualities and one of his great deficiencies." Morris Udall, a friend of Anderson's who has worked with him on legislation, disagrees with some of this. "John is a practitioner of realpolitik," Udall says. "I worked with him on the Alaska pipeline, on the Alaska-lands bill, on election reform, and I found him to be pragmatic and practical; he understands that you have to make compromises. That he has survived within his party in the House says something."

Now, talking to Anderson in his home, I ask him how he responds to those who say that he is too independent, too stubborn, even a bit too arrogant to be a good President, to be able to govern effectively.

He replies, "I think in normal times I would have a very difficult time of it, because people don't easily adapt to new ideas. What I've got to bank on is that under Carter things have come to such a state that even cynical people in the House or Senate will consider new approaches. And I will have, by having been elected, accomplished a miracle—and it will take a miracle to elect me—and then they would judge that I had accurately gauged public opinion. And if it was a national-unity government that drew on the best in both parties, and if you put that together with having achieved the miracle of being elected, then, yes, I think it might charm some of the folks who populate the Congress. But it won't be easy. And if Congress doesn't express an interest in cooperating, a President has to go over their heads. Carter hasn't really done that, except for tootling up and down the Mississippi last summer talking about his windfall-profits tax."

I ask Anderson if he would enjoy working with the levers of government, trying to make the machinery work, taking on the interest groups, and so on.

He replies, "You've got to do it differently from the way Carter has. I remember the series of meetings that Carter had on energy where one day he called in the producer groups and one day he called in the public-interest groups. We've got to break that approach—of perpetuating what has been called the war of the parts against the whole. We have to create new coalitions. To simply sit there and try to manipulate the traditional levers of power—no, I don't think I'd do that. I'd make a bigger mess of that than Carter. You have to create a situation where some of the interest groups put down some of their own concerns for the sake of a higher interest. Carter takes on Mobil Oil, which is a safe enough target. Carter hasn't told the interest groups, Listen, you're just a part of this country, you can't dictate policy for two hundred and twenty-two million people. The President has to be active and visible. I'm not just talking about the Rose Garden strategy. God, who listens to Carter anymore? We listen to him for news about Iran. But you don't have a feeling of him as a father figure, speaking to and for the whole country and leading it. He tried to do that on the fifteenth of July of last year.'' That was when Carter gave his ''malaise'' speech. ''I think it's the only time he tried to do that. I think he came a cropper by suggesting it was the people's fault. Oh, he took a little of the blame, saying he had been managing the government instead of leading it, but he didn't project a vision. I don't know what it is about the poor man. He can't do that.''

Anderson and I talk for a while about his policy positions. On economic policy: ''Basically, it's a pretty draconian budget policy, not excepting defense. Also, there would be an incomes policy, where you would expect labor and management to cooperate in holding the line by using the tax code to apply penalties and incentives. Reagan is a throwback to Adam Smith, with the idea that all you have to do is cut taxes. I believe that government has to play a role.'' He adds, ''We should have saved the automobile industry from itself, by requiring higher miles-per-gallon standards.''

On foreign policy: ''Just because we are the leaders of the Western world, we can't expect the allies to go against their interests. We are going to have to concentrate on enhancing the mutuality of interests of the Western alliance, so that they can see that it is in their interest to follow the lead of the United States. There has got to be much closer coordination of economic policy, in order to produce the necessary political cohesion.''

About the Soviet Union: ''Instead of thinking the Russians are plotting world conquest, I think they're terribly insecure. They haven't reached their economic goals for some years; they see our economy three times larger than theirs; they're worried about becoming net importers; they're worried about having access to raw materials. I think we have to sit down and talk to them about not having a struggle for access to raw materials. Just as we're having a Law of the Sea Conference, we should try to construct an international regime where materials will be available to all nations. I see a need for far more internationalism and talking to the Soviet Union in those terms, rather than just resigning ourselves to a climate of constant confrontation. I think Carter hyped Afghanistan. I think we ought to balance our condemnation with hints that if the Russians are ready to talk about other things, we're still ready—rather than shelve SALT, build the MX missile, and, as Reagan says, 'rearm America.' I just can't abide this notion that we're headed into a dark age of confrontation and all we can do is spend on the arms race and arm other nations. That's not the approach I would take.''

I ask Anderson about the fact that he began in Congress as a conservative and over the years became more liberal.

''That has occurred,'' he replies. ''It was the awakening of John Anderson, the exposure to a lot of facts and a lot of conditions in the country that in my insular background I wasn't aware of. I'm a product of rural Middle America. I didn't think the cities were all that relevant to my existence.''

I ask him to clarify his political philosophy now, and he replies, ''Pretty conservative as far as the necessity of a new self-discipline in managing the budgetary affairs of the government, but liberal in the concept of trying an idea that's new, even if it's outrageous, and the willingness to take some new approaches. That sounds sort of vague, but there's something there.''

Some of the positions that Anderson has supported in the past will undoubtedly become issues in the campaign. One that already has is the constitutional amendment he sponsored early in his congressional career, which, while it prohibited the establishment of a state religion, would have had the United States "devoutly" recognize "the authority and law of Jesus Christ." Of this he has said, "It was a dumb thing to do." He says that some of his recent votes "have been cast rather grudgingly, just because I was a member of the leadership of my party." He asserts that that is why he originally signed on as a sponsor of the Kemp–Roth bill—which Reagan espouses—to cut taxes by thirty percent over three years. "I had grave reservations," he says.

Anderson says that he is uncertain at this point about his plans for the coming weeks. The whole thing has to be invented. We talk about his intention of running an unconventional campaign.

Anderson says, "It can't be the old, conventional partisan bickering, where one week I attack Reagan and one week I attack Carter. No, I have to convince the American people that I have more to say. That's a tall order, but that's the excitement of the challenge."

CHAPTER 8

The Final Round

THE LAST stage of the primary contests for the Democratic Presidential nomination had, in what was already a strange political year, its own form of strangeness. It was not just that the outcome of the final primaries was in question; it was also uncertain what that outcome would mean—whether, after the long, bitter struggle between Jimmy Carter and Edward Kennedy, the nomination would finally be settled. In addition, the fall campaign had backed into the primary campaign, presenting at times the picture of a free-for-all: Kennedy running against Carter; Carter running against Kennedy, Ronald Reagan, and John Anderson; Reagan, apparently not at all displeased with Anderson's presence in the race, running against Carter; and Anderson, of course, running against both Carter and Reagan.

The final round of primaries offered Kennedy his only hope of keeping the nomination contest alive, for whatever purposes he had in mind, and presented others who were so inclined with what might be their last chance to substitute some other nominee for Carter. Carter was far ahead in the delegate count; but more than a third of the number of delegates needed for the nomination remained to be chosen, and primaries were to be held in eight states, among them three of the nation's largest, on the final date—Tuesday, June 3rd. The Kennedy people knew that it was impossible for them to catch up mathematically, but they—and some others—argued that there was a difference between the "arithmetic" and the "psychology." They argued that if Carter did not do well in the three big primaries—California, Ohio, and New Jersey (how well he had to do in how many of these states depended on who was making the judgment)—this, on top of

Carter's defeats in other industrial states, might lead the Party to deny him the nomination. All manner of schemes for having the Party nominate someone other than Carter, or Kennedy, had been floating about. So, for all the Carter people's professions of a lack of interest—their insistence that the nomination contest was over and they were concentrating on the contest to come in the fall—they knew that they not only had to win some on the last Tuesday but to win well, so as to get on with raising money for the Party and preparing for the fall campaign. Meanwhile, a three-way contest between Carter, Reagan, and Anderson was already under way.

On Thursday afternoon, May 22nd, Edward Kennedy is at the Martin Luther King, Jr., Hospital in Watts. He arrived in Los Angeles yesterday afternoon for this, his second-to-last campaign swing through California before the primary. (He will make other stops here as he crisscrosses the country in the last days of the campaign.) In a speech before an A.F.L.–C.I.O. convention in Cincinnati yesterday, Kennedy said that if Carter was the nominee he would come in third in November, behind Reagan and Anderson. (Anderson, who has met the requirements for getting on the ballot in every state whose deadline has come up since he announced he was considering an independent race, and who is planning suits in states with earlier deadlines, said in Los Angeles yesterday that he is in the race to stay. "There's no doubt in my mind. Sure I'm in. Sure I'm in.") Kennedy must do what he can now to get attention. He is relentlessly carrying on his campaign—his schedules are heavy, and there are few days off—which was widely dismissed as hopeless at several points this year, but the question is whether very many people are paying attention. He is followed by a press corps much diminished from earlier in the campaign, and several of the reporters are along simply in case something dreadful should happen to him.
Kennedy keeps pressing his argument against the Carter Administration, but that is no longer news. So he must take other tacks, like saying that Carter would come in third in November (this to give Democrats pause) or, as he did last week, challenging Carter to debate him and saying that if, after a debate, Carter won a majority of all the votes on June 3rd, he would concede Carter the nomination. This was, of course, a no-lose proposition for Kennedy, but it also offered Carter a possibility of getting Kennedy to step aside. The White House, as was to be expected, dismissed the proposal out of hand.
Carter was certainly no more likely to share the stage with Kennedy at this point than he was earlier in the year. (In the conservative counts, Carter is given between thirteen hundred and fourteen hundred delegates, and Kennedy between seven hundred and eight hundred—sixteen hundred and sixty-six are needed for the nomination.) The President's political advisers have begun thinking of ways of trying to get Kennedy out of the race after the primaries are over, so that he won't take his campaign to the Convention. Three days ago, in what some Carter people had hoped would be part

of this process, Carter visited his campaign headquarters and suggested to his people that they join him in extending a "healing and friendly hand" to their political opponents. But then, apparently unable to resist his own combative instincts, he suggested that Kennedy had waged a campaign of "false promises . . . empty slogans . . . distortions of issues."

Of the three big states up for grabs twelve days from now, California is considered Kennedy's best bet. Among other things, Carter has never done well here, and has not built up much of a base in the state. According to some in the Carter camp, the President and Hamilton Jordan feel politically estranged from California, a feeling that no doubt contributes to the estrangement. The Carter people are still debating whether or not the President should make a trip to California before the primaries. The one state where Carter is scheduled to go, Ohio, is the one where he is considered most likely to do well and where his campaign is making the greatest effort. Ohio is relatively conservative in its politics, compared with the other large industrial states, and four years ago Carter carried it in the primary and in the general election.

The race is considered very close in both New Jersey and California. As of now, it seems inevitable that, whatever happens on June 3rd, the Party's system of proportional representation will enable Carter to win enough delegates to get the nomination. But Kennedy is striving to make that only part of the equation. One of Kennedy's problems is that so many people regard the contest as over that he must constantly explain why he is still bothering, and why the voters should still bother. Some Carter people maintain that history will show that the nomination was settled last month, when, though Kennedy carried Pennsylvania, he did so by less than a percentage point. Had the margin of victory been greater, they say, the chemistry of the rest of the contest would have been different. Kennedy's strategy, after all, was based on winning in the industrial states, and his victory in the New York primary on March 25th had thrown a fright into the Carter camp. Moreover, after the Pennsylvania primary and the Missouri caucuses, both of which occurred on April 22nd, the Carter people claimed that they had gained forty more delegates than Kennedy had. They also maintained that if, on the basis of intense campaigning in Pennsylvania, Kennedy could manage little better than a tie, he was not a very strong candidate even in the industrial states. Four days later, Kennedy won the Michigan caucuses, but by only one delegate. Carter then won a string of victories—in Texas, North Carolina, Indiana, and Tennessee—while Kennedy won only the District of Columbia. This was as expected, and therefore it didn't affect the psychology of the contest, but it did affect the delegate count. Last week, Carter carried Maryland and Nebraska—a Kennedy victory in Maryland had been considered quite possible—and earlier this week Carter carried Oregon. Next week, there will be contests in Kentucky, Idaho, Arkansas, and Nevada, all of which Carter is expected to carry. So Kennedy has not had a big victory since the one in New York.

One question, of course, is how Kennedy, who had done so well against Carter in the polls until he challenged him, got to this point. Some of Kennedy's advisers think that his political fate was settled in the first month of the campaign. First—on the day the hostages were seized in Iran, and one year before the election—there was his unsuccessful interview on CBS, of which so much was made. Then there was the uncertain start of his campaign: the apparent lack of a clear rationale for his candidacy; the difficulty of a sudden transition, even for a Kennedy, from the Senate to a national, closely watched campaign. His tendency to stumble around at times in his campaign speeches then was made much of, as were his critical comments on the Shah of Iran. The theory of some of Kennedy's associates is that this was the period when most people made up their minds about Kennedy. The polls showed him taking a nose dive during that time. The extent to which Chappaquiddick was re-examined in the press, and the impact of that re-examination, came as a surprise to almost everyone. Chappaquiddick, plus the Kennedys' marital troubles, developed—with the help of the Carter campaign, especially in its advertising—into the "character" issue. One man I know, who favors Kennedy, believed all along that he should not run, because, as this man put it, "the American people will see him as someone who does not have his life together." Peter Hart, Kennedy's pollster, has a theory that the people don't open what he terms "their windows" very often—that is, there are only certain times at which they make judgments. He thinks that the windows on Kennedy were open in November, and that it was difficult to change people's impressions after that.

According to this line of thinking, even when Carter's competence came back into question in the public mind, when his handling of the crises in Iran and Afghanistan came under increasing criticism, and when the economic issue, which was supposed to be Kennedy's strongest one, came to the fore, too many people had made up their minds about Kennedy. "People were not able to connect with him," one of Kennedy's aides said to me recently. Even some of his advisers say that his style did not help: that he came across on television as shouting; that his way of attenuating words, in sarcasm, came across somehow as vaudeville, raising the question of whether he was a serious man, and so did the nervous laugh with which he commented on his losses on Tuesday nights. According to a number of the people around him, Kennedy is well aware of the shouting problem and has tried to deal with it, but with limited success. He has a big voice, and it had long been a key part of his political style to arouse his audiences—sometimes even electrify them—with that voice. But the style did not serve him well on television, which tends to magnify. Kennedy's old-fashioned oratory is ill suited to modern communication.

Patrick Caddell said to me recently that he thinks that even had it not been for Iran and Afghanistan, from which Carter was presumed to have benefitted so much, Carter would have defeated Kennedy. He said that it would have been an even more slashing campaign than it has been, with

Carter arguing, I'm a moral man and you're not, and Kennedy arguing, I'm a leader and you're an incompetent. Caddell believes that the personal aspects are more important to people than anything else when they make up their minds about the Presidency—that this is a phenomenon that was produced by Johnson and Nixon, and one from which Ford was the first to benefit—and that the impact of the issues is minuscule. "Character will always be first," Caddell said, "and Carter would have won on character." Caddell pointed out wryly that the news has been so bad—especially on the economy—that surely his point has been proved. Some of the networks' "exit polls" on primary days showed that Democrats favored Kennedy on the questions of who would handle the economy better and who was a better leader, but that when it came to the question of "honesty" or "trust," they favored Carter. Another factor, which also had to do with these things but went beyond them, is that a great many people simply don't like Kennedy. It is often forgotten that his brothers aroused a similar feeling, though perhaps not to the same degree. Of course, there are those who believe that Kennedy's politics are all wrong for this period, but this hypothesis cannot be tested, given the other clouds on his campaign. And, of course, one cannot consider in a vacuum what happened to Kennedy: there was also the considerable skill with which the White House used the tools of incumbency.

Today, Carter was in the state of Washington on an official trip to inspect the damage caused by the eruption of Mount St. Helens. Rosalynn Carter was in Los Angeles this morning and has gone on to Oakland. And now Kennedy, looking exhausted and uncomfortable, is in the Alberta King Child Care Center (named for Martin Luther King, Sr.,'s wife, who was murdered). Kennedy's face is pale and blotchy; his body seems chunkier than usual; his suit is rumpled, and the breast pocket is coming loose, and another jacket pocket has been unartfully mended; the leather of his shoes is cracked and worn. Most campaign events are set pieces, but this one is a bit too stagy, and Kennedy doesn't seem to know what to do; of course, the young children, who are seated around low tables painting plaster-of-Paris objects, haven't a clue who he is. Kennedy wanders around for a while, talking quietly to the children ("I'm Ted") and admiring their work. Kennedy is actually very good with children. Then he sits down slowly—as if bothered by his chronic back trouble—and listens while the center is explained to him by some of its officials. He seems distracted at first, unable to bring himself to focus on what is being said, but then, when the officials show some nervousness about performing before the press, he seems to come to, and, the skilled politician, helps them out. Then he gives a little talk about the need for expanded child-care programs.

Following that, Kennedy goes out into a courtyard to address a crowd of hospital workers about the importance of "bringing health care into the communities" and of national health insurance. Now he speaks strongly and firmly. He says, "I travel across this country and I hear those voices that say we can't do this, we can't provide decent health care, now is not the time to pass national health insurance." And he tells the crowd, "I remember the letter that Martin Luther King sent from the Birmingham jail when he said, 'Now is the time.' " Then he says, "I wish Mr. Carter had come right here to the Martin Luther King Hospital, right out here on this platform"—and he steps to one side of the platform. "There'd be room for us, right out here." He points to the other side and then to his side. "He'd be right over there, and I'd be right over here. And we would ask him why it is that we in this country cannot have a President of the United States who's committed to provide a decent quality health care to the citizens of the nation." He says, "I believe that the people of California are entitled to that kind of a dialogue and that kind of debate. Not only on health care but on all the other important issues."

In a suite at the Biltmore Hotel, in downtown Los Angeles, Kennedy gives a series of television, radio, and newspaper interviews. It is an accepted rule of politics that California, because of its size, is a difficult state to organize politically, and that one campaigns there through "the media." So each morning Kennedy tries to do some radio and television interviews, and late each afternoon does some more. Far more people are hearing these interviews than are hearing his speeches. Besides, this is a way to get free air time. Invariably, he is presented with the delegate count and asked why he is staying in the race. This afternoon, he answers that question as he usually does: "I wish the Carter-Mondale committee was as concerned about the rate of unemployment as they are about the delegate count." Whenever possible, he gets in a line to the effect that "Mr. Carter ought to come to California and debate these issues." He points out that he was willing to debate Carter when he himself was ahead in the polls, and that the President was willing to debate for a time after the hostages were seized. On November 6th, two days after the CBS program, the White House accepted the Des Moines *Register*'s invitation to debate, and withdrew on December 28th. By that time, Carter was ahead of Kennedy in the polls. Again and again, Kennedy points out in these interviews—and also in his appearances—that Hubert Humphrey debated George McGovern (in the California primary in 1972), that Robert Kennedy debated Eugene McCarthy (in the California primary in 1968), and that John Kennedy debated Lyndon Johnson (at the Democratic Convention in 1960). "I stand in that tradition," he says. Now he says, "The people of Southern California have to make a decision whether they want four more years of Carter economic policies," and he says that there have been twenty-five thousand jobs lost in the Los Angeles area in the last month alone. He says, "The people here in California are entitled to listen to Mr. Carter explain to them why they have an inflation rate in the Los Angeles area of twenty-six percent. And why he is asking for a ten-cents-a-gallon gasoline tax. Now he ought to come out here to Los Angeles and respond to the questions of the people."

He says, "My candidacy speaks for those men and women who have been made unemployed. My candidacy speaks for the elderly people who today have worked a lifetime in the plants and factories of Los Angeles, now living on Social Security, and can't make ends meet. My candidacy speaks for the sixty-five hundred students in Los Angeles County that will not be able to get scholarship assistance because of the reductions and the cutbacks this year. My candidacy speaks for the unemployed. Now, those individuals and groups in our society are entitled to be heard. Their needs are entitled to be addressed." He says that these problems can't be dealt with by speeches calling for Party unity—that if in 1968 Robert Kennedy and Eugene McCarthy hadn't tried to change the Vietnam War policy the divisions within the Party would still be there, and that if in the late 1940s Hubert Humphrey hadn't brought up the subject of discrimination the divisions would still be there, and that "the serious economic challenges" the country is facing cannot be swept away by speeches about Party unity. In one interview, he says the Democratic Party cannot afford to nominate a "pale carbon copy" of Ronald Reagan. Asked about what he would do in the event he did not win enough delegates to justify continuing his campaign, he replies, "I learned many years ago from my father that if you start thinking about coming in second place, you're not going to come in first place."

There is probably a great deal to this. The question of why Kennedy does not get out of the race has been raised repeatedly since he lost the Iowa precinct caucuses by a two-to-one margin, in January. Kennedy and his advisers have more than once considered whether to fold the campaign. But it is not very difficult to understand why Kennedy is staying in. Among other things, as he suggests, quitting was not in his upbringing—quite the contrary—or, probably, in his genes. Moreover, it appears that he really has come to believe that he is, as his aides say, fighting for what he believes the Democratic Party should stand for. It is a more intense form of a fight that he and Carter have been engaged in for quite some time. This is not a scrap between a couple of old pols who realize that it is in part a game; it appears that Kennedy and Carter really dislike each other and what each thinks the other stands for—and that this dislike has deepened as the campaign has gone on. And though Kennedy doesn't talk about it much—he has an abhorrence (again the upbringing, no doubt) of appearing a "crybaby"—it seems that he does resent the Carter campaign's efforts to make such an issue of his "character."

So, having started the thing, Kennedy would have a hard time stopping it. And when he goes into a hall or a gym to address a crowd there are people cheering him. The polls may show him being the choice of only thirty-odd percent of the Democrats as of now, but that still means, to him, that there are millions and millions of people who feel that his candidacy is important. People with less to go on have satisfied themselves that their candidacies were important, that they were a voice. Moreover, who could say? There was always the possibility—a possibility that kept failing to materialize—that somehow the bottom would fall out from under Carter. Kennedy has long since shown that he is a resilient man. Many people seem baffled that he has remained equable and good-humored as he has gone through this campaign, but those traits are deep in his nature, and they are also, it seems, part of his code of being a good sport. One of his aides says that there is an Irish fatalism to him. And given the other losses he has sustained, losing an election is not such a big thing. But, whatever happens, he seems determined to live up to what he sees as his own obligation to family tradition, and to rescue what honor he can from the exercise. This will require some difficult decisions down the line.

Now, asked in one of the interviews whether if he loses in California on June 3rd he will carry his candidacy to the Democratic Convention, he replies quickly, "Yes, I will, because I believe very deeply in the issues I'm speaking to," and he adds, "I think the struggle is over the heart and soul of the Democratic Party." By now, Kennedy looks good. He seems to have organized himself: the juices have started flowing, and he is focussed; his complexion is its normal ruddy color, and the blotches have disappeared. He ends the last interview by saying, "The people of California can say they do not want to be taken for granted by the Carter Administration, and what they can clearly say is that they don't want four more years of incompetency. And what they can clearly say is that they want America to regain control over its own destiny in our economy, in energy, and they want a restoration of American prestige and influence in the world."

Early tonight, Kennedy attended a fund raiser in East Los Angeles sponsored by Mexican-Americans. ("The people in this country are entitled to competency in the government, and they're entitled to a commitment to the improvement of the quality of life," he told them.)

Now he speaks to students gathered in an auditorium at U.C.L.A. Wearing his glasses, he reads his speech. It is a sober one and a tough one, indicting the Carter Administration's record, offering some of his own solutions, including wage and price controls, and stating, "The issue of debate raises a question about the integrity of our system itself: Should we choose a President on the basis of the record, the positions, and the purposes of the candidates? Or are we to grope toward that choice without knowing how the incumbent explains his past—or what he offers for the nation's future? What is at stake in 1980 is not just the character of the candidates but the character of our politics and our country." He continues, "This election raises another question that transcends any specific issue: Do we still have faith in our own best impulses and ideals?" He reads carefully and clearly, and he is applauded and mildly cheered from time to time, but he doesn't get this audience worked up. Kennedy's problem is that he gets an audience worked up when he gets worked up, and then he shouts; tonight he is obviously trying not to do that. Though he knows it is a problem, he is inclined to shout when it is late at night and he is tired, or when he gets before an audience he can't resist working up; when he is subdued, so is his audience, as if it senses he is holding something back.

Two days ago, in Newark, Kennedy gave a speech in which he spelled out a detailed plan for "the reindustrialization of America"—for revitalizing the economy and improving productivity, through various incentives aimed at modernizing certain industries. The idea of "reindustrialization" is coming into fashion, and is something that Jerry Brown has talked about. (Brown has not only dropped out of the Democratic race—he seems to have disappeared.) Tonight, Kennedy gives Brown credit for the idea.

As Kennedy responds to questions, he speaks with more feeling. He states one of his recurring themes: "I believe a President can make a difference. I believe that Franklin Roosevelt and John Kennedy made a difference. And when Lyndon Johnson said, 'We shall overcome,' those words stated by a President of the United States were a powerful message that went all over this country, that this country was committed to the elimination of discrimination." He says, "We have no magic solutions, but I do believe we can make meaningful progress on the basic questions of the quality of life in this country, and move this country closer to the ideal of economic democracy and social progress and social justice. And that is what I am committed to." Kennedy seems to actually believe what he is saying—a phenomenon that should not be noteworthy. At one point, he remarks that he and Carter come from different philosophies, and that is true. They are men of different temperaments and different outlooks, and they come from different political traditions. It is possible that Kennedy really cannot understand Carter. Carter's way of handling the Presidency is antithetical to Kennedy's view of how it should be handled. And the range of their differences on issues is far broader than were, say, McCarthy's and Johnson's or Robert Kennedy's and Johnson's. Kennedy says now, as he often does, "I'm tired of listening to a President and to an Administration that wrings its hands and says no one can do any better. I come from a different tradition."

Kennedy has broken out of the numbing approach he had at the beginning of his campaign, when all he seemed to have to say was that with him things would be better. He was critical then of Carter's handling of economic and foreign policy, but his grenades didn't seem to land anywhere. He redefined his approach after his devastating defeat in Iowa. The speech he gave at Georgetown University in late January had its own problems, but it did mark Kennedy's self-liberation. After that, he returned to the liberal Democratic politics with which he is comfortable, talking of human needs and of programs to meet them. He talks a lot about programs, sometimes using government terminology—for example, "COET" (crude-oil equalization tax)—with which few are familiar.

He talks these days of his answer to inflation, offered in the Georgetown speech—of placing controls on prices, profits, dividends, interest rates, wages, and rents—and says that while it may not be perfect, it is preferable to putting people out of work and slashing the budget for health, education, and housing. And now he has combined this with a sharpened definition of his difference with Carter on the subject of "leadership." He does not talk so much about gasoline rationing, the other major domestic proposal he made in his Georgetown speech. One of his aides explains that this is because the two proposals, added up, sounded like too much big government. Kennedy says that he favors "moving toward" a balanced budget. And he says at U.C.L.A. tonight, "I favor strengthening our conventional forces. But I oppose a helter-skelter militarism that will succeed only in impressing us with our own overkill. I favor a defense second to none. But I also favor a firm commitment to control nuclear weapons before they consume the world in nuclear fire."

There is a sense of unreality about this campaign. It sometimes seems as if Kennedy were talking into a cave. The President may be highly visible on television, but his physical absence from the campaign is almost palpable. Kennedy may reach out to jab at Carter, but it seems that he can't touch him. It is beyond the question of a debate. Of course, Carter has had to try to govern, and to take responsibility for his policies. But how would he have done if he had appeared before union members, campus audiences, ethnic groups, week after week, defending his record and answering questions? Like as not, he would have won, but the feel of the contest would have been different. We shall never know. Out where the campaign is happening, there is a faint aura of illegitimacy about the Carter candidacy—which could have been avoided. Out where the campaign is happening, it sometimes seems that it isn't happening at all.

On Friday, I have a conversation with Kennedy on the plane en route to Oakland and San Francisco. I ask him if he has found the campaign frustrating.

"I'm not interested in thinking back over the period of the campaign," he replies. "There are ten days to go. There's not really time to think about the campaign, not really a chance to think about that. I would hope that I've benefitted from the experiences of the past. I'm thinking now about the remaining days of the campaign. And then, after June, I'll look to the future." A politician in the midst of a race, like an athlete in a championship match, has to concentrate on the task at hand, can't afford to spend much time reflecting on what happens if he doesn't succeed. His psychic and physical energies cannot be deflected. And Kennedy is not inclined to reflection or introspection in any event.

I ask Kennedy how he thinks the President has been so successful in his approach.

"I think he's been effective in convincing a significant segment of the Democratic Party that no President can make a difference today, and therefore, no matter how bad things get, it's not his fault—nobody could have done better. He's built on the previous experience of the American people —the Nixon period and the Ford period. People weren't called upon to do very much; not much was expected of them. So that was the climate, the atmosphere, in which the campaign started. I think he's been able to convince a lot of Americans that no one can do better and no one has to be very much alarmed at the current challenges of our time.''

"Do you think that's how you ended up this way?" I ask.

He replies, "I'm sure there are a lot of other factors that contributed to it. Raising my voice on TV and all kinds"—he trails off—"of . . . other . . . things. I'm not as concerned about those matters, nor have I given much thought to them. I'm sure I'll have a time in my life—but not now."

I ask him how he will measure the imperatives for him after June 3rd—to keep going, or to stop in the name of Party unity.

"I'm sufficiently realistic to know that there are dates and events beyond June 3rd," Kennedy replies. "But my energy and focus are on this period. There'll be two months, plenty of time to consider the situation. But I'm committed to going to the Convention and making the effort for the nomination." There is no reason not to take him at his word at this point. Recently, I asked one of his closest associates whether, when there is increased pressure on Kennedy after the primaries to step aside and let the Party heal, Kennedy might not yield, and the associate said simply, "That isn't going to happen. The divisions are too deep."

Now I ask Kennedy if he cares whether Reagan or Carter is elected, if the choice comes to that.

He replies, "I'm thinking about my own situation. I've spoken about what I consider to be the realities of the fall. If it's Reagan and it's Carter, it's also going to be John Anderson, and I don't think Carter can win under those circumstances. I think the Party has to face up to what the central challenges of the Party are. As I've pointed out in my campaign, it isn't just a campaign, it's a cause. That's why I think the talk about unity without responding to these central questions is just empty."

Kennedy's campaign aides are already focussing on the state conventions that will be in the final stages of selecting delegates after June 3rd. They foresee great public-relations and psychological value if Kennedy is able to reverse some of the results of earlier stages of the process—as he did last month in Vermont. In March, on the same night that Kennedy was winning the Massachusetts primary, Carter won a non-binding preferential primary in Vermont, which was of great public-relations value to him. On April 22nd, in the town caucuses, Kennedy received a majority of the delegates to the state convention, to be held tomorrow. Some Kennedy aides say they think Kennedy still believes that he has a chance to get the nomination: that if he does well enough on June 3rd the realization will sink in that Carter is quite weak and that the Anderson candidacy could cost the Democrats the election. Moreover, the Kennedy people, like a great many others, expect that following the Republican Convention, in July, which will be a harmonious one, Reagan will be far ahead of Carter in the polls. At this point, the thinking goes, there will be further doubt about the efficacy of nominating Carter, even if technically he has enough delegates to win.

The key test would be a vote on a rule that would bind the delegates to vote on the first ballot for the nominee to whom they are pledged. Since the candidates' organizations are involved in the selection of their own delegates, the Carter people say they believe that the risks of rebellion are minimal; and in any event they have already begun a careful process of making sure that their delegates stay committed. The Kennedy people have begun to poke around for uncertain Carter delegates. The thought that Carter might be too weak a candidate, and also that Kennedy was unacceptable to too great a portion of the Party, was what gave rise to the talk earlier this spring of nominating a third man. The names of Vice President Mondale, Edmund Muskie, and Henry Jackson began to be bandied about. At one point, it became difficult to get across the street in Washington without someone's coming up and saying, for example, "Do you think Muskie could get the nomination?" (The inquirer in that case would often be someone who was associated with Muskie.) The Mondale people were aware of the talk, but circumspect. Muskie, of course, is now Secretary of State. Neither he nor Mondale is in a very good position from which to lead a rebellion, if either should be inclined to do so. In private conversations, White House people have insisted that any attempt to unhorse Carter would leave the Party in ruins. Jackson sharpened his criticism of Carter, and found new adherents among the liberal elements of the Party as a result of his warnings against "overreacting" on Iran and Afghanistan. Yesterday, Jackson gave a speech in Chicago in which he said that because working people believed the Democratic Party had "reverted to the economic policies of Herbert Hoover," Reagan might win in November. When, in early May, Governor Hugh Carey, of New York, called on both Carter and Kennedy to release their delegates and have an open Convention, few thought it a selfless act. There was some buzzing in the congressional cloakrooms about the possibility of a third man, but nothing serious took form. The problem is that the sequence of events which would lead to the nomination of someone else would require concerted action on the part of a collection of Democrats—not a customary occurrence. Moreover, elected officials tend to have a preference for the regular order. And then, people also considered that Carter is one of the most tenacious politicians in memory.

At a press conference at the Oakland airport, Kennedy talks about the effects on the Oakland area of the recession and Carter's budget reductions, and about Carter's refusal to come to California to debate the issues.

A reporter tells Kennedy that yesterday Mrs. Carter said in Oakland that in 1976 Kennedy had refused to debate his Republican challenger for the Senate.

Kennedy replies that he did debate.

"She was wrong?" asks the reporter.

"Yeeesss," Kennedy replies, smiling. (Later, I was told by people in the Carter campaign that they knew that the information given Mrs. Carter was incorrect.)

This afternoon, Kennedy met with senior citizens at a housing project in a black section of Oakland and then went to San Francisco, where he gave more television and radio interviews and, this evening, attended a fund raiser at the Empress of China Restaurant, in Chinatown. To provide a "visual," the campaign arranged for Kennedy to be greeted by a Lion Dance, performed by some young Chinese, to the accompaniment of cymbals and drums, outside the restaurant, on Grant Avenue. As the dragonlike thing, with a blue, gold, and green head, wriggled about and the drums banged and the cymbals clanged, Kennedy looked puzzled and stroked his chin. Only about forty people turned up for the fund raiser, but, despite the embarrassment, Kennedy managed to squeeze out some enthusiasm. (However disheartened a politician may be by the turnout for a fund raiser, he must try to make it worthwhile for those who bothered to arrange it and those who paid to come.)

But tonight, at the United Irish Cultural Center, in the Sunset District of San Francisco, Kennedy is given the kind of reception a politician dreams of, and of which there have been very few for him in this campaign. The hall is jammed and an overflow crowd is downstairs. A big green-and-white sign says, in Gaelic, "A Hundred Thousand Welcomes." As Kennedy enters, a band strikes up, and a singing group called the Boys of the Old Brigade sings "The Boys of Wexford." Kennedy, reaching the stage, joins in. Tonight, he forgets about the stricture not to shout, relaxes other campaign inhibitions (he holds a baby during some of the singing), and simply allows himself to have fun. The crowd, ecstatic, shouts, "We want Ted!" Kennedy, pleased, stands and claps and sings along as the Boys of the Old Brigade sing some other Irish songs. This is his kind of event—the kind that he got used to in Boston and that has eluded him this year. Irish labor and political leaders are on the stage. Joe O'Sullivan, a retired president of the San Francisco Building Trades Council, who arranged this event, is presented with an Irish Man of the Year Award.

"Let's hear it for Joe one more time!" Kennedy roars gleefully as he begins his remarks. And as he goes through some introductions he turns to O'Sullivan from time to time and says, smiling, "How'm I doing, Joe?" or "Anybody who can do a rally like this, I'll do whatever you say." To the crowd, he says, "Being at a magnificent Irish Cultural Center like this tonight makes me think it's time to elect another Irishman as President of the United States."

The crowd cheers.

"I want to know, are we going to play 'When Irish Eyes Are Smiling' on June 3rd?" he asks.

The crowd wholeheartedly yells "Yes!"

"And I'll tell you something, Joe," Kennedy continues, shouting, his fist pounding the air. "It's time we grew some shamrocks in the Rose Garden." The crowd cheers again. And then he just lets go. His voice ringing, he says, "I believe, as you believe, that the Presidency of the United States can make an important difference." He cries out, "We have a President now that doesn't really believe that a President of the United States or an individual can make a difference. I reject that suggestion. That runs alien to everything that I believe, everything that I grew up with. I believe that individuals can make a difference, and anyone that doubts that ought to know Joe O'Sullivan. There are men and women like Joe O'Sullivan who are making a difference every day of their lives, to the young and to the old. There are schoolteachers in this room this evening. There are parents that are bringing up young families. There are people who are working with young children and with our senior citizens—all individuals that are making a difference in the quality of life for the people of this great nation of ours. And I say to you that a President of the United States can make a difference. A President of the United States can make a difference. We can read the history of this country and see it so clearly. Franklin Roosevelt made a difference when he pulled this country up by its bootstraps when it was facing the Depression in the period of the nineteen-thirties. Harry Truman made a difference when he converted us from a wartime economy to a peacetime economy. John Kennedy made a difference, Lyndon Johnson made a difference. And Presidents of the United States, I believe, can make an important difference." He talks about unemployment and inflation, and he pounds the lectern, saying, "I wish, my friends, that Jimmy Carter would come here to this hall tonight and debate those issues. Why won't he come to face the Democrats of California? Why won't Jimmy Carter come to California? What are you afraid of, Jimmy Carter?" He works the crowd, shamelessly and successfully, and he is giving them what they want. This may be terrible television, but it's as if he didn't care now: he's having fun, they're having fun, the hell with it. He concludes, "Are you going to be with me on June 3rd?"

The crowd roars "Yes!"

And then a woman sings "The Irish Soldier Laddie," changing a line to "I will march with Kennedy," and the crowd joins in.

Monday, May 26th, Memorial Day. The San Bernardino County Fairgrounds, in Victorville, California, about seventy miles northeast of Los Angeles. Ronald Reagan is to attend the Western Deserts Gospel Sing here today. Victorville, surrounded by dry land containing mostly scrub brush and Joshua trees, is in what is known as the "high desert," an elevated region of the Mojave Desert. From the fairgrounds one can see the San Bernardino Mountains, snow still covering some of the peaks. The air is cool and clear. Victorville is a stop on the direct route between Los Angeles and Las Vegas, which is three hours away. This is considered very conservative country—old Western and heavily religious. Roy Rogers has a ranch, Happy Trails, near here, and there is a Roy Rogers museum in Victorville. There are a number of churches and gospel-singing groups in the area. On the fairgrounds, various gospel-singing groups are performing on various stages, families are picnicking, and in various booths people are purveying ribs, fried chicken, cotton candy, records and tapes of gospel singing, and Jesus bumper stickers. One begins to picture Ronald Reagan and Jimmy Carter competing for the "born again" vote next fall. Recently, Richard Wirthlin, Reagan's pollster, said that Reagan expects to keep Carter from "cornering the market" on "born again" Protestants, who, Wirthlin said, constitute about a third of the population and are significant not only in the South but also in such important states as Ohio and Illinois. The evangelical movement is getting increasingly involved in politics, and many of the evangelical ministers who have radio or television programs have been speaking out for Reagan. While Reagan is here, Carter is visiting the U.S.S. *Nimitz,* the aircraft carrier from which the failed mission to rescue the hostages in Iran was launched, and which conveniently returned to port in Norfolk today.

George Bush pulled out of the Republican race today, leaving Reagan the sole contender and therefore all but officially the nominee. Actually, Bush handily defeated Reagan in Michigan last Tuesday, and Bush and his aides had expected that such a victory would keep his campaign alive until the end. They were proud that out of a crowded field Bush had ended up in a two-man race with Reagan. Howard Baker, who had seemed so promising to so many, never really got his campaign going, and dropped out on March 5th. John Connally, having gambled nearly twelve million dollars and gained one delegate (in Arkansas), was left like a beached whale after the South Carolina primary, on March 8th; he dropped out the following day. Robert Dole also dropped out in March, and Philip Crane dropped out in April. Bush was the only Republican other than Reagan to win any primaries. As in the case of the Kennedy campaign, sources of solace in a political race shift. After Bush won Iowa, he was all the rage. But he foundered in New Hampshire when Reagan, who hadn't bothered to campaign much in Iowa, came on strong, and when people began to get the impression that Bush hadn't anything to say. Reagan's polls indicate that Bush's decline in New Hampshire began after the first Republican debate, not the second, more famous one, in Nashua. Bush's staff now feels that it should have run "issue-oriented" advertising earlier in the course of the New Hampshire primary. It seemed that whenever Bush himself turned up on television, he was talking about "momentum." Then Bush had some bad breaks. He won Massachusetts, but the media attention was on John Anderson, who came in a close second. Earlier this year, Bush aides told me they hoped to have Anderson out of the way by the time of Massachusetts. Bush's people maintain that if Anderson had not still been in the race, Bush would have won or come close to winning in Illinois, and would have won Wisconsin—

and perhaps the nomination. They say that they could have won in New Jersey and Ohio, and even done well in California. "Reagan did not have the nomination locked up," says David Keene, Bush's political director.

Whether this is daydreaming or not, we'll never know. Campaigns are filled with "what if"'s. As it is, Bush came surprisingly close to Reagan in Texas and defeated him in Pennsylvania. By that time, Bush had developed a half-hour "Ask George Bush" format for television which was effective enough that even some Reagan people say the race might have been closer if he had used it earlier. Bush would have liked to stay around to the end, on the theory that (1) you never know, and (2) doing that well would stand him in good stead four years hence. Since he and his aides expected the news of his Michigan victory to bring in the contributions to keep going, Bush was shocked when ABC and CBS, in their late-night election coverage, led with the fact that their projections showed Reagan with enough delegates to win the nomination. The money didn't come in, and Bush, told the cold facts by his advisers this past weekend, decided—very reluctantly —to get out. He had been on the road almost constantly for a year and a half, and it is hard to stop.

Reagan arrives at the fairgrounds shortly after noon and holds a press conference, in an open stable, to give his reaction to Bush's withdrawal. Bales of hay, six deep, have been piled behind where Reagan is standing. Reagan reads a graceful statement, commending Bush for being a "superior campaigner," and thanking him for "his expression of support for my candidacy." Reagan looks ruddy and well. He is asked a few questions about his Vice Presidential selection. He isn't saying, of course, even if he has an idea who it will be: the Vice Presidential selection is the thing most likely to keep people interested in the Republican Convention. Then a reporter asks Reagan if he considers himself a born-again Christian. Reagan shambles around a bit, saying, "Well, I know what many of those who use that term mean by it. But in my own situation it was not in the religion of the church that I was raised in, the Christian Church. But there you were baptized when you yourself decided that you were, as the Bible says, as the Bible puts it, that that is being born again. And so, it was, within the context of the Bible, yes, by being baptized." In answer to a question about how his campaign will change now that he has the nomination, he explains that though the schedule may let up some, he's going to press his campaign against Carter: "That's the only person I've been campaigning against in the campaign so far."

Because Reagan went after Carter rather than his fellow candidates, he will have an easier time finding the Party unity he wants. His candidacy has already been blessed by his former rivals, and he is planning to attend a number of "unity dinners" in the coming weeks to help them pay off their campaign debts. He is also planning to meet with some news organizations in the East, in a clear attempt to persuade them that he is a reasonable fellow. In January of 1979, Senator Paul Laxalt, of Nevada, Reagan's campaign chairman, arranged for Reagan to meet with just about every Republican senator. "That allayed a lot of their doubts," Laxalt says. Reagan, who seemed so improbable to so many for so many years, is now the Republican nominee. His next task is to convince as wide a range of people as possible that he is not improbable—a task that the Carter people are already planning to make as difficult as possible.

Reagan is asked what, after having tried for the nomination for so long and having almost got it four years ago, his emotions are now.

"What are my emotions right now?" Reagan replies. He pauses. "You know, the honest answer is, I don't think it's quite sunk in yet. I've been campaigning so long and so hard that it surprises myself. I haven't been fidgeting around, I've been sitting quietly catching up with the news clippings on the plane. I think maybe someplace along the line later today I'll go home all by myself and let out a loud yell."

On the stage at the rodeo field, Dale Wade, the manager and bass guitarist of a gospel group called June Wade and the Country Congregation, who has produced this event, announces that Reagan is about to arrive. "Tell him that Victorville loves him," Dale Wade says. "Tell him that Jesus loves him." The large crowd—about five thousand people—gathered in the bleachers cheers as Reagan arrives and takes a seat in a front row to watch the performance. Many in the crowd wave red-white-and-blue streamers. Dale Evans, on behalf of Roy Rogers, accepts an award. June Wade and the Country Congregation sing a song they dedicate to Reagan—"It's a Long, Lonesome Walk to the Top of the Hill." June Wade and the other woman in the group are wearing long white dresses. The stage is framed in pink, turquoise, and gold cardboard, and a large wooden wagon wheel is at the rear. Written on the rim of the wagon wheel is "Western Deserts Gospel Sing," and Reagan's name is at the base. Dale Wade, who repeatedly says "Praise God," introduces a number of people, including the chairman of the board of his record company. Reagan sits with Miss Victorville, who is wearing a white suit and a tiara, and a man in an Abraham Lincoln costume. Reagan smiles, signs autographs, and applauds as June Wade's group sings some more songs. Then Dale Wade introduces Reagan ("A man I very much respect and admire for his Christian testimony and for what he stands for, no matter where he is"), and Reagan goes to the stage and is given a plaque, "in appreciation for your Christian testimony and recognition of gospel music."

Then Reagan gives an unusual speech. Referring to a line in the Gettysburg Address, he says, "We are engaged in a great conflict to see whether that nation or any nation so conceived can long endure," and goes on, "That is really what is at stake and what is at issue today; whether this nation can continue. This nation under God." He talks, as he often does, about the "loss of confidence, a great concern and worry on the part of the American people." He attributes the loss of confidence to inflation. He cites "our lack of confidence with regard to the energy crisis" and the "doomcriers in the land who tell us that we will never again have things as good as we've had them, that we must learn to live with scarcity." He says, "I don't believe that," and he is applauded. He says, "I think that this country is hungry today for a spiritual revival—one nation, under God, indivisible," and he is applauded. He says, "There are people in our land today who want to take 'In God We Trust' off our money. I've never known a time when it needed to be there more." He says that the people who built America "didn't have an urban-renewal plan or an area-redevelopment program."

More than any other political speaker one can think of, Reagan is fond of making his point through illustrative stories. The stories are sometimes quite long, and sometimes convoluted. He tells them vividly, and they have the ring of scenes in old-time movies. Now he tells of the Reverend Muhlenberg, a Revolutionary War minister, who was preaching a sermon. "A messenger came down the aisle and handed him a note. He stopped his sermon, and he opened the note and read it. And then his congregation was amazed to see him remove his ministerial robes and he was wearing the uniform of George Washington's Army. And he said to his startled congregation, 'There is a time to preach and a time to fight.' " Reagan says that he has been "talking throughout the country about regaining our ability to defend ourselves." He says, "Of the four wars that have taken place in my lifetime, none of them happened because this nation was too strong. We backed our way into the wars because some people thought there was nothing that we were willing to risk our lives for." He cites the leader of the minutemen, who said in Lexington, "If they mean to have a war, let it begin here." And he asks, "Should he have said, 'Oh, no, let's get out of the way, this is too much trouble'?" And then he says that Carter refers to the Vietnam War "as a time of moral poverty," and he continues, "When fifty thousand people, young Americans, give their lives to protect the people of a small country, a defenseless country, against godless Communist tyranny, I think it is an act of collective moral courage, not moral poverty." (This seems to be a change. Reagan often says in his speeches that there will be "no more Vietnams." When I asked him last February what he meant by that, he said he meant that "never again must this country ever ask young men to fight and die in a war we're afraid to let them win," and when I asked him if he was saying we should or should not have gone into it, he said, "I was one who never believed we should have gone in.")

He says that he was reading some literature on the way here by "some of those organizations that think we should be more like the Soviet Union, that we should adopt more of their principles and so forth." (Reagan frequently begins a story by saying that he was just reading something or just talking to someone.) Then he makes a reference to his military service during the Second World War. (Reagan has written that he was disqualified for combat duty, because of nearsightedness, and was assigned to the 1st Motion Picture Unit of the Army Air Forces "to train combat camera crews, make training films, and photograph highly secret projects.'') ''When the general orders would come in, I'd stick them under the blotter, so that at the end of the day when I had time I could read them. Because in them were always the citations for heroism and bravery.'' And then he says that he read a news item about how the Soviet Union gave a medal to a Spaniard living in Moscow and he wondered why, and he found out that this man had lived in Cuba for a few years and had also been in jail in Mexico, and that ''he was the man who buried the axe in the head of Leon Trotsky.'' Then he says he remembers that the United States gave the Congressional Medal of Honor for an act he had read about during the war. ''It was a B-17 coming back from a raid over Europe all shot up with anti-aircraft fire. The ball turret that hung, as some of us can remember, under the belly of the plane had been hit; it was jammed. The ball-turret gunner was wounded; they couldn't get him out. And as they were coming over the Channel they were losing altitude, and the captain ordered 'Bail out.' And as the men started to bail out, the wounded boy in the ball turret realized he was being left to go down with the plane. And understandably he cried out in terror. The last man to leave the plane saw the captain sit down on the floor, take his hand, and say, 'Never mind, son, we'll ride it down together.' A Congressional Medal of Honor posthumously awarded to a man who was willing to give his life just to bring comfort for the few minutes remaining in the life of a fellow companion.'' He says, ''The contrast between the two governments is spelled out in what we give, or gave, our awards for: theirs for murder and ours for the greatest sacrifice that a man could make.'' And he concludes with what he says is a line Tom Paine uttered ''in those dark days'' of the Revolutionary War: ''We have it in our power to begin the world over again.'' And he adds, ''We have it in our power, with God's help, to continue doing just that.''

As always, Reagan's delivery is smooth; his head is often slightly tilted to the side. His speech is an amalgam of Christianity and militarism—the preacher-soldier—and goes over well.

Tuesday, May 27th. Today, in the city of Industry, in the San Gabriel Valley, outside Los Angeles, Reagan returned to his more familiar speech. He praised the free-enterprise system and deplored government inroads into it. He said that the federal government was created to do only three things: preserve order, protect the national security, and provide us with a stable currency. He said some of his familiar lines: ''I believe the time has come for a turnaround in which we bring government back down to within the limits.'' Balancing the budget is ''like protecting your virtue—you just have to learn to say no.'' He pointed out that he has been criticized for his call for a tax cut of thirty percent over three years, and he continued to defend it. This is something that is being thrashed out among his advisers: some are more inclined toward a traditional monetary and budget-balancing approach. From talks with Reagan advisers, one gets the impression that they are reaching for a way to blend the two approaches. Some of his congressional supporters, who went around the country in 1978 pushing the Kemp-Roth thirty-percent-tax-cut idea and found that the public was skeptical, wish that Reagan would talk about budget cuts first, then tax cuts; they think this would be more generally accepted.

Using an argument that Democrats used to make against Republicans, Reagan criticizes the Carter Administration for adopting "the old-fashioned course that you can't control inflation unless you create a recession and have unemployment." And today Reagan said, as he often does, of the energy problem, "The answer is very simple indeed: Get the government out of the energy industry and turn it loose again." Some of his congressional advisers also wish that he would moderate that rhetoric. When I asked Reagan advisers at the Los Angeles headquarters today whether in the fall campaign Reagan would continue to say that there is more oil under the ground than has yet been extracted, as he did today—"Geologists in that industry have told me that there is more oil and natural gas yet to be found than we have so far used, and I am inclined to believe that they are correct and that we'd better get at the business of finding it"—they replied that the Governor would offer "a broad energy program" for the fall.

Reagan said today that the United States was reaching what the military terms a "window of vulnerability" to Soviet missiles, that he thought for the Soviets "it's a window of opportunity," and that "the President under those circumstances might be faced with the choice of surrender or die." He also said, "There will be no more Taiwans, no more Vietnams, no more betrayal of allies and friends."

Reagan has his lines and his anecdotes down well now, and though he has shown, in debate and in response to reporters' questions, that he can be spontaneous and deft, he chooses not to change what he says very much. He comes across as self-confident, and he is universally described as a nice man. He does have an Irish temper, some of his aides say, and can be quite impatient. Reagan does not come across as an extremist, in part because of his style, in part because he has the reputation of having been a moderate governor, and in part because many listeners have a tendency to assume that he does not really mean what he says—that much of it is said for effect. It is likely that, as people around him maintain, he knows that things are more complicated than he suggests, but to what extent does he know this? He does have an exploitative side, which the nice-guy demeanor smooths over. Every politician exploits people's emotions, or tries to; the question is, Which emotions, and to what degree? Reagan picks at things that are bothering people, making them angry; he talks in a soothing style, but he is not a soothing force.

When one talks with Reagan's advisers, one gets the clear impression that there will be an attempt to have him give more thoughtful speeches in the fall campaign, presenting more detailed domestic and foreign policies. They say that a different kind of campaign will be required from the one that carried him through the primaries. All sorts of lists of task forces and advisers have been drawn up, and all sorts of position papers are being written. But there's no way of knowing yet which new people will actually end up having an intellectual influence on Reagan. Some of Reagan's advisers are uneasy about his sometimes loose use of "facts" and statistics—though they say that "the media" have made more of this than the public has—because they fear that it contributes to a larger problem: an impression that Reagan may not have a clear grasp of what is going on in the world. One of Reagan's advisers has told me he realizes that it is going against Reagan's nature to try to get him to stop using so many statistics. "He loves those numbers," this man said. There is an attempt by some of Reagan's advisers to liken him to Eisenhower. One of them suggested the similarity in a conversation today, and said that now, in a period of nostalgia, Eisenhower is enjoying a new fashion. Reagan, it seems, deliberately plays the politics of nostalgia, by harking back to the good old days, when things were simpler. The trick is how to do this without seeming out of date and out of touch. This is a more serious problem for him than his age. Reagan has taken to deflecting the age question by joking about it.

The advisers say that the stress in the fall campaign will be on Reagan as a competent manager, and that Reagan will offer his own ideas for managing the government. They say that they believe Carter's record makes him very vulnerable, but they also expect the White House to make full use of incumbency, as it has against Kennedy, and to try to make Reagan the issue, as it has Kennedy. The Reagan people are obviously pleased with the presence of John Anderson in the race, and eager to paint him as a liberal (just as the White House is eager to portray him as a conservative). One indication of how far ahead the Reagan people are thinking about the implications of Anderson came in the course of a conversation I had today with William Casey, the campaign director, when he took from his desk a memorandum explaining the number of seats in the House of Representatives, and in which states, the Republicans would have to win in order to control a majority of the state delegations—and thus be in a position to select the next President if the election should end up in the House.

This afternoon, Reagan gave an indication of how much Anderson's presence means to him, and showed his deft touch, and also his sly side, when he was asked to respond to Jody Powell's comment today that the President would not debate Anderson in the fall. Reagan was asked about this by reporters as he was entering a house in Pasadena where one of his precinct phone banks is. "Of course," Reagan said of the President, "he's reluctant to debate within his own Party." Then he got another lick in by saying, of Anderson, "I see no reason why, if there is a debate, he shouldn't be included." Then, when he was asked why he thinks Carter doesn't want to debate Anderson, he replied, nonchalantly, "Maybe because he thinks they might be appealing to the same voters."

Reagan may have won the nomination yesterday, but he acts as if nothing has happened. Today, Gerald Ford endorsed Reagan, and tonight, at a fund-raising dinner at the Beverly Hills Hotel for California Republican legisla-tors, which Reagan and his wife, Nancy, are attending, a state senator announces that Reagan has just won Kentucky by eighty-three percent, Idaho by eighty-four percent, and Nevada by eighty-three percent. Yet Reagan gives essentially his standard speech. He says that he remembers when the President "told us we had to give up the Panama Canal because he said no one would like us if we didn't." He goes on, "I remember he has said we should have the SALT II treaty because no one would like us if we don't ratify it. And I think it's time we tell him that we don't care whether they like us or not." He makes many of the same points he has been making for months now. He has been speaking quietly, and the audience is attentive but not aroused. And then he says that it is time for the Republican Party to broaden its base, to reach out to "good solid blue-collar Democrats who will no longer follow their Party's leadership," to "go into the minority neighborhoods and the ethnic neighborhoods, not as our opponents have gone into them over the years, insulting and demeaning them, by offering only handouts, as if this was what was necessary to secure their support," but "to go in and say, 'Look, we know that you want what everyone else wants: opportunity, a chance at jobs for the future, a chance to educate your children, and raise them for a better life for them than we have had previously, to be treated with the dignity of an individual sharing the same hopes and aspirations that all other Americans share.' " He says, "And if we do that, I think we'll find that a lot of voters that up until now the Democrats have taken for granted will be ours."

Columbus, Ohio, May 29th. With the last primaries five days off, Carter is making his first avowed "political" trip of the campaign. After the Presi-dent, through a combination of design and accident, got himself into a policy of remaining in the White House as long as the hostages were held, the problem arose of how to get him out. His advisers believed that travel was necessary in order to nail down the nomination as firmly as possible, to have the President start explaining himself to the country and trying to rally it (with a view to the fall), and also to get him back to campaigning. They feared that he had become rusty. (This is another instance in which politi-cians are not unlike athletes.) To the President's advisers, that breathtaking week in late April—in which there occurred the failed mission to rescue the hostages in Iran, the resignation of Secretary of State Cyrus Vance, who had objected to the raid, and the quick replacement of Vance by Edmund Muskie (to divert attention from the raid and Vance)—seemed as good a time as any for the President to announce that he would now travel. People would be too distracted to focus on any one thing, and there was an osten-sible new context. The President's explanation, at a White House briefing for civic leaders that week, that the problems had become "manageable enough now for me to leave the White House," caused his advisers some embarrassment and himself some unnecessary criticism; there were also problems when he ventured forth to Philadelphia the following week and took some swipes at Vance. (His remarks were a display of the mean streak that some of Carter's aides had feared would show up when he campaigned.) The trip to Philadelphia was billed as "non-political"—and thus came out of the government's budget, as opposed to the campaign's—but, of course, the media in Philadelphia reach New Jersey, which has no major television stations. As it happened, the strategy behind the handling of the events after the raid worked. For one thing, the raid turned out to be popular, and helped the President's standing in the polls. Caddell says, "People wanted the President to do something, and something happened. It's that simple. It dissipated the growing anger and pressure over the crisis. It's the one reason no one in the country cared whether Cyrus Vance was leaving—especially once Muskie was chosen." One of the President's advisers says, "Maybe one of this Administration's greatest talents is its ability to contain disaster."

After an extended internal debate, it was decided that the President would not campaign in California. For one thing, the President's campaign began to run into budget problems. Fund raising has fallen short. A decision was made to reduce the Vice President's and the First Lady's travel schedules and to increase the budget for advertising. The decision to stress advertising at the expense of campaigning was a controversial one among those involved in campaign policy, some of whom felt that the advertising was essentially negative, and that the President's team, including the President, should be more active in campaigning and putting forward a positive case. In the first months, Carter's spokesmen could go around the various states saying how much the Administration was doing for them, in terms of jobs and programs. Now, as a result of budget cuts and the recession, there was less to brag about. Iran and Afghanistan no longer worked in the President's favor. There was internal disagreement over how effective the campaign of Carter the person versus Kennedy the person continued to be. And some Carter people felt that Kennedy's pounding away had, in fact, begun to hurt. Another reason it was decided that Carter would not go to California was the fear that the trip might not be successful—because of Carter's basic lack of popularity in the state, because of the political apathy that was believed to prevail there, and because there was a fear of demonstrations. The Vice President and Robert Strauss strongly urged the President to go, but the final judgment, shared by Powell, Jordan, and the President, was that it would be far worse to go and then lose the state than not to go and to lose it.

Ohio was considered Carter's best state; Ohio was likely to give Carter a good reception; and Ohio was, after all, the "heartland" of America and the state where Carter was most likely to prevent Kennedy from winning all three of the big states on June 3rd, thus denying him the argument that the only major industrial state the President had carried in the primaries was

Illinois. So the President would go where he was likely to do best. Moreover, Ohio, which Carter carried against Ford, will be one of the crucial states in the fall. Already, a substantial amount of money has been put into advertising in Ohio—much of it for ads, produced by Gerald Rafshoon, showing "man in the street" interviews in which people make negative comments about Kennedy. Caddell argued that these were having a strong impact, and recently the Carter budget for Ohio was increased. As of a week ago, the Carter camp expected to win Ohio by eight to fifteen percentage points, and considered the two other big states close and hoped to win them. (The Kennedy campaign, recognizing a probable loss in Ohio, is concentrating the candidate's time and its limited resources on New Jersey and California.) The Carter campaign strategy of spending a lot of money early in the hope of getting Kennedy out of the race did not work, but the strategy of spending everywhere, in order to pile up enough delegates, did. The Carter people are very impatient with all the talk of how Carter must score a psychological as well as an arithmetical victory—and they blame the media for such talk—but now they feel that they must deal with it. One of the President's strategists said to me recently, "The challenge early on was not to do it nicely but to do it at all. Now we want to do it nicely." But once it was decided that the President would campaign, and where, there remained the question of what he would say. One of the President's advisers said to me two weeks ago, "All of a sudden, everyone is talking about what we are going to say about a second term."

Here, in the middle of this Midwestern state, a rally is to be held for the President at a plaza in front of the Nationwide Insurance building at noon. Noon is a good time to get people out for a rally, and the Carter campaign has been working on this event for some time; the day is hot and sunny, and a huge crowd has gathered. Carter is, after all, the President. Much has been made in the press of the fact that Reagan is holding a rally a few blocks away, and people commuting between the two sites report that Carter's crowd is larger. Some people in the crowd say that they are Republicans but have come to see the President.

The plaza is good for giving a picture of a dense crowd, and the tall, modern building in back of it is decorated with bunting and a large American flag. Behind where the President will stand is a large green-and-white sign saying "SUPPORT PRESIDENT CARTER." The Presidential seal is on the lectern where he will speak. There are five bands here, and their music has been helping to build the crowd's anticipation. An announcer tells the crowd, "Air Force One is safely on the ground, and the Presidential motorcade is on its way right now," and the crowd cheers. The announcer keeps telling the crowd what "an historic occasion" this is. Carter is no mere candidate: he is the President and the symbol of the Presidency, which obviously still counts for a lot. Just as the President arrives, red, white, and blue balloons are released into the air—a sight that one associates with Richard Nixon and Republican Conventions. But this is obviously an excellent "visual" for tonight's television programs. The President is wearing a dark-blue suit and a white shirt. He looks good from a distance, but up close he has been looking pale and tired lately. He grins his wide grin and waves, palm out, in all directions to the crowd. This event has to make him feel good. Senator John Glenn, Democrat of Ohio, introduces Carter. (Ohio's other senator, Howard Metzenbaum, also a Democrat, is supporting Kennedy.) Glenn, who has been a friend of the Kennedy family, endorsed Carter a week ago, after some pressure was brought on him to do so. Today, Glenn says that "there have been disappointments" but that the people's choice "has been very clearly expressed," and it is "a time to close ranks."

Carter begins by saying, "I've been waiting a long time for this moment." He is applauded. He says, "And there is no place in the world I would rather be right now than in Columbus, Ohio." He is applauded again. He thanks Ohioans for having provided him the primary victory in 1976 that insured his nomination, for putting him over the top at the 1976 Democratic Convention, and for making a difference in whether he or Ford won in 1976. And he thanks them in advance for providing him a majority of the Democratic delegates next Tuesday. (This past Tuesday, Carter easily won the Kentucky, Arkansas, Idaho, and Nevada primaries, and he is only a few delegates short of the sixteen hundred and sixty-six that he needs. The Carter camp claims that he has sixteen hundred and sixty-two, and the Associated Press gives him fifteen hundred and eighty-four.) Now Carter launches into his argument about why he should be re-elected. He cites Franklin Roosevelt, who said that he would not campaign for his re-election in 1944 but would correct any errors that his opponents made about him and his Administration, and he says, "Although I will, of course, campaign this fall, now is a good time to set the record straight, not only about my own record but also about the strength and the achievement of the United States of America." Then he asks the audience a series of questions, to each of which he gives the answer: the United States. Which nation has the highest productivity per worker? (This to offset the fact that productivity in the United States is declining, as the President has publicly noted elsewhere. Last year, the growth rate was negative.) Which was the only major developed nation to meet the goal of reducing oil consumption by five percent in 1979? (The actual reduction was about two percent; five percent is the amount by which consumption fell below anticipated consumption.) Which nation had the greatest increase in industrial production? Which nation added more than nine million new jobs in the last two and a half years? (This to offset the fact that unemployment is rising—in the last three months, there has been an increase in unemployment of almost a million people. Actually, the President slipped: his jobs figure, which he has referred to on other occasions, covers the last three and a half years.) "Which nation is strongest and at peace? The United States." And then Carter gets to his main theme. "We do live in a time of challenge; we do live in a time of change; we do live in a time of danger. But in every area of change, in every area of challenge, in every area of danger, because of our courage and strength, America is turning the tide."

His voice comes over loud on the amplifying system—he is pumping unaccustomed enthusiasm into his delivery, as if he knows how important this debut is. The crowd reaction to the President is warm but not exceptionally enthusiastic. In the course of his remarks, the President removes his jacket, and the crowd applauds. It may just be that he is hot, but he has shown that he is one of them.

Using the phrase over and over, he says that "we're turning the tide" in energy, on inflation, on interest rates, in foreign policy, in military strength. And, in what seems like the beginning of an attempt to portray Reagan in a certain light, Carter says, "As long as I'm President, our nation will be ready and determined to use our great strength for peace," and his voice rings out as he repeats the phrase "for peace." He says that the nation's new energy plan—it's not clear what he's referring to—is "more ambitious than the space program, the Marshall Plan, and the interstate highway system combined." He says, "It will replace foreign oil with American ingenuity and with Ohio coal." (A White House aide informs me later that the President was referring to the money that will accrue to the government from the windfall-profit tax over eleven years—two hundred and twenty-seven billion seven hundred million dollars. Congress has advised that sixty percent of the money be used for income-tax reduction, and the rest for energy research and development, mass transit, energy assistance to low-income people, and so on, but none of that is binding.) He says, "And I tell you flatly, with the perfect knowledge that if I make a mistake it is going to hurt me, I make this prediction: that in the second half of this year, beginning in the summer, the inflation rate is going to go down, too, and you can count on it."

There is only a brief reference to Iran, and none at all to the hostages. He says that he realizes that not all the decisions he has made have been right or popular, and he says that they certainly have not all been easy ones. But, he says, "We have been tested under fire, we have never ducked nor hidden. . . . We have done what was right and we have always told the truth." Although Carter has done his share of shading the facts, the polls indicate that the people feel he is an honest man, and that is one of his political assets. He ends on a note of uplift: "As long as I'm President, the government of the United States will be committed to those fundamental principles that hold our ever-stronger nation together: freedom, democracy, compassion, and human rights. We'll remain committed to the full promise of America—the land of equal justice, the land of full opportunity, and the land of liberty for all Americans." After he concludes, he sits in the open back of his limousine, waving to the crowds, as the motorcade pulls away.

The speech is actually a tryout, and the theme was not arrived at until earlier this week. The problem was to find a speech that could be based on the record and could hold out some promise for the future, and would also be believable. A basic speech defending the record had been floating about, but the President's aides felt that there was a need for something a little more positive, and for a rhetorical peg; thus they arrived at "turning the tide." Some of the President's advisers worried about the "credibility" of the President's message, and are not yet convinced that this is the one he should carry into the fall. It is as if he were asking where Reagan gets off saying things are in such bad shape, but Carter ends up saying that things are getting less bad than they had become under *him*. (One of the President's advisers remarked to me, "Our campaign has gone from 'Why Not the Best?' to 'It Could Be Worse.' ")

While the White House was figuring out what the President could say, it was continuing to try to figure out how to get Kennedy out of the race. A committee has been estabished under Richard Moe, Vice President Mondale's chief of staff, to work on this problem. Yesterday, Mondale himself called a Democratic senator who is close to Kennedy to suggest that the senator urge Kennedy not to prolong the fight. Strauss has been casting some lines out. The Carter camp wants people in Congress to point out to Kennedy that the longer he stays in, the more divided the Party will be, and the greater the jeopardy to Democrats in the House and the Senate who are running for re-election. The trick is how to bring pressure on Kennedy without bringing so much pressure that it stiffens his resistance.

Cleveland. Following the rally in Columbus, the President spoke to a fund-raising luncheon there, gave some local interviews, and then flew to Cleveland. (In Columbus, I encountered Strauss outside the luncheon, and he said to me, of the rally, "That was good, wasn't it? I thought it was important to bring the President somewhere nice and safe. No way he wouldn't get a goddam good crowd here today. No way that won't look good tonight. No way they can make a negative out of it. It'll be a positive. It'll look good in New Jersey and California, too. We've got eight states to look good in tonight. He'll look much better than the boy [Kennedy]. Did you see the boy on TV this morning? He looked bad—tired.") There is quite a difference between a President's campaign and anyone else's. Air Force One is an impressive-looking plane. The President's motorcade is very large, as is his staff contingent—even when, for budget reasons, it is being held down. The Presidential seal is on each lectern where he speaks. The logistics are smooth, and transcripts of the President's public utterances are produced in no time.

Now, shortly after five, the President arrives at an auditorium in Parma, a town just outside Cleveland, for a meeting with senior citizens and community leaders. He came here as a candidate in 1976. Parma is a heavily blue-collar, Eastern European community. To the extent that there is a race between Carter and Kennedy in Ohio, it is in this northern, industrial area, where the recession has hit. The southern part of the state is conservative and more rural, and safe for Carter. Parma is being sued by the Justice Department for racial discrimination in housing.

At closer range, the President's face looks pasty, and there is a puffiness under his eyes. This auditorium is quite warm, and he frequently dabs his forehead with a handkerchief. (Eventually, he removes his jacket again, and his shirt is wet.) He gives a condensed version of the speech he gave in Columbus, saying, "I thought, just in a short period of time, I would try to put the challenges that we face in perspective, because quite often in our great country there is too much of an overemphasis on the negative side of life." With this audience, he stresses that "our nation is a nation of immigrants." He says, "We do have problems. Our country has problems that we can handle. The challenges that face us today are not nearly so severe as the ones that have been faced in the past." He says that more than a third of the budget goes for programs for senior citizens. (According to the Office of Management and Budget, the figure is about twenty-six percent, and is arrived at by including, in addition to Social Security, Medicare, and so on, such things as public housing, veterans' pensions, and retirement programs for federal workers and the military.) He takes some questions from the audience. Rafshoon's film crew is filming this scene, just as it filmed the rally in Columbus, for use in forthcoming campaign ads—a practice that gives new meaning to the term "media event."

After a few questions, the President tells the audience, "As I look in your faces, it is an inspirational thing for me to know what you mean to our nation, and what our nation means to you. . . . We need have no fear of the future. In my judgment, the greatest nation on earth, with your help, will be even greater in the years to come." No more talk about a "crisis of confidence," no more lecturing the country for being self-indulgent, as he did in his famous "malaise" speech last July. (Like other thematic innovations—"the New Spirit," "the New Foundation"—that one was quickly abandoned.)

Carter's next appearance is at the Olivet Institutional Baptist Church, in a run-down black neighborhood on the east side of Cleveland. This place is a long way from Parma, in several respects. The church itself, a rectangular building, seems fairly new, and has white walls, blue-and-red glass windows, and pale wood panels on the stage. Awaiting Carter's arrival, the choir on the stage is singing robust hymns. Then, on cue, it goes into "The Battle Hymn of the Republic," and as it begins the chorus—"Glory, glory, hallelujah!"—the President enters. He stands on the stage, his feet wide apart—a characteristic Carter stance—and joins in the singing. Rafshoon's crew, crouching, moves back and forth among the members of the choir, filming the President and his audience.

Carter then sits in one of the chairs on the stage. George Forbes, the president of the city council and a leader of this district, makes some remarks in Carter's behalf. (Louis Stokes, the congressman from this area, is for Kennedy.) Then the Reverend Dr. Otis Moss, the pastor of the church, tells the audience of a recent trip he made to Washington, during which various black government officials told him how much the Carter Administration had done for blacks. The pastor has been to the White House twice in the last two weeks. Carter greets the dignitaries and the audience: "Ladies and gentlemen, brothers and sisters." He is applauded. Carter learned in Georgia how to speak in black churches, and he put that ability to good use four years ago. He reminds the audience that he was at this church in 1976. Tonight, he talks about "our brother, Vernon Jordan," who was shot in Fort Wayne, Indiana, early this morning. This is Carter's first mention of Jordan in any of his appearances today. He says that just a few minutes ago he spoke on the phone to Jordan's wife and his surgeon, and he asks for a moment of prayer for "our brother, Vernon Jordan." He remarks, offhandedly, that he believes the attack on Jordan was "an assassination effort." (At this point, there is no public information about what happened, and later in the evening Jody Powell tells reporters that the President has no additional information.) He talks of his "close personal relationship" with Jordan. It is true that the two men have known each other a long time, but, as Carter acknowledges here, they have also had serious, and public, disagreements about the Administration's policies toward blacks. Carter says that he was unable to see Dr. Moss the last time he was in Washington, because he had to inspect the volcano in the state of Washington. ("I flew over it, and I was impressed then with the power of God.") He quotes Martin Luther King, Jr., and he says that when Moses led the people out of Egypt they didn't reach their destination immediately. "They turned against Moses. They began to complain about the manna and the quail. . . . They forgot about the freedom that they had found, and they forgot about the slavery that they had escaped." And then he says, "The American people, and particularly the black people, have not yet reached the promised land. But we are on the road toward the promised land." And he is applauded.

He talks about how much more the government is doing now for blacks than it was four years ago, repeating as a refrain, "But we haven't yet reached the promised land." He explains that the one new major domestic program the Administration is seeking would provide two billion dollars to train people who might be ready to drop out of high school. (The full funding would not occur until the fiscal year 1982.) He mentions the important black officials in his Administration, and also mentions Andrew Young, who resigned under pressure. He says that he has appointed more black federal judges than all the previous Presidents put together. He says, "This is a time of controversy . . . a time of challenge . . . a time of impatience . . . a time of inconvenience. But it is also a time of opportunity." He says, "A President has got to face a lot of things: rampaging rivers, exploding volcanoes, Republicanism that might come back next November." He says, "We never thought it would take this long to reach the promised land." And he concludes by quoting the Bible.

And then, after addressing a large fund-raising dinner in Cleveland—at which he talks once again about the challenges and opportunities; praises the United States for being strong and at peace ("a nation not selfish, not divided, not trying to take advantage of other people"); praises the progress that he says has been made on energy; says that our alliances are stronger than ever; points out that refugees are fleeing to America, not from it; and concludes, "We've got the greatest nation on earth and it's going to be even greater in the future"—the President returns on Air Force One to Washington.

June 3rd. Tonight, Carter wins enough delegates to give him the nomination. He has carried Ohio, and also West Virginia and Montana. But Kennedy has carried California, and also New Jersey and Rhode Island (both of these states heavily), as well as South Dakota and New Mexico. Carter's margin in Ohio and his lead in the delegate count are not as great as his campaign aides had been predicting. For Reagan, of course, the evening is just a formality, and we see him on television looking very pleased and calling on Democrats and independents to join him in "unifying America." (Tonight, the networks include John Anderson in their election roundup; their exit polls showed substantial support for him, as have other recent polls.)

The Carters are shown at a victory rally in Washington, smiling but not looking very happy. The President tells his campaign workers, "I have one deep feeling in my heart, and that is thanksgiving to all of you who turned what eight months ago was a prediction of absolute defeat into a wondrous victory tonight." There is that: his case was widely written off as hopeless when this all began. He says, "And I am now dedicated to bringing our Democratic Party back together, after we have faced two formidable candidates who ran tremendous campaigns on their own, to reach out a hand of friendship and cooperation for them and their supporters." And Kennedy is shown addressing the crowd at his Washington headquarters. Having had a good day, he and his campaign workers appear jubilant. It has come to that. Kennedy speaks defiantly: "Today Democrats from coast to coast were unwilling to concede the nomination to Jimmy Carter. And neither am I. . . . We are determined to move on to victory at the Convention and in the election next November."

CHAPTER 9

The Republican Convention

DETROIT, SUNDAY, JULY 13TH. The Republican National Convention officially opens tomorrow, but in fact it has already begun. Ronald Reagan will, of course, be the nominee, but that does not settle a number of other questions. This Convention is a showcase for Reagan: an opportunity to convince the nation—indeed, the world—that he is "Presidential." This was described to me a couple of weeks ago by his campaign director, William Casey, as the overriding goal of the Reagan team. As Reagan's staff sees it, there will be two tests for Reagan here: the way he goes about choosing a running mate, and his acceptance speech. The ideas that the Reagan people will attempt to establish here this week, according to Peter Hannaford, a public-relations man who has been a close adviser to Reagan for years and is in charge of what is written for him, and Peter Dailey, a California advertising man who has been signed up as Reagan's media adviser (he handled Nixon's advertising in 1972 and worked for a while on Ford's 1976 campaign), are that Reagan is not a rigid conservative, not just an actor, not simplistic—that he is competent, pragmatic, and thoughtful, and that he is looking to the future. Hannaford said in a conversation I had with him yesterday, "The acceptance speech will be a thematic speech, impressionistic. It will be different from his stump speeches. There will be no laundry list of statistics or facts and figures—people are aware of that side of him."

The statistics have caused Reagan some trouble, of course, as have slips on other matters. The staff has now begun to take care to see that Reagan is carefully briefed before each stop. Hannaford continued, "The speech will be broad enough in scope that everyone feels included. It is an inclusionary speech. Governor Reagan wanted it to be indicative of his theme of renewal and rededication of the country. He wants it to be a forward-looking speech, striking the theme of a coalition of people with different backgrounds who share the same values and want a sense of steadiness and stability. He will stress five summary words: 'family,' 'work,' 'neighborhood,' 'peace,' and 'freedom.' "

I asked Hannaford how this fitted in with the poll data the campaign had gathered.

He replied, "It's all quite compatible with the data we're finding: a strong desire to enter a period of stability, of steadiness, of consistency—coupled with economic fear."

The Reagan campaign organization is not in very good shape, considering the time it has had to get in shape—the nomination has been in hand since May 26th. And Reagan, who apparently tends to take a relaxed view of such matters, has allowed things to drift. In politics, a head start can be of great advantage; the Reagan people appear to be frittering. The campaign staff is ridden with tensions among the different generations of aides. Though some of the Reagan advisers are more conservative than others, the frictions have less to do with ideology than with the nature and duration of the various people's ties to Reagan. Lines of authority are fuzzy at best. A plan for the fall campaign is only beginning to evolve. The indecision that has marked the Reagan group lately—sometimes with damaging consequences—was demonstrated twice in recent weeks; over whether Bill Brock should be replaced as chairman of the Republican National Committee and over Reagan's failure to address the convention of the National Association for the Advancement of Colored People. (Brock is a conservative, but not as conservative as many of Reagan's followers. The fear of those who wanted him ousted—the more right-wing members of the Reagan camp—was that if Reagan lost the election Brock would fire the Reagan people who were being added to the National Committee's staff, and thus they would lose their opportunity to take control of the Party's machinery.) After much public to-and-fro, Brock was kept on. And now Reagan is to address the National Urban League in August. Some of Reagan's own people are worried about the lack of planning for the fall, and about the lack of lines of authority within the staff, and about Reagan's reluctance to assert himself. "He's very good with people," says one loyal aide. "But he's not so good with persons."

The tendency to let things happen characterized the Reagan campaign's approach to the consideration of the platform here last week. Some people within the Reagan camp are disturbed by the platform committee's removal of the Party's long-standing support of the Equal Rights Amendment (it substituted a section saying, "We acknowledge the legitimate efforts of those who support or oppose ratification of the Equal Rights Amendment") and its addition of a section supporting an anti-abortion constitutional amendment and of another one saying, "We will work for the appointment of judges at all levels of the judiciary who respect traditional family values and the sanctity of innocent human life." The platform committee also added a section calling for repeal of the fifty-five-mile-an-hour speed limit. Other Republicans, especially Party officials and elected politicians, are appalled. They place some blame on the Reagan staff, saying that the political people were preoccupied elsewhere or asleep at the switch, and that the "substantive" people who were on the scene failed to see the political implications. (In fact, Reagan opposes the Equal Rights Amendment and favors a constitutional amendment to prohibit abortion.) The platform committee also adopted an amendment, offered by Senator Jesse Helms, of North Carolina, calling for military "superiority" over the Soviet Union.

What happened on the platform committee, and the reaction to it among other Republicans here, is indicative of what sort of group or what sorts of groups are gathering here in Detroit. Both political parties have a group on the periphery—the Democrats on their left, the Republicans on their right —that comes to the Convention interested more in issues than in politics. The candidate is less important than the causes; these groups are unresponsive to arguments that what they seek to do might hurt the candidate's chances of winning the election. They disdain compromise. When the Democratic Party is tending leftward, as it was in 1972, the people on the periphery tend lefter; when the Republican Party is tending rightward, as it is this year, the people on the periphery tend righter. And in both instances it is these people who head for the platform committees. And there is a new element at the Republican Convention this year: the fundamentalist religious movement, which has recently got increasingly involved in politics. It is a new form of an old element in American political life. These fundamentalists constitute a kind of counter-reformation—against the growing public acceptance of such things as abortion and homosexuality, against the changing role of women. They seek prayer in the schools, they are disturbed about sex education, and they object to textbooks that they feel do not uphold traditional values. They are upset and they are absolutists, and their power comes from their numbers and from their method of communicating —through the "electronic ministries." Their strength is enhanced by their alliances, ideological and political, with the New Right.

The New Right, as opposed to the old conservatism, has its roots in social protest, in the politics of discontent, and it fastens on social issues—abortion, busing, homosexuality—as well as such issues as gun control, the Panama Canal, and military spending. These groups seek to implant their social and moral views in law. The New Right is technically nonpartisan but essentially Republican, and tries to appeal to blue-collar workers. (It also constituted some of "the Wallace vote.") Therefore, it plays an important part in Reagan's attempt to build a "new coalition." Actually, Nixon and Agnew tried much the same thing, with some success. But now the groups that can contribute to such an effort are better organized and financed and use more sophisticated political techniques. They are raising enormous sums of money to spend on political campaigns.

One political fundamentalist group, called the Moral Majority, is headed by Dr. Jerry Falwell, an electronic evangelist who claims twenty-five million viewers for his program, "The Old Time Gospel Hour," and who will be here in Detroit. Falwell's organization has a number of delegates at this Convention, and it controls the Alaska delegation. Donald E. White, an Alaska delegate who served on the platform committee, says that the fundamentalist crusade is pro-life, pro-family, pro-morals, and pro-America. Reagan must come to terms with these people. The Reagan campaign has already made it clear that it plans to compete with Carter for the "born again" vote.

Though in some instances these groups' interests may overlap with those of more traditional conservatives, the two strains are culturally distinct; the fundamentalists and the New Right have little in common with the traditional conservatives (the Tafts and the Buckleys). The new strain is essentially small-business and rural—it has a strong streak of populism—and is suspicious of the boardroom, and it makes the boardroom nervous. It is actually more radical than conservative. As of now, Reagan is astride this uneasy, even unwitting coalition, each element seeing in him the vehicle for achieving its purposes. Reagan enjoys strong support from business, and his closest friends in California are businessmen of substantial means—people such as Justin Dart, the head of Dart Industries, and Holmes Tuttle, the head of Holmes Tuttle Enterprises—who persuaded him to go into politics and gave him financial backing. Reagan is gifted at talking, in his speeches, to the "common man," at speaking to his grievances. But he socializes with magnates, and they are among his closest advisers. Such moderates as are here have pretty much given up. They are outgunned, and they know it, and they have talked themselves into accepting Reagan. Some of them—especially the elected officials—talk, at least privately, with bewilderment about "those nuts" who they feel have taken over this Convention. In fact, the moderates gave up years ago. They considered the gritty work of political organizing beneath them, and were accustomed to having the Party panjandrums arrange matters to their satisfaction. But as participation in politics spread, the panjandrums could no longer maintain control. The conservative movement, including the segment that developed into the New Right, went out and organized, almost unnoticed—and produced the nomination of Barry Goldwater in 1964. Now they are about to have their next triumph. The moderates could have been more of a force this year had they rallied around one particular candidate. They control the governorships in several important states, including Michigan, Illinois, Ohio, and Pennsylvania. But they lay low until it was too late. (An exception was Governor William

Milliken, of Michigan, who went on the line for George Bush and helped him win the Michigan primary.) Another problem the moderates have is that it is hard to say what, exactly, they stand for. The conservatives have no such difficulty.

At this Convention, there are old Reagan people and new Reagan people —who are not quite comfortable with each other. The old Reagan delegates are more "political," more adjusted to the idea of compromise, than the new Reagan delegates. The old Reagan aides are suspicious of the new ones. There are some people now working for Reagan who worked for Goldwater and then for Ford (against Reagan in 1976). They are flexible. Some of them also worked for Richard Nixon, who will apparently go unmentioned in the course of this Convention, as he did in 1976, and as will Nelson Rockefeller, the last Republican Vice President. But this Convention has drawn—as onlookers, circulators, socializers—a number of people who worked for the Nixon Administration and have since retired to private life, and people who socialize in Republican circles but seemed to hide out four years ago. And this Convention, inevitably, has drawn people who are ready to go back into the government.

Although Reagan has known since late May that he would be the nominee, he has postponed the decision about the Vice Presidential candidate for a number of reasons, his aides say: it would be hard to keep the decision a secret; it provides the only source of suspense at this Convention; and, according to one aide particularly close to Reagan, "he realizes he'll be watched for the way he does this, and the place to be watched is at the Convention."

Another reason, apparently, is that Reagan is having trouble finding a running mate who appeals to him. Reagan's aides have been saying their polls show that the only possible choice that helps him is Gerald Ford, who has insisted that he will not run. "There's nobody outstanding in that crop," one of Reagan's most trusted advisers said to me this morning, referring to the most frequently mentioned prospective candidates: George Bush, who lasted longest against Reagan in the primaries, and who, though conservative, has support among the Party's moderates; Howard Baker, senator from Tennessee; Richard Lugar, senator from Indiana; Jack Kemp, congressman from New York; Guy Vander Jagt, congressman from Michigan; Paul Laxalt, senator from Nevada; Donald Rumsfeld, who was White House chief of staff and Secretary of Defense under Ford; William Simon, who was Secretary of the Treasury under Nixon and Ford; and Anne Armstrong, former Ambassador to Great Britain. Mrs. Armstrong appears to be on the list for symbolic reasons, as she was in 1976. There is a strong argument that it is in Reagan's interest to have made the decision by now. He could, as one man who advises Republicans said to me, get off the plane when he arrives here tomorrow and say, yes, he has decided whom he will select, and will announce it later in the week. "The Convention is not the real world," this man said. "People start coming in and out of the candidate's suite and bringing pressure, reacting to the moment."

Ford arrived in town yesterday. He criticized the E.R.A. platform plank on his arrival, and there is much talk here about what he said on "Issues and Answers" today about the Vice Presidency. Ford is presumed to be for Bush—at least, some of Ford's closest associates as well as some of Bush's (in some instances, they are the same people) believe this to be the case. Ford said that Reagan should pick someone who would "broaden the base" and would "have some greater background than he has in Washington, D.C." He spoke most highly of Bush and Baker, described Lugar and Kemp as fine fellows but "newcomers," and gave a bit of the back of his hand to Rumsfeld and Simon.

Simon is not considered a serious possibility now; he has never been in politics, and some members of Reagan's staff feel that his personality is too abrasive. Rumsfeld, it turns out, has a number of enemies: several of his colleagues in the Ford Administration considered his elbows a bit too sharp. Baker is considered out because many members of the conservative wing of the Party, particularly the Southerners, have an emotional negative reaction to him. These days, they say it is because he supported the Panama Canal treaties, but they were just as emotional about him four years ago, before he had had occasion to vote for the Panama Canal treaties. Their feeling seems to be that he is a Southerner who is not quite Southern, and a man who is too opportunistic. A Southern delegate said to me today, "There's a perception that he's very much a compromiser—a perception in the South that he's inclined to compromise on issues that Southerners feel emotionally about."

Baker started trying to be the Vice Presidential candidate in 1968. After he was passed over last time (Ford did not want to take on the right wing at the Convention), he said, "If I ever run for national office again, it won't be for Vice President." And so this year he ran for the Presidency but got nowhere. When he found himself back in the Vice Presidential speculation, he apparently decided that he really did not want to go through that again, or at least didn't want to appear to be going through that again, and so he has said that he is not a candidate for Vice President. The Reagan people have decided to take him at his word.

It is one of the ironies of this Convention that Ford, who defeated Reagan in a tough fight four years ago, has become the power broker. Just as Reagan had to be appeased by the platform in 1976, it is assumed that Ford has to be appeased by the Vice Presidential selection. According to people who know Ford well, he doesn't think much of Reagan—he resents the fact that in the 1976 Presidential campaign Reagan didn't exert himself on Ford's behalf, and he finds Reagan, as one Ford associate puts it, "thin." In his autobiography, Ford criticized Reagan's "penchant for offering simplistic solutions to hideously complex problems." This March, when he reconsidered his earlier decision not to run in the primaries, his associates convinced him that it was too late. But Reagan needs Ford—Ford's approval would give Reagan legitimacy among moderates—and so Ford's word on the Vice Presidency is considered of great importance. (Ford is conservative, as is Bush, and Baker is not exactly liberal, but all things are relative.) The press, with no other real story to chase, is playing along with the Reagan people's desire that the selection of the Vice Presidential candidate provide suspense at this Convention. But unless this is all an elaborate charade—and it does not seem to be one—is this any way to pick a potential President? This struggle over the Vice Presidency is, of course, one for very big stakes. Even if Reagan does serve out one or two terms, whomever he selects has a good chance at the Presidency after that. It's an odd way to pick a President, but everyone knows that that might be what, in effect, is happening.

Monday. Guy Vander Jagt, who is to be the keynote speaker, has breakfast this morning with a group of reporters. Vander Jagt is the chairman of the National Republican Congressional Committee, which works to get Republicans elected to the House. All of Reagan's potential running mates will speak before the Convention, and their thoughts and their oratory will be directed at him. The Reagan people have been saying that among the criteria is how these people perform at the Convention and how the Convention reacts to them. Vander Jagt talks with a deep voice, and he has a broad head and a tan, leathery face. He is asked what he thinks his chances are of being selected as Reagan's running mate.

"I have a very strong feeling that I remain on the list," he says. "It's a little bit like a fella that has his eye on a girl, and he's concluded that she's kinda interested in him. She hasn't said anything; it's in her eyes, a glance."

Vander Jagt has never met with Reagan alone. He is asked, "In order to get that feeling, you have to at least see the girl once in a while, don't you?"

He replies, "There have been communications between me and the Reagan camp. I just get good vibes."

Vander Jagt was a strong supporter of Ford in 1976. "Has Reagan been growing on you?" he is asked.

"Very much so," he replies.

He is asked if he would attach any conditions to becoming the Vice Presidential candidate.

He replies, "I would agonize for about a tenth of a second and then I would accept enthusiastically."

On the Convention floor this morning, floor whips and political representatives of the Reagan forces are decked out in the same sorts of red and yellow golf caps that the Ford forces wore four years ago. I ask Trent Lott, a congressman from Mississippi, who is wearing a red golf cap, what they are worrying about. "Nothing," he replies. "But if you assume nothing will happen, then something will. Besides, we're all here. We have to do something." In fact, the Reagan Convention operation is being run by the same man who ran Ford's four years ago—William Timmons. Timmons, who is forty-nine, worked for Goldwater's nomination and then for Nixon's, handled congressional relations for the Nixon White House during Watergate, managed the alarmingly precise 1972 Republican Convention, and now has his own Washington lobbying firm. Timmons was tapped only recently to handle the Convention for Reagan and also to be the political director for the Reagan campaign. He has had precious little time to work on strategy for the fall.

Monday afternoon. Reagan is to arrive shortly at the Detroit Plaza Hotel, which is the Convention headquarters and also the headquarters for the Reagan campaign. This hotel is a baffling structure of circles within circles: circular spaces within a cylindrical building; on the lower level, a revolving circular bar; and, on the lobby level, still another circular bar, with semicircular seating areas, or "pods." Candidates' arrivals are one of the set pieces of political conventions. Leaflets have been distributed advertising Reagan's arrival here, and a large crowd of people, most of them young, began to gather on the lower level (where Reagan will make an appearance) a good hour and a half before his arrival time. Many of them were brought to Detroit by the Reagan organization to paint signs, demonstrate, and cheer. A jazz band entertains them and raises their level of excitement, and a man in a white suit leads them in practicing cheers. At one point, the man cautions them, "When Reagan gets here, please do not raise your signs, because it might block the television cameras." The crowd yells when Mike Curb, the lieutenant governor of California and the program chairman of the Convention, announces that Reagan has arrived in the hotel and is on his way.

Then Reagan, with his wife, Nancy, alongside, appears on the platform. He is wearing dark trousers, and a white jacket with brass buttons and with a white handkerchief in the breast pocket. Reagan has an engaging stage smile in any event, but now he looks genuinely happy, as he should. Mrs. Reagan is dressed in a beige Adolfo suit. One of Reagan's closest aides has told me that she is smarter than Reagan, and tougher. Now Reagan tells the crowd, "Nancy and I were just flying by and thought we'd drop in and see what's going on." Then he says, "I had a dream the other night. I dreamed that Jimmy Carter came to me and asked why I wanted his job. I told him I didn't want his job. [Pause] I want to be President." Reagan's timing is, as usual, perfect. The crowd yells with delight. Reagan refers to "the need for a crusade in this country today." He speaks to Detroit and, by extension, the urban workers and the unemployed to whom his campaign will attempt to appeal. He says he's glad that the crusade will begin "right in this city," and he refers to "the economic hardships brought about by the economic programs of this Administration." He mentions unemployment and lower productivity, and says, "We are determined to change this and make America great again." It is a brief little speech, and then he is gone.

In one of the upper lobbies of the Detroit Plaza, I have an interview with

Mike Curb, about the program he has planned for this Convention. Curb, who is thirty-five years old, has a baby face, large blue eyes, and dark-brown hair. He is conservatively dressed—in a way that reminds one of his political antagonist, Jerry Brown. Curb started his own record company some sixteen years ago, along with a moral-uplift singing group called The Mike Curb Congregation. Curb tells me that his big successes were with Donny and Marie Osmond and with Debby Boone's recording of "You Light Up My Life." Curb points out that Pat Boone led the Pledge of Allegiance this morning, and says that Debby Boone just had a baby or she would have been here. Curb talks earnestly and with enthusiasm.

"We've tried to consolidate the Convention program into four very solid programs," he tells me. "Tonight, you have not only President Ford but two members of his Cabinet. They'll talk about how good it was in their time, so he can talk about the future. Tuesday night, we will go all the way from Barry Goldwater to Dr. Kissinger—the whole spectrum of the Republican Party. If Governor Reagan is going to win in November, we have to have a united Party. I'm very optimistic." He speaks of the number of people who have tried to get on the program; this has been a problem. The Convention managers have tried to favor Republicans running for election or re-election this year.

At the end of the program tonight, there will be an hour of film and entertainment. As for the entertainers who will appear, Curb says, "We have tried to have entertainers of substance—not just familiar faces but people who represent something to the American people. For example, Jimmy Stewart." In tonight's film, there will be a brief clip from *Mr. Smith Goes to Washington,* and then Jimmy Stewart will be shown talking about the Republican Party. He is a Reagan supporter. Curb says, "I think Jimmy Stewart fills the role that John Wayne did in '76." (John Wayne put in some appearances for Reagan in 1976.) Curb continues, "Michael Landon is another example. He'll be in the film tonight. He has been speaking out on issues about his feelings as an American—has been speaking out for Reagan." Then he mentions Richard Petty, a seven-time national auto-racing champion. Petty will be in the film and then speak to the Convention. Curb says, "He's a household word in the Southern region. He's interested in government, interested in politics. Richard Petty will tell why he believes it's important to elect a Republican." Dorothy Hamill will also be in the film and will speak. Curb says, "She let it be known she was willing to come here. She wants to speak directly about her views and express her enthusiasm for our chances this year. I brought in Donny and Marie Osmond. They had all their hits with my company. They're very popular in Middle America. They're from Utah. They have a youth image. They believe strongly in Governor Reagan. They said they wanted to present a song called 'Go, Ronnie, Go.' " He explains that Susan Anton and Efrem Zimbalist, Jr., will be co-hosts of the event tonight. "Susan Anton has a great youth following and great enthusiasm. Efrem Zimbalist has a more traditional Republican following, and he's also very enthusiastic. They'll be excellent co-hosts, because they'll do it with conviction.'' Curb says, ''The emphasis we put on that rally for the Governor when he arrived was young people. I think it is impressive to people to see young people supporting Governor Reagan. Tonight, we'll end the program with several thousand young kids singing a song called 'Together . . . A New Beginning.' '' The theme of this Convention is ''Together . . . A New Beginning.'' Mike Curb wrote the song.

Monday night. The Joe Louis Arena, the Convention site. Usually, keynote speeches come at the beginning of Conventions. That is the point: to get the Convention going, stir up the delegates. But this year's keynote speech is not scheduled to occur until tomorrow night. Ken Rietz, who is program director for this Convention, compared tapes of the 1976 Convention proceedings with what the networks showed, to see what was likely to get on the air. It was decided that tomorrow night's program might be a bit weak, and so the keynote speech was put off until then. Anyway, tonight is to be Ford's night. Aware that the networks will cut away from the proceedings on the rostrum, the Convention planners are arranging ''counter-programming,'' through Peter Dailey: the networks will be provided with people to interview—officials of the Convention, famous political figures, delegates. All these, of course, will be expected to say nice things about Reagan and the Convention and to stress certain themes. The major theme, William Timmons told me a couple of weeks ago, is to be that Jimmy Carter is ''dumb, dangerous, and deceptive.''

Tonight, William Simon gives a strong speech castigating Carter's economic policies, and he is applauded frequently. Carter has provided this Convention with plenty of material, but Simon seems to be suggesting that things were better under Ford than they actually were. Inflation was lower then, but there was also the worst recession since the Second World War, and unemployment reached nine percent, a figure it has not reached since —as yet. The Republicans did then just what they accuse the Democrats of doing now: they fought inflation with unemployment. Inflation has been rising, with some brief respites, since the Vietnam War, and no Administration has found a steady solution to it. There were budget deficits under Gerald Ford. (In the last full fiscal year he was in office, the deficit reached sixty-six billion dollars.) Then Rumsfeld gives a speech attacking Carter's foreign and military policies. Rumsfeld even borrows some of Edward Kennedy's material, saying that the Carter Administration has been the ''surprised'' Administration: surprised in Afghanistan, surprised in Iran, and so on. But somehow Rumsfeld's speech falls flat—it seems to be a problem of the delivery, for certainly he is saying things that appeal to this Convention.

On the Convention floor, Guy Farley, a delegate from Virginia, is working to get a petition circulated that calls on Reagan to select Jack Kemp as his running mate. Farley is a lawyer from Warrenton, near Washington, a born-again Baptist, and a leader of the New Right in his state. He tells me that this is his first Convention. He served on the platform committee, where he helped write the Party's new position on the E.R.A. (including the language designed to appease E.R.A. supporters) and the plank calling for a constitutional amendment banning abortion. He also supported the provision specifying that judicial appointees "respect traditional family values and the sanctity of innocent human life." Farley is a soft-spoken man with blue eyes and curly gray hair. He used to serve in the state legislature and is expected to run for lieutenant governor of Virginia. Farley says to me, "I felt very strongly about the pro-life issues. I don't like to use the term 'born again,' because it has been abused. I consider myself a Christian. I think what we did in the platform committee will help Reagan in the fall. People don't vote against someone because he is pro-life; they vote for him."

Ford is greeted enthusiastically, and he looks well. Ford has become a sentimental figure, as some other ex-Presidents have. His Administration looks better in retrospect than it was—a development to which Carter has made a substantial contribution. Ex-Presidents are granted a certain benignity. Gerald Ford's transformation in the public eye from the somewhat limited but tough partisan congressional leader into a likable President began when, amid great relief, he took over from Richard Nixon. His very uninterestingness made him seem safe. He begins his speech on a somewhat surprising note. "Some call me an elder statesman," he says. "I don't know. I don't mind telling you all that I am not ready to quit yet. I've got news for this Convention and Jimmy Carter—this Republican is going to do everything in his power to elect our nominee to the Presidency of the United States." He says, "So when you field the team for Governor Reagan, count me in." He reminds the Convention that in 1976 Carter used economic statistics to condemn his record, and now Ford throws the current statistics at Carter. "By his own statistics, Mr. Carter has failed. There is no alternative—he's got to go."

Ford still speaks somewhat woodenly, but with more animation than usual. He has worked hard on this speech, practiced it with advisers. Moreover, it seems, according to his associates, that he really is angry at Carter —angry at him for defeating him and then doing, as Ford sees it, a worse job. Ford is described as genuinely upset by what is happening to the country—this is no routine partisan speech. And he is going over very well here. His lack of enthusiasm for Reagan is now overcome by his distaste for Carter. "You've all heard Carter's alibis: inflation cannot be controlled; the world has changed; we can no longer protect our diplomats in foreign capitals, nor our workingmen on Detroit's assembly lines; we must lower our expectations." And then he says, "Baloney." He criticizes Carter for the grain embargo and the boycott of the Olympics. Kennedy has made the same criticisms. There are only so many arguments. Ford says that we should have had the foresight and the military strength to prevent the invasion of Afghanistan. He does not say how. There is not much content in this speech—it is a pep talk about America and a condemnation of Carter, and he gives it vigorously and he excites the Convention. But nostalgia is not a policy.

The Republicans are having a fine time with the image that Carter himself has implanted as someone who is trying hard but who may not be up to the job. Carter is not a commanding figure, so when he suggests that things are complicated he can be seen as appearing helpless. His speech, given a year ago tomorrow, suggesting that he might not have been up to the job and that he would try to do better—his "malaise" speech—has been hurled back at him by speaker after speaker here, as it has been, in other contexts, by Edward Kennedy. But to insist that Carter is not up to the job is not a prescription for what to do. Carter is a tempting target, but beating him over the head is not a policy. Moreover, the questions facing this country *are* complicated. The rhetoric here, like most political rhetoric, ascribes things to "fault"—somebody else's fault. It docs not concede that there are uncontrollable forces, events that affect things. There is no history. Nothing is beyond control. There is an answer for everything. A simple answer.

Today, the news broke that Billy Carter, the President's brother, had registered as a foreign agent for the Libyan government and had received two hundred and twenty thousand dollars from it.

Tuesday morning. George Bush is addressing the California delegation in the Mackinac Ballroom of the Detroit Plaza. He is a member of one of the "caucus teams" that the Convention managers are sending around Detroit today to talk up Ronald Reagan to the various delegations. The theory was that this would give the delegations something to do, let them see some of the sturn of the Convention up close, and give the delegations' home-town papers something to write about.

Bush says, "Let me say just a few words about the Republican foreign policy and Governor Reagan's foreign policy—they're the same, incidentally, totally the same." Bush's voice is still nasal, but it seems to have a lower timbre than it did earlier this year. And he speaks with more assurance and less motion—he does not jump around, as he used to. Bush is carrying on a new campaign here. During the primaries, he had some problems with the Reagan foreign policy. Now it's all fine. He was critical of Reagan for advocating a blockade of Cuba in response to the Soviet invasion of Afghanistan, and for suggesting that the United States should issue a deadline and ultimatum for the hostages' return. He said that Reagan's foreign-policy statements contained "inaccuracies and inconsistencies." He opposed Reagan's endorsement of the Kemp-Roth proposal to cut taxes by thirty percent over three years as inflationary, calling the proposal a false "blueprint for paradise" and "voodoo economics." He criticized him for making "phony promises" and "flamboyant statements" and offering "simplistic answers." Yesterday, Bush told some of the delegates he met with that the positions Reagan had articulated were "excellent," "strong," and "exciting." He tells this group, "There is no may-laise in the United States . . . no unwillingness to be strong abroad. I believe that the perception of the United States has to be changed almost instantly." He says, "I want to go back to something President Ford was criticized for in some quarters—Mayaguez. But something happened; something changed. People felt the United States would do something."

Bush is developing as the most generally acceptable Vice Presidential choice at this Convention: he has strong ties to the Party's moderate wing, to its all-rightniks, and he does not give offense to the Southerners the way Baker does. He is also favored by some members of the Reagan staff as the best choice politically. But it is apparently the case, according to a number of people around Reagan, that Reagan and his wife are not much impressed with Bush. It is apparently true that Reagan draws large conclusions from the debate in Nashua, New Hampshire—which is becoming one of the seminal events of the 1980 campaign—at which Bush froze when the other Republican candidates, with Reagan's encouragement, tried to participate in the scheduled Reagan-Bush debate. The Reagans concluded, according to someone who was with them at the time, that the incident showed that Bush is not "gutsy." The Reagan camp also feels, I'm told, that while Bush came close to defeating Reagan in Texas, with better judgment and more guts he could have won. (This is an odd thing to hold against him; clearly the Reagans are just as glad that he did not beat them.) They feel, it's said, that Bush's success in the later part of his campaign was due to his good organization, not to Bush. Candidates—and their wives—have a way of ending up resenting those who opposed them in the primaries, as if to have done so were not quite cricket. When people ask Bush's associates how they might be helpful in getting Bush the Vice Presidential slot, it is suggested that they talk up Bush's candidacy to the Reagan people and to Reagan himself. I remarked to an associate of Bush's today that it was interesting that Bush seems to be able to bridge all the factions of the Party. He smiled and replied, referring to the fact that Bush had been criticized in the early part of his campaign for not taking clear positions on the issues: "Early on, it hurt a little."

At ten forty-five, Henry Kissinger is holding a press conference at Cobo Hall, a large exhibition hall next to the Joe Louis Arena. He has just met with Reagan, and arrived here with his usual flying squad of security agents. Kissinger is in an odd position at this Convention. Four years ago, he was the object of an attack by Reagan and his followers: for pursuing détente and a SALT agreement, for Ford's refusal to meet with Aleksandr Solzhenitsyn. He was, in fact, made into the symbol of the differences over foreign policy between Ford and Reagan. Tonight, Kissinger will address the Convention. Ford has urged him on Reagan as an adviser; in order to please the right, the Reagan people did not include him in their list of foreign- and defense-policy advisers, but in order to please the moderates they are allowing him to speak tonight—in some quarters his approval of Reagan would be considered a big plus. The idea of having Kissinger on the program is attributed to, depending on whom one asks, (1) the Republican National Committee, (2) the Reagan people, (3) Timmons. But once the idea surfaced, it would have been difficult to head off. One of Reagan's aides said to me over the weekend, "I wish he would just go away." Kissinger has gone from Republican candidate to Republican candidate this year offering his services. One Reagan aide has told me that Kissinger has made a point of staying in touch with Reagan over the last four years. Kissinger may have served Nixon and Ford, but he carries the aura of his patrons, the Rockefellers, and of the Trilateral Commission—a private organization of businessmen, lawyers, academics, politicians, and others seeking cooperation between Europe, Japan, and North America—which the right wing is convinced is part of a conspiracy. (Bush was a member, too. Earlier this year, Reagan, in answer to a question about the commission, described it as "a group of multilateral corporations and international bankers . . . not directed towards the general problems of the people of this country.") Richard Allen, Reagan's principal foreign-policy adviser, worked for Kissinger for a while in the Nixon Administration, but the two men soon had a falling out and Allen left. Allen is still not very fond of his former boss. But Kissinger has also had ties to the conservatives. He has been a friend of William Buckley's for some time. Of late, Kissinger has been sounding more and more hard-line, cultivating the right, working himself back into its graces. Some conservatives who had nothing good to say about Henry Kissinger's policies a few years ago now quote him approvingly.

Reagan, like candidates before him, has gathered unto his campaign the "experts." Like Carter four years ago, he has had a particular need to do this; he must build in protection against charges that he is unschooled in the issues. The people who can do him the most damage are the "experts" in his own party. Every Administration produces a new crop of "experts"— people who may never have been heard of before but who gain credentials by virtue of having served in an Administration. From then on, they become talk-show guests and sources for journalists, and are drawn upon as advisers. If a candidate doesn't wish to be discredited by the experts—to have them suggest that he doesn't know what he's talking about—he tries to co-opt them. Like as not, the experts are willing to oblige, seeing another opportunity to serve in the government or to have access to power. The candidate, wishing to appear knowledgeable, drops the experts' names, and has them serve on advisory committees. Thus, when Jimmy Carter talked about arms control during his quest for the nomination he dropped the names of Paul Warnke and Paul Nitze, even though the two men were in bitter disagreement over the issue.

Reagan's lists of experts include ninety-one in all for foreign and defense policy and a hundred and six for economic and domestic policy. The great majority of the foreign- and defense-policy advisers come from the right of the Republican spectrum. Some of Reagan's foreign-policy advisers were opposed to the SALT agreement that was being negotiated by Ford, and played a role in causing it to founder. The domestic advisers are, as has been noted, divided over Reagan's tax proposals. An attempt is now being made to work out a defensible explanation of how Reagan can cut taxes by thirty percent over three years, increase military spending substantially, and balance the budget—all of which he has pledged to do. Reagan's own staff has been concerned that Reagan have a program that will hold up under scrutiny and has called in Ford's economic advisers, under Alan Greenspan, who was chairman of the Council of Economic Advisers. The group is to meet with Reagan at lunch today.

Some of Reagan's more traditional economic advisers find the theory that underlies the Kemp-Roth proposal—the economist Arthur Laffer's theory that lowered taxes will pay for themselves through the stimulus to the economy—a bit exotic and questionable. Reagan, coached by Kemp, a Laffer enthusiast, had said in the campaign that he was simply talking about the sort of thing John Kennedy proposed in 1963. The more traditional advisers are inclined to believe that although that approach may have worked then, the economic system was not inflation-ridden then and such an approach now would exacerbate inflation. So they are working on a set of numbers which they hope will be unassailable, suggesting that with some tactical adjustments Reagan can offer Kemp-Roth (the platform committee has gone ahead and endorsed it), a version of the accelerated depreciation allowance sought by business, and a somewhat smaller increase in the defense budget than envisioned in the platform. The idea is that he could pay for it all by not expanding existing programs or enacting new ones: federal outlays would grow more slowly than federal income, which would increase with growth in the economy and with the increased taxes people would continue to pay because inflation would continue to push them into higher income brackets.

Now Kissinger, at his press conference, is asked what he thinks about the platform. It not only calls for "military superiority" but rejects the recent SALT agreement and calls for the construction and deployment of all manner of new weapons; its language about the Soviet Union is reminiscent of the Cold War era; and it deplores "the current drifts toward neutralism in Western Europe." Kissinger was the architect of the SALT I agreement, but has taken an ambivalent position on SALT II.

Kissinger replies, "While I have read the Republican platform, I have not learned it by heart." He cracks, "Of course, I am working at it with great dedication." He says, "I believe it is the aim of the Soviet Union to establish a predominant political position in the world."

He is asked if he discussed with Reagan any position in a Reagan Administration when they met this morning.

Kissinger answers in a manner suggesting that such a discussion would be beneath him: "I made it clear before the appointment that I didn't think this was the appropriate time to discuss a position. I'm not here as a job seeker.'' He says that he supports Reagan.

He is asked, ''Would you exclude any position if an interesting position was available?''

''That would depend on the circumstances that exist,'' Kissinger replies.

He is asked if he believes that Reagan has the proper experience and background in foreign policy to be President.

He replies, slowly, ''In many ways, no one can have the experience before he is in office.'' He says that, ''based on my relatively brief conversations,'' Reagan does have the qualifications.

He is asked if he found any issue on which there was less than substantial agreement between him and Reagan.

Kissinger replies, ''We discussed primarily those issues that had given me some concern. I felt that the Governor's position, as it was explained to me, was one that I find compatible with my own. We discussed the 'superiority' in the platform. It was my understanding that we will not play a numbers game in every category of weapons but that we will maintain a military establishment that will deprive any possible opponent of the opportunity for military aggression.''

He is asked if he supports Reagan's call for a blockade of Cuba.

He replies, ''It is difficult for anybody to deal with the complexities of a hypothetical situation.''

Kissinger is subdued, treading carefully.

He is asked his views on East-West relations.

Kissinger replies, ''I have stated my position on the subject, which is based on strong defense, determined resistance to expansionism, reciprocity to reduce the dangers of war. Those are my positions, and it's my understanding that they are compatible with Governor Reagan's.''

This afternoon, Reagan attended a meeting with unemployed auto workers—as part of his effort to use the locale of this Convention to broaden his constituency—and had meetings with elected officials about the Vice Presidential nominee. ''I assure you, it's not decided,'' one of Reagan's closest aides said to me today at Reagan's headquarters, on the sixty-ninth floor of the Detroit Plaza. (At that point, Reagan was meeting with Ford, and, of course, it was later revealed that in the course of the meeting Reagan asked Ford to consider running with him.) The aide said to me that Ford had definitely not been ruled out, and also that there had been a ''clear drift'' to all the discussions that Reagan had with the elected officials, many of them conservatives. ''They want to win,'' this man said to me this afternoon.

(The ''clear drift'' of the meetings, I was told later, was that Bush was the best bet, with this caveat: ''Of course, if you could get Ford, *that* would be the ticket.'' Ford's speech of Monday night ''was a hint to some that he might join the ticket,'' a Reagan aide recalled. ''Some of us were just turning and looking at each other.'' William Casey had had a memorandum prepared on the implications of the Twelfth Amendment to the Constitution, which prohibits electors in the Electoral College from voting for both a President and a Vice President from their own states. This could have presented a problem for the electors from California, where both Reagan and Ford reside. There were ways to get around this: Ford could have claimed residence in some other state, for instance, but he had said that this would be a "cheap political gimmick." Once it seemed conceivable that Ford might join the ticket, Casey became a strong backer of the idea of naming Ford. According to Casey, some of Ford's friends had been indicating for months that Ford could be persuaded to join the ticket, so the idea had been on the table for a long time. Its most active proponent was apparently Bryce Harlow, who has alternated between serving in Republican White Houses and lobbying in Washington for Procter & Gamble. The idea went off the table for a brief spell after Reagan paid a call on Ford at Rancho Mirage, near Palm Springs, in June and Ford said, publicly as well as privately, that he was not available. But then the idea got back on the table shortly before the Convention, some of Ford's friends having told the Reagan people that they still thought that Ford might be persuaded to join the ticket. So, coming into the Convention, the Reagan people wanted to make another try for Ford, and remained undecided about what to do if that didn't work. Besides those on the public lists, a couple of other names were under consideration —such as Albert Quie, the governor of Minnesota and a former member of Congress, and George Shultz, a former head of the Office of Management and Budget and a former Secretary of the Treasury, who was suggested by Casey. Over the weekend, Reagan's businessmen friends Dart and Tuttle, and also Reagan's lawyer, William French Smith, were promoting the Ford idea. Some Reagan aides were concerned that too much time and energy were being devoted to something that would not work out.)

In and around all the to-do about the Vice Presidency, sporadic attention has been given to the fall campaign. Richard Wirthlin, Reagan's pollster, has prepared a strategy, which, not very surprisingly, is now described as a "national campaign." Campaigns rarely advertise that they will write off certain states; among other things, the opposition must be made to worry about and spend resources in as many states as possible. The Reagan campaign, according to what is being said here, will concentrate heavily on the Eastern and Midwestern industrial states. There will also be major forays into the South, and although the West is presumed to be Reagan's, it will not be ignored. The thought is that some Western trips might be got out of the way before Labor Day.

One of the Reagan aides I talked to today said that there would be an attempt to make Reagan's appearances in the fall campaign "more structured and controllable" than they were in the primaries, with concentration on radio and television appearances. "You're not going to remake Ronald Reagan," he said. "You have to get a combination of new material and things he's comfortable with." Inevitably, the Reagan camp talks of making Carter the issue, just as the Carter camp talks of making Reagan the issue. It is clear from conversations with the Reagan people that they know Reagan can talk himself into embarrassing situations that he must then talk himself out of. But Reagan does a good job of getting himself out of tight spots (at least, he has thus far)—in part because he is clever, and in part because of his personality. The genialness, the smoothness make the difficulties seem to slide right off him. Reagan's aides stress the importance of his not responding to the Carter campaign's attacks; they do not want him on the defensive.

A lot of people have speculated that this election may be decided by Reagan's making some major boner—just as they thought the primary contest would be—or that the Carter campaign may succeed in painting him as reckless. The Carter campaign will certainly try, and it is gathering the material right now on Reagan's past pronouncements, but one problem it will have is that Reagan just doesn't *look* reckless. The big question, a number of people agree, is whether through a series of impressions the public will be getting—indeed, has already begun to get—Reagan will come off as a plausible President. Public opinion can be shaped by a major event or two, but it can also be formed by cumulative impressions. This is what happened to Lyndon Johnson, it is what happened to Richard Nixon, and it is what has been happening to Jimmy Carter. Reagan is very familiar, and very famous, but an impression of him as President does not yet seem to have formed.

One of Reagan's closest aides said to me this afternoon, "You have to be very careful with the facts that you give him, because he absorbs things so quickly that if you give him something wrong it's hard to get it out. He's like a computer on facts and figures." According to people who know him well, Reagan is apparently not so good at remembering names. A number of people who have worked with him describe him as bright and quick, but they do not describe him as thoughtful and contemplative. Some come right out and use the word "shallow." What comes across is that Reagan is shrewd but uncomplicated. I am told that he talks about issues in private conversation just as he does when he is onstage or in interviews (in which he talks as he does when he is onstage). Otherwise, when he relaxes, he often talks about the movies. In men's company, he engages in what would politely be termed locker-room humor.

The Reagan campaign has already made certain moves in anticipation of moves on the part of the Carter campaign—proposing a one-year tax cut now, predicting an "October surprise." There is some question whether it was intended that Reagan go as far as he did the other day, when he said in a "60 Minutes" interview, "I think very definitely the Soviet Union is going to throw a few bones to Mr. Carter during this coming campaign in order to help him continue as President." One of the people closest to Reagan said to me this afternoon, "That isn't something we all sat around and talked about." Reagan's genial demeanor may mask the fact that he is, once in combat, a very tough competitor. One man who has worked with him closely says, "He's as fierce a competitor as anyone around." The records of 1976 and 1980 would indicate that this is so.

At the conclusion of one of the conversations on the sixty-ninth floor this afternoon, I asked a man who has been with Reagan a long time how he felt now that Reagan was about to win a nomination he had begun seeking in 1968. He looked out the window at the Detroit River and said, "You know, when you're in it, it seems unreal. We always believed that because we're Westerners we weren't going to get it."

Tonight, Goldwater is on the rostrum. Goldwater started it all in several ways. Reagan's political career began when he made a televised speech for Goldwater in 1964. Now Goldwater, aged and ill, is treated like a beloved grandfather, even though some of the far right thinks he sold out when he endorsed Ford four years ago. "We believe the citizen is sovereign," Goldwater says. "There must be a change from weakness," he says. But the fire has gone out.

On the last night of the 1976 Republican Convention, I had a talk with Weston Adams, a lawyer from Columbia, South Carolina, who was a Reagan delegate. "We're not going to lose next time," he said to me then, and he told me that the conservatives were going to form a network, get going, and take over the Party. When I find Adams on the Convention floor tonight, he says, "My prediction came true." He goes on, "Last time, we had the nomination taken away from us. Ronald Reagan was the sentimental favorite of that Convention; he had it taken away from him by the Presidency. My prediction was that we would get organized and would not be denied the nomination. Ronald Reagan's riding the popular sentiment for conservative values. Now we've come in line with the American mainstream."

He replies, "I worry that he might be branded by his enemies as too far right, like Goldwater. Goldwater was not as careful as Reagan. He set his traps for himself, for his enemies to use to destroy him. They're two very different men. Goldwater was a kind of Patrick Henry of the conservative revolution. But revolutions consume the instigators. Samuel Adams and Patrick Henry never became President. Another thing that worries me—if we don't pick someone perceived as moderate to run with Reagan, John Anderson might draw votes away from Reagan. That's why we have to pick someone like Bush."

I ask him what his people did in order to fulfill the prophecy he made four years ago.

"We started right after the 1976 election; we were in contact with Reagan people throughout the country. He had his operatives out, and we were in contact with those people. In fact, you could say that we never stopped the Reagan campaign. We were making suggestions among the groups in the various states; we were recruiting people, organizing. What the opponents never realized was the network of Reagan people who had been together for a long time and kept in contact. What it amounts to is Reagan had his own party.''

John Connally makes his speech to the Convention. His Presidential campaign was a spectacular bust, but, for Connally, talking confidently—jaw jutting, voice booming—is as natural as walking down the street. He, too, borrows liberally and happily from Kennedy's rhetoric.

The program begins to run very late. Too many speakers have been scheduled, and too many of them are talking too long. Many of them are saying the same things.

Jack Kemp's people stage a demonstration when he is introduced to speak. Whatever happens to Kemp at this Convention, it is clear that he and his forces are preparing for the future. All week, his backers have been pushing hard: receptions, Reagan/Kemp buttons and boaters, press releases. John Rhodes, the Minority Leader of the House and the chairman of the Convention, tries to gavel the demonstration to an end. ''We are rapidly running out of prime time,'' he says. Kissinger, waiting to give his speech, must be going crazy. And Vander Jagt is scheduled to speak after Kissinger. Kemp is boyish and enthusiastic, which can give the impression that he lacks depth. A number of people say Kemp is smarter than he's often given credit for. Kemp does say some simple things in his speech, but he is at least also grappling with ideas.

Finally, Kissinger gets to speak. He gives a somber, strong condemnation of Carter's foreign policy. It is as much a political speech as a foreign-policy analysis. Even Kissinger, the historian, a man who understands complexity, seems to be suggesting, as other speakers here have done, that just about everything that has gone wrong in the world is Carter's fault. If the people at this Convention really believe that everything that happens in the world is within a President's control, and if Reagan is elected, they are in for a shock.

On the rostrum, Kissinger concludes, ''The time has come to close ranks. We all now turn to Ronald Reagan as the trustee of our hopes. . . . Under his leadership, we will overcome the storms ahead; we will hold our heads high and we will build that better world at peace that fulfills the dreams of mankind and the high ideals of our people.''

The keynote speech has been put off until tomorrow. There has been near-pandemonium under the rostrum. While Kissinger and Vander Jagt waited their turns, some thought was given by the Convention managers to letting Vander Jagt precede Kemp and Kissinger, but then Kissinger threatened not to give his speech at all. So Vander Jagt placed a call to William Casey, in Reagan's suite, and, through him, got word from Reagan that the Vice Presidential choice was still open, and that Reagan would watch Vander Jagt's speech even if it was given after midnight tonight, or put off until tomorrow night, and Vander Jagt decided that he would prefer to give the speech at a better hour tomorrow.

Wednesday. At nine-thirty this morning, Lyn Nofziger, who is in charge of press relations for Reagan, is holding a briefing in the Detroit Plaza. Reagan is supposed to make his Vice Presidential decision by tonight. I have already been told that the matter is in a state of great uncertainty. The whole thing seems quite disorganized. The list of possibilities has narrowed: Kemp is too conservative if the point is to broaden the base, and, besides, he is considered to be campaigning too hard; Lugar didn't help himself with his speech on Monday, which was dull; Rumsfeld, like some others on the list, apparently never was a serious possibility; Reagan likes Laxalt personally, but Laxalt is another conservative from the West; Bush is still in the picture, and so is Vander Jagt, of whom the Reagan people don't seem to have much of an impression one way or the other. But some in the Reagan camp are still not satisfied with the list of choices, and are wondering if there is anyone they haven't thought of. But the talk now is about Ford.

Nofziger is a wry, rumpled man with sprouts of dark hair coming out of a bald head, and a constant five-o'clock shadow. He is more of an ideological conservative than some of the other people around Reagan—though he has been telling people that he thinks Bush would be Reagan's best choice. The press likes Nofziger, because he understands its needs and tries to help. Now Nofziger announces that Reagan will have lunch with caucus-team members in Hamtramck. Hamtramck is, of course, a Polish community. Reagan is touching a lot of bases. Yesterday, he not only met with unemployed auto workers but also attended a reception sponsored by the Convention's black caucus.

Nofziger is asked why Reagan is going to lunch in Hamtramck.

"He thought it would be good to get out of the hotel," he replies.

Nofziger is asked if any meetings are planned today between Reagan and Ford.

"Not at this time."

"Has there been any progress in narrowing down the list?"

"Not at this time."

Throughout the day, Reagan aides are cancelling appointments and saying things like "The Vice Presidential thing is at a critical point." One man who is in on the discussions says, in a hotel hallway, "The Vice Presidential thing is still boiling."

How does Reagan make decisions? Much has been written about his tendency, as Governor of California, to delegate, and to have a collegial sort of government with his Cabinet. The problem is that in Washington the Cabinet officers soon tend to represent the constituencies of their departments, and strong direction is needed from the White House. Former governors who have seen government in a state capital and in Washington say it's not at all the same thing. Not only do states have no foreign or military policy but state Cabinet officers, they say, are more amenable; interest groups are not as strong at the state level; and often the state legislatures do not develop as much power as the Congress. In today's Washington *Post,* John Sears, who was Reagan's campaign manager in 1976 and directed the 1980 campaign until he was fired the day of the New Hampshire primary (Sears went too far trying to consolidate his power and alienated too many of the old Reagan hands), writes about Reagan's decision-making. Sears may not be without some bitterness, but still his piece is interesting and has the ring of truth. Sears describes the life of an actor: "Your place of business is a set designed to look real. You get into a costume, people bring your coffee, you're made up. A crew in charge of cameras, lighting, scripts, and other details moves about. You don't question what they're doing. Someone explains today's scene. You perform. Then you do the same thing over and over again until the director is satisfied." Then he writes that Reagan's decisions rarely originate with Reagan. "He is an endorser. It is fair to say that on some occasions he is presented with options and selects one, but it is also true that in other instances he simply looks to someone to tell him what to do. . . . There are indeed limits to the advice that Reagan will accept. . . . If his advisers are adequate, there is nothing to fear from President Reagan. But he can be guided, and Presidents who are too easily guided run the risk of losing the confidence of the people."

Tonight, the Ford talk is caroming around the Convention hall. All day, there have been rumors of meetings. And now all the talk in the hall is about the interview Ford has just given Walter Cronkite, in which he said, "If I go to Washington—and I'm not saying that I am accepting—I have to go there with the belief that I will play a meaningful role across the board." When Cronkite observed that if Ford joined the ticket, "It's got to be something like a co-Presidency," Ford did not correct him, and went on to say, "That's something Governor Reagan really ought to consider. . . . We have a lot of friends in Washington. . . . And for him to not understand the realities of some of the things that might happen in Washington is being oblivious to reality."

So Ford is really considering joining the ticket. It must be remembered that Ford was itching to become President again, but he must understand the gossamer nature of "understandings" between Presidential and Vice Presidential candidates on any "new, enhanced role" for the Vice President. Still, Ford has always been dutiful about coming to the aid of his party. When Party leaders go to him, as they apparently did today, and tell him that he can save the republic, their entreaties are difficult to resist. Ford, of course, became President only as a result of a bizarre set of circumstances. He served as President for a little under two and a half years and lost his bid for election.

Ford obviously takes his role as former President very seriously. The apotheosis suits him fine. Ford might be better off left as a sentimental, nostalgic figure. As an actual candidate, he would be reduced in size, and might again, literally and figuratively, start bumping his head on helicopters.

Ford might do Reagan more good by campaigning for him as a former President.

But the politicians, and some people for whom Ford's acceptance might mean a return to power, may well have other priorities. For the Party leaders, what they see as the "dream ticket" of Reagan and Ford might help them gain not only the Presidency but also more seats in Congress. And for some of those Republicans looking toward succeeding Reagan as the Party's nominee—politicians make this sort of calculation—Ford would be preferable to a potential rival. Will this Convention consider it such a dream ticket when it learns that, in the bargain, it might get Kissinger, who, along with Greenspan, is negotiating with Reagan's people on Ford's behalf? How could Reagan and Ford campaign as a "team"? Ford has already criticized the platform for abandoning the E.R.A., and he has other differences with Reagan. Could Ford really play the role of the subservient candidate? There are reports emanating from the negotiations that the Ford people are suggesting that, among other things, Ford might be given responsibility for the management of national security and economic policy. What is going on here? Are they making a distinction between delegating power and sharing power? Are they rewriting the Constitution? There are real questions to be addressed about the management of the Presidency, but this is not the time, or the circumstance, for that. The whole episode has a disconcerting ad-hoc feel to it—the feel of other occasions when politicians, in a panic to deal with some immediate problem, start improvising. Worst of all from Reagan's standpoint, he is sending out a signal that suggests something that could be very damaging to him: that he doesn't comprehend the nature of the Presidency. It's understandable, from his point of view, and as a result of the urging of the Republican politicians, that he should make a last-minute attempt to get Ford on the ticket. But even if he succeeds, the ticket will have been damaged by the way it was put together.

Shortly before eight-thirty, Vander Jagt finally gets around to giving his keynote address. It may be too late for him to impress Reagan now. He says, "Whether it is Monday or Tuesday or Wednesday, I think I have to be the luckiest guy in America to be able to have this opportunity to try to give expression to your hopes and dreams for America." His old-fashioned oratorical style seems self-conscious. As he continues, he gets a good reaction from the audience, but he isn't saying very much. He is making noise.

When it comes time for Bush to give his speech, there is a large demonstration for him. The demonstration was, of course, designed to impress Reagan. The Bush people once thought that he had been given the ideal time to speak: Wednesday night, when interest would be building, just before the balloting for the Presidency. Now they must wonder. Bush must be sick. The man he had counted on to press his case with Reagan is now reported to be negotiating for his own spot on the ticket. Bush still manages to smile his engaging, crooked smile, and give his speech. He speaks more slowly and forcefully than usual. It is a gallant performance under the circumstances, but he doesn't seem to have anything to say. Like the other hopefuls, he plays to the distant emperor. He praises Reagan and condemns Carter, and says that under the leadership of Ronald Reagan "the strength of the American dollar will be restored . . . the crushing burden of federal bureaucracy and the excesses of regulation will be lifted from the back of America's free economy. . . . Americans overseas will once again be able to count on their government to protect their safety . . . a policy of peace-through-strength will assure that no power on earth, be it great or small, will miscalculate the resolve of the American people and its leaders." He says that we "must strengthen the intelligence services of this country" and that "we must stop apologizing for the United States of America around the world."

By shortly after ten, CBS has announced that Ford will be Reagan's selection as running mate, and that the two men will appear in the hall later tonight and Reagan will announce that Ford will run with him. All night, in the hall, delegates, elected officials, and reporters have been going up to each other and asking if "it's really happening," and the commonly accepted answer has been that, amazingly enough, it is. No one is sure where the information is coming from; it is just one of those pieces of information that get passed along as fact.

When Senator Laxalt concludes his speech placing Reagan's name in nomination, the demonstration—long planned—is tumultuous. Besides, these people have reason to celebrate. They have waited sixteen years for this. And Reagan is not just a candidate; he's a cause. He is not just another political figure to them; he's a beau ideal. He has their hearts. The roll is called, and Montana puts it over for Reagan, and the place goes crazy.

At the Mississippi delegation, Trent Lott says, when I ask him what he would think if it turned out to be true that Ford was on the ticket, "I'd be in a state of shock. Then I'd be very enthusiastic. Then I'd have to sit down and think about the political realities of it. Reagan is sixty-nine and Ford is sixty-seven; that might not go over so well. I still can't imagine Ford taking it, unless he thinks there isn't a viable alternative. Some in the Mississippi delegation are saying that if Reagan is going to do that type of thing, why doesn't he go with Bush—that he would offer the same attributes."

By eleven-thirty, there begins to creep into the hall some question as to whether "it's really happening."

A man in the Ohio delegation says to me, "It's a damn indecisive guy who the night before is still working it out. You get to that point and you're still negotiating—I just can't believe it. It's all the same: Kissinger, Vance —what's the difference?"

A rumor starts up that Ford will take the Vice Presidential nomination and after the election will resign in favor of Kemp.

At eleven thirty-four, Rhodes announces the results of the balloting: Anderson, thirty-seven (boos); Anne Armstrong, one; Bush, thirteen; abstentions, four; Reagan, one thousand nine hundred and thirty-nine. The jubilation starts all over again: people jump on their chairs, blow horns, dance, shout. Trent Lott now tells me that Reagan's Convention managers have asked the floor whips to prolong the demonstration, so Lott, a subdued, tailored man, gets up on his chair, cheers, and waves his Reagan banner in the air. The floor is all banners, Confederate flags, cheers, rebel yells, and the sound of the band, with the drum playing an insistent, urgent, almost tribal beat.

I go to the Florida delegation to ask L. E. (Tommy) Thomas, who ran the Reagan campaign in his state this year—as he did in 1976—and is the chairman of the delegation, how he feels.

"Sick," Thomas replies. "I don't like the Ford thing. I think it's a bad team. Reagan doesn't need him. Ford doesn't like him. The first thing in a Vice President should be loyalty. And we damn sure don't need co-Presidents."

I ask Margaret Heckler, a congresswoman from Massachusetts and a leader in the fight for E.R.A. and against the constitutional amendment prohibiting abortion, how she feels about the possible Reagan-Ford ticket.

"I love it," she replies excitedly.

Word starts sweeping the floor that there may be some hitch in the Reagan-Ford arrangements.

The band plays "It's a Grand Old Flag."

A delegate from North Carolina says to me, "Isn't this a shocker? Reagan said the man had to be philosophically compatible. What are they going to do about the E.R.A., SALT, the Panama Canal thing?"

The band plays "Anchors Aweigh."

Now, apparently, Reagan is coming to the Convention hall. There is some question whether Ford is.

The band plays the Marine Hymn.

The Convention managers are having no trouble prolonging the demonstration. But no one here knows what for. Some key Reagan people have been going on and off the Convention floor, looking worried. Some delegates are doing a snake dance. A network reporter tells me that Reagan and Ford are both coming to the hall.

Suddenly, someone rushes by and shouts, *"It's Bush!"* The Reagan lieutenants are fanning out over the floor saying, "It's Bush." No one seems to know what else to say, except to pass the word along. Some people don't believe it. At this point, they aren't inclined to believe anything. A Reagan lieutenant says to me, over the din, "About an hour ago, it became not Ford. It's been very complicated—the most incredible political story."

Finally, at twelve-ten, the band, conducted by Manny Harmon, who also played at the 1976 Convention, plays "God Bless America," the signal that the demonstration is to stop.

I ask Guy Farley what he thinks.

He replies, "Well, I'm speechless."

It is hard to remember a night like this in politics. Reagan has ended up where he probably should have, but by a remarkable route. He, Ford, and Bush have been tarnished in the process. The whole thing suggests a picture of Reagan passively, without much thought, dealing out his Presidency; of Ford being tempted by a combination of duty and pride, and being egged on by people who were not necessarily thinking of his interests; of Bush having been embarrassed. It is a picture of some chaos. If they wanted Ford, why didn't they think of these things ahead of time?

The Reagans appear on the rostrum, Nancy Reagan dressed in red. Reagan gives his assured, modest wave and smiles his open-mouthed smile. Then he speaks to the Convention. "I know that I am breaking with precedent," he says. "But in watching at the hotel the television and seeing the rumors that were going around and the gossip that was taking place here, I felt that it was necessary to break the tradition." He talks as if the "rumors" were self-generated—as if his actions had had nothing to do with them. "It is true that a number of Republican leaders, people in our party, officeholders, felt, as I am sure many others have felt, that a proper ticket would have included the former President of the United States, Gerald Ford," Reagan says. He sounds hoarse and tired. He says, "We have gone over this and over this and over this, and he and I have come to the conclusion, and he believes deeply, that he can be of more value as the former President campaigning his heart out, which he has pledged to do, and not as a member of the ticket." He then says that he will recommend that the Convention nominate as his running mate "a man who told me that he can enthusiastically support the platform across the board," George Bush.

Thursday. Robert Strauss, chairman of the Carter-Mondale re-election committee, is on the CBS morning news, smiling. He says, "You know, I've messed up a lot of things. They messed one up last night."

At 8 A.M., a weary Nofziger briefs weary reporters. It is to be a day of briefings and backgrounders and television appearances of various participants in the events of the last two days—all putting out their versions of the story. There were many participants, and there will be many versions of the truth. In a way, it doesn't matter; what matters is that these people got themselves into such a situation at all.

(As the stories emerged later, some suggested that Ford had "overreached" in his demands—or that Ford's representatives had overreached —and that Reagan had to call the whole thing off. But there is no evidence that at any point—and this is also based on conversations I have had with Reagan aides since the Convention—Reagan called it off because he felt Ford's price was too high. It is true that the Reagans were a bit stunned to see Ford discussing the matter on television with Cronkite and not disputing the idea of a "co-Presidency." Some of the early stories—coming out of the Reagan camp—suggested that Reagan's putting a deadline on the matter, sending word to Ford that he needed a decision that night, was his way of bringing the matter to a close, because he thought the demands had got out of hand. But that does not appear to have been the case, either. In one of the briefings, Ed Meese, Reagan's chief of staff, told reporters, "We were still discussing it, to tell you the truth, when the President made his decision." Meese also said, "The Governor was waiting for his response, and if it had been affirmative they would have discussed it again and gone to the arena." Another Reagan aide has said to me, "Had the same set of circumstances existed a night earlier, we'd have kept talking. But we couldn't talk any longer." Reagan did want to bring it to an end Wednesday night, but the overriding reason for doing so seems to have been that, especially with the possibility of a Reagan-Ford ticket such a public matter, he did not want to take the chance of beginning the next day with a Ford rejection. The embarrassment—humiliation, even—would have been too great; moreover, there would have been little time to get on with arranging for his next choice. A press conference to announce his running mate had long been set for 11 A.M. Thursday. It is also true, I am told, that Reagan did plan to go to the arena with Ford. According to one man who was in the Reagan room Wednesday night, at about eleven Reagan, still planning to go to the hall with Ford, looked at his watch and said, "Come on, Jerry, call up. We've got to get over to the hall."

In the various versions that emerged, it became clear that in the discussions between Ford's representatives, among them Kissinger and Greenspan, and Reagan's representatives, Casey, Meese, and Wirthlin, various ideas were explored: that Ford would, as one of Reagan's associates later put it, serve as "a kind of superdirector of the Executive Office of the President"—which includes the National Security Council, the Office of Management and Budget, and the Council of Economic Advisers; that Ford might serve as Secretary of Defense as well as Vice President; that Ford might have a veto power over certain appointments; that the White House staff would report to the President through Ford. The Reagan people drew up a list of possible arrangements—typing and retyping it themselves, because they did not feel they could entrust such a thing to secretaries—and they later described this as just a list of "talking points." Eager to play the whole thing down, they began to describe these negotiations in terms suggesting that it was just a bunch of guys "batting back and forth" some ideas, a "brainstorming session" to figure out a way to make the Presidency work better—which in itself would be a rather odd thing to have been doing at that particular moment. Of course, while the Reagan people wanted to get their side of the story out, they also wanted to say nothing that might annoy Ford; and the Ford people wanted everyone to understand that Ford and his representatives weren't reaching for power—just a "meaningful role" for the Vice President. Ford himself ruminated aloud at a lunch on Wednesday with editors of *Newsweek* that the arrangement might follow "a format where you have a head of state and a head of government." He gave as examples Britain and France. The trouble is, this isn't Britain or France.

It is not necessarily the case that the Constitution was being redrafted; if the President maintained ultimate authority and responsibility, various types of arrangements could be made. A number of people, including Kissinger, said later that the whole thing could have been worked out if time hadn't run out, which raises the question of whether they ever understood what it really was that they were doing, or that that was no time to be doing it. Moreover, the discussions were not about simply the placement of boxes on the organization chart; they were about an exquisitely delicate set of arrangements between two men who not only had never worked together but actually didn't much like each other. And both would come with entourages that were not brimming over with mutual esteem.

Some of the Reagan people, including Allen, were nearly apoplectic when they got wind of the role Kissinger was playing, and made efforts to insure that he would not, as a result of these dealings, end up with power in a Reagan Administration. It developed that in the one conversation Reagan and Ford had with each other about this whole business Ford suggested that Kissinger be brought back as Secretary of State and Greenspan be made Secretary of the Treasury. In one of the briefings Thursday, a Reagan aide described this as a discussion of "the kind of people" Ford might like to see in a Reagan-Ford Administration, and later both Kissinger and Greenspan were at pains to deny that they had sought these posts. Kissinger went to great lengths to tell the press in subsequent days that he had been recruited as a go-between by the Reagan people. The Reagan people say that this is not quite the case: that they simply called Kissinger in after Reagan first broached the idea of the Vice Presidency to Ford in Detroit, as one of the people who would talk to Ford about the idea. It is also clear that both Kissinger and Greenspan were urging Ford to join the ticket. And so, after Ford, at about eleven-thirty, told Reagan that he didn't think it would work, Reagan told his staff that he wanted to call Bush. In his conversation with Bush, he suggested that Bush be willing to say that he supports the platform across the board. While Reagan is given much credit for his instincts in deciding to go to the hall to quell the rumors, in reality he had always planned to go. One of his closest aides says, "He had always felt that going to the hall Wednesday night, once he made the decision, would be an interesting thing to do.")

At this morning's briefing, Nofziger says, "We have a fine ticket. George Bush is the only person he asked."

He is asked by Tom Ottenad, of the St. Louis *Post-Dispatch*, what he would say about the "obvious criticism" that the whole affair did not make Reagan look good.

Nofziger replies, "I would say somebody's misreading the whole thing, Tom."

Later, he is asked, "Lyn, what does this whole thing say about the Reagan campaign?"

Nofziger replies dryly, "It says it's a very well-run operation and we know what we're doing and we're moving ahead to victory in November."

At eleven-ten this morning, the Reagans and the Bushes arrive at Cobo Hall for a press conference. These press conferences to present the candidate's choice have become another Convention set piece. Today, of course, the interest isn't in who it is but in how on earth it all happened. Mrs. Bush is a handsome woman, and is admired for her directness. Nancy Reagan seems stony today. Reagan and Bush simply look like different types. It's a cultural difference. Reagan looks ineradicably Western, and Bush, though now a Texan, Eastern. This was a sort of shotgun arrangement, and it is known that Reagan resisted selecting Bush, but people who know both men say they will get along well enough: that Reagan is easygoing, and that Bush will do what he is asked. At the press conference, Bush seems tense. He recounts that Reagan called him last night. He can't remember exactly when, and says, "It's irrelevant." He says, "I accepted enthusiastically and I look forward to assisting in every way possible." Last night, he was shown on television saying that he would "work, work, work" for the ticket, and that he "loves" the platform.

Most of the questions are to Reagan, about the Ford affair.

He is asked, "Isn't it clear then, Governor, that Mr. Bush was your second choice?" (Bush is smiling, uneasily.)

Reagan replies, "I think the situation is unique."

Bush is asked if it doesn't seem clear that he was the number two choice for the number two spot.

He replies, "Absolutely not. It's unique. What difference does it make? It's irrelevant. I'm here."

Bush is asked his positions on E.R.A. and abortion. (Bush has supported the E.R.A. and opposed a constitutional amendment prohibiting abortion.)

He replies, "My view is that the big issues, the major issues in the fall . . . are going to be economic and foreign affairs. I oppose abortion and I'm in favor of equal rights for women." And then he says edgily, "I'm not going to get nickeled and dimed to death by detail. I'm not permitting myself to get bogged down in accentuating, and permitting you to accentuate, the differences with the Governor during the campaign, which have been minimal."

Bush is asked how he felt last night speaking to the Convention—whether it was a night of anguish.

He replies, "It wasn't a night of anguish. But at the time I was not oblivious about the speculation that someone else would be anointed. . . . That does not exactly get you up for the speech."

Bush is asked about his repeated insistence in the course of his campaign that he did not want to be Vice President.

He replies, reasonably enough, "Could you ever imagine a person running for President and saying he wants to be Vice President?"

On the Convention floor tonight, Philip Crane, congressman from Illinois, who made an almost-forgotten run for the Republican nomination this year, is telling a reporter of his annoyance that he was not asked to address the Convention; in retaliation, Crane says, he turned down an offer to second Bush's nomination.

He is asked who his first choice for the Vice Presidential nomination was. He replies, *"I* was my first choice."

At nine-fifty, Bush has been nominated by the Convention as Reagan's running mate. The band, signifying Bush's assortment of bases, plays "The Eyes of Texas" and "Boola-Boola." One would not have expected to hear the Yale song at this Convention. Bush, standing on the rostrum with his family, looks overjoyed. With reason. He started out, as he was fond of saying early this year, as an asterisk in the polls. Bush is expected to help with the traditional white Protestant Republican base, the suburban vote that might have been lost to Anderson. The choice of Bush is also intended to reassure the Party regulars, and to indicate to the country at large that Reagan is no right-wing ideologue. The text of Bush's acceptance speech is only two and a half pages long, and shows signs of a good bit of cut-and-pasting. He was told to keep it short. This is Reagan's night. (Four years ago, Walter Mondale gave a lengthier and more substantive speech to the Democratic Convention—his role was to reassure the liberal constituency.) One of the obviously inserted lines is "I enthusiastically support your platform." Bush compares Reagan to Eisenhower—a comparison the Reagan staff has been trying to establish for some time now. He says, "It's up to each and every one of us to help carry Ronald Reagan's message of a strong, free America the length and breadth of this land." He calls on "disillusioned Democrats and independents" to join in the mission.

The demonstration for Bush lasts longer than Bush's speech. The Convention managers are dragging it out again: they're waiting for Ford to get to the hall, so that he can appear with Reagan.

The movie that precedes Reagan's acceptance speech is designed—as Peter Dailey, Reagan's director of advertising, told me last weekend it would be—to show "his strong basic Midwestern ethic; that he comes out of the heartland, was a hardworking young man at an early age, that he was a union leader, and that he had a strong record as governor." And now the orotund-voiced narrator of the film says that "the Reagans were a thrifty, hardworking, close-knit family" and that "young Dutch always had to work for spending money and to help out his family." The film says that as head of the Screen Actors Guild, Reagan was "tireless in his efforts to improve the lot of every working man and woman," and it also says that he "prevented a takeover of the film industry by organized crime." (This is a switch. When he was head of the Guild, Reagan was known for his anti-Communist activities. His aides were unable to explain to me later just what Reagan did to fight organized crime.) It quotes the head of the California state A.F.L.–C.I.O., John Henning, saying that Reagan signed into law large increases in unemployment benefits. "He believes in the boundless opportunities of the American idea," says the announcer.

The Reagans come to the rostrum, and the Convention erupts again. The crowd is not just cheering, it's screaming. Eventually, Reagan gives his speech. Before he begins his prepared remarks, he says, "My first thrill tonight was to find myself, for the first time in a long time, in a movie in prime time." He states his basic theme—that he wants "to build a new consensus with all those across the land who share a community of values embodied in these words: 'family,' 'work,' 'neighborhood,' 'peace,' and 'freedom.' " In a primitive way, he is using the symbols of national piety, using words that get a conditioned response. "Family" seems a safe enough term—one that is perhaps literally on the verge of replacing "motherhood" —but it also has special meaning to his fundamentalist and New Right following. He is using these people and they are using him. ("Neighborhood" is a code word, too.) Reagan is a vessel into which a lot of people are pouring their ambitions. He is the telegenic, easygoing ex-actor in whom people are finding, or hoping to find, what they want. There seems to be something unformed about him. Why, for all his familiarity, does he remain a remote figure? Why is his staff so protective of him, and why is it explaining him so much? One wants to avoid overdoing the actor element, but it is there—is one of the central things about him. He has spent most of his life playing roles, learning how to please people, stir certain emotions. There can be little doubt that Reagan has developed some beliefs, but that is different from having given hard thought to hard questions, from having a grasp. There is a passivity to his nature that is reassuring in some respects but could also become the instrument of purposeful people.

Now, with this acceptance speech, which his staff has long considered crucial—it is the occasion for the first nationwide look at him as a potential President—Reagan brings his skills to bear. He delivers it in a style suited to television—well modulated, soothing—as opposed to one, which he has used on the road, designed to whip up the audience at hand. This is not the occasion for "red meat." It is time to try to assure the national audience that this is a pragmatic, steady man who has ideas about government and who is reaching beyond the constituency that got him where he is tonight. Predictably, he condemns Carter's record, and he excoriates what he calls Carter's " 'trust me' government." He does draw on material he has used before: about the Pilgrims who arrived at Plymouth and formed a "compact;" about the people who "pledged their lives, their fortunes, and their sacred honor to found this nation;" about Abraham Lincoln calling on Americans "to renew their dedication and their commitment to a government of, for, and by the people." More stirring symbols. "Together, let us make this a new beginning," he says. He calls on the people to restore the old values and virtues. He is cheered when he says, "I pledge to restore to the federal government the capacity to do the people's work without dominating their lives."

This speech was designed to demonstrate that Reagan is not simplistic; yet he suggests that the cause of inflation is "a government which has utterly refused to live within its means"—and nothing else. After a nod in the direction of energy conservation, he criticizes the Administration for telling us "to use less." He says, "America must get to work producing more energy," and he talks, as he did throughout the campaign, about the large amounts of oil as yet untapped. He has backed off, though, from his controversial statement that there is more oil underground than has yet been used, and he talks, as his aides have said he would, about other energy resources. He comes down hard on regulations, but he also says, "We will not permit the safety of our people or our environmental heritage to be jeopardized." There is no guide here to what choices he would make.

He talks against big government in a rather orthodox fashion, and says that his first act as President will be to impose a federal hiring freeze. (Such a thing is largely symbolic when it comes to grappling with the size of government, and, in any event, a partial hiring freeze is already in effect.) "Everything that can be run more effectively by state and local government we shall turn over to state and local government, along with the funding sources to pay for it." He does not say whether there will be any national standards for the transferred programs, or federal protections for their recipients. He does not deal with the fact that this would enlarge state and local governments, which have already been growing at a faster rate than the federal government. There is no question that the federal government should be made less cumbersome, but he does not seem to know what a difficult chore that will be. "We will simply apply to government the common sense we all use in our daily lives," he says. Can he really think that? He reaffirms his backing of a thirty-percent tax cut over three years, and gives the rationale that several of his economic advisers reject, and he espouses accelerated depreciation allowances. He tells minorities, "We have to move ahead, but we're not going to leave *anyone* behind." He pledges to put the unemployed back to work and to provide training for those who do not have skills. He promises to stimulate new job opportunities in the inner cities.

He attributes the presence of a Soviet combat brigade in Cuba and the invasion of Afghanistan to America's strength being at its "lowest ebb in a generation," and says that Americans are still held hostage in Iran because "the Carter Administration lives in the world of make-believe." He says, "We are not a warlike people," thus trying to head off Carter's grabbing the "peace issue" and any attempts to paint him as reckless. "We resort to force infrequently and with great reluctance—and only after we have determined that it is absolutely necessary." He says, "We are awed—and rightly so—by the forces of destruction at loose in the world in this nuclear era." He says, "The United States has an obligation to its citizens and to the people of the world never to let those who would destroy freedom dictate the future of human life on this planet." Does anyone disagree?

He quotes Tom Paine, as he often does—"we have it in our power to begin the world over again"—and also, as he is fond of doing, Franklin Roosevelt's 1936 "rendezvous with destiny" speech (Reagan was, of course, once a New Deal Democrat.) And, as he has done before, he quotes the part of Roosevelt's 1932 acceptance speech which called for the elimination of unnecessary functions of government and said that government must be solvent; but he does not quote parts of that speech which called for the expansion of government activity.

And then, voice quavering, he adds something that is not in the prepared text. "I'll confess that I've been a little afraid to suggest what I'm going to suggest," he says. "I'm more afraid not to." Then he pauses, and says, "Can we begin our crusade joined together in a moment of silent prayer?" It is a perfect Reagan touch, drawing on the symbols of prayer and patriotism. It is hard to think of another politician who could pull this off—or would try to. He bows his head, lifts it, and says, emotionally, "God bless America."

CHAPTER 10

The Democratic _____
Convention _____

NEW YORK, SATURDAY, AUGUST 9TH. With only two days remaining before the Democratic National Convention officially begins, and with what could well be the deciding vote scheduled to take place on the first night of the Convention, several camps are here maneuvering. On Monday night, the delegates will vote on whether to adopt a new rule binding them to support, on the first ballot for the Presidential nomination, the candidate to whom they were pledged in the primaries and caucuses. Highly persuasive, morally compelling cases can be made on both sides of the theoretical argument over this rule—and it does raise a serious question—but the struggle going on here has very little to do with political theory. If the rule is adopted, President Carter, who goes into the Convention with more than enough delegates pledged to him, will be the nominee. (He has nineteen hundred and eighty-two; sixteen hundred and sixty-six are needed for the nomination. Edward Kennedy has twelve hundred and twenty-four.)

Adoption of the rule is being opposed by a number of different forces— and that is their problem. Their motivations are stumbling over each other. The Kennedy forces have been working for some time for the rule's defeat, which would provide the last, if unlikely, chance to wrest the nomination from Carter. Recently, they have been joined, in a sense, by a number of people who want to obtain the nomination for almost anyone other than

Carter—or Kennedy. In a public-relations coup of sorts, these people have rallied around the idea of what they term an "open Convention." Under the "open Convention," the delegates would not be bound, and perhaps someone other than Carter would be nominated. That this might involve brokering of the sort that some of the idea's backers would find abhorrent in other circumstances does not trouble them excessively right now. Nor does the Carter side seem terribly bothered by the idea that it is seeking to impose on the Party a rule that would not allow the delegates to take into account changed circumstances—would not allow them to act as a deliberative group rather than as robots. Some people see the new rule as the logical extension of reforms that the Party has already adopted; others see it as reform gone so far as to be self-defeating. It grew out of a series of reforms initiated in the late sixties, and was designed to insure that the delegates to the National Convention would constitute a "fair reflection" of the results of the primaries and caucuses. This new rule, which was offered by White House representatives in Party deliberations following the last election, was adopted by the Democratic National Committee, which is dominated by Carter people, as part of the delegate-selection rules for the primaries and caucuses but has not yet been adopted as a Convention rule.

Aside from the politics, a number of delegates are concerned over the principle of the issue. One argument is over whether, since it was in effect during the delegate-selection process, it must govern the Convention. Another is over whether it belonged in the delegate-selection rules in the first place, since it deals with behavior at the Convention. Many dispassionate people think that it goes too far, offering no flexibility, and sets a bad precedent. The problem in such matters is how to strike a balance. It is probably fair to say that those who are arguing the principle that the Party rules must allow flexibility would be screaming bloody murder if it were *their* delegates who might be shaken loose.

The drive for an "open Convention" gained new impetus as a result of a number of coinciding elements. First, there was the Billy Carter affair, which broke in the course of the Republican Convention last month, and which was characterized by a series of revelations, sudden recollections, and new questions. It wasn't Watergate by any means, but it felt like it at times—even in the reaction of the politicians. There was the panic on the part of Democratic members of Congress who returned from a July recess having found that Carter was in terrible shape in their states or districts and fearing that they would go down with him. (At this point, Carter's popularity rating is at twenty-one percent in the Gallup Poll, the lowest for any President in the poll's forty-five-year history, and he is twenty-eight points behind Reagan in the ABC News–Harris Survey.) For many of these people, the Billy Carter problem presented an opportunity. In the Senate cloakrooms, there was talk—reminiscent of Watergate times—of a delegation's going to the President to ask him to withdraw, or, at least, release his delegates. But the senators recognized that they were confronted with one of the most tenacious politicians in memory. Eventually, Robert Byrd, the Senate Majority Leader, who was trying to protect his flock, and who has never been very fond of Carter—the Carter people failed to cultivate Byrd appropriately, and Byrd is a very proud man—called for an "open Convention." (Of the thirty-four senators up for re-election this year, twenty-four are Democrats, and several of them are in very tough races.) Two Fridays ago, about fifty House members, most of them relatively junior, gathered to try to figure out how to extricate the Party from Carter. They also considered how to make the effort seem more noble than a "dump" movement, and out of that came the call for an "open Convention." And, finally, alternative nominees and people working on their behalf made some moves. A Committee to Continue the Open Convention opened an office on Capitol Hill and has now established a headquarters in the New York Hilton. Some backers of Secretary of State Edmund Muskie and Senator Henry Jackson, of Washington, had had such a move in mind for a while. The committee is headed by Edward Bennett Williams, a close friend of Muskie's. Representative Michael Barnes, of Maryland, the spokesman of the committee, worked in the 1972 Muskie campaign, as did Keith Haller, his administrative assistant and one of the committee's staff coordinators. Actually, associates of both Muskie and Senator Jackson have been watching for an opportunity, and have been making some moves—as have the principals. Muskie's statement of lack of interest, issued at the behest of the White House, was not totally persuasive to a number of people, including many at the White House. Jackson, no fan of the President, has been openly critical of him for some time. There are people at the White House who think that Byrd, too, has the idea that the Convention might somehow deadlock and turn to him. Hugh Carey, the governor of New York, several weeks ago called on both Carter and Kennedy to release their delegates, and no one doubts that he would be pleased to step in if he could find a place to put his foot. These kinds of situations give all sorts of people ideas. A Jackson Can Win Committee has established a headquarters at the Biltmore, and a Muskie committee has set up shop on the third floor over J. J. Applebaum's, a new delicatessen on Seventh Avenue. (One of the owners is a brother-in-law of one of the committee workers.) Muskie, as he must, is keeping a discreet distance. The Jackson, Muskie, and Open Convention people are cooperating with one another, and there is talk—depending on whom you talk to— of a Muskie-Jackson ticket, a Jackson-Muskie ticket, a Kennedy-Jackson ticket, a Carey-Somebody-or-Other ticket.

But the Jackson, Muskie, and Open Convention people, to the extent that they are distinguishable, say that the game is hopeless unless Kennedy gets out; they say they are finding too many people unwilling to try for an "open Convention" if it means that Kennedy might be nominated—and Kennedy is not about to get out. And there are problems with each of the alternatives. There had been talk of Vice President Walter Mondale, but even if Mondale were of the temperament to challenge the President, reality ruled such a challenge out. Jackson, because of his foreign-policy views, would inflame the left wing of the Party; and in 1976 he won only two primaries. Muskie is a man with a low irritation threshold who ran an unimpressive campaign in 1972.

There has been the question of whether a nomination wrested from the President at the Convention would be worth having. And there is also the problem of bridging the gap between, on the one hand, the would-be candidates, would-be power brokers, and worried politicians in Washington and, on the other hand, the delegates. The Carter delegates are not only pledged to the President but bound to him by a number of different ties. Carter's support at this Convention is a curious amalgam of delegates he aggregated through assiduous use of his incumbency and through his own brand of un-Party politics—of personal ties and alliances of convenience. The potentials of incumbency have grown with the growth of government, and the Carter group has broken ground in the development of those potentials. Carter never has been much of a Party man, and he still is not. Many of the delegates are people with personal ties to him—people who themselves are not Party activists but in whose homes he has stayed, whom he has cultivated. The other major element in Carter's constituency at the Convention is the officials—mayors, state chairmen, and so on—and union leaders who threw in with him, even when his fortunes were low, because he was the President. It was in their interest—the White House saw to that—to stick with the President. If someone else became the nominee, many of them figured, they could transfer their loyalties at the appropriate time. What they did not figure on was that their short-term commitment would breed its own success and become, along with whatever amount of discomfiture, a long-term commitment.

For more than two years now, Carter and Kennedy have been fighting over the constituency of the Democratic Party. When it came to an out-and-out fight for the nomination, Kennedy's politics may have been more satisfying to union leaders, but there had grown up a cat's cradle of arrangements between the White House and labor which would have been very awkward for many unions to pull out of. The leadership of some unions —most notably the United Auto Workers, which felt betrayed by Carter's apparent loss of interest in national health insurance and in tax reform—did go with Kennedy, and Kennedy did receive the support of a number of other labor groups, but the majority of the most politically active unions supported Carter. The National Education Association, which in 1976 gave its support to Carter in exchange for a pledge to obtain legislation establishing a Department of Education, has more delegates here (three hundred and two) than any state except California. Carter delivered on his promise, and the N.E.A., which has developed a highly sophisticated political organization, was crucial to Carter's successes in the caucuses and primaries this year. I recently asked a White House aide what the N.E.A. wants now, since it has won the department. He replied, without hesitation, "Influence. It has the department; now it wants to run it."

The large number of amateurs attending this Convention—it is estimated to be the first Convention for about two-thirds of the delegates—indicates what has been changing Party politics, and also explains why Carter is likely to hold his delegates. And it suggests why a number of people are searching for a formula for selecting delegates which satisfies both the need that gave rise to the reform impulse twelve years ago—the need to open the Party to wider participation and dilute the influence of "the bosses"—and the need to have the Convention bear a closer relationship to the Party. The reforms reduced the number of officials who can attend Conventions without running as delegates. A Democratic senator said to me last week, "We have to find a new equilibrium. The people who attend the caucuses or get selected as delegates are not the people who've traditionally been involved. You have a group of people who have been solicited, cultivated, one on one. Their allegiance has been obtained on a basis that has very little to do with substance, program, philosophy—it's the personal contact, the picture on the piano. It's an extension of the Mayor Daley school of personalized politics. This gets into the question: What is a political party? What relevance should be given to genuine sustained involvement and to people who have responsibility for the Party's fortunes? These people at the Convention are like mayflies: they live twenty-four hours, have their day in the sun, go to the Convention, and bring back their souvenir programs. But they are not genuine custodians and stewards of the Party trust. Others are left with the real work of fashioning a coherent program and generating public appeal. Officeholders, who have the greatest stake, are not only outside of it but aggressively seek to stay outside of it. If they did get in, and took sides, it would alienate a substantial number of people. Most senators and congressmen don't even know who the delegates are. The senators who have the most at stake in the selection of the Democratic nominee are powerless to affect it. If a group of us went to call on Carter to 'open' the Convention, he could properly dismiss us—we have no troops."

What all this also means is that the Convention is increasingly dominated by the candidates. One man who had long been involved in the reform movement said to me recently, "The fundamental problem is that this is essentially not a Party Convention—it's a Presidential-candidate Convention. The delegates to the '68 Convention were, far more than is the case now, regular Party—chosen by Party officials in the state. If this were the '68 Convention, Carter would not be the nominee. Now most of the delegates have been vetted by the candidates' organizations. That's one great failure of the reforms—we've taken the Party out of the selection process and we've substituted Presidential parties in its place. The benefit is that the delegates are more likely to represent the balloting; the difficulty is that when you have a close contest you have more partisanship among the candidates' backers, and you have less flexibility. A lot of the changes since '68 I'll still defend, but now we've reached the point where the delegates are just hand-chosen agents of the candidate. I think, inevitably, we'll have to look at the rules again, and the issue will be: How do you bring the Party back into the process? The task will be to find some middle ground that doesn't undemocratize the system but makes the Party at least the author of the system.''

About two weeks ago, the White House realized that it had a serious problem on its hands, and it moved to head off the movement toward an ''open Convention.'' (Actually, the Carter team, although outwardly confident, had been nervous about its delegates for some weeks.) Robert Strauss came back from his annual summer vacation at the races in Del Mar, California. Mondale was called back from a vacation in New Jersey, and Mondale's staff was recalled from various parts. Delegates were canvassed and canvassed, and waverers or people who might reach the waverers were phoned by the President, by Mrs. Carter, by Mondale, by various other officials. Some senators who were backing the President held a luncheon on Capitol Hill—to demonstrate that there *were* senators who were backing the President. On Friday, August 1st, four hundred delegates were invited to Washington for a pep talk by the Vice President and then the President. (This had already been in the works and was the third such occasion. It was considered an inexpensive way of reinforcing the President's delegate strength. For many of the delegates, it was their first time in the White House.) On the same day, Hamilton Jordan and Patrick Caddell had lunch with some county leaders from New York State—who, it was feared, might feel obliged to go along with Carey—and the President himself talked to Meade Esposito, the Democratic leader of Brooklyn. The county leaders are now expected to stick with Carter. And on that same Friday some seventy-five members of Congress were brought to the White House to express their continued loyalty to Carter. Then, on the following Monday, the President held a press conference to deal with the problem of his brother. Some of the people around the President had considered the idea that the Carter forces should not fight for the new rule: the thinking was that to make such a fight might make the President appear weak—worried about his delegates' loyalty—and that to win the nomination by forcing the delegates to vote for him might be a victory with too high a cost. But the President is said to have felt particularly strongly that the rule should be adopted.

In a sense, the Kennedy forces maneuvered the Administration into this position. The side without enough votes for the nomination often tries to establish a test vote on an issue prior to the Presidential balloting—and on the highest ostensible grounds it can think up—in the hope that somehow this will change the chemistry, alter the atmosphere of the Convention. (In 1976, the Reagan forces, under the guidance of John Sears, did the same thing.) If the Kennedy side were to win the rules fight, the Convention might be seen to have been transformed—and this the Carter people decided they could not risk. Thus, at his press conference last week the President denounced the move to an ''open Convention'' as one that would return the Party to ''the old brokered-type Convention,'' and he characterized the effort as essentially Kennedy's. While the President's performance in dealing with the Billy Carter problem left some questions unanswered, it was generally judged to be an effective one, which was all that mattered at the moment. All these efforts succeeded in taking the steam out of the "open Convention" movement. Now the Carter people are fairly confident, but are leaving nothing to chance in the next two days.

Kennedy arrived in New York yesterday, and, sounding as strident as he ever has, shouted, "The four years we've had already are four years too many!" This will be a hard thing to back off from, if the need arises. He seemed almost crazed, a caricature. A number of people, including some of Kennedy's friends, and even some of his staff, have become puzzled about what he thinks he is doing. Leaving aside the style in which he is doing it, the question is not so puzzling. Kennedy and his people are aware that the odds against his getting the nomination are long indeed, but they have travelled all year on the theory that at some point the bubble around Carter would burst. It isn't surprising that Kennedy may not realize the extent to which support for Carter is not transferable to him, may not realize how much antipathy there is to him. In politics, as elsewhere, one can become so obsessed with reaching one's goal—so certain that if only x will happen the goal will be reached—that any number of things that happen will be assumed to be x. Publicly and privately, Kennedy has been saying that he expects to win; in reality, he has been hoping that something would break.

The Billy Carter affair and the panic on Capitol Hill gave the Kennedy people a new sense of optimism. Moreover, it was difficult for Kennedy to get out—as various people had counselled him to do along the way—because, as was clear from the outset, this was not any old political fight. Relations between Carter and Kennedy, never good, had become worse. And Kennedy had come to believe that his was not simply a candidacy but also a cause—an instrument for moving the Democratic Party closer to what he saw as its proper ideological home. If Kennedy did lose, Carter would need his following, and there remained the platform, and even Carter's policies, to be affected.

Kennedy made it a point not to complain in public, but he and his people believe that the contest for the nomination was not a fair fight: that Carter manipulated the hostage issue, hid behind foreign affairs, and did not engage in a debate even in the larger sense. Kennedy remains determined to get that debate, one way or another. Several months ago, one of his closest advisers told me that, whatever happened, Kennedy would give one hell of a speech at the Convention—that there was no way the Carter people could prevent him from appearing there, and in prime time. The Kennedy people point out that as the campaign began to focus on the issues Kennedy had been stressing, Kennedy began to do better. They point out that Kennedy defeated Carter in a number of the industrial states—states that Carter needs to win in November if he is to be re-elected. They argue that the farmers were misled when the Administration told them they would not be adversely affected by the grain embargo that was imposed after the Soviet Union's invasion of Afghanistan. There remains bitterness over the personal nature of the campaign against Kennedy—the emphasis on "character." To a degree, it seems, the Kennedy people just cannot believe that the Democratic Party will renominate Carter. And it is not against the rules to carry a nomination contest into a Convention. So Carter may have the delegates, but Kennedy still has a hold on Carter. The Carter camp, beyond winning, wants as uncontentious a Convention as possible. Only eleven weeks remain between the end of the Convention and Election Day.

The Carter group has actually been working on the fall campaign for some time. Some people have been out in the field since April—under the auspices of the Democratic National Committee, since federal funding for the fall campaign is not obtainable until after the nomination. (One of the arguments the Carter campaign uses against the nomination of anyone else at the Convention is that election campaigns are now such large and complicated undertakings that no one could put together a campaign starting this week.) The campaign's high command has been meeting at eight o'clock each morning in the White House office of Jack Watson, who has replaced Hamilton Jordan as chief of staff so that Jordan can give even fuller attention to the campaign. Patrick Caddell says that his current survey data indicate that Reagan has more serious problems than Caddell had thought earlier this summer. "He has more serious problems with his ideological setting than I believed," Caddell told me in a conversation we had this morning. "He has problems with the question of war and peace, with people not knowing how he would handle things in office." Caddell's findings indicate, he says, that Reagan is substantially worse off than Carter was four years ago at this time—but also that Carter is worse off than Ford was. (Following the Democratic Convention in 1976, which preceded the Republican Convention, Carter led Ford by thirty-three points, and the election turned out to be a very close one.)

One of the things that will be stressed in the acceptance speech—its tone is still being decided on—is that this election really presents a choice, that it matters. Hamilton Jordan is said to be concerned that not enough people think it does make a difference who is elected. I have been told that the decision is for Carter not to go after Reagan personally—not, in the phrase of one campaign aide, to "do a Kennedy"—but he will stress that one has to be concerned about Reagan, because Reagan will set America off in a different direction. Caddell says, "Reagan and the people around him want to take America off the course it's been on for half a century—it's on that that Carter can make his case. Their platform should be taken seriously. We also have to get across that Carter has gained experience on the job—that we've made a down payment and ought to cash it in, that he'll be in a better position to function in the second term."

The President will try in his speech to get the focus on Reagan, as a way of pulling the Party back together; it is also recognized that the President will have to have something to offer for the future. The theme that Carter used on his one day out on the campaign trail during the primaries, in Ohio, that "we're turning the tide" on our problems, has been retired. Several of the President's aides weren't very pleased with that theme. Carter lost about eight points across the board in the primaries after his trip to Ohio. The President's advisers are also aware that the President needs to offer something that deals with the economy. Some believe he has needed to do so for quite a while. He is planning to offer a program for "reindustrialization," which is becoming a highly fashionable concept. Jerry Brown talked about it in his campaign; Kennedy talked about it; and business and labor like the idea. But the Administration has got bogged down in the policy and politics of the program, and the whole thing has been put off. Even if it had been ready, White House aides worried that if the President unveiled the proposal before the Convention it would seem "political," and Kennedy would denounce it as inadequate. So the President mentioned the program in a recent speech to the National Urban League, will mention it again in his acceptance speech, and will offer it when it is ready.

The President's advisers believe that the Republicans did score points against Carter in the course of their Convention, and they want to use this opportunity to fight back. Over three hundred members of the executive branch are here—to talk to delegates in their caucuses, to give interviews to everyone from a network newsman on the Convention floor to a reporter for a local newspaper. Specific areas of the country where the President needs to do well have been selected for such press treatment, and the officials' schedules have been fed into a computer. The Convention planners did an analysis that indicated that the networks carry only eight or nine minutes out of every hour of the proceedings on the podium. The Carter people want to fill in the difference to the maximum extent. A complicated operation has been established to "track" the floor reporters—thus turning the whole idea inside out—and, by offering them bigwigs at opportune moments, keep them from dwelling on things that the Carter people would just as soon not have dwelt on. "We are going to try to massively use the media," one of the President's advisers has said to me. "More than is usually done." Gerald Rafshoon has prepared "talking points" for the Administration officials to stress in their interviews. ("In this pivotal election, President Carter and Governor Reagan are going to force a big choice on the people of the United States." And "Jimmy Carter . . . moderate in ideas . . . deliberate in actions . . . rich in Presidential experience.") A Presidential adviser has said to me, "More time and energy have gone into the massive scheduling and press operation than into the floor fights. We haven't talked about it much—but we're going to take the networks for a ride."

At eleven o'clock, Paul Kirk, the Kennedy campaign's national political director, is holding a press conference at the Starlight Roof on the eighteenth floor of the Waldorf-Astoria. Kirk has been one of Kennedy's more cautious and low-keyed advisers. He was against Kennedy's getting into the race and, earlier this year, urged him to get out. But lately, either because he is caught up in the last, desperate effort or because he is playing out a public role, he has been getting quite worked up and insisting that Kennedy will be nominated. (Other Kennedy aides have been—at least privately—more cautious.) Now Kirk, talking enthusiastically, like a football coach, tells the press that the Kennedy forces are picking up a great deal of support on the vote on the rule. "I think we may be on the threshold of one of the major political stories of recent political history," he says. He says that the press may be about to witness "the most spectacular story of turnaround." The Kennedy camp's optimistic theory has been that if the rule was rejected on Monday this would be followed by victories on the platform on Tuesday, and then the Convention would take on a life of its own, in which anything might happen. (It is because the Carter people have also recognized this possibility that they have fought so hard on the rule.) Kirk outlines this theory and then says, "So we look forward to the nomination on Wednesday night and the acceptance speech on Thursday night, and to helping you write the biggest story in recent political history." Kirk says that the states that are considered "soft" on the rule—Pennsylvania, Illinois, Michigan (a list with which the Carter people agree)—are, not coincidentally, ones that Carter needs to carry in November, and ones where, in the current polls, "Reagan cleans Carter's clock." He says that Kennedy and members of his staff are calling people in those states and others and "asking them whether they want the Party to walk to the gallows."

"Has Kennedy ever considered withdrawing?" Kirk is asked.

He replies, smiling, "You gotta be kidding."

The problem is that the more the Kennedy people stress the point that Kennedy can still win, the more it chills the efforts of others to defeat the rule. Word is going around that some Kennedy people are sending a message to the other campaigns that they should join with Kennedy's in trying to defeat the rule, and that if Kennedy doesn't make it, they might.

At twelve-thirty, Hugh Carey and Edward Bennett Williams hold a press conference on behalf of the Committee to Continue the Open Convention and announce that they are "very, very close" to having enough votes to defeat the Carter forces on Monday. At the committee's headquarters at the Hilton, calls are being made to round up more support. An effort is under way—by Muskie people, Jackson people, Kennedy people, Open Convention people—to develop a "favorite-son strategy." Such a strategy might fit the ambitions and tactics of a number of people. The idea is that Senator Adlai Stevenson, of Illinois; Senator Birch Bayh, of Indiana; Senator Jackson; Governor Carey; Governor Richard Lamm, of Colorado; Secretary of State Muskie; maybe Senator Lloyd Bentsen, of Texas (and some others, perhaps), would be nominated as favorite sons, so that no one could get the nomination on the first ballot. If these people—or their followers—thought they could get the nomination, or were at least tempted by the publicity of having their names placed in nomination, there might well be more support for the effort to defeat the rule. And if the rule was defeated, who knows what might happen?

The movement to "open" the Convention represents a confluence of a multitude of motives. Stevenson is making some calls to members of the Illinois delegation. The different camps seem to have conflicting information about who might be "loose" or who has taken what position on the rule—partly because of wishful thinking, partly because of sheer confusion, partly because of the fact that a number of people are trying to figure out how this thing will turn out before they take a position. Many of them do not want to have been on the wrong side if Carter is the nominee. They do not want to make a move that doesn't work, so they may not make a move. Several governors are waiting until the eleventh hour. "I've never seen a situation where more people had their finger to the wind," Keith Haller said to me this afternoon. But the essential fact is that the Open Convention people are winging it, while the Carter people have power, computerized lists, and a seemingly infinite capacity for making phone calls—including phone calls placed by the President of the United States.

Close associates of Muskie who are here in New York are lying low and assuring people that they have nothing to do with the efforts to draft Muskie, but a number of people, including some in the White House, have noticed that Muskie does not seem to have instructed his boosters to cut it out. (Muskie, Edward Bennett Williams, Arnold Picker, who is the principal fund raiser for the Open Convention Committee, and two of Muskie's closest associates dined at a Washington restaurant a couple of weeks ago.) At twelve-thirty today, at the same time the Open Convention Committee held its press conference, King Golden, the chairman of the Draft Muskie Committee, held a press conference at the headquarters over J. J. Applebaum's and called on Kennedy to get out of the race. Golden is a young lawyer from San Diego who worked in the youth division of the 1972 Muskie campaign. At the Muskie headquarters, young people are making calls on some twenty phones. The Muskie people had not much focussed on the question of the "open Convention" until they realized that the only way Muskie could get nominated was through defeat of the new rule. Golden is now trying to reach Joseph Brennan, the governor of Maine, to try to persuade him to call a press conference and urge Kennedy to withdraw. Brennan supported Kennedy during the primaries; Muskie, quietly, helped Carter. The strain between Muskie and Kennedy goes back some way: Muskie, a Catholic, was the first senator to come out for John Kennedy, and he was, by his lights, a supporter of Robert Kennedy in 1968. According to a close friend, he then very much resented the fact that in 1972 Ethel Kennedy supported George McGovern. And, according to someone who knows Muskie quite well, he would still very much like to be President, and would not be displeased if fate should arrange such an outcome. He is also said to recognize that there are serious limits to how much, at this point, he can affect fate.

The Jackson people have been trying for some time to get a few prominent people to come out for Jackson—in particular, Governor Carey and Senator Daniel Patrick Moynihan, of New York. One of Jackson's supporters said to me this afternoon, "It's like trying to nail gelatine to the wall; everyone is ready to do something if someone else does." Jackson, for a change, is turning down appearances on television; he does not want to seem to be running for the nomination unless there's a serious possibility he can win it. The supporter said, "Scoop's not going to get out there without others being there."

Sunday. Robert Strauss is having breakfast with a group of reporters.
He is asked, "Will Kennedy be on the podium Thursday night?"
"I don't know," he replies.
"Are you worried?"
"I'm not worried," Strauss replies. His offhandedness is not convincing. "Our position is very simple. I said yesterday we want to leave here with a united Party. A part of that is the support of Senator Kennedy—and many others. We hope for that. We have compromised and reached out on several issues." He points out that in the negotiations that preceded the Convention, Kennedy was accorded an opportunity to speak about the platform on Tuesday night, in prime time. "I said, 'Let's give it to him—he's campaigned for nine months.' I used the word 'valiantly.' "
Kennedy may have lost the fight for the nomination, but he still has a strong base in the Democratic Party, and Carter needs his people. He needs to have the constituency groups, especially labor, fired up to work for the November election; he needs to avoid losing disenchanted Democrats to John Anderson; he needs to present a tableau of unity on television. Given Kennedy's competitive temperament and his disdain for Carter, there is every reason to believe that he enjoys, and will make the most of, the grip he continues to have on him.
Now Strauss says that the most important thing on his mind is "how we tell our story in a positive way." He says, "The whole world isn't going to chisel in marble what takes place on that podium." But Strauss seems genuinely perturbed. He is of the old fight-and-shake-hands school of politics, and he fancies himself one of the leading referees, and the fight between Carter and Kennedy has got beyond him. He is frustrated by his inability to bring it to a close. He says, somewhat agitatedly, "If you have any wisdom and judgment at all, you know you don't get carried away by personalities and pettiness in a political fight. The good guys know—whether they are for Kennedy or Carter, or for Reagan or the Democrats—that politics is tough enough and the town that we live in is tough enough that you don't cut each

other's throats. They know that you scream at each other one day and go out for lunch on another day.'' He points out, accurately enough, that some of the fights that will take place this week ''are structured just to make it tough for us.'' He says, ''If we were in the forties in the approval ratings, it would be like shooting fish in a barrel.''

Strauss has a point. If Carter's electability were not in real question, the outcome of the Convention would have been settled some time ago. Beneath all the noise and the maneuvering of recent days, there have been some difficult questions. One question is whether, after the primaries and caucuses are completed, it is fair to take the polls into account. Especially Jimmy Carter's polls, which may have set a new record for mobility. On the other hand, electability used to be a—perhaps the—major criterion of party Conventions. The few primaries that were held were meant to be advisory to the party leaders—who didn't always follow the advice. And who is to decide who is electable?

There are a lot of attempts to read Kennedy's mind these days—even by people who work closely with him. For all his surface gregariousness, Kennedy is an Irish internalizer, not given to sharing his feelings or thoughts very widely. Yet it is hard to see how he has any real choice but to end up playing the good sport. He is a Democrat, after all, and unless he is finished with public life he can't be seen as having torn up the Party; now that he has won widespread praise for the resilience and good humor he showed in his campaign, he can't end up appearing to act like a bad loser. One of Kennedy's associates says, ''His position is very difficult. He wants to do what's best for the Party but not something that does not look credible, or that seems opportunistic. He'll have to persuade people that embracing the candidate is not opportunistic, that he's not doing something he doesn't mean. That's what people criticize the most in politicians—they never seem to mean it. He'll have to find a way back for his followers—a large percentage of whom can't abide Carter. That's why his Tuesday speech is so important. My guess is you won't hear much criticism of Carter and you will hear a lot of Reagan.''

On Sunday afternoon, the Illinois delegation is caucusing on the lower level of the St. Moritz, where it is staying. The various state delegations have been arriving today and will be caucusing today and tomorrow. Representatives of both sides in the rules fight will be addressing them. Illinois, where Carter triumphed in the primary, has been causing the Carter people their worst headache. And Illinois is being watched by other delegations; if the President loses substantial support there, other delegations might follow. This afternoon, the Vice President will appear at its caucus. Carter's triumph in the Illinois primary last March—he won a hundred and sixty-three delegates to Kennedy's sixteen—stemmed in part from the endorsement of Kennedy by Mayor Jane Byrne, of Chicago, who was then extremely unpopular. But the Mayor is a force: after running against the old

Daley organization, she turned around and made peace with it, and a number of the city's politicians have decided that it is in their interest to make an accommodation with her. One Illinois politician here has said to me, "Even if she is unpopular, if you've got a street you want paved or a building you want to build or a few friends you want to get jobs for—and the last is the most important—it's worthwhile to be in her favor."

Moreover, in Illinois the Carter people tended more than they did in other states to select as delegates people who were involved in politics. In part, this was because the slates had to be drawn up by the first of the year, at a time when Carter's prospects did not look good. He had been low in the polls, and the Mayor and the Cook County organization had endorsed Kennedy. It was widely assumed that Illinois would be a Kennedy state. The thinking was that it was important to get people on the ballot whose names carried some weight. But these were people who knew how to deal and who had their own agendas. When they saw that Carter needed them on the rule issue, they started dealing. The question of the rule provided an opportunity for people to waver, or to appear to waver. One of Carter's campaign officials says, "When you're down, everybody wants to do business." Al Majerczyk, a Chicago alderman, who is believed to control four votes in the Illinois delegation, helped the Carter forces in the primary, because he was anti-Byrne, but he has since come to terms with the Mayor. He has told the Administration he's got about nine people who need jobs—not such big jobs, he adds, but jobs. The Mayor of Chicago has some thirteen thousand jobs at her disposal; the President of the United States has about three thousand. A Carter campaign official says, "They don't understand that there is no federal sewer department." Other Illinois delegates have been under pressure from the Mayor's office. One woman has asked the Administration for a job. A few have said that it is not good politics for the President to impose the rule. A few even oppose it on principle.

Carl Officer, a black, and the mayor of East St. Louis, Illinois, on which the Administration has bestowed a substantial portion of the federal treasury, told the White House that some of his delegates might not support the rule. East St. Louis has been gerrymandered into a black island with little tax base, and the White House was fearful of Kennedy support there. Jack Watson, who used to head the office that maintained liaison with the state and local officials (an office that became of great value in the campaign), and Eugene Eidenberg, who was formerly Watson's deputy and is now the head of the office, have been working with Mayor Officer. A man named Clarence Darrow (his grandfather was a cousin of the famous one), a state representative from Rock Island, who is running for re-election, began to express sympathy for the idea of an "open Convention." The Vice President phoned him and persuaded him that the President needed his support. A state representative whose ward committeeman is the vice mayor of Chicago—ward committeemen are the most powerful, as compared with township or state committeemen, because they pass out the patronage—

was believed to be feeling pressure from the Mayor's office, but a few days ago he came around. Sal Pullia, a Democratic committeeman for Proviso Township, was viewed as susceptible to pressure from the Mayor. One campaign official talked to him and reported that he was a difficult case. Congressman Martin Russo, who has been helping the Carter campaign, talked to him and reported that his vote might be obtainable if Mondale talked to him. Mondale talked to him and got his vote. Some of the trouble has to do with the question of who will play what role in the fall campaign in Illinois. Jerry Cosentino, from suburban Chicago, who is the state treasurer and is assumed to be planning to run for higher office, wants to run the Carter campaign in Illinois in the fall—a job the Carter people don't want him to have. Cosentino has threatened to lead a move for an "open Convention" if he does not get the role he wants. Tim Kraft, the national campaign manager, has been negotiating with him, Hamilton Jordan has been negotiating with him, and Vice President Mondale has seen him. As of now, he is telling people he does not know how he will vote tomorrow.

At five o'clock, Mondale appears at the Illinois caucus. He makes some jokes, including one about Stevenson, and he says that he travelled some twenty thousand miles on the campaign trail this year and one of the things he learned was that "Illinois is one of the great, vibrant Democratic states in this nation." He says, "We're going to be meeting tomorrow in an open, turbulent, sweaty, controversial Convention. We don't hide our controversies; we are an open party." He says that the Convention will accurately reflect the choice of the people. Mondale waves an arm up and down and speaks strongly, but his voice is thin, so what amounts to a shout from him does not come across as a shout: "We are the least bossed Convention— oh, boy, are we unbossed." He gives the reasons for the rule; says that the Democrats will win in November; and talks about how much the Administration has done for jobs, education, Social Security, the cities, women, minorities, energy. And then he takes on Reagan. He is not just making the case for the vote tomorrow; he is making the case for the Administration, and telling these people that there is a real chance for the Carter ticket to win. Much of this is the sort of thing he said during the primaries. Illinois is one of the most important states in the fall election. As for Reagan, Mondale smiles and says, "Boy, do we have an opponent. I'm going to have more fun this fall than I've had in a long time," and then he spiritedly takes on Reagan on various issues.

The focus of this Convention is on Carter and Kennedy, as it was in the primaries, but there is also the story of Mondale and Kennedy. In the course of the year, Mondale began to let it seep out that he would like to be President after Carter. Mondale has one of the ablest political staffs in the country, good relations with the Democratic constituency groups—better relations than Carter has—and a network he has kept intact. Other, younger Democrats have been grooming themselves for future Presidential contests —adjusting their politics, getting themselves mentioned, and all that—but from Mondale's perspective Kennedy has been the biggest obstacle. Mondale concludes, "Illinois is going to be one of the great battlegrounds of this campaign. Let's get this family together. Let's unite, and let's keep a good President." He adds, smiling, "And, by the way, a marvellous Vice President." The audience laughs and applauds; Mondale seems popular with them—more popular than Carter.

Late this afternoon, it was announced that the Kennedy and Carter camps had reached agreement on more planks in the platform. At one point, there had been eighteen minority planks, but both sides had planned all along to give in on some—the Kennedy side because it did not want to annoy either the Convention or the public by pressing too many issues, the Carter side because some of the Kennedy proposals seemed so unexceptionable that it would be embarrassing, and probably futile, to oppose them. Both sides know that the big fight will come over a Kennedy proposal to add to the platform a twelve-billion-dollar jobs program. The Kennedy people have defined the platform fight as well as the rules fight: they are deliberately offering something that they know the Administration must oppose and that the Democratic constituency groups might well support. The Administration also acceded today to a Kennedy proposal that two hours before the start of the nominating speeches the candidates state in writing their positions on the platform. The President was resistant, and his people agreed mainly because they thought that if they opposed the proposal they might well be defeated, and that since this would come before the fight on the rule to bind the delegates, it could be seen as a test vote. Carter may come to regret this concession, but he may have been truly stuck. Convention strategies are often—perhaps usually—not grand ones but a series of small, ad-hoc decisions.

The Jackson people have decided that it's over—that Carter has the votes on the rule. Some of them are quite annoyed at Carey, from whom they thought they had a commitment to endorse Jackson, but who said today on "Issues and Answers" that he was not backing any particular candidate. A Jackson man said to me tonight, "This kind of situation does not bring out the best side of people."

Tonight, the Pennsylvania delegation is caucusing in the State Room of the Roosevelt Hotel. Kennedy narrowly won the Pennsylvania primary in April; he has ninety-four delegates to Carter's ninety-one. Pennsylvania is another delegation that has the Carter people worried. Once again the politicians in the delegation are making the most of the opportunity presented by the rules fight. Dr. Cyril Wecht, the Democratic Committee chairman of Allegheny County and also a county commissioner—a powerful figure— endorsed Carter (after considering endorsing Kennedy, according to the Kennedy people), but recently he said consideration should be given to an "open Convention." He was called by Strauss, by Jordan, and by the President, and then he decided that, having given it full consideration, he was not for an "open Convention." Waverers—or ostensible waverers—are asking for everything from tickets to the Convention for friends to the release of someone from prison.

Dan Horgan, who used to be executive director of the Democratic National Committee, is working Pennsylvania for the Carter forces. Horgan, who is from New Jersey, has worked in politics a long time, and understands it. "There are a hundred and eighty-five liars in here," Horgan cracks. He tells me, "If Kennedy was going to do something, he'd have to get fifty votes out of here. There's only a couple of places to do something—this is one of them. There was a moment ten days ago I was scared to death. The Open Convention guys didn't get it for three reasons. The congressmen said on a Friday that they hoped to have a whole lot more names on Monday. I thought they'd have a whole lot more names on Monday. They didn't. Second, they didn't get Byrd in time. And then Kirk made a bad mistake. He said that if there was an 'open Convention' Kennedy'd win. That was the wrong mistake. In politics, you must never make the wrong mistake. If he hadn't done that, they could have broke off pieces from the Muskie movement, the Jackson movement. If Bob Strauss had been on their side, it woulda happened. But he was on our side, thank God."

The room is hot. At nine-fifteen, Kennedy arrives. He has been chasing around to caucuses and meetings all day, and he looks pale. One of his close aides insists that Kennedy is enjoying this. "You have to enjoy it to drag yourself around eighteen hours a day. We're trying to get back to the old Democratic idea that politics is fun." Kennedy is still looking for a break in what he and his people see as a static situation. They believe that the "open Convention" move has stalled but also that some break, somewhere, could still change things. Kennedy speaks with a full voice, but he refrains from shouting. "Even though we may differ in the next few days," he says, "we're going to be together in the fall against Ronald Reagan." Kennedy says that "the economy is the issue," and says, "You and I listened the other night to the Republican candidate for President of the United States. . . . He was talking about prosperity. He was talking about jobs. He was talking about putting people back to work and giving them new hope. That's the speech a Democrat ought to be making, not a Republican. We will not surrender the economic issue." He says, "The most important social program in this country is a sound economy." He says that the delegates supporting him "are not bound in any way, other than by their conscience," and about half the people in the room jump up and cheer. He says, "If by any poooor judgment of the Convention they provide a closed rule . . . I want them to vote their conscience on the great issues of the platform and then on the nomination, and I'm still very confident that, voting on their conscience, we'll gain the nomination and go on." And then he is drowned out by cheers.

What he has just said doesn't follow, of course. Kennedy is giving it a last try, however futile that may be, but he is also edging his way out, saying that, whatever happens, he will be a good Democrat. Every Convention has some question that comes to dominate it—some "Will he?" For years, the "Will he?" of Democratic politics was "Will Kennedy accept the nomination?" Would he agree to a nomination that was presumed to be his for the asking? Now the "Will he?" is "Will he go on the podium and accept defeat?" Of course he will. He can't not.

Kennedy is followed, after a while, by Strauss. It's entertaining to listen to Strauss talking righteously about the need to protect the Party from the brokers. Strauss used to consider the reformers a bunch of troublemakers. In 1976, before Carter's nomination became inevitable, Strauss, then the Party chairman, used to tell people with great relish that the Convention would probably deadlock and then he would gather a group of people in a room—he even named some of the people who would be there—and settle the matter of the nomination.

Now Strauss, talking to the Pennsylvania delegates, is the honeyed voice of reason. "There are people going to be looking in on television, my friends, and they're going to be saying, 'Can we trust the Democratic Party?'" He continues, "I say to you that one of the things they're going to grade it on is: Have you kept faith with the contract that the men and women who placed their confidence in you and elected you on, for one primary purpose—to cast their vote for the Presidential nominee they prefer." He tells them, "I don't happen to like the damn rules, if you really want to know what I think about them, but we told the people these are the rules we follow, and as far as I'm concerned they're a solemn agreement with the people who elected you." He concludes by appealing to them as Democrats. "Whatever happens in this Convention, let's remember we're in a tough game. . . . Let's leave here and make up our mind that there's nothing in the world that will unite a bunch of Democrats like Ronald Reagan."

Late Monday afternoon. The debate on the rule is scheduled to begin at six-thirty, and the vote will be taken an hour later. Just off the Convention floor, Robert Torricelli, who used to be on the Vice President's staff and who worked on Illinois for the Carter-Mondale campaign, looks worried. "It's still not one of our stronger states," he says. This is the time for the delegates to play out their acts of uncertainty—thus getting attention and who knows what else, and driving both sides crazy. Mayor Byrne has flown into town to work for votes against the rule. Her interest in the matter has energized Thomas Hynes, the Cook County assessor, who broke with Mayor Byrne and the organization and backed Carter in the primary, to help the Carter forces, because he, like some others, does not want the Mayor to get credit for helping to "open" the Convention. Jerry Cosentino professes not to have made up his mind yet; it was arranged that he would meet privately with Kennedy this morning when Kennedy addressed the delegation. The Carter people have given him floor passes, and tickets to a fund raiser, and offered him a spot on the podium.

Richard Newhouse, a black state senator from the South Side of Chicago, is also saying that he is still undecided. Newhouse wants more relief for the Wisconsin Steel Company, in Chicago, which has laid off about thirty-five hundred workers. He is also complaining about what he says is his lack of access to high-level officials. This afternoon, Newhouse told a Carter official that he might use the rule vote to protest the national economic situation. Now a Kennedy whip tells me that Mayor Officer, of East St. Louis, has told the Kennedy people that he might vote with them.

The Carter people are still worried about the loss of a substantial number of votes from the Chicago area. Intrastate rivalries have been brought to the Convention, where competitors are vying for larger roles. Roland Burris, the state comptroller and the only statewide elected black official, is in a rivalry here with Cosentino, because both men are seeking higher office. Burris, too, has been offered a spot on the program. (Burris has also asked that Mrs. Carter attend a Goodwill Industries dinner in Chicago in early September, at which he will be named Man of the Year.) Also, in an attempt to please various factions, the Carter people divided the chairmanship of the delegation among four people (two men and two women), one for each night. Cosentino and Burris were the two men. Cosentino wanted to be the sole chairman and was put out. The Carter people think Cosentino can affect up to thirteen votes here. Now, on the Convention floor, William Green, the mayor of Philadelphia, who is a Kennedy supporter and the chairman of the Pennsylvania delegation (the Carter people tried to prevent his becoming chairman, despite the fact that Kennedy won the primary), says, "My guess is that if there is a lot of movement in other states there will be a lot of movement here. It'll balloon if things happen in Illinois; otherwise, there will be a modest number of defections from Carter." Dan Horgan says, "I don't think we've got more than five who might split with us."

At the Illinois delegation, toward the back of the hall, it is chaotic. Philip Klutznick, the Secretary of Commerce, who is from Chicago, is here, working the delegates. Edward Quigley, a ward committeeman from the West Side of Chicago and a Kennedy delegate, has a message to call Mayor Byrne on the Kennedy phone at the Illinois delegation, but he can't get the phone to work. He tells me, "I'm a ward committeeman, and I got six delegates." Paul Simon, a congressman from southern Illinois and the leader of the Kennedy forces in the state, is predicting that his side may pick up thirty votes on the rule.

Patricia Driscoll, a Carter delegate, says, "Cutthroat politics is what it's all about." She points in the direction of Donna Matteo, and says, "Ask her."

Miss Matteo, a young woman in a peach dress, is a Carter delegate from

Chicago. She says that the Byrne people offered her a job in an unspecified city department. She tells me that the offer was made today, "by a close personal friend of mine," and that she refused.

Now Quigley pulls Cosentino, a stumpy, broad-faced man, aside for a chat.

I was told earlier that Anthony Scariano, a former state legislator and a Carter delegate, was opposed to the rule because he had always been against the principle of loyalty oaths and for the principle of open meetings. A number of other Carter delegates, Congressman Russo, and Vice President Mondale have all called him, to no avail. "I have very strong feelings about Conventions," Scariano tells me now. "Delegates should not be locked in on a loyalty basis. Phil Klutznick was just here lobbying me, in a very nice way. I told the Vice President last week, 'Why have a Convention if the delegates are locked up? They don't bind the Electoral College in most states; why bind delegates to a National Convention?' " Then, having spelled out his reasons of principle, Scariano adds, "I'll vote for Carter. But if we had a stronger, more attractive candidate on the scene, I would switch. That's something Carter doesn't understand—that a lot of people are for Carter not because they love Carter so much but because they love Kennedy less."

Then, I ask Scariano, if the Convention were "open," would he go for another candidate?

"I certainly would," he replies. "Morris Udall or Mondale, or perhaps even Muskie. I want to keep that option open. Why shouldn't I extend it to everybody else?"

I ask him if the Carter people have given up on him and are leaving him alone.

He replies, "Oh, my God, no."

Now Eugene Eidenberg, a tall, partly bald forty-year-old man with a mustache, talks to Cosentino. "You O.K. on the rule?"

Cosentino replies, "Yes."

Eidenberg asks, "What did you tell your people?"

Cosentino replies, "I told them that they were all on their own, and that I have some principles about me, and that I told the President I would vote for the rule. But don't bother me anymore." To me, he says, "What they put me through for three weeks!" Eidenberg is not satisfied with Cosentino's reply, and moves to assure Cosentino's friends here that Cosentino is being paid attention.

Now Eidenberg goes to have a chat with Sue Morris, a Carter delegate and the wife of the mayor of Waukegan. She had told Carter campaign officials that she didn't think Carter was doing enough about the economy, and that she would not vote with them on the rule until she was convinced that Carter would do more. The Vice President called her but was apparently unable to persuade her.

Another uncertainty is Vince Demuzio, a state senator from the Springfield area, who is upset that there is not more in the platform about the disposal of toxic wastes. It has been worked out by the Kennedy forces that if Demuzio votes for the "open Convention" Kennedy will give a speech on the Senate floor on the subject of toxic wastes. That's what Kennedy has to offer. At the state's caucus this morning, Stuart Eizenstat, the President's chief adviser for domestic policy, promised Demuzio a letter setting forth the President's policy on the subject, and Demuzio has also met with three White House officials who deal with the toxic-wastes question, and a member of the Carter-Mondale campaign staff indicated to Demuzio that the Administration would work for new legislation on the subject.

Now a group of black delegates from various states, with Richard Newhouse as one of the leaders, has gone to talk to Jordan and Strauss, in a Carter trailer, to demand a session with them tonight or tomorrow; its agenda is jobs, Justice Department action against the Ku Klux Klan, and access to high-level Administration officials. They are promised a meeting tomorrow.

Outside the Carter trailers, Tom Donilon, who is twenty-four years old and is in charge of keeping track of the delegate count for the Carter-Mondale campaign, is in shirt-sleeves, and looks worried. He sends Richard Moe, the Vice President's chief of staff, on a mission to Maine. The Carter people got word that Governor Brennan was starting a Muskie movement in the state delegation. Jordan has got the President to phone Muskie, who is vacationing in Maine, to have him phone the Maine delegation and tell them to call the thing off. Strauss himself told some Maine delegates that if they went against the President on the rule they would embarrass Muskie. It's hot and crowded back by the trailers. The whole Convention is overcrowded, in fact. The number of delegates has doubled since 1960: as the reforms broadened participation and required more representation of minority groups and women, rather than throw anyone out the Party just grew.

Inside the Convention hall, Edward Bennett Williams is addressing the delegates. "Can it be that in the name of reform we are suspending freedom?" he says. But few are listening. An argument over Party principle is in reality a bareknuckled Carter-Kennedy fight. On the floor, one of the congressmen behind the "open Convention" move is depressed. "The Kennedy people would rather go down in flames," he says. "He should have withdrawn. People have been talking to people very close to Muskie, and I think he would have made a move if we could have got this Convention open." Communication about matters such as these is usually indirect and obscure: people deal in codes and signals and grunts; people tell people what they want to hear. The congressman continues, "We pushed all the buttons we could in the last few days; we tried to get all sorts of people to announce their candidacies in order to stop Carter."

Off the floor, Paul Kirk has come out of the Kennedy headquarters, a corner room adjacent to the Carter trailers, and announced—obviously trying to influence what is happening on the floor—"We had a big victory yesterday with the platform, and today the momentum carried over to the caucuses. There'll be a big surprise here in New York, just as there was in March." (That was when Kennedy won the New York primary.)

As the debate over the rule proceeds, the hall grows more emotional—but not very emotional, given what is at stake. This will be, in effect, the balloting on the nomination. But there is a kind of limpness here. Dianne Feinstein, the mayor of San Francisco, speaking from the podium, and speaking forcefully, says, "We don't change the rules after the game has been played." She refers to the fact that people argue that the polls are bad, and therefore someone who won twenty-four out of thirty-four of the primaries should be denied the nomination. Conditions change every minute, she says. "You could change candidates every month."

Through it all, P. J. Cullerton, an elderly man, sits quietly. He is a Chicago ward committeeman and a Kennedy delegate. His arms are resting on a gold-handled cane, and he is wearing diamond cufflinks and a Piaget watch bordered with diamonds. He tells me he has been to every Convention since 1932. He was around when Richard Daley, the late mayor of Chicago, was in a position to throw a delegation to one candidate or another. "I'm for the 'open Convention,' " Mr. Cullerton tells me. "I like to have a little flexibility at Conventions."

Carter officials are all over the floor. I run into Reubin Askew, the former governor of Florida, who is now the President's Special Trade Representative. He tells me that he is on the way to the Florida delegation. "Just going there to hold some hands," he says. Landon Butler, who is in charge of White House liaison with labor groups, is talking to labor delegates. At Illinois, Chip Carter, the President's son, has been by to have a chat with Marjorie Winkelhake, a Carter delegate from Urbana, who opposes the rule on principle.

Several aides to Mayor Byrne—one an administrative assistant and another her patronage chief—turn up and stroll around amid the delegation. Richard Newhouse returns, and a number of people ask him how he is going to vote. He tells them, "I'm not saying anything." Then he tells Eidenberg, "I have it under advisement."

Thomas O'Neill—lieutenant governor of Massachusetts, a Kennedy man, and the son of the Speaker of the House—is hovering around the Illinois delegation. O'Neill has been working for the past few days trying to pry Illinois loose. He shakes his head and says to me, "What motivates the political mind sometimes escapes me." He says, "Every time we get someone on the philosophical value of the thing—openness connotes a nice thing—the Carter Cabinet descends."

Eidenberg asks Jesse Jackson, who has happened along, to talk to Richard Newhouse. This is the kind of thing the Carter people know how to do: they fan out their troops and use all the resources at their command, and they work relentlessly. They have spotted problems quickly and dealt with them quickly. It is the same thing that they did all through the primaries.

But they don't seem to know how to apply the same methodicalness and clarity of purpose to governing.

The balloting begins. The delegates' votes are marked on yellow sheets, which are then collected by the state whips. California passes. A mob forms around Richard Newhouse. He votes for the Carter position. Illinois passes; the tally is not complete. Eventually, it is, and the vote is a hundred and fifty-three for the rule binding the delegates and twenty-six against; the Kennedy forces picked up only ten votes. Five Carter supporters from Chicago defected; Sue Morris, Marjorie Winkelhake, and Anthony Scariano also voted against Carter. Vince Demuzio stuck with Carter. The Illinois vote cannot be announced until all the states have been called. Most of the states' votes are exact or very nearly exact reflections of Carter's and Kennedy's delegate strength. Kennedy picks up a few votes here and there, but there are no big breakthroughs. Before the end of the roll call, it is clear that it's all over.

The casting of the final ballots is just a formality. Kennedy picked up only eight votes in Pennsylvania. The vote to "open" the Convention is thirteen hundred and ninety to nineteen hundred and thirty-six. After all that, Kennedy and the "open Convention" forces picked up only about fifty Carter votes. The Kennedy people on the Convention floor, realizing what has happened, shout, "No, no, no!" But not very emotionally, and not for long. Neither side seems very emotional tonight.

Outside the Carter trailers, Jody Powell, who looks unaccustomedly relaxed, says the President called up a little while ago and spoke only to Tom Donilon, the delegate counter. Powell is asked about the black delegates who came back for a talk earlier this evening. He replies, "We were doing what I assume the other side was doing. If there were delegates who still had questions or were wavering, we brought them back for a chat."

Donilon appears. Now he is wearing a jacket; his babyish Irish face has the pallor of someone whose life for many months has consisted of computers and telephones. He is asked what the President said. Donilon replies, "He asked me if he could take Rosalynn off the phones to the delegates."

At about ten o'clock, Kennedy appears on television to comment on the vote. (In the Convention hall, a boring film about the writing of the platform is being shown, and none of the networks have it on.) First we see the Kennedy family, and Kennedy's close friend John Douglas, a Washington attorney who served in the Justice Department with Robert Kennedy. Kennedy's sisters campaigned for him enthusiastically, as they did for their other brothers; this year must have been a baffling one for them. This is the end for Kennedy—an end that has been postponed, or prolonged. The focus by this time is so much on how long he stayed in, whether one admired or disapproved of his tenacity, that it has almost been forgotten with what expectations the whole thing began.

Now Kennedy appears, looking solemn, grim. He essays a little joke.

"I'm deeply gratified by the support I received on the rules fight tonight—but not quite as gratified as President Carter." He continues, "I'm a realist and I know what this result means. I have called President Carter and congratulated him. The effort on the nomination is over. My name will not be placed in nomination." Then, for the first time in a long, punishing campaign, a campaign that delivered him more blows than most people can take, his disappointment shows. He has difficulty composing himself: he is clearly fighting to keep his face in control, and his voice trembles slightly. He says, "I continue to care deeply about the ideals of the Democratic Party. I continue to care deeply about where this party stands, and I hope the delegates will stand with me for a truly Democratic platform. Tomorrow, I will speak to the Convention about the economic concerns that have been the heart of my campaign."

The time has come to end the campaign, and Kennedy knows it, but he still doesn't let go of Carter. The Carter people had hoped to effectively end the contest with Kennedy tonight, so as to get on with putting the Party together, and to make Reagan the opponent for the rest of the week, but few thought that he would withdraw. On the Convention floor, the delegates are largely unaware of what has just happened.

Tuesday. Late morning. Robert Strauss, sitting in his suite on the forty-ninth floor of the Sheraton Centre (formerly the Americana), the Carter headquarters, looks tired. He has just met with Jordan and Moe. "We're trying to work on the platform thing," he tells me. "I have a call in to Senator Kennedy, and I'm waiting to hear from him. Hamilton has a call in to Kirk, and he's waiting to hear from him. We have a very simple problem and a very difficult one. There are certain political things a President can give on and ones he can't. He can't accept a twelve-billion-dollar jobs program. What I'm trying to work out is how do we work out these differences politically—to say that there are differences between us but they pale when you put our positions alongside Ronald Reagan's. I don't think people want to see an arrogant President who refuses to deal politically or one who caves. We're going on the floor tonight with a lot of people with political constituencies who find it very difficult to reject some of the Kennedy planks—and they're adroitly drawn, to make it difficult to reject them. I've been meeting with some mayors and some black leaders to see if we can submit some language Senator Kennedy can live with. The problem is, if I were him I'd want to go through with a real tough speech and have a roll-call vote, to validate my candidacy from last November to now. If I were advising him, I would advise him to do that."

The Carter people have come up with a draft statement saying there may be differences between Carter and Kennedy on how to provide more jobs but they agree on the goal. What is going on now is a replay, on a larger stage, of the fight that Carter and Kennedy carried on at the midterm Party Conference, in Memphis, almost two years ago—a fight over the constituency of the Party. The Carter people insisted then, as they insist now, that the interest groups assembled were not and are not reflective of the Party as a whole, to say nothing of the country. Carter's problem now is that he may have been able to hold labor unions on the question of the nomination but he will not be able to hold them on an issue that is put in terms of jobs. Whether Kennedy's proposal is the solution to the unemployment problem —and honest people differ over that—is irrelevant at the moment. This is a political fight, revolving around symbols more than substance.

Now Strauss says to me, "I want the right noise and the right music to come out of here. We handled last night well. We were able to identify problems almost within the hour and deal with them. I called a man in Wyoming for a half-vote while the roll call was going on. I called him when they were three states before Wyoming. We were working to make it as neat as possible. If you have a little tiny run in your stocking, it's not a big problem. If you have a big run, it's a big problem. It's best if you have no run at all. Our instincts after the vote were to make a very brief statement. That was a good decision—not to get up in those anchor booths and gloat. We're cautioning our people not to sound anti-Kennedy tonight. We're telling them that what happens in that hall is what the people in the anchor booths think happened, and the other side is going to structure a squabble as best they can. The same people in the media who were working Kennedy over last week will have lumps in their throats tonight. The American people will hear lumps tonight. I want tonight to be as mild and sweet as it can be. I've told our people, and I believe, this will not be a good night. This will be a Kennedy night. I'm a realist. Tonight will belong to Kennedy. It'll be 'the gallant fight' tonight. Our victory will come on Thursday night. Those are the political realities as you figure out how to get from here to November 4th."

Tonight, the Convention floor is decked out with blue-and-white Kennedy posters and blue balloons. Strauss was right. This is to be Kennedy's night. In a sense, Kennedy and the President aren't arguing over very much, and, in a sense, they are arguing over a great deal. Given the spectrum of American politics, the details of what each of them is proposing are not very far apart. But their approaches to government, their political viscera, are very different indeed. And the substantive differences between the two men have become exaggerated by the situation they're in. Kennedy's politics had been more liberal than Carter's, but Kennedy got into the race essentially because he didn't think much of Carter's leadership and also because Carter was very low in the polls. That Kennedy hadn't figured out a rationale for his candidacy which he could explain to the public was what got him started off so badly and was one of the factors that doomed his candidacy. It took him a while to find how to explain what he meant by "leadership." His search for a rationale led him to give the speech at Georgetown University, in late January, in which he staked out policy differences with Carter. It often happens in campaigns that the candidates search for differences, or create them, and, having found them, exaggerate them; they have to have something to talk about, after all. But Kennedy and Carter are very different kinds of men, out of different cultures and political traditions, and that, more than programmatic details, defines the differences between them.

On the way into the Convention hall tonight, I encountered a young woman who has worked for the Kennedys for many years and who worked on this year's campaign. "At least he's alive—that's the big thing," she said.

Once again Administration officials have fanned out across the Convention floor. At the Pennsylvania delegation, Stuart Eizenstat, looking worried, as he usually does, is talking earnestly, which is how he usually talks, to K. Leroy Irvis, a black, who is a Carter delegate and the minority leader of the Pennsylvania House of Representatives. Irvis points to a paper that has been circulated containing what is termed "compromise economic language" on the economic plank. It talks of how much concern the Democratic Party has shown for jobs over the years, mentions programs already under way and the one that the President is to offer soon, and says, "The Democratic Party is prepared to offer economic solutions which are equitable, which are realistic and significant, which will reduce unemployment while we also continue to fight against inflation." Irvis says to Eizenstat, "If you want my support, I want stronger language than what I see here. Don't waste my time. I don't like the specific twelve-billion-dollar figure, but I don't like this Pablum."

Eizenstat says that Jesse Jackson endorses the language, and that "we've worked with Lane Kirkland."

Behind them, a Kennedy floor whip is frantically shouting, "Lane Kirkland has not agreed to this compromise!"

In fact, Kirkland, the president of the A.F.L.–C.I.O., has unleashed his troops to work for the Kennedy minority report. Kirkland is dubious about the economic program the Administration keeps promising that it will offer, and he wants labor to put on a show of strength here. He still hopes to extract from the Administration a program substantial enough to offer some hope, and to fire up labor to work for Carter this fall. "We can go only so far with an anti-Reagan campaign," Kirkland has said to me. "That's a lousy way to campaign. Carter's got to have something to offer to working people."

Labor, obviously for bargaining purposes, has put forward a twenty-five-billion-dollar economic program. In recent weeks, Kirkland tried to mediate between Kennedy and Carter, to see if some agreement on an economic program could be worked out, perhaps in a way that would allow Kennedy to get some of the credit and then step aside—something like the "compact of Fifth Avenue" that Richard Nixon and Nelson Rockefeller reached just before the 1960 Republican Convention. Kirkland believed both sides to be interested. But political realities kept the thing from coming to pass. The

Kennedy people's position, which they outlined both to Kirkland and to Carter's representatives, was that they were interested in more than simply platform language—they wanted to see a program. And though the White House said that it was willing to compromise, it seemed more interested in striking a deal with labor which would have had labor campaigning for the Carter approach rather than acting as a mediator. A couple of weeks ago, the President dined privately with Kirkland. A White House aide said to me, "We're working on an economic plank that labor will sign on to and Kirkland will agree to. If we succeed in doing that, it will have the effect of isolating Kennedy."

But the Carter side had decided not to try to come up with an economic program yet. And the Kennedy people got a new burst of hope from the Billy Carter problem and the move for an "open Convention." Besides, the Kennedy people wanted to save something to fight about at the Convention, and knew that the jobs plank was their strongest weapon.

This afternoon, Ray Marshall, the Secretary of Labor, read to Kirkland the "compromise" language that is being circulated tonight, and Kirkland found it more forthcoming than the Administration's previous offerings, but by that time his people were going all out for the Kennedy jobs proposal, and were taking the opportunity to show that, by God, there was a labor presence at the Convention that had nothing to do with Carter or Kennedy. Kirkland told the Administration that he would not reverse field unless the Kennedy people were willing to do so. The Kennedy people had no interest in compromising, and from the looks of things tonight they do not need to. This morning, Paul Kirk told Richard Moe that the Kennedy side was going ahead with its twelve-billion-dollar jobs plank and if the Carter people wanted to come along, fine. The "compromise" is being offered in the name of some blacks who back Carter. Bill Clinton, the governor of Arkansas and a Carter supporter, has urged the Carter people to accept the Kennedy plank—in light of Kennedy's withdrawal, of the likelihood that Kennedy will give an emotional speech tonight, and of labor's support for the plank. He told them that the President could still demur slightly in his statement on the platform.

This afternoon, there was a roll-call vote on another Kennedy proposal —one saying that a jobs policy "is our single highest domestic priority." It carried by three hundred and seventy votes. Pennsylvania, with its ninety-four Kennedy delegates and ninety-one Carter delegates, voted for it a hundred and fifty-six to twenty-nine. A Carter whip says to me tonight, "This one's going to be worse." Not only is labor working hard for the Kennedy jobs proposal, but Pennsylvania, Illinois, Michigan, and Ohio have been hit especially hard by the current recession. Carter floor whips have told Jordan, Strauss, and Donilon that the Administration can't win this fight and shouldn't try to. A good number of the whips are labor representatives, and have refused to help the Administration on this one. The N.E.A., Carter's most loyal union, has released its members to vote as they wish. Shortly after seven, Strauss and Jordan called the Carter floor leaders and state whips off the floor and gave them a pep talk. They said that they were not going to abandon the Administration's economic policy or trade away the platform, even though they might lose. Strauss told them, in effect, "I know it's hell out there, and it's going to be a bad night for us, but the next two nights will be good. If this plank carries, the President will disavow it tomorrow night, so we should all get behind him and try." Late this afternoon, Strauss talked to several important Pennsylvania delegates off the floor and asked them to support the President on the economic plank. They told him that they couldn't go back to their people, who were closely aligned with the labor movement (some are elected officials dependent on labor), and pressure them to reject this plank. Strauss said he was sure they'd do what they must, and thanked them.

On the podium, Neil Goldschmidt, the Secretary of Transportation, is talking about the "compromise," and saying that it is acceptable to the President. He is booed. Now the Carter whips are handing out another paper, containing a brief outline of the Carter Administration's objections to the Kennedy proposal and saying that a vote against it will be a vote for the "compromise." Goldschmidt is saying, "We are not here to apologize . . . not to excuse mistakes—for some have been made." Ray Marshall and Charles Schultze, the chairman of the Council of Economic Advisers, are lobbying the Michigan delegation. William Miller, the Secretary of the Treasury, is working the floor. Even Alonzo McDonald, the White House staff director, who is more familiar with business-management techniques than with politics, is roaming the floor. The Convention floor is a hot mass of rumors, people, noise. The Kennedy people and the labor people are spoiling for a fight against the Administration, rebelling against the Carter style of government. It is too cool, too moderate, too bloodless for these people.

This is the sweaty heart of the Democratic Party. Carter is remote from it, unable, for various reasons, to identify with the style and substance of the traditional Party, and the Party people smell that in him. He is a Southern politician who never had to fight the Republican Party or identify with the ethnic groups, and he can't persuade these people that in his bones he is one of them. Kennedy, with his jobs proposal, is trying to show Carter, as he did in Memphis, who really owns the Democratic Party. Carter may have whipped Kennedy in the primaries, as he said he would, but Kennedy wants to whip him now. Now Andrew Young, speaking on behalf of the Administration, is telling the Convention, "I remember people looking at the Voting Rights Act and saying, 'It isn't enough.' " At the Ohio delegation, Martin Hughes, the delegation chairman and an international vice-president of the Communications Workers of America, is telling Tim Hagan, the chairman of the Cuyahoga County Democratic Party and the head of the Kennedy forces in Ohio, that he has asked his people to identify all the labor votes in Ohio, and he says that he thinks he can get at least twenty-four Carter delegates to join with the seventy-seven Kennedy delegates on this vote.

Barbara Mikulski, the tiny congresswoman from the streets of Baltimore, introduces Kennedy. She was to have nominated him tomorrow night, but this will have to suffice. There are screams, shouts, cheers as Miss Mikulski finishes her introduction and, with the band playing "MacNamara's Band," Kennedy comes onto the podium. It is the first real emotion of the convention. He nods in acknowledgment of the cheers—no big gestures now— and finally begins to speak. He starts out joking that "things worked out a little different from the way I thought," and then goes into his speech. "My fellow Democrats and my fellow Americans: I have come here tonight not to argue for a candidacy but to affirm a cause." His tone is somber, and the audience listens attentively. In fact, I cannot remember a Convention floor being so still. "I am asking you to renew the commitment of the Democratic Party to economic justice." He speaks slowly, firmly—does not shout, as he often did during the primaries. "This is the cause that brought me into the campaign and that sustained me for nine months, across a hundred thousand miles, in forty different states," he says. (He is identifying his campaign and also pointing out, subtly, that Carter stayed in the White House.) "We had our losses, but the pain of our defeats is far, far less than the pain of the people I have met. We have learned that it is important to take issues seriously but never to take ourselves too seriously."

Kennedy's unusual resilience, his actual disinclination to take himself too seriously—his capacity for recognizing the ridiculousness of various situations—are a large part of what kept him going. Now, in a number of ways, he reminds the audience of what he says is the historic cause of the Democratic Party, the commitment that has "defined our values, refined our policies, and refreshed our faith"—the commitment to "the common man." He says that it is not just an economic but "also a moral issue that I raise tonight." He recites the principles behind his economic proposals—that unemployment should not be used to fight inflation, that employment will be the first priority—and says that these "have been the soul of our party across the generations." Kennedy has been talking about these things for months now—saying, as he says tonight, that he believes in "the ideals of the Democratic Party" and in the potential for a President "to make a difference"—but never so well as now.

Kennedy has always been one of the Party's most commanding speakers, but, as was widely known, he can also stumble around and talk in semi-coherent half-sentences—and did at the outset of the campaign. Then he seemed to lose confidence in his speaking ability. Many of his formal speeches were stiff, and to the end he could not control the shouting, though he knew it was a problem. He also gave some bell ringers—but these were not news, and the country rarely saw them. The news was when he stumbled or shouted. Perhaps it didn't matter; perhaps it was always the case that his personal life was too flawed for the country to accept him. We shall never know, because there were so many elements in his defeat. Perhaps, as the Carter people insist, his politics were wrong even for the Democratic

Party; but that is not clear, especially tonight. Now he is taking this one last opportunity to show 'em—show 'em he can speak, show 'em who can seize the Democratic Party and bring it to life—and to throw the issues in Carter's face one more time. But he does not dwell on Carter; the challenge is implicit.

As Kennedy settles into his speech, his delivery gets stronger; a speaker knows when he has a hold on his audience, and grows more confident. He takes on Reagan. He quotes some Reagan statements, and says that "that nominee is no friend of" labor, the cities, the senior citizens, the environment, and so on. He quotes Reagan as saying, "Fascism was really the basis of the New Deal," and says with great indignation, "And that nominee, whose name is Ronald Reagan, has no right to quote Franklin Delano Roosevelt."

The audience roars its approval. Kennedy is even setting the style for campaigning against Reagan. Then he defines his liberalism—something he had not seemed to do all year. "The commitment I seek is not to outworn views but to old values that will never wear out. Programs may sometimes become obsolete, but the ideal of fairness always endures. . . . It is surely correct that we cannot solve problems by throwing money at them, but it is also correct that we dare not throw our national problems onto a scrap heap of inattention and indifference. The poor may be out of political fashion, but they are not without human needs. The middle class may be angry, but they have not lost the dream that all Americans can advance together." He has touched on the core of the Democratic Party's problem—a problem of definition. He skirts some of the hard questions—the questions imposed by limits, by resource constraints, by the growing anger at what are seen to be the failures of government, and by the fright and frustration of the middle class. But he does suggest that a number of politicians these days are confusing what is fashionable with what is right; he is reaching in there and reclaiming the moral base and the heritage of the Democratic Party. He is reminding these people what they are supposed to stand for. Bell ringers may not answer hard questions, may not deal in studied analysis, but they can move people, and the ability to move people is the beginning point of leadership. Tonight, he does not mention wage and price controls, which he advocated in his Georgetown speech, and which are included in one of the platform amendments that will be voted on after his speech, and he does not mention gasoline rationing, which he also advocated at Georgetown and then dropped, because his advisers thought he was advocating too much "big government." He does talk about tax reform, an idea that Carter used to advocate but has dropped. But the focus is on providing jobs, an unexceptionable goal. "There were some who said we should be silent about our differences on issues during this Convention," he says. "But the heritage of the Democratic Party has been a history of democracy. We fight hard because we care deeply about our principles and purposes." He is reminding them that not everything can be glossed over.

Kennedy's speech, while it is well written, contains more than a little soaring rhetoric, melodrama, and sentimentality, and it works. He has created and defined this moment. He is ringing emotional chimes that the audience seems to want to hear. It is like listening to a great aria for its own sake, even though one knows what is to happen next. Kennedy has absolutely taken over this hall. Perhaps if he were still a candidate the audience would not be so receptive, but we shall never know. It is clear that this will be seen as one of the memorable moments of any Convention. This must be giving him satisfaction; he knows that Carter cannot do this.

This speech must be paining Carter, and Mondale. Kennedy summons up scenes from his campaign—recalls Leonard Trachta, the Iowa farmer who did not know whether he would be able to pass on his farm to his children, and who became a staple of Kennedy's Iowa campaign, and the elderly woman in Oakland, during Kennedy's campaign for the final round of primaries, who told him she could not afford a telephone. He congratulates Carter on his victory, quickly, and says that he is confident the Democratic Party will reunite. And then, in a dramatic finale, he evokes the memory of his brothers, quoting lines from Tennyson that they quoted ("I am a part of all that I have met"), and closing with a line that calls up twenty years of memories: "For all those whose cares have been our concern, the work goes on, the cause endures, the hope still lives, and the dream shall never die."

The applause goes on and on. Kennedy comes back to the podium to acknowledge it a few times, waves briefly to the crowd, and is gone. The cheers of "We want Ted!" continue. Tip O'Neill—whose heart must be with what Kennedy has just said—cannot bring the Convention to order. So he stops trying, and lets them get it out of their systems. On the floor, William Green tells me he estimates that Pennsylvania will now support Kennedy's economic plank a hundred and eighty-five to nothing. Just before Kennedy spoke, the Carter whips in Pennsylvania took a quick vote and found that they had five votes out of the hundred and eighty-five delegates. An aide to Mayor Richard Caliguiri, of Pittsburgh, who is a Carter supporter, went off the floor and suggested to Hamilton Jordan that the Carter delegates be released on the economic plank. "We're going to kill the five we're sitting on," he said. Jordan said that the Carter campaign's position was no but that they should do what they wanted. The aide returned to the floor and told the delegates they were free. There is a report that Minnesota, Mondale's state, will overwhelmingly support Kennedy.

O'Neill and Kennedy people and Carter people on the podium are on telephones. It is clear that negotiations are taking place. After the demonstration has gone on for about thirty-five minutes, O'Neill finally gavels the Convention to order and calls for voice votes; a last-minute decision has been made, given the emotion on the floor, given the drubbing the Administration would take, to skip the roll call on Kennedy's economic proposal. The ayes for the plank drown out the noes, and O'Neill says, in his big voice, "In the opinion of the chair, the ayes have it." He swiftly and firmly moves through the vote on three other proposals, and—in clear contradiction of the sound in the hall—rules that the noes have it on the Kennedy proposal for wage and price controls. It is obvious that a deal has been struck and the Administration has decided to cut its losses.

Wednesday. Tonight, the Convention hall is decked out with green-and-white Carter posters and green balloons. But the attention is still on Kennedy. The big question is how Kennedy will react to Carter's reaction—required in writing before the nomination tonight—to the platform. Kennedy, in his headquarters at the Waldorf, is still in command of events. Carter arrived here this morning (his arrival at Newark Airport was taken, as it was probably intended, as a slap at Carey), and all day there have been meetings of Administration officials and meetings and calls between Administration officials and A.F.L.–C.I.O. officials (including Kirkland and Douglas Fraser), and Hamilton Jordan has been shuttling between the Sheraton Centre and the Waldorf, where he discussed with Kirk the President's possible reaction. Kennedy still has a lock on Carter, because he has not yet endorsed him, and the "Will he?" about his appearance on the podium endures; Kennedy demonstrated convincingly last night that he will have a great deal to do with how much enthusiasm the delegates have for Carter when they leave New York. Once again he has maneuvered Carter into a situation where Carter is caught between the demands of the Democratic constituent groups and what he deems to be the mood of the electorate at large. One of the last meetings between Administration and labor officials was in the hotel room of Kenneth Young, Kirkland's executive assistant, on the eighteenth floor of the Sheraton Centre. There is to be a meeting of the A.F.L.–C.I.O. Executive Council next week, and Kirkland needs to have enough to offer so that the Council will endorse Carter.

Some of Carter's advisers suggested today that Carter essentially accept the Kennedy plank, but there were two sticking points: the twelve-billion-dollar figure and, more important, the strong disinclination to appear to be giving in to Kennedy. One of Carter's advisers said to me today, "We have a problem here. We don't have the ideological control over the delegates we had in '76. This time, we were the incumbents, and we had to turn to the Party regulars—elected officials, labor—and they have their own agenda."

This Convention is beginning to get on people's nerves. It's too hot out, the streets are too jammed, and Madison Square Garden is too difficult to navigate. The multitudinous guards seem to take pleasure in directing you from one spot to another by the longest possible route. It has sometimes seemed that one got from the Statler, the Convention headquarters, to the Garden, across the street, via New Jersey. And inside the hall there are too many boring speeches. Slots on the podium have become a form of patronage. Tonight, Roland Burris gets his moment: he introduces John Y. Brown, the former president of the Kentucky Fried Chicken Corporation and present governor of Kentucky, who shouts on about nothing in particular. (Jerry Cosentino, apparently annoyed that Burris has been given a spot on the program, has now refused to speak.)

The only speaker who has anything interesting to say tonight is Jerry Brown. Brown's unconventional style did not go over well this year, and he folded his campaign after the Wisconsin primary, in April. Brown, as might have been expected, did not have staying power. He came across as too exotic, too cold, a bit contemptuous of people, a soloist. He seems even more of a loner than Carter. Now the press reports are that Brown is going to try out a new style: the conventional politician, the party man. As a first step, he will campaign for the Carter-Mondale ticket. Brown begins tonight by praising Kennedy "not only for his moving speech last night but also for a long career dedicated to the cause which binds us all together," and he quotes Franklin Roosevelt. Roosevelt is getting quite a workout this summer.

Brown attacks Reagan, which is apparently to be his role in the campaign. And then he turns to some of the new, harder questions. At least Brown is interested in ideas: "How will we—as but four percent of the world's teeming population—prosper past the next four or five Democratic Conventions?" He talks about pension funds as a source of investment capital. He says that "we have not found jobs for all those that want them, because we have not adequately focussed on the work that must be done," and he spells out some suggestions. "We cannot sustain a way of life that uses one-third of the world's basic resources for but a few percent of its people," he says. Not many politicians are willing to talk this way.

The President's statement on the platform has been released, and copies of it are being circulated on the floor. After struggling all day, the Administration came up with this wording on the Kennedy jobs plank: "I accept and support the intent behind [it] and plan to pursue policies that will implement its spirit and aims." In the statement, Carter also talks about how much his Administration has already done to create jobs and about his forthcoming economic program, and he deals with the question of spending by saying, "The amounts needed to achieve our goals will necessarily depend upon economic conditions, what can be effectively applied over time, and the appropriate concurrence by Congress." Lane Kirkland has let it be known that he approves. Now, again, the wait is for Kennedy. The Carter people decided not to disavow a plank added by the Convention yesterday which called for the withholding of funds from Party candidates who did not support the Equal Rights Amendment. Despite the fact that a number of people think this a poor principle—other groups could impose similar restrictions —the Carter people decided that its political impact would not be nearly so negative that they should risk the wrath of its supporters at this Convention. Another plank adopted yesterday called for federal funding of abortion; in his statement tonight, Carter reiterates his opposition.

Just outside the Carter trailers, I ask Gerald Rafshoon what impression he is trying to create for tomorrow night. He replies at once, "Excitement." The President is still working on his acceptance speech—which he has had weeks to prepare. Rafshoon has concerned himself with the Convention program, the speakers, and the floor interviews. "We have some kids taking down everything that happens on television," he tells me. "If Tom Brokaw is talking to some Kennedy people, we get Neil Goldschmidt over there."

There is not much excitement when Bob Graham, the governor of Florida, makes the nominating speech for Carter. (Graham was selected to nominate Carter because, according to a Carter adviser, he wanted to do it, Carter badly needs Florida in order to win in November, and Graham has been very helpful to Carter for some time. Among other things, he and his political organization helped Carter win the Florida caucus test vote in October—an event that was the first public indicator that Kennedy would have no easy time of it.) When Graham finishes, the delegates cheer dutifully. In the Ohio delegation, the labor delegates, holding the green-and-white posters, pump their arms up and down as if doing calisthenics. The Kennedy delegates look disconsolate. The Carter whips, acting as cheerleaders, try to keep the cheering—"Jimmy! Jimmy!"—going. The demonstration doesn't last very long—about ten minutes—and the seconding speeches don't get much reaction.

As the balloting proceeds, Kennedy receives almost as many votes as he would have if he had remained in the contest. On the Convention floor, Bill Clinton, the governor of Arkansas, a Carter supporter, is uneasy. He tells me that he is discomfited by the number of votes for Kennedy. "We've reached out, but not far enough," he says. When, shortly after midnight, Texas puts it over the top for Carter, there is a great cheer and the band strikes up "The Eyes of Texas." This Carter victory has been a long time in coming, but still there is some excitement at its arrival. The story of Carter's renomination is a remarkable one. However they did it, they did it. But on the Convention floor only a small percentage of the delegates seem truly worked up. By the end of the balloting, Kennedy has received the votes of all but seventy-eight of the delegates originally pledged to him: the final tally is Carter twenty-one hundred and twenty-nine, Kennedy eleven hundred and forty-six.

Kennedy has issued his statement, which has been awaited all night. It seems a grudging one. It says, simply, "I congratulate President Carter on his renomination. I endorse the platform of the Democratic Party. I will support and work for the re-election of President Carter. It is imperative that we defeat Ronald Reagan in 1980. I urge all Democrats to join in that effort."

Gerald Rafshoon, being interviewed on television, says that for Jimmy Carter "that's a badge of courage, to be unpopular."

Thursday. Hard to believe, but the talk has started up again about whether Kennedy will run four years from now. Kennedy's people have let it be known that he will be on the podium tonight. One of his top aides says that it was a close call. They may have thought it was, but Kennedy had no choice. In a talk I had with the aide this afternoon, he explained the thinking that had gone on in the Kennedy camp for some time. They knew that the numbers were against Kennedy's nomination. They felt that an "open Convention" would have made it easier for them but not necessarily that they would have won under those circumstances. They recognized that the "open Convention" movement, having picked up steam, seemed to stall during the week before the Convention began. They tried to do what they could to affect the movement—among other things, Kennedy had talks with Jackson and Byrd before the Convention—but they knew that the final impetus for an "open Convention" had to come from elsewhere, and it never did. They felt that some important Party leaders or delegation leaders, or an important delegation, had to break with Carter. They knew that calls for an "open Convention" by such people as Byrd and Carey would not suffice—that there was a distinction between, on the one hand, the congressional leaders, and even the governors, and, on the other, the delegates. They thought up until the last moments that the break might come in Illinois.

The plan had been to go ahead with the nominating process even if the Kennedy forces lost the vote on the rule. But the margin of the defeat on Monday night clarified their thinking. After the roll call, Kennedy talked to John Douglas, to Paul Kirk, who was at the Garden, to some of the aides who were with him, and to one of his sisters, Jean Smith. A statement was drafted, and he withdrew. As for the decision on whether to appear on the podium, the aide said "it was a near thing." He said that Kennedy "felt a very strong obligation to the people who had worked for him in the primaries." He continued, "Unless there was movement on the issues, he couldn't go up there and act as if it were just a game and he were just an old pol. Maybe it was inevitable, but from the conversations he was having I know he had not made up his mind until last night." The big question last night, of course, was how to respond to the President's response to the platform; from the Kennedy point of view, the principal problem was that Carter did not accept the jobs plank as Kennedy intended it. Several drafts were written; one would have expressed regret at Carter's failure to endorse the plank, stressed the importance of defeating Reagan, and refrained from endorsing Carter. But there were practical considerations: the Convention was proceeding, and there was talk that some of the Kennedy delegates would walk out. For both selfless and selfish reasons, the Kennedy people did not want that to happen. They did not want to cause a rupture in the Convention, and if there was a rupture they didn't want to be held responsible for it. As the evening went on, Kennedy decided that he would disregard Carter's response to the platform and issue a simple statement endorsing the platform, mentioning the importance of defeating Reagan, and endorsing Carter.

Kennedy apparently believed for a long time, and up to the end, that Carter had not been true to Democratic principles, that the economy was in a shambles because of Carter, that Carter would be a weak foe against

Reagan—that, simply, Carter would not be nominated, because it wasn't right. The Kennedy people had thought all year that events would catch up with Carter, but they did not reckon on the cohesion of the Carter delegates. A Kennedy aide says, "Everything happened as we said it would. We won all the states we should have after New York, except Ohio, which was damn close. The economy was getting worse, and he was going down in the polls. It all caught up with Carter—except his delegates stuck."

There has been a lot of talk, inevitably, in the past couple of days about whether the Democratic Party can "reunite" after this week. Delegate after delegate is asked about this on television. But the division here is of small dimensions compared with that of 1968 or 1972. Moreover, the statements the delegates make here now don't mean very much. One Kennedy aide likened the reactions of the disappointed delegates to angry letters that one should put in the drawer for a while. Time will cool some people off, and the Carter forces are hoping that Reagan will bring others around. The problem that the Carter people are facing is not so much the division at the Convention as it is lack of enthusiasm for Carter. (John Anderson has come to town to try to pick up the support of some of the Kennedy people, which is somewhat embarrassing. Anderson seems to be floundering.) In a conversation I had with Hamilton Jordan late this afternoon, he said, "The thing people have got to remember is that next Monday morning everyone who was here will wake up and realize that no matter how unhappy they are with Jimmy Carter, the alternative is Ronald Reagan. A lot of groups, in their own self-interest, will come together and unify the Party."

After a great deal of discussion among the President's advisers, it has been decided that he will campaign with what might be termed a "semi–Rose Garden strategy." There were those who wanted him to stay in the White House for the most part, on the theory that that would make him seem more Presidential than campaigning would. Several of the President's advisers, including Jordan, essentially accept Caddell's theory that it is the challenger to the President who becomes the issue, who must explain himself—as Carter did in 1976, and as Kennedy did this year. Therefore, it was argued, the President should be left to being President, and the opponent should be left out there running around and being subjected to the scrutiny of the press. The other side argued that Carter could win re-election only if he was seen to be out there fighting for it.

Tonight, Bill Clinton, who is thirty-three, gives what is probably the most thoughtful speech delivered here all week. Clinton addresses himself to some of the hard realities, and to the question of why so many people are alienated from the political system. "They cannot be moved by the symbols and accomplishments of the Democratic Party of the past," he says. He is addressing the difficult transitional period that government is facing—Kennedy did not do that—and he does it in substantive terms. Carter is experiencing that transitional period, but he cannot explain it.

The hall has been deliberately packed tonight. Party officials want to make it as difficult as possible to move through the aisles, so as to prevent any unwelcome demonstrations.

Mondale's acceptance speech is well received. He has managed to get through the Vice Presidency without making many enemies. His political instincts are more liberal than Carter's, and he has somehow conveyed this without seeming disloyal. In his speech, he touches on the symbols of the Democratic Party and pays tribute to its leading figures, including Kennedy and Muskie. He gives his own definition of the Party: "We believe in the fundamental decency of the American people. And we believe in strong, efficient, compassionate government." He does his own version of what Hubert Humphrey, his mentor and patron, did to Goldwater at the 1964 Democratic Convention (a scene that was shown in a film tribute to Humphrey last night): he says, in a litany, various things that "most Americans believe" and adds after each, "But not Ronald Reagan." The audience enjoys it and joins in.

Mondale has a lot of Hubert Humphrey in him (the voice is different, but even the speech cadence is similar), but he is a more modern man, and also more contained. Mondale has a good sense of humor, but he is not as jolly as Humphrey was. Over the past four years, Mondale has become more comfortable addressing a large audience, more confident. In his speech, he makes fun of Reagan's proposal to cut taxes by thirty percent over three years. He, like Kennedy, throws some of Reagan's quotes back at him. He goes at Reagan hard, and somewhat excessively. He lists what he says are the accomplishments of the Administration: the number of jobs that have been added to the work force (he does acknowledge that "there are still too many Americans unemployed"); increases in spending for health care, housing aid, food stamps, education; appointments of minorities and women. He calls it a "progressive agenda" and a "good, solid, progressive record." He talks about what a complex job the Presidency is, and then taunts Reagan for having sat in Detroit "drawing up a plan to divide the Presidency and weaken its power—for convening "a Constitutional Convention in his hotel room." The Democrats plan to make use of the strange events occasioned by the possibility of a Reagan-Ford ticket.

Mondale says that real defense spending fell thirty-five percent under the Republicans. This is odd: four years ago, Carter vowed to cut defense spending. (All but seven percent of the reductions under the Republicans represent the ending of the Vietnam War; moreover, some of those cuts were imposed by the Democratic Congress.) Mondale says that in recent years Reagan has advocated the sending of troops to Ecuador, Angola, Rhodesia, Panama, Cyprus, Pakistan, North Korea, and the Middle East— the Administration has been planning to use this against Reagan for some time—and he says that the American people "want a President who's steady, who's sober, who's experienced, and who's demonstrated he knows how to keep the peace." This will be another line of attack against Reagan in the fall. He makes a strong argument for the SALT agreement, and gets big applause. He ends on an upbeat note about his pride in America. "Don't let anyone tell you we're less than we've been," he says. "And don't let anyone make us less than we can be."

Rafshoon's film, which precedes the President's speech, shows the Washington Monument, the Jefferson Memorial, and the Lincoln Memorial, with the narrator telling us, "No one who's not had the responsibility can really understand what it's like to be the President," and then we see Carter walking into his office. We are shown some of America's grandest sights, and then paintings of earlier Presidents, and the narrator tells some of the terrible things that were said about those Presidents. The film that was shown at the Convention four years ago emphasized Carter's freshness— we saw him walking in the peanut fields in bluejeans. Now we are getting the awful-burdens-of-the-Oval-Office routine. We are shown scenes of Carter, during his one day on the campaign trail, in Ohio, speaking at the black church in Cleveland. We see a number of officials and plain folks praising him; we even see Cyrus Vance, who resigned, praising him.

The film stresses the Camp David agreement between Israel and Egypt —of which we have heard, and will hear, much in this year's campaign. A Carter aide has said to me, "Can people picture Reagan getting Begin and Sadat together?" These propaganda films, which both parties have come to use now, make one uncomfortable. There is a scene of Carter sitting at his desk in the Oval Office—actually, he seldom uses the Oval Office—in contemplation, Rodin-like. Then the President is announced, and the band plays "Hail to the Chief." No walk through the audience—even if he could get through the aisles—like the one of four years ago. And "Hail to the Chief," retired in a fit of populism at the beginning of Carter's term, has sensibly been brought back. It's good for Carter and good for the country: we need our symbols.

Carter's speech is surprising in several respects. He comes on stronger than usual; now it is he who is shouting. He praises Kennedy and virtually pleads with him for his support. It may be no accident that he fumbles the line "Ted, your party needs—and I need—your idealism and dedication working for us." The way Carter says it, it comes out, "Ted, your party needs. And I need your . . ." It must have been a difficult line for Carter to bring himself to say. But he stands there as a supplicant. Candidates like to talk about how they have travelled the length and breadth of the land, but Carter didn't do that this year, so he says, "During the last Presidential campaign, I crisscrossed our country and listened to many thousands of people." He says, "I have learned that only the most complex and difficult tasks end up in the Oval Office." He makes one of the arguments that will be made for re-electing him: "I have learned that for a President experience is the best guide to right decisions. I am wiser tonight than I was four years ago.'' And then he makes one that will be used against Reagan: "The life of every human being on earth can depend on the experience, judgment, and vigilance of the person in the Oval Office.'' Since his aides do not think the case has been made that it matters who wins this election, Carter now says, "This election is a stark choice between two men, two parties, two sharply different pictures of America and the world. But it is more than that. It is a choice between two futures.'' He describes the future under him as one of economic security, justice, and peace, and the one under Reagan as one of despair, surrender, and risk. He talks of the "fantasy America'' that the Republicans describe, and says, "It is a make-believe world of good guys and bad guys, where some politicians shoot first and ask questions later.'' He goes on and on attacking Reagan. Last summer, one of Carter's closest advisers told me that Democrats made a mistake when Reagan ran for governor of California by trying to paint him as a dangerous man. The Carter people seem to have forgotten that. And Carter's style is a totally new one: scrappy, the fighting bantam rooster. Perhaps he is trying to evoke Harry Truman; the Carter people would like Truman's 1948 victory to be a precedent. There is something troubling about Presidential candidates' redefining themselves—as both Reagan and Carter are doing—just a few months before the election. Now Carter defends his record, gives a preview of his new economic program, and makes many of the same points that Mondale has just made—including the one about cuts in defense spending under the Republicans. He says that if the Republicans are serious about their tax-cut proposals and their pledges to make large increases in defense spending and to balance the budget, while still maintaining Social Security, Medicare, Medicaid, and pension programs, "then a close analysis shows that the entire rest of the government would have to be abolished.'' (The Office of Management and Budget has worked up a set of figures that purports to support this claim.)

The audience applauds, and cheers from time to time, but it is cheerless. Carter just does not give a lift to occasions; he does not seem to know how to. He doesn't evoke very much in people, because he doesn't give very much. He is a withholder. The smile is up front, but he is somewhere back in the weeds. The loner in him has left him a lone figure. He obviously has difficulty with people, which is why he is surrounded by so few. Carter has brought himself to have more meetings with politicians and make more phone calls to them, in order to get things done, but he remains a stranger to them. One senator said recently that he does not enjoy talking on the phone to a President who he knows is reading from a card. Carter is a masterly technician of technical politics but not of the politics of moving the nation. And one of Carter's most loyal advisers says that the Carter campaign is seen by the public as having been manipulative, and is paying a price for that. One gets the sense that, even now, Carter is still groping for a definition of his Presidency—that he tries one thing and then another. There is no question that, as his own people keep saying, he works very hard at his job. And they are probably also correct in saying that some part of his problem has to do with the unpleasantness and the frustration of the times, and with the problems that are resistant to solution, and even with the current tendency to tear down people in public life. It is not a pleasant time to try to govern, or to be in politics. There are things in Carter's record which he can legitimately defend; his problem is in some part a stylistic one —an inability to communicate what he is doing—and in large part an inability to steer a steady course. In leadership, it is important not only to do the right thing but also to be able to communicate it. Style of leadership has a great deal to do with how a democracy works.

The demonstration for Carter is kept going until Kennedy can get to the podium. (Even the balloons won't drop.) Carter is the pursuer still. In the meantime, Strauss has called to the podium just about every elected official in the vicinity of New York, and the Cabinet, and a small mob is there by the time Kennedy arrives. A great cheer goes up. Kennedy waves his fist in the direction of the Massachusetts delegation and, eventually, shakes hands with Carter. Much will be made of the fact that he does not engage in the traditional victor-vanquished, arms-clasped-in-the-air salute, but his restraint isn't surprising. The Kennedys don't go in for that sort of thing— they aren't public huggers or touchers. Besides, it's a hacky gesture. It would be patently phony under the circumstances. Perhaps there is a touch of arrogance in his behavior at this moment—we can't know. We also can't know what scars this year has left him with. It was no normal political fight, and it cannot end normally.

The band plays "Marching Along Together," and Kennedy leaves the podium. The part of the crowd shouting "We want Ted!" drowns out the others, and Kennedy makes one more appearance on the podium. Then he leaves, and the Carters and the Mondales stand there, waving to the crowd. The arrangements for the final moments seem to be an attempt to recapture the hope and optimism with which the Democratic Convention ended four years ago. As then, the Reverend Martin Luther King, Sr.—Daddy King— gives the benediction, and, as then, the orchestra plays "We Shall Overcome," but the effect isn't the same.

CHAPTER 11

Reagan _____

PHILADELPHIA, SUNDAY. SEPTEMBER 7TH. Ronald Reagan is here for the first of five days of campaigning that will take him not only to Pennsylvania but also to Indiana, Illinois, Wisconsin, Ohio, and New York. It is commonly agreed that the large industrial states are the main battleground of the Presidential election.

For Reagan, this week marks the beginning of an important period, in several respects. His campaign organization is still pulling itself together; the Reagan camp has been frustrated in its efforts to make Jimmy Carter the target; and Reagan himself has got into unwonted difficulties. While some Reagan aides say that the various controversial remarks Reagan has made in recent weeks have been blown out of proportion by the press, they are beginning to realize that Reagan's problem, and theirs, is that a campaign for the Presidency is of a different nature from one for the nomination. And a major factor in that difference is that the press intensifies its scrutiny of what the nominees say—and so does the public. Things that could be got by with earlier in the year—that even helped to win the primaries—are watched by a larger and more critical audience. Reagan himself is said by his closest aides to be annoyed by the attention that the press has paid to what it sees as his "gaffes" but also to accept the idea that he must be more careful. Up to a point. Both he and some of his longtime advisers are of the opinion that he has been quite successful in politics by saying what he believes. A candidate and his less objective aides tend to overlook the role of fortuity in the candidate's success; Reagan was a skilled candidate in the primaries, but he was also lucky. Still, he and his entourage now realize they have a problem. So they have arranged for Reagan's speeches to be written in time for them to be cleared by a number of people; have revised the scheduling and advance work (Ron Walker, who was chief advance man for Richard Nixon, has just been brought into the Reagan campaign in the same capacity); and have decided to try to, in the words of one aide, "control the environment." Reagan is to be less accessible and less spontaneous. Stuart Spencer, the president of the California public-relations firm of Spencer-Roberts, will now travel with Reagan, to help ward off mistakes. Spencer managed Reagan's campaigns for governor in 1966 and 1970, and was an important figure in Gerald Ford's campaign four years ago. He joined the Reagan campaign this summer, and last week he was asked to join the travelling entourage. Reagan and his wife, Nancy, are said to have seen the need for the presence of a senior, experienced adviser.

Some of Reagan's aides, however, and Reagan himself, feel that some of what were widely seen as gaffes were not mistakes at all: his restatement, at a press conference, of his belief that the United States should maintain an official relationship with Taiwan, a policy that would violate the agreement between the United States and China (this issue, which had theoretically been taken care of by Reagan's aides in the Party platform, was raised again on the eve of the departure of George Bush, Reagan's running mate, for China, and served to undermine both the trip and Bush's credential as the former head of the United States liaison office in China); his suggestion, in a press conference before he spoke to an audience of evangelicals in Dallas, that the Biblical theory of creation should be taught in the schools along with the Darwinian theory of evolution; his reference, in a speech before the Veterans of Foreign Wars, to the Vietnam War as a "noble cause." The Reagan entourage, apparently unanimously, does see as a mistake his charge that when Carter began his fall campaign, on Labor Day, in Tuscumbia, Alabama, he did it in "the city that gave birth to and is the parent body of the Ku Klux Klan." But there remains considerable internal disagreement about whether Reagan should have issued an apology, as he did, after the fuss arose over it. (The Carter Administration, of course, did its best to stir up the fuss. Carter himself made an indignant statement to reporters: "Anyone who resorts to slurs and to innuendo against a whole region of the country based on a false statement and a false premise is not doing the South or our nation a good service.") The word that an apology should be issued came from the campaign organization's headquarters, in Arlington, Virginia; the travelling entourage resisted, on the ground that an apology would only perpetuate the story, and the travelling staff still thinks that the apology was a mistake.

Some of those in the campaign continue to hold the view that what Reagan said about China and Vietnam was simply what he had said all along, so why all the commotion? A Reagan aide has said to me, "On the China thing, his view is, damn it, he's not going to be seen as backing off previous positions." That Reagan had said these things before was true enough (though the Vietnam statement was a new form of a sentiment that Reagan had expressed in the primaries), but now more people were listening. In the opinion of some of Reagan's aides, a number of these incidents accomplished the purpose of solidifying Reagan's original political base.

The purpose of this week's travels is to expand that base. And so the Reagan campaign came here to Philadelphia from Washington this afternoon. Reagan's advisers have, they hope, battened down the campaign organization and buttoned up the candidate—and they are holding their breath. They say, oh, well, these things happened early in the campaign, and they point out that Carter made mistakes in the early part of his 1976 campaign. "Who gives a damn about them, compared with the economy?" one aide said to me. "I can't believe that the guy out there who's been laid off gives a damn about a two-China policy, or even knows what you're talking about." Stuart Spencer says that in 1966 Reagan remarked to him, "Politics is just like show business." When Spencer asked Reagan what he meant, he explained, "You have a hell of an opening, you coast for a while, you have a hell of a closing."

The Republican Convention, Spencer says, was a very good opening. But Reagan's aides are clearly apprehensive. When I asked one of his most important advisers last week what they planned to do about the recent problems, he replied nervously, "I don't know. How do you control the things that come out of a man's mind?" An aide travelling with Reagan said to me today, "One of my jobs this week is to keep him out of trouble." Another aide said, "The problem is, he has an inclination to answer any question he's asked. He started doing a lot of question-and-answer sessions back in 1966, when he first ran for governor, to show he wasn't just an actor reading lines, and he likes to do that. Left to his own devices, he would do a lot of Q. and A.—he has confidence in himself."

It is a warm and sunny afternoon. Reagan is to address a crowd at Super Senior Sunday, a fair put on by senior-citizens groups in Philadelphia. (Chip Carter, one of the President's sons, and Keke Anderson, John Anderson's wife, will also make appearances here today.) Reagan is seated amid a large number of people gathered on the steps in front of the Philadelphia Museum of Art—the steps are better known because Sylvester Stallone ran up them in *Rocky* than because they provide the foreground for a striking Greco-Roman building. As the crowd awaited Reagan, something called the Glenn Miller Orchestra played such tunes as "In the Mood." Then, with the orchestra playing "Chattanooga Choo Choo," Reagan and his wife arrived at the site aboard a trolley. Reagan is dressed in a brown plaid suit, with a white handkerchief in his breast pocket; Mrs. Reagan is in a beige silk print dress. The microphones won't work, and while everyone waits, the orchestra plays "In the Mood" again. Reagan smiles and moves his head up and down in time to the music. After a while—at Nancy Reagan's suggestion, it seems—the Reagans get up and dance, going into a subdued jitterbug. Reagan does look the matinee idol now. He looks well—tanned and healthy. Finally, the microphones are repaired.

Reagan's speech today is to be about Social Security. The Carter campaign has charged that Reagan has advocated making the Social Security system voluntary, and this afternoon Carter campaign workers are here passing out copies of a press release, issued two days ago in Washington, that contains some quotations from Reagan indicating that he suggested that people be allowed to buy their own voluntary retirement plans instead of participating in Social Security. Of course, for a Presidential candidate to suggest that Social Security be voluntary could be fatal, and Reagan has not gone near such an idea this year. He has said in the past that as President he would appoint a commission to study ways to improve the fiscal soundness of the Social Security trust fund. (The retirement trust fund is now expected to be bankrupt in less than three years unless many billions of dollars are raised; the estimates are from thirty billion to a hundred billion dollars. Neither Reagan nor Carter has offered a solution to the problem.)

In his speech today, which he reads, Reagan refers to the fact that the steps have been made famous by *Rocky:* "They symbolize determination, hope, a belief in a dream." He attacks the record of the Carter Administration. He says (incorrectly) that one of the cuts the President suggested when he called for a balanced budget was in the way Social Security payments are adjusted for inflation. He also says that a study "authorized" by Carter called for a tax on Social Security benefits. (This was a recommendation made in 1979 by an advisory council that reports every four years. The recommendation was never endorsed by the President and is specifically rejected in the Democratic platform.) He says that as President he "will defend the integrity of the Social Security system." He does not say how. He decries waste in the federal government and closes by telling the audience, "I will not apologize for our generation—we have known four wars in our lifetime; we have known a great Depression that changed the face of the world." He does not seem entirely comfortable reading the speech, and falters at times; Reagan appeared more at ease with the more informal stump speeches in the primaries. He ends by quoting a line that, as he points out, John Kennedy intended to include in an address he did not live to make: "We in this country, in this generation, are, by destiny rather than choice, the watchmen on the walls of world freedom." As Reagan makes his way back to the motorcade, he pauses briefly to reply to a question from a local radio reporter. Lyn Nofziger, Reagan's press secretary, steers Reagan away.

After the speech, I ask a Reagan aide why Reagan quoted John Kennedy. "Show me a quotable recent Republican President," he replies, and he adds, "J.F.K.'s a hero, and helpful if you're going after blue-collar votes— the same way Franklin Roosevelt is."

Lately, the Reagan campaign has tried to focus on one theme each week, but that idea has all but officially been abandoned. (One week was spent on the arms race, which some Reagan aides think was not such a good idea. Besides, the realities of campaigning, the unexpected events, including some of his own missteps, made it hard to stick to one theme.) The focus this week is to be on the ethnic voter and the subject of economics. On Tuesday, in Chicago, Reagan is to give an economics speech, promised some time ago, on how he will do the various things he has pledged: cut taxes, increase military spending, and balance the budget. The objective this week will be to keep up the attack on Carter, and not to get on the defensive. Reagan's polls indicate that Reagan is ahead of Carter right now in almost all the major industrial states except New York. But John Anderson has just been endorsed by the policy committee of the Liberal Party in New York (his endorsement by the Party will follow), which should help Reagan. A Reagan aide said this afternoon that he had sent a bottle of champagne to Anderson's campaign manager.

The consensus among the Reagan people now is that the election could be quite close. Their strengths, they say, lie in their candidate, in Carter's record, and in Reagan's state organizations, which are made up of people who have been working for Reagan for a long time—some since 1968. "Now they smell victory," one aide says. Reagan's aides say that their worries are about Carter's use of incumbency and about events beyond their control. One political adviser says, "I worry about the damn hostages." Another political adviser has said to me that historically Republicans are a couple of points ahead of Democrats at about this time but then get beaten as the Democratic voters "go home." He said, "This year, they don't have to go home. They've got John Anderson."

This evening, Reagan makes an appearance at the field house of St. Joseph's University. One purpose of this event is to work on getting out the vote in the Philadelphia area. Reagan's polls show him slightly ahead of Carter in Pennsylvania—which Carter carried in 1976, largely on the strength of the vote in Philadelphia—but the Republicans are behind the Democrats by about eight hundred thousand registered voters as of now, and are concerned that in November the traditional Democratic vote might "go home." The Republicans have established an elaborate get-out-the-vote program, and they have more money to spend on such activities than the Democrats do. The Republican state parties and the National Committee, which are better off financially than their Democratic counterparts, are permitted by law to contribute to the national campaign. The Republicans are also expected to benefit more than the Democrats from the "independent" committees that can be formed to raise and spend money for the Presidential campaigns. Tonight's appearance is before a group that is part of what is called Commitment '80, a joint project of the Republican National Committee and the Reagan campaign to get out the vote. Tonight's gathering is of people in the Philadelphia area who want to get involved in the project. It also gives Reagan an opportunity to be on local television, live.

The master of ceremonies drags out the introductions until, as he puts it, "the live television comes on," and then, at the appointed moment, he introduces Reagan, to large cheers. As Reagan begins to speak, some young people in the audience hold up a large sign protesting the use of nuclear weapons and start shouting. Reagan looks at them and pauses—one wonders what is coming and how much his staff is worrying. Then, summoning up one of his jokes, he says, "You're taking up my time, and it's the first time I've had a chance to be on prime time since they shut off the late, late movies." (He began his Convention acceptance speech with a variant of this joke.) As he tries to continue his remarks, the shouting also continues, and Reagan looks at the demonstrators and pauses again. And then, appearing angered, he says that the message his hecklers are trying to get across "is that Christ is betrayed by nuclear weapons." He goes on, "Well, let me say something. Is there anyone in the world who has not believed that Christ is betrayed anytime we find ourselves embroiled in that greatest of man's stupidities—war against our fellow man?" The audience cheers and applauds. That's the skillful Reagan—fast on his feet, adept at turning situations to his advantage. The polls show that the question of war and peace is one on which Reagan has trouble, and Reagan now uses his opportunity further, saying that he is opposed to the SALT treaty but that he would "sit at a table with our adversaries for as long as it took" to negotiate a better agreement. Then he proceeds to the remarks he apparently planned to make.

He says that St. Joseph's, a private university, illustrates another difference between him and Carter. He points out that Carter opposes tuition tax credits, and adds that the new Department of Education "is planning all manner of things to limit and restrict institutions of this kind, because their faith is totally in public education only." (After his appearance, Reagan's aides were unable to offer any explanation of what he had in mind.) He tells the audience that the election is not really one between Democrats and Republicans, because "there are just millions of Democrats who are as unhappy with what's going on as we are." He talks of "the hands I've shaken," saying, "There's a great and high percentage of black hands, and there's an awful lot of hands that are callused." He talks to this group about the importance of its work in the campaign: "I still believe campaigns are won out there in the precincts with somebody knocking on a neighbor's door." And then, as he often has, he tells a long, vivid anecdote, the point of which is to say that this election will determine whether we can provide for our children "the same freedom that we knew in this country when we were their age." This is a theme Reagan used throughout the primaries; often his rallies had a group of children there as props. And then he repeats the theme words of his campaign: family, work, neighborhood, peace, and freedom. "That's what we represent," he says.

On his way out of the field house, Reagan greets some of the people in the crowd and answers their questions. The "pool reporters," who are supposed to stay near the candidate and report to the others what happened, are kept out of earshot by Reagan's staff.

Monday. Kokomo, Indiana. This morning, Reagan paid a call, obligatory for Presidential candidates, on John Cardinal Krol, of Philadelphia. During the meeting, Nofziger told reporters that what Reagan had in mind when he said last evening that the Department of Education was planning new restrictions on private schools was that since it is a new Department the people in it will "justify their existence by adopting restrictive regulations," and Nofziger added, "We understand there is a study being made in the Department in which the government rather than the schools themselves would handle the accreditation." (The Administration denies that such a study exists.) Then Reagan flew to Kokomo—his chartered plane has been named LeaderShip 80—for a lunch-hour rally here at the Kokomo Mall. (Mrs. Reagan left the trip after the visit to Cardinal Krol.) This is a sort of drop-by in Indiana—one of two planned visits to the state, which Republicans have traditionally carried.

The locale of this visit fits the Reagan political plan. Unemployment in Kokomo, which is tied to the automobile industry, is over nineteen percent. Kokomo is a Democratic city in a Republican county. The mall is within sight of Delco Electronics, a General Motors division, where about a tenth of the workers have been laid off, and a Chrysler plant, where about a third of the workers have been laid off. At the mall, Reagan is introduced to the crowd—in a reference to the fact that he headed the Screen Actors Guild in the late 1940s and early fifties—as a "leader in the labor movement." Reagan is wearing a tan suit and looks sporty. It's another warm and sunny day. A daytime fireworks display that the Reagan campaign had planned for the end of Reagan's speech has been called off. The Reagan people hint that the Democratic city officials who ruled it out were taking orders from higher up. ("They're trying to ruin our rallies," a Reagan aide told me.)

Reagan is to give what is developing as his stump speech for the campaign. The speech is different in style and politics from the one for the primaries: less ridden with statistics, more cautious, and aimed at Democratic and independent voters as well as Republicans. One of Reagan's aides said to me today, "The stump speech in the primaries was basic Reagan." The idea is that he will have one or two stump speeches, and on days when the campaign wants the speech to make news there will be an insert on some subject. Reagan's charge last week that the Carter Administration was guilty of a "cynical misuse of power" in letting it be known in August that the United States had developed a technology—"Stealth"—that would make a plane invisible to radar was such an insert. With that charge, Reagan managed, as had been intended, to shift the focus from himself to Carter, and put the Administration on the defensive. The fact that there was a project to develop such a technology had been in the military trade journals for years; whether the "Stealth" announcement told the Soviet Union anything it did not know, or gave it an advantage, is debated. Reagan said that the announcement gave the Soviet Union "a ten-year head start" on developing ways to counter the system. Defense Secretary Harold Brown, announcing the new technology, said that it "alters the military balance significantly;" actually, the deployment of a "Stealth" plane is about ten years away. But it is altogether likely that the Administration did have politics in mind when it announced the project. (Such things have happened before. In 1964, Lyndon Johnson, who was being charged by Barry Goldwater with not having maintained a sufficient defense, announced the existence of a new reconnaissance plane, of over-the-horizon radar, and of two anti-satellite systems.)

Reagan begins by telling the crowd that he's from Illinois but when he became a sports announcer after graduating from college he came to Indiana to broadcast a football game. He croons a line from "On the Banks of the Wabash, Far Away" and then goes into his stump speech. (Reagan was known as a very good sports announcer; it's said that he had a remarkable ability to describe a game vividly play-by-play, even if all he knew about it was what he read on the wire. Reagan was inventing a lot of it, it's said, but he gave his listeners the feeling that they were hearing a firsthand account.) In his speech, which he reads, Reagan says, "All across this land, I've found a longing among our people for hope, a longing for a belief in ourselves and the vision that gave birth to this nation. For the values of family, work, neighborhood, peace, and freedom. They're at the heart of the American dream. Jimmy Carter would have us believe that dream is over . . . or at least in need of some kind of drastic change." Then he goes into a condemnation of the Administration: "For the first time in the history of our country, we face three grave crises at the same time—each of which is capable of destroying us. Our economy is deteriorating. Our energy needs are not being met. And our military preparedness has been weakened to the point of immediate danger. The Carter record is a litany of despair, of broken promises, of sacred trusts abandoned and forgotten." And then he lists unemployment, "inflation running at eighteen percent in the first quarter of 1980," black unemployment, budget deficits, "the highest interest rates since the Civil War," productivity falling during six straight quarters, tax increases. Then he says that Carter "tries to tell us that we're only in a recession, not a depression," and that "when the American people cried out for economic help, Jimmy Carter took refuge behind a dictionary," and then he says, "Well, if it's a definition he wants, I'll give him one. A recession is when a neighbor loses his job. A depression is when you lose yours. And a recovery is when Jimmy Carter loses his."

When Reagan first said that the country was in a depression—in a speech in Columbus, Ohio, eleven days ago—a number of people thought that it was another gaffe. Reagan had inserted the term in his prepared speech at the last minute (just as he had previously inserted the description of the Vietnam War), and Alan Greenspan, one of his economic advisers, who was along on the trip and had not been informed, told reporters that he could not support Reagan's definition of the economic situation. But Reagan and other advisers obviously think that the charge is good politics, because it puts Carter on the defensive. (For all his easygoing style, Reagan has demonstrated once more that he can be a tough opponent. He has a temper, and he sometimes uses it to effect in his campaigns—"I am paying for this microphone, Mr. Breen.'' He has also demonstrated that he is shrewd, and has a certain sly side.) Reagan goes on now, with indignation, about the economy. Reagan is good at projecting indignation. He says he will offer an economic program that will lower taxes and cut the cost of government. He says, ''There's enough fat in the government in Washington that if it was rendered and made into soap, it would wash the world.'' Referring to the economic program that Carter announced ten days ago, Reagan says that Carter has now offered ''his *fifth* new economic program.'' (Three of those programs were the annual budgets required by law.) But he does land on another of Carter's vulnerabilities—his ever-changing policies. Carter's new program included tax cuts for both individuals and businesses, to stimulate investment and growth. ''Well, it won't work,'' Reagan says. ''It's cynical. It's political. And it's too late. The damage is done, and every American family knows it.'' Then he draws on Edward Kennedy. (It was expected during the primaries that in the fall Reagan would use some of Kennedy's material against Carter, and, as the Reagan aide said, ''Kennedy'' is a good name to use with blue-collar workers.) Reagan cites Kennedy's charge that Carter was constantly being surprised, and he lists a number of ''surprises,'' and says, ''Well, I'd like to think that he's due for one more surprise.'' And the next words—''a surprise on November 4th'' —are nearly lost in the applause. He closes by quoting the line he quoted yesterday from the speech that John Kennedy ''never got to speak . . . because of the tragedy that took place.'' Reagan's voice is tremulous today, just as it was yesterday, when he says that line.

This is an eerie campaign. It's not just that Reagan is cordoned off and protected from the press; it's a question of why his aides feel he must be protected from the normal give-and-take of political life—of what it is that they are afraid will be revealed. They are not simply protecting Reagan from the press; they are trying to protect him from himself. They behave as if they were a group of trainers who have a beautiful racehorse on their hands —one that must be given constant care. The aides' protectiveness conveys, unwittingly, a certain patronizing view of Reagan—as if they dared not let him loose. It seems to be more than a matter of gaffes, though that's part of it—or should be, not just because the gaffes might affect his electability but because they raise questions about his judgment. Other Presidential campaigns have been carefully ''packaged,'' allowing as little spontaneity or chance of accident as possible. (For instance, Richard Nixon's in 1968.) But not all of them. It is natural and not unreasonable for the people in a Presidential campaign to view the press as a minefield, but not all people in public office are incapable of dealing with it, and the ability to deal with it is one requirement of the Presidency. Jimmy Carter is also running a carefully controlled campaign, of course; and Gerald Ford, who had once been one of the most accessible people in public life, ran such a campaign in 1976. (Nixon hid out in 1972, and everyone knew why.) But there is a difference between a campaign for re-election by a President and a campaign for the

Presidency by someone who has never held the office. A President has had to govern; he has a record; he has been subjected to intense scrutiny for quite a while. The challenger asks for attention. The President has to do things; the challenger can simply say, without taking account of certain realities, what he would do. When a President makes a mistake in a campaign, it can affect the nation; when a challenger makes a mistake, it affects only his own fortunes. Reagan's campaign is now designed to be as unrevealing as possible. That is in itself revealing.

At about three o'clock, Reagan's plane lands in Chicago, and Reagan, as is the custom in campaigns, waits to emerge from the front of the plane until after the press has disembarked and the cameras have been set up to record his arrival. During such intervals, candidates usually get last-minute briefings on who will greet them and what to expect. Today, Reagan is to be met by James Thompson, the Governor of Illinois; Dennis Voss, co-coordinator of Illinois Ethnics for Reagan; and a Polish-American dance group in Polish costumes. (Reagan is not good at remembering names, and the last time he was here he greeted Thompson as Dave. Gary Schuster, of the Detroit *News,* has reported that this time, during the interval before Reagan left the airplane, Nofziger ran to him and said, "Don't forget, Governor, it's Jim, Jim, Jim, Jim, Jim, Jim Thompson, not Dave.")

Reagan is to walk through a Lithuanian neighborhood in southwest Chicago. Actually, he will go down one street, for only two or three blocks; this event is essentially one for the cameras. Such neighborhood walks have been Presidential-campaign set pieces ever since ethnic politics came into fashion in recent years. The whole business of courting ethnic groups, which is conducted on a bipartisan basis, involves more than a little exploitation of these people. After the walk, Reagan will meet with some Polish-American leaders at the Palmer House, where he and his entourage are staying tonight. He begins his walk at the intersection of Washtenaw Avenue and Lithuanian Plaza Court, and from there he and Thompson, with a retinue of Secret Service agents, policemen, aides, the press pool, and some people dressed in Lithuanian costumes—the whole group cordoned off by ropes—walk down the middle of Sixty-ninth Street, past two-story houses, past the Kaunas Park Inn, past the United Lithuanian Relief office, past the Liths Soccer Club. Thompson steers Reagan to one side of the street and the other, and Reagan reaches over the ropes to shake hands with the cheerful crowd that has come out to see him. This is a conservative Democratic neighborhood—Ford won the area four years ago. Reagan is strong downstate and needs to win votes in the Chicago area. Ford narrowly carried the state in 1976, and Carter is fighting hard for it this year.

Reagan ends up at Ramune's Restaurant and Delicatessen, where he is scheduled to stop for coffee. He sits at the counter, with leaders of the Lithuanian community on either side, sampling an array of pastries which has been proffered. This, too, will make fine pictures, and Reagan's staff shuttles the national and local press through the delicatessen so that they can record the scene. Thompson asks Anna Konkulevicius, a co-owner of the place, who is in Lithuanian dress, what she wants Reagan to do as President. She replies, "Free Lithuania and oppose the Communists." Reagan remarks, "Someday they will be free." While Nofziger and others herd the press through, shooing off anyone who tries to ask Reagan a question, Reagan chats somewhat absently with the people on either side of him. He doesn't seem to be much interested in them or to be making much of an effort. One can't help considering what someone like Sargent Shriver, an enthusiastic type, would have done in this situation. (I remember Shriver, as the Vice Presidential candidate, walking through an ethnic neighborhood in Philadelphia in 1972, going on about how much he enjoyed it, and expressing delight with the new fashion of ethnic politics.) Most politicians I can think of—even Jimmy Carter, who is warm when he chooses—would have at least feigned more interest in these people, and many would have been actually interested in them. It's hot in the delicatessen, and Thompson mops his face with a yellow towel. Reagan looks composed—he sits there smiling, looking like the easygoing good guy—and slightly bored. He is posing.

All politicians pose at times, of course, but one cannot avoid the thought that with Reagan the whole thing might be an act. Even when one resists thinking about Reagan's prior career, watching him over a period of time forces the thought that with him it is always a performance, that everything he does and says is for effect. Most politicians let down their guard in public at some point; Reagan seems always to be onstage. His remoteness from people, except for his wife and a few close friends, is striking. It begins to seem no accident that, though he is now in a profession that puts a premium on such a thing, he does not remember people's names. He does not seem to try to learn them; it appears to be of no interest to him. He does not engage in the normal give-and-take with people who accompany him on these trips—not even, it seems, with his aides. He is secure in his circle of rich friends, and one gets no sense of his reaching out beyond that, of his being curious about people, of his talking to people because it might be interesting. It's not just that he's on guard but that he is remote. His eyes don't engage, he doesn't engage. It's not the coldness that Carter shows at times—it's more impersonal than that.

Reagan does not seem to be a thinker, or to be in search of ideas. He has some views and a sense of the way the world ought to be, and some political instincts, and he collects snippets that reinforce his views, help him make his case, vary his routine. Carter does have curiosity and thinks things through and has a lot of beliefs; his problems stem from a lack of commitment and an overmanipulativeness. Ford was and remains popular because there is a realness about him. There does seem to be a certain unformedness about Reagan, a lack of inner structure. Again, the thought is inescapable: this is characteristic of many movie stars. A friend of mine once described another star as a "boy-man." Someone I know once asked Fred Zinnemann, the movie director, what a certain very famous female star was really like. Zinnemann replied, "What makes you thinks she's like anything?" People who have interviewed Reagan, or talked to him about issues, have come away with the impression that he is a pleasant man but also that he was performing. When he is asked what he really thinks about an issue, or means when he talks about it, he is more likely than not to answer by telling an anecdote related to the issue—which is the way he has tended to talk about issues in his campaign appearances, at least until now. Talking to Reagan, one gets the sense that he does not realize that he is evading, is not dealing with the issues. One gets the sense that an anecdote is his way of dealing with the issues.

When Reagan begins to answer a question from a local radio reporter ("What did you think of your welcome here?"), Nofziger and another aide almost have apoplexy. *"No interviews!"* Nofziger shouts, waving his arms and diving for the reporter. "Just let me reply to this one," Reagan says to Nofziger calmly, and then he says, "Most heartwarming. Anyone who wouldn't be thrilled is unconscious."

The Crystal Room of the Palmer House, 9 P.M. Gerald Ford had dinner with Reagan tonight and, as Reagan's aides hoped, will now meet with the press. The last time the two men met was at the Republican Convention, after they and their respective aides failed to reach an agreement on the terms by which Ford might run as Vice President. Four years ago, Ford beat Reagan for the nomination. Now Reagan, the nominee, needs Ford, just as Carter, the nominee, needs Kennedy. Ford has agreed to campaign for Reagan, just as Kennedy has agreed to campaign for Carter. The Reagan aides planned that the two big stories out of today were to be Reagan's meetings with Cardinal Krol and with Ford. One of the aides said to me on the plane to Kokomo, "The story about Ford is that he's there—just like the meeting with Kissinger last week." (Kissinger met with Reagan at the house the Reagans are renting for the duration of the campaign in Middleburg, Virginia, near Washington and also near the Arlington headquarters.) Reagan keeps to a leisurely schedule, in part to dictate which events will make news. The big event tomorrow is to be Reagan's economics speech. Advance texts of the speech were distributed to the press on the plane en route to Chicago, and a "fact sheet" explaining Reagan's economic proposals will be handed out shortly, and there is to be a briefing by some Reagan advisers. One of the admitted goals of this whole exercise is to make Reagan seem "Presidential." Thus, as in the case of Presidents, the advance texts, background papers, background briefings.

Ford arrives at nine-fifteen. His arrival is low-key—he just walks in, smiling. He may be an ex-President, with all the benefits and honors that the station bestows, but tonight he is just another man. Perhaps because of that, he seems somewhat shrunken. He seems to have left his apotheosis in the other room. Ford says that he "just had a delightful dinner" with

Reagan, and that the two men talked over their campaign plans. Ford says that he thinks he can be most helpful to Reagan in the large industrial states, "where the Carter economic policy has brought about a disaster."

He is asked if he believes that Reagan fumbled on the subjects of Vietnam and evolution. He walks around the question by saying that he will not comment "on non-issue comments by others, whether they're President Carter or Governor Reagan." He says, "I'm going to talk about the issues."

In answer to another question, he says, "I have an interesting campaign schedule. It's going to be my last hurrah." One wonders. Ford may not run for President again, but the dutiful Republican in him keeps returning from the sidelines to go out on the road. Besides, Ford, who put in years of travel for his colleagues when he was in the House of Representatives, seems to like it on the road, and to get restless after he has played a certain amount of golf. Now he says that he will spend fifty-three of the next sixty days on the road—that's a more rigorous schedule than is planned for Reagan—and will fly sixty thousand miles to campaign in thirty states, and he lists the numbers of congressional, senatorial, and gubernatorial races he will help out in, in addition to his efforts for the Reagan-Bush ticket. He attacks the Carter Administration for announcing the "Stealth" program.

Stuart Spencer is standing off to one side, his arms folded; he looks satisfied. Then a reporter asks Ford if he thinks it is credible to claim, as Reagan is claiming, that in one term an Administration can cut taxes by ten percent a year for three years, make a substantial increase in military spending, and balance the budget. Ford replies, "I don't believe that Governor Reagan has said in this campaign that he's committed automatically and categorically to the ten-percent reduction. My understanding is that he has committed himself to a one-year tax reduction." He is referring to the one-year tax cut that was offered by congressional Republicans, with Reagan's support, in June, to get the jump on the Administration. One year was settled on because a number of Republicans do not agree with the idea of proposing substantial cuts for three years. But Reagan committed himself to the three-year program many times in the primaries, and it is contained in the Republican platform, and the speech text, which the reporters here are holding, commits him to it again. Good old Ford. Actually, it's not his fault; he just hasn't got the news.

Another reporter asks him, "Mr. President, how do you feel about a ten-percent tax reduction in each of the next three years?"

Ford digs in further: "I wouldn't commit at this point to a categorical attempt to see tax reductions for each year of the next three years."

Spencer does not change his expression. Another reporter asks Ford why he wouldn't commit himself categorically to three years of tax reduction.

Ford replies, "Because I don't think at this stage we can see down the road what the economic situation will be in thirty-six months."

Asked, toward the end, what he means by "last hurrah," Ford says that after this campaign "I'm going to retire and take life easy and do a lot of things that I haven't been able to do for the last thirty-some years." He says, "After January 20th, when we have a new President inaugurated, I'm going to relax and resume my skiing on the snowy slopes of Colorado and improve my golf game—at least, I hope I'll be hitting fewer spectators on the circuits—and I will have a great time. Betty and I are going to really enjoy ourselves."

There are a number of surprises in Reagan's economic proposals. The most striking surprise is that they jettison the theory that originally lay behind them—the theory that the economic growth that would be stimulated by a thirty-percent cut in taxes over three years would make up for the loss of revenue (the "Laffer curve"). Reagan used to say that he would be able to cut taxes substantially, increase defense spending substantially, and balance the budget because of the stimulus that would come from the tax cuts. The task of coming up with a numerical justification of Reagan's program, to prepare him for the hard questions that would inevitably arise in the Presidential campaign, fell to a committee headed by Alan Greenspan. Greenspan is actually a very conservative man, but, compared with some of the people who had been advising Reagan, he is conventional. The orthodox economists around Reagan considered it significant that Laffer did not attend a luncheon Reagan held with his economic advisers during the Republican Convention. Tonight, Greenspan, one of the advisers who are conducting the briefing, says that to defend Reagan's tax cut simply on the assumption that it would make up the lost revenue would be "a risky proposition." So much for that. The names Kemp and Roth don't appear in Reagan's speech. Reagan mentions the names of his more conventional economic advisers. Laffer is gone. Reagan has entered the orthodox conservative economic mainstream. He has been pushed into a new policy by his new advisers.

Another surprise in Reagan's economic proposals is that the spending for defense is so modest—given the seemingly vast increases called for in the Republican platform, and given Reagan's rhetoric. William Van Cleave, a former Pentagon official, who is a Reagan defense adviser, says that the Reagan budget contemplates an increase of five percent in real terms (over inflation) in each of the next five years, which would come to the same amount that has been approved by the Senate Budget Committee (two hundred and seventy billion dollars by 1985) and is not dramatically higher than the budget envisioned by the Carter Administration. Reagan's new program also jettisons his earlier proposals to eliminate the windfall-profit tax and inheritance taxes, and its accelerated depreciation allowance is much reduced from the one included in the one-year tax-cut bill offered by the Republicans in June. It is estimated that the items Reagan dropped would have cost the Treasury a hundred billion dollars. The Reagan defense plan at this point is just a number to be fed into his economic plan. "We're working very hard indeed on coming up with defense proposals," Van Cleave says. Greenspan says he assumes that the cost of Reagan's defense proposals will probably be "somewhat higher" than the figure in the table contained in the background materials, which is designed to show the budgetary effect of Reagan's program. This raises the question of what, if anything, the table means.

It seems clear that Reagan's economic advisers have taken these steps, and some others as well, in order to come up with some numbers that would fit the general outlines that Reagan has prescribed. Reagan's economists also used the most optimistic of the forecasts of the level of revenues by fiscal year 1985, and then added to that some more revenues that they say will result from their program. This way, they arrive at a balanced budget by the third year, and show surpluses after that. The Reagan program relies on an overall rate of growth—about four and one-half percent starting in two years—that is generally considered optimistic. (The rate of growth over the past five years has averaged three and three-tenths percent.) The Reagan program also assumes a rate of inflation of close to nine percent for the next five years (and inflation helps swell revenues). Reagan's pledges to cut government spending are modest, given his past rhetoric, and they are vague ("waste and fraud"), but they are also optimistic about what can be done.

The "fact sheet" has the look of something that was got together in time to have something to present. The staff was still working on the figures this afternoon on the plane. There is common agreement that taxes should be cut, to offset some of the tax increases that are pending as a result of inflation—which pushes people into higher income brackets—and of higher Social Security taxes. The differences are over how much to cut them and who should be the beneficiaries. Reagan's income-tax cuts for individuals are larger than those recently proposed by Carter and would offer more relief to people in the higher income levels. Reagan's proposal would index taxes for inflation after the first three years; Carter opposes indexing. Ironically, Carter's proposals, aimed at "reindustrialization," offer more than Reagan's in the way of help for business. Overall, Reagan's cuts are far larger than those envisioned by the Senate Budget Committee, but they would not reduce the size of the national tax burden in relation to the gross national product. Greenspan says, "We would much prefer to cut it. It turns out that that is very difficult to do." (Reagan is also apparently abandoning the idea, which he once said should be seriously considered, and which is alluded to in the Republican platform, that the United States should return to the gold standard.) Reagan and his advisers have redefined the Reagan proposals, thrown away the premise, and come up with some numbers to prove that the revised proposals will work. This is all happening in a vacuum. The Administration has already issued a fact sheet of its own, attacking Reagan's proposals, but it assumed that Reagan would stick to his old ones, so it misses its target. There will be a war of numbers this fall, and there is a question whether or not anyone will be able to make sense of them.

Tuesday. Shortly after noon, at the Palmer House, Reagan gives his economics speech at a luncheon of the International Business Council, a

Chicago-based trade organization. Like other campaign audiences, this one is a prop; but in this instance Reagan and his people clearly have a very large purpose in mind. Today, Reagan is wearing a gray suit, the most "Presidential" outfit of all the ones I have seen him in this year. He reads the speech from a TelePrompTer, skillfully, and barely acknowledges the audience's presence. His audience is the television cameras. Watching and listening to Reagan now, one could almost think for a moment that this is an address from the Oval Office—which is the intention. Reagan's tone is conversational. Stuart Spencer said to me earlier this week, "He knows what that camera's doing out there. He knows that the microphone picks up your voice when you're talking like this." Spencer was talking in a conversational tone. "He's the only politician in America who really understands those things." Reagan's speech is a harsh attack on Carter's economic policies and a general explanation of his own proposals. "Mr. Carter's American tragedy must and can be transcended by the spirit of the American people, working together," he concludes. "Let's get America working again. The time is now." And he adds to his prepared remarks some comments on his record as governor of California. As usual, he exaggerates his achievements. But he is attempting to show that he is indeed qualified to be Chief Executive, that he can look like one and talk like one, that he can deal in big substance. It is an effective performance.

After this, Reagan will go on to Milwaukee, Cleveland, Buffalo, and Erie —for more walks through ethnic neighborhoods, more appearances before blue-collar workers, and more attacks on Carter. Reagan's aides believe that their candidate is now on the offensive.

CHAPTER 12

Anderson _____

New York, Wednesday, September 24th. John Anderson is holding a press conference at the New York Hilton, in the early afternoon. Anderson's campaign, for all its recent good fortune—his opportunity to appear with Reagan in the League of Women Voters' debate, in Baltimore, on September 21st (Carter stayed away), his endorsement by the New York State Liberal Party, the certification of his eligibility for federal funding—now has a number of problems. The main one is that Anderson continually has to try to explain the campaign's rationale, since the rationale has changed from the one the campaign began with. When Anderson launched his independent candidacy last spring, he said that the purpose was to offer people an alternative to Carter and Reagan in case both their candidacies collapsed, and he also said that if it appeared that his candidacy would lead to the election of Reagan he would drop out. But gradually—perhaps inevitably—Anderson reached the point where, for both external and internal reasons, he would not, could not, drop out. Yet it is widely agreed that his candidacy could cost Carter the election. And so now, when Anderson is asked about this at press conferences and interviews, he says that he is not "a spoiler," because the two other major candidates are so wanting that "what's to spoil?" He also insists, as he apparently feels his situation requires, that he intends to win, and his speeches and other statements are dotted with "as President I will"'s.

But few people around Anderson expect him to win—they have other agendas—and it seems clear that Anderson does not really expect it himself. Some of Anderson's key advisers are beginning to say, though not for attribution, that he cannot win, and—also perhaps inevitably—they are suggesting that the candidate is at fault. (This is a phenomenon common to losing campaigns.) Anderson's second major problem—and it is connected with the first—is that he has not been as successful as he had hoped to be in conducting a "campaign of ideas." His advisers attribute this in part to what they say is the addiction of the press to the "Who's ahead?" aspect of political campaigns, and in part they are correct. But it is a fact that Anderson has somehow not been able to take command of the situation and the opportunities that his campaign has presented. And he has slipped into doing what he said last spring he would not do: he is spending a good bit of the time attacking Reagan and Carter. There are indications that he has decided that this is the way to get attention.

Now, at the press conference, Anderson repeats a charge he made earlier today—that Carter was engaging in "self-serving demagoguery" by saying, as he did on Monday in California, that the November election would decide "whether we have peace or war." (This was a variation on a theme that Carter has been using since his acceptance speech at the Convention, in August.)

A reporter points out that Anderson once described Carter and Reagan as behaving "like two tarantulas in a bottle," and asks Anderson if he has now "joined them in the bottle."

Anderson replies, "I feel a little bit like the little kid on the block who is being ignored while the two bullies go at each other. It seems to me as I read the press and as I watch television that all of the attention right now is being devoted to the charges and counter-charges between Jimmy Carter and Ronald Reagan. Maybe I just better remind people that there is a third man in the race."

He is asked whether he thinks that Carter is deliberately making such charges against Reagan in order to divert attention from him, and he replies, "Oh, there isn't any question but that he and his campaign manager, Mr. Strauss, from the beginning set out as a very deliberate, conscious, continued, contrived campaign strategy to ignore the fact that two million people have signed petitions to put me on the ballots in all the states, that we had raised millions of dollars and were conducting a campaign in all parts of the country, and were a legitimate candidate." And he says that what Robert Strauss wants to do is repeat the idea that Anderson is a spoiler "over and over and over again, until it becomes part of the political vernacular of this campaign." He concludes, "But I just hope that in time the people will realize that this is just a slogan."

That Anderson is in a position to determine the outcome of the 1980 Presidential election whether or not he wins a single state is little disputed, and that he might end up in such a position was why some of his friends urged him not to take the independent route—which led to his assertions that he would not allow such a thing to happen. Anderson said at the outset that he was beginning a process that he could stop at any time, but, for reasons ranging from the practicalities of running at all to human nature's resistance to stopping, he has ended up in a process that has become increasingly difficult to stop. Anderson's friends believe that his campaign for the Republican Presidential nomination began as a sort of what-the-hell exercise—he had decided to retire from the House of Representatives and wanted to go out with some notice. Some of his friends believe he started on the Presidential campaign wishing to strike a blow against the Republican Party's right wing, represented for him by Reagan, after being nearly defeated in the Republican primary in his congressional district by a conservative challenger in 1978. At the outset, Anderson captured attention by coming across as different from the others—and he was, to some extent—but there also seemed to be a certain self-consciousness in the way he set himself apart. (In Iowa, he supported the President's embargo on the sale of grain to the Soviet Union, and in New Hampshire he supported gun control.)

Among those who thought they saw Anderson's possibilities early this year was Tom Mathews, a partner in a direct-mail consulting firm with such clients as the American Civil Liberties Union, the Sierra Club, Planned Parenthood, Common Cause, and organizations supporting abortion rights and handgun control. (The firm also works for a number of liberal politicians.) Mathews estimates that his major clients, numbering about a dozen, have a total of about a million and a half members, who donate some forty million dollars a year to various causes; he says that his firm has available to it about four million names, on mailing lists that it acquires from "list brokers"—people who rent out lists of names that come from such sources as rosters of subscribers to certain magazines and members of and contributors to certain organizations and causes. This is about the same number of names Richard Viguerie has; Viguerie, who maintains his own lists, deals in right-wing causes.

The role of the list entrepreneur is a new phenomenon in American politics; he is a new member of the cast of characters. And the list entrepreneurs don't simply raise money for candidates and causes; they can build political movements. At the end of January, Mathews, with Anderson's approval, financed and sent out a mailing to raise funds for Anderson, the theme of which was "The politicians and press don't think you count. . . . I do believe you count." This was very much along the line of the "Everybody's organized but the people" mailings that Mathews used to send out for Common Cause. In fact, in 1973 Mathews tried to persuade John Gardner, then the chairman of Common Cause, to run for President, but Gardner declined. Since then, Mathews has held to the theory that there is out there a great center, disgusted with both parties and ready to be organized politically. Perhaps, he thought, it could be organized around Anderson. The response to the Anderson mailing was uncommonly high. ("We knew we'd struck oil," Mathews says.) So, shortly before the Massachusetts primary, in early March, Mathews went to Boston to see Anderson and told him that he was sitting on top of a political phenomenon—that he could have the financial support of tens of thousands of people in the political middle, that millions of dollars could be raised—but that he could not remain a Republican if the phenomenon was to occur. Anderson was apparently fascinated and shaken by the idea—"That's a shattering concept," he said—and he and Mathews agreed to meet again.

Anderson went on as a Republican, lost the Massachusetts and Vermont primaries but did well enough to get attention, and then, in mid-March, lost in Illinois, his home state. In March, a few days before the Wisconsin primary, on April 1st, there was a meeting, at the Pfister Hotel in Milwaukee, of Anderson; Mathews; David Garth, the political-media expert; some members of Anderson's campaign staff; and Norman Lear, the television producer, who had become interested in Anderson. Anderson had gone to see Garth the previous fall but had found him too expensive at the time. Mathews and Garth made the case that Anderson's only chance to have an impact on the election was as an independent. Garth has said to me, "I didn't like Carter, I didn't like Reagan. John Anderson interested me. And the kind of challenge he was mounting had to come from the right of the spectrum. If there is to be a third, independent force, it can't come from the left—the two parties would gang up on it. But they can't gang up on a moderate, centrist campaign. In that sense, Anderson was ideally profiled for the role." Following that meeting, Mathews went to see Garth in New York, to find out whether he was interested in working on an independent campaign (he was), and talked to some lawyers in Washington about helping with the legal complexities of getting Anderson on the various state ballots. At a meeting in Malibu in April, Mathews spelled out to Anderson how an independent campaign could be launched, and Anderson replied, "When do we button this thing up?"

Then, after Anderson launched his campaign, everything changed. The focus of what campaign existed was on getting Anderson on the ballots, and Anderson himself virtually dropped from view. One reason was that so many resources were going into the ballot effort that there was no money for ads, and another was that—as Garth had predicted—the Party Conventions took up so much of the oxygen. When Anderson did make an interesting speech, it was barely covered. "We were out of sight," Garth says. "I couldn't find *me*." But there was still another reason: Anderson had become largely indistinguishable from any other politician seeking the Presidency, and what had become known as "the Anderson difference" was gone. Moreover, by the end of the summer the campaign was about a million dollars in debt. At the end of August came a "crisis" meeting in Washington; it was decided that Garth would take over the campaign full time, and that Mathews would travel with Anderson, to try to make some sense of the scheduling, and to handle some political problems and the press. (Anderson's campaign staff is composed of a number of people who are more earnest than experienced; press relations had not been very good, and Anderson tended to get cranky with the press.) It was decided that somehow Anderson had to find the voice that had captured imaginations at the outset, and that he had to recognize the paradox of his campaign: the only way he had a chance of winning the Presidency was by not focussing on winning the Presidency; like the Zen archer, he had to let the arrow shoot itself. "The campaign had nearly expired," says Mathews.

Then came some breaks: Anderson's success, after some efforts in various directions, at coming up with a running mate—Patrick Lucey, the former Democratic Governor of Wisconsin and an ally of Edward Kennedy's; the League of Women Voters' announcement that Anderson would be included in the Presidential debates if he stood at about fifteen percent in the polls (this focussed attention on how Anderson stood in the polls and led to the fuss over whether Carter would participate in the debate, which focussed more attention on Anderson); the decision of the Liberal Party in New York to list Anderson on its Presidential line; and the Federal Election Commission's certification that Anderson's campaign would be eligible for federal funding if he received as much as five percent of the vote on November 4th. The F.E.C.'s ruling meant that Anderson could borrow against that assurance—and, consequently, would have to stay in the race in order to pay off his debts.

In working up a platform, the Anderson people tried to put together something that would appear to contain ideas without appearing to have tried too hard to contain ideas. Ideologically, the platform goes down the aisle between the two parties. It calls for tax incentives to labor and management for wage and price restraint (an idea that Carter once proposed and then gave up on); for a reindustrialization program that would provide tax incentives and bonuses to rehabilitate troubled industries and increase productivity; for an Urban Reinvestment Trust Fund (the funds to come from federal excise taxes on alcohol and tobacco), to encourage the rebuilding of cities; for a Community Transportation Trust Fund (also from federal excise taxes), for mass transit; and, of course, for the fifty-cents-a-gallon tax on gasoline which Anderson has been espousing. The platform stresses energy conservation, defends foreign aid, and offers specific proposals for dealing with the pending deficits in Social Security finances. Anderson's staff prepared a number of speeches based on the platform, but Anderson largely ignored them. Anderson's loner quality has made him difficult for his would-be managers to manage, and while that may be just as well, it frustrates them considerably.

Candidates do need advice. It is difficult to tell when advice becomes manipulation, and apparently Anderson thinks it does very soon. "He's exasperatingly, maddeningly self-directed," says one of his would-be advisers. Another describes him as "impenetrable." Independence from manipulation by image makers is a healthy thing, but Anderson's general approach raises the question of how he would do at such a collegial enterprise as trying to run the government. Anderson's speaking style has been uneven, often leaving his audiences flat—and not just because he was saying that they would have to do hard things, face difficult realities. Anderson is a very well-informed man, and he can come across as a clear thinker, impressive, and even charming; he is not humorless when he is at ease. But he can also come across as didactic, humorless, preachy, and not the sort of fellow you would like to have around all the time. To a lot of people, that was how he came across in the League of Women Voters debate. When he does do something that sets him apart—such as telling aerospace workers at TRW that he opposes the MX missile (TRW has a research contract for the new missile), or stressing that, unlike Carter and Reagan, he is not proposing cuts in individual income taxes—he seems self-conscious. He sometimes seems to be saying things for the purpose of setting himself apart. When the politics of "differentness" is forced, it is simply another form of politics. Anderson seems compelled to keep telling us that he is different. He recently told an audience in California, "I simply will not cater to popular opinion at the expense of any of the things I have stood for."

The political problem of his campaign, which some of the people around him recognize, is that Anderson has not succeeded in reaching beyond the relatively educated, affluent voters who (along with some college students) form the core of his constituency—beyond the people on Mathews' lists—to the great mass of voters. Some of his associates say he has not had time to do this; it may also be, some say, that he does not have the personality to do it—that the same qualities that cause him to be a loner show up in his campaign persona and tend to be off-putting. Some politicians can reach from the intelligentsia to the factory worker; in fact, a politician must be able to do this, not only to win but also to govern this country. Anderson, however, does not seem to be able to. This raises the question of what the Anderson campaign is about.

At some point in the last couple of weeks, as a result less of any specific incident than of the roiling of the campaign, Anderson stopped thinking that it made any difference whether Carter or Reagan won. The mixture of conviction, self-justification, anger, and bruises that leads to such a reaction is difficult to sort out. But it is clear that Anderson and the top people in his campaign now do not care who gets elected. They now define the campaign as at least a vehicle for "shaking up the system." Garth has said to me, "The shock to the American system from this campaign could be very important. He's trying to talk reality and give people as close to the unvarnished truth as I've ever seen given. People are cynical about the system, because they see too many politicians acting out of cynicism. People say we're destroying the political system. What system are people defending? No one gives a damn about it. His campaign serves as a real warning to the system: that either you do better than Jimmy Carter and Ronald Reagan or you can't bask in the security of the two-party system—that when fifty percent of the people in this country don't give a damn about politics, you are on the very edge of instability.'' Mathews says, ''If he even slightly takes some of the fatuousness out of our political system it's important. Maybe he's a pioneer and he's breaking ground.''

But there are other thoughts about what the Anderson candidacy might lead to. There is a possibility that what has been begun with Anderson will go on with or without him, and probably without him—a very strong possibility that an effort will be made to take the constituency that has been built around his candidacy and either turn it into a new party or use it to try to take over one of the existing parties.

In other respects, too, the implications of the Anderson campaign go well beyond Anderson. The tension between keeping some flexibility in the system by providing the wherewithal for independent movements and risking the disruption that such movements could cause is just beginning to be considered. Chastising the two major parties is a different matter from breaking up the two-party system. An effort to take over one of the existing parties is one thing: the major parties have, at some points in history, changed their definitions and their bases. But starting additional ones or launching independent candidacies has other implications. For one thing, anybody can do it. The techniques are becoming more sophisticated. And the next person who makes such an effort may not be as benign a figure as Anderson. Moreover, it risks further fractioning, even paralysis, of the political system. ''We are lurching toward fragmentation,'' says Robert Teeter, the Republican pollster and analyst. ''And all the things we are doing in the name of people's right to run independent candidacies lead us to it.'' And then, it raises the question of how someone elected without an established political base can govern. The ability to command ''the media'' is at once an insufficient and a potentially dangerous basis for governing. It is beginning to occur even to some people to whom independent movements once seemed appealing that the noble, issue-oriented, well-meaning independent voters who disdain the parties and fear that in trying to shore up the role of the major parties we might ''go back to the bosses'' have not faced the fact that the alternative might be to go forward toward Italy. ''Except,'' says one man in Washington who has been involved in political reform, ''that if we built a multiparty system we would do it infinitely more skillfully and destructively than Italy. It would be Special Interest, Inc.'' A politician who is tied to a large party structure, whatever its failings, and whatever his willingness to ignore it, has at least some protection from the cross-pressures; a politician without such ties has no instrument to rally behind him.

Following the press conference, Anderson makes a stop at a center for the elderly at the northern tip of Manhattan, adjacent to the Bronx. The press bus gets lost, and we arrive just as Anderson is leaving. There have been a number of logistical mishaps in this campaign. After Anderson returns to the Statler, where he and his entourage are staying, I have a talk with him in his suite, on the seventeenth floor. He is hoarse from campaigning, and, a slight man, looks thinner than usual. I ask him how he thinks he's doing, compared with how he felt when he started on this venture last spring.

He replies, "I honestly think that we have gone much farther than I ever believed possible then. I was never under any illusions about the difficulty of my quest—bereft of party organization and funds. But I continue to be reinforced and assuaged by the knowledge that I am serving a very useful purpose: giving people hope. Those feelings will be dismissed by the cynical as delusions, but I'm not given to delusions."

I ask Anderson how, if his quest is futile, he gives people hope.

He replies, "I think the people who support me—I guess the young excepted, who tend to be more idealistic and unwilling to concede the insurmountable heights we're supposed to be assaulting—believe it is helpful to have an independent candidacy, to challenge the two-party system. And the longer the candidacy goes on, the more unworthy the two other candidates seem. I don't want to sound querulous, but Reagan lacks balance: he's for giving everything to the oil companies; the Russians are behind everything. And Carter stands for a failed Presidency, and his campaign is nothing but a desperate attempt to cling to office. I had given him credit for being steady and cool; now I think the fear of defeat has caused him to lose his cool. The statement he made the other day about war and peace reveals an instability of his character that could affect his Presidency. He has gone far beyond normal political hyperbole. I don't think it's a very pretty picture."

I ask Anderson when he crossed the line into not caring whether Carter or Reagan is elected.

"I don't know, but increasingly, as I went around the country, it wasn't just the siren call and the admiring throngs," he replies. "I felt it was really selling people short to say that John Anderson would decide by his participation or non-participation who the next President should be. There's nothing wrong for there to be three candidates. For me to calibrate that I take more from this fellow than the other fellow, and this fellow is worse than the other fellow—it was a pretentious thought to begin with that I might drop out of the race and decide which candidacy should succeed. For me to decide that my candidacy is going to affect things one way or the other is pretentious." In effect, Anderson has turned his original formulation upside down. "And, what the heck, if I dropped out, a lot of these people wouldn't vote at all. I guess, as a result of my personal experiences, I have given the American people more credit for their ability to make their own decisions, and have come to believe that it's not up to one single man to decide who's going to be elected. This is what I tell myself—and I could be wrong: I tell myself that my candidacy will give millions of people a candidate whom they believe and whom they trust—particularly young people, to whom I feel a particular responsibility. It's very important that they not feel turned off by the system. I think history will prove what I've been saying—that not since at least 1968, with the McCarthy movement, have they been so excited about a campaign. I think that's an important thing I can do for the political system—give those people a chance to participate."

I ask Anderson if it worries him that his candidacy could cause the election not to be settled on November 4th, and require it to be decided in the House of Representatives next January. (This could happen if the electoral votes were very closely divided between Carter and Reagan and if Anderson carried a single state.)

Anderson pauses. Then he says, "Not really. No. The Constitution did make provision for this. I've said before that Gerald Ford served as an unelected President for almost two and a half years and no one challenged his mantle of leadership. Whatever the opportunities for mischief in having the House elect the President, you can't challenge the legitimacy of the process. The Constitution provides for it. No, I'm not struck dumb with terror by that prospect. I think the system would survive."

CHAPTER 13

The President _____

DETROIT, WEDNESDAY, OCTOBER 1ST. Shortly before 10:30 A.M., President Carter is to arrive at the airport here for a campaign trip that will take him to a Ford automobile plant nearby, and following that he will go on to Flint, where he will hold a "town meeting," and then to Niagara Falls, New York, for more campaign events this evening. On Monday, he went to New York City for an appearance before the International Ladies' Garment Workers' Union, at which he reaffirmed his support for aid to New York City; made an appeal for the Jewish vote, which is a real problem for him, by saying that Israel's expulsion from the United Nations would "raise the gravest questions" about the further participation of the United States; and expressed his strong support for the Equal Rights Amendment, which Ronald Reagan opposes. (The Carter campaign's polls find that the E.R.A. is an issue that works especially well for Carter.) Tomorrow, Carter will make appearances in Ohio and Pennsylvania.

The President is travelling more during this fall campaign than he and his aides had planned, largely because they don't know what else to do. While campaign officials and Carter aides have recently been saying for public consumption that they are optimistic, they have been worried. They have had the sense for some time that the Carter campaign is stalled—is in what several of them term a "lull." Even as they made a case for how Carter could win, they were anxious. They concede that at this point Reagan is leading in electoral votes; that he has arrested the slide that began with his gaffes earlier in the campaign; and that Carter has suffered a slight decline in his standing. A number of the President's aides attribute this to the flurry that started in mid-September over some Carter statements that drew attention to his tendency to show a certain mean streak when he campaigns. (The tendency has been apparent since 1976, and even earlier; what happened this fall was that there became a sufficient number of examples of it to form a critical mass, and there was sufficient disenchantment with Carter, and with the whole campaign, that the subject received a good deal more—disproportionate—attention.) Carter's aides recognize that what they have sought to make the central theme of this campaign—that there is a real difference between Ronald Reagan and Jimmy Carter, and that it matters greatly who is elected—has failed to take hold.

This was among the things that the President and his top campaign advisers discussed at a meeting in the family quarters of the White House yesterday afternoon. Such meetings are held on the average of once a week. Campaign officials and White House aides who work on the campaign also meet each morning at eight o'clock at the Carter/Mondale Re-Election Committee headquarters, on L Street, a few blocks from the White House; and each afternoon at two a number of officials meet in the office of Richard Moe, the Vice President's chief of staff, to frame responses to something that may have arisen in the campaign that day. This is an outgrowth of a group that met every afternoon during the primaries to frame responses to Edward Kennedy.

The original plan for the fall had been what the President's advisers called a "limited Rose Garden strategy;" the theory was that Gerald Ford had done well in 1976 when he stayed in the White House and left Carter, the challenger, out there scrambling around. Now, however, Carter's aides feel that the President does not get attention when he does "Presidential" deeds at the White House, and so he must go on the road. The problem, of course, is that Carter wore out the White House as a backdrop during the primaries. But there are positive reasons as well for having the President travel. His visits do get ample local coverage—the Carter people have become quite skilled at assuring that—and it has been found that his political fortunes are usually boosted in an area he has visited. Some of the President's trips are in connection with efforts to raise money for the Democratic Party, which is far behind the Republicans in this. But at the heart of Carter's campaign are problems that are a reflection, and an extension, of problems that have troubled his Presidency: for reasons of personality and style, and as a result of his approach to the Presidency, Carter has failed to build a committed constituency. Says one of his campaign aides, "We've got the age-old Carter problem—that we have never had a broad base of enthusiastic support. His support is wide—cuts across a lot of groups—but not very strong." In effect, what Carter has to do in this campaign, after four years of the Presidency, is go out in the country and start all over again.

Carter has been trying to establish the theme that it does matter whether he or Reagan is elected by saying in his campaign appearances that this election presents "a choice between two futures." Last summer, Patrick

Caddell outlined this approach in a memorandum to the President, and he drew a diagram to illustrate it. The idea was to get people thinking about the future—on the theory that the present might not be a very advantageous ground to fight the election on—and to show that, by making hard decisions now, under Carter, on such issues as energy and the economy, the country could have a good future, whereas if it accepted Reagan's "simple solutions" it would have a bad future. Carter and his aides have had a hard time finding a way to make a positive case for his re-election.

The "good future–bad future" theme was launched in the President's acceptance speech at the Democratic Convention, and Carter has been using it on the road ever since. The "good future" means economic security, justice, and peace, and the "bad future" means despair, surrender (to the oil merchants, to economic misery), and "the risk of international confrontation." It was the way he stated this theme in California last week— saying that the decision made in November "will help to decide whether we have war or peace"—that got him into trouble. Jody Powell did tell reporters afterward that this was an "overstatement," and then issued a list of Reagan quotes to show that Reagan had suggested the use of military force in nine situations in recent years. (Sometimes it is not clear what Reagan was suggesting, but the list does indicate a pattern of thinking.) The President's aides are upset that the press paid more attention to the President's statement than to the list, and they say that the question of Reagan's judgment in international crises is a valid issue (and Caddell's polls indicate that Reagan is vulnerable on it) and that they intend to pursue it. So much might not have been made of Carter's statement about "war or peace" if the press and the President's political opponents had not been on the lookout for statements that illustrated Carter's inclination to lash out—just as, shortly before, the attention had been on Reagan's gaffes.

These things go in fashions during Presidential campaigns. And the nature of press coverage contributes to the impression that is created. The one controversial line is likely to be what is mentioned in the brief network report on a campaign. Once the press, generally speaking, feels that the attention should be on a certain aspect of a candidate's campaign (his gaffes, bumbles, foibles, overstatements, stammerings), that's where the attention goes, and stays—until a new subject comes into fashion. Meanwhile, like as not, the public has got a distorted impression of what is going on. Gerald Ford was not always bumping his head on helicopters and liberating Eastern Europe; Edward Kennedy was not always inarticulate; Ronald Reagan was not always making gaffes; Jimmy Carter is not always being mean. The 1976 campaign—or any campaign within memory—was not exactly a minuet. Carter has got into trouble lately not only because of his inclination to meanness at times, which has worried White House aides, but also because, with his penchant for hyperbole in all manner of circumstances (there is hardly a foreign leader or a Democratic politician who is not his "close friend"), he is sometimes loose with his language; because, frankly, a lot of people in the press, like a lot of the public, are down on Carter—are disillusioned with him, find him a not very likable man; because there is despair about the choices the public has and the kind of campaign that is taking place. What Carter has said is not as reckless as has been portrayed. And when Carter makes such a statement, Reagan has an opportunity, which he seizes, to react more in sorrow (just as Carter did when Reagan made his remark that Carter had begun his fall campaign "in the city that gave birth to and is the parent body of the Ku Klux Klan"), and say that the people are owed an apology—which he does very well. And meanwhile the attention remains on Carter's, rather than on Reagan's, campaign. None of the President's advisers defend the statement he made at the Ebenezer Baptist Church, in Atlanta, suggesting that Reagan had injected the issue of the Ku Klux Klan into the campaign (this isn't quite what happened)—a charge that Carter linked with criticism of Reagan's talking about "states' rights" in Philadelphia, Mississippi, in August. Having made these charges, the President said, dramatically, "Hatred has no place in this country. Racism has no place in this country"—and immediately got himself embroiled in a furor over whether he was calling Reagan a racist.

White House aides complain that the press does not pay enough attention to some of Reagan's controversial statements. They have been trying to think of ways to draw attention to Reagan's courtship of right-wing evangelicals without having Carter himself offend the "born again" vote. They say that the press does not pay attention when anyone other than the President criticizes Reagan, and so the President has to do it. The Carter people also complain that Reagan has been allowed to get away with exaggerating his achievements as Governor of California. The problem here is that most journals at some point—probably back during the primaries—did examine that record, and they can't keep on doing it. Carter's aides, remembering their own campaign strategy of four years ago, are concerned that Reagan has convinced people that he was a good governor and that people will conclude that if he was a good governor he would be a good President. (Caddell's polls indicate that people do believe Reagan was a good governor.) Gerald Rafshoon has made some "man-in-the-street" commercials to counter Reagan's claims. The main effort, though, is to heighten concern about Reagan as President. Says one Carter strategist, "The most important thing is to make people think of Reagan and the Presidency." Therefore, Rafshoon has made a series of commercials showing an empty Oval Office as a narrator says, "When you come right down to it, what kind of a person should occupy the Oval Office?" and then asks if it should be "a man who, like Ronald Reagan," said, or proposed—and then the commercials cite, depending on the issue, Reagan's positions on military interventions, China, urban aid, aid to New York City (which Reagan opposed until just the other day), and so on, and all these positions are contrasted with the positions Carter has taken.

The President's campaign team had hoped Reagan would be "blown away" by this time, but now they assume that, barring any dramatic event, the election will stay uncertain to the end. They do, however, feel vindicated in their decision, which was one of the most difficult they had to make, to have the President avoid the League of Women Voters debate with Reagan and John Anderson. They take some pleasure in Anderson's recent drop in the polls—and in the fact that Anderson's standing did not improve after the debate—and, stressing how badly he is doing, seem to be trying to talk him out of the race. Their hopes for a Carter victory rest on the Democrats' becoming more united now than was widely predicted at the time of the Convention this summer; on this becoming an increasingly partisan campaign, causing Democrats to "come home" (and there are more Democrats than Republicans); on Carter's record coming to be more appreciated and questions about Reagan's suitability for the Presidency taking hold; on the advantages of incumbency coming to bear. The Carter people have been hopeful that the sheer effort the entire Carter team—the Cabinet, the Vice President, the First Lady, other members of the Administration, and especially the President himself—is putting into the campaign will pay off. One campaign official says, "At some point, stamina counts for something." Still, several of the President's chief strategists—in particular Hamilton Jordan and Caddell—are aware that the campaign needs a new approach, and they have been searching for one.

Lined up to meet the President at the Detroit airport today is the usual set of dignitaries—in this case, the mayors of Detroit and surrounding cities—and a row of new cars. Fuel-efficient 1981 models are parked on the runway, with signs atop them giving the name of the company: a Chrysler K car, a General Motors Buick Skylark, a Volkswagen made in America, a Ford Escort, and an American Motors Eagle. The automobile industry has been both the cause and the symbol of Michigan's high unemployment, and these cars represent the hope for a recovery, so the politicians come here to associate themselves with them. Carter narrowly lost Michigan four years ago, and it is one of the states that are being fought over hardest. Both sides claim they are ahead here.

A month ago, Reagan, who had opposed the recent government loan to Chrysler, came to Detroit and praised the Chrysler K car. Just before the opening of the Republican Convention in Detroit last July, the President stopped here at 7 A.M. en route to Tokyo to announce a series of actions he was taking to help the automobile industry. Yesterday, the White House announced a tripartite agreement between steel companies, steelworkers, and the government to help the steel industry. (Among other things, it will hold down the importation of steel—a policy that reverses a decision Carter made earlier this year and that could make cars, and many other things, cost more.) Automobiles and steel, of course, affect the economies of a number of states—particularly the ones the President will be visiting this week. (A White House aide said to me yesterday that the steel agreement would have "a big impact" in Ohio, Pennsylvania, and New York.) Douglas Fraser, the head of the United Auto Workers, has flown here with the President. Fraser supported Kennedy for the nomination, but now his union is working hard for Carter's re-election—as are many other labor organiza-

tions. Aside from the campaign organization itself, labor is the most important component of the President's re-election effort: getting people
registered, "educating" union members, and, on Election Day, getting out
the vote.

Now the President, dressed in a navy pin-striped suit, alights from Air
Force One, which is always an impressive prop—blue, silver, and white,
with "United States of America" painted on its side and a flag on its tail—
and greets the dignitaries, after which he goes over to inspect the cars. As
the photographers snap away, he stops at each car, listens to a company
executive describe it, peers under the hood, asks questions. The President
of the United States is blessing the new cars. The Reagan people may be
good at arranging settings for their candidate, but how can a challenger beat
this? Jody Powell, standing off to the side, has just received word from
Washington that Reagan has said in an interview that he would scrap the
SALT II treaty (he said something to this effect in Philadelphia earlier this
fall) and went on to say that "the one card that's been missing in these
negotiations has been the possibility of an arms race." Powell is happily
telling reporters about it, but what use the President will make of this development has not yet been decided.

After about fifteen minutes of car inspection, the President leaves in a
motorcade for a Ford plant in Wayne, a suburb of Detroit. The plant had
been shut down about half the time during the first six months of this year,
and then this summer it was closed for six weeks while it was converted for
the production of the new cars. The plant is currently working two shifts in
order to get the cars—the Escort and the Lynx—on the market. Models are
in the showrooms, and the cars will go on sale Friday. Obviously, it doesn't
hurt to have the President here today. Carter, wearing protective plastic
glasses, tours the noisy plant in the company of Philip Caldwell, Ford's
chairman; John Latini, the plant manager; and other company officials. He
shakes hands with workers, gives them friendly smiles, and manages to look
interested as the new models are explained to him. All the while, of course,
he is surrounded by Secret Service agents and a large retinue of photographers. And then, as the pièce de résistance, the President gets in a red 1981
Escort, fastens his seat belt, and drives the car a few yards, off the assembly
line. He doesn't often get to drive anymore. White House aides make sure
that the photographers are in place.

Outside the plant, the President makes some remarks to a waiting crowd.
Two high school bands are on hand to play "Hail to the Chief," which they
do rather lugubriously, and then Fraser and Caldwell, labor and management, praise the President for what he has done for the automobile industry.
(Fraser says, "My dear sisters and brothers, for your own sake and for the
sake of your country, re-elect Jimmy Carter." Caldwell reminds the crowd
of the President's trip to Detroit last summer, and praises his new tax
proposals to help industry and his "new approach to cost-effective regulations.") The President steps to a blue-topped lectern with the Presidential
seal, which appears everywhere he does. He looks tired, and much aged

from when he was doing this sort of thing fours years ago, but he is not as pale as he sometimes is. It's a warm, sunny day, and he seems to enjoy being out here campaigning. "I've just seen some of the best-designed, best-built, most up-to-date automobiles in the world," he says. He follows his prepared text only in part—and this may be why on occasion he gets in trouble. He tells the crowd, "I remember as a boy in Georgia living on a farm studying the magazine ads as the new models for each year were revealed, and then as soon as I could get a chance to go to the county seat, over in Americus, Georgia, I would go there and look with wide-open eyes at the new American cars in the local automobile dealerships." He praises the automobile industry for having met consumers' demand for more fuel-efficient cars. (He does not mention how long it has taken the industry to get around to making such cars.) And he says, "Today, as President, I urge American consumers to go into the showrooms around this country and test-drive these new American cars. There's not a better-built, safer, more durable, or more efficient car today than these new American models." He tells the crowd he will make certain that the thousands of new cars and trucks the government will buy in the next few months are American-made. The crowd applauds. (It is already law that the government give preference to cars and trucks made in America.) He says, "I pledge to you that as President I'll use the full resources of my own office to insure that the American automobile industry has access to the capital it needs to retool, to compete, and to maintain its rightful share of the American automobile market." The President's recent tax-cut proposals are tilted in favor of the ailing automobile and steel industries.

Carter talks about steps he has taken to reduce foreign competition. (The Japanese have cooperated by announcing that they have asked their automobile exporters to "exercise prudence.") He talks about the new partnerships that have been established between industry, labor, and government to deal with the automobile and steel industries. Where we are headed with these arrangements is something that is yet to be sorted out. The advantage is that they provide a way of bringing conflicting interests to the table (industry, labor, and environmentalists were involved in the negotiations concerning steel) and getting something done; the disadvantage is that the interests of the consumer might not be adequately represented. The subject of "reindustrialization" is all the rage, but it means different things to different people: it can mean bailing out sick industries, worthy or not; it can mean placing bets on new industries; it can mean paying off political I.O.U.s. Now the President brings in Franklin Roosevelt—perhaps he and Reagan are competing over who mentions him more often—and points out that Roosevelt and the automobile industry cooperated during the Depression and during the Second World War. And then he closes—sounding a bit like John Connally during the primaries—by saying, "I intend to be your President when a constant stream of ships full of American-built cars are unloading in Tokyo and Yokohama, and I want your help to make that come true." The audience applauds warmly. It's the President's birthday, and so he is given a several-tiered cake, and the crowd sings "Happy Birthday," somewhat awkwardly. Carter returns to the microphone and remarks, smiling, "You make cars better than you sing."

Ronald Reagan may talk, however vaguely, about the tax breaks and the jobs he will propose and provide; Carter can propose and provide them. Actually, Carter didn't have much to do with the automobile industry's eventual decision to build cars that were more fuel-efficient—he, like Gerald Ford before him, urged the companies to make the change, but the main inspiration came from OPEC and the consumers—yet he can drape himself on this progress, and he can offer help.

One Carter adviser said to me some time ago that the Carter people felt that Ford didn't make very imaginative use of incumbency in 1976, and that they intended to do better. These trips offer good examples of what is possible. And there are many others. So much was made earlier this year of the Administration's use of well-timed grants and other federal projects that this approach is being played down—but not abandoned. Whenever such examples of federal munificence are announced, or discovered, Administration officials are careful to say that they had been "in the works." But, of course, the officials were aware that an election was coming, and what its date was. A large number of projects will be announced before the election. The Carter people did not invent this device; they just perfected it. Chicago, for example, was the recipient early this fall of quite a bit of federal good will. The Administration was concerned about the press attention that this got in Illinois, because, while it is pleased to have the support of Mayor Jane Byrne, it knows that she remains controversial and engaged in a bitter political struggle with Richard M. Daley, who supported Carter in the primaries. Campaign trips to Illinois are highly delicate matters. These local struggles affect Presidential politics all the time. Vice President Mondale ushered the aircraft carrier U.S.S. *Saratoga* into Philadelphia yesterday for a five-hundred-million-dollar overhaul at the Philadelphia navy yard. Standing on the deck of the carrier, the Vice President said that because of the project "thousands of jobs that would have been lost will be saved and thousands of new jobs will be created." (There are, of course, some other not very subtle uses of incumbency, such as the Administration's recent decision to allow price supports for dairy products to rise, reversing an earlier Agriculture Department policy. A similar decision was made just before the Wisconsin primary. The Carter people didn't invent this device, either—though now, because of campaign-finance laws, no contributions can be involved.) But it is probably generally true, as some Carter officials say, that federal bounty is less important to the campaign at this stage than it was during the primaries. At that point, Carter had to rally elected Democratic officials against the Kennedy challenge, and while there are no longer many elected officials who can turn out a big vote, such people can be helpful in primaries and caucuses, where the turnout is usually quite low.

The Carter people are counting more heavily now on the benefits from the careful cultivation of special-interest and ethnic groups which has been going on for quite some time. The Administration worked with many of these groups in the formulation of policies, appointed many of their representatives to key Administration posts, and installed people in the White House to look after their concerns. All this was not done simply in the interest of enlightened government. There are good reasons for grass-roots involvement in policy making and for being conscious, in making appointments, of the various segments of society. But the Carter Administration appears to have gone beyond such considerations and into an intensely political exercise. And White House people are making extensive efforts to see that the exercise pays off. For example, toward the end of last year the Administration announced a program to help rural areas and small towns, and the direction of the program was placed in the same White House office that coordinates assistance to mayors and governors. In all, about thirty people in the White House, some detailed from other agencies, are working on it. "The result is that there are hundreds of organizations all over the country that are pursuing rural economic-development projects," a White House official says. Along the way, these groups have been invited to the White House for "consultation." A couple of months ago, women leaders from rural areas came to the White House; a couple of days ago, farm workers' organizations met there. At the Democratic Convention, delegates representing rural areas were gathered for a meeting with Jack Watson, who used to head the White House liaison office and is currently the President's chief of staff. One White House aide says of this program, "It's translatable into political payoff. We've briefed our campaign field people on it. It's just fundamental politics. These rural groups can work on registration and getting out the vote, and they have a stake in Jimmy Carter's staying in office." This man explains, "What's going on at this point is not so much constituency stroking—with such a short time to go before the election, there's no time for that. If we're going to reap the harvest of what we've done for the last three years, we'll do it now. If we haven't sown the seeds yet, forget it. One of the real secrets of this Administration is that we've worked at constituency development: if you look down the list of organizations and constituency groups, you'll find policies to match. We've gone out to constituency groups and said, 'What are your needs?' " The National Education Association got the Administration to create the Department of Education, and the education profession in general got the largest increases in spending for education to have taken place in any administration. Mayors and governors have been treated solicitously. The Administration has tripled the size of federal procurement for minority contractors. The White House aide says, "The story of this Administration is that we've made the guts of government work in ways that pay off."

One theory behind the care that has been taken in making appointments, it was explained to me, is that in a time of economic difficulty the appointment of minority-group members to the executive branch and the judiciary gives the Administration something to talk about. There is a White House aide whose sole job is to deal with ethnic groups, one whose job is to work with labor, one who works with blacks, one who works with Hispanics, one who works with women, one who works with Jews, one who works with consumer groups. The head of the Council on Environmental Quality, which is within the Executive Office of the President, has been working with environmental groups. One weekend in September, representatives of several of these organizations—Friends of the Earth, the Sierra Club, the Fund for Animals, the Audubon Society, the Wilderness Society—had a day-long meeting in Washington to decide what they were going to do politically. According to a White House official, they considered endorsing Anderson, on the theory that if Anderson did well enough to throw the election into the House of Representatives, they would have substantial bargaining power. But then, according to the White House official, "cooler heads prevailed," and it was decided that leaders of these groups (twenty-two of them) would come to the White House and meet with the President on September 10th and announce their endorsement of him—which they did. (The endorsements were made in the names of the individual leaders, not of the organizations, either for policy reasons or, in some cases, because the organizations are tax-exempt.) A few days later, the environmentalists met with representatives of the Carter campaign to discuss where to concentrate their efforts to do the most good. The Sierra Club, for example, which has a political-action committee, is expected to concentrate its efforts on New York and California. (Last week, the President designated the Channel Islands, off Santa Barbara, a marine sanctuary—a matter of great importance to the Sierra Club—and the word went out over the environmentalists' network right away.) A similar sequence of events was followed with senior citizens' organizations and consumer groups. All these organizations have strong networks that can be helpful in the campaign. One White House aide says, "It does translate into activity at the grass-roots level. That's what it's all about."

The Carter campaign has put together an ad-hoc ethnic campaign committee, which, according to a Carter aide, represents just about every ethnic group in the country. "All those groups are out there working for us," the aide says. Unlike the national environmental or consumer groups, this person explained, the ethnic groups are organized more on a community basis, and can be quite helpful in specific areas. This person said that the President should do very well with the Polish National Alliance, an organization based in Chicago, to which the President made a speech a couple of weeks ago. (And last week Stanislaw Walesa, the father of Lech Walesa, the leader of the recent strikes in Poland, met with the President at the White House. On Labor Day, Walesa had stood alongside Reagan with the Statue of Liberty as a backdrop. Now he said he was grateful to Carter for the economic help the United States was giving Poland, and that he would support him. Walesa is not, however, a citizen.) Work is going on with groups of Italian-Americans, Greek-Americans, Lithuanian-Americans. "And don't forget the country-and-Western fans," a White House aide said. "Willie Nelson!" Willie Nelson is a favorite of the President and some of his aides, and his political utility has not been overlooked. They thought it was quite a stroke to have Willie Nelson sing the National Anthem one night at the Democratic Convention.

All this constituency courting may explain a good deal about Jimmy Carter's politics, and also about his Presidency. One White House aide put it this way: "People ask, 'Where's the theory? Where's the glue?' We built the record of this Administration bit by bit, group by group. We weren't unaware of the political benefits, and it fits Jimmy Carter's style. It's the way he ran for election four years ago. He's inductive rather than deductive. We've worked with the individual groups and tried to solve constituency problems. If we have failed, we have failed to draw it together and give people a picture of what it all adds up to. Therefore, people say, 'What's he done?' It's all of a piece with his politics." Carter ran for the nomination in 1976 by trying to pick off this group and that one, and this was part of what led people to decide that he was "fuzzy." He carried what many see as the habits acquired in a campaign for the nomination into his campaign for the Presidency, and then right into the White House. There was something for this group and something for that one, something here and something there, and no one, including Carter, could say what it all added up to. Some people who have observed him at close hand think the problem of definition goes back further than the first campaign for the Presidency; they suggest that it stems from a tradition in Southern politics of deliberately blurring the picture, of consciously avoiding definition.

Flint. At one point last summer, Flint had an unemployment rate of twenty-six percent, and its unemployment is currently just under twenty percent. Reagan challenged Carter to come here, and he and his aides decided to take up the challenge. Carter will hold a "town meeting"—a favorite device of the Carter campaign. His aides feel that this kind of event gives him a chance to demonstrate his intelligence and his command of the issues —and it has other advantages. Carter is better at doing these meetings than at giving set speeches; moreover, such meetings are preferable to rallies, where the press will make a crowd count and note the degree of enthusiasm. The questioners can be relied on to ask less pointed questions than the White House press corps does, and the audience can be depended on to be appreciative. Also, these meetings tend to be held in gyms, where the applause and the cheers resonate well. The President's aides say that the audience is selected by lot from people who send in coupons that have been printed in the papers along with an announcement that the President is coming to town (thus stirring a bit of pre-visit excitement), but there are indications that certain groups are urged to have members in attendance. Before the President arrives at a meeting, a Carter organizer selects the questioners at random, but with an eye out to see that different ages, races, sexes, and ethnic origins are represented. Carter aides say that the questions are not screened. A local television station usually broadcasts the entire town meeting, as will happen in the case of today's event, and there is extensive local and regional coverage. Also, while he is in an area the President will often give an interview, lasting perhaps half an hour, to from one to four local TV and radio reporters. And he usually gives a newspaper interview as well, to be run in question-and-answer form in a local paper. Following today's town meeting, Carter will give such an interview to a reporter from the Detroit *Free Press*. Jody Powell has explained to me that these television and newspaper interviews give the President an opportunity to talk about his record, which the President's aides are convinced the national press will not cover when he talks about it in campaign appearances.

Today's town meeting is held in the gymnasium of the Flint Northern Community High School. A band plays "Hail to the Chief" when the President enters, to great applause. In his opening remarks, Carter tells the audience he is pleased to be in Flint on his birthday (cheers) and praises the cars he saw earlier today (more cheers). He urges Americans to buy American-made cars (applause) and says, "I will not rest as President until our automobile industry is completely competitive and has its tax laws written and economic assistance provided and investment capital ready and the protection of American workers that's necessary for us to make our entire American automobile industry competitive in every sense of the word." He talks about the "new partnerships" between government and labor and industry. And he talks again about the cooperation between the automobile industry and Franklin Roosevelt.

He says once more, "I intend to be President when a constant stream of American ships filled with American-built automobiles are unloading every week and every month in Tokyo and Yokohama, and I want you to help make that pledge come true." (Cheers, applause.) The President answers questions about the Cuban-refugee problem, and he points out that the Administration first cut the number of refugees (the "open arms" policy was causing serious political trouble, especially in Florida, a key state for Carter), that Cuba has now ended the refugee flow, and that refugees who have not yet been settled will be sent to Puerto Rico. (Puerto Rico has no electoral votes.)

One questioner gives a little speech about the importance of Flint. The President says that he agrees, and he points out that he is here (applause), that he and Mondale came here together on the night before the 1976 election (applause), and that this is his fifth visit here (applause). He also says that he knows the citizens of Flint have been hurt by the fact that the automobile industry was too slow to change its models—"my heart goes out to those who suffer"—and that his Administration is working to put Flint back on its feet.

Carter is asked "what the future is for our senior citizens," and he replies that that depends a lot on what happens on November 4th, and then goes on to talk about the importance of keeping the Social Security system sound.

He says that Social Security payments must keep up with inflation, and adds, "We need a nationwide comprehensive health program for our people." (Carter hasn't been talking about national health insurance much lately, but in 1976 he did promise the U.A.W. that he would back such a program.) There are more questions about what he will do for the automobile industry and for Flint, and questions about the current fighting between Iran and Iraq. The President's aides are not unaware that the war presents a situation in which the President can appear "Presidential." The pity of it is, for him and for the country, that incumbents have so exploited international situations for political purposes—Carter didn't invent this device, either, but he certainly makes use of it—that the public is highly skeptical of anything that is said or done about such crises.

Carter is positive and definite in giving his answers. From the time he came on the national scene, it was clear that he enjoyed appearing knowledgeable (whether he knew just what he was talking about or not), like a schoolboy who has studied his lessons. As President, he has a lot more information to draw on. Carter is a studier. He gets to the office between 5:30 and 6 A.M., and often spends several hours in solitude, accessible to no one. He is an almost obsessive self-improver. Even his recreations—tennis, jogging—are ones that call for self-improvement.

Now a little girl asks him a question that is almost too good to be true: "My daddy is a Republican and my mom is undecided. What is the difference between the Republican and you so I can tell my parents how to vote?" The President tells the little girl that that is an excellent question and says that the Democratic Party "has always been the one that cared most about human beings," and he talks about this at length, identifying himself closely with the traditions of the Party. His opponent, he says, was against Medicare and Medicaid, and he cites suggestions Reagan has made in the past that there should be a voluntary aspect to Social Security—this is a favorite issue of the Carter campaign—and he summons up quotes of Reagan's against aid to New York City and to Chrysler. And then he says that every President since Harry Truman has been for arms control but that "my opponent is against the SALT treaty that we're trying to get ratified now, and he believes we ought to have a nuclear-arms race to convince the Soviet Union that we are the most powerful nation on earth." He concludes, "With an arms race there would be no way for the Soviet Union to agree to balanced reductions in atomic weapons."

This is as much as the President and his aides plan to make of this material today. They do not want to distract attention from the automobile events, which they think went well; they want to see how Reagan's SALT statement plays in the press; and they would prefer to have more time to prepare a response. Moreover, by waiting a day, they figure, they can make it a longer-running story. More use will be made of the SALT issue in the coming days.

The President answers questions about the draft ("There's not going to be any draft; the registration is to prevent the need for a draft''—a comment he does not explain); about a proposed submarine communications system; about the Ku Klux Klan (''a despicable and obnoxious blight on the free society of America''); about federal jobs programs. The questioners introduce themselves, and the President usually addresses them by their first name; toward the end, he takes his jacket off—a Carter trademark—in a move that suggests he is having a fine time and feels at home. He is applauded. When a truck driver involved in hauling American-made trucks asks about getting trade assistance because of the importation of Japanese trucks, the President says that he will talk to the Secretary of Labor and call the driver back personally (applause).

The President closes the session with a statement that incorporates one of his major campaign themes. He mentions the difficult problems the country is facing, cites the progress that has been made on reducing the imports of oil, and says, ''The point is our nation has faced much more serious challenges and much more serious problems in years gone by than any that I have seen since I have been in the White House—the Great Depression, the First World War, the Second World War, Watergate, the Vietnam War. Those kinds of things have shocked this country and endangered our very existence and our nation's security.'' He continues, going into his upbeat message, ''We've got problems now. I don't want to underestimate them. There are no easy answers. But our country, when we were united and when we understood the problem or the challenge or the obstacle, has never failed, and I don't have any doubt in my mind as President of this country that the United States of America, a united people, as we face the future together we will not fail.'' Then he adds another Carter trademark: ''And you can depend on that.''

Carter had an upbeat message four years ago, and he gave it with more assurance. Of course, he didn't have as much reality weighing him down then. There are advantages to being the incumbent, but there are also advantages to being the challenger—as Carter is finding out. There was a boldness about the Carter of four years ago, particularly in the early part of the campaign, that is missing now. Something seems to have gone out of him. In fact, the boldness seemed to leave him soon after he got to the White House; an uncertainty, sometimes indecisiveness, began to show through. In 1976, he drove his campaign staff; after that, he became more malleable. He did some bold things after he got to the White House, but not as many as his campaign, particularly in the early stages, might have led one to expect. When some of his initiatives began to falter, so did he. He gave the impression in 1976 that when he got to Washington he would move the furniture around, but, as things turned out, he didn't seem to know how to manage that. The uncertainty led to a series of regroupings in which he and his aides tried to redefine his Presidency: he would take on ''Washington;'' he would try to cooperate with Congress; he would be a populist; he would try to cooperate with industry—all of which culminated in the retreat to Camp David in the summer of 1979. There followed the spectacle of the comings and goings of politicians and thinkers and the "malaise" speech. This was followed by the firing of Cabinet officers and word from the White House that the Administration would be taking dramatic new initiatives—and that was the end of it. The picture that emerged was not of a President who was in charge. Carter does not have a commanding presence, and his efforts to appear to take charge have flopped. The cause and effect—the mixture of the lack of a commanding presence and the lack of confidence—is impossible to sort out. And there has been so much zigging and zagging on policies that he, and the policies, have seemed lost at times. He has made it difficult for other politicians to support his policies—they never know when they might get left in the breach.

As a matter of fact, Carter's record is better than his leadership style, and it is the leadership style that keeps the record from being appreciated. Most objective observers would agree that Carter has taken on some difficult, even miserable problems, and doggedly worked them through. Energy is about as difficult an issue as there has been for some time, and his Administration has made some real progress on it. The record on the economy is not outstanding, of course, but this is a problem for which solutions are elusive. Other Presidents might have found reasons to avoid taking on the Panama Canal problem. (Other Presidents did avoid taking it on.) The Camp David accords on the Middle East were a result of Carter's doggedness. There are a number of less dramatic problems on which the President has plugged away and got things done. Deregulation of certain industries and Civil Service reform do not sound very exciting. Recitations of the list of his legislative achievements tend to make the audience nod off. The various kinds of things he has done do not lend themselves to an all-embracing theme, such as "the New Deal." Any fair judgment of Carter will have to take into consideration how much was within his control. His Presidency coincided with historical forces that, however frustrating, the United States could not command. It is not unprecedented for a President to be paralyzed by Congress on certain issues, but these days the potential for paralysis is more highly developed. And, even at that, Carter's record with Congress, measured on a box-score basis, is not so bad—though his relations with Congress are nearly terrible.

But what Carter has achieved has been discounted by his inability to get it across, and by the intensely political character of so much of what he does, and by the zigzags. He is constantly blurring the picture. History, if it is fair, will probably say of Carter that he was able to get some things done but that he wasn't able to lead, that he wasn't able to get the confidence of the people—which is an important failure. Carter is not an able speaker, or even, in one sense, an able politician. He can work at this and work at that, fix this and that, but he lifts no spirits, kindles no imaginations, does not get people thinking in new ways. He does not appear to be a man totally without a compass, but in reaching for the political fruits of so many of his acts he cheapens them, and demeans the Presidency. Carter does not come across as the kind of man who would wreck the country for his own aggrandizement, but he does often come across as someone who would go to great lengths to get ten percent more of the Chicano vote, or what have you.

One gets the impression of a man who is terribly serious about policy but keeps undermining himself. And in the process he undermines the motivation of those who might help—in Congress, among outsiders. People get pumped up about taking on this problem or that, and then Carter takes the air out of them. Part of the trouble is that he is a poor presenter of what he is trying to do. He does not know how to carry people along. He has little taste for the sweatiness and earthiness of politics; he seems to undervalue the emotional and psychological links between people that make things happen, and he seems to believe that arguments speak for themselves—that if you've made your argument, that's all you need to do. He doesn't seem to understand that people in political life act—or don't act—because of loyalty and affection and a whole range of psychological factors, a web of relationships which builds up. Or, if he understands this, he doesn't much act on it. Perhaps he can't. Some people who have been watching him think that the cold side of his nature and the engineer in him have taken over increasingly, after efforts to reach people through a speech—to inspire— have failed. Though he can be quite charming, his inturned personality is such that he often deadens political meetings—even small ones, at which legend has it that he is so good. He has established several alliances of convenience but acquired few true allies. He has few friends. He came to Washington a loner and he remains a loner. Though he can command the spotlight at will, and though we have seen much of him, he gives off little sense of who he is or what he thinks or where he think he's going. This has placed a pall over his Presidency, and over his campaign for re-election.

Niagara Falls, New York. A few days ago, it was decided that the President would do a favor for Jerry Wurf, the president of the American Federation of State, County, and Municipal Employees, who has been helpful to the Carter campaign, by coming here to address the annual convention of one of the union's New York State employees locals—a large one, numbering some two hundred and twenty-five thousand members. The New York local—the Civil Service Employees Association, an outgrowth of the old state patronage system—is far from solidly Democratic, and is powerful in upstate New York. But it has endorsed Carter, and he is also helping himself in coming here. The President's campaign strategists decided that while the President was in this area he could help himself further by signing two documents of great importance to citizens here. If signing ceremonies at the White House no longer cause much of a stir in the national media, they can still make a splash at the local level. And so, in a room at the Niagara Falls International Convention Center, the President signs an agreement, reached in August, between the federal government and the state of New York, to help relocate citizens living in the area of the Love Canal, which has been used as a toxic-waste dump, and a bill to provide federal funds for cleaning up the nuclear waste left by a nuclear-fuel-reprocessing plant situated near here. Both documents are indicative of a new kind of problem that government has to deal with. New York's governor, Hugh Carey, and its two senators, Daniel Patrick Moynihan and Jacob Javits, and other politicians are on the stage with him, and local political and labor leaders are gathered in the audience. Carey and Carter are not enormously enthusiastic about each other, but signing ceremonies bring together all manner of people to share the credit. The Carter campaign is still hoping that Javits, who lost his bid for renomination by the Republican Party and is now listed on the Liberal line along with John Anderson, will drop out of the race. And they are all on the stage, smiling.

In the ballroom of the convention center, the President opens his remarks to the Civil Service Employees Association by saying, "If I can't be at home with Rosalynn and Amy, I can't think of any place I'd rather be than here with you." (Applause.) He has been given a warm welcome. "Happy Birthday" was sung to him for what seemed like the thousandth time today, and Carey gave him an "I ♥ New York" T-shirt and a gold Tiffany "I ♥ New York" lapel pin. William McGowan, the union's president, has told the audience, "Brothers and sisters, James Earl Carter is our candidate, and we're going to work our butt off for him." This union has a great many members who work in mental hospitals, and the President tells the audience about the "lifetime of commitment" that he and his wife have made to the cause of mental health, and announces that yesterday he appointed McGowan to serve on the President's Commission on Mental Retardation. He praises Wurf, makes a joke about Wurf's outspokenness, talks about the progress that has been made on energy, about his visit to Detroit and about the steel agreement, praises public-service workers (no more talk about "bloated bureaucracy"), and talks about some of the things that still have to be done. He mentions welfare reform and ratification of the Equal Rights Amendment. He says, "I cannot agree with every proposal you make and also agree with every proposal that other groups in this country make. . . . I cannot promise you that there'll be unlimited federal resources to meet every demand that's presented to my desk in the Oval Office. I can't promise that every new program will be passed through the Congress without delay, even if you and I agree that it ought to be done. I cannot promise you that there will not be difficult challenges in the future and tough decisions to be made." But, he tells them, "we share the same ideals and the same goals and the same hopes in the future."

And then Carter spells out what he thinks "the consequences might be if the wrong decision is made" in the election. He attacks—using Reagan quotes—positions Reagan has taken in the past on the minimum wage, the New Deal, the Occupational Safety and Health Act, unemployment compensation, Medicaid and Medicare, and aid to Chrysler and to New York City. He quotes Reagan as having said that the Humphrey-Hawkins bill was "a design for Fascism." (Reagan said this in an interview in which he also said that "Fascism was really the basis for the New Deal.") Carter's aides have decided that the President should pull back from trying to paint Reagan as a bad man—they realize that Reagan is thought of as a "good guy"—and should try instead to ridicule him, using more of his quotes and proposals as material rather than generalizing.

But Carter doesn't quite carry it off. His timing is bad, and his delivery doesn't get his message across. One can't help thinking what other politicians might have done with the same material: Edward Kennedy offered one example at the Democratic Convention, and Vice President Mondale in his campaign appearances is more successful at this than Carter. Carter twits Reagan for having had to change his tax-cut proposal, but when he makes the point that even Gerald Ford opposes a three-year tax cut, which Reagan is offering, he muffs it. And when he attacks the substance of Reagan's tax proposals he seems to exaggerate the deficit that would result. He misleads his audience about a Reagan proposal to transfer the operation of some federal programs to the states, suggesting that Reagan would have the states pay the full costs of programs like welfare. (Reagan does not propose this. He did appear to be proposing such a thing for a while during the 1976 primaries, but after the Ford people landed on that he switched and talked about transferring the administration of some programs to the states, along with the funds to pay for them. There may be problems with this proposal, too, but Carter misrepresents it.) Carter is making a case more against Reagan than for himself. He speaks strongly, for him, but his delivery still lacks strength. He concludes by telling the audience that "New York State can make the difference in the entire election outcome for the nation, and what happens in this region and what happens in your own communities all over this state can spell out the difference for the future of the country." Earlier this week, Carter said that he could not win if he didn't carry New York, and that appears to be true. The applause for him at the conclusion of his remarks is less enthusiastic than it was at the beginning.

On the plane back to Washington, I have a talk with Jody Powell. Powell is as close to Carter as anyone other than Mrs. Carter, spends more time with him these days than any of his other aides, and in many ways both affects and reflects his thinking. I ask Powell if he is concerned that the President hasn't given any excitement to this campaign, or got across a positive feeling that he should be re-elected.

"Yes," Powell replies. "That's certainly a problem. He's not the sort of person who has people storming the barricades."

"Why is that?" I ask.

Powell replies, "Part of it is his nature and personality. He isn't a spellbinding orator. It's not his style; he doesn't put a lot of stock in it. A lot of politicians have found out—Ed Muskie in 1972, for one—it's hard to evoke the sort of committed, storm-the-barricades attitude if you are a centrist, moderate, middle-of-the-road candidate." (There is a story that in 1972 one of Muskie's campaign advisers told him that his problem was that the people didn't have any sense of his "vision," and Muskie is said to have replied, "Well, what is it?") Powell continues, "There is a fairly good rule in politics that the extremity of the position and the fervency of the support have a fairly close correlation. If Howard Baker had won the Republican nomination, his support would have been much less fervent than Ronald Reagan's, but he would have been a much more formidable candidate. I'm not concerned about it, because as long as I've known Jimmy Carter—and before I knew him—people have talked that way about him, and he keeps on winning elections."

Then do you feel, I ask Powell, that Carter is making the best possible case for his re-election?

He replies, slowly, "No—no—no." He continues, "We're getting there, though. He's got to work things through in his own mind. He's got to work on his ad libs. That's one of the prices, frankly, of not being on the stump in the primaries. Reagan's been on the road forever, and he was campaigning in the primaries. The question is, How do you sum it all up? The whole point is to get people to understand, as the President has said over and over again, the very serious differences between what the next four years would be with Jimmy Carter in the White House and with Ronald Reagan in the White House. The question is, How do you make the point in a way that doesn't distract people from what the point really is?"

What about making the positive case for why it should be Carter?

Powell replies, "The problem there is that nobody would cover that. Nobody is going to write two paragraphs about Jimmy Carter saying, 'These are the things I've done that ought to make you vote for me.' People aren't going to report that. It's not a conspiracy against Jimmy Carter that they don't report it when Jimmy Carter says it. They don't report it when anybody says it."

The Carter campaign is conscious of criticisms that it is not dealing with "the issues," and so it has been decided that, beginning October 12th, Carter will give fifteen-minute radio talks on Sundays. (The original plan was that they would last a half-hour.) The talks are supposed to be thoughtful and issue-oriented. The idea is that, though not many people will listen, the press will report that Carter is giving these talks. Moreover, since there is little news on Sundays, there is more likely to be coverage of the talks in the Monday papers than if they were made on any other day.

As the plane circles for its landing in Washington, Powell says, "There may be different approaches, but the bottom line is how do you put the hay down so the mules can get at it." He pauses, and adds, "We ain't there yet, but we'll get there."

CHAPTER 14

The Election

WASHINGTON, WEDNESDAY, OCTOBER 15TH. The election, just under three weeks away, refuses to get itself decided. The polls generally put Jimmy Carter and Ronald Reagan at about dead even in the popular vote, which is where they were on Labor Day. The percentage of voters who say they are undecided is unusually high. But Reagan starts out with an advantage in terms of the electoral vote: most of the West, which voted solidly Republican in 1976, is conceded to be his, and he is also believed to be making some inroads into Carter's Southern base. The race is presumed to be very close in most of the key states. John Anderson is not expected to carry a single state, but he could still affect the outcome. (In 1976, Eugene McCarthy, with only nine-tenths of one percent, or just seven hundred and fifty thousand votes, cost Carter four states.) Anderson is believed to be drawing most of his support from people who would otherwise vote for Carter, but in some areas he also draws support from Republican moderates who might otherwise vote for a Republican nominee. About three weeks ago, when Anderson was staying at about fifteen percent in the polls, the Carter camp quietly decided to put out the word to its people in the field to take on Anderson directly: the President and the Vice President would not say anything about him, but those speaking on behalf of the ticket were to criticize him; the attack would also be carried out in material printed on behalf of the campaign. And Gerald Rafshoon made some radio ads attacking Anderson.

Carter is still having trouble getting the hang of how to go after Reagan. Last summer, some prominent California Democrats warned the Carter people that Reagan would be very hard to pin down. He's a great deflector, they told them; they said, in effect, "You hit him with something, and he'll say 'I didn't mean it, I didn't say it, I was different then.' " An official of the Carter-Mondale campaign said to me over lunch today, "He may not have been a great actor as actors go, but he's a great actor as politicians go." He went on, "One of the biggest frustrations of this campaign has been our inability to lay a glove on the guy. We've now decided to try a new approach: to try to paint Reagan as a 'flip-flopper.' " Reagan has changed his position lately on a number of positions—including his new support of aid to New York City, and of a governmental bailout of the Chrysler Corporation, both of which he used to oppose—and has redecorated several other positions. There is nonetheless a certain piquancy to the idea of Carter's attacking someone else as a "flip-flopper"—and Carter's own vulnerability on that score may make it hard for him to be persuasive. The Carter campaign official told me, "The 'flip-flop' approach is to get us away from the 'mean streak.' "

The President's campaign aides, headed by Hamilton Jordan, believe that what they see as the central issue of the campaign—the contrast between Carter's philosophy and Reagan's and, therefore, to them, the crucial nature of the election—has got lost in all the dust about "meanness." The campaign official said today, "The focus on Carter's 'mean streak' was dominating the coverage of the campaign, and the thing that we thought was important—the differences on the issues—wasn't getting through. It's crucial for us to get the Democrats back, so it's in our interest to have the differences discussed." The greatest furor over the "mean streak" came after the President said in Chicago last week—in line with his attempt to establish the theme that this is a crucial election—that the voters would "determine whether or not this America will be unified or, if I lose the election, whether Americans might be separated, black from white, Jew from Christian, North from South, rural from urban." (Reagan said to the press the next day, in a sorrowful manner, "I think he owes the country an apology.") Actually, Carter had said much the same thing at a dinner in Washington a week earlier, but the remark had gone largely unnoticed then. And a number of people, including some Republicans, felt that what Carter said in Chicago was well within the bounds of political rhetoric, and, given some of the things Reagan had done, was not entirely without basis.

But by the time Carter made the statement again the journalistic vogue was to focus on his capacity for "meanness" in a campaign. Moreover, Carter invited criticism by the way he has pursued what has come to be called the war-and-peace issue—he has said that this election offers a choice between peace and war—and he has undermined himself by appearing to cast the argument in those terms. What the argument really has to do with is Reagan's grasp of and judgments about international situations. By using a broad brush, Carter got some paint on himself. He cited a number of instances in which Reagan seemed to be suggesting military intervention in certain situations, and said, "If you've got a strong military and you are jingoistic in spirit and just want to push everybody around and just show the macho of the United States, that is an excellent way to lead our country toward war."

The President's aides believed that Carter was making some headway on the war-and-peace issue—and so did Reagan's—but the furor over the "meanness" eventually reached such a pitch that Carter's aides advised him to back off and try another approach. "Everyone agreed that a real break had to be made," the campaign official said to me today. However, Carter's aides did not expect him to be as contrite as he was in an interview with Barbara Walters—which was arranged by the Carter people so that the President could announce that he was going to change. Carter came across in the interview as a chastened schoolboy promising to be good from now on; he seemed, as he often does, weak. The campaign official says, "The idea had been for him to go on there and say, 'This is ridiculous. The important thing is that there are deep differences between me and Reagan, and we are now going to campaign on those.' But he got sidetracked in an apology. It didn't go as well as everyone thought it would." (Some of the President's advisers have been arguing for another change in tactics: they say that perhaps they missed the boat by trying to compare this election to 1964, and that perhaps the analogy should be to 1968—not that they should appear to be saying that Reagan is Nixon but that they should make the point that the attitude that defeated Humphrey was that he was "not pure enough.") After the interview, Carter continued his criticism of Reagan's suggested interventions and attacked Reagan for having said, in the interview published October 1st, that he would set the SALT II treaty aside and that "one card that's been missing in these negotiations has been the possibility of an arms race." Carter said that Reagan's "opposition to the SALT II treaty, his opposition to Medicare, his opposition to many of the programs that are important, like the minimum wage or unemployment compensation, his call for the injection of American military forces into place after place after place around the world indicate to me that he would not be a good President or a good man to trust with the affairs of this nation in the future."

But Carter has two problems in trying to make the attack take hold. While his essential character has not changed, the public's impression of it has. He has never been attractive in combat, especially when cornered. But though Carter's tendency toward "meanness" had been apparent for some time (his mother once described him as "a beautiful cat with sharp claws"), and there were ample indications that he could be petty and cold, Carter had got across to the public the idea that he was a nice man. When the idea suddenly hit that he might not be such a nice man after all, the public reacted with the sort of disillusionment about which it can be unforgiving. This disillusionment undermines whatever Carter says. His other problem is that Reagan does come across as a nice man; Reagan's style is one of geniality, of affability. Reagan seems a less complicated person than Carter, and this helps Reagan. Carter's charges seem to slide right off him. And Reagan aids this process by simply shrugging and saying things like "Carter is reaching a point of hysteria that is hard to understand."

Reagan has said some fairly rough things about Carter—he has accused him of incompetence, and said that his record is disastrous and has weakened the country, and a few days ago he called Carter "the greatest deceiver ever to occupy the White House"—but the focus has been on the nature of Carter's attack. And the Carter campaign's attack has been kept up in other ways. In a speech at Notre Dame the other day, Secretary of State Muskie said that the kinds of suggestions made by Reagan for military intervention could keep the United States "endlessly at war all over the globe." A Rafshoon advertisement has a California "man in the street" saying that Reagan "would have gotten us into a war by now," and another calling him "scary." One advertisement cites Reagan's statement about an arms race and has Carter saying, "We are not dealing with just another shoot-out at the O.K. Corral." Most politicians try to make their opponents, rather than themselves, the issue, and Carter has good reason to try to make Reagan, rather than his own record, the focus of this campaign. He did a similar thing in the case of Senator Edward Kennedy. In this instance, the problem is not that Carter is trying to make Reagan the issue but that he isn't doing it well. His attacks are humorless and shrill; the pitch is too high. Even his voice is a problem—especially compared to Reagan's. Carter's is a hard voice to listen to for very long when he's exercised. Four years ago, he talked soothingly. And this country seems to have gone squeamish about political invective, which it used to enjoy. (John Sears, Reagan's former campaign manager, has written that what is being said this year pales beside some of the things Truman said about Dewey in 1948.) But perhaps that's because Carter doesn't employ it deftly.

Reagan has been treading carefully among his various constituencies and has demonstrated his talent as an adjuster. It has been part of his strategy all year to try to attract blue-collar voters, but in the primaries he also had to stay in good standing with his conservative followers—whose interests sometimes coincided with those of blue-collar voters (on cultural and some economic issues) and sometimes diverged (on other economic issues)—who could get him the nomination. His current goal is to hold his conservative base, continue to appeal to blue-collar workers, and try to expand his appeal to reach independents, Anderson supporters, and Southerners disaffected from Carter. (George Bush, his running mate, who, while a fairly conservative man himself, comes across as a moderate, has been assigned the task of trying to help expand the Reagan base.) Reagan has made a number of expensive promises lately: in Tampa, to increase Social Security benefits for those over the age of sixty-five who choose to continue working; in Youngstown, to aid the steel industry; to raise military pay; to build more naval ships; and, in a speech before the National Maritime Union, to increase the merchant marine. He has received the endorsement of the Teamsters and the National Maritime Union. His campaign literature distributed to union members does not mention his suggestion, made last spring, that "we should look very closely" at whether unions ought to be subject to anti-trust laws.

Reagan's visit early this month to the Reverend Jerry Falwell, the fundamentalist minister and founder of the Moral Majority, was another attempt at deft footwork. The idea, according to a Reagan strategist, was to touch base with the important fundamentalist constituency (which can be particularly helpful against Carter in the South) and also to mollify the Jews. In that setting, Reagan was to stress his belief in the Judeo-Christian ethic, and he did. But that got lost in the controversy—which it is hard to believe is going on—over whose prayers God hears. Not long ago, Falwell associated himself with the comment of the Reverend Bailey Smith, the president of the Southern Baptist Convention, that "God Almighty does not hear the prayer of a Jew." Recently, Falwell met in New York with Rabbi Marc Tanenbaum, of the American Jewish Committee, and dissociated himself from the remark. In between, Reagan showed up at Falwell's headquarters, in Lynchburg, Virginia, and took the occasion both to condemn the "expulsion of God from the classroom" and to express his commitment to the separation of church and state; he did also refer to Judeo-Christian values and to the B'nai B'rith, and when he was asked by reporters on his arrival at the Lynchburg airport whether he shared the view of the ministers about whom God does and does not hear, he said, "No, since both the Christian and Judaic religions are based on the same God, the God of Moses, I'm quite sure those prayers are heard." He went on, "But I guess everyone can make his own interpretation of the Bible, and many individuals have been making differing interpretations for a long time."

Yesterday, Reagan, who is having difficulty with the women's vote, announced, in his first press conference in a month, that one of his earliest appointees to the Supreme Court would be a woman. Reagan's problem—which both sides' polls pick up—is generally ascribed to the war-and-peace issue and his position against the Equal Rights Amendment, but there may also be something else: an impression that he represents the Hollywood cowboy ethos.

Reagan's one major departure from the tight packaging of his campaign produced the only note of levity that has been injected into the conflict thus far. It happened at a time when Stuart Spencer, the California public-relations man, was absent: one night in Steubenville, Ohio, Reagan launched into a rambling discourse on pollution, saying such things as that Mount St. Helens had produced more sulphur dioxide than ten years' worth of automobiles, and repeated his previous statement that trees were responsible for ninety-three percent of the nation's nitrogen oxides. The following day, in Youngstown, he said that air pollution had been "substantially controlled" (even as Los Angeles was suffering from a smog alert). The Carter Administration, of course, jumped all over his statements, and when Reagan appeared in California a few days later some students attached to a tree a sign that said, "Chop me down before I kill again." The day after Reagan made his remark about air pollution, he said, "I didn't say anything about it being substantially under control."

The Reagan people have been assiduously trying to build protection against Carter's reaping political credit from any break in the hostage situation in Iran. They have been warning again and again of an "October surprise." This strategy was devised in June, a Reagan campaign official tells me. The idea was that when Reagan aides and campaign surrogates were asked what they thought might happen in the election, or were given any other opportunity, they would talk about the possibility that the Carter people would produce an "October surprise." William Casey, the campaign's director, used the term in his talks with reporters during the Republican Convention, in July. The theory was that it was a nice catchy term and would make its way into the media—as it has done. The Reagan campaign has also established a special working group to make plans for dealing with the political consequences of a hostage release.

The President's campaign may have been successful in its effort against Anderson—but at a price. Anderson's standing has dropped in the polls, and today the League of Women Voters announced that it would take a new look at his poll ratings this week and would withdraw its invitation to him to participate in the Presidential debates if his standing was no longer significant. (The criterion is that a candidate has to have fifteen percent in the polls in order to qualify.) The Anderson people have failed in their attempts to borrow from banks against federal funds that he would be eligible for after the election if he received at least five percent of the vote; the Carter Administration did what it could to discourage the banks from making the loans. Lately, Carter has been chiding Reagan for refusing to debate him unless Anderson was also included. Carter has been doing this more out of necessity than out of preference: though he seems to have got away with his refusal to appear in last month's debate between Reagan and Anderson, he has felt constrained to try to shift to Reagan some of the blame for the fact that there has been no Carter-Reagan debate, especially since Carter has been avoiding a debate all year. So the President appears to want to debate Reagan because he must appear to want to debate Reagan, but neither he nor his people are keen on having a debate now. They figure that a debate helps a challenger (just as the debates with Gerald Ford helped Carter in 1976); they fear Reagan's talents as a performer; and they figure that since they are gaining on Reagan there is no point in taking a chance.

Monday, October 20th. The Reagan side has decided to accept an invitation to debate, because, these people say, while they have a margin over Carter now, it may not be a sufficient margin—or "cushion," as they put it —to protect them against developments in the final days of the campaign. William Casey said to me, "We feel we're ahead, and we're building our lead again, but we have to figure that in the last two weeks the incumbent can dominate the nightly news. And we haven't been in the top half of the nightly news lately. Carter has been in the top of the news in connection with Iraq and Iran, and we were in the latter half of the shows. Carter could charge that we were ducking the debate; his campaign has more surrogates to put out there, and the whole governmental apparatus to work for him; and we don't know what he has up his sleeve. So we may be ahead, but we don't know what kind of cushion we need."

Richard Wirthlin, Reagan's pollster and an important campaign strategist, was one of two Reagan campaign officials who opposed the idea of a debate. (The other was William Timmons, the deputy director for campaign operations.) Recently, there had been a number of stories saying that the Reagan campaign had "stalled," and that the—dread word—"momentum" had shifted to Carter. A number of polls indicated that the race continued to be quite close, and some indicated that Carter was moving ahead in the industrial states. Wirthlin does not agree with these assessments. Over lunch today, he told me his soundings showed that as of two days ago Reagan held a six-point lead over Carter: Reagan about forty-three percent; Carter about thirty-seven; undecided eleven; Anderson ten. Ten days ago, however, he, too, had felt that Reagan was running into trouble in some of the industrial states—Illinois, Ohio, Pennsylvania—and had so informed the strategists travelling with Reagan. What worried the strategists was that once the idea that Reagan was encountering problems filtered out through the press, it might become a fact.

In political campaigns, there are times when it is best to be seen as running behind—but not many. If a candidate is seen to be ahead, this affects his organization, his supporters, and, most important, the press coverage, which affects all else. For this reason, campaign spokesmen are inclined to put the best face on the facts.

There had been not only a lot of press comment recently to the effect that Reagan was "slipping" but also some advice—the press is liberal with its campaign suggestions—to the effect that Reagan needed to debate; and some of Reagan's field directors sent word to campaign headquarters that they were worried that Reagan was "sitting on his lead." Wirthlin says that he favored a debate at an earlier point but later worried about the time that it would take away from the campaign so late in the game. However, other members of the Reagan entourage were strongly in favor of a debate. Wirthlin did try to assure them that Reagan was still in the lead, but when he was asked whether Reagan would have enough of a "cushion" for the end of the campaign he could not say. All agreed that Reagan had much to gain from a debate. "Most of the pluses that Reagan takes out of a debate are image-related," one of Reagan's advisers said to me. "He can demonstrate strength and also compassion. He comes across as reasonable in debates. He'll come across warm and easygoing. It'll be hard for Carter to make the 'warmonger' label stick. Reagan won't be able to match Carter on detail, but that won't matter very much." For these reasons, and in case there should be a last-minute break in the hostage situation, the Reagan people are pushing for the debate to be held the night before the election. Wirthlin said to me today, "Given the political environment, the election is going to hang or fall on that debate."

Wirthlin's counterpart, Patrick Caddell, also opposed a debate, and others around the President had misgivings, but Carter was trapped. The reaction would be too negative if Carter ducked another debate, they concluded. "There's no way out of it now," one Carter adviser said to me yesterday. Some Carter advisers thought that a debate held distinct advantages for Carter: it would give him an opportunity to illustrate the differences between him and Reagan on the issues and to point up Reagan's changed positions on various issues. Another advantage, as some see it, is that a Carter-Reagan debate would further damage Anderson. The Carter people may be underestimating Reagan's talent for political theater—a talent that Carter happens to sorely lack. Reagan has used that talent to dominate every political debate he has participated in, starting well before this year. No matter what happens, though, there is something wrong with the idea that the process of choosing a President should come down to a single television event. The press will be unable to resist casting the event in terms of "who won," turning it into one great sporting event. A debate does offer insights into the candidates' characters, but it tests only some of the things that are important in the White House.

Wirthlin maintains that the public polls indicating that Reagan and Carter were about even in key states were taken just when Carter was getting off his "meanness" horse and Reagan had committed his gaffe about air pollution, and that they therefore represented only a fleeting moment in a long campaign. He feels that the race was tightening up in the key states—that Democrats were beginning to "go home"—but says that Reagan was never behind in them. But because major newspapers published the view that Reagan was stalled and in trouble, that view became gospel. Moreover, Wirthlin added in our conversation, "When we looked at the South, we saw that the results we had been looking for were there." Reagan had fallen behind in Alabama after he made his remark that it was the birthplace of the Ku Klux Klan, but now he was five points ahead there, according to Wirthlin's polls; and his polls also indicated that Reagan was ahead in Missouri, Louisiana, and South Carolina, and had a good chance in Mississippi. According to Wirthlin's polls, Reagan and Carter were now about even in Kentucky and Tennessee—"two states we hadn't even considered," Wirthlin said. "We're back in the ballgame," he added. "I've got to believe Pat Caddell knows the same thing I do." There are a number of ways that Reagan, who starts with the West (with the possible exceptions of Oregon and Washington), can win a sufficient number of electoral votes—two hundred and seventy. "We can win this election without taking Ohio, Pennsylvania, Illinois, or Michigan if we can crack the South, and I think we can take two of those states," Wirthlin said. "Carter and Reagan are even in Michigan and Ohio, but we're in a little trouble in Pennsylvania. There's a possibility that we can carry Connecticut, Maine, New Hampshire, Vermont, and Wisconsin. The whole house of cards could come down on them."

There has been an argument within the Reagan camp over how aggressive Reagan should be. Several of his advisers have wanted him to attack Carter more. Wirthlin's view has been that Reagan first had to build what Wirthlin terms a base of credibility: his polling during September had found that a great many people said they didn't know very much about Reagan. Only recently—during the second week of October—did the number of people who made that response fall below thirty percent. This put Reagan in a position to go into what Wirthlin calls "the attack mode"—to hit harder at Carter's record. As a Reagan aide puts it, "The theory was that before people moved away from Carter, which they wanted to do, they had to have a better sense of what they were moving to." Reagan could then begin to attack Carter's record more strongly, and the campaign advertising would also be more aggressive against Carter. The surrogates would stress Carter's indecisiveness, his "mean-spiritedness," his "vacillation" in foreign policy, and his manipulation of the Presidency for political ends. "I think now we can begin to raise questions about Carter more directly," Wirthlin said to me today. "The Governor's tone will probably become more confrontive. You'll see TV ads that deal more specifically with Carter's record."

There has been some disagreement within the Reagan camp over the ads, which have thus far emphasized Reagan's record as governor—at least, as the Reagan people tell it. Some of his political advisers thought there was too much emphasis on Reagan's record and not enough on Carter's. But the tone of the ads was part of Wirthlin's strategy of getting people to see Reagan as a benign manager, not as an aggressive partisan. Some people in the Reagan camp thought that the ads were too mild and that they were run too often. "I'm sick of them," one Reagan campaign official has said to me. But Wirthlin's polls showed that the governorship ads did well for Reagan. The Carter camp's polls showed the same thing.

Wirthlin's polling also has indicated that a high percentage of people—about forty-four percent—considered Reagan "dangerous": they respond affirmatively when they are asked whether Reagan is best described by the phrase "He is most likely to get us into an unnecessary war." In part, the Reagan people think, this is related to the fact that Reagan comes across as the stronger leader. ("There are a few political perceptions that are unmitigated assets or unmitigated weaknesses," Wirthlin says.) In part, however, they concede it has to do with the statements that Reagan has made in the past about areas in which he might intervene with military force, including his suggestion, in January, that one option for reacting to the Soviet invasion of Afghanistan was a blockade of Cuba—a suggestion to which George

Bush, among others, took great exception—and his recent comment about the SALT treaty and an arms race. Some people around Reagan have suggested to me that one of the factors at work here is that many of the people who are supposed to advise Reagan on foreign policy have their roots in the world of defense and strategic planning, and that when Reagan himself is dealing with foreign-policy issues he tends to think in terms of strategic weaponry—the B-1 bomber, and so on. And in part it has been because Carter's attacks have taken hold. The Reagan people see the debate as one way to put to rest the notion that their candidate would be a "dangerous" President.

Last night, Reagan gave a half-hour television address on the subject of foreign and defense policy. The address was skillful, as was to be expected. Reagan began, "I'd like to speak to you for a few moments now not as a candidate for the Presidency but as a citizen, a parent—in fact, a grandparent—who shares with you the deep and abiding hope for peace." Reagan, it seems, is trying to turn his age to advantage by playing the role of the genial grandfather. (He concedes that his sole grandchild, who is two years old, barely knows him. When the child didn't seem to recognize him at the Republican Convention, he quipped, "He only sees me on television.") Reagan's age has been used to make him seem comfortable, reassuring—a man in his twilight years wanting only to do good for his country. Wirthlin says his polls indicate that people think of Reagan as more vigorous than Carter or Anderson—presumably because he is seen on television, where it counts, in motion: going up and down airplane ramps, out speaking to workers. And, with his apple cheeks, full head of hair, and large physique, he looks healthy. So the age issue seems to have gone away.

In his address last night, Reagan criticized Carter's "litany of fear" and paraphrased Franklin Roosevelt: "The only thing the cause of peace has to fear is fear itself." He said, "We must build peace upon strength. There is no other way." And he said, "Our economic, military, and strategic strength under President Carter is eroding." He said, "Only if *we* are strong will peace be strong." He said, accurately, that "the present Administration has been unable to speak with one voice in foreign policy," and he promised that his Administration's policy-making would be "more coherent." He spoke in general terms about restoring relations with our allies and conducting "a realistic and balanced policy toward the Soviet Union," and about a "realistic policy for the Western Hemisphere." (The idea for a "North American Accord" with Mexico and Canada, with which he began his campaign last year, and which then sort of disappeared, was resurrected in the speech.) He called for investment by the private sector, with government assistance, in the development of Africa (there has been precious little recognition of the existence of the Third World in this campaign by either candidate), and he advocated strengthening the Voice of America, Radio Free Europe, and Radio Liberty. He said that we needed to curb international terrorism through efforts by the Central Intelligence Agency and through making it clear that we will refuse to make concessions or pay ransom. As for arms control, he said, "I would assign a high priority to strategic-arms reduction," and "As President, I will immediately open negotiations on a SALT III treaty." He said that the SALT II treaty had been blocked by the Senate; in fact, because it was so controversial and because of outside events, mainly the Soviet invasion of Afghanistan, the treaty was never brought up on the Senate floor. He called for "restoring the margin of safety" in defense—which appears to be the same thing as superiority.

Sometimes Reagan leans against a desk; on one occasion, he walks to a wing chair and stands beside it. For a man with his abilities, he actually seems a bit awkward. One of Reagan's staff members is bothered by some of Reagan's ads, saying that he becomes stiff and unnatural when they are being filmed. Still, he is smooth in his delivery, and he looks Presidential. In last night's speech he used the word "peace" forty-seven times. He said, as he has often said in his campaign, that "I have known four wars in my lifetime—I don't want to see a fifth." He ended, as is his wont, with a long anecdote, the gist of which was that young people were "what this campaign is all about." Young people have been one of his symbols: sometimes on hand as props at his rallies, often referred to in his speeches. When reporters asked Reagan advisers, who were available for a background briefing yesterday, what much of the speech meant, they could not say. Reagan did not explain, among other things, how it is that the Russians would allow the United States to gain "a margin of safety." (He has sometimes said that they could not afford to keep up.) Nor did he explain what would happen between the time the SALT II treaty was scrapped and any new agreement was reached. The pending treaty, which both sides have pledged to observe during the approval process, prevents the Soviet Union from deploying a number of weapons systems it is ready to go ahead with.

In a fumbling way, Reagan and Carter have ended up making this election campaign one that focusses on the big issues. They are not arguing over things like window valances put up for the director of the Federal Bureau of Investigation, as happened in 1976. They are arguing over the economy, over foreign policy and national-security policy, and over the role of the government in our society. Both sides are distorting the issues and taking cheap shots, however, and neither candidate is offering a very clear picture of what he would do. Carter seems not to know what he would do with another four years, and Reagan seems to feel (with some reason) that in a campaign clarity leads only to trouble. Are we reaching a point where the larger the question, the less we are to know of what either candidate would do? Or is it just these candidates?

"We've designed the campaign to finish very hard," Wirthlin said today. "We've husbanded our advertising money for the end of the campaign—the Carter people spent a lot of theirs early—and we'll have five million dollars to spend on ads in the last two weeks. We have enough money for three thirty-minute television programs on Election Eve; we have five hundred thousand volunteers; we have five million pieces of literature to distribute."

When I asked William Casey what the plan was for the next two weeks, he began by saying, "We haven't done as well as we might have on how bad Carter's record is. We've dealt with the defense issue, because we had to. Carter's attack has increased the perception that the Governor may be dangerous; it had to be responded to. That's the only cloud we see on the horizon." Then Casey said he expected that the Consumer Price Index to be published this week would show an increase in inflation. "Between that and the debate, we'll ride the economic issue all the way home," he said. "With more resources for advertising, more volunteers, more enthusiasm, if we get our issues across now we'll go sailing in."

Today, Reagan travelled around with Henry Kissinger; former Secretary of State William Rogers (whom Kissinger, when he served as national-security adviser to Richard Nixon, relegated to the sidelines); Elliot Richardson, the former a-number-of-things; and Anne Armstrong, former Ambassador to Great Britain and now deputy chairman of the campaign. Reagan is wrapping himself in Republican respectables—they don't come any more respectable than Richardson—and the respectables are pleased to oblige. Kissinger said that he approves of Reagan's approach to SALT, and NBC showed Rogers saying of Reagan, "He is not a warmonger."

Yesterday, Carter, in his second radio address, said that "peace is my passion," and continued, "Over the last twenty years, we have taken some tentative steps away from the nuclear precipice. Now, for the first time, we are being advised to take steps that may move us toward it." Today, before he took off to campaign in Pennsylvania, Ohio, and New York, he read to reporters a statement saying that Reagan was "extraordinarily naïve" about nuclear arms and "does not understand the serious consequences of what he's proposing." And the President said that if the hostages were freed he would release Iranian assets held in this country. Reagan, who is also campaigning in Ohio today, and in Kentucky, too, referred to the President's statement and said that there were a number of things "I don't understand." He listed inflation, unemployment, the Soviet troops in Afghanistan, and, raising the until now forbidden subject, he said, "And, lastly, I don't understand why fifty-two Americans have been held hostage for almost a year now."

Monday, October 27th. The much-discussed public unhappiness with the two major candidates running for President this year is based partly in reality and partly in myth. One myth is that there are a number of people stacked up like a cord of wood somewhere who could easily be good Presidents. But there are a great many highly intelligent, competent people, in the private sector and in public life, who would be hopeless Presidents. Politics requires certain skills, and both Carter and Reagan have some of those skills. Another myth, which seems to persist, is that there is a savior out there who can move into the White House and set everything right. The percentage of great Presidents in our history is not high. The men who designed our political system did not place their hopes in the idea that we would have great leaders; in fact, they were wary of the idea of saviors. Moreover, there is a tendency, untempered by experience, to hold Presidents responsible for everything that happens, and this can lead to the dashing of hopes. Little account is taken of the possibility that there are forces or events that are immovable or beyond control. Everything that goes wrong in the world is attributed to Carter. Of course, it is not out of the question that there will be a more popular set of candidates down the road; there probably will be. Much of the frustration with the choice this time is laid at the door of "the parties," as if some disembodied (and anachronistic) group had got together and selected these people. We are who selected these people. The campaigns that the two men are waging come out of their own particular personalities and characters, and were foreshadowed many months ago.

Robert Teeter, the Republican pollster, said in a conversation I had with him last week that this election is, to an unusual degree, a national one. Teeter, who polls for a number of Republicans running for the Senate and House and covers a number of states for the Reagan campaign, explained that when the polls shift in one of the swing states they tend to shift, and largely to the same degree, in all the swing states. "The things that affect this campaign are things that are going on nationally, and the focus is on the Presidential candidates—not the Vice Presidential candidates, the First Lady, and so on," he said. Teeter's assessment, like that of Reagan's campaign aides, is that Reagan is a few points ahead of Carter across the board —but that the race is quite close in most of the important states—and that Reagan enjoys a lead in the electoral vote. The most interesting thing, in his view, is that the electorate has hardly moved at all since the fall campaign began. He pointed out that both candidates have been holding somewhere between thirty-six and forty-one percent of the voters, and that eventually one of them has to pick up several more percentage points to win. "Reagan has all the people his natural appeal could reach, and Carter has all the people who say, 'I'll never vote for Ronald Reagan,' " he said. "They have to do something a little different to get the last seven or eight percent. That's where the debate comes in." Teeter, who is based in Detroit, added, "In the Detroit vernacular, 'You've sold everyone a Chevrolet who's going to buy one.' "

The New York Times–CBS News poll that was published last week showed Carter and Reagan about even —Carter thirty-nine percent, Reagan thirty-eight percent, Anderson nine percent, and undecided thirteen percent. Yesterday, the Gallup poll gave Carter forty-five percent of the vote, Reagan forty-two. The poll has a margin of error of four points, meaning that the figures could be four points higher or four points lower—and that could make quite a difference. Moreover, these surveys do not tell us about the electoral vote, where Reagan has the advantage. Time and Newsweek polls, like the recent Times–CBS poll, gave Carter a one percent lead. The NBC News—Associated Press poll gave Reagan the lead (forty-two to thirty-six, a slightly lower margin than before), and the ABC News–Harris poll gave Reagan a lead of forty-five percent to forty-two.

It is clear from conversations with Carter aides that they are worried. Caddell told me a few days ago that Florida, which is a critical state for Carter, seemed lost. (The President has continued to campaign there, though.) Other aides say that they are worried about Texas, Wisconsin, Pennsylvania, South Carolina, and Ohio. Yet they insist that they see possible victories in several states that Ford carried last time (Connecticut, Maine, Michigan, Illinois, Washington, Oregon, Virginia, and New Jersey). The degree of the President's trouble is indicated by the fact that he has had to spend time in Massachusetts and New York, which should be safe for him by now if he is to win, and that he will have to spend still more time in the South.

Within the Carter camp, there is quite a bit of resentment of Mayor Edward Koch, of New York, whom they consider to be excessively friendly to Reagan and insufficiently energetic on the President's behalf. The Carter people are preoccupied with the Jewish vote. Some have worked hard to get the Administration to issue a categorical statement that the F-15 fighter planes sold to Saudi Arabia will not be outfitted with bomb racks and re-fuelling equipment, which would produce a threat to Israel; the Administration had promised the Senate that these would not be provided, but Defense Secretary Harold Brown and Carter's national-security adviser, Zbigniew Brzezinski, were reported to have recently recommended them. The President did tell an interviewer not long ago that such equipment would not be provided, and the President's aides went to great lengths to bring this to the attention of reporters. (The President's comment was said to have come as a surprise to foreign-policy and defense officials.) The Carter people profess themselves perplexed by the problem with Jewish voters, in light of the Camp David agreement. But they know that the problem arises out of mixed signals from the Administration over its policy toward Israel—the hapless United Nations vote last March, and hints seeming to come from Brzezinski's office that after the election the United States will be tougher toward Israel.

Some also recognize that the problem between Carter and Jewish groups is in part cultural (the groups were suspicious of him in 1976) and in part a result of Carter's inability to talk to all manner of groups in a way that reaches them. In fact, the only place he seems to be successful is in black churches—and in those he draws on his own experience. Carter was helped out in Texas last week, particularly among the Chicanos, by Senator Kennedy, who has played the good soldier this fall, making several appearances on Carter's behalf, some at his side. (Inevitably, this set off the quadrennial speculation about whether Kennedy would run next time—usually, such speculation does not begin until after the election—and Kennedy has teasingly fuelled the speculation along.) The President's aides are hoping that the President will also get some mileage in farm areas out of a recent agreement to sell a great deal of grain to China. (Such sales, of course, raise the price of grain, and therefore of food, in the United States, but that is not the sort of thing that weighs on Administration officials—whichever party is in power—at election time.)

Carter has been pointing to the fact that farm prices have risen during his Administration, and has said that he hoped they would go higher. Unfortunately for him, the last Consumer Price Index to come out before the election has shown prices to be going up by about one percent, or at an annual rate of twelve and seven-tenths percent. The highest factor in the increase was the price of food. Carter, who, with good reason, has largely avoided the subject of the economy during the campaign, responded to the new inflation figure by saying that it indicated the strong inflationary forces in the economy and predicting that Reagan's proposal to cut tax rates by ten percent a year for three years "would be like pouring gasoline on a fire." The President gave a speech on the economy to the National Press Club two weeks ago, but it received very little attention. He does have a program to revitalize the economy—not a very exciting one, but a program—and he talked about it in the speech, but he does not seem able to implant it in the national consciousness. He doesn't even seem to have tried to. Carter simply has trouble getting himself across: it is not just a matter of a lack of presence, though that is a real problem, but also one of a lack of clarity in what he is trying to say.

On television Friday night, Reagan was quoted as calling inflation "a continuing tragedy of immense proportions." The hard fact is that there are forces at work which will make it difficult for whoever is elected to get inflation under control, and neither candidate has offered a plan that is likely to do so. When Reagan campaigned in the South last week, he stressed his intention of increasing military spending and suggested that a total ban on trade with the Soviet Union was "a very viable option." (Reagan opposed the embargo on the sale of grain to the Soviet Union which Carter imposed after the Soviet invasion of Afghanistan.) The simplistically termed war-and-peace issue stands on its head in the South: Reagan is believed to be helped there by his strong pro-defense, anti-Soviet militance, and Carter to be hurt by his stress on peace, arms control, and moderation in dealing with the Soviet Union.

Both sides are clearly nervous about the hostage question. Amid signs out of Iran that the release of the American hostages might be imminent, Carter officials are trying to dampen hopes that the hostages will be released before the election, in case they aren't, and the Reagan people are trying to diminish the credit that will accrue to Carter if they are. After charges concerning the hostages went back and forth between Reagan and the Carter campaign for a couple of days, aides at Reagan's headquarters in Arlington, Virginia, suggested that he stop talking about the issue. When Reagan was asked by reporters to explain his comment that he did not understand why the hostages had been held so long, he replied, "I believe that this Administration's foreign policy helped create the entire situation that made their kidnap possible. And I think the fact that they've been there that long is a humiliation and a disgrace to this country.'' Asked if he had any ideas of his own for releasing the hostages, Reagan replied, ''I think I've had some ideas, but they're— You don't talk about them.'' Mondale and then Carter landed on this, saying that if Reagan did have any ideas he ought to offer them, and likening Reagan's statement to Nixon's ''secret plan'' in the 1968 campaign to end the war in Vietnam. Carter accused Reagan, of all things, of turning the hostage issue into ''a political football.'' One of Reagan's aides told me, ''We had decided to spend all week on the economic issue, but we got sidetracked by the hostage issue,'' and added, ''He does have some views, as a matter of fact, but you don't hint at them and then say, 'I won't say what they are.' ''

Reagan did get back to the economic issue, decrying ''Jimmy Carter's demonstrated inability to govern our nation,'' and saying that ''nowhere has his inability to handle the job of the Presidency been more apparent than in his handling of the American economy.'' He also said, ''In this campaign, Mr. Carter has not answered for the economic misery he's caused.'' On Friday night, Reagan gave a half-hour address on the economy, attacking Carter's record and repeating his pledge to cut tax rates by ten percent for three years, and this time suggesting that he might balance the budget by the fiscal year 1982. (When he spelled out his program in Chicago in September, he said that the budget might be balanced in fiscal 1983.) He ended his televised address with a story he had read in a Fort Wayne newspaper about a little girl who could not buy roller skates, because the price kept going up. He concluded, ''That's right, Andrea, what Mr. Carter has done to this country's economy just isn't fair.''

Henry Kissinger held court in Washington last week and explained to reporters that the hostages might be returned soon because there is a logic to returning them now from Iran's point of view. This, of course, diminishes any credit that might come Carter's way. But Carter has made his own contribution toward undermining any such credit, through his exploitation of the problem. Still, the Reagan people's nervousness about a hostage release is evident in their conversations. One aide said to me on Friday, ''I think absent a hostage release, with just a credible performance in the debate, Reagan wins the election. But the hostages will probably be released, and I don't know how that will cut.'' And then he asked, as he undoubtedly asked everyone he spoke to, ''How do you think it will cut?''

On Saturday, one of Reagan's closest aides said to me that as a result of the foreign-policy address on TV Reagan had picked up four points from the undecided voters. ''He talked to millions of households, and that's bound to have an effect,'' this man said. The Reagan people have always put great faith in Reagan's televised addresses. Some have been landmarks in his political career. ''He can give his views unfettered by the press,'' the aide said of these final campaign addresses. ''And the undecideds are at a stage where they are willing to listen. That's the point of the televised speeches now. Our research tells us that people find him believable. You're talking about moving only four or five percent of the people in something like eight states at this point. Starting Sunday night, we'll have a lot of new ads on. We'll now get the benefit of our ad people's having saved most of their money. There will be a message of hope from Reagan, some negative ads about Carter, and ads using Jerry Ford, Betty Ford, Nancy Reagan, and Eugene McCarthy.'' The Reagan people are delighted that McCarthy endorsed Reagan last week. McCarthy, who, of course, ran as an independent four years ago, had reportedly been critical of Reagan recently, and had appeared in ads for Anderson and for Ed Clark, the candidate of the Libertarian Party. The Reagan people feel that McCarthy helps defuse the "war issue."

"We've got to stay on the subject of the economy," the Reagan aide continued. "Over sixty percent of the people think that inflation is the biggest issue. I can't understand why the press is so interested in the war-and-peace issue. We can't let the media and Carter draw us into staying on that one. The media are far more interested in it than the people themselves are." Then he turned to the subject of the hostages: "In the last four or five days, it began to hit us that the hostage thing might happen. If it does, I don't have any idea how it will affect the campaign. It depends on when they return, what condition they're in, what the deal is, when the deal was made. If we've done one thing well, we've talked about the 'October surprise' enough to get the idea implanted." As for the debate, this man said, "I think that if it's a draw Reagan wins. He'll be there standing next to the President of the United States, and that goes a long way toward allaying fears. People will see him as Presidential. It's clear that after the debate with Anderson a great many people saw Reagan as calm, in control; that debate helped Reagan—it went a long way toward allaying fears about him. What it all comes down to is that people don't want to vote for Carter but aren't sure about Reagan. The half-hour television shows and the debate will give that crucial four or five percent of the voters reason to think it's O.K. to vote for Reagan."

Some of the Carter people are apprehensive about the debate—fearful that Reagan's style will win out. Caddell has warned the President that he has only a twenty-five percent chance to "win" the debate, and that such debates are vehicles for challengers. The Carter people are engaged in diminishing people's expectations about the President's performance, and the President himself has taken to saying such things as "A lot of people say he's better at making speeches than I am, and I guess they're right."

Tuesday, October 28th. Everything about the debate is out of proportion: the relationship of the event to the campaign; the buildup it has received. It has become the world heavyweight championship and the Super Bowl combined; the only thing missing is Howard Cosell. For days, we've been told on the television news how the two candidates—like two contenders for the heavyweight title—have prepared (Reagan, for three days, in the garage at his rented estate in Virginia, rehearsing, complete with videotape replays; Carter, more sporadically, at Camp David and in Cleveland, and getting in some campaigning in between). Tonight's news showed Carter jogging early this morning in a cold rain in Cleveland. It was an unnerving sight. This is being described in the press as a sudden-death event. It's no way to decide an election. There is much talk about whether either candidate will commit the big gaffe that will decide everything; but the gaffe, such as the one Gerald Ford made over the question of Eastern Europe four years ago, is the exception. And a single gaffe shouldn't decide an election, either. Debates are not a bad idea as one element in an election process; they do offer the voters a sustained look at the candidates. But if there are to be any debates there should be several, allowing more time for a number of questions to be explored, and reducing the impact of any single event.

Carter looks tired tonight, his eyes puffed; Reagan looks to be in robust health. Reagan takes the opportunity offered by the first question—on the differences between the two candidates concerning the use of military power—to say, "I believe with all my heart that our first priority must be world peace." He and Carter both seem to be proceeding on the assumption that if they say the word "peace" frequently, that answers everything. Reagan repeats some of his stock campaign lines, such as "America has never gotten in a war because we were too strong." He also says, "I'm a father of sons; I have a grandson." He fumbles a bit in his answer; he seems uncustomarily—but understandably—tense.

Carter, in his first answer, does his Presidential routine: "I've had to make thousands of decisions since I've been President, serving in the Oval Office." And he says, "I have learned in the process"—a mistake, it appears, because the remark comes off as apologetic. He makes an unsubtle dig at Reagan, saying that "there are no simple answers to complicated questions." As he did in his acceptance speech at the Convention, he cites the lowering of spending for defense under the Republicans, leaving out the fact that most of the decrease was a result of the ending of the Vietnam War and also the fact that some of the cuts were imposed by a Democratic Congress. "There are always trouble spots in the world, and how those troubled areas are addressed by a President alone in that Oval Office affects our nation directly," he says.

Reagan, justifiably, takes up the points about defense, but then he does some distorting of his own—about weapons systems that he says Carter stopped or delayed. (This litany is one that critics of defense policy have recited over and over, until the repetition has given it the aura of truth.) Carter argues that the rate of inflation is seven percent for the previous quarter, down from about eighteen percent in the first quarter (this is true), and says that his Administration has added nine million new jobs (this is also true), and Reagan points out that the current rate of inflation is twelve

and seven-tenths percent annually and that eight million people are unemployed (figures that are also true). What is anyone learning from all this?
Reagan gets off another of his stock sentences: "We don't have inflation
because the people are living too well; we have inflation because the government is living too well." He distorts, as he has in the campaign, something that Carter said in his recent speech on the economy. In explaining
some of the historical causes of inflation, Carter cited "the failure to raise
adequate revenues at a time of greatly increased public spending, like the
Vietnam War." (Lyndon Johnson's insistence on paying for the war and the
Great Society without raising taxes, so as to avoid drawing attention to the
cost of the war, led to an inflationary cycle.) Reagan gleefully mentions this,
leaving out the reference to Vietnam and so making it appear that Carter is
urging more taxes.

Neither man really tells us what he would do about inflation. Reagan
continues to avoid citing any government programs that he would cut in
order to meet his goals of reducing taxes, increasing defense spending, and
balancing the budget. They hurl statistics back and forth (Carter pointing
out that, despite Reagan's claims that taxes were rebated to the people,
taxes were also increased during his governorship). They are like a couple
of grown men trading "So's your old man" charges. Reagan uses another
stock campaign line: "Why is it inflationary to let the people keep more of
their money and spend it the way that they like, and it isn't inflationary to
let him take that money and spend it the way he wants?" Like many of
Reagan's lines, it scans well and explains nothing. He uses other such lines
tonight, saying, for example, that the Department of Energy has a budget in
excess of ten billion dollars and "it hasn't produced a quart of oil." (He has
pledged to abolish the Departments of Education and Energy.) Reagan
paints, graphically, a somewhat different picture of his experience in the
South Bronx early this fall from what actually took place. He is very good
at describing scenes, whether or not they are real.

Carter talks about some of his programs—about what has been done for
cities and for various minorities—but, as in the campaign, he can't seem to
get his points over. Carter comes across like a teacher we don't really want
to listen to: he's not interesting to listen to, it's no fun to listen to him, he
doesn't engage us. What will be important about this event will be what the
press says happened. Carter uses a question about terrorism to talk about
his sympathy for Jews. He describes the Palestine Liberation Organization
as a "terrorist" group. He is following a plan laid out for him by Caddell in
a long memorandum, which advised him to touch base with the constituencies he needs to reach. Caddell suggested that Carter not attack Reagan but
envelop him—argue that his proposals are simpleminded, that he doesn't
seem to have a grasp of the issues, that he doesn't explain what he would
do, and that he is "dangerous" in the sense that his positions on military
involvement are "dangerous." The two men argue about SALT. Reagan
says he wants to negotiate with the Soviet Union "to have not only legiti-

mate arms limitation but to have a reduction of these nuclear weapons to the point that neither one of us represents a threat to the other." He gives no indication of what he means by that.

Reagan fluffs his lines more than usual. Carter uses the words "dangerous" and "disturbing" several times to describe Reagan's positions. He says, "This attitude is extremely dangerous and belligerent in its tone, although it's said with a quiet voice." Reagan says that he does not advocate "nuclear superiority;" he does not mention "margin of safety." Carter's reference to his daughter Amy in connection with nuclear arms—saying she told him that it was the most important issue—is embarrassing. He tries to explain in graphic terms just what is being talked about when one refers to nuclear weapons. Carter obviously feels he has a good issue in nuclear proliferation, which he talked about a great deal in 1976, but he is less persuasive on the issue now, having made such an effort in September to get Congress to overrule the Nuclear Regulatory Commission and permit the shipment of nuclear fuel to India.

On the subject of energy, Reagan says he's not sure that the price of fuels will go up, and, in accord with what he has been saying all year, remarks, "I do believe that this nation has been portrayed for too long a time to the people as being energy-poor when it is energy-rich." He criticizes the setting aside of public lands from exploration for oil. This is a big issue in the West: Reagan has lent his support to a Western movement called the Sagebrush Rebellion, which seeks the return of federal lands to the states. He condemns regulations that hold back the mining or burning of coal.

Carter keeps up an attack on positions that Reagan has taken in the past, and he does have Reagan on the defensive a good bit, and scores several substantive points, but at times he comes across as carping, pinched, and humorless. Reagan, on the other hand, comes across as smooth, genial, with the silky voice that has carried him so far, the slight nods of the head. On occasion, Reagan simply denies that he has said things he is on record as having said—that nuclear proliferation is "none of our business," that the Social Security system should be made voluntary. (Neither man says what he would do to insure the solvency of the system.) He turns Carter's attacks on his record into suggestions that Carter is simply a desperate distorter. His "There you go again" remark to Carter, delivered with a smile and a shrug, is—like other Reagan lines in other debates this year—a theatrical coup. And it has the ring of something thought out in advance: it telegraphs a "What can you expect?" attitude; it suggests that of course everything that Carter is saying is a distortion; and it ever so gently and deftly cuts Carter down to size, removes his "Presidentialness." The suggestion is that no one would say that, after all, to someone we really considered Presidential.

In his remarks, Carter tries, as he has been trying all fall, to depict himself as the linear descendant of the earlier leaders of the Democratic Party, and he says that he does not believe Reagan wants war but that the question is one of judgment and "a belligerent attitude which has exemplified his attitudes in the past." Oddly, it is Carter who seems the more wedded to a script tonight: there seem to be few spontaneous remarks, and he passes up several opportunities to call Reagan to account for misstatements. The debate does show that there are substantial differences between the two men. Toward the end, Carter gets in an appeal to the South ("I'm a Southerner") and to women (the Equal Rights Amendment). Carter's strategists hope that he is reaching the Anderson voters by stressing the issues of peace, women's rights, and control of nuclear weapons, which are presumed to be of concern to independents and suburbanites. In his closing remarks, Carter, strangely, thanks "the people of Cleveland and Ohio for being such hospitable hosts during these last few hours in my life," and he repeats his message about how much he has learned. And he tries to end on a note of uplift. The Carter people may have miscalculated in choosing, after a lot of discussion, to let Reagan speak last. Their thinking was that it would be better to have Reagan give the first answer, on the theory that that was the moment of maximum nervousness and the one that would shape people's impressions.

In his closing remarks, Reagan lands on Carter's greatest vulnerability—and touches the nerves that are bothering people—by suggesting that when people vote, "It might be well if you would ask yourself: Are you better off than you were four years ago? Is it easier for you to go and buy things in the stores than it was four years ago? Is there more or less unemployment in the country than there was four years ago? Is America as respected throughout the world as it was? Do you feel that our security is as safe, that we're as strong as we were four years ago?" He cites his experience as governor of California, giving his version of it—he has done this again and again, in an attempt to show that he is executive material and should be considered Presidential—and he concludes by saying, as he has said all year, that he would like to "have a crusade," a crusade "to take government off the backs of the great people of this country."

Reagan's task tonight, as it had been established by the press (with the help of Carter), was to not look threatening or "dangerous." Of course, he didn't, because he doesn't. Reagan's easygoing manner has served him very well; looking genial is what he does. When, in his appearances, he is stern, he is not threateningly stern, and when he expresses anger he speaks to the anger in people without really seeming angry himself; he seems appropriately indignant. By the test that had been established for Reagan in the debate, he merely had to be himself to come out ahead. Carter had the harder task, or set of tasks: to pin down the elusive Reagan, and to offer compelling reasons he should be re-elected. Carter was not as successful at his task as Reagan was at his.

Much of the television commentary afterward has to do with the fact that neither man made a major blunder. But while it is true that neither placed Sri Lanka in Latin America they left a lot of loose facts strewn around the stage and said much that needs further exploration. But the commentary has to do with how they looked and what their tactics were far more than with what they said. The ultimate absurdity is a telephone poll by ABC in which, for fifty cents, people can phone in and say who "won." The network keeps stressing the fact that the poll is unscientific, but still ABC makes a big thing of the result, which is that people thought Reagan "won," and this fact will imprint itself upon the post-debate consciousness.

Thursday, October 30th. Each side has been busy sending forth the word that its candidate "won" the debate. Last evening's CBS news showed Carter citing the New York *Times* of February 1st, containing the remark about nuclear proliferation ("I just don't think it's any of our business") which Reagan denied in the debate that he had said; and Carter talked about this in his appearances. Both candidates will be dashing about the country in the next few days and hitting many of the same states. In a conversation I had with Richard Wirthlin today, he said, "The debate was a real plus for us. We needed to do two things: drive very hard on the economy, and smooth the rough edges Ronald Reagan has accrued, rightly or wrongly. In doing that, we may have come across more defensively, but it was necessary. We came off well on the war-and-peace/leadership/competence set of issues. We measured a control group at two points in time. We think the debate gained us two points."

Wirthlin's polling indicates that the number of people who said they thought Reagan would get the United States into an unnecessary war dropped from forty-four percent to forty percent—still uncomfortably high for the Reagan people. But more important to them is that, by a ratio of two to one, people said that Reagan came across as a strong figure. "The changes indicated that we could use the peace issue against Carter, especially in the South—the peace-through-strength theme," Wirthlin said. "Carter used the theme of 'The South shall rise again' in 1976—he appealed to Southern pride. We'll try to offset that. We've been making some peace-through-strength ads in the last couple of days. We test-marketed the theme in Texas, and it went very well." Having saved advertising resources for the end, the Reagan people plan to saturate certain markets—in particular, Michigan, Ohio, Illinois, and Pennsylvania. Wirthlin said, "Carter can still win this election, but he has to fashion something new that will give him a big boost, and I don't think it will be the hostages—either they won't be released or, if they are, it won't be so effective, because there is so much skepticism. If he uses his precious time to build up leads in Texas, Michigan, Ohio, and California, and get a change in the momentum, he could come close to beating us. So what we have to do is keep our two Southern flanks—Texas and Florida—intact." The Reagan people have added Arkansas and Louisiana to Reagan's schedule, in the hope that he might carry them, and have dropped Kentucky and Tennessee, in the belief that they cannot be won. "Then we have to focus on the industrial states and keep our California base together,'' Wirthlin continued. ''And in the end we'll come back to the upbeat message of the Convention acceptance speech— the can-do America.''

The Carter people are worried about the South. ''The fact that the President still has to spend time there indicates his problem,'' one Carter campaign official says. Carter plans to end his campaign in Oregon and Washington, where his aides believe he has a good chance, and in California. Carter officials maintain that polls indicate that Carter is only three or four points behind Reagan in California, and say that Governor Jerry Brown says Carter has a good chance to carry the state. They are planning to spend more than a hundred and eighty thousand dollars on advertising in the state in these last few days. All this may be being done because Carter is in trouble in states he needs, such as Texas and Florida, but the Carter people swear that that is not the case.

Tonight, the news programs, which is where most people follow the election, contain a lot of bad news for Carter. A report on the Billy Carter case by the Justice Department's Office of Professional Responsibility was leaked to the press and it says that the President was uncooperative in the investigation. Interest rates are going up and the stock market is going down. There are pictures of the Iranian parliament, the Majlis, in an uproar. The networks also show us Carter in Michigan, saying that after he is re-elected he will meet with the Prime Minister of Japan on the subject of automobile imports. (Reagan will appear in Michigan with Gerald Ford on Saturday; Mrs. Carter and Mondale will be there over the weekend; and Carter is scheduled to return to the state on Sunday.) In Philadelphia, the President appeared at Pilsudski Hall with Stanislaw Walesa, the father of the strike leader in Poland. And John Anderson is shown being interviewed on CBS, still having to explain his candidacy and saying that it is ''within the realm of possibility'' that he will win.

Friday, October 31st. The Carter people are saying, out of necessity, that it is very close but they think when people contemplate a Reagan Presidency they will vote for Carter. And to a degree that is impossible for others to measure they believe this. By saying that the election is close, they are alerting all potential Carter voters that they must get to the polls. Of late, Carter has taken to talking about what happened to Humphrey in 1968. Early this afternoon, Robert Strauss, Carter's campaign chairman, said to me on the phone, ''We're a little bit of an underdog right now, but it's not serious. Reagan got his plus out of the debate early—he got a bit of a bump in the polls. I think we'll get ours when the Democrats go to vote. Carter talked to our constituents in the debate. That's not the sort of thing you win a debate on, necessarily, but it's how we get our Democrats back.'' Strauss sounded agitated. ''It's close; it's very, very close. I think over the weekend people have to contemplate a Reagan Presidency, and we have to get our vote out. Carter has to light something up this weekend; that's hard as hell to do. The more the press writes that Reagan has it, the better. People have to focus on Reagan as President. Front-runners have never done well this year, and Reagan is not very appealing to Democrats.''

I asked Strauss what Carter could do this weekend to be effective.

"Carter can't do a goddam thing but keep doing what he's doing," he replied. "I think he should put himself in the underdog role. He runs better as an underdog—and it makes people think about Reagan." The Carter people are going by the theory they followed during the primaries: that when people considered Kennedy as President—which was what the Carter people tried to get them to do—they voted for Carter, and when it seemed that Carter was winning they began to turn to Kennedy. In developing these theories, political strategists may be extrapolating a theory from evidence that might lead to a number of different conclusions; sometimes they extrapolate a theory that meets their needs.

The Carter strategy this fall has been to make the question "Who should be President?" and also to try to make this a contest between the two parties rather than a referendum on Carter's record, and to prevent too many people from basing their vote on general dissatisfaction with things as they are. But this election has turned into a negative referendum—on Carter and his record. People have found out that Carter is not so nice as they once thought—and voters who feel betrayed tend to be angry voters—and his record isn't exactly outstanding. But, in the eyes of a number of people who are not necessarily for him, Carter got a bit of a bad ride in this election. His exaggerations got exaggerated, and it became an article of faith that he had branded Reagan a "warmonger" and a racist and a lot of other things; and Reagan had only to smile and look like a nice man to make Carter's case look all the more off. Carter has not actually said that Reagan would deliberately start a war (or called him a "warmonger"), but his sloppy and overeager attempt to make the case against Reagan has left the impression that that is what he has said—and he undoubtedly didn't mind if people drew such conclusions about Reagan. The issue has been framed all wrong, in the campaign and in the public mind, by both sides.

The Reagan campaign argument, expressed more through Reagan's surrogates than by Reagan himself (so as to avoid further problems for Reagan), is that Carter's uncertainty and vacillation have led to our current international troubles. With "certainty" and "strength," they say, such things as Iran and Afghanistan would not have occurred. It's an easy argument to make, and there are no facts with which to refute it. It explains everything away. There is no history, no nationalism, no tribalism, no local tension— nothing that cannot be controlled. Reagan has been able to capitalize on the attacks that have been made on Carter for some time by those who say that our defenses are weak. In this instance, as in others, Carter has the harder argument to make, and, given his difficulty in getting his points across, when he tries to explain that things are more complicated than this, it gives the impression of hand wringing. There is also an argument that while, as is always the case, there are elements of our military that need tending to, we are sufficiently strong to deter the Soviet Union. But it's a harder argument to make, and Carter doesn't make it very well—to the extent that he tries to make it at all.

The implications of Reagan's policies, domestic and foreign, have barely been discussed. Reagan may win the Presidency because, among other things, he has no record to defend and he seems nice. His approach is optimistic. Besides, Carter, like other Democrats before him, has never figured out how to run against Reagan. The advantages of incumbency are rivalled by the disadvantages—especially in bad times, whatever their cause. The incumbent has a record, while the challenger can criticize the record and offer hope. That Carter doesn't seem to know how to talk about his record may have a deeper source than sheer inability to talk commandingly. He didn't have a clear picture of what he wanted to do when he ran for office, and he didn't seem to have a clear picture of what he wanted to do once he was in office. It would require more than a well-devised speech and a strong voice for him to be able to make it clear now what he plans to do. He has never seemed to be able to explain his real achievements, and making his opponent the issue only feeds the impression that he has no idea what he would do if he were re-elected. He has made no real case as to why he should be re-elected other than that he is not Reagan. At the end of this election campaign, Carter is just about where he was when he began: essentially without a political base, without any enthusiastic following. His support stems mainly from some alliances of convenience that his Administration has made with certain interest groups—or, at least, with their leaders—and from concern about Reagan. It says much about Carter, and his campaign, that at the end his strategists are counting on concern about Reagan to pull him through.

Tonight's news programs lead off with stories about Iran: American officials are waiting for the parliament to meet on Sunday; yesterday, debate was blocked because of the absence of a quorum. Once again we are waiting for the Iranians to do something. Some people with ties to the Reagan camp are spreading the word that a deal has been made—was made some time ago, in fact—and at least some of the hostages will be released Sunday night. People who write Carter off as a hopeless incompetent are suddenly crediting him with having achieved the most complicated of feats with the most exquisite timing. Toward the end of the campaign, candidates take on the look of what may be their fates—somewhat as dogs take on the look of their masters—and for the past couple of days Reagan has been looking like a winner (confident, buoyant) and Carter like a loser (strained, dispirited). Carter looks as if something had gone out of him; given how much politics obviously means to him, that something could be very large indeed. Yesterday, Reagan called the Carter Administration "a tragicomedy of errors." He said the Administration was one of "ineptitude," and was "a shambles." And on tonight's news we see Carter, at an airport in Florida, holding up a 1961 album of Reagan speeches opposing Medicare as "socialized medicine." (In the debate, Reagan said that he was not opposed to the idea of Medicare but supported other legislation. The legislation he supported was backed by the American Medical Association.) On television tonight, we see the President of the United States looking tense and worried, playing "show and tell."

Saturday, November 1st. A Carter campaign official said to me on the phone today, "Whenever I'm asked, I say we're going to win. Honestly, I don't know. I was awake three hours last night trying to figure it out. The strategy here is to poor-mouth. Jordan and Caddell and Powell are convinced that if we go into the weekend appearing to be behind, that gets people to focus on Reagan and it gets out the vote." Hamilton Jordan and Patrick Caddell are telling their colleagues that Carter was at roughly this same point in 1976—that Ford pulled slightly ahead over the weekend, and then when people focussed on what another Ford term would mean, they swung over to Carter. Yesterday, the President told a rally in mid-Florida, "Without your help, I cannot win." He said, "If the election were held today, the issue would be very much in doubt." The Carter campaign official went on, "They express great confidence around here that they are going to win. My own view is that, beneath that, they're scared. I think that the President, for the first time, thinks he might not win. The odd thing is that after the debate our reports from the people in the field were that Carter's approach had worked—the Democrats were coming back. We did a phone-bank survey in Washington State that showed the same thing. It was when the instant analysis began to sink in that we started having problems. The real question this weekend is what we can do, if anything, to refocus on Reagan. We held meetings on that yesterday and this morning. There's not a sense of panic here—there's a sense of concern." Carter officials are worried about the turnout in Philadelphia, and have dispatched two important figures from the Kennedy campaign to talk to William Green, the mayor of Philadelphia, who had supported Kennedy. Kennedy himself is to appear in Philadelphia with Carter tomorrow night. "We're continuing to dance our ballet in Chicago," the Carter campaign official said. The campaign is still caught between the forces behind Mayor Jane Byrne and those behind Richard M. Daley. The official continued, "We're constantly trying to reassure Ed Koch."

I asked him who was trying to reassure Koch.

"Damn near everybody," he replied.

In a conversation late this afternoon, Caddell said, "What's happening is this: Last weekend, the undecideds were starting to move to Carter. He was showing a fifty–forty favorable-unfavorable rating among the undecideds, and Reagan was thirty-two favorable and fifty-nine unfavorable. And the undecideds looked like Democrats—looked like our vote. We had a two-point lead in the head-to-head with Reagan; Gallup showed a three-point lead and the *Times*–CBS poll showed a one-point lead. It looked good going into the debate.'' He told me, ''We learned in '76 that people are driven by who they think other people think won the debate—by what they hear about who's the winner. That especially helped Carter in '76. That's why we wanted this debate as early as possible—because we'd be seen as losing, and we'd need more time.'' Caddell's figures indicate that, following the debate, Reagan got a boost, and by Thursday night he was four points ahead. ''It was a confluence of things,'' Caddell said. ''It's not just the debate—it's also the hostage thing. Thursday was the day the Majlis adjourned for lack of a quorum. It looked as if nothing would happen. That was the worst case in my book. Once the balloon of optimism about the hostages goes up, it has to stay up.'' Caddell continued, ''Historically, going back to 1948, there has always been an incumbent-party surge toward the very end of a campaign; the 1964 and 1972 elections were exceptions, because they weren't close to begin with. Humphrey, as the nominee of the incumbent party in 1968, had a last-minute surge. Ford had one in 1976. In 1976, I thought on Sunday that we had lost the election. Early this week, it looked like that surge was happening to us. Now the mass of undecideds is still out there.'' Richard Wirthlin, who is travelling with Reagan, is saying that the undecided voters are breaking three to two for Reagan.

I asked Caddell what the strategy was now, and he replied, ''Our strategy now is to let Reagan get out in front—encourage him to —and have Carter take the position of the underdog. Even if we weren't behind, we'd want to play the underdog. I've yet to see a bandwagon this year. Starting tomorrow, we'll have another election, with people seeing that Reagan might win and Carter pushing the Party buttons. The hostage thing is the big wild card. As of now, that's where we are.''

Today, in Texas, Carter cited his priorities for a second term; it was about time. (The priorities are energy self-sufficiency; higher productivity and employment, through tax cuts for businesses; national health insurance; cleaning up toxic wastes; and several foreign-policy goals.) Actually, Carter had sprinkled these things through his appearances, but he had never seemed to pull them together—even in his own mind. He also said, ''In four years as President, I've learned a great deal. I have learned that it is not always enough to be right. We must set priorities, or the most important work may not get done.'' Actually, the White House staff talked for years about setting priorities, and made lists, and even drew up calendars; but something always went awry. Carter continued, in what sounded like a little civics course in the Presidency (a course that he may have absorbed too late), ''We need to make our programs understood and then build a consensus for them.'' Gerald Rafshoon has made a new ad, showing Reagan's conflicting statements about nuclear proliferation, and the Carter campaign is also making much use of an ad featuring Harry Truman. ''I need you,'' Carter told his audiences. He also denounced ads that have been run in the South by fundamentalist groups, suggesting that he is not a good Christian and that he has encouraged homosexuality.

Today, Reagan appeared with Ford in Grand Rapids, Michigan, Ford's hometown, and the two men tore into Carter's record. Ford, the old partisan campaigner, is really going at it this fall; he doesn't like Carter, and he has been telling people that he and Reagan, whom he once dismissed as "simplistic," have become "very compatible." Reagan said today that Carter had failed because of "his total inability to fill Jerry Ford's shoes." The Reagan camp is projecting that Reagan will win three hundred and twenty electoral votes.

Sunday, November 2nd. Phones rang early around Washington this morning with the news that the Iranian parliament had listed conditions for the hostages' release and that Carter had flown to Washington from Chicago in the middle of the night and was meeting with Administration officials at the White House. The pictures on the television screens show a preoccupied President walking from his helicopter to the Oval Office, being greeted by the Vice President, being handed a piece of paper by Zbigniew Brzezinski. Very Commander-in-Chief-looking. No one quite knows the meaning of the conditions (that the United States pledge not to interfere in Iran's internal affairs; that Iran's assets be unfrozen; that the Shah's wealth be returned; that all court claims against Iran be dismissed), or whether they are negotiating positions, or whether they can be met. The White House has announced that the President will respond in accordance with two interests: national honor and concern for the hostages. White House aides are urging the press to be cautious about whether this might be the breakthrough.

The hostages were seized on a Sunday one year ago. Our politics has been in thrall to the Iranians ever since. Carter has been trying to ride the crocodile. Sometimes he has been able to manipulate the problem to his own temporary advantage, but it has always been there as a menace to him. The hostage crisis became to many a symbol of what they saw as a decline in our power. And it has added to an impression of Carter as hapless. This had to do very much with his style: the term that came to be used about him in private conversations was that he was a "wimp," and he began to be portrayed in cartoons as peanut-size and looking bewildered. When he tried to explain the point of being patient, the futility of force, he could not do it forcefully. When he used force, he botched it, and was never able to explain to critics on any side why the plan made sense. Carter is an articulate man; yet he has not been successful at explaining himself. Now Carter is caught in a swirl: hopes are undoubtedly rising that the miserable business of the hostages will end quickly, but he cannot appear to be "caving in" to the Iranians, and he also cannot afford to have the balloon collapse before Tuesday—which happens to be the calendar anniversary of the seizure of the hostages.

The Reagan camp is being very careful. Reagan, coming out of a church in Columbus, Ohio, says to reporters, "This is too delicate a situation. . . . I'm not going to comment." The comments were left to his surrogates, Ford and Bush, who are on "Meet the Press" and "Face the Nation" (the Reagan side got the better of the Carter people in the TV bookings on this weekend before the election), and their reactions clearly follow a plan laid out by the Reagan camp. They say that the matter is very sensitive, that Ayatollah Khomeini is trying to manipulate the election (this avoids saying that Carter is trying to manipulate it, which might seem a bit graceless at this moment; anyway, that idea has already been planted), and that, of course, we must not let the Ayatollah decide the election. Henry Kissinger, interviewed on ABC, says, "I am accusing the Iranian government . . . of now trying to tell the American public how to vote."

Reagan's surrogates also say that the United States should not take sides in the Iran-Iraq war, and should not release the spare parts that Iran has already paid for and that have been impounded as frozen assets. (Carter has said they would be released.) By taking these positions, the Reagan people were able to appear cooperative and at the same time set themselves apart and establish some criteria by which Carter would be judged. The terms that the Iranians specified had been floating about for some time, and Reagan said in September that as far as possible they should be met. Under some circumstances, such a move by a candidate would be criticized as interference in international negotiations, but Reagan's statement went largely unremarked on. Last month, Reagan said that he would not object to allowing other countries to sell Iran spare parts if the hostages were returned. Ford, on "Meet the Press," went a bit further than Bush, saying that he did think "it seems like a coincidence that this great activity has all of a sudden taken place." Last week, Ford had said, "There's a lot of cynicism, a lot of skepticism out there among people." When he was asked by reporters if he shared those feelings, he replied, "I do."

At six twenty-two, Carter appears on television, looking exhausted but, this time, in command. He avoids appearing too eager for a settlement by saying that the United States has two fundamental objectives: "protecting the honor and the vital interest of the United States, and working to insure the earliest possible safe release of the hostages." He says that "as we understand the parliament's proposals"—no official version of the demands has yet been received—"they appear to offer a positive basis for achieving both of these objectives." The statement is dignified, careful, and firm. He adds, "Let me assure you that my decisions on this crucial matter will not be affected by the calendar." The President and his aides struggled over the statement, in an effort to have its tone contain just the right blend of optimism and caution. Some of the President's aides were reluctant to have him say anything at all.

Early this evening, Caddell tells me by phone that his survey last night showed that the President was now about dead even with Reagan. He says he was elated. "The most important thing is that we have regained about three-fourths of the support we had lost on questions that indicate how people feel about the candidates and what they feel are the most important factors in making their decision," he says. Among these questions are whom people have more confidence in to handle an international crisis (Caddell says that Carter's lead on this has gone back to where it was before the debate) and who is more qualified to be President. And the importance of the economy is a factor in the decision. Caddell says that Reagan holds such a lead over Carter on the question of who is better able to handle the economy that every time the economy gains a little weight in the decision Carter loses a number of points. That's why the Carter people have tried to keep the focus on who is better able to handle an international crisis. Caddell says, "We were getting killed on Thursday and Friday. Now a whole new election is taking place." He will have the results of a new poll later tonight. He adds, "I just wish we hadn't debated."

Monday, November 3rd. William Casey says to me, "I think we're in unbelievably good shape. We're way ahead in all the polls; and our own polls, which are more exhaustive than the public ones, show us eleven points ahead—across the board and comparably in the states. Whatever shake Carter gets from the hostage thing—and I don't think it will be that great—we have enough of a cushion. And our polls show that people are increasingly skeptical about Iran." The Reagan pollsters asked such questions as "Do you think the Iranians are trying to manipulate the American election?" (the Reagan people had spent some time saying they were) and "Do you think Carter should try to manipulate the return for political purposes?" and "Do you think we should make any kind of deal in order to get the hostages back?" The answers are not very surprising.

The final Gallup poll, which was completed Saturday, has Reagan forty-seven percent to Carter forty-four and Anderson eight—this result being within the statistical margin of error. The Gallup report said, "Never in the forty-five-year history of Presidential-election surveys has the Gallup poll found such volatility and uncertainty." The Harris poll has Reagan forty-five percent, Carter forty, Anderson ten. The *Times*–CBS poll said that Carter and Reagan were running about even in the popular vote, but the *Times* story on this poll points out that Reagan appeared to continue to hold a "sizable" lead in the electoral vote. (The *Times*–CBS poll also found that Reagan got more benefit from the debate than Carter did.) An NBC survey has given Reagan two hundred and eighty electoral votes.

The President has gone back on the campaign trail, having missed some stops yesterday. California has been cancelled and Detroit has been added, on the assumption that a stop in Detroit is more likely to help in Michigan than a stop in Los Angeles is to help in California. The Carter campaign official whom I spoke to on Friday and Saturday said to me this time, "I'm fairly cheerful. Caddell's poll showed us as up on Saturday. I think we got a little bit of lift out of yesterday. Whether it's enough, who knows? Maybe people will see that the President's policy of patience has paid off. Maybe they'll see that the situation is delicate. Maybe people will look at it and say, 'I wonder how Reagan would have handled it.' Another positive thing: it looks like the weather is going to be good tomorrow. That should help our turnout. We want high numbers."

On tonight's news, Ayatollah Khomeini tells the militants, "I cannot thank you enough" for seizing the Americans. The news reports are full of stories about the difficulties involved in meeting the Iranians' terms. We see Carter asking Democrats to "come home" and appealing directly to Anderson supporters by citing issues on which he and Anderson agree. We see Reagan, along with Bush, Ford, and Bob Hope, at a rally in Peoria, asking the questions with which he closed the debate. We see Anderson saying that the people who have supported him "are not going to shrivel up and die."

At four minutes past eight, the Reagan campaign puts a twenty-minute ad on ABC; a half-hour version will run on NBC and CBS later this evening. The Reagan campaign people say they are outspending the Carter campaign three to two at this period. Also, the Republican National Committee has more financial resources at hand than its Democratic counterpart has. The Reagan campaign's own expenditures are further supplemented by those of numerous "independent" committees that have been established to support the Reagan effort and are not counted under the campaign-finance law. The law limits each Presidential campaign to spending the twenty-nine million four hundred thousand dollars in federal funds that has been provided, but under a court ruling, individual committees may spend as much as they want in support of or in opposition to a candidate as long as there are no direct ties to the candidate's campaign. Several of the "independent" groups that have been established for Reagan are headed by his allies, and there are indications that their "independence" is a bit shaky. The spending by "independent groups" has rendered the campaign-finance law meaningless.

At eight twenty-four, the Carter campaign runs its one long ad for this evening. The ad is mostly a hodgepodge of snippets from the film that ran at the Democratic Convention (pictures of statues of Presidents; other politicians praising Carter; lots of footage of the signing of the Camp David accords on the Middle East), and then it shows Carter, seated at his desk, removing his glasses and wearing a sweater. We are back to that. Carter says, "Because I've learned, I am going to be an even better President in my second term." He spells out his "vision" for the future—something that he failed to do in the campaign. He deals with his history of zigs and zags by saying, "When one approach has not worked, I have not hesitated to refine it or change it. But the *goals* have not changed." He closes by quoting Franklin Roosevelt.

Reagan's half-hour ad has Reagan sitting in a chair talking, with Bush sitting alongside. Bush says just a few words, and Reagan's appeal is masterly. And classic Reagan. "What kind of country, what kind of legacy, will we leave to [the] young men and women who will live out America's third century?" he asks. "Many Americans seem to be wondering, searching—feeling frustrated and perhaps even a little afraid." He speaks of "government that has grown too large, too bureaucratic, too wasteful, too unresponsive, too uncaring about people and their problems,'' and he says, ''I believe we can embark on a new age of reform in this country and an era of national renewal.'' He talks of reducing taxes and regulations and of reforming the way the government is run (he ''will make Cabinet officers the managers of the national Administration, not captives of the bureaucracy or special interests in the departments they are supposed to direct'') and of putting Social Security on a sound footing; of crime; of his record as governor of California; and about the America that can still be. Our days of greatness are not at an end, he tells us. He quotes John Wayne as having said, shortly before his death, ''Just give the American people a good cause, and there's nothing they can't lick.'' He says that Wayne was his friend, and that ''Duke Wayne did not believe that our country was ready for the dustbin of history.'' He tells a long, involved story about the prisoners of war in North Vietnam which he told all through the 1976 campaign. Once again he shows his talent, which goes back to his days as a sports announcer, for graphically describing a scene. He fluffs his lines a few times, and those mistakes are left in the tape, as if to offset any idea that this is just a slick actor. He summons up a number of patriotic symbols—Reagan is a master at this. The speech is deliberately emotional. He recalls the astronauts who were killed. He talks, as he often does, about the settlers of America setting out to build ''a city upon a hill.'' He calls up the memory of Arthur Fiedler on the Bicentennial Fourth of July. He talks of the Chicago Cubs outfielder who grabbed a flag at Dodger Stadium from some demonstrators who were trying to burn it in center field, and recalls that the crowd stood up and sang ''God Bless America.''

''I find no national malaise,'' Reagan says. Carter will never live that speech down: first Kennedy threw it back at him, and now Reagan does. Americans are ''frustrated, even angry,'' Reagan says. He has been remarkably skilled at speaking to that anger and frustration. ''We understand the limitations of any one nation's power,'' he says. ''But let it also be clear that we do not shirk history's call.'' And then, speaking with strength, he goes down a list of people and says, ''Let us speak for them''—people ''who seek the right to self-determination,'' people ''who suffer from social or religious discrimination,'' victims of police states and torture and persecution. He speaks to ''our allies,'' and to a long list of countries: to the people of Great Britain, to the people of France, to the people of Latin America, Australia, the Philippines, Taiwan, Korea. He is already playing the world leader. This is a remarkable political performance. He quotes a man who died at Bunker Hill. And then he closes with the kinds of questions with which he closed the debate. The last one is ''And, most importantly— quite simply—the basic question of our lives: Are you happier today than when Mr. Carter became President of the United States?''

Tuesday, November 4th. On the radio this morning, Carter is heard addressing a crowd in Plains, where he has gone to vote. His voice breaks as he talks, and it does not sound the way it sounded when he wept with joy on greeting his fellow townspeople after the election four years ago. "I've always had confidence in the American people," he says. "I've tried to honor my commitment"—long silence—"to you."

At one o'clock this afternoon, Caddell tells me over the telephone, "It's over. The bottom has dropped out." His latest poll indicates that Carter could lose to Reagan by as much as ten points. He says that on Sunday night Carter was behind Reagan by five points, and that the answers he got to questions about the hostages (about when people thought they would come home, about whether the terms seemed reasonable) began to make him nervous, and that the responses grew more negative last night. A higher percentage thought it would be a long time before the hostages were returned; a higher percentage thought that the Iranians' terms were unreasonable. "On Sunday night, we began to see some worrisome numbers about the decline of America's position in the world," Caddell says. "People were jumping all over the place this weekend. I was waiting to see where they'd land. Last night, they landed against us." Caddell says that what he calls "the internals"—the questions that are asked about the two candidates such as who is most qualified to be President and who is most trustworthy —are still breaking in Carter's favor. "It's a fed up vote," he says. He says that the campaign has been successful all year in "keeping the wolf from the door"—that is, in preventing the anger and frustration of the people from coming into the election and engulfing Carter—but that "now the wolf is racing through the house." He continues, "We worked all year, and then didn't have anything to do with it at the end. It just rode off on its own." Not long after midnight, Caddell told Hamilton Jordan that they were facing a seven-to-ten-point loss already, and that it had what Caddell describes as "all the makings of being somewhat open-ended"—that is, the bottom was dropping out. The two of them and Rafshoon phoned Jody Powell, who was then travelling with the President, and after Carter concluded a rally in Seattle and was back on the plane Powell told him.

Shortly after eleven this morning on the West Coast, Richard Wirthlin learned that Reagan would carry Kentucky, which the Reagan people had written off, and he told Reagan that he had better get his acceptance remarks ready.

By one minute after seven NBC has given Indiana, Florida, and Mississippi to Reagan. Carter's Southern "base" has collapsed. All that work on Florida gone in an instant. At seven-thirty, NBC gives Alabama, Virginia, and Ohio to Reagan. It's very early to know about Ohio. Carter has been given only Georgia. Birch Bayh, the Democratic senator from Indiana, has been defeated. Bayh's elections have always been close ones, and Indiana is normally a Republican state, but, still, it begins to seem that the Reagan tide will sweep many people before it. By one minute after eight, on NBC, Reagan has Connecticut, New Jersey, Pennsylvania, Michigan, Illinois (so go the industrial states), and North Dakota. A minute later, he is given

South Dakota, Kansas, Missouri, Tennessee, Oklahoma, and Texas. This isn't an election, it's an earthquake. Carter is being handed a staggering defeat. At eight-ten, Carter gets the District of Columbia, which goes Democratic no matter what. At eight-fifteen, NBC projects Reagan the winner. Reagan's margin in the popular vote is not as great as the electoral-vote landslide would suggest, but the states keep falling into Reagan's column. Reagan takes the West, of course. Other Democratic senators are being defeated. It seems that a great national the-hell-with-'em is taking place. But, interestingly, Barry Goldwater is in a tight race to reclaim his Senate seat.

At nine forty-one, we see Carter aides and Cabinet members gathered on the stage of the Sheraton-Washington Hotel, waiting for Carter to come and give his concession statement. The polls haven't closed in the West, but he is going to go ahead and get it over with. Robert Strauss looks stricken. There are a lot of sad faces on that stage, including some now familiar ones —Jordan, Rafshoon, Powell. They came out of nowhere, and now they have been blown away. Carter played on national anxieties in 1976, and now those anxieties have grown and turned around and whacked him. He was up against someone even better than he had been at speaking to what was bothering people. He invented himself, but the invention didn't hold up. His political situation had seemed hopeless several times—as it did a year ago. Then, on the same day—November 4, 1979—two things happened: Kennedy stumbled, and the hostages were seized. Carter managed to put both Kennedy's vulnerabilities and the hostage crisis to good use, but eventually it all collapsed on him. He manufactured what popularity he had out of events and out of other people's vulnerabilities, and that wasn't enough to sustain him. He will have plenty of time to ponder how it would have been at the end if he had not made so much of the hostage crisis at the beginning. And whether he had any choice. His was a technical campaign and a technical Presidency: he methodically welded the pieces together. But mechanics was not enough, and the pieces would not stay together. The networks are telling us tonight that according to their exit polls the result stems largely from dissatisfaction with the economy, especially inflation, and there's probably a great deal to that. The country just got angry, and Reagan skillfully focussed that anger by looking the people square in the eye and asking them, "Do you really want four more years of this?"

Carter enters the room to "Hail to the Chief," which he once disdained as too magisterial, but which he used all he could during the campaign. He'll probably miss it. The Presidential seal, which went everywhere with him, is on the lectern. But the symbols can't help him now. Suddenly, they seem like relics he is hanging on to. We adjust quickly. Carter seems to have pulled himself together for this difficult moment, and he makes his statement with dignity, and even a rare human touch, saying, "I can't stand here tonight and say it doesn't hurt." How must it feel to be so resoundingly rejected? Mrs. Carter, by his side, appears to be having the harder time composing herself, and she looks a bit angry. Carter says that he has phoned Reagan and told him he wants to have the best transition in history. He says, "I've not achieved all I set out to do," and adds, "But we have faced the tough issues." This is what he kept trying to tell people during the campaign, but it didn't work. "The great principles that have guided this nation since its very founding will continue to guide America through the challenges of the future," he says. "We must now come together as a united and a unified people to solve the problems that are still before us, to meet the challenges of a new decade." He is gracefully playing out his role in one of America's great dramas: the peaceful transfer of power. He sounds better than he ever did in the campaign.

Mondale, who is in Minnesota, appears a few minutes later. Mondale came out of the campaign with his reputation intact, perhaps enhanced, and he is already looking ahead to 1984. Now he praises the democratic process and says that today "the American people quietly wielded their staggering power."

There remains something awesome about our democratic process: even in years less dramatic than this one, and despite all the polling and predicting and analyzing, we never know what will happen until the people exercise their choice. At ten forty-five, Anderson makes a concession statement. He says, "I was not destined to be the next President of the United States— that is a decision deferred." And he smiles as his followers begin to shout "Eighty-four!" He quotes Abraham Lincoln: "Disappointed, yes; bruised, no." As of now, Anderson is getting about six percent of the vote—enough to receive federal funding for his campaign—and is affecting the outcome in several states.

At eleven fifty-five, Reagan comes onstage at the Century Plaza Hotel in Los Angeles, with his wife, Nancy, beside him. He looks overjoyed, as well he might. He says, "There's never been a more humbling moment in my life." He quotes Abraham Lincoln telling newsmen on the day after his election to the Presidency, "Well, boys, your troubles are over now; mine have just begun." Reagan says, "I think I know what he meant," and he adds, "but I don't think he was afraid." Reagan says, "I am not frightened by what lies ahead, and I don't believe the American people are frightened by what lies ahead." He says, "We're going to put America back to work again."

Wednesday, November 5th. After the earthquake, the sorting out is going on. People awoke today to find not only that Reagan had been elected in a landslide electoral vote but that the Republicans had taken control of the Senate—something that not even the Republicans had dreamed possible— and had picked up a sufficient number of seats in the House to insure that the prevailing ideology will be conservative. Moreover, the Republicans who will gain positions of power in the Senate—the committee and subcommittee chairmanships—are for the most part very conservative Republicans. The transfer of power may be orderly, but the atmosphere in Washington is that of a place that has suddenly been taken by a conquering army.

The army seems as surprised as anyone. Would-be Administration officials are jockeying for position in a Reagan government (actually, they have been doing this for some time, but now things get a bit less delicate); Capitol Hill figures who had long dwelt in the minority twilight suddenly find themselves committee chairmen (and the angling for subcommittee chairmanships has begun). There are lives to be sorted out; thousands of people are out of jobs; hostesses are revising their guest lists; lawyers and lobbyists are updating their Rolodexes. A taxi driver I know who does chores for some people who work in the White House is glum about the idea of losing his entrée there. But mainly there is a great deal of trying to figure out what happened. As usual, a lot of sweeping judgments are being made. Facts that do not fit the generalizations are dismissed. The myth becomes larger than the facts, and the myth is simpler than the facts. What happened last night was a very big thing, but there is no one simple reason for it.

Of course, Reagan won decisively, but his popular margin was not proportionate to his electoral margin. He won by a margin of ten percent of the votes (fifty-one percent to Carter's forty-one percent, with seven percent going for Anderson)—a lower margin than was enjoyed by Eisenhower (over Stevenson) in 1952 and 1956, not to mention Johnson (over Goldwater) in 1964 and Nixon (over McGovern) in 1972. The electoral-vote count is four hundred and eighty-nine to forty-nine. Carter carried only six states (Georgia, Hawaii, Maryland, Minnesota, Rhode Island, and West Virginia) and the District of Columbia, but little notice has been taken of the fact that Anderson received more than the difference between Reagan and Carter in thirteen states (Alabama, Arkansas, Connecticut, Delaware, Kentucky, Maine, Massachusetts, Mississippi, New York, North Carolina, Tennessee, Vermont, and Wisconsin). There is no way to know how many of those votes would have gone for Carter, of course, or whether many of these people would have voted at all, but it is clear that Anderson cost Carter at least several states.

Much is made of the fact that nine Democratic senators, most of them liberals, were defeated, but it is also a fact that ten Democrats, most of them liberals or moderates, were re-elected to the Senate and that two Democrats were elected to it for the first time. Several Democrats who were defeated were prominent liberals—Frank Church, of Idaho; John Culver, of Iowa; George McGovern, of South Dakota; Gaylord Nelson, of Wisconsin; and Bayh—but, again, the picture is not so simple. Not only had Bayh's elections always been close, but he, like McGovern and Nelson, had served three terms, or eighteen years, and Church had served four terms, and their opponents were able to say that that was time enough (just as Bayh had said about his opponent in 1962).

And there was a kind of double-jeopardy incumbency at work this year.

The Republican pollster Robert Teeter, who advised several Republican candidates this year, suggested that they make the argument that if the people wanted to change things they not only had to get rid of Carter but also had to change the direction of Congress by voting against the incumbent. Teeter says that Robert Kasten, in Wisconsin, and Dan Quayle, in Indiana, did not defeat Nelson and Bayh on a liberalism-versus-conservatism basis. "They beat them because they said that it was time to change things in Washington," he says. Moreover, McGovern, culturally and politically, does not quite fit South Dakota's politics now, and the same is true of Church and Idaho. Iowa may be closing out, at least for the time being, its brief period of electing Democrats to statewide office; and it has a record of never re-electing a Democratic senator. But even these conclusions are tempered by still other facts. All the Democratic senators who were defeated ran better in their states than Carter did, with the exception of Herman Talmadge in Georgia. The Idaho vote was forty-nine percent for Church and fifty percent for his opponent, while Carter got twenty-five percent to sixty-seven percent for Reagan. There are always a number of immeasurable factors in any defeat. Nelson was regarded in Wisconsin as being inattentive to the state, and he seemed to realize too late that he was in a difficult fight. It is safe to say that at least some of these people would have won if it had not been for Carter.

The precise force of the Reagan tide cannot be measured, but there can be no question that one existed. Some of the Democrats who were re-elected had a lower victory margin than had been anticipated. Caddell says that a drop in Democratic support toward the end could be seen in the senatorial races as well as in the Presidential race. In addition, the turnout was the lowest it had been in thirty-two years. Teeter says he does not believe that what happened in the Senate races was ideological. "I don't think people said, 'We need some conservatives in there,' " he told me. "Ideology is not important to voters. They don't think of themselves as liberals or conservatives, or of politicians as liberals or conservatives. When you ask them whether they are liberal or conservative, and they tell you, and you ask them what that means, they talk about life-style—pot, family, and so on. The problems change more than the people. The voters are in favor of what they see as pragmatic solutions to these problems. When the problems were civil rights, housing, education, people accepted what seemed pragmatic solutions—more government action. When the problems became inflation, high taxes, government spending, people again voted for pragmatic solutions, and in this case that meant less government."

There were also, of course, the intensive efforts of various conservative and anti-abortion groups to defeat selected liberal senators, and there was the sustained and well-financed effort of the Republican Party, which spent over nine million dollars on television ads—quite effective ones—against the Democratic Congress. (The Democrats had no counterpart ads.) The National Conservative Political Action Committee spent over one million dollars on six Senate races; the Moral Majority says that it spent three million dollars against liberal senators. In several states, anti-abortion groups handed out leaflets at Catholic churches on the Sunday before the election. And there are other facts that get in the way of the "conservative tide" theory: Elizabeth Holtzman, a very liberal Democrat, would doubtless have won in New York if Jacob Javits, who had been defeated in the Republican primary, had not appeared on the ballot (along with Anderson) on the Liberal Party's line. Warren Magnuson, of Washington, was defeated by a moderate Republican, not only because he had been in the Senate a long time—six terms, or thirty-six years—but also because he is old and has trouble moving about. Barry Goldwater, who barely survived his challenge (by one percentage point), got in trouble in part because he is obviously ailing, as is Javits. Anti-incumbency turned up in some other forms: Talmadge was defeated largely because he had been "denounced" by the Senate for misuse of his official finances. All but one of the members of Congress who were involved in the Abscam scandal were defeated. John Brademas, of Indiana, the House Majority Whip, had been facing close elections for some time. Several Democrats from the West who were defeated blame Carter's early concession.

And looming over all this was not only the strong Reagan sweep—or the enormous Carter defeat—but also the nature of the Reagan-Carter contest. Time and again during his Presidency, Carter had made things difficult for other Democrats—by getting them to support a position that he then changed, by taking positions that were difficult to explain. Even Democrats who kept their distance from Carter couldn't escape the effects of his management of the Presidency, or of the pounding that he and his policies took at the hands of Reagan. It is difficult for a party to have an agenda if its incumbent President does not seem to have one. And this comes back to the nature of the Reagan victory.

The Reagan earthquake was set off by a number of elements, only some of which could be called ideological. It was something far more complicated than a "conservative tide." One very large ingredient, of course, was Carter's failure: his inability to lead; his inability to be competent or to project what competence he had; his poor judgment about people. There was the capacity of the contemporary world for frustrating people—as Americans, as taxpayers—and people's inclination to lay their frustrations at the door of the Oval Office. The frustration lands on the incumbent because he is there. And Reagan was deft at exploiting that frustration. But now he will have to deal with the elements that fed it; not all of them will go away with Carter. Every decade, the world seems more complicated and more unmanageable, and this is unlikely to change. There was Reagan's enormous skill as a media politician, who had his own shrewd instincts, and who was also well packaged and well coached. None of these elements were ideological; they were just neutral facts. There was also a reaction to a whole range of social and moral issues—including race (which embraces affirmative action and busing, Cuban refugees and illegal immigrants), the sexual revolution, women's rights, homosexuality—on which a substantial number of people felt that things had moved too fast. A movement such as the Moral Majority cannot get going unless it unlocks something that is there. There was Reagan's skill, and his party's, at reaping the benefits of people's unhappiness with "government" and anyone who had anything to do with it (much as Carter, less powerfully, ran against "Washington" and "the bloated bureaucracy" in 1976), even as Reagan dodged and weaved (as Carter did four years ago) about just what steps he would take to deal with the problem. And there were enough governmental absurdities and failures to make government a vulnerable target. Running against "the rascals" and "the government" is a fairly sturdy American tradition. And there is a new degree of cynicism about politicians, fed by much of the press, which suggests that not a one of them is any good.

Increasingly, and with more sophistication, the various segments of our society—business, labor, farmers, maritime workers, postal clerks, doctors, uniformed firemen—organize themselves to make demands, and they feel increasingly aggrieved at government when their demands are not met. But no President can meet the demands of all these groups. (Carter did a great deal for the National Education Association, and so the N.E.A. supported him.) There are the constraints on resources, fiscal and physical, that any President has to grapple with in the face of these demands. So a great deal of what happened, in the national race as well as in many local ones, was anti-incumbent. Robert Teeter, who polled for Ford in 1976, points out that four years ago, in what was, in the end, a very close election, the question came down to whether people wanted four more years of the incumbent, and they said no. Teeter says, "The direction of the country is more conservative, but not because people think of themselves as ideologues. It's a feeling that the wheels have come off the federal government, and they just have to try to get it back in control. There was also frustration over the hostages, over refugees, over international trade—people were anti-Japanese, anti-German, particularly in the industrial states. All the frustrations were there, and, besides, the odd things that the government does —some of the nutty regulations—seemed to catch up with people this year, because they were hurting economically. And, all that aside, the most important issue of the campaign was Jimmy Carter's record."

There is disagreement between the Carter and Reagan camps over exactly what happened at the end, but there may be an element of truth in what each of them says. Caddell says that it was the last-minute developments over the hostages. He and others in the Carter camp point out that the television news programs on the eve of the election led off with the hostage story (still in suspension) rather than with the story of the election itself; that the country was presented with Ayatollah Khomeini thanking the militants; and that all this let loose pent-up frustration and anger over a number of things, especially the economy—the frustration and anger the Carter people had been struggling to stave off. The Reagan people say that the big element was people's sense of Reagan's leadership in contrast to Carter's record. Actually, it seems that both sides are talking about essentially the same thing. What is harder to reconcile is their disagreement over what the polling data indicated in the last days of the campaign. But here, too, the differences are not so great. These polls have a margin of error of three points or so in either direction, and they involve a good bit of guessing. Wirthlin and Teeter dispute Caddell's assertion that Carter pulled even during the final weekend, but it is a fact that most of the public polls said that as of Saturday the race was very close. There are suggestions that some of the polls were based on faulty data about the makeup of the electorate—that some may have assumed that there were more Democrats in the electorate than there are. (All the polls weight their samples in terms of how they think the electorate will finally look—a process that allows for a number of misjudgments.) It just might be that a lot of people didn't choose to tell the pollsters what they really thought, or weren't sure what they thought until the end.

As it happened, both camps ended up with about the same estimated margin of victory for Reagan on Monday, and both were just about right. Caddell insists that what happened is "ahistorical": that since the beginning of the postwar period Presidential elections that were close all along stayed close to the end. He says that there was a great deal of movement at the end of the 1978 congressional campaign, which might have been a harbinger of what happened this year. Wirthlin and Teeter maintain that there never has been such a substantial and sudden drop as Caddell maintains took place. (A *Times*–CBS poll published November 16th indicates that about one of every five registered voters changed his mind in the last four days, and that the reasons were the hostages and the economy.) The public polls, with one exception, stopped counting by early in the weekend, so if there was a substantial shift in the last days before the election they would have missed it. The exception was the Harris poll, which kept going until Monday night, and showed a five-point lead for Reagan.

Interestingly, the Reagan pollsters did not find an increase in Reagan's lead until two days after the debate—that is, not until people got an impression of what people's impression of the debate was. Reagan, according to Wirthlin's figures, went into the debate on Tuesday with a five-point lead, and showed a five-point lead on Wednesday; on Thursday, it was seven points; on Friday, nine; on Saturday, ten; on Sunday and Monday, eleven. The Reagan camp thought on Monday that Reagan would win with three hundred and ninety-five electoral votes. "I think the debate established the basis for our pulling it away," Wirthlin told me. "It took the edge off the 'dangerous' image and enabled us to go hard at Carter over the weekend, and end up Monday night with a vision-of-the-future speech."

When I asked Wirthlin what he thought made the election come out the way it did, he replied, "I think the thing that turned the vote was that the issue became leadership—Reagan's leadership in framing and coping with the most important issue, the economy."

Many of the state polls, of both parties, on senatorial races also turned out to be wrong, and this lends credence to the idea that an avalanche occurred at the end.

One man I know who works within the White House explains what happened this way: "There was an illusion created—it just occurred—at the time of the Democratic Convention, and continuing through the period of Reagan's mistakes early in the fall, that we were building on the base of the Democrats. It was an illusion because the base wasn't there. The nature of the 'support' that we had and were building on was such that it could be blown away. When you move up from the twenties to the thirties in the polls, you're building on people who were not there anyway. The pollsters may not have misread the situation. The people who said they were for us were very tenuously for us, and the slightest breeze blew them away."

Of course, the important thing in politics, when it comes to determining the behavior of politicians, is not necessarily what happened but what people think happened—what become the accepted truisms. The truisms guide behavior. There is little question that most of those Democrats, and even those moderate Republicans, who remain in Congress will poke their heads out of the trenches very cautiously. The right wing and the Moral Majority took a couple of opportunities this year to show that they could affect Republican primaries by getting someone sympathetic to them nominated, rather than a more centrist Republican, and they are already issuing threats about moderate Republicans and liberal Democrats whose terms expire in two years—in part, to affect their behavior between now and then.

There is another reason the behavior of Congress will change to a greater degree than the simple numerical shift between the parties would dictate. Several of the Republicans who have been elected to the Senate are not the traditional conservative Republicans; Robert Taft would not recognize them, and they are quite unlike Gerald Ford or Robert Dole. They are right wing, nihilistic, counter-reformationist. They are culturally distinct from several of the conservatives already in Washington as well as from the moderate Republicans. Their political origins seem to be the same pressures that have given rise to the "single issue" groups: as government seems less and less responsive in solving problems, people feel that they have to apply more and more pressure at a single point. One place to do this is in the nominating process, where participation is usually low and well-organized groups can, therefore, have a major effect. These newly elected senators will join some like-minded men who are already in the Senate and form a critical mass. Furthermore, those who are already there have shown that they do not play by the old rules of the club; comity is of little interest to them. Howard Baker, who will be the new majority leader, has his work cut out.

And so has Reagan. He has inherited an assortment of constituencies

whose interests will be difficult to reconcile. Some of the right-wing senators, for example, will seek to do things that would seriously upset Reagan's
blue-collar constituents. Reagan has an opportunity to clear out some of the
more senseless things that government does. Carter had the same opportunity, but before long he got lost in the maze of the special-interest state.
Reagan became more moderate as his campaign went on, but now he will
have to control—or mollify, at least—his right flank. Much is made of the
fact that he was a more moderate governor of California than his campaign
for the office suggested he would be. But it was also a fact that the California
legislature was Democratic. If he wants to be a moderate President, he will
have to be agile—as he has been this year. Conservative groups are already
busy reminding him of their contribution to his election. This kind of maneuvering goes on with every new President; these groups are behaving just as
liberal ones do when a Democratic President starts moving to the center.
There are certain laws of physics that hold true in politics.

Thursday, November 6th. On television, Reagan is holding his first press
conference as President-elect, and it is all very Presidential. A disembodied
voice sounding just like the one at the White House announces, "Ladies
and gentlemen, the President-elect of the United States and the Vice
President-elect." Reagan and Bush arrive onstage at the Century Plaza
Hotel looking healthy and happy. Reagan loses no time about showing that
he is taking charge: he briskly announces the names of those who will
conduct the transition for him. He is asked how much consideration he is
going to give to the new conservative groups, including the Moral Majority,
and his answer is skillful: "I have told the people who have supported us in
this campaign that I'm going to do as I did when I was governor of California
—that I am going to be open to these people. You want a President of all
the people, and I am going to want to seek advice where I think that I can
get advice from those who are familiar with a particular problem." He says
that he believes in "linkage" between negotiations on arms control and
"the policies of aggression of the Soviet Union." He says he realizes that
the Departments of Energy and Education, which he had said during the
campaign that he would abolish, have "legitimate functions which have
always been performed by government and that should continue to be."
(During the campaign, he managed to convey the impression that by abol-
ishing them he would do away with everything that these Departments did.)
He is coming across as being in command. Another new beginning, another
fresh start.

There is a certain dewiness to every new President—even a sixty-nine-
year-old one. Reagan is more relaxed than he was during the campaign, and
shows a certain charm that he did not allow himself to display then. During
the question period, he calls on a number of foreign correspondents. (Lou
Cannon, of the Washington *Post,* has written that this was by design, to
send reassuring messages to foreign leaders.) He firmly states his support of

Howard Baker as majority leader. (Some conservatives were threatening to try to block Baker. Today, Strom Thurmond, who is to replace Edward Kennedy as the chairman of the Senate Judiciary Committee, announced that he would press for legislation to reinstitute the death penalty for certain federal crimes.) Reagan says that he thinks the economy was "the issue of the campaign."

When Reagan is asked if he still feels wedded to the Republican platform, he replies, "I am—I ran on the platform; the people voted for me on the platform. I do believe in that platform, and I think it would be very cynical and callous of me now to suggest that I'm going to turn away from it. Evidently, those people who voted for me—of the other party or of independents—must have agreed with the platform also." Asked what he would say to reassure those who feel potentially disenfranchised by his political views, he replies, "Well, I don't think that anyone is disenfranchised by my views."

Appendix

FOLLOWING ARE memorandums that were prepared by Richard Wirthlin, Reagan's pollster, for the Reagan campaign, and by Patrick Caddell, Carter's pollster, for the Carter campaign, and that were given to me after the election.

Wirthlin's first memorandum was written at midpoint in the primaries. He believed then that Reagan had the nomination won, but that there were problems that needed attention and also that it was time to begin planning for the fall campaign. The second memorandum suggests strategy for the period between the end of the primary period and the convention—what to do during the "doldrums," when the primaries are no longer dominating the political news and a campaign might be affected by whatever winds are blowing. The third and fourth suggest strategies for trying to hold the campaign to a given subject—a "focused impact theme"—during a given week, in these instances foreign affairs and the economy. Wirthlin's fifth memorandum lays out strategy for the final weeks of the campaign.

The first of Caddell's two memorandums proposes strategy for the general election, and the second lays out strategy, in the context of the final weeks of the campaign, for the debate with Reagan.

A few excisions were made in both sets of memorandums.

—E.D.

The Wirthlin Memorandums

Memorandum I

Some Initial Strategic and Tactical Considerations for the 1980 Presidential Campaign

DRAFTED MARCH 28, 1980

PRESENT STATUS OF THE CAMPAIGN

To date, Ronald Reagan won ten of the thirteen direct primary contests held. He narrowly lost two of the others (Massachusetts and Connecticut), and his name did not appear as a candidate on the third (Puerto Rico). With over a third of the 998 delegate votes needed to nominate now locked into the Governor's column and with his best states only now starting to come up on the primary calendar, the general election campaign, from our point of view, starts today.

The purpose of this paper is to stimulate thought and discussion among the senior staff and the Governor that will evolve into a detailed campaign plan built on the (agreed upon) goals, objectives and strategies.

Several critical lessons that emerged from our primary politicking can be most helpful in developing an effective strategy for the general election campaign. These are:

- Never before has the electorate been as volatile in switching support from one candidate to another. While there is evidence of more than usual interest in the campaign, the loyalty of the voters runs thin indeed.
- The primaries have clearly revealed Carter's basic vulnerability. In spite of the number of wins he has strung together, Kennedy's surge in Connecticut and New York attests to the incumbent's weakness. Additionally, exit interviews taken in Wisconsin and Kansas show that even

351

those who vote for Carter do so less out of allegiance to him than in protest to Ted Kennedy.

- In the process of walking through and beyond the hot coals of the Iowa setback, we learned once again that our most effective asset is providing the electorate with in-depth exposure to Ronald Reagan.[1] His personal, political power reflected strongly in the pro-Reagan vote switching induced by debates and the positive impact the Governor wielded when he campaigned in the critical primary states right through the day of the election (Illinois, South Carolina, Florida, Wisconsin and Kansas).
- The strong political allegiance the Governor generates was further evident in the number and loyalty of the volunteers he attracted when the program was mounted specifically to recruit, motivate and utilize them in New Hampshire.

Potential liabilities also surfaced in the primary campaigns:

- It has become evident that the dynamics of the primary and Reagan's campaign have created a certain degree of tension between the Reaganites and the Party. This arises from a number of sources. For one thing, our support cuts across party lines more effectively than that of the other Republican hopefuls. Further, most of the "organizational Republicans" have supported one or another of Ronald Reagan's opponents over the last six years, and have viewed the Governor himself as an "outsider." Thus, it is not surprising that the success of his campaign has created stresses and outright resentments within the party structure.
- I do *not* believe that the press conspires to make the Governor look incompetent, dangerous or uncaring. Nevertheless, as he has progressed from one of many contenders to the most likely Republican nominee, and possibly the next President of the United States, the electronic and print media have become more critical and more damaging politically to our general election goals.
- Similarly, the voter himself now views Ronald Reagan in different terms than he did earlier. In the primary, the vote can be used by franchised citizens to protest or to experiment or to stop a "dangerous" candidate. While some of these same motives may be extant in the general election, the vote decision focuses heavily on the judged success or failure of the incumbent's administration and the potential leadership capability of the challenger.

What portends for maximizing the possibility of Ronald Reagan's securing the presidency will be discussed in the sections which follow.

Once the strategic considerations are reviewed and agreed upon by the senior campaign staff and the Governor, the campaign plan will be used to establish the frame of reference for the specific functional and tactical elements of the campaign —its organization, scheduling, issue research, the press, the convention, attitudinal research, the candidate, the media, finance, opposition research, and the volunteer elements. Certain tactical considerations are included in this initial paper because they appear to be of urgent concern.

[1] See p. 109.

THE MAJOR THRUST OF THE CAMPAIGN

When an incumbent president seeks a second term, then the election generally becomes a referendum on the successes and failures of his administration. Jimmy Carter can be defeated if this proves, as it has in the past, to be the major thrust and focus of the 1980 presidential election.

Hence, Jimmy Carter's leadership, his incompetence, and his failures must be the major targets of our campaign.

Kennedy's success in New York and Connecticut revealed the political potency of making Carter's administration and leadership the issue. (Kennedy sent the right message, but in Wisconsin and Kansas it was delivered by the wrong messenger.)

We can set the stage for a similar campaign by purchasing a half-hour of prime-time television in May or June to launch the general theme of quality of leadership —showing where Carter has taken us since 1976 and what the promise for America might be for the 1980's should Ronald Reagan be elected. But this tactic must be supported by the electorate viewing the Governor—unlike Ted Kennedy—as a favorable and credible alternative to Jimmy Carter.

Specifically, we must position the Governor, in these early stages, so that he is viewed as less dangerous in the foreign affairs area, more competent in the economic area, more compassionate on the domestic issues and less of a conservative zealot than his opponents and the press now paint him to be.

To accomplish these objectives early in the campaign, it is essential that we start developing new material on four issues:

- the general issue of leadership;
- a non-ideological issue (such as the values and aspirations themes or urban problems);
- the economy;
- and, a "peace-oriented" foreign policy position.

Once that image foundation is solidly established then we can confront, expose, and decry the major failures of the Carter administration in the closing months of the campaign.

Care must be exercised so that the Governor's criticism of Carter does not come off as too shrill or too personal. We *can* hammer the President too hard, which will spawn backlash. Furthermore, given the potential problems Carter faces with both foreign affairs and the economy, he himself will provide us with additional targets between now and November.

Nevertheless, the Governor must never attack Jimmy Carter's personal integrity.

THE POLITICAL-INSTITUTIONAL POWER BASE

It is absolutely critical, in light of the stresses and strains that the primaries have generated and the fact that liberal and moderate Republicans are disproportionately represented in the power centers of the Party, that we immediately begin to reach out, secure, and extend our support among the following key elements within the Party:

- Republican National Committee
- Other 1980 presidential contenders
- President Gerald R. Ford
- Incumbent Senatorial, Congressional and Gubernatorial Republicans

Republican National Committee

For the interim period we will have four channels into the Republican National Committee.

First, Fred Biebel [a former state party chairman of Connecticut] and Jerry Carmen [a former state party chairman of New Hampshire], as past Eastern chairmen, enjoy entree with both the R.N.C. and the state committees. They will accomplish the following objectives:

- Identify early the nature and scope of any stresses or strains between the established party organization and the Reagan loyalists and resolve these as quickly and as amicably as possible. This goal will be the primary responsibility of Fred Biebel.
- Jerry Carmen will work in conjunction with Fred, but his major responsibility will be to insure that the new Republican National Committeemen and women and state chairmen are Reagan supporters. It is critical that while we maintain a strong sense of party unity, on the one hand, that we do not, on the other hand, lose this critical power base regardless of the nature, course or outcome of the presidential election.

The second liaison channel will be with the Project 80 Committee [a party committee established to plan for the 1980 election]. We will fold into our general campaign plan pieces of the work already undertaken by Project 80 where the specific staff papers suggest strategies, tactics, and action plans that are congruent with the goals and objectives of the campaign as we view them.

The third liaison will be provided through the offices of Paul Laxalt [senator from Nevada and the campaign chairman] and Tom Evans [congressman from Delaware]. They will interface with the Committee from our interest position in the House and the Senate and will also provide us with general strategic counsel regarding the Republican National Committee.

Fourth, we should identify early the resources that we need to have from the Republican National Committee to run an effective fall campaign. Furthermore, it is essential that we exercise directly power and control over those particular resources.

Other 1980 Presidential Contenders

We have already secured the verbal support of almost all those candidates who initially sought the Republican presidential nomination. John Connally, Howard Baker, Robert Dole and Phil Crane have committed to support Ronald Reagan.

It is essential that we not only use their endorsements adroitly with the media but also take full advantage of their "support" in raising money and bolstering our organization with key men from their campaigns who have proved to be effective. It is equally critical that we give them a position of prominence in our organization, such as through the Executive Advisory Council or the National Agenda Council, to tie them closely and meaningfully to our campaign. All these men can serve as excellent surrogates through the summer and into the fall.

Even though it appears that John Anderson will bolt the Party and run as an Independent, we should avoid, and in particular Ronald Reagan must shun the strong temptation to unload on Anderson. It is clearly in our best interest to preach party unity now as strongly as we did earlier. If Anderson should decide to run an independent candidacy, we have lost nothing by making it as easy as possible for him to stay within the Republican ranks. If we treat him benignly during the primaries and he still decides to leave the party, then the onus of spoiler falls squarely on his shoulders alone.

Plans should be prepared now to garner the full and active support of George Bush, once he recognizes that his candidacy has lost its viability. Of course, that decision might possibly come as late as the convention in Detroit, although I doubt this. His support and resources should be absorbed by our campaign adroitly and enthusiastically.

President Gerald R. Ford

Of all Republicans, Gerald R. Ford potentially can hurt us or help us more than any other. He is respected a great deal by the electorate at large, and even more so in the Republican ranks. Because he considered his own presidential candidacy on his belief that Ronald Reagan could not win, his whole-hearted and active conversion to our cause will carry a significant political impact

While it is important for Bill Casey [the campaign director] to begin to develop the ties to Gerald Ford, the clincher will come only when Gerald Ford and Ronald Reagan sit down amicably, one on one, and resolve for the near-, and hopefully long-term, the major difficulties that arose out of the 1976 election.[2] It is essential that prior to the convention Gerald Ford is given an official position in our campaign. Having him assume the chairmanship of the National Agenda Council could provide one such possible opportunity.

Incumbent Senatorial, Congressional and Gubernatorial Republicans

Hardly a week passes without additional Senatorial and Congressional support coming our way. Furthermore, a number of the liberal/moderate governors are actually opening up lines of communications with our campaign. These Republican incumbents can provide a most valuable base for our campaign. They can help us develop good state campaign plans, provide political resources to enhance our success in their states, and as spokespersons for the Governor's political interest in the fall. We need the organizational mechanisms to assure that we take advantage early of these resources.

[2] Such a meeting occurred at Ford's home in Rancho Mirage, California, on June 5th,1980.

THE ELECTORAL POWER BASE

Survey research conducted in the primary states shows that Ronald Reagan won *not* because his ideological positions were congruent with the electorate, but rather in spite of a rather substantial ideological gap between himself and the average Republican. The extent of the gap was remarkable. In Illinois, Wisconsin and Pennsylvania, Ronald Reagan's distance from the individual's ideological position was greater than the distance between the individual and Congressman John Anderson.

While ideology does not cut strongly in the primary contests, it will be a major vote determinant in November. As the following table shows, the best predictor of vote between Reagan and Carter turned out to be a combination using ideology and party. Note that we have no opportunity to win the general election unless we pull substantial numbers of moderate ticket-splitters into our column.

VOTER TYPES AS PREDICTOR OF REAGAN-CARTER VOTE
(May 1979)

		Reagan	Carter	Undecided
Conservative Republicans	(22%)	85%	12%	4%
Moderate liberal Republicans	(7)	69	25	6
Conservative ticket-splitters	(13)	50	41	9
Moderate ticket-splitters	(17)	50	40	10
Conservative Democrats	(14)	37	58	5
Liberal Democrats	(22)	25	68	7
Non-Republican Blacks and Hispanics	(6)	17	78	5

Without question, the electorate must view Ronald Reagan in less extreme conservative terms in the fall if we are to win.

This can be done without altering any issue positions. By rounding out the total perception of Ronald Reagan as a more human, warm, approachable individual, and by stressing some issues and leaving others for the opponents to develop, we can "moderate" the arch-conservative characterization of the Governor.

In 1976 and in the earlier primaries in 1980, the more exposure individuals were given to Ronald Reagan through the 30-minute television statements and the debates, for example, the less "dangerous" he was perceived to be. It is essential that we build upon this advantage prior to the convention. The Governor, in short, must use a technique he developed effectively when he was Governor of the State of California—going to the people directly and not relying upon the 30- or 40-second news clips, or the editorial thought pieces for the voters to build their impression as to what kind of man he is.

Secondly, in rounding out the multi-dimensionality of our candidate, it is imperative that we expose the *real* Ronald Reagan. A warm, compassionate, caring individual runs counter to the prototypical view most Americans hold of conservatives.

Possibly the best single vehicle to achieve this particular objective of the campaign is the convention. But prior to that time, we should give careful attention to the nature, thrust and source of our own paid media to present to the voters of America the depth and warmth of Ronald Reagan.

Where Must We Win to Win?

In assessing the electoral power base, we should always keep in focus the major goal of this campaign. It is not to acquire at least "50% plus one" of the votes cast in the fall for Ronald Reagan. It is to secure at least 270 electoral votes. Thus, properly targeting the states forms the key strategic element in winning the presidency. These target states are listed in Attachment A. Note the following: the seven largest electoral college vote states constitute 39% of the total electoral vote. Thus, a Western-Sunbelt strategy will *not* provide us with sufficient votes to win. We must pick up states in the East and heavily in the Midwest to beat Carter. Carter is still politically popular in the South. Thus, to win we must focus attention and target a good portion of the top nine largest states. These include: California, New York, Pennsylvania, Texas, Illinois, Ohio, Michigan, New Jersey and Florida. 52% of the total electoral votes are found in these top nine states.

For the top 15–20 target states we must develop individual campaign plans. For the top ten targeted states a Reagan campaign manager will be given the responsibility of that state to see that the resources are properly allocated to bring home a victory. In each of the top ten states, a campaign plan similar to the one that will be eventually developed for the general campaign must be created to provide goals, objectives, strategy, tactics and action steps so that we can monitor our progress and allocate the resources best designed to win those key states—and, thereby, the fall election.

OUR MOST VALUABLE RESOURCE: RONALD REAGAN

Care must be given to the candidate's schedule, his press relations, and speeches to maximize his positive political influence on the campaign.

Scheduling

Governor Reagan has come through three very tough weeks of campaigning with flying colors. Despite this, I feel it is absolutely necessary that we now carefully review scheduling strategy to maximize the potential impact of our most valuable political asset—the Governor himself. I would suggest that we:

- Provide the Governor with more time to read briefing papers, newspapers, etc.
- Keep the briefings as complete, but as short as possible; limit the number of individuals who attend those sessions to three or a maximum of four.
- Give the Governor senior staff coverage on the road. One of the following should be with him on every tour: Anderson, Meese, Hannaford, Allen, or Wirthlin.
- Watch scheduling when we fly to the East and avoid appearances before 10:30 A.M. on the first or second day out. The Governor definitely is an "afternoon person."

Every trip should be evaluated on the basis of its impact and its effectiveness in achieving the general strategic objectives described above. We should have someone who is politically sensitive with the Governor on every trip. We need someone to evaluate the schedule in terms of providing enough time for the Governor to absorb the briefings and new materials that he is going to be hit hard and heavy with over the next couple of months.

Personnel: Press Secretary/Press Option

The three-pronged attack of a recent *Wall Street Journal* article (March 28, 1980) can do us much damage. It specifically alleges that:

- Ronald Reagan could some day commit a fatal blunder such as George Romney's "brainwash remark" because of "poor staff work caused by the continuing disarray of Mr. Reagan's decimated campaign staff."
- The Governor is unable to adroitly limit the damage of an awkward answer.
- He continues to use old material even when a major new statement is promised.

The above holes can be covered, in part, by our acquisition of more press muscle, with the addition of more personnel.

They will be especially helpful in cutting our losses when an awkward statement is made. But equally as important, it is absolutely essential that we quickly:

- Provide in the schedule sufficient time for extensive and good briefings every day or we will expose the candidate to more unnecessary shots from the press.
- Increase, through such briefings, the candidate's sensitivity to the particular audience, and prepare him in advance for questions that it might generate.

Speeches

What Ronald Reagan says will determine the outcome of this election more directly than any other single factor. As mentioned above, we should have him develop the theme of leadership over the next three months. I strongly urge that we buy the half-hour of prime-time to help raise money, to create a video tape to use in secondary markets, and to show the volunteers at fund raisers.

Ronald Reagan is the only candidate I know of who can sit at a desk, look directly into the camera and hold the attention, interest and grab the emotions of a television audience. We should use this asset now to expand our general electoral base.

We also need, relatively early, to work out our economic theme, not only to save us from the downside risks of someone going back over the last ten years and putting together a collage of statements the Governor has made on the economy to "show" his disjointed approach, but also because it will be the major issue for us to follow throughout the campaign. In developing the economic theme, we must also attempt to fold in the tone of his being more compassionate and concerned. The latter objective, however, requires some special themes and stand-alone speeches. I would suggest that we start working on an urban policy speech which will do more than anything else to allay the concerns that some of the minorities and moderate liberal ticket-splitters have about the Governor's sensitivity to some of our big city problems.

SUMMARY

Ronald Reagan can be inaugurated the next President of the United States in January 1981, but this will not happen by chance. It is hoped that this paper will stimulate the thought and discussion necessary to turn the key strategic considerations into the specific action steps that will achieve that goal.

ATTACHMENT A
Reagan Base, Carter Base, Battleground States

Reagan Base (16) (77)

Nevada – 3
Idaho – 4
Montana – 4
Wyoming – 3
Colorado – 7
New Mexico – 4
Utah – 4
Arizona – 6
North Dakota – 3
South Dakota – 4
Nebraska – 5
Kansas – 7
Indiana – 13
New Hampshire – 4
Vermont – 3
Alaska – 3

Battleground: New England (2) (12)

Maine – 4
Connecticut – 8

Battleground: Mid-Atlantic (4) (88)

New York – 41
Pennsylvania – 27
New Jersey – 17
Delaware – 3

Battleground: Farm Belt (2) (20)

Missouri – 12
Iowa – 8

Carter Base (10) (78)

Georgia – 12
Alabama – 9
Massachusetts – 14
Minnesota – 10
Rhode Island – 4
District of Columbia – 3
Hawaii – 4
West Virginia – 6
Arkansas – 6
Maryland – 10

Battleground: Outer South (7) (95)

Texas – 26
Oklahoma – 8
Florida – 17
North Carolina – 13
Virginia – 12
Kentucky – 9
Tennessee – 10

Battleground: Deep South (3) (25)

South Carolina – 8
Louisiana – 10
Mississippi – 7

Battleground: Pacific (3) (60)

Oregon – 6
Washington – 9
California – 45

Battleground: Great Lakes (4) (83)

Ohio – 25
Illinois – 26
Wisconsin – 11
Michigan – 21

Battleground States Within Size Classes

Large States[3]

California (45)	B +
Texas (26)	B
Ohio (25)	B –
Illinois (26)	B –
Michigan (21)	C
New York (41)	C
Pennsylvania (27)	C

Medium States

New Jersey (17)	B
Florida (17)	B
Virginia (12)	B –
Missouri (12)	B –
North Carolina (13)	C +
Tennessee (10)	C
Louisiana (10)	C
Wisconsin (11)	C –

Small States

South Carolina (8)	B +
Oklahoma (8)	B +
Iowa (8)	B
Maine (4)	B +
Washington (9)	C +
Connecticut (8)	C –
Mississippi (7)	C +
Oregon (6)	C
Kentucky (9)	C –
Delaware (3)	C –

First Cut State Targets
April 11, 1980[**]
(Rank-ordered by assessed winability within size classifications)

Large States (122)

* California – 45
* Texas – 26
* Illinois – 26
* Ohio – 25
  New York – 41
  Michigan – 21
  Pennsylvania – 27

Medium States (58)

Florida – 17
New Jersey – 17
Virginia – 12
Missouri – 12

Small States (28)

Oklahoma – 8
South Carolina – 8
Iowa – 8
Maine – 4

* Must win.
** Based on national data, secondary data, and local newspaper polls.
[3] The grades reflect the probability of a Reagan win.

Recap

Base Support	77
Large States	122*
Medium States	58
Small States	28
	285

Targeting Tools

1. Candidate's time
2. Surrogates' time
3. Media expenditures
4. Voter registration drives
5. Demographic/special voter targeting
   - Ethnics
   - Youth
   - Born Again

* Includes only (*) states.

Memorandum II

TO: **GOVERNOR RONALD REAGAN, BILL CASEY, ED MEESE**

FROM: **RICHARD B. WIRTHLIN**

DATE: **MAY 26, 1980**

SUBJECT: **STRATEGY FOR THE DOLDRUMS**

On May 20th, all three networks declared that you had the necessary 998 delegates to win the nomination. Today, George Bush withdrew from the fray.

Finally, the Republican primary race ends.

We now face, however, a period of approximately six weeks of no political contests —a period of the political doldrums. Even though the political winds will blow with little force until the convention, we can, nevertheless, effectively use this period to steer our campaign considerably closer to its goal of electing you the President of the United States.

During the doldrums, we face the risk of the media picking, willy-nilly, its own stories (some of which will be very negative). Or we can, given the press focus on you now as the nominee, write to some extent, our own media script.

Additionally this period must be used to organize, consolidate and prepare for the general election and the convention which represents the most crucial political event for us until the fall, and also block out the general goals, objectives and action plans of the campaign we intend to use from now through November. Specifically, we should attempt to achieve the following objectives during the doldrums:

- Position you so that you are viewed by the media and the public as true presidential timber.

- Control as best we can the focus, thrust and scope of media coverage.
- Continue to unify the Republican organizational structure from the Republican National Committee down to the state levels and strengthen and expand our organizational influence at all levels.
- Prepare to maximize the favorable political impact of the convention.
- Create the basic internal organizational structure for the coming campaign.

I. Presidential Perceptions

The primary election process afforded both opportunity and risk—the opportunity to gain positive and needed exposure for you that cast you in the role of a winner, and laid to rest the myth that you are too old to seek the presidency.

Contrarily, the primaries also generated the risk associated with an almost unrelenting drumbeat of critical scrutiny by the press and by your primary opponents. The need for exposure also led to the innumerable press availabilities, given the paucity of our paid media and organizational resources, and dictated the heavy schedule of long trips almost entirely structured by the primary calendar rather than by the need to maximize your political strength nationally.

Over the past five months you have run the primary gauntlet almost every Tuesday capped by an appearance on television. This has led to your now being over-exposed —not in the sense that people have seen too much of you, but rather they have seen too much of you in this same role, either accepting victory with a smile or defeat gracefully.

Now that the election process has selected you as the Republican candidate for the presidency, I believe that we can and should exercise much more discretionary power over the kinds of public exposure you are given between now and the convention.

Campaign Gimmicks

Primary campaigns by their very parochial nature strongly tempt the candidate to don funny hats, etc. Given the seriousness of the times and the desire of the electorate to have a strong leader, we must now put that kind of political gimmickry far behind us. In sum, each and every trip scheduled between now and the convention should be closely scrutinized against two specific criteria.

- How does this trip and/or event help us in achieving our campaign objectives in the general campaign? and
- Is this the best possible use of your time given the other tasks you must accomplish between now and the convention?

The fund raisers and the editorial boards are probably essential. Everything else, however, should be subjected closely to the above two guides.

While your effectiveness rating (according to NBC) still ranks considerably above Carter's (Carter 9% very effective, Reagan 22% very effective), that rating slipped measurably during the April period when the press charges were coming hot and heavy.

Bill Casey's 10 guidelines provide some good pointers:

1. To maximize your effectiveness and avoid distraction, confusion and unproductive wrangling, *stay away from specific and arguable statements* which are *not relevant in policy terms.* For example, all that is relevant in making oil policy is that there is a hell of a lot of oil to be found in Alaska. Don't get caught up in conflicting predictions as to whether it can turn out to be more than in Saudi Arabia or not. Don't take the risk that the press will convey or the public grasp qualifiers like "potential."

2. Stay away from *unnecessary predictions*. It is enough to justify getting the government out of the way of our oil explorers if that will reduce our dangerous and costly dependence on Middle East oil. It is not necessary to carry the difficult burden of an argument that this will make us self-sufficient in five years.

3. *Make policy arguments comprehensive*. The combination of coal, oil, nuclear and synthetics will solve our energy problem more surely and more permanently than oil alone. The combination of tax cuts, expenditure cuts, reduction of excessive restrictions and paperwork, getting greater accountability by eliminating layers of government will reduce inflation more quickly and surely than tax cuts alone.

4. *Support proposals by citing more than one beneficial result*. A tax cut will not only increase the incentive to work and invest. It will also increase buying power in families and shift effort from public payrolls which produce restrictions and paperwork to private payrolls which produce goods to satisfy family needs and to pay our way in the world.

5. *Don't get drawn into a numbers game.* Economists can argue but no one knows how fast tax cuts will generate enough new revenue to make up for the revenue lost by lower rates. In campaigning it is sufficient to set a direction. Only when in office will anyone have the up-to-date information necessary to make a decision on how fast to proceed and what policy mix to use. To stay out of an endless numbers game which no one can win and will lose the interest of the public, set a direction (production rather than contraction) and specify a variety of policy instruments which are available to move there (tax cuts, expenditure cuts, fewer restrictions, less paperwork).

6. When specific *data* will sharpen a proposal or an attack, *attribute it to a specific source* or be ready to cite a recognized authority.

7. Stay away from statements or positions that are *too technical* for public understanding, i.e., the gold standard.

8. Stay away from statements that can be *made to look warlike or provocative;* (blockade Cuba), particularly when they are based on a judgment about what someone will do or think in the future (the Russians are not ready to confront us yet).

9. Stay away from statements that can be twisted to an attack on the *patriotism or character of an opponent,* i.e., the Soviets want to see Carter win.

10. *Don't hesitate* to say "I'm not prepared to address that question yet," or "I'm still studying and discussing that issue with my advisors."

Lastly, and perhaps most important of all, you should never get involved, Governor, in responding directly to charges about your use of facts. If Carter or his crew can ever structure the campaign so that you are spending time in answering their charges rather than developing your own case against them, at that juncture they will have won the election.

Your surrogates and your staff should answer these questions.

In short, at this point we do not simply need exposure, but rather we need to generate the right *kind* of exposure. This means that we must pick and choose our forums and maximize the favorable coverage we get during the doldrums.

Past campaigns provide clear evidence that excellent and more controlled media coverage can be generated with a presidential candidate at "home" rather than on the road. In a post-election round-up session at Harvard University [following the 1976 election], Alan Otten [of the *Wall Street Journal*] asked the Carter people the following question, "While you were putting your organization in place, why wasn't Carter himself moving around the country more?" Powell responded, "First I thought he was overexposed, and second, the type of publicity we were getting was the best we had gotten during the whole campaign period, certainly better than we would have gotten out on the road. If we could have stayed in Plains until October, as Ford stayed in the White House until October, we would have won by five or ten points."

I think, Governor, we can take a page straight from their book. If we develop the strategy for generating the type of publicity that we need between now and November we can deal to our strength rather than what the media might want to "toss our way." Press coverage of our campaign to date has been too random, too open, and in short, you have been too accessible. For reasons discussed above, this was necessary. But we are in a much different ballgame now. Rather than having to speak to the Republicans of a given state, in this the early stage of the general campaign we should address on almost every instance the general electorate.

Later the campaign's focus must of course narrow to certain key states. You do not need, Governor, the press conferences or the press availabilities to make news. You are now in the position where virtually anything you say becomes news.

With this in mind, let's review the calendar of events for the next six weeks, to identify how we might maximize the favorable news coverage you generate and minimize the kinds of risks that all candidates run when they extend virtually an open door to the press.

June 3

While the media and our opponents have conceded the election to us we really need to cap that event on June 3rd. I have not seen the planned schedule of events, but anything we might do to give this some good, strong media hype would be well-advised. Might it be possible to have the other candidates in the race join you that evening? Your statement to the press should be carefully crafted and cover at least the following key points:

1. Thank those who have worked so hard in the organization, especially volunteers who spent literally hundreds of thousands of hours in your behalf in the campaign.

2. An expression of gratefulness that you have been given the full support of all the Republicans who sought the office with you.
3. A call at this point to the Democrats and the Independents who may not have participated in the primary process to join your campaign to help open up a new era of hope for the 1980's.

Editorial Boards

On June 16th through the 21st we meet with the editorial boards of the major news magazines and some of the major newspapers. You should be carefully and thoroughly briefed for this meeting. I would suggest that that briefing cover not only the likely issues that the editors might raise or other issues that you might want to cover, such as your position on freedom of the press, but the staff should also prepare for you an outline of the particular biases, both positive and negative, that Time Magazine, the Hearst Newspapers, Newsweek, the Washington Post, etc., have reflected in their coverage of this campaign year. Furthermore, someone should prepare for you a brief biographical sketch of the key men and women with whom you will meet. This sketch should include their backgrounds, interests, and what their political inclinations might be.

Without question, these meetings are critical in establishing rapport and allaying some of the basic fears that the Eastern press has concerning your campaign. How successful we are in accomplishing these two objectives will strongly influence the kind of treatment you will be given by them from now through the election period.

Radio Address

During this period of the political doldrums when interest is at a low ebb, we can gather and control some of the media focus by making perhaps one major new speech in a forum of our choosing. I recommend that we buy ten minutes of national radio time towards the later part of June or the first part of July, and prepare a speech on the topic of leadership which would, in brief, contrast the failures of the Carter Administration with the hope that your own administration could bring to the new decade of the eighties.

This speech might also tie into some of the Fourth of July themes and may be given the first part of July to tie that theme in well. It is important that we work out a good, effective distribution of this speech to the press. We will likely get more coverage through the secondary press channels than even through the delivery of the speech itself on the radio.[4]

The Unity Dinner

On June 13th, you will hold the Unity Dinner here in California which will be televised on the 20th. Planning sessions have already been instigated with Pete Dailey [a Reagan media adviser] concerning the nature, thrust and political purposes of that event. While there are some dangers and risks in that kind of coverage, I'm confident we can overcome those and make this a positive media event for us. Specifically, the Unity Dinner will be well-used if it's structured to have the other major candidates launch some attack themes against the Carter administration. You would close the event with a strong appeal not only to Republicans to close ranks,

[4] Reagan gave a twenty-minute radio speech on leadership on July 2nd and 6th.

368

but also would welcome to your campaign Independents and Democrats whom we will need in the fall to win the election. One of the most appealing themes to this particular group is that your leadership would bring more order and certainty in what people now view as a very uncertain environment. People are not expecting economic miracles, but they do expect that an economic environment can be established in which they can cope more effectively than they do now.

Republican Governors

On the same day that the Unity Dinner event is televised (June 20th), you have a scheduled meeting with the Republican governors. The statement that you give to that group should be crisp, sharp, and directed toward some specific problems in which they are uniquely interested. While we have a good idea of what [Ohio] Governor Jim Rhodes' concerns are in this regard, the staff should interview the other governors to get an idea of the topics that would be most relevant for discussion with them. It is important that we structure that meeting so that when those governors are interviewed by the national and their own, local press, they will have some specific material in hand that they can use in support of your candidacy.

Gerald Ford

I think it would also be wise if we could encourage Gerald Ford to make some visible gesture of support soon. If nothing more, at least one direct visit between you and Ford prior to the convention would be very much in order. We should have clearly in mind what we would want Ford to do in our campaign. Without question it would be most beneficial to have him associated with our effort early. We should move on this quickly as I understand that the Independent Expenditure Committee wants to use Ford to raise funds. While that activity would be helpful to us, it is clearly in our best advantage not to have him go that route but be locked into our effort early and directly.

The Mexico Visit

Your visit to Mexico July 2 through the 7th, should be reserved for well-deserved rest and relaxation. However, would you consider meeting, either at the beginning of that visit or its close, with President Lopez Portillo? It could well be in our political interest to refurbish the North American Accord theme. As you know from the research I presented it did have very favorable impact on several key Independent and Democrat subgroups. If we should decide to begin discussing this issue once more, your visit to Mexico would provide a media forum from which we could launch more discussions about closer relationships with Canada and Mexico. This decision, however, should be made relatively soon so that if you do decide to visit Portillo, we can also touch the proper bases with the new Trudeau administration in Canada.

There are also, Governor, a number of activities we consciously should play to the press during this entire period of the doldrums that will provide us with positive stories.

The Selection of the Vice-President

For example, the press is intrigued with the process of our selecting a Vice-Presidential nominee. It would be well worthwhile to give the media some insight into the process. Specifically, as we begin discussing Vice-Presidential contenders with party leaders, opinion makers, and then with some of those who may be considered potential Vice-Presidential candidates themselves we should not attempt to hide that process. While I don't believe we should overly impose on individuals by having them visit you in Pacific Palisades in tandem, nevertheless, it would not hurt at all having you caucus with some of the major figures in the Republican party— Senators, Governors, past officeholders who might also be considered Vice-Presidential nominees, either in your home or when you visit the East. This process should be good for one or two stories a week from, say, the tenth of June through convention time. However, the final choice is the one mystery that we want to hold secure until the Convention.

A secondary benefit of having you meet with individuals who could be considered Vice-Presidential contenders and/or members of your cabinet is that the process provides those visitors with a natural forum to make statements after the meeting that reference some of the elements of your programs and policies that we want the press to begin to cover.

A related but somewhat distinct ongoing activity that will provide us with the same kind of controlled and positive media exposure can be generated by additional meetings with your policy groups.

In addition to the discussions about foreign policy and the economy, we also need to be viewed publicly as showing an interest in and a knowledge about urban policy, and energy and the environment. Experts in these fields should also be heard.

Getting our message out through the "company we keep" can be most advantageous to us in this early stage of the campaign. Such meetings I believe will also in part offset a concern that we have selected so many advisors so early; some of them may view themselves as sitting on their hands and might go to the press in a disgruntled mood. We do need to keep these individuals busy and involved and made to feel a part of what we're doing. Providing such meetings perhaps with yourself, but also with other senior members of the campaign staff and then issuing statements to the press afterwards provides an excellent vehicle that will reinforce the points you want to make on policy and, additionally, establish the fact that you are surrounding yourself with men of stature, competence and ability.

The Politics of Politics

A third kind of ongoing material we can give to the press having positive impact relates to the press' almost insatiable desire to understand the "politics of politics." For example, I think we made much too little of our bringing Pete Dailey on board. Perhaps in the next week or two we might issue a major statement on Pete's activity and the kind of men he is assembling to handle our media activity. As others are added to the team we should provide the press with ample material on their backgrounds and expertise. This will bring respect and understanding of the seriousness of our intent to beat President Carter in the fall.

Miscellaneous Activities

I believe we can generate with comparative ease at least three or four stories a week that we can control. Some of the prime targets for such stories might be to have those who participated in your administration speak of its strengths and accomplishments. We should, for example, seek out Democratic legislators to review the things you accomplished as Governor. A list of those who were not directly part of your administration or who were not too partisan but who can speak with a great deal of credibility about your accomplishments should be developed and employed. Now is the time to reinforce the good things that were accomplished by you as Governor. This will begin to establish a reservoir of favorable response which will be able to withstand some of the criticism and distortion that is bound to come our way before the election closes in November.

Additionally, we can get triple impact from any major policy positions you might take from now through the November election. I would strongly suggest that if we decide to resurrect the North American Accord idea, that you make a lengthy statement on your position. Then we can orchestrate support of the idea through surrogates, perhaps two or three days thereafter. The cycle would then be closed by holding a press conference a few days later in which you spend 15 minutes of a 20-minute press conference to deal specifically with the North American Accord. The press, of course, would be apprised beforehand of the structure of the press conference. By following this three-step procedure we can keep the issue alive, and get double or triple the coverage that we would get by simply issuing policy statements without proper back-up.

In closing this section which is related to some of the things we might do to focus and control the thrust and scope of the media coverage, a word of caution is in order. I do not believe we should meet with each and every special interest group that wants an audience. Such meetings are almost always more detrimental than helpful from a media perspective to a presidential campaign. The press, when hearing of such meetings, always assumes the worst, that some kind of deal has been cut. If for overriding reasons those meetings are held, then you should be thoroughly apprised beforehand of the specific purpose of the meeting and whether any requests are going to be made so that we can screen out any group bringing undue pressure upon you during this very critical stage of the campaign.

III. UNIFICATION OF THE REPUBLICAN PARTY TOP-TO-BOTTOM
The Republican National Committee

We should keep two major objectives in mind as we deal with this committee over the next six weeks. We must:

- First, control the Republican National Committee's personnel, budget and work plans;
- Second, do so without fragmenting the party.

The extent to which we are able to accomplish the latter objective hinges on Bill Brock's full cooperation. If he is not willing to grant us sufficient control to use the Republican National Committee to indirectly assist the Presidential campaign effort, this must be determined sufficiently early and several weeks prior to the Convention so that appropriate changes can be made in an orderly fashion to minimize any disruptiveness. If that decision must be made, I would strongly urge that we plan for Brock to have some other role in our own campaign.

Republican Governors, Senators, and Congressmen

We need to expand and extend our base of support among this key group. You should make calls, Governor, to key members of this group to enlist, reinforce and strengthen those who can be effective spokespersons for the campaign. Given Carter's propensity to attack us, we are going to need every defender we can enlist. A number of them are, I am sure, going to be found among the ranks of incumbent Republican officeholders.

Furthermore, we should begin to establish liaison with all strong Republicans running against Democratic incumbents. It would be wise to meet with them perhaps at the end of July to coordinate our campaigns with their campaign staff where that is feasible and advantageous to us.

State Parties

We are in the process, Governor, of evaluating each state party that may become a target state for us in order to correlate our activities and determine early where we need to bolster the organization with our own people. Not only is it important that we run our voter identification programs, victory squads, and get-out-the-vote efforts through the state party where feasible, but we need to also establish some local press activity in the key states to ensure that we get the biggest bang possible for our non-paid media effort in the key-swing states.

IV. POST-CONVENTION SPEECH

We should begin now to plan for the first major speech you give after the Convention. It is my belief that this speech should be our long-awaited economic policy speech. Our campaign has suffered to some extent by the press' expectation that you would deliver a major economic speech prior to the end of the primary season. There is no question whatsoever that concerns about inflation, unemployment, and the economy generally will be major concerns of the electorate right through November.

We need now to bring direction, focus and coherence to your position on the economy. You have made hundreds of statements over the last 15 years about the economy. Those statements must be brought into focus under a strong, credible economic policy statement. Not only will this provide us with the platform that we can use effectively to launch additional economic statements at later junctures in the campaign, but also it will protect us from the charge that some of your Republican opponents made which will undoubtedly be echoed by the Carter crowd that you propose "Voodoo economics." Such a speech on the economy is the single most critical thing you should do in this immediate post-Convention period.

V. REPUBLICAN CONVENTION

We should continue to plan in order to maximize the political impact of the Republican Convention. While a good deal of planning has been underway for over a year on the Convention, it still lacks to some extent the thrust that is so essential for us to develop if we are to take full advantage of the Convention mechanism. We have several good people actively working on this problem presently.

The Convention should have two major objectives:

- To reinforce the perception held by the American electorate that the Republicans are united this year (the most cardinal point in this regard is to minimize the rancor and disputes that might arise out of the discussions of the platform), and
- build the Convention around those visual and verbal impressions that will maximize your support among *all* voters.

I would urge that we reserve a day toward the end of June on which the various elements of the Convention can be presented to you to confirm how closely the Convention matches these salient objectives.

VI. BUILD THE BASIC ELEMENTS OF THE REAGAN FOR PRESIDENT GENERAL ELECTION ORGANIZATION

While it will take until the first of September before the organizational structure will be in place, it is important that prior to the Convention we have all the key persons in place.

In every presidential campaign that is initiated after the nominee is chosen, there is always a shake-down and realignment of personnel. It is important that such realignment occur early so that we can go with the first team from the end of August right through the November campaign. We need time now to construct that team and to outline clearly the areas of authority and responsibility in order to minimize duplication and to ensure that all of the key areas are covered carefully and systematically.

Lastly, we need to develop a campaign plan. By the twelfth of June we will have prepared for your perusal, Governor, a general campaign plan which will outline the general strategic considerations that we believe will determine who wins and who loses in November, what the present attitudinal environment of the electorate might be, and a careful and candid assessment of your political strengths and weaknesses as they are compared against Carter's.

From this document we will prepare a shorter version of twenty-five or thirty pages which will be given to those responsible for:

The paid media
The press
The volunteers
The relationship with Republican National Committee
The state organizations

Those having the prime responsibility for these areas then will be asked to develop in conjunction with us, the specific tactics and action plans they intend to employ which are consistent with the general campaign plan.

These individual and modular plans will act not only to give a direction to the campaign but will also serve as a basis upon which to judge the progress and effectiveness of the campaign at various critical stages. On this basis we can build the budget, schedule your time, and focus the media effort against the most basic and critical criteria—which of these activities will maximize the vote for Ronald Reagan in the fall.

Memorandum III

TO: GOVERNOR REAGAN, AMBASSADOR BUSH, SENATOR LAXALT, AMBASSADOR ARMSTRONG, WILLIAM CASEY AND DEPUTY CAMPAIGN DIRECTORS, REAGAN BUSH COMMITTEE

FROM: RICHARD B. WIRTHLIN

DATE: AUGUST 9, 1980

RE: FOCUSED IMPACT THEME: FOREIGN AFFAIRS

Given the difficulty we experienced last week in effectively coordinating and implementing the focused impact theme of urban affairs to satisfy some very specific campaign objectives, I thought it might be helpful to all of us if I outlined and distributed the campaign objectives, strategies and tactics associated with the next focused impact theme of foreign affairs, which we will mount in mid-August.

FOREIGN AFFAIRS THEME

Campaign Objectives

1. Block out early Ronald Reagan's foreign affairs position as one that is reasoned, strong, and safe.
2. Recognize and attempt to resolve the perceptual dilemma that large numbers of voters now wrestle with: on the one hand, Reagan would be a strong and decisive leader in foreign affairs (which "we" applaud), but on the other hand, he would be too quick to push the nuclear button (which "we" fear and abhor).

374

Strategies

1. While voter concern about foreign affairs now occupies the major worry of only one in ten Americans, for us it represents a key strategic issue for three reasons:

    (a) An international crisis between now and the election could skyrocket foreign affairs to the top of the saliency list.
    (b) Carter fully intends to direct an attack against us in this area because he believes it is one of our major political weaknesses.
    (c) By projecting Reagan's *peace* posture early, we can, if it is handled properly, reinforce a major perceptual strength (decisive leader) and alleviate a major weakness (dangerous).

    Clearly, the nature of these three reasons dictates early action (August 17th through the 25th).

    The major theme that must be reinforced these eight days through Reagan, Bush, and the spokespersons' speeches and color events reflects in the announcement speech:

    > We are not a warlike people. Quite the opposite. We always seek to live in peace. We resort to force infrequently and with great reluctance— and only after we have determined that it is absolutely necessary.

    > Of all the objectives we seek, first and foremost is the establishment of lasting world peace. We must always stand ready to negotiate in good faith, ready to pursue any reasonable avenue that holds forth the promise of lessening tensions and furthering the prospects of peace.

    In sum, the campaign must establish Reagan as a leader capable of returning the U.S. to a position of world leadership—*not* in the role of the world's policeman —but through our own strength and through closer cooperation with our allies.

2. Specifically, Reagan's position must be:

    (a) *Strong:*   Americans heavily back improving our defense position, because they do believe it would increase the chances of establishing peace. They yearn not necessarily to be "liked in the world community, but to be respected *again* . . ."
    (b) *Reasoned:*   Nevertheless, the rhetoric must *not* be strident or threatening. Recognizing the complexities of the world as it is and developing rational options to deal with those complexities must be an inherent part of our foreign affairs position.

3. Reagan can maintain his position of "strong leader" but pull the sting out of the "dangerous" charge by:

    (a) Always speaking in terms of promoting international stability with an aim toward world peace. Rather than a "defense posture," we should use the term "peace posture."

(b) Avoiding any reference to "the arms race" but stressing the need to re-establish "the margin of safety."

(c) Emphasizing the need for and the advantage of strengthening our ties with proven allies.

Tactics

1. Appoint a project director to coordinate all aspects of this project as outlined in the tactics that follow.

2. Launch the Foreign Affairs Focused Impact project with the Reagan-Bush press briefing prior to Bush's Far Eastern trip August 16th. Develop some specific talking points that the principals should stress in discussing Japan, Taiwan and the People's Republic of China.

3. During this period deliver the three themes—Peace, Strength, and Friends (Allies).

   (a) *Peace:* August 18th, VFW Chicago.[5]
   Remember, our audience is *not* veterans; it is the 45 million Americans who will hear pieces of the speech, and more precisely our *key* audience are those 19 million American voters who now say that Ronald Reagan (not Carter or Anderson) is best described by the phrase, "Is a dangerous person to have in the White House" and the 29 million voters who pick Reagan from the triad as "most likely to start an unnecessary war."

   This speech should be cautiously positive about the prospects for peace and be forward looking in tone.

   It should not dwell too long on the distant past, nor get too embroiled in the semantics of detente.

   The theme can include a list of actions by the Carter Administration which have created international instability and increased the risk of war. But, this should be done in a reasoned and non-strident way.

   The Governor's position on peace-time draft registration should *definitely* be worked into this speech. The VFW may not agree with him on this issue and he may openly recognize that in his initial comments about this topic, but those voters under 35 *will*—and this is the best issue we now have to break that age cohort's belief that Reagan is a military hardliner. Additionally, veterans and most Americans *do* agree with Reagan's rationale (increase pay for members of the volunteer army and strengthen the reserves) for opposing peace-time draft registration.

   This need not be a long speech—12 minutes maximum, but it has to deliver the message: Ronald Reagan if elected President will improve the chances of our having an enduring peace in the 80's.

[5] This was the speech in which Reagan inserted the line calling the Vietnam War a "noble cause" (see p. 262).

(b) *Strength:* August 20th, American Legion

This theme "preaches to the choir" to this immediate audience. We must keep in mind that the general audience (the U.S. electorate), while strongly opting for enhanced defense capability, wants that objective achieved without militancy or excessive bluster.

The major thrust should be to round out what we mean by "the margin of safety."

We should avoid talking about specific military hardware, but we can take on the Carter Administration for gutting Ford's five-year defense plan—and highlight the *dangers* those cuts have now imposed.

(c) *Friends:* We need to speak to the issue of *Allies*. Two opportunities—an 8-minute insert into the Religious Roundtable meeting or a longish press release about the need for strong and loyal allies to be issued the same day (August 22nd).

These three speeches need to be reviewed by all of us before they are put into cement.

4. The color events during this period (August 17th–August 25th) must be consistent with our major theme and strongly reinforce it visually. Most Americans (60%) *see* the news on TV, they don't hear it or read about it.

Some suggestions: a visit to a closed defense plant, or shipyard, etc. Care must be taken to assure that *the* site being dramatized represents what we want it to —an *un*necessary cutback. Boston's roots in the Revolutionary War has some interesting possibilities—Paul Revere, Bunker Hill, the Minute Men, etc. We need to get a full list of all possibilities soon and make some choices so that these events can be well advanced.

5. We should begin lining up our surrogates and those available through the RNC's Speakers Bureau now. Is Ford available on the 16th? If so, he could take Carter apart for his "dangerous" cutbacks on defense spending, etc. Some other possibilities to speak out on the issue in our behalf after the 21st are: Rumsfeld, Haig and other selected members of our Advisory Council. The surrogates should be thoroughly briefed on the Governor's position and we should suggest to them some attack lines.

6. Prepare for each speech some specific talking points for the press.

7. Tape and edit the "Peace" speech for re-broadcast on national radio August 23rd or 24th.

8. Prepare for release (if they are ready) some of our policy papers.

9. Work out the specific objectives we want to achieve in the press briefing session between the Governor and Bush and brief both accordingly.

10. Circulate the speeches and research papers through the communication channels used by those who would be most likely to be interested and favorably disposed toward those views.

Memorandum IV

TO: **GOVERNOR REAGAN, AMBASSADOR BUSH, SENATOR LAXALT, AMBASSADOR ARMSTRONG, WILLIAM CASEY AND DEPUTY CAMPAIGN DIRECTORS, REAGAN-BUSH COMMITTEE**

FROM: **RICHARD B. WIRTHLIN**

DATE: **AUGUST 13, 1980**

RE: **FOCUSED IMPACT THEME: THE POCKETBOOK**

Not many political truisms endure. One, however, has held: a candidate is elected President because he correctly identifies the central issue of his time and generates the public expectation that he is capable of effectively dealing with that issue.

Kennedy and Johnson recognized that civil liberties and social concerns dominated the national issue agenda in the 60's and responded with the New Frontier and the Great Society programs. As the racial and social revolution yielded to Vietnam in the late 1960's, Richard Nixon's foreign affairs positions took him to the White House. The war issue of the early 70's was replaced by the political reform issue in the post-Watergate era. Jimmy Carter ascended to the presidency by running on personal integrity and against Washington bureaucrats.

The pocketbook issues—inflation, unemployment, the energy crisis, recession and taxes—dominate the issue agenda in this 1980 presidential election. How we respond to these issues will, in no small degree, determine whether or not Ronald Reagan assumes the presidency in January 1981.

The purpose of this memo is to block out the campaign objectives, strategies, and tactics associated with the focused impact program (August 27 through September 10) that directly bear on this strategically critical campaign issue.

378

THE POCKETBOOK THEME

Campaign Objectives

1. Between the end of August and early September present to the American voters a comprehensive economic plan which will serve as the major linch-pin of the entire Reagan/Bush campaign effort. This plan must go beyond the isolated and independent treatments of the various pocketbook issues and provide a consistent and complete proposal for effectively dealing with the nation's economic ills.
2. The Reagan economic plan must satisfy three major criteria: it must be comprehensive, credible and proprietary.

   - *Comprehensive*—the program must go beyond the isolated treatment of the pocketbook issues—inflation, unemployment, balanced budgets and taxes—to present a complete proposal for curing the economic ills. Voters are fully aware of the dual economic demons of inflation and unemployment and desire a proposal which copes with both.
   - *Credible*—the plan must withstand the critical scrutiny of the professional economists. It must be internally consistent. While many of them may not agree with the assumptions we make in drawing up the plan, they must agree that, given our assumptions, the conclusions drawn will hold.

Although voters may not understand economic theory or the relationship of economic factors, they do understand that economic issues are complex and not subject to facile resolution. A Reagan proposal, while remaining straightforward, must convince the voters that it deals with the full spectrum of economic complexities.

We cannot back away from the economic objectives clearly supported by the Governor over the last 18 months—a tax cut, a balanced budget and increased defense spending—but we must show two things clearly. First, that it is possible to achieve our triple objective; and second, that our economic program *will* reduce inflationary pressures and increase jobs.

   - *Proprietary*—the Reagan economic plan must be identified as his and must not reference, in whole or in part, others.

Strategies

1. The lack of a comprehensive Reagan economic plan has led to the promulgation of independent economic policies which now must be synthesized into a general economic framework. In order to achieve credibility, both with the voters and the press, Reagan must announce an all-encompassing economic plan which reconciles the following seemingly contradictory Reagan objectives:

   - The need for a massive income tax [rates cut] for businesses and individuals,
   - increases in the defense effort to catch up with the Russians, and
   - securing a balanced federal budget.

2. Deal to Reagan's strengths and Carter's weaknesses by allocating a major part of our early campaign resources to the economic issue agenda.

President Carter's handling of inflation, the energy crisis and taxes has been rated low throughout his term in office and has recently sunk to all-time lows. Further, voters see the nation as teetering on the brink of economic ruin and perceive Carter as both contributing to the problems and being incapable of finding solutions.

Contrarily, voters do believe that inflation can be managed by a strong President. They hold that a competent President can keep prices from continually rising (74%) and that the federal budget can be balanced over the next 5 years (77%).

Over half of the electorate now identifies inflation as *the most important problem* the United States faces today.

Most critically of all, fully 56% of the voters say that Reagan, not Carter (14%), "offers the best hope to reduce inflation." Thus the pocketbook issue cluster and, specifically, the inflation module strongly reinforce our strengths and Carter's weaknesses. We must, therefore, do all we can to keep the electorate's attention focused on this issue as the campaign builds and, thereby, keep Carter on this "hook" right through to November.

3. It is important that we utilize the Governor, the Ambassador [Bush], and our major surrogates to deal with the pocketbook issue in a coordinated and consistent fashion, particularly during the period of August 27 through September 10. Some of the topics the major surrogates can develop, in addition to reinforcing the primary elements of Reagan's economic program, are jobs, reindustrialization, and making the federal government system more responsive and responsible.

4. In developing the themes and speech elements on the economy, we should keep in mind that there are certain specific demographic targets that will respond even more strongly than the population at large.

The aged are most concerned about inflation, while the young and minorities worry about jobs. Targeting our comments to these two groups will help reinforce key elements in the electorate that we need to strengthen.

Furthermore, a number of other related economic issues can be tied to specific geographic regions of the country. For example, the automobile, coal, construction and steel industries have been more severely wounded by the recession in certain areas than in others. These targets of opportunity should be recognized and hit.

Tactics

1. Appoint a project director with the requisite authority and responsibility needed to coordinate and implement all aspects of this focused impact project as outlined in the tactics that follow.

2. We should launch the pocketbook focused impact project with the Governor's speech to the Ohio Teamsters' Conference on Wednesday August 27. The primary thrust of that particular speech should be productivity, jobs, and Reagan's program for revitalizing U.S. industries.

3. The Labor Day speech, which is now staged for Ellis Island in New York[6] on September 1, must be very forward-looking in thrust and economy-related in theme. Because the backdrop provides visual ties to roots that touch the heritage of many Americans, that reference should be used primarily as a vehicle to get into the major theme: the economic promise that America held for those who came to its shores over the last 200 years and how that promise can be more effectively realized today and throughout the 80's if we put a bloated federal government on a diet and make it more responsive and responsible.

This speech and the Ohio Teamsters' speech need not be long—no longer than 15 minutes.

4. The third speech to be given, possibly at the B'nai B'rith on Wednesday, September 3 might be used as the platform for the Governor's centerpiece economy speech. This speech would outline the major elements of his economic program, show how those elements interrelate and are consistent, and demonstrate that the program will deal effectively with the major economic ills now besetting our country.[7]
Unlike the foregoing two speeches, this speech should run 30 minutes. While some reference must be given in the speech to the problems of Israel, nevertheless, it might well be possible to utilize this as the major platform to launch discussion of the Governor's economic proposals. Clearly if the press are primed and forewarned that it is at the B'nai B'rith that the Governor will present his major speech, it would be given proper coverage. However, should it be decided not to use this forum to focus on Reagan's Economic Plan, a strong pocketbook theme must still run through whatever other remarks the Governor gives at this forum.

Should we decide not to use the B'nai B'rith to present the Governor's Economic Plan, another suitable forum needs to be identified very quickly so that we can coordinate the time, the place, and the message of the Governor's speech with the things that are going to be done by Ambassador George Bush during this same period.

5. At present, there are proposed visits during the period September 7–10 in Philadelphia, Indiana, Iowa, Illinois, Wisconsin, Michigan, and Ohio. While the primary purpose of these visits is to raise funds, I would think it wise that, should those dates hold, we block out on each day a color event and a major statement to highlight some of the specific applications of the Governor's economic program to an identified economic problem. For instance, we might use Ohio to focus on the economic problems of energy. The automobile industry, of course, has high saliency in Michigan, light industry in Wisconsin, and steel in Illinois. The senior citizen group in Philadelphia provides an ideal audience for us to reinforce our position on Social Security and take a crack at Carter on his inability to control inflation.[8]

6. George Bush could be well scheduled during this period to cover our southern bases with the same economic message the Governor delivers in the North.

[6] Reagan gave this speech at Liberty State Park in Jersey City, New Jersey, with the Statue of Liberty as a backdrop (see p. 295).
[7] This speech was not actually given until September 9th, in Chicago (see p. 274).
[8] See p. 263.

Florida and Texas would be two states in particular that should be covered. Cutting back government waste can be strongly emphasized in this region of the country.

7. The forums for all of the speeches described above and those that will be scheduled for the surrogates should be carefully selected to give us strong visual impact that reinforces the major points being covered as dramatically as possible.

8. The economic focused impact program should rely more heavily perhaps than any other on the proper use and orchestration of surrogates. It is critical that we use Ann Armstrong, Paul Laxalt and Jerry Ford, among others, to carry the general theme forward. Once again, Ford might be used to take Carter on frontally (using perhaps the same vehicle he did at the convention—the misery index) with good effect.

   In addition, however, this is the time when our economists should be out on the point in discussing the sophistication of the Reagan program and reinforcing its credibility and comprehensiveness. Greenspan, Shultz, Lynn, Walker, Weinberger, etc., should now be folded into the program to put them before the right audiences with the right messages during this critical period.

9. Two radio programs on the economy should be mounted nationally. One of these could follow the Labor Day speech during the week of September 1–5; the other must address how Governor Reagan plans to cope with the three critical needs of reducing taxes, increasing defense spending, and balancing the budget.

10. Requisite policy papers should be prepared to augment and enrich the various points the Governor makes in his economic speeches. These can be used by the surrogates and hopefully will be picked up by the press to give depth and strength to the proposals that he will discuss during this critical week.

11. Less technical talking points should be prepared for all the surrogates before Labor Day for use in post–Labor Day speeches.

Memorandum V

TO: RONALD REAGAN, NATIONAL CAMPAIGN
DIRECTOR, CO-CHAIRPERSONS AND DEPUTY
CAMPAIGN DIRECTORS

FROM: RICHARD B. WIRTHLIN

DATE: OCTOBER 9, 1980

RE: STATUS OF THE CAMPAIGN AND SOME
STRATEGIC CONSIDERATIONS

During September the national polls read the 1980 presidential race between Reagan and Carter as almost a "dead heat" with only a few points separating the two major party nominees. Over the last ten days that gap has widened in our favor. Nevertheless, the contest remains tight.

Although Carter is a tough campaigner, an astute politician with a politically adept staff, he is an extremely weak incumbent President seeking re-election. His vitriolic personal attack on us clearly backfired. But, we should still expect, Governor, that he will continue to press his campaign of *fear* and divisiveness. He cannot run on his record. He is *not* an attractive incumbent; his record excites no one, least of all the Blacks who believe they elected him and the Southern White Protestants who did, in fact, elect the Georgian. To win therefore, Carter must re-constitute his electoral coalition because the 1976 Southern, big city coalition has dissipated during the term.

In effect, Carter has been unable to convert his 1976 electoral coalition that brought him into the White House into a governing coalition to run the country during his first term, secure his re-election for a second. The Border South, especially Virginia, Florida and Texas, are clearly in doubt for Carter, and we breathe down his neck in the Southern states of: Missouri, Louisiana, Mississippi, Tennessee, and Kentucky. There is nothing certain about Pennsylvania and Ohio in the Great Lakes region either.

Recent surveys even suggest that Anderson's candidacy, while unable to get untracked nationally, will seriously affect Carter's chances in Massachusetts (Reagan: 27%; Carter: 26%; Anderson: 24%) and perhaps New York.

Where will the election be won or lost in the last week?

Closely associated with the notion that Carter is a very "beatable" incumbent is the idea that our electoral base is larger than Carter's. Hence, the marginal gain necessary for an electoral victory is smaller.

The stinger is, however, that the states that remain competitive and at stake are the large electoral states where the winner can make up ground quickly regardless of the original base.

Specifically, our win coalition hinges on the states of:

- Texas
- Florida
- Ohio
- Illinois

plus "clinchers" in several possible combination wins in:

- other Great Lakes and Northeastern states
- Southern and/or small states.

(See "Win Scenarios" in Table Section.)

The unsettling prospect for the Democratic incumbent is that his poor job performance has so damaged his re-election possibilities that the people are not inclined to vote for him. He is described as "a failed President . . . a total disappointment." Of all incumbent presidents in recent history, *Carter is the most beatable*.

We, notwithstanding, have *not* been able to capitalize fully on Carter's unattractiveness. The Governor's consistent marginal lead is a mere shadow of what it was following the Republican Convention. The Convention is unquestionably a political anomaly spurred by a media "hype" unique to presidential year political coverage. But the current 5 to 8 point lead may well prove to be an insufficient margin even against this "small, mean-minded, do-anything-to-win" incumbent.

To guard against the volatility of the vote and the uncertainty voters may have about us, the primary task during the last two weeks of the campaign must be to solidify the vote.

The strategy from the Convention until mid-September was to appeal to the Republican/conservative political base.[9] From mid-September until mid-October the prin-

[9] This was during the so-called "gaffe" period, when several of the things Reagan did were done in order to secure that base (see p. 261).

cipal political objective was to reach out to the undecideds and middle America. We broadened our appeal to the moderates, independents, and soft Anderson voters. Now during the last thirty-odd days of the campaign a serious effort must be made to secure the coalition, deal to strengths and avoid giving any voter a reason not to vote for Reagan. The danger is that our present margin will not stand up as the campaign moves toward election day. Hence, we must build the current margin to a national 8 to 10 point lead during the remaining four weeks. The margin is necessary to offset the return of some traditional Democratic voters to their political allegiances regardless of their dissatisfaction with Carter, and offset the impact of a likely October Surprise.

The Anderson factor remains as uncertain and elusive as in June when the campaign plan was written. The current political judgment is that Anderson has not been able to get a national campaign going and his problems with financing remain acute, perhaps paralyzing. What persists, however, is that Anderson's impact varies state-by-state, and that as the campaign closes on election day, the impact appears critical in only a few states. Nationally it appears unlikely that Anderson will be able to rise above the 8–10% range with the highest concentration of his vote coming in New York, Massachusetts—the Northeast generally—some Great Lakes support and Northern California. Otherwise, the Anderson appeal is spotty, largely insignificant in the Mountain states and the South.

Where should we expect the national ballot to be October 20th?

The slippage in our vote has halted. We have regained momentum now after several weeks of positive campaigning.

Carter is going into a rough period. From all indications the press has picked up on the "meanness" theme and it is likely this will hurt. But Carter's most serious problems stem from the "smallness" of the electoral base of solid and lean states upon which to build his base.

By October 20th, the national ballot, assuming current trends continue, should be averaged (across the different national studies) at approximately:

Candidate	Percent	Oct. 20
Reagan	42–44	43
Carter	34–36	35
Anderson	8–12	8

I review below the "Seven Conditions of Victory" we must meet to unseat Jimmy Carter.[10]

SEVEN CONDITIONS OF VICTORY

We Can Beat Jimmy Carter 21 Days from Now If We:
    (1) Without alienating our base, expand it to include more:

[10] Wirthlin originally drafted this campaign plan in June.

- Independents,
- Anderson voters, and
- disaffected Democrats

to offset Carter's larger Democratic base and the incumbency advantage.

We must shed every overt Republican symbol.

Nevertheless the last week we must allocate our resources to deal to our coalitional, *conservative* strength, and bring the focus of the campaign back to the economic issues.

We should *not* break any major new issue ground except in the foreign policy and highly targeted "social" issue areas. The thrust of our speeches to accomplish this condition must be directed toward:

- inflation,
- jobs,
- economic growth, and
- a more responsible and more efficient federal government

(2) Allocate all campaign resources carefully against the target list of battleground states.

We must remember that the successful outcome of many months of effort hinges on just the few percentage points we garner marginally in less than ten states.

Sufficient media funds should be available to purchase heavy spot market exposure in a few key states during the final two weeks.

The time commitments of Ronald Reagan and George Bush must be assessed and assigned against state target priorities.

Event schedules should be kept free of low-mileage meetings or events and provide sufficient personal time to *recharge* during the closing days of the campaign.

(3) Focus campaign resources to reinforce the Governor's image strengths that embody the presidential values a majority of Americans think are important:

- leadership,
- competence,
- strength, and
- decisiveness

At the same time, we must minimize the perception that he is dangerous and uncaring.

A major foreign policy speech (not a defense speech) blocking out "Reagan's Peace Plan" addressed to a national audience should do more for us in this regard than any other single campaign event. The statement on women issued today also helps in this regard.

Ultimately the voters will choose the man they believe best suited to *lead* this country in the decade of the 80's. Hence, in addition to the above general "leader perceptions" we need to reinforce, we must also give the voter the opportunity to get a glimpse of the quality, skill, and experience of the men and women that a Reagan Administration would attract to implement his ideas and programs.

(4) Reinforce through our media and spokespersons (not necessarily through the Governor) Carter's major weaknesses—that he is:

- an ineffective and error-prone leader,
- incapable of implementing policies,
- mean-spirited and unpresidential,
- too willing to use his presidential power politically, and
- vacillating in foreign policy and creating a climate of crises.

A sharp contrast must be drawn between Carter's political promises and his performance.

Given Carter's proclivity to mount personal and vindictive attacks, we have the opportunity to play it very cool and come out of those exchanges more "presidential" than "President" Carter.

In sum, the voters do not want Carter, but are not yet quite sure of us. His outbursts help. They may be muted, but they will continue.

(5) Neutralize Carter's "October Surprise," and avoid fatal, self-inflicted blunders.

(6) Position the campaign to pick up as much of the Anderson vote as possible as Anderson fades in the stretch.

It appears Anderson has not achieved the national momentum necessary to sustain a viable candidacy. Anderson's national base may be no larger than 6–8% and significant in only New York, Massachusetts, and the Northeast generally.

Furthermore, on November 4th, many loyal Anderson voters will be confronted with the reality of "throwing away" their votes if they stay with Anderson. In all probability many of these voters will opt not to vote for Anderson, and will cast a vote for either Reagan or Carter because they are vehemently against one of the major candidates.

Now, Carter carries more negative baggage than Reagan. Every effort should be made to appeal to these voters, giving them every reason possible to vote for Reagan. The target Anderson states—Illinois, Connecticut, Pennsylvania, Ohio, Michigan and New England generally.

(7) Maintain control of the thrust of our campaign by refusing to let it become event-driven especially in the last two weeks of the campaign. Be prepared to end the campaign either on a hard note or a high note depending on the momentum and level of support we achieve next week.

The Caddell Memorandums

Memorandum I

RE: **GENERAL ELECTION STRATEGY**

DATE: **JUNE 25, 1980**

FROM: **PATRICK H. CADDELL**

This is a first cut at a general election strategy. My approach here is to set forth some approaches as we intensify, reshape, and refine our general election plans. By definition, it is sketchy at some junctures. For a start, we have almost no survey data at our disposal except for recent primary data from selected states. We have no general election data on Carter, Reagan, Anderson, Issues, General Attitudes, States, etc. except that gleaned from public polls. There is great urgency to correct this deficiency. Therefore, much of this memorandum is premised on hunch, experience, and theory.

This memo is an attempt to give some early attention to the need for strategy/themes which we neglected to address until late in the 1976 campaign—much to our woe. Too often we substitute priority setting and high tactics for real conceptual strategy. It is a problem that I suspect concerns us all.

I. WHERE WE BEGIN

President Carter faces an extremely difficult reelection. Struggling against a persistent defeated primary challenger, we face a united Republican party with a challenger posed to our right attempting to crowd our center. To our left, we face an Independent candidacy raiding our unhappy left leaning base and threatening the key electoral vote rich industrial belt. For a candidate who has often appeared a "remainderman"—taking the votes left over—a two front assault is of great concern.

The issue structures could not be worse. After a long period of runaway inflation

388

which badly battered the President's standing we face what could be a worse *political* problem—unemployment. While there is a view that better unemployment/ recession be an issue in a general election against a Reagan than in a primary vs. a Kennedy, I think there is another factor deserving attention. While inflation is very destabilizing to the political environment, its potency as a *direct* voting issue has been exaggerated, in part because the public tends to distribute blame widely and remains skeptical that any specific official or individual could truly solve inflation. *On the other hand, unemployment/recession, in the past, has been blamed more specifically on Presidents and there is a history of presidential action solving the problem.* It has always had great potency as a voting issue—although almost exclusively directed against Republicans.

Energy costs continue to rise. There are rumblings in the cities, which if they explode, could tear at the always fragile urban Democratic coalition between blacks and blue collar whites. To the public, American foreign policy appears in disarray —the hostages are still captive, the Russians seem on the move and while there is a deep apprehension over armed conflict, a sense of political and military decline pervades the public mood.

The country's general mood remains much as it has since late 1978. The public is anxious, confused, hostile, and sour. Pessimism remains high. An unhappy electorate has reflected its overwhelming skepticism by awarding every candidate in 1980 a negative personal rating. The public mood this year is reflected in the success of negative approaches and negative campaigns.

More to the point the American people do not want Jimmy Carter as their President. Not forced to choose a specific candidate, voters by almost 2 to 1 would reject Carter as President, a remarkable turnaround from 1977, 1978, and much of 1979. Indeed, the saving grace for us has been the unfavorable reaction to other candidates. The "lesser of evils" theme has provided the major boost against Ted Kennedy in the primaries. At the moment, the same sentiment makes reelection viable —even perhaps by a substantial margin. This negative election is quite rare in American history—indeed the 1976 choice was a comparatively positive one.

The "lesser of evils" success to date should not obscure a fundamental truth—by and large the American people do not like Jimmy Carter. Indeed a large segment could be said to loathe the President. *Ironically, the President in past years has received lower job ratings than he has now. However, he has never, never had favorable/unfavorable personal ratings as low and as negative as he receives today.* It appears that the basic positive feelings that voters had toward Jimmy Carter— that served as a safety net—have badly eroded. (This is one of the most crucial areas that must be assessed by immediate survey research.) Such a set of attitudes integrated with the general public mood could be a serious danger; allowing the electoral situation to alter in an erratic, and radical fashion.

We can see glimpses of the problem as reflected in primary survey results. One must keep in mind that the respondents are *not* general election voters, or even Democrats, but screened *hard core* primary voting Democrats!

	Calif.	*Ohio*	*N.J.*	*W.Va.*	*Montana*	*Nevada*
1. Carter Favor/Unfavor	52–44	65–32	54–41	62–35	59–39	55–42
2. (Soft) Carter Job Approval/disapproval	41–51	52–41	45–48	54–40	46–47	44–48

	Calif.	*Ohio*	*N.J.*	*W.Va.*	*Montana*	*Nevada*
3. (Hard) Carter Job Ex-good/OF-poor*	28–71	35–65	32–68	40–59	–	34–64
4. Energy/Ec programs— wrong/correct or worse if given time	43w/35r	39–45	46–40	38–41	44–39	42–38
5. Carter qualified to be President—Yes/No	47–42	58–32	49–41	56–34	52–39	52–39
6. Carter has vision to provide solutions Agree/Disagree	36–55	42–45	42–50	44–42	38–50	39–55
7. Nobody could really have done more than Carter Agree/Disagree	35–59	41–52	40–54	–	–	–
8. Carter shown can't handle Presidency, we'd be better off trying a new Pres.—Agree/Disagree	58–35	48–43	55–39	47–46	50–41	59–32
9. Want Democrats to nominate someone else Agree/Disagree	57–38	48–49	54–40	42–50	56–38	55–41

*OF indicates only fair.

These numbers are stunning—even more so when one realizes who these people are and that Carter carried 4 of these 6 states against Kennedy:

- In every state at least ⅓ of the primary voters gave Carter a negative personal rating.
- On the "soft" job question, Carter got a disapproval in five of the six states. The 4 point job scale questions (excellent, good, only fair, poor) were abysmal.
- Substantial percentages disagreed that the President was qualified for the office.
- The vision question failed miserably in almost every state. This question showed a big gain in late 1979–early 1980 and has tumbled dramatically since February.
- The protest question is staggering. The notion that Carter can't handle the job and a new President is needed passed everywhere—often by huge margins.
- Finally, even while giving him the nomination, majorities in 4 and almost 5 states want the party to nominate someone else.

Again we must remember these are *hard core primary Democrats!*

Two further comments: (1) as an analyst, I dread to imagine the results when we *test* the whole voting population including Independents and Republicans; (2) one can imagine how deep Kennedy's problems are to be defeated by the President. Indeed renomination has been, in many ways, a miracle.

Some Negative Perceptions of the President

- Doesn't seem to have a clear view of where he is going and why, doesn't seem to understand our problems or have solutions to them.
- Does not think in terms of vision or quality of life and articulate these.
- Administration decision process is often incapable of bold, rapid action; in seeking the "safe" course, often miss opportunities when timing is critical.
- Not really on top of job.
- Not decisive.
- Not in control of government. Doesn't seem to want to use his power and authority.
- Boring, not exciting.
- He is politically expedient; seems inconsistent, swings one way and then another.
- Is a poor communicator—often press considers speeches too poor to report seriously.

A Few Causes of Poor Perceptions

- The primary struggle.
- Overexposure on political matters, transparent political techniques.
- Inability to communicate a vision of what life in America should be and a well articulated, logical program to get us there.
- Inability to articulate goals and programs effectively.
- Serious White House, Administration, campaign problems. Error rate high. Poor execution.

Lest anyone think these points are the fantasy of some congenital pessimist—let me point out that every one of these points is taken directly from the Ford campaign memo [a memorandum written for the Ford campaign in the summer of 1976] of August 1976! It is amazing how much they apply to us. In fact, except for the growing dislike problem, Jimmy Carter, particularly in the polls, takes on more and more the Ford 1976 profile.

The Carter problem is exacerbated by several factors:

- Carter's greatest strength has always been his empathy, concern and compassion for ordinary people. Yet over the last few months he has appeared consistently as remote, cold, and indifferent to people.
- Carter has fostered perceptions of manipulation, calculation, almost deception in behavior to maximize political advantage.
- Carter is additionally seen as passive, defensive, always overwhelmed by events, rarely leading, always reacting.
- Most significant is the rapid turnover in public opinion. As I warned last November, the quick rise of Carter in the polls [was] fueled by a rationalization on the part of voters that he had really been changed and steeled by crises he faced—that he was a *different* Jimmy Carter. Our open end qualitative polls reflected that exact sentiment. The danger arose that

such a rationalization, if overturned by a perceived return to the "old" Jimmy Carter, could result in an unprecedented degree of anger and bitterness as voters were forced to conclude that Carter had tricked or deceived them. I fear that danger has been realized.

These factors are critical, for they strike at the very foundation of Jimmy Carter as a public man. They undermine the great Carter virtues: warmth, concern, openness, honesty, decency, and truthfulness. They lessen the value of the attributes that almost saved Ford in 1976.

II. WHERE WE BEGIN/WHERE WE HAVE BEEN—THE STATES/THE CONSTITUENCIES

Jimmy Carter approaching the 1980 general election appears in profile to be much more the 1976 Gerald Ford than the 1976 Jimmy Carter. That is an important point for in some ways it suggests the road down which we must traverse. Given Carter's greater personal negative, one might wonder why Carter still leads Reagan—the answer lies in the fact that Reagan is not Jimmy Carter 1976 either in profile or strength. However, that truth is compensated by the additional Anderson threat in key northern industrial states.

What follows is a rough guess, *without data,* of the electoral vote situation without Anderson and with Anderson. Even though we do not know the situation in most of the states it is still a revealing exercise.

CARTER VS. REAGAN
(needed to win—270)

Safe		Marginal (+)		Swing		Marginal (−)		Lost	
Massachusetts	14	New York	41	California	45	Indiana	13	Kansas	7
Georgia	12	Pennsylvania	27	Illinois	26	Virginia	12	Arizona	6
Minnesota	10	Michigan	21	Texas	26	Oklahoma	8	Nebraska	5
Maryland	10	No. Carolina	13	Ohio	25	Colorado	7	Idaho	4
W. Virginia	6	Missouri	12	New Jersey	17	Mississippi	7	Utah	4
Arkansas	6	Wisconsin	11	Florida	17	New Mexico	4	Wyoming	3
Hawaii	4	Tennessee	10	Louisiana	10	New Hampshire	4	No. Dakota	3
Rhode Island	4	Kentucky	9	Washington	9	So. Dakota	4	Alaska	3
D.C.	3	Alabama	9	Iowa	8	Montana	4		
		Connecticut	8	Oregon	6	Nevada	3		
		So. Carolina	8			Vermont	3		
		Maine	4						
		Delaware	3						
	69		176		189		69		35

245			189			104	

If one looks at likely states Carter is only 25 votes short—Reagan 166. If one uses the formula (all safe + ¾ of marginal+ + ½ swing + ¼ marginal−) Carter would get (69 + 132 + 94 + 17) = *312* electoral votes to *226*. My own guess is that that would be a *conservative* estimate.

The picture drastically changes if we add Anderson:

CARTER VS. REAGAN VS. ANDERSON
(needed to win—270)

Safe		Marginal (+)		Swing		Marginal (−)		Lost	
Georgia	12	Massachusetts*	14	Penn.*	27	California*	45	Kansas	7
W. Virginia	6	No. Carolina	13	Texas	26	New York**	41	Arizona	6
Arkansas	6	Minnesota*	10	Michigan*	21	Illinois*	26	Nebraska	5
Hawaii	4	Maryland*	10	Florida	17	Ohio*	25	Idaho	4
Rhode Island	4	Tennessee	10	Missouri*	12	New Jersey*	17	Utah	4
D.C.	3	Kentucky	9	Wisconsin*	11	Indiana	13	Wyoming	3
		Alabama	9	Louisiana	10	Virginia	12	No. Dakota	3
		So. Carolina	8	Washington	9	Connecticut**	8	Alaska	3
				Oregon	6	Oklahoma	8		
				Maine*	4	Iowa*	8		
						Colorado	7		
						Mississippi**	7		
						New Mexico	4		
						New Hampshire	4		
						South Dakota	4		
						Montana	4		
						Nevada	3		
						Vermont	3		
						Delaware**	3		
	35		83		143		242		35

118		143		277

* States decline 1 step [from one category to another with the addition of Anderson].
** States decline 2 steps [from one category to another with the addition of Anderson].

Thus we find that Anderson impacts not so much on the *popular* vote yet but his impact on state alignment is great. As the map graphically indicates, the changes are almost all in the Northeast and industrial midlands and they are massive. Fifty-two electoral votes (New York, Connecticut, Delaware) shift from Carter to Reagan, 121 votes (California, Illinois, Ohio, New Jersey, Iowa) from even to Reagan, 75 votes go from Carter to swing (Pennsylvania, Michigan, Missouri, Wisconsin, Maine) and 34 votes from safe Carter to marginal Carter. Thus Carter/Reagan switch with Carter having 118 votes safe or leaning, Reagan 277—much more than needed. By the formula Reagan leads 308 to 230. While Carter has a good shot at the swing and marginal Reagan states, it will require some real effort to diminish both opponents.

Constituencies

In 1976 Carter won (as I explained in detail in my December 1976 memo) by taking the South and holding enough big states for the edge. In the South we carried the electoral vote 127 to 12. In the Northeast we won 108 to 36, in the industrial midlands we carried 58 electoral votes to Ford's 68. And although we won no electoral votes, except Hawaii (losing 125 to 4) we did run quite well, for a Democrat, in the farm belt and far west states. In the big states (New York, Ohio, Pennsylvania) Carter's victory was secured, not in the heavy Democratic cities—indeed the margins were too small—but in the suburbs of NYC, rural/S.E. Ohio, and central Pennsylvania, where Carter heavily cut into the Protestant, small town, high status Republican vote. Except for blacks, Carter's showing with traditional Democratic groups, particularly upwardly mobile Catholics, was not very good.

Looking at constituency groups one must be alarmed. Carter is having problems again with Catholics, Jews, liberals, the young, et al., particularly in the Northeast. If we look at the 1980 primaries, Carter basically repeated his 1976 performance—winning the South, doing well in the Midwest and being defeated decisively in the Atlantic Eastern states and California. For the most part the primaries won in 1976 were won again in 1980, those lost before, lost again. Once more Pennsylvania, even though a narrow 4500 vote loss this time, broke the back of the opposition.

In 1976 we were basically on our left in the general election. We were able to hold enough liberals, Jews, Catholics, etc. to win while Ford ate us up with Independents *and* Catholic suburbanites. We do not appear so fortunate in 1980.

First, although Reagan's blue collar strength has been much exaggerated in the primaries, he can hurt us with this group particularly in the blue collar metropolitan suburbs. In addition, the bad economic news has got to hurt and hurt badly. It could be seen not only in Reagan or Anderson defections but in lowered turnouts as well.

Second, Anderson cuts deeply at the moment into our liberal, young, upper class, suburban support. He cuts away people who would never vote Reagan but *who may well stay* with Anderson because they perceive Carter to be a pale imitation of Reagan.

Third, I'm not sure the Jews will vote for Carter no matter what.

Fourth, one has to be concerned about the black vote—particularly the turnout.

Fifth, it is hard to imagine that Carter will surpass or even match his 1976 showing in the non-traditional Protestant, small town, rural communities of the North and Midwest, particularly farmers.

All of this raises some serious concerns. From this perspective, victory looks difficult. If Reagan cuts into blue collar conservative Catholic Democrats; Anderson pinches off liberals, Jews, and suburban independents; Carter does not surpass his 1976 showing among non-traditional groups—how does Carter win?

The answer is by no means hopeless. It requires a major strategic thrust with a conceptual plan as will be touched on in the next section. For this part (states and constituencies) a few points of targeting are important. First, Reagan is *not* going to take all the Ford 1976 vote. I suspect a lot of moderate upper income Independents and independent Republicans will have a difficult time with Reagan. This was evident in the primaries against Bush/Anderson. In fact the "equal" Anderson draw comes from many of those people. Unfortunately, the electoral break seems to be against us. Second, with the right strategy, signals, and actions, many of the Democrats can be shored up.

Our approach must be as follows:

States

1. The South must be secured. We need a base and the home region must be it.
2. Our major focus must be on the northern big states (Ohio, Pennsylvania, Illinois, Texas, Michigan, New Jersey, Missouri, Wisconsin). This should be our major thrust.

3. We must take either New York or California.
4. To add small state targets of opportunity to our small base states.
5. The more key states Anderson is not on, the better.

In numerical terms our goals must be as follows:

1. *The South*—Of the 139 electoral votes in the South we must win at least *110*. Texas and Florida become crucial. If we win everything else (including Mississippi, Louisiana, and most unlikely Virginia) and lose Texas we can meet this goal. If we win Texas we can lose Florida and Virginia but nothing else.

2. *The North*—In the Northeast and industrial Midwest there are 270 electoral votes. Assuming we can win Hawaii in the West (4 votes) and get the 110 in the South, we need 156 electoral votes in these two regions to win.

   A. *Good Small/Medium States*—If we win Minnesota, Missouri, West Virginia, Maryland, Delaware, the District of Columbia, Massachusetts and Rhode Island—all highly doable except perhaps Missouri—we gain 62 votes, leaving 94 votes short.
   B. *More Difficult Small/Medium States*—In the more difficult small/medium states (Connecticut, Maine, Wisconsin, Iowa, Indiana, New Hampshire, Vermont) are 51 electoral votes. If we take a minimum of 15 votes we are short 78 votes.
   C. *Big States*—Now things get difficult. New York, New Jersey, Pennsylvania, Ohio, Michigan, and Illinois have together 157 electoral votes. We need ½ (78) of those votes. If we take New York (41) we then need any combination of two of the others (the smallest, Michigan and New Jersey gives 38—one more than necessary for victory). Thus we would need half of the big states. Without New York, things become very difficult. Winning Pennsylvania, Illinois, and Ohio would give exactly 78 votes. Losing any one of these would then require winning both New Jersey and Michigan. Winning the two states (Ohio and Penn.) won in 1976 plus Michigan (73 votes) would still leave us five votes short.

3. *California Option*—Winning California (45) would easily replace New York or 2 other states and probably assume election. If both New York and California were won *no* other big state would be needed!

4. *Cushion states*—There are a few Western states that might be winnable and thus provide either cushion or insurance. Most prominent are Oregon (6), and Washington State (9). There are very outside chances at South Dakota (4), New Mexico (4), Colorado (7), and Oklahoma (8).

This obviously is a tall order with little room for error. The South is crucial. Indeed if we can meet the 110 vote goal then with some small state breaks we could win with only New York (or California) and Pennsylvania. Thus we *could* win as follows:

	Electoral Votes	*Running Total*
1. South	110	110
2. Good northern small/ medium states and Hawaii	66	176

	Electoral Votes	Running Total
3. Wisconsin & Connecticut	19	195
4. New York (California)	41 (45)	236 (240)
5. Pennsylvania	27	263 (267)
6. Washington State (9) or		
Iowa (8)		271–272 (275–276)

An additional big state a la Michigan puts us close to 290–300 electoral votes as in 1976.

Constituencies

1. We must work to solidify blue collar and middle class Catholics.
2. We must solidify blacks and browns.
3. We need to improve with Jews, liberals, upper educated young and cut them away from Anderson.
4. We must move to targets of opportunity in *key* states. Among them are:
   a. Protestants
   b. Middle class/upper middle class moderate Independent/Republicans
   c. Small town/rural voters

Everything we do must be directed at these targets of solidification and opportunity. Much of what we can do will depend on our strategic/conceptual/thematic moves to affect large public perception and the definition of the general election itself.

Summary

In short we must have essentially a Southern strategy *and* a Northern blue collar, liberal, suburban strategy. Blacks and Catholics become essential, Jews and browns important.

III. SOME ADVANTAGES/SOME DISADVANTAGES

As we begin a conceptual strategy it may be helpful to enumerate some hard intrinsic advantages and disadvantages we face at the outset. The lists are by no means all inclusive.

Advantages

1. *The President*—An excellent politician, when in fighting trim perhaps the best campaigner in the business. He is at his best when his back is to the wall. Great under pressure. Best on his feet and in Q & A. Also he *is* the President of the United States.
2. *The White House*—The 800 pound gorilla is on our side if utilized properly.
3. *Experienced Campaign Team*—In a world of the blind the one eyed man is king. In the candidate, chief surrogates, and top campaign people we have a group that has accumulated painful general election experience and that works in relative harmony.

4. *The Center*—With Reagan to the right and Anderson to the left, Carter starts in the vast center. General Elections are usually won there.

5. *No surprise*—Because he is known, Carter is less vulnerable (although not invulnerable) to major negative attacks raising new fears or doubts.

6. *Opponents*—Our opponents are not intrinsically all that strong or powerful.

Disadvantages

1. *No Base*—Except for a weakened South, Carter has no real base, particularly when it comes to Democratic constituencies. Little enthusiasm.

2. *Four Opponents*—Carter has not one, but four opponents:

1. Reagan
2. Anderson
3. Kennedy
4. The Government

The last two might be neutralized or converted to allies. The other two hammer from different directions.

3. *A Divided Party*—vs. a united Party of 1976 in reverse.

4. *Spending*—We will be outspent perhaps as much as 2 or 3 to 1.

5. *The Record*—While it can be argued that Carter's record can be a plus, the perception of that record is quite negative and harmful.

IV. STRATEGY—FROM "WHY NOT THE BEST" TO "IT COULD BE WORSE" ("AND TOMORROW COULD BE BETTER")

A. A Primer on Presidential Politics—Passing the Barrier on Acceptability/Defining the Election

Jimmy Carter begins this election as an underdog. Indeed if things were to continue as they have we could well lose the election. However, there are a number of factors which make a Carter reelection not only possible, but likely. Indeed if things can be managed well, with a little luck Carter could win by a landslide.

The truth is this: If he is to win, Jimmy Carter is just as likely to win by a landslide as by a slim margin.

Much of this belief can be found in the peculiar and unique nature of Presidential general elections. It is that nature, more than anything else that destroyed Edward Kennedy's chances when the nomination process became a General Election.

The vote for President is unlike that cast for any other office. That small point is responsible for so much of the befuddlement by the press, politicians, and consultants at grasping the true shape and decisionmaking process in a Presidential election. Presidential election experience is rare and thus they fall back on the bulk of their own experiences; experiences whose superficial similarities distort the true understanding of the matrix of forces at work.

In truth, the public expends an enormous energy on its choice for President. First, the public *cares* a great deal who is elected, despite much ballyhooed nonsense to the contrary. Second, the public is bombarded by enormous amounts of information.

These two factors interact to produce a complicated structure of assimilation and decisionmaking. In general my experience indicates that people fairly well sort the strengths and weaknesses of the candidates in reaching what is *always* a rational decision. (Unfortunately, because there are no in-depth public polls taken *during* the actual process when the dynamics interact, the theory of Presidential elections has been developed often after the election when the waves have washed away the sands of evidence.)

The vote for President is rarely a frivolous one. It is consciously and subconsciously weighed, debated, and struggled with by almost every voter.

In this process there are two critical points in the election. And while there are events, mistakes, actions, strategies that play to alter the result, most of the actual Presidential vote decisionmaking is resolved in these two stages.

Stage ONE—Acceptability Threshold

From my research and experience in the last two Presidential elections and from historical research, I am fairly convinced that a moment exists for every non-incumbent challenger in which a majority of the public decides that the person, even if he is not their choice, is qualified and able to be President. In short, can the candidate sit in the Oval Office. The passage from prospective candidate to possible President of the United States is invisible and perilous. In this judgment, unlike a primary, doubt is almost always resolved against a challenger. A successful traversing of the threshold does not ensure election, it only means that the election can then be joined with the challenger having a chance of success—the result still depends on the campaign itself. However, failure to pass the minimum threshold of relative acceptability, competence, and qualification will always doom the challenger. From that failure there is no recovery, no matter what the campaign's course.

The moment itself is harder to define. Clearly, it begins at nomination—when the candidate becomes a possible President of the United States of America—when the scrutiny becomes intense. Sometimes the decision is instantaneous (like McGovern in 1972 after the Convention/Eagleton affair or Goldwater before the convention). Its ending is less clear and more open ended. For JFK the first debate probably settled the question and while not giving him the election over Nixon (the polls only changed a few points); it did make Kennedy an acceptable choice to at least a majority of the electorate despite his youth, inexperience, etc.

It is over this period that a challenger is most vulnerable. A major mistake can be fatal. Even mistake-free, the candidate is in great danger. 1976 is a perfect example.

In June, Carter had a twenty-five point lead over Gerald Ford. Yet pre-Convention an indepth survey analysis indicated that Carter would probably lose. It was the Convention that gave Carter the *chance* to win—particularly the acceptance speech. While people focused on the Ford acceptance speech, it was the Carter acceptance speech that was more decisive—at the first critical moment of focus it made Carter a President for many people—including a number that did not vote for him. Even with the speech and a thirty-five point lead, Carter was vulnerable. For many still considered him a risk. That was the true crisis of the *Playboy* interview, not that Carter talked about "lust," not the interview itself but rather the concern that was raised about his judgment. Ironically, even though the first debate was a "loss" it may have saved the campaign for it reassured people. Indeed, the debates were crucial, for collectively they made Carter "safe" for enough people to make victory possible.

If one understands this theory it is clear why incumbency is such a general election advantage. Only a sitting President (and interestingly, to a degree, a Vice President) is exempt from the process. Even if a President is viewed as wrong, or incompetent —amazingly he is by definition "safe." He has proven that he will not blow the world sky high. As a rule of thumb, a political party would be insane not to renominate a sitting President no matter how unpopular he seems at the time. 1976 should be instructive to all. (Indeed, it is amazing how little the press and politicians ever learn.) Carter began with a 35 point lead over a sitting but unelected President. He began at Labor Day with an 18 point lead. Yet the election was razor close. Pundits talk about how Carter "kicked away" or "blew" this great lead. In truth, given the "safety/risk" question the election was always destined to be close—in many ways it was a miracle that an unknown one-term Southern Governor was even elected.

Stage TWO—Defining the Election

A general election for President is a different campaign physically from any other campaign, particularly a nomination campaign. Despite the easy assent most would give to that point —the truth of the matter is that there is no way anyone who has not been through one can understand the experience. The scrutiny from the press and public is 100 times more intense and constant than in the primary season. The crush and demands of a fifty state campaign are incomprehensible. In 1976 Carter, who was perhaps the best primary candidate in history, was totally at sea when he hit the road in September. It took him a whole month for him to get his sea legs. (JFK had a similar experience in 1960.)

Mistakes abound. Most come from inexperience. Some come from arrogance and hubris. The most common mistake is the natural tendency of campaigns to repeat the primary nomination effort. This is understandable—it worked already and besides it is the only relevant experience anyone has. The tendency is exacerbated by the human nature mindset of the campaign team to wit: "We won, we know what we're doing, we don't need anyone else." This happened in the 1972 McGovern campaign, in the 1976 Carter campaign, and it has already begun in the 1980 Reagan campaign. If we are smart, it can be an enormous advantage for it makes the Reagan campaign predictable and it makes ambush feasible.

If pitching is 75% of baseball, then 75% of elections victory revolves around the definition of the campaign. *He who sets the definition of the campaign usually wins.* In other words, the conceptual definition—the basis upon which the election is decided—is the key to victory. Yet this strategic imperative is often ignored or events take over and set the definition. It is a difficult task, particularly at the Presidential level where extensive voter perception, events, and historical tides play such an active role. In 1976 neither side set the definition—in fact neither side was all that cognizant of the framework. In that year Carter rode the thematic outsider/ values restoration to nomination. In the general election the framework became "risk vs. safety"—was the risk of the unknown Carter who promised real change worth replacing the more limited but safe incumbent Ford? In the end a majority of the decisive votes resolved that the risk was worth it. In retrospect, had either candidate been able to impose a different stronger definition the result might have been quite different.

It can be done. In 1960 Kennedy succeeded in making his hinge point—the need to get moving—dominate over the stability of Nixon even though the country was prosperous and at peace. In retrospect, it was quite an accomplishment.

At the moment, the 1980 campaign is adrift—searching for a definition. In a vacuum, the public and events may move to construct a definition that may or may not be advantageous to our prospects. That is too great a risk to take. It is imperative that we find a definition that is efficacious and seek to impose it from the outset. And that means more than a theme or slogan—although they can be helpful. It is unlikely Reagan will attempt the effort for I don't think he or his people conceptually understand the process. This is our opportunity.

In sum, it is crucial to grasp the structure of Presidential politics. The unique structure of Presidential general elections tends to work to our advantage. If we formulate and execute a strategy on an understanding of the two stages, the acceptability threshold and the election definition, then not only can we win but we might win by a landslide.

B. A STRATEGY—SOME BACKGROUND POINTS

In approaching a strategy that takes into account the two items above, there are several assumptions that need to be kept in mind.

1. The Need for a Positive Thrust

Although 1980 has proven to be a negative year—as 1978 would have indicated— there still exists the need for a strong Carter positive message.

PEOPLE MUST BE GIVEN A POSITIVE REASON TO VOTE FOR JIMMY CARTER. In short, the voters must have some sense that four more years of a Carter Administration will not be merely a rehash of the last four. While we may be able to win on the basis of a negative campaign alone, I think such a course will be savage, unenjoyable, and has all the potential for electoral disaster. Frankly, there must be a limit to the public's patience in simply leveling our opponents. At some point enough people may well decide that nothing can be as bad as what they have now and opt for the chances of change.

Indeed, one of our Anderson problems is that too many of our voters have decided that the "lesser of evils is still evil" and perceived so little hope in Carter's Presidency that the prospect of a Reagan Presidency fails to alarm them. They find themselves unable to vote for Carter who they view as only a marginally better alternative. I suspect that for some the ogre of a Reagan win can be raised sufficiently to move them towards Carter. However, I also suspect that some positive raison d'etre for Carter would bring them over more easily and in greater numbers.

A similar case can be made for much of the public at large. The road for them to Carter will be made a lot smoother if they can perceive a positive thrust that makes the rationalization easier. Jerry Rafshoon has prepared an excellent memo on themes/media strategy that embodies much of our shared thoughts. It lays out some excellent themes and approaches and I will not try to reproduce it here. However, as Jerry would agree, this media approach will not work, will not be credible, unless some *real* and *tangible* actions by Carter, as President, signal these themes as valid. The media cannot promise a better tomorrow if the evening news constantly undercuts and discredits that idea by portraying an Administration that is unimaginative, defensive, inept, timid, and unsuccessful. Such a condition as persists today puts the campaign in an exceedingly impossible situation.

Given the reality of the economy and other issues the immediate news is not going to be good. We must be in a position to suggest that the present difficulties are a transition, that the future can and will be brighter. Unfortunately, simply saying that this is so will not work. There must be a clear set of actions that give credibility to the idea. The need is for a few large and bold strokes that point to the long term rather than a lot of small incremental actions that will surely be lost in the storm. Bleeding daily as we are doing can lead to political death. Simply attempting to bandage the wounds is unlikely to accomplish much either. We would be far better off with larger bold efforts that are directed to the long term.

Too often the response to our problems is to argue that we need to "sell our accomplishments better." There is an understandable frustration over the failure of the press and public to appreciate and credit what are a number of real Carter Administration accomplishments. However, to believe that an exposition of the same will solve our problems is to pursue a siren song. I suspect that even if everyone in America was made aware of these accomplishments our problems would remain. In truth, there are several problems with this approach:

First, it is not believable. Too much "bad real news," inflation, unemployment, Iran, etc. undermines the willingness to receive such information.

Second, given the large apprehensions about the country and the world, the litany of accomplishments does not seem significant enough in their totality to ease the doubts and concerns. In isolation, they do not really spell a necessarily better future.

Third, we have tried this road before. Time after time this offensive has been rebuffed. This was vividly clear during the President's campaign trip to Ohio. The "turn the tide" theme was attacked, derided, and lampooned by commentators, cartoonists, and politicians alike.[11]

In truth, it did not do much for the electorate either. In all the key states on June 3rd, including Ohio, we *declined* after the President's foray. In Ohio our lead dropped from a solid fifteen points to barely six on primary day. In short, the approach was not *credible.*

It is the last point that is most instructive. Accomplishments *do* have a role. However, they must have both credibility and context. It is the context that will provide credibility. What we must do is take actions and announce goals for the long term future that have enough appeal to grab public attention and support. Only then with some receptivity established can we go back and show how the accomplishments of the last four years have laid an unglamorous foundation for these future oriented actions/proposals. We must establish the future's beachhead and *then* fill in with past efforts and successes.

As I have suggested, the moves must be bold and large. Only such efforts can hope to survive the predisposition of negative response in the current politically supercharged atmosphere. Only that scope will permit us to show that the President has learned and grown. We must point not just to the next four years but to the 20 year span left in this century. The efforts should point toward the United States and world we envision at the turn of the millennium. Obviously, the economy is an obvious target area. There are others. The whole area needs to be explored separately as I will do in a separate writing.

[11] See page 179.

In sum, the need for a positive thrust is overwhelming. It holds the final key for victory. More importantly, it is the road that leads to a potential landslide if one is possible. Without it victory will not only be desperate but itself in jeopardy.

2. The Two Candidate Problem

We face a problem in having two opponents trying to cut us. Because they come from different directions they will require different tacks. Unfortunately, those efforts are not particularly complimentary. However, it seems to me that if we await Labor Day to deal with both then we may find ourselves in the position of having too much on our political plate with which to deal. Therefore we must make a concerted effort to "defeat" one of them before October. For a host of reasons that will become clear I recommend that we take Reagan on first and attempt to "beat" him by October 1. If necessary then we can turn our public focus toward Anderson.

3. Ideological Positioning

Given the nature of our opponents and our constituency problems, some attention needs to be given this area. Throughout his national political career Jimmy Carter has essentially dominated the center of American politics. So adroitly did he do so that liberals tended to view him as a liberal, conservatives as a conservative, etc. This positioning, while denying him hard core supporters, did permit maximum flexibility—Carter could slide left or right to meet any immediate challenge.

There are now two complications to this situation. First, Carter is in jeopardy of losing the center to Reagan. Surveys already indicate that Reagan is placed by the electorate as closer to them on general issues than Carter. Second, in a general election sense Anderson is assaulting much of Carter's natural liberal base whose normal certainty would allow Carter to move right toward Reagan. These factors are further complicated by the fact that Carter, to win, must hold the more conservative South *and* the more liberal blue collar Northeast. An all out move to secure one area could lead to an alienation of the other.

Therefore, I would suggest the following approach:

First: To the extent possible we cannot afford this to be an ideological/candidate position election. We need to find some other grounds.

Second: Vigorously seize the center back from Reagan—particularly in foreign policy. Push him back out to the right and away from the center, particularly in the North.

Third: While not abandoning general position on domestic issues find several "safe" issues that the President can move hard left on in the North and Midwest. This also requires wooing back Kennedy and party liberals.

Fourth: Play up the Democratic Party as the umbrella to hold over the diverse regional areas.

C. THE ELECTION DEFINITION—"THE PRESIDENCY—A SERIOUS BUSINESS"

If we approach the question of election definition—on what basis the electorate should cast its vote—and take into account the ideological, issue, and opponent problems we have then one area stands out like a beacon—the Presidency itself. In fact, what I propose is that we link the Presidency itself to the 1976 definer, safety vs. risk, in putting forth a 1980 election definition.

What I suggest is that we make an effort to raise the public's consciousness about the office—"the hardest job in the world," "the most demanding," "complicated dealing always with complex problems," "awesome burden," "the place where life and death are decided," "war and peace," etc. ad nauseam. We would want to send a number of subtle and not so subtle messages:

- No office for an amateur or ideology
- A place that needs a cool head (and hard)
- Needs someone smart, understands complex issues
- A job that demands incredible stamina and energy.

There still exists in this country a reverence and awe for the office. We must take advantage of this. If we succeed at this definition several things can be accomplished:

— We can point people forward deciding the election on the basis of who can better sit in the Oval Office, more directly—who is SAFE to sit in the job rather than just issues, positions, or record.

— By making the job complicated and impossible we can build some sympathy for the President's problems and hence his record.

— More importantly, we can force all the concerns about Reagan (and Anderson to an extent) from the periphery of concern to center stage; age, impulsiveness, rigidity, simplicity, intelligence, and experience.

— We can put all the burden on our challengers to *prove* they could do so much better that such a risk would be advisable.

Such an effort would require a free and paid media effort to educate and teach the latent attitudes people have about the Presidency. Indeed our message becomes one of "when you vote for President—vote like your whole world depends on it."

D. RONALD REAGAN—MAKING THE CHALLENGE THE ISSUE—EARLY

If we accept the theory of the Acceptability Threshold and the need to dispose of one candidate, then Reagan becomes the obvious choice.

To begin with, he can get elected and Anderson cannot. If he gets knocked out early then we can mop up afterwards.

Most importantly, we know when Reagan gets nominated he will be put under intense scrutiny as he attempts to pass the Acceptability Threshold. Our near total energies should be put in the period July to September into two tasks: (1) rebuild Carter/Develop positive thrust and (2) deny Reagan the Acceptability Threshold. Thus we must make people not only concentrate on President Reagan but we must help make that as uncomfortable a notion for them as possible. If we succeed at beating Reagan early then we will have won even if the survey numbers take some time to reflect the victory.

To this end we have several things working for us:

1. *Reagan himself*—His tendency to shoot from the hip, to confuse complicated ideas.

2. *Reagan Mistakes*—Reagan will make mistakes. Every candidate in a general election situation does. However, he has more than the average propensity to err. Worse he is stubborn in the face of attack. Already in the primaries he has taken positions or made statements—Cuba blockade, farm parity, minimum wage, that would have been full blown disasters if he had been a general election candidate.

There are two gaping problems in this area:

a) The *Press* has so far been fairly easy on Reagan—ever since they proved wrong about his demise after Iowa. Part of this reflects their dislike of the President.

b) We have failed to take advantage of Reagan slips. Several weeks ago he flip-flopped on the Mideast with Ghorbal and it went unanswered. His tax cut plan was allowed to energize without attack on our part. We cannot continue to give him a free media ride. We must be prepared to both *force* and *exploit* mistakes.

3. *Reagan Staff*—John Sears devised a first rate strategy and like Bismarck was dropped. The strategy worked anyway, though. However, there is now a question whether anyone around Reagan has the ability to formulate a first class political strategy. As I indicated earlier, they are not likely to bring on any experienced talent either. In addition, they are inexperienced in general election politics and I think unlikely to understand the structure and forces of a Presidential general election until they are actually in it.

Reagan cannot be made an evil person—unlike a decade ago, age has taken the harshness off the image. He is seen as a likeable, friendly grandfatherly figure. He is not a nut. His simplicity and view of the world has great superficial appeal. He describes problems well. However, he is vulnerable on a number of points and they are the ones we must exploit.

1. *Is Reagan Safe?*—He has made over the years and in his campaign some incredible and often naive statements. There is plenty to work with here from domestic issues (for example, on the environment—"If you've seen one tree, you've seen them all") to foreign policy (blockade Cuba). He can be hammered on many, all raising the point—"Would you trust this man to be President?"

2. *Shoots from the Hip*—His impulsiveness in action and statement can be turned to the question of whether someone who shoots from the hip so often can be trusted as President.

3. *Over His Head*—A simplicity of view and experience that raises real questions of whether he can handle the complex problems of the Presidency. If attacked right, this can be carried over even to positions that have superficial appeal but which raise on another level greater doubts.

4. *What Are His Solutions?*—In an electorate where doubt and suspicion has placed every candidate in the position of *proving* that he can solve problems, Reagan is vulnerable on the grounds of raising problems but having weak or suspicious solutions.

5. *Positions/Ideas*—In his record and his campaign he is open to assault on a host of positions and ideas not the least of which is Kemp/Roth. Enough concern can be raised over these to inflict substantial damage.

6. *Backers/Advisors*—Reagan has around him scores of people who have positions and records that are scary. Many have made statements even recently that could get Reagan into hot water. This whole area raises the idea of whether Reagan knows enough about what's going on to really be in charge.

7. *He Is a Republican*—We must remember that not only is Reagan a Republican, he is a right-wing, big business, rich man Republican. For all his warmth, he is no friend to working class or middle income or minority Americans.

8. *His Record as Governor*—We cannot let him get away with the idea that he was a good Governor. If we can create enough doubts about his record then he will suffer badly (as Carter did when the Ford people undermined Carter's record in 1976). This is particularly true as this is his only elected government experience.

9. *Age*—While this is not a salient issue to most people it is a latent concern for most. Anything that indirectly raises concern over his stamina, etc. can be harmful and give people an excuse to move away.

E. ANDERSON

In many ways, Anderson is an appealing target. His Congressional record even as late as 1978 raises quite a contrast to the 1980 candidate Anderson. This candidate of retroactive virginity has many potential vulnerabilities. Nonetheless, we must take care in the approach.

Strategically, Anderson is hurting us now. While in popular vote he draws fairly equally from both Reagan and the President, the electoral vote story, as discussed earlier, is quite different. However, he does serve a temporary purpose. He is a holding place for many people who do not want to vote for Jimmy Carter now. However, if Reagan is hurt badly he could be the holding place for upper income suburban Independent Republicans who may well want to defect from Reagan.

Anderson cannot be elected President. For starters, he has very high negative ratings. He would have difficulties even if he were popular but this factor alone will shut him down. In addition, Anderson has not worn well this year; he should have won both Illinois and Wisconsin where he led initially but in both he slid precipitously in the last weeks. Actually, Anderson is in the "Twilight Zone," neither high enough to get the brutal scrutiny that would hurt him or low enough to be ignored. Actually, if he were higher in the polls I suspect the scrutiny would force a faster fall than likely in his "none of the above" positions. As it is he will decline probably more slowly—particularly since he is the press candidate of the moment.

This is not to underestimate the Anderson danger. It is very great. If he holds at the end a small core—they are likely to be our voters in crucial states. Also, as stated before, a lot of these people want to be for Anderson—they are appalled by the President and do not find a Reagan Presidency that much worse. More than anything else this calls for a positive Carter thrust.

If the time comes, I am convinced that Anderson is vulnerable even more on his character than his record. He is trying to suggest that he is more righteous, more holy, than other politicians—that he is not a politician. Yet I suspect he is highly vulnerable on the charge of opportunism—of pandering. The Mideast is only one example. Unlike other candidates, his very effort at being "better" means that any chink in that armor, any damage to that image becomes instantly fatal.

I think our initial approach should be as follows:

1. *Ignore Publicity*—I think we have learned our lesson here. Having dealt with the debate question we should obviously let him alone in public.

2. *Ballot Access*—However, here we should continue an all out assault. Keeping him off key ballots is worth the hullabaloo. Actually, people don't care that much about internal political machinations and ballot fights are unlikely to draw the kind of attention and sympathy that the debate did. In those states we need to win we should undertake every effort to keep him off the ballot, legally and politically. This is particularly true in the big northern industrial states like New York and California.

3. *Liberal Groups*—So far this effort has been disappointing. We need to reenergize labor and liberal groups to go after Anderson on his record, his statement to continue as a Republican, etc. They might have the lead and be targeted in *key* states to liberals, suburbs, young, universities, upper income, etc. We should seek to help *target* those efforts and they should be extensive.

Further, this provides an immediate effort for those groups and individuals whose support for the President is unenthusiastic and will have to develop gradually.

To this end, I recommend that right after the conventions we set up a separate citizens or Republicans/Independents committee for the President. It should be separate from our official campaign/DNC campaign. Many of our anti-Anderson efforts could be channeled here.

4. *The Early Campaign*—Given the high education level of Anderson voters, their large urban clustering, and their liberal disposition, I would recommend a mail/literature campaign highly targeted to those areas where we need to break down the Anderson vote. Highly targeted, it would be far less expensive than a broad effort.

V. STRATEGIC/TACTICAL CONCERNS

There are a number of other strategic/tactical factors that must be addressed. I would like to touch now only a few that are the most pressing.

A. WHAT KIND OF CAMPAIGN?

We have had a number of internal debates about the kind of campaign we run and the components of such a campaign: media vs. field, strategy vs. tactics, Presidential activity vs. Presidential campaigning, etc.

This author has some very strong views. First, we must recognize that we face a complicated and risky *General Election* for President. It will be resolved by big images, big events, big decisions. Real events and the perceptions that arise from them will be far more important than the campaign. Free media (hard news) will be vastly more important than paid media which in turn will be light years more important than field operations which will be infinitely more crucial than special groups. We cannot and must not follow our instincts and try to run the 1980 General Election as we ran the primaries or as we ran the 1976 General Election.

The 1976 General Election was at best a mediocre effort. As one of the principals of that effort with a large share of the blame, I am quite willing to say this. We tried to run a national primary campaign, which was our experience. We did not run a conceptual strategic campaign, we did not attempt to lay out a conceptual framework of messages, issues, signals, or definitions. Rather than a Conceptual Strategy, we had a Strategy of Tactics. We are not in a position to do this in 1980. We must learn from our experiences. In some cases, we must learn new experiences.

Our most vital need is to devise and control the messages and images of this election. Everything must be subordinated to this effort. In recent weeks, the huge logistical demands of the campaign have sucked up our time. Yet, we have missed several opportunities to strike major blows whether on Reagan's Mideast flip, Anderson's Iran apology statement, or Reagan's tax cut plan. We must be prepared to respond and initiate coordinated efforts at these and other targets of opportunity. Conceptual strategies are very difficult, they are abstract at best. Yet we must do it. It is at that level that victory and defeat will be decided.

We need a strategy group—fully supported that is designed to be at the core of the campaign/White House efforts. It must have the primacy of time, effort, and resources. Everything else must be subordinate to this.

The campaign itself is made up of many pieces. Yet if we look at the factors that influence Presidential vote some guidelines become possible.

FACTORS INFLUENCING PRESIDENTIAL VOTE

I.	Real Events, Perceptions, Carter Actions, Reagan Actions, Anderson Actions, Free Media, etc.	65–70%
II.	Paid Media	25–30%
III.	Field Operations	3–5%
IV.	Other—(Phases of the Moon, Weather, Astrological Charts, World Series Outcome, Stock Market)	0–2%

Areas I and II make up 90–95% of the factors influencing the outcome. Almost ⅔ have little to do with the physical campaign (except trips, speeches, etc.). These areas that fall into the campaign are the paid media, research, and polling (the latter is used to drive I and II).

Such a delineation suggests that not all campaign efforts or dollars are created equally—some are clearly more important than others. To this end I would strongly suggest that in planning our efforts we recognize the time/resource primacy of these areas. For the budget it suggests that the marginal dollars spent on areas I and II are far more valuable by 6, 7, 8, 10 to 1 factors over field dollars for example. Clearly the budgets and resources for those areas should be maximized—general economies and reductions cannot be across the board. Those needs, media, polling, research, travel, etc. must be met in full first.

There has been some discussion about Field/Get-out-the-vote efforts which can play a key role in a close election. Without belaboring the point, it seems that much of the 1976 field budget necessarily went to overhead. In 1980 it would seem practical that major registration, targeting, and GOTV [get-out-the-vote] efforts be made at *key groups in key areas of key states* to boost the turnout in those places where we were hurt in 1976 and face problems in 1980. In such a way, we can make even more effective whatever dollars, large or small, we have in 1980 for field operations.

B. The White House/The Campaign

The effective integration of the Government (particularly the White House) and the campaign can be decisive. We cannot hope to maximize our advantages if they simply overlap—they must be integrated. The White House cannot deal with the campaign just on obvious campaign matters. For the White House is the campaign.

Everything the President says *is* the campaign—not just political statements.

Everywhere the President goes *is* the campaign—not just political events.

Everything the President does *is* the campaign—not just campaign items.

Therefore, in all ways the White House and Government must be a part of the campaign.

C. The President's Initial Efforts—Back to the Rose Garden

During the summer it is crucial that the President concentrate on being President. Besides fundraising, the President needs to concentrate on a few things: (1) the substance of the Government—to provide a consistent positive thrust; (2) rebuilding his image as a warm, straightforward person of empathy; (3) rebuilding his tattered relations with the press; and (4) thinking through his concept of a second term.

The number of campaign or even official trips/events that look campaigny need to be reduced. A town meeting or two might be in order. He should refrain from attacking his opponents—that is the work of others.

The President needs to let Reagan get out front, particularly in September, and go through what he did in September 1976. When we do campaign, town meetings rather than speeches should be the order of the day.

The best candidate the President can be early is to be a bold, vigorous, compassionate President.

D. Surrogates

This is one of the most crucial and deficient areas in the campaign. If the President is not to carry the early campaign, especially the attack, then these efforts must come from his surrogates. Frankly, we have made poor use of our surrogates particularly the Cabinet and key senior White House aides. That is due in part to the nature of primaries and partly to poor central planning on our part.

The role model for our surrogates should be the 1972 Nixon campaign. In that effort, the surrogates—particularly the Cabinet—were used to savage McGovern. Every speech or idea generated by McGovern was attacked by the appropriate Government official. Soon he was fighting Government officials rather than the President—a hopeless task. Even when it is clearly a political act when the Secretary of the Treasury attacks a candidate for economic foolishness, it makes news and it hurts, and raises doubts.

What this requires is several conditions:

(1) A highly centralized effort that coordinates the surrogates' schedules, decides who is to carry the message, clears the decks of other competing activity, etc.

(2) Surrogates cannot be sent off on their own. In 1972 the Nixon White House decided not only the subject of the attack, they *wrote it* ensuring that what they wanted got delivered.

(3) A process for deciding what departments do and whether it should be a White House announcement is crucial.

By all logic such a component belongs in the strategy coordinating body.

In addition, we need to, to the extent possible, utilize Party and Congressional figures to complement the surrogate efforts. This should prove easier in a general election than in primaries.

E. THE CONVENTION

This will be our single best mechanism for sending our message via free media to the country. It is a chance if utilized properly to both send negative and positive messages. However, it must be organized to do so. Already some planning is proceeding in this area.

1. *Speeches/Themes*

Once we can decide exactly what themes we want to promote then as many speakers as possible can be utilized to send those messages. This is particularly true of the Keynote, the Platform speeches, the nomination speeches, and the Vice President's acceptance speech.

2. *Access/TV Media*

We are endeavoring to institute a system whereby all key officials will be coordinated both during and outside the Convention. We will want to utilize Cabinet/White House Staff/Government officials to spend time giving interviews to key media outfits in key states. Again the effort would be to decide a message and have them get it out.

While the Convention is on television we would want to control senior officials and campaign officials so that we could maximize on floor interviews at proper moments, again to send out the desired messages.[12]

3. *Acceptance Speech*

This speech is most crucial. It will be the President's greatest opportunity to impact the electorate. It is a speech that must be removed from the normal White House speech process, developed and heavily practiced.

---

[12] See page 229.

Memorandum II

Debate Strategy

PATRICK H. CADDELL

OCTOBER 21, 1980

I. OPPORTUNITY AND RISK

The debate on October 28th offers some opportunities and is fraught with great risk. The risks far outweigh the possible advantages. Yet, if we can maximize our efforts we can turn the debate into a decisive act *in our favor* toward election.

This debate is very different both in possible impact and in the campaign mosaic. Tomorrow (October 22) marks the anniversary of the third and final 1976 debate. The first debate you have with Governor Reagan will come almost a full week later and mark the beginning of the last week of the campaign. No debate in 1960 was held as late. Because it is the first debate and so belated, it will dominate the political scene perhaps until election day itself—certainly at least into the final weekend. There is no historical precedent for gauging its importance.

We know from our debate research and the 1976 campaign that debates serve to reinforce supporters, regardless of the winner, rather than to convert or move voters. Millions have no problem voting for the "loser" in a debate. History shows little actual vote movement caused by a debate itself. However, because this unique debate takes place in an election populated by two unpopular candidates, and marked with great volatility, one cannot discount the possibility that it will actually serve to convert as well as reinforce, particularly with soft, undecided, and minor candidate voters.

Further this debate will take place smack at the point when history suggests major movement toward the incumbent party begins. Certainly while the election has been "bogged down" for weeks, we see clear voter positioning and massing that suggests such a movement is about to begin. There is a possibility—by no means certain—

that the expectation of the debate will hold up the start of that movement. There is also the possibility that the debate itself could either enhance or retard that likely movement. That is our great risk in the debate. Those are clearly the reasons the Reagan campaign opted for a debate and sought one as late as possible.

A. Positive Potential for Carter

I see four potential positives for us in these debates:

> *First, excitement.* This campaign has lacked the excitement and crackle of past campaigns. This has been particularly true with our minority voters, blue collar voters, and normally certain liberal voters. The debate—late, singular and dramatic—could certainly inject a dose of interest and excitement so far missing—despite our poll findings earlier in September which revealed far fewer (52%) "very interested" in debates than the 81% recorded in September 1976.

> *Second, Anderson loss.* This debate sans Anderson is certainly likely to drive down and accelerate the slippage of Anderson voters. It should force *liberal, Democratic, Kennedy* Anderson voters to focus on Reagan vs. Carter and could snap them back toward their natural second choice—the President.

> *Third, Carter Positive Exposure.* Except for the Billy Carter Press Conference (a negative issue, at best) and the Acceptance Speech (overshadowed by Kennedy stories) this debate offers the first in-depth exposure of the President to the American people since the crisis days of last winter. This should be a real plus for the President.

> *Fourth, Reagan Doubts.* The debate could serve to reinforce the enormous doubts and uneasiness that exist about Ronald Reagan. This, however, is the chanciest of the four positive Carter potentials—although by far the most important.

B. The Risk for Carter

At the outset there are greater risks for the President than opportunities. There is a 75% chance that Carter will "lose" the debate even if he "wins" on points, a la Anderson. There is only at best a 25% chance that the President will "win" in real and hard terms. Everything we know about debates, 1980, 1976, 1960, leads to this conclusion.

Debates are the vehicles of challengers. In a general election for President the incumbent or the semi-incumbent figure (usually a Vice President) is already well known to the electorate. No matter how unpopular, he is experienced and relatively "safe." The challenger, no matter how popular, engenders doubt, particularly on the nuclear/foreign policy question. In Presidential campaigns, doubt is usually decided in favor of the status quo. Hence the historical late incumbent party advantage in competitive general elections. Debates give challengers in-depth exposure impossible in news coverage. The debates allow the challenger the opportunity to reassure voters even when they do not out-debate incumbents. They are the best device for a challenger to reach and cross the Acceptability Threshold.

Without the debates I am certain that Jimmy Carter would have lost in 1976; the in-depth assurance gained from the debates allowed him to head off the incumbent surge in the last 48 hours. I suspect strongly that without the debates John Kennedy would also have lost. In 1980 we have already seen how the Anderson-Reagan debate allowed Reagan to reassure a number of voters, to move his favorability up, and in combination with some Carter difficulties to surge back ahead in the race reversing the rapid decline he was then experiencing.

If Reagan got so much out of a debate with Anderson then the possibilities in an appearance with the President are that much greater. In addition, the doubts about Reagan are so great that even a less than excellent appearance coming so late can help him even more than normally because of the public's low expectation levels. (One thing that mitigates a little against Reagan in this sense is the actor stigma.) From this perspective one can argue that Reagan is exactly right in seeking such a dramatic late debate.

Thus Reagan can win even if he loses the debate on "points" to Carter. That is exactly when happened in the Anderson-Reagan debate. Anderson "won" but really lost—being a minor candidate he needed a spectacular showing to propel him into major candidate status. Instead he got a slight win. Reagan while "losing" actually won. He got a chance, albeit in part because of the lack of follow-up or press criticism, to reassure some voters.

Anderson failed in part because he did not understand debates. He did not exploit openings left by Reagan to do real damage to Reagan. His attacks were mild one-liners rather than hard in-depth blows. He was more interested in promoting his own ideas in a vacuum than in challenging Reagan. In retrospect only a total destruction of Reagan offered Anderson any hope—looking all right was fatal. We must understand this lesson well if we are to TRULY WIN.

We can think of our debate as a football game with each team having one chance to move the ball and score. However, we get the ball on our five yard line. Reagan starts with the ball on *our* 40 yard line—already in near field goal range. Mild success can put Reagan in certain field goal range. A moderate sustained drive can give him a touchdown. The President must move 95 yards for a touchdown without losing possession. He must move 70 yards or more to get a field goal. He can easily gain more total yards and yet lose the real score. Thus grinding out yardage up the middle is not much of an option. Only excellent precision, bold strategies, and high risk plays are likely to yield a real score.

I AM CONVINCED WE CAN "REALLY" WIN. WE WILL NOT WIN, HOW-EVER, ON KNOWING MORE FACTS, ON SPOUTING STATISTICS, OR LOOKING GOOD. ONLY BY A WELL CONCEIVED STRATEGY, BRIL-LIANTLY EXECUTED, CAN VICTORY BE ACHIEVED. IT IS POSSIBLE BUT WILL REQUIRE A TRUE UNDERSTANDING OF THE SITUATION AND OF THE EFFORT REQUIRED. THIS MEMO IS ABOUT THAT STRATEGY.

II. WHERE WE BEGIN—THE POLLS

The election is now close but massing for movement. For a month the election has remained within tight parameters—the candidates go up and down but only within limits. Recently, we completed a panel study that re-interviewed a large cross section of people surveyed just prior to the Baltimore debate [between Anderson and Reagan]. In the last two Presidential elections our October panel study has shown small overall changes in the overall vote numbers but massive internal movement with as many as one-third of the electorate changing position. We were stunned to find in our panel study that about 95% of both Carter and Reagan voters in mid-September had landed back with the same candidate by mid-October. However, we also knew that national surveys taken between the original and the panel had shown 6–8 point shifts—thus the conclusion that while movement had occurred (we see that most in the volatile changes in the statistical regression tests), most people had simply returned to their positions by the 10th of October. In short, for weeks nothing *really* happened although there had been movements post-Baltimore debate to Reagan followed by a small Carter bounceback.

Our most recent data, both in person and telephone, suggest this is about to change. There have been definite *attitudinal* movements away from Reagan and toward Carter particularly on key questions such as Reagan qualified, Reagan vision, Carter vision, Carter safe, "close to me on issues," "international crisis." Although the vote showed little movement the internals point to a real Carter movement in the making leaving aside the debates. This, again, would follow historical trends, particularly 1976.

Briefly I would like to show in capsule the key Carter, Reagan, and comparative attitude results.

A. *Comparative Semantic Differentials* (1–7 scale opposite adjectives)

	Warm	*Cold*	
Carter	64%	16%	(+48)
Reagan	43	32	(+11)

	Effective	*Ineffective*	
Carter	32	49	(−17)
Reagan	48	26	(+22)

	Trustworthy	*Untrustworthy*	
Carter	65	20	(+45)
Reagan	48	26	(+22)

	Decisive	*Wishy-Washy*	
Carter	32	50	(−18)
Reagan	56	24	(+32)

	Dedicated	*Opportunistic*	
Carter	57	24	(+33)
Reagan	44	35	(+9)

	Strong	*Weak*	
Carter	36	45	(−9)
Reagan	59	22	(+37)

	Thoughtful	Impulsive	
Carter	57	22	(+35)
Reagan	40	38	(+2)

	Qualified	Unqualified	
Carter	46	36	(+10)
Reagan	48	30	(+18)

Thus Carter has big positive edges on Warm, Trustworthy, Thoughtful, and Dedicated with a slim positive margin on Qualified. He receives negative margins (although less than July by far) on Effective, Decisive, and Strong. Reagan conversely gets his strongest edges on those three qualities although his best margins never reach Carter's on *his* best adjectives. Reagan has no negative scores but runs quite poorly on soft adjectives like Warm, Trustworthy, Dedicated. His barely even score on Thoughtful represents a giant drop since July.

These results provide a sense of the broad public images of both men although as we shall see in the direct comparisons these scores are not necessarily related. For example, we will see that although on the Semantics Reagan has a (+18) score on Qualified while Carter has a (+10) that when asked who is better qualified Carter wins 50% to 35%. Thus Qualified *in a vacuum* means something different for Carter than for Reagan in the public's eye. Nonetheless Carter does best on the "soft" or human dimensions while Reagan has a mediocre showing. Carter does very, very badly on "hard" and job related measures while Reagan in a vacuum does best on these scores.

B. *Specific Carter Questions—Positive/Negative*

1. Job Approval 40%; Disapproval 52% (*miserable,* but slightly better on field survey—44–48).

2. 4 Point Job Rating: 3% Excellent; 26% Good

29% Positive

44% Only Fair; 26% Poor

70% Negative

(Not good at all but "poor" is down from 37% in July.)

The Carter job rating is the biggest drag on the election. It costs the President on the average of 15 negative points in his Favorable/Unfavorable rating and 5 points in direct vote loss to Reagan according to the Regression Analysis.[13] That is quite a handicap weight—without it altogether Carter would be at least 10 points ahead—maybe in the LBJ–Nixon landslide range. (Historically, these attitudes on job seem to remain in place once the campaign gets underway—Ford in 1976 showed no job rating movement in September/October although some personal Favorable/Unfavorable movement.)

[13] Regression analysis is a statistical analytic model which attempts to determine which factors are truly affecting choices, and the relative importance of those factors. For example, if two factors, such as effective and honest, have the same number, regressive analysis may tell which factor is more important.

3. *Agree/Disagree Opinions on Carter* [14]

Positive	A	D		*Close*	A	D	
Stands up what believe even if unpopular	58%	27%	(+31)	Understands me	48%	39%	(+9)
Keep out of War	50	27	(+23)	Economy/Ener. wrong/right	41	43	(+2)*
Cares	58	36	(+22)*	Can't handle Pres	46		
				Better than credited	47		(+1)
Learned/better next term	56	37	(+19)**	Shown Qualified Yes/No	45	48	(-3)**

Negative	A	D	
Can't handle new President	52%	43%	(-9)**
Safe Choice	40	54	(-14)**
Vision	34	57	(23)**

Reduce Unemployment 2nd Term			
	Y	38	
	N	41	(-3)
	DK	21	

Reduce inflation 2nd term			
	Y	34	
	N	49	(-15)
	DK	17	

* Most important now for attitude on vote formation.
** Very important.

C. *Reagan Questions*

1. Governor of California—18% Excellent; 36% Good
                                                                  54% Positive

                                              25% Only Fair; 12% Poor
                                                            37% Negative

(Positive margin still high at 17 points but was 38 points before media ads started, still a big Reagan help.)

[14] These are shorthand terms for questions Caddell's survey asked. For example, "Cares" stands for "Jimmy Carter really cares about people like me: do you agree or disagree?"

2. *Reagan Agree/Disagree*

Positive	A	D		Close	A	D	
Not qualified	35	56	(+21)**	Not know talk about	44	46	(+2)
Too old to be Pres.	43	50	(+7)	Cares	43	43	(0)**
Generally shown				Does dumb things	44	43	(−1)
Qualif.	47	42	(+5)				
Handle Foreign							
Affairs	42	37	(+5)				
Reduce Inflation	37	34	(+3)*				
		(30 DK)					
Reduce							
Unemployment	37	34	(+3)				
		(30 DK)					

Negative	A	D		
Is risk	51	44	(−7)*	
Not trust in crisis	49	41	(−8)**	
Understands me	40	48	(−8)	
Vision	38	48	(−10)**	
Has well defined				
program	35	50	(−15)	
Too simplistic	56	36	(−20)*	
Wonder judgment	59	35	(−24)	
Criticizes, not say				
what will do	60	34	(−26)**	
Keep out of war	23	51	(−28)**	(26 DK)
Shoots hip	64	27	(−37)*	

* Important.
** Very important.

A quick perusal leads one to wonder how Reagan is even in the race at all. There are several reasons. First, the Carter perceptions. Second, on the biggest factors, California Job, Qualified, Vision, Reagan does well—better than Carter. Although we are beginning to see key negative movement on Qualified and Vision, as well as on Job. Third, many doubts about Reagan are not yet salient. Fourth, some positive attributes Strong, Effective, etc. not in Agree/Disagrees. Still, the vulnerabilities are breathtaking.

D. *Candidate Comparisons*

Carter Wins	C	R		Close	C	R	
Religious	67	7	(+60)	Speak out Issues	33	33	(0)
Equal Rights				Hostages	29	32	(−3)
Women	64	15	(+49)*	Get things done	39	42	(−3)**
Moderate	59	21	(+38)				

Keep out of war	49	18	(+31)*			
Trustworthy	50	33	(+17)***			
Tells Truth	39	19	(+20)			
Cares	42	24	(+18)*			
Understands me	41	24	(+17)	*Reagan Wins*	*C*	*R*
Better Qualified	50	35	(+15)*	Strong Defense	28	51 (−23)
Understand 80's	42	30	(+12)*	Inflation	30	46 (−16)***
Foreign Policy	47	37	(+10)	Unemployment	31	42 (−11)***
Handle Internat.						
Crisis	44	35	(+9)***	(Negative won by Carter, thus		
Respect More	44	35	(+9)***	Reagan gain)		
Close on issues	44	37	(+7)***	Weak	41	18 (−23)

(Negatives won by Reagan, thus
   Carter edge)

Says wrong thing, wrong time	16	48	(+32)
Slick	20	36	(+16)
Worry him in White House	32	40	(+8)
Dirty campaign	12	20	(+8)
Mean	9	16	(+7)

* Important.
** Very important.
*** Very, very important.

The candidate comparisons speak volumes on the problem of the election. Carter wins almost every direct comparison. Of the four *** issues on his side of the ledger, the margins are at the bottom of his list—thus they are most important but Carter wins by least. Only Trustworthy is high. A number of Carter issues have little saliency or impact yet—like "moderate." Reagan wins only a few but they are all crucial and he wins by good margins to go with his competence perceptions. Again, however, Reagan is vulnerable.

E. *Ideologies* (7 point scale)

	Liberal 1,2	*Moderate* 3,4,5	*Conservative* 6,7
Voter	16	55	25
Carter	22	62	13
Reagan	9	30	56

Thus, Carter is much closer to the electorate than Reagan. (Remember Carter wins Moderate 59–21!) One-third of the voters place Reagan at extreme conservative slot "7." Yet he "wins" issues like defense, economy, etc.—a real Carter opening here.

F. *Some Issue Results*

1. Most important issue

	Inflation	*Unemployment*	*Foreign Affairs*
First Response	48	15	25
Second Response	31	25	28

2. *Foreign*
   (a) U.S. Position in the world

	Excellent	*Good*	*Only fair*	*Poor*	
Mid October	4	23	50	21	A slight decline,
July	4	28	49	18	War in Gulf?

   (b) Iran/Iraq
   1. War loss of U.S. Power ... 25
      Don't get involved ... 66
      Don't know ... 10

   2. Likely lead to wider war:
      Very likely ... 33 ... 71
      Somewhat likely ... 38
      Not very likely ... 14 ... 24
      Not at all ... 10
      Don't know ... 4

   3. Carter handling:
      Strongly approve ... 22 ... 56
      Approve ... 34
      Disapprove ... 16 ... 30
      Strongly disapprove ... 14
      Don't know ... 10

3. *Economy*

   (a) U.S. Economy Rating Today:

	Excellent	*Good*	*Only fair*	*Poor*
	1	7	31	59
	(8)		(90)	

   (b) U.S. Economy One Year from Now:

	Better	*Same*	*Worse*
	48	8	25

   (c) Personal Economic Situation in 1 year:

	Better	*Same*	*Worse*
	54	22	16

   (d) Economic Scale:

	Optimist			Pessimist		
	1	*2*	*3*	*4*		
October	26	28	30	16	(54–46)	[+7] gain
September	22	28	30	19	(50–49)	

(e) Large Tax Cut: Good time   29
                     More harm than good   56
                     Don't know   15

III. TARGET GROUP—DEBATE

First, all the debate research indicates that two groups are most affected by debates:

1. College educated
2. Women

This is crucial for us to remember. We are not carrying college educated although we did well there in 1976. Many of these voters were and are Anderson voters. Women remain our key group. Unlike 1976—we are carrying women and losing men—we are the incumbent. As we learned in 1976 women can be moved by the challenger as we successfully attempted to do in the Third Debate and the last week of the campaign. Reagan gained with both groups after the Baltimore debate. Indeed, for a month we have seen the most volatility with housewives—the key group every time Reagan moved. Bob Ableson [a Yale professor who was a consultant to the Carter campaign] has been concerned all along that toward the end these women would be influenced by their husbands—i.e. toward Reagan.

THUS, OUR FIRST AND PARAMOUNT TARGET GROUPS ARE THOSE INFLUENCED BY DEBATES: COLLEGE EDUCATED AND WOMEN.

College Educated

This suggests that Complexity of Problems, Economic Issues, and a deep understanding of issues will be important for the College Educated. We also know in general they have become more conservative—inflation and tax concerns—on economic matters. Economic Revitalization will appeal to them. On social issues they have become more liberal in recent years.

Women

These voters will be concerned with a number of "our" issues. First and foremost Peace and control of nuclear arms. They will be concerned with "soft issues" and "human issues"—Human Rights, Women's rights, justice for minorities. We will want to contrast to Reagan's negativism. Also, they are, as college educated, future oriented and concerned with the complexities of the 1980s.

There is another target group to consider. In our most recent field survey we grouped out those voters who were (1) for Reagan but not very certain to vote for him; (2) uncertain Anderson voters; and (3) the Undecideds. This group totaled about ⅓ of the electorate. They are a very important group for us—any gains must logically come from this group. They also represent some real opportunities for us. These voters:

— See inflation as #1 issue but rate foreign policy, not unemployment, as #2 concern.

— As a group they are heavily Democratic and Independent.

— They are flat middle of the road. Sixty-seven percent at 3,4,5 position of ideology scale. Sixty-nine percent put Carter there as well. However, only 36% give Reagan such a middle of the road position and over ½ put Reagan on the more conservative side of the scale.

— On comparative questions they give us good edges (when they give at all). This is most true on International Crisis, Keep Us from War, Cares, ERA, Respect More, Understands 1980s, Tells the Truth.

By group these voters are:

— 57% women, 43% men
— 23% white collar and clerical workers
— ⅓ are high school graduates, only 42% college educated
— 27% are union households
— 20% are Kennedy primary Democrats
— 22% are 26–35 years of age, 21% over 65, only 28% middle aged

Thus compared to target group one they match as women. However, they are more lower middle Democrats, less college educated.

Our Regression Analysis reveals some crucial information. The Carter Competence, Cares, and Inflation do not cut as hard with these voters. There are four things that do *matter:*

1. Party—there is a 77 point Democratic edge here.
2. Reagan competence—very important to them, Reagan slightly positive.
3. Reagan cares—hurts Reagan slightly, much more important factor than to all other voters.
4. Carter has learned, be a better President—scores very high. Carter has real edge. Will be an important theme.

Thus, if we mix our targets we would find the following:

1. All women—(soft issues as discussed, Reagan's lack of concern; Carter learned) Carter moderate—not Reagan
2. College educated—(harder issues and SALT, Economic issues—inflation/taxes—complex issues—Future 1980s—Reagan not understand, not up to job, Carter learned) Carter moderate—not Reagan

3. Lower middle/middle Democrats—young and old (Democratic Party, programs, Reagan Republican, not competent or concerned, Carter learned) Carter moderate—not Reagan

As one can see, these targets blend fairly well. Some common themes run through. However we should avoid a crucial mistake—you cannot talk to all at once. There has to be a balanced effort to go in-depth for one group on one issue and another segment on another question. To do all at once will weaken impact and thrust. Balance will be key. There are some unifying themes though, "Carter learned," "Moderate," "Peace," "Reagan not concerned," "Reagan not understand or grasp," "the Future."

We should direct question preparation/rebuttal proposals aimed at these target groups.

A further note on target groups. In the course of the debate we want to hit two spread groups at least once. They would not get the constant focus accorded the above groups:

4. Jews—Maybe Israel, Moral Majority, Anti Right Wing, Social Program
5. South—A native emotional identification

IV. A STRATEGY

Let us begin by understanding how each of the two candidates can "win"—in a real sense—this debate.

Reagan wins if:

• He assures people—about Ability, Judgment, Simplicity, Grasp of Issues
• Turns War and Peace to a Character issue rather than a Policy issue
• Shows compassion—concern for people
• Avoids mistakes of substance, avoids being pinned down
• Makes 4 years Economic failure the issue, Carter record

Carter wins if:

• He reinforces Reagan Doubts—Ability, Judgment, Simplicity, Grasp of Issues
• He makes Foreign Policy/war concern grow
• He shows that he has "learned—be a better President"
• He hurts Reagan on California Record
• He hurts Reagan on Inflation/Economics
• He hurts Reagan on Compassion/Concern
• He proves better President given credit for
• Carter dominates issue of Future—makes it basic

Thus, Reagan can win if he solves his own problems. Carter cannot win by solving his own problems—he must deny Reagan as well.

A. THEMES

If we combine the survey data, the target audiences, and our understanding of debates, the theme points of the debates begin to emerge. I have clustered ten positive theme points and then ten negative theme points and from those can draw seven basic themes that underlie our approach in the debates.

Carter Positive Themes

1. *I have learned—will do better 2nd term*—Almost 60% of the electorate believes this about Jimmy Carter. That is the door through which converts and undecideds must walk in voting for the President. We know that the regressions suggest that this is crucial for the target voters. It involves some mea culpa but it also points to the future. Above all themes it has primacy.

2. *Took unpopular positions—but they were right—I am the President*—Sometimes makes mistakes, sometimes things didn't work out but took right and balanced positions, risked popularity (energy, grain embargo, windfall profits, etc.) but did right thing, nature of job—continued responsible tradition of Truman, Eisenhower, Kennedy, Johnson, Nixon, Ford. Some payoff seen Energy, USSR. Use Incumbency.

3. *Man of Peace*—Arms control, Mid East, Africa, Human Rights, used prudence and strength—No Wars.

4. *Policies—some successes*—We do not need to attempt to correct three and one-half years of perception in one debate, not possible. Can point to some successes beginning to pay off.

   (a) Economy getting better—learned about inflation—jobs created.
   (b) Energy—fought first program. Took heat on higher prices; don't like either. That is why fought windfall profits tax (guess who doesn't). Have cut back on imports, production highest—Balance—Solar, Synfuels, etc.
   (c) Foreign Policy—Mid East—first time—Israel Security. Africa—fought for Human Rights, has had impact. USSR—might predict success of grain embargo—Soviet's Shortfall—Olympics—No War. China opening great—one-fourth of mankind. Arms Control—crucial issue—life/death. Handled crisis without conflict.
   (d) Government—Civil Service Reform, employees, etc.

5. *Understand the complex problems 1980s.* Changing nature of issues, Economy, Rebuild, Peace, Energy—Pollution, etc. World in 2000. Progress being made.

6. *A Moderate*—Moderate man, looks for balanced approach. Angers extremes but most Americans would agree. Continuation of line of 15–35 years of predecessors—same road. Airplane must have two wings—not one. Balance Energy—Conservation *and* Production, Foreign Policy—Arms Control and Defense, Economy —Jobs and Inflation/Control prices and Rebuild—Enterprise, Government and Labor. Cities—Private Enterprise *and* Government.

7. *Man of Compassion, Concern, Cares, Understands People—A Democrat*—Personal qualities—warmth all crucial how approach issues. A Democrat in the Democratic tradition—of justice for all—ERA, Civil Rights, Appointments, etc.

8. *Personal Leadership Qualities*—Trustworthy, Dedicated, Prudent, Qualified, Intelligent—inspire respect. All crucial for office and country. Restate open and honest Government. Town Meetings, etc.

9. *Has Vision—Eye to the Future*—Where we go next. What America can become. Energy—Rebuild. Energy—Technological Explosion, Conservation, American Energy, etc. The World—Peace, Human Rights, Friendships. Control Nuclear Arms. Society—Harmony, unity.

10. *Safe*—All add up to sensible, safe choice. Not extreme. In Tradition. Dependable. Can best be entrusted with awesome complex power in dangerous world.

Reagan Negative Themes

From the outset we must concede that Reagan is a well intentioned, good man. The issue is policies—what he advocates, what he understands, who he hears.

1. *Reagan Does Not Understand . . .* —This is the constant refrain for us. Does not understand the issues. Does not understand the process. Does not understand the consequences of proposals. Does not understand the risk. Does not understand the complexity of the problem. Does not understand the facts.

2. *Reagan Simplistic*—A constant refrain—"That sounds good—but it is too simplistic." Does not grasp complex ideas, will not work—lacks depth approach, misses intricacies—no easy answers come to Presidency. "I have stood where you do—but it's not as easy—different in the office."

3. *Policies—Domestic—Criticizes but what would he do?* Not bad intentions—does not understand. Policies wrong, radical/out of mainstream, disastrous.

Economy—Kemp/Roth Tax Cut—has not learned from our problems—overheated economy. Highly inflationary—numbers. Answer to Rebuild, Revitalize.

Energy—Too simplistic, wrong. Oil companies—Windfall Profits Tax. No conservation. Consequences of policy—today. No problem? Doesn't understand reserves, world demand.

Government—Return Welfare/Education to states. How fund? Cost to states, tax impact. Radical. How cut, where, specifics?

Social Programs—OSHA, CETA, etc. Impact. Social Security.

4. *Policies—Foreign Policy—Criticizes but what do?* Reagan not warmonger, wants peace—but not question of intentions but policies. Instinct—Interventionist. Arms control endangers country—naive, fails to understand 15 year process. Nonproliferation—consequences. Human Rights?

China—does not understand how crucial US position.

MidEast—policies do to Egypt? Stability important to Israel.

Latin America—Panama, aspirations, etc.

Africa—South Africa—Rhodesia idea.

Military superiority, what mean? what do?

5. *Reagan Judgment, Comments, Hip Shooting*—Nature of Office. Comments, words are policy. World reacts. Judgment—instinct, prudence necessary. Careful, Thoughtful—not need impulsive actions, words. One man not advisors.

6. *California Record*—Misrepresents record. Taxes—three increases, largest in history. Employment—property taxes led to Prop. 13. Mental Health—compassion. Not like Presidency.

7. *Ideologue—Not Moderate—Radical Approach*—Takes one approach of ideologue, not the way most Americans would act. Offers policies that would be sharp

departure from 30 years of bipartisan policies. Risky. Does not seek balance. Energy —only production. Economy—no rebuilding inflationary tax cut. Government—not sole cause of problem. Foreign policy—just toughness.

8. *Insensitive to people, does not understand people—A Republican*—Would hurt ordinary people, help business. Not a racist but insensitive on states' rights. Same ERA, same Labor, same Hispanics (prisoners used to pick lettuce during strike), Older Americans—health care, Medicare. Moral Majority—offend thousands of Catholics, Jews. New kind but still a Republican—tradition.

9. *Does not understand complex 1980s—Future*—Old ideas, old approach, not understand technology with energy. Rebuilds Economy. Kind of world 80s will be. Not grasp dangers or opportunities.

10. *A Risk*—Summary. Policies, risky. Simplistic. Lack of Understanding. Overturn 30 years of progress. Radical departure. People around him.

SUMMARY OF THEMES

These twenty themes points can be grouped into seven large themes—4 positive—3 negative.

Carter Positive

1. *Have Learned—Be Better*
2. *Policies—Right/Impact; Continuity/Democrat*
3. *Peace*   = SAFE
4. *Qualities—Moderate, Democrat, Compassion, Vision*

Reagan Negative

1. *Not Understand/Simplistic/Ideologue*
2. *Criticize—What of Policies—Domestic/Foreign/California Example*   = RISK
3. *Insensitive—Comments/Lack of Compassion/Republican*

B. A DEBATE DEVICE—SYMMETRY OF ANSWERS

I believe the method of how we answer the questions will be crucial. Every answer must have a symmetry of structure that covers the difficult ground of both positive and negative themes aimed at the right target audience. A device with consistency and symmetry has appeal, for it orders answers/rebuttals into a pattern that hammers the central messages into the consciousness of the target group.

We want to be obviously responsive to the substance of questions—for we know that the President has enormous and impressive grasp of the issues. Also, we know from 1976 that substantive answers are best—that they pull over leaners. In addition they contrast well with Reagan. *We want to be precise, drawing on depth of knowledge. This does not mean use of dull statistics or programs.* Nonetheless, we need a structure that permits the themes to emerge time and time again.

Here is the symmetric device:

1. *Determine Target Group*—not all at once.

2. *Learned/Be Better/Took Unpopular but Right Stands*
   (a) I have learned much. Gained experience. Means a better second term.
   (b) I took the best policy mix available. Sometimes didn't work out as well as hoped. Many times did and will pay off. I did the right thing even when unpopular—that's what being President is all about. Generally worked out.

   EXAMPLE: Energy—people scoffed at Moral Equivalent of War. Fought hard. Did not like higher prices—not anticipate OPEC. Made some mistakes, paid political price. Got Energy program to work—not one but two. Now not using as much, took time but impact great—what if we had not. Paid price of popularity, had to be done. But also why fought for windfall profits tax—oil companies—why they get it, as opponent proposes? Now can move on with conservation and production—solar, synfuels—make American energy.

3. *Continuity*
   My actions built on 15–20–30 years of bipartisan/Democratic tradition. One President inherits and passes on. Building over time. I continued that (like predecessors), I took moderate and balanced approach as they and you would do. Followed Democratic instructions, help people, partners, etc.

   Cannot afford to throw away 10/20/30 years of building work on some radical departure of approach as represented by my opponent. Must stay on road to progress.

4. *Attack Reagan's Predictable Answers*

   • My opponent is well intentioned. He does not understand the problem. He does not understand the consequences of what he proposes.
   • He has not learned from our efforts/successes.
   • Use current campaign quotes—don't need old ones.
   • My opponent's approach, some good, but is too simplistic—does not recognize reality, complexity.
   • My opponent criticizes but what would he do? What would be impact? How would he do it? How would he pay for it?
   • (Rebuttals) My opponent has not answered the questions. He is not being specific. He has not explained. He has ducked issues. In Oval Office you cannot duck the issues. He hasn't answered the questions—he just hasn't given any details.
   • I have stood where you do, Governor Reagan. It looks easy from the outside, I've learned that's not the way it works. You don't realize X, Y, Z, etc.

5. *Future/Same Road*
   My proposals look to the future. We must move into the 1980s new challenges, new opportunities, new approaches. America 1985 and 2000. We

must follow same *progressive* road to future. My policies built on experiences, learning, principle, continuity offer better next four years, better decade.

C. A Word on Format/Approach

1. *Format*—Bob [Strauss] and Jody [Powell] have negotiated a format that will permit the President to do what he must in this debate. It provides for substantive answers/followup and substantial rebuttal—counter-rebuttal. The 90 minute program is divided into two segments.

(a)   First half—Baltimore Format with followup.

Q to A	.30 minutes
A answers	2.00
Follow up Q to A	.30
A answers	1.00
Same Q to B	.30
B answers	2.00
Follow up Q to B	.30
B answers	1.00
A Rebuts	1.00
B Rebuts	1.00
(reverse order)	

(b)   Second half

Q to A	.30
A Answers	2.00
Same Q to B	.30
B answers	2.00
A Rebuts	1.30
B Rebuts	1.30
A Sur Rebuts	1.00
B Sur Rebuts	1.00

(c)   Closing statements

A	3.00
B	3.00

In the first half the press helps and in the second we can pursue Reagan on our own. The same-question format is somewhat restrictive but the 9–10 minutes per topic with 3 shots allows an exhaustive pursuit of an issue, a chance to get beyond Reagan's stock answer and the arena to employ our device of the symmetrical answer.

2. *Attacks—The President's role is not to debate Ronald Reagan.* We are letting the American people compare responses to similar questions. Reagan is the foil for the President.

We want to give Reagan enough rope to hang himself with foolish, simplistic answers, and not let him get away with meaningless, high sounding homilies.

We do not want to try and "nail Reagan down" on specifics. The road is littered with smart, clever politicians who thought that because Reagan isn't too intelligent and because Ronald Reagan isn't too substantive they could pin him down. Ronald Reagan may not be a genius and he certainly has no deep grasp of substance but he is very hard to pin down and he is, to quote Marty Franks [in charge of research for the Carter campaign], superb at slipping punches.

There is a temptation to try to pin Reagan down by firing direct challenges at him (I challenge Governor Reagan to name one area of the world where he has ever recommended military restraint). *Examination of his past debates, however, shows him to be skilled at evading challenges with a variety of diversionary tactics.* (To the above for example, he might say, "Anyone who knows me knows how much restraint I can have. Why in this campaign I've been provoked many times by the hostile tactics of my opponent and I've been restrained. As President, I would apply that same good judgment to hostile provocations from abroad.")

IT IS IMPOSSIBLE—BOTH TO LOOK PRESIDENTIAL AND TO CHASE REAGAN. No one looks dignified chasing after butterflies and no one looks in command when their punches are missing. (Remember how good the young Mohammed Ali looked leaning back against the ropes while assorted heavies exhausted themselves trying to make contact.)

We do not need to catch Reagan and couldn't if we wanted to. A better method is:

TO EDUCATE THE AUDIENCE ABOUT REAGAN'S ELUSIVENESS, CAPITALIZING ON THE SIMPLISTIC AND RAMBLING NATURE OF THE RESPONSES REAGAN HAPPENS TO GIVE.

Better:

"Governor Reagan has not been specific. He has ducked that issue. Well, in the Oval Office you can't duck the issues."

"My opponent's response may sound good but it doesn't answer the question. He hasn't given any details. He has not explained where the money comes from, etc."

"Well I wish that issue were as simple as you make it sound. There is much more to it though. My opponent does not understand the consequences . . ."

These responses on evasion (as distinct from his *proposals*) should not be given too somberly or waspishly, however. Ideally the audience should be politely drawn into an amiable game in which each of Reagan's responses is watched closely to see if he ducks or doesn't understand another issue.

There is a useful byproduct of the strategy of letting Reagan wander and then calling attention to it. All the vague and loose ends left over from the debate by Reagan can be the stuff of the final week's campaign.

3. *Quotes*—We need to study the Reagan list of quotes. While I would not give up all his old quotes I would always use them in tandem with a current 1979–80 campaign quote. And by God we should use them. Remember, this debate will be the first time most people will have heard these things!

Further I would have quotes from FDR, JFK, Truman, and others to use if Reagan gets off on his Democratic act.

4. *Some Other Points*—These are several answers or points I am most anxious to see used by President Carter either to make a specific point or touch a specific group. They follow in rough paraphrase:

(a) *CRISIS ANSWER—FOREIGN POLICY*

In the last four years I have been President (according to the _____ group), _____# (we need to get this)[15] of armed conflicts have broken out in the world. In every one of those conflicts, I *alone* have had to determine two things (1) America's interest and (2) America's involvement. Each of those armed conflicts carried the seeds for larger war and for American involvement in those wars. I am thankful to say that not once in those ____ (# of wars) did America become engaged. America did not go to war. Success is often measured in Foreign Affairs by what does *not* happen as much as what does happen.

My opponent does not want war. No reasonable person does. However, it is policies and ideas that concern me. Time after time, he has advocated American military intervention. This year alone he has advocated military intervention in Pakistan, the Middle East, etc. In preparing for this debate I have found not an instance when he has cautioned restraint over the past ten years. When we had a fishing dispute with Equador, he advocated sending a naval task force—in a fishing dispute with a tiny country!

This year after the invasion of Afghanistan by the Soviet Union, I imposed a grain embargo on the Soviet Union. It was an unpopular political act—I know that—it could well cost me this election. But it was the right thing to do and it has worked. Just last week President Brezhnev gave a speech pointing out just how much the embargo has hurt the Soviet Union. I called for a U.S. Boycott of the Moscow Olympics and the United States led _____(# of countries) in refusing to give the Soviet Union a propaganda victory while Soviet troops were ruthlessly suppressing the brave Afghan people. It was not an easy decision to ask our athletes to sacrifice years of training. It was not popular. But that boycott humiliated the Soviets. It worked. The Soviets have lost face and friends everywhere because of our tough actions. They were tough actions that did not lead to war.

My opponent refused to support the Embargo. He did not support the Olympic Boycott. Instead he advocated in response to a Russian invasion in the Middle East that we blockade Cuba! and days ago when asked what he would have done if the Russians attempted to force the blockade he said and I quote "(Quotation on Russians would not)" Well, what if they had? Would we have had an armed confrontation? Would we have had war? What would that have done to help the situation in Afghanistan?

I don't know. But a President cannot play fast and loose with this kind of awesome military might. Reagan has a pattern of advocacy steps that would invite military confrontation. A President must use caution, prudence, and thoughtfulness in his acts and his words. The Oval Office is not the place for quick judgments, hip shooting, impulsive statements. I have followed

[15] The memorandum leaves these facts to be filled in later.

the pattern of my predecessors in these crises—Presidents Eisenhower, Kennedy, Johnson, Nixon, Ford. Governor Reagan has a different approach that concerns me and should concern every American. Only a very poorly informed person would confuse steadiness, prudence, and flexibility in crisis with timidity and vacillation.

(b) *HUMAN RIGHTS*

Human Rights is extremely popular. I would like to have the President raise that banner in the face of Reagan and proclaim its success. I would like to challenge Reagan's position on this issue.

(c) *STANDING WHERE YOU STAND*

From earlier the idea that—I was a challenger. It looks simple. It's not —it's difficult in this job. I have learned things don't work that easily.

(d) *WELFARE/EDUCATION PROGRAMS*

We want to engage on this subject particularly as it opens the door to property taxes.

(e) *SOUTH*

We need to find a way to identify the President emotionally with the South in this debate.

(f) *JEWS*

Again we need to deal directly with this question and alert them to Moral Majority.

(g) *FLORIDA REFUGEES*

As an example of tough decisions (unpopular politics vs. Reagan's simplicity) I would like to find a place for this example:

— Refugees presented difficult problem, how to handle, cannot turn back; yet cannot be allowed to be overwhelmed, laws neglected.
— Took action, unpopular. Balance actions. Made no one happy. May cost me Florida in the election. Did right thing.
— Complicated problem. Complex difficulties. Complex, but balanced answer particularly to question of criminals, mentally incompetent, etc.
— However, Governor Reagan simplistic position—difficult—let them all in and worry about sorting them out later.

(h) *ERA—AN ISSUE OF ECONOMIC JUSTICE*

Given the target audience, our poll edge, etc. the President must find a way to work in the ERA—economic justice, equal rights argument and Reagan's position. If necessary he must bring it up himself. This is crucial.

V. ISSUES

A. SALIENCE

The Reagan camp has taken a major risk by agreeing to meet us in a debate. *Debates can have major impacts on reassuring voters and they can have major impacts on the saliency of different issues. Thus the Reagan camp can win the battle of "war and peace" and lose the war.* That is, if the debate results in higher saliency on issues of war, peace, nuclear arms, etc., Reagan can be a loser even if he narrows the President's lead in these areas. Why?

In 1976 contrary to conventional wisdom, the foreign policy debate did not really hurt Ford despite the Polish gaffe. The debate lowered his edge over Carter on issues of crisis management and foreign policy but it *increased* the salience of the issues enough to increase the edge that international issues were giving him! So Reagan can decrease our gap on international issues and still lose votes by getting more attention in the voting booth onto these issues.

Thus on *issues* we want to do the following according to the polls:

Foreign Policy

1. *Keep us out of war*—We have a huge lead on this issue but the saliency is still low so if we can raise the saliency we will get more votes. The more the debate is on the subject, the better. *Arms Control must be linked directly to war.*

2. *International Crisis*—This has a high saliency but our edge while rising is far below war. If we can increase the gap then we can pick up a lot of votes.

3. *Foreign Affairs*—This issue has moderate to low saliency and we have a moderate ten point edge. If we can both increase saliency and our margin we can pick up more points.

Thus, the best thing for us is to have the debate focused as much on foreign policy, crisis, war and peace. Also Human Rights. We must make every effort to push every possible question to this area when possible. We particularly will want to move it when possible toward war and peace over crisis, which is more a competence test. We should pronounce it the preeminent Presidential Issue Area.

Domestic—The Economy

This is a very tricky area as the survey data show. We are paying an enormous electoral price for the state of the economy although people do see things getting better.

1. *Inflation*—This issue has a very high saliency. Reagan is also besting the President decisively on the issue. It costs us enormously. Thus we don't want to increase the saliency—although it is hard to imagine it being more important. We must go right to Reagan on this issue—hurting him on this issue—trying to close the gap.

There is some risk that we will not close the gap much but still raise saliency. Thus we would be on better grounds on foreign policy but we will have to be especially aggressive on this subject—particularly Kemp/Roth.

2. *Unemployment*—Saliency on this issue has been declining recently. Reagan

still holds a wide lead on this issue although not as great as on inflation. We need to find a way to approach the issue that closes the gap. Frankly we would be better off fighting on the already high salient grounds of inflation and trying to slide off unemployment.

3. *ERA—Social Issues—Helping Poor, Elderly, Etc*. We have very large leads in this area but except for a moderate low saliency on ERA the others are insignificant. We should seek to exploit our advantage by raising and pressing these issues. Reagan has no credibility on these issues so if we can raise the saliency all the better.

Negative Issues

1. *Defense*—There is one issue we want to avoid like the plague—Defense. It has nothing to do with our position. At the moment, its saliency is very low—almost insignificant on the regressions. However, Reagan has his largest margins on this issue, +23 points. Thus heavy discussion here is only likely to raise saliency—more than our closing the gap—costing us votes at a rapid clip.

2. *Changing the Government*—This issue has no significance and Reagan has a moderate to huge edge. This issue has no future focus.

The chart below spells out the issue picture:

GROUP I	Issues Moderate/Low Saliency Large Carter Edge (+ +) *Keep out of War* *ERA* *Social Issues—Elderly, Poor, Race, etc.* *Human Rights*	Go after big—Best Group— raise saliency and thus harvest votes.
GROUP II	Issue High Saliency Moderate/Small Carter Edge (+) *International Crisis*	Go after in big way to raise margin—thus votes.
GROUP III	Issue Moderate/Low Saliency Moderate/Small Carter Edge (+) *Foreign Policy*	Some gain here in raising saliency—edge a secondary target.
GROUP IV	Issues High Saliency Large Carter Edge (+ +) *None*	Go after—gains somewhat hard to get—helps.
GROUP V	Issue High Saliency Large Reagan Edge *Inflation*	Possible target—close edge without raising saliency can provide Carter votes.

GROUP VI	Issue Moderate Saliency Large Reagan Edge	Troublesome—tough going— to close edge in way that
	Unemployment	outstates loss from saliency.

GROUP VII	Issue Low Saliency Large Reagan Edge	Avoid—saliency increase outstrips any gain margin
	Defense *Managing Government*	closing swing Reagan votes.

Other Qualities—VOTE EFFECTS

Of course the factors influencing vote extend beyond issues to candidate qualities —personality, leadership and Party provide votes. Without going through an elaborate chart I would like to point out those non-issue comparatives and qualities that if exploited properly can give or cost votes.

1. *Big Carter Gains—Saliency Increased* (comprise factors of moderate salience but large Carter edge)

   (a) *Party*—Enormous Carter edge
   (b) *Carter learned*—A door if saliency raised for voters to move
   (c) *Carter cares*—A Carter plus if saliency raised
   (d) *Better qualified*—An abstract hard to raise in saliency but if so by performance means votes

2. *Big Carter Gains—Edge Increased* (comprise factors of high salience, but only moderate Carter edge)

   (a) *Close on issues*—Always crucial, moderate helps here, gets things done, Cares important (hostages show up here along with issues)
   (b) *Respect more*—Abstract but important
   (c) *Get things done*—At moment an even division—heavy weight but no impact

3. *Carter Gains—Changing Perceptions* (comprise factors of high saliency where Carter hurting by negative perceptions—positive change yields votes—best area for Reagan to attack)

   (a) *Carter job performance*—Frankly, hard to change in a debate
   (b) *Carter vision*—Movement here has big impact
   (c) *Carter safe*—Very negative—movement here has real impact

4. *Carter Gains—Reagan Perceptions* (high or moderate saliency—drive Reagan down—high gain)

   (a) *Reagan competence*
   (b) *Reagan qualified*
   (c) *Reagan vision*   (Hurt Reagan here and Carter
   (d) *Reagan risk*   votes go up)
   (e) *Reagan keep out of war*

With the critical addition of Party, the issues listed here are the same as the principal positive and negative thrust points outlined in this section.

Other Qualities Affecting Favorable/Unfavorable Rating

There are a number of qualities that do not move vote directly but which move favorable/unfavorable ratings and which go directly to vote decision (i.e., if I drive your favorable rating down and your unfavorable up, it will be directly reflected in vote).

All of the qualities listed in the above section (Agree/Disagree—such as vision, safe, risk, etc.) also contribute to favorable/unfavorable rating although their independent impact on vote is more crucial. In addition to those we find the following qualities to have significant impact on the candidate ratings:

1. *Ronald Reagan*

   (a) *Not trust in crisis*—high saliency and Reagan negatives hurt his rating. If that became more negative, it would drive rating down.
   (b) *Simplistic*   moderate saliency and vast negative Reagan margin. Increased saliency will drive down rating.
   (c) *Shoots from hip*
   (d) *Wonder about RR judgment*—all big negatives—only moderate saliency
   (e) *How much more Reagan do than Carter*
       and
       Hasn't told what do, but criticizes too much

A. Target Group Issues

If we again look at the target groups we find that the issues/qualities that most affect them are:
   1. Party—heavily pro-Carter
   2. RR Competence—slightly pro-Reagan
   3. RR Cares—hurts Reagan
   4. JC Learned—very pro-Carter
   5. Inflation—quite pro-Reagan but lower saliency

Thus movement on saliency or margin or both, will have significant impact.

All and all, the targets become quite consistent with the presentations in Section IV.

B. "Feminine vs. Masculine" Issues/Human vs. Technological

The issues raised in the debate can also be seen as human issues—peace, human rights, women's rights, justice for minorities. *These are "feminine" issues and it is wise not to be too combative on them. There is not a need to be harshly critical of Reagan, the audience knows who to trust on these issues. Women are especially drawn to Carter's positions in this area, as these are matters of human compassion.* This partly accounts for the Carter advantage among women. It would not be wise to risk offending his audience by too tough tactics here, except on the issue of peace which has wider and more deadly implications for the Reagan candidacy.

On the other side, Carter trails Reagan among men. Partly this is a matter of a perceived lack of Presidential decisiveness on masculine issues. It could therefore be desirable to press for advantage on certain such issues. Energy and pollution are two possibilities. These issues have their soft or human side too, but they are, to a major extent, technical. The President should present his own views and programs forcefully here (I have an engineering background and happen to know something about these matters), and press hard against Reagan.

On energy, explain why Reagan's view that there is no problem is naive and why one can't simply assume that indefinite producing capability is attainable. Need for some environmental balance.

On pollution, chide Reagan again for trying to pretend the problem isn't there and for being so ideologically hidebound about the Federal regulation in this area.

Reagan will come hard on the defense issue. To the extent we are on this issue, which hopefully is minimal, a style of rejoinder is to adopt the technological stance as for other "hard science" issues. The United States doesn't get stronger by producing every possible weapon in every imaginable quantity. You have to plan defense technology years in advance so you don't find yourself with billions sunk into poor weapons. You have to pick and choose and you have to have a good balance of strong capabilities. That's the course I have been following as President.

C. A Specific Issue—The Economy

There are a number of points that we want to touch in this area:

- Disappointment, some mistakes but also some unexpected shocks like OPEC—use to get to energy. Inflation worldwide problem.
- Things are getting better, latest figures.
- Some things gone better, job creation.
- Have learned from experiences. Know need for building production base, hence Economic Revitalization program—retool, refit, and rebuild.
- Reagan has criticized but what does he offer? What is Reagan's solution? Tax cut that is *inflationary,* Kemp/Roth. (Pound inflation aspect—Ford used inflation, taxes, and Carter Georgia record to good effect in first debate according to Tell Back research.)
- Rich man's tax cut.
- Inflationary impact overwhelming, not even stated.
- Reagan's numbers don't add up.
- Otherwise vague on inflation, unemployment.
- Description by Bush, Business Week, others—Ford impact.
- Reagan has not learned lesson about need to build, not have inflationary tax cut.
- Carter deals with the future. Already better. Learned. Vision of Future.

VI. CARTER POSTURE

The President wants to project the manner of a calm experienced President. The Incumbent. As to substance, depth, and grasp of complexity, this debate offers the

President the opportunity to sell in a wholesale way what he excels at in a retail setting (town meetings, press conferences, etc.).

A. President as Educator

The President must eschew obfuscation. Carter should talk *to* the audience on debate night using this opportunity to wear his hat as *GREAT EDUCATOR,* explaining in conceptual terms what the job of President entails. He should imagine he is talking to a high school class—not preaching to them—but guiding them to understand so they can reach solid, informed judgments.

B. Footprints

To increase the sense of a strong Carter we must continually leave personal and policy footprints, a record to which we can refer. Say:

> I strongly believe
> I have always stood for
> I have always had a firm commitment to
> As I said again and again

C. Biography

One reason for Reagan's television effectiveness is in part because of his aw-shucks nice guy style. To meet the public's desire for intimacy—at a distance—the President should take one or two opportunities during this debate to give the audience some "biography." Some ideas:

1. *Camp David*—an incident that happened there, maybe the Gettysburg story for the South.
2. *Trips*—incidents.

VII. REAGAN

We can pretty well anticipate Reagan's approach. While we might get surprised we are very likely to get the same Reagan that has always appeared in debates. Indeed, one finds in examining old transcripts that he always tends to use the *same* answer! This provides an important planning opportunity. It means that we can prepare the President for a likely Reagan answer to get both his own answer and lines of attack in the rebuttal.

A. "Tapes"

As we know, Reagan has these little "tapes" of answers for approaches. His negotiators tried to fight off follow-ups or probes for obvious reasons—there's little beyond these tapes. We must get beyond those tapes.

I'm sure the Reagan people expect us to go right after him—direct, tough, mean.

Reagan will be prepared to deflect these as I indicated in the strategy section. That is why we must not *pursue* him on specifics but rather on general lack of understanding and avoiding the issue.

B. QUESTIONS

Reagan has a habit of answering or trying to answer questions put to him. This is how he often gets into trouble. The follow-up questions should be helpful here. Further, particularly in the second half of the program in the double rebuttal period, we may want to throw out one or two *carefully* chosen questions to Reagan particularly to get at his true beliefs.

C. TRUE BELIEFS

Reagan is an actor. He usually will put forward that which is prepared for him. However, there are a few things—things he has stood for all his life (like Taiwan). He is not likely to back away from these if challenged hard. To the extent that we can get to these we should try. Here is a sampling:

China—Taiwan connection
Nixon—opposed resignation—supported pardon
Russians
Free Enterprise—the answer to all things
Oil Companies
Environment

Research has shown that many people think he takes these positions for political gain—that he does not really believe them. This is a favorite theme from the press. The truth is that he *believes* some very strange things and if you get beyond the "tape" answer he will defend those positions just as he has advocated them for years in front of the faithful.

After all, he is an actor.

D. REAGAN PSYCHOLOGY

Reagan is trying out for the biggest part of his life. That's the way he sees it. Whatever the veneer he will go into the beginning of this debate nervous, even scared. Remember Jimmy Carter at the first debate? *This is an advantage that the President must move to exploit in the first ten or fifteen minutes. We should plan well the opening of the debate.*

VIII. SETTING EXPECTATIONS

Setting expectations is a critical game in debates particularly with the press. It is also with the public—usually the candidate expected to do well will "lose"—does not meet expectation. To this extent we want to emphasize the Reagan edge—Actor, etc. My guess is that the public will expect a slight Reagan edge.

The more crucial and dangerous game is that with the press. They have an inor-

dinate role in convincing the public not only about who won on "points" but more critically, on the nature of the debate itself.

The Baltimore debate is an example. Even though the public saw a narrow Anderson win (or margin provided by Carter voters) the press said *both* did well, no mistakes, etc. *Thus, the press* helped reassure the public about Reagan. If they had pursued the several Reagan errors—not knowing about the urban Homesteading Act, Reagan not having inflation figures and either not knowing or lying—then the impact of the debate would have been quite different. It is likely that the public would have been less reassured and that Reagan would not have gotten a boost from the debate.

Thus we cannot let the press go into the debate with the simple notion of looking just for a winner and loser. Nor with the idea that both will do well. *Not only must we "win" on points, more importantly we must win substantively and have the press judge the debate on that criterion.*

We must make an all-out effort to educate the press to the questions of:

(1) Will Reagan be specific?
(2) Will he flip-flop?
(3) Will he know what he is talking about?
(4) Will he be simplistic with no depth?
(5) Will he err?

We have to emphasize that such is the criteria we are looking to for "winning" and hurting Reagan. It must seep into their psyche as well.

Jody, Bob, and everyone else must begin with urgency to push this line. We want to win on substance—not style—on who will be a better informed President, not on ease of delivery. Otherwise given the abominable coverage this year, the press will let Reagan slide off saying he looked good, didn't screw up, or got his points across. That could be disastrous.

This is a crucial area. It cannot be over-emphasized.

IX. POST DEBATE

A. Winning

We must have post-debate follow-thru a la the expectation section. We must push the idea of victory of substance, depth, specific answers. We cannot accede to the idea of just who won or lost. "We won but we won because . . ." We must hit Reagan hard, immediately, for not answering, lack of knowledge, etc. This will obviously be easier if the press is pre-conditioned themselves. Of course if there is a substantive mistake, this will be easier.

B. Follow Up

We must pursue the debate themes immediately afterward. Particularly if the salience of our issues increases. This gives us several days of pro-Carter anti-Reagan material.

C. ADS

We may well want to run radio ads—stressing that we won—and the reasons why at the moment the public is still trying to form its decision. Again we could stress Carter's "learned," "vision"—Reagan's "risk," "simplistic," "not understand," etc. This could have a real impact. Jerry needs to pursue it if he thinks it is technically feasible. It could help offset much of the press.

X. PREPARATION

This is a very crucial area. In 1976 we poorly prepared the President for the first debate and did a much better job the second and third times around.

Frankly we must not let our concern over demanding his time keep us from properly preparing Jimmy Carter. Nor must we let him be overwhelmed. Here are my suggestions.

A. *Minimize players*—Everyone will have ideas. Many will be good. However, only a handful can really effectively shape a debate. We need an input process but we do not need a cast of thousands.

B. *A debate of strategy, not fact*—*This debate will not be won on facts.* The President, unlike 1976, knows everything there is to know about government. He needs to lightly brush up on that. He needs to brush up on Reagan some. He does not need hundreds of pages of briefing books.

What he needs to do is approach the debate from a political strategy point. Frankly I think this document is that strategy approach. *To win the President must* PREPARE *and* PRACTICE *an execution of this strategy.* It requires less facts than knowing the strategic and tactical *imperatives for every and any* situation.

C. *Preparing*—To this end I would suggest the following:

1. We need to review likely questions—given the same question format and the limited number of questions—this will not be very difficult.
2. We need to review Reagan's past forums, debates, interviews, etc. Since the tapes are always the same, it is likely that it will be fairly easy to anticipate Reagan's approach.
3. Then we need to formulate our (a) target groups, (b) our positive themes and (c) our negative themes in line with the symmetric answer approach discussed in Section IV.
4. We need to wargame this debate, both without and with the President. This is particularly true as it relates to the rebuttals. This is new territory and needs to be planned carefully.

    Sam Popkin,[16] who knows Reagan well in this area, should probably come to work with Marty [Franks] and David [Rubenstein, deputy director of the domestic policy staff].

[16] Popkin, a professor at the University of California at San Diego, had advised the Carter campaign on debate strategy in 1976, and researched for the Carter campaign in 1980, and acted the part of Reagan in Carter's rehearsals for the 1980 debate.

5. We need to review the 1976 debates, particularly 1 and 2. The first to see how Ford dealt with us so effectively and the second to see successful attacks on an incumbent. Also we should review the Tell Back analysis CSR [Cambridge Survey Research] had done on the Anderson-Reagan debate. The President should probably see this as well. We should perhaps see the Robert Kennedy–Reagan debate from 1967.

D. *Practice*—The President must practice. He must be urged to resist his usual instinct to read and study alone. Frankly, that is one reason the first debate in 1976 was lost. The President spent a lot of time studying in Plains for that first debate and damn little strategizing. We did exactly the opposite in the San Francisco Debate and it showed. We had a strategy and the President executed it brilliantly.

I would recommend that the President practice with only a few of us. Also, that we consider gaming out with the President the crucial but dangerous rebuttals. It will take some of the President's time, but the pay-off will be substantial.

E. *Travel*—The President should go to Cleveland by mid-day Monday. In 1976 he prepared and focused better on the road—there were also fewer distractions.

F. *Schedule*—I would strongly recommend the following schedule:

1. While the President is on the road Friday we pull together the research, answers, etc. and merge with themes. That would begin Thursday.
2. On Friday a handful of us would go to Camp David to pull most of this together.
3. On Saturday the President would return—relax and begin to review the material and see the relevant tapes. Some initial discussion could take place.
4. On Sunday we would begin intense sessions of strategizing and practice.
5. On Monday in Cleveland we should strategize and practice *again*.

Index

446

About the Author

ELIZABETH DREW is a journalist in Washington and the author of three earlier books—*Senator, American Journal: The Events of 1976*, and *Washington Journal: The Events of 1973–74*. In addition to being widely respected as a writer, Ms. Drew is known for her appearances on "Agronsky and Company" and other nationally televised public-affairs shows. From 1971 to 1973 she hosted her own television interview program on the Public Broadcasting Service. She has received several awards for her work, including the Award for Excellence from the Society of Magazine Writers, The DuPont-Columbia Award for Broadcast Journalism, and the Medal for Distinguished Service to Journalism from the University of Missouri's School of Journalism. Ms. Drew has been awarded honorary degrees by Yale University, Hood College, Trinity College in Washington, Reed College, the Georgetown University Law Center, and Williams College.

WILSON
and His
PEACEMAKERS
American Diplomacy at the
Paris Peace Conference, 1919